Essentials of Practical Real Estate Law

Third Edition

The West Legal Studies Series

Your options keep growing with West Publishing

Each year our list continues to offer you more options for every course, new or existing, and on-the-job reference materials. We now have over 140 titles from which to choose. We are pleased to offer books in the following subject areas:

Administrative Law	Family Law
Alternative Dispute Resolution	Federal Taxation
Bankruptcy	Intellectual Property
Business Organizations/Corporations	Introduction to Law
Civil Litigation and Procedure	Introduction to Paralegalism
CLA Exam Preparation	Law Office Management
Client Accounting	Law Office Procedures
Computer in the Law Office	Legal Research, Writing, and Analysis
Constitutional Law	Legal Terminology
Contract Law	Paralegal Employment
Criminal Law and Procedure	Real Estate Law
Document Preparation	Reference Materials
Environmental Law	Torts and Personal Injury Law
Ethics	Will, Trusts, and Estate Administration

You will find unparalleled, practical teaching support.

Each text is enhanced by instructor and student supplements to ensure the best learning experience possible to prepare for this field. We also offer custom publishing and other benefits such as West's Student Achievement Award. In addition, our sales representatives are ready to provide you with needed and dependable service.

We want to hear from you.

The most important factor in improving the quality of our paralegal texts and teaching packages is active feedback from educators in the field. If you have a question, concern, or observation about any of our materials or you have written a proposal or manuscript, we want to hear from you. Please do not hesitate to contact your local representative or write us at the following address:

West Legal Studies, 5 Maxwell Drive, Clifton Park, NY 12065-2919

For additional information point your browser at

www.westlegalstudies.com

THOMSON

DELMAR LEARNING

Essentials of
Practical Real Estate Law

Third Edition

Daniel F. Hinkel

THOMSON

DELMAR LEARNING

Australia Canada Mexico Singapore Spain United Kingdom United States

WEST LEGAL STUDIES

ESSENTIALS OF PRACTICAL REAL ESTATE LAW 3E
Daniel F. Hinkel

Career Education Strategic Business Unit
Vice President:
Dawn Gerrain

Director of Editorial:
Sherry Gomoll

Acquisitions Editor:
Pamela Fuller

Developmental Editor:
Melissa Riveglia

Editorial Assistant:
Sarah Duncan

Director of Production:
Wendy A. Troeger

Production Manager:
Carolyn Miller

Production Editor:
Betty L. Dickson

Technology Manager:
Joseph Saba

Director of Marketing:
Donna J. Lewis

Channel Manager:
Wendy E. Mapstone

Cover Design:
Dutton and Sherman Design

Library of Congress Cataloging-in-Publication Data

Hinkel, Daniel F.
    Essentials of practical real estate law / Daniel F. Hinkel.—3rd ed.
        p. cm.—(West Legal Studies)
Includes index.
    ISBN 1-4018-1471-9
1. Vendors and purchasers—United States.
2. Real property—United States. 3. Conveyancing—United States. I. Title. II. Series.

KF665.H52 2003
346.7304'3—dc22   2003062518

NOTICE TO THE READER

Publisher does not warrant or guarantee any of the products described herein or perform any independent analysis in connection with any of the product information contained herein. Publisher does not assume, and expressly disclaims, any obligation to obtain and include information other than that provided to it by the manufacturer.

The reader is notified that this text is an educational tool, not a practice book. Since the law is in constant change, no rule or statement of law in this book should be relied upon for any service to any client. The reader should always refer to standard legal sources for the current rule or law. If legal advice or other expert assistance is required, the services of the appropriate professional should be sought.

The Publisher makes no representation or warranties of any kind, including but not limited to, the warranties of fitness for particular purpose or merchantability, nor are any such representations implied with respect to the material set forth herein, and the publisher takes no responsibility with respect to such material. The publisher shall not be liable for any special, consequential, or exemplary damages resulting, in whole or part, from the readers' use of, or reliance upon, this material.

To: John Henry

Contents In Brief

Contents

Chapter 5
DEEDS   95

Chapter 6
LEGAL ASPECTS OF REAL ESTATE FINANCE   112

Chapter 7
TITLE EXAMINATIONS   164

Preface

This text was originally written as a reduced-essential version of a larger text *Practical Real Estate Law* by Daniel F. Hinkel. *Practical Real Estate Law* covered every aspect of a modern real estate practice. That text, because of its detail and comprehensive coverage, totaled more than 600 pages, and some instructors teaching courses designed for six- to ten-week terms had found it difficult to complete *Practical Real Estate Law*. The students who were attending the shorter courses suggested that the text be shortened and that some detail be deleted. Consequently, the editors at West Publishing Company asked me to consider a way to revise and reformat the material in *Practical Real Estate Law* to reach the varied audience of the day. The result was *Essentials of Practical Real Estate Law*, first published in 1993.

It is time for a new edition of this book. Many things have happened since the last revision in 1998. Lawyers and their clients keep revising and updating legal forms. Technology and the increased use of the Internet provide real estate attorneys and legal assistants with new tools and procedures for conducting a real estate transaction.

Essentials of Practical Real Estate Law, Third Edition, retains the liveliness and readability of the parent book. Each chapter gives definitions of key and important terms where they first appear in the text, and there is a comprehensive glossary at the back of the book. There is a self-study examination at the end of each chapter to reinforce the student's understanding of that chapter's material.

Based on comments and suggestions from various teachers, students, and reviewers of the second edition of this book, the text has been revised. Chapter 1 introduces the student to the concept of property ownership and the various types of ownership that can exist are discussed. Chapter 2 introduces the student to the situation in which real property is owned by more than one person and discusses all the forms of concurrent ownership. Various encumbrances to the ownership of real property, with special emphasis on easements are discussed in Chapter 3. In Chapter 4, basic contract law is discussed and standard provisions found in real estate contracts are explained. Chapter 5 contains a discussion of deeds, complete with many examples and sample forms. Real estate finance with emphasis on notes and mortgages, complete with many examples and sample forms, is discussed in Chapter 6. Chapters 7 and 8 are devoted to title examinations and title insurance. Chapters 9 and 10 are devoted to real estate closings, with Chapter 9 containing a full discussion of the substantive issues of real estate closings and Chapter 10 being devoted to forms and examples of closing documents, including a sample of a residential real estate closing transaction. Chapter 11 acquaints the student with condominiums and cooperatives. Chapter 12 is a full discussion on the methods of describing real property and contains sample surveys and legal descriptions. Chapter 13 includes a discussion of leases, complete with residential and commercial lease forms.

CHANGES TO THE THIRD EDITION

Forms

All forms where needed have been updated and new forms have been added to the text.

Expanded Coverage

New materials have been added in Chapter 3 that discuss environmental concerns of real property. New materials have been added in Chapter 4, expanding the discussion of the role of a real estate broker. New material has been added in Chapter 12 that discusses how to describe real property. The chapter also contains a full discussion of surveys, complete with many survey examples and assignments for students to work through. Chapter 13 is a new discussion of landlord-tenant law with an emphasis on commercial leases. The chapter also contains a discussion of residential leases, including an introduction to the Uniform Residential Landlord and Tenant Act.

Case Material

A number of cases have been introduced in many of the chapters to illustrate important points of law and to give students experience in reading actual cases and applying actual disputes to chapter material.

Personal Profiles

A number of personal profiles of legal assistants working in the real estate field have been added. These profiles add a human interest component to the material.

STUDENT LEARNING FEATURES

- **Chapter objectives** open each chapter to focus the student's attention on the key concepts.
- **Terminology** is emphasized in each chapter. The terms appear in boldface and are defined in the text where they first appear. They are also listed at the end of each chapter as a reference. Finally, a comprehensive glossary is located at the end of the text.
- There is a **self-study examination** at the end of each chapter to help the students reinforce their understanding of the material contained in the chapter. The answers to the self-study examinations are located in the Appendix.

SUPPLEMENTAL TEACHING MATERIALS

- The **Instructor's Manual** is available online at **www.westlegalstudies.com** in the Instructor's Lounge under Resource. Written by the author of the text, the *Instructor's Manual* contains the following:
- *Introduction and Chapter Outline*—Each chapter contains a short summary of the topics covered and a chapter outline.
- *Teaching Ideas*—Each chapter contains teaching ideas for the instructor with ideas for adding to the text with material relevant to your state.
- *Answers to Review Questions and Case Problems*—The manual contains answers to the review questions and case problems found at the end of each chapter.
- *Test Bank*—A test bank with true-false questions and multiple-choice questions is prepared for each chapter.
- *Transparency Masters*—A number of transparencies that can be used as teaching aids are included.

- **Online Resource**™ The Online Resource™ can be found at **www.westlegalstudies.com** in the Online Resource™ section of the Web Site.
- **Web page**—Come visit our website at **www.westlegalstudies.com**, where you will find valuable information such as hot links and sample materials to download, as well as other West Legal Studies products.
- **WESTLAW**®—West's online computerized legal research system offers students "hands-on" experience with a system commonly used in law offices. Qualified adopters can receive ten free hours of WESTLAW®. WESTLAW® can be accessed with Macintosh and IBM PC and compatibles. A modem is required.

- **Strategies and Tips for Paralegal Educators,** a pamphlet by Anita Tebbe of Johnson County Community College, provides teaching strategies specifically designed for paralegal educators. A copy of this pamphlet is available to each adopter. Quantities for distribution to adjunct instructors are available for purchase at a minimal price. A coupon on the pamphlet provides ordering information.
- **Survival Guide for Paralegal Students,** a pamphlet by Kathleen Mercer Reed and Bradene Moore, covers practical and basic information to help students make the most of their paralegal courses. Topics covered include choosing courses of study and note-taking skills.
- **West's Paralegal Video Library**—West Legal Studies is pleased to offer the following videos at no charge to qualified adopters:
- *The Drama of the Law II: Paralegal Issues Video* ISBN: 0-314-07088-5
- *The Making of a Case Video* ISBN: 0-314-07300-0
- *ABA Mock Trial Video—Product Liability* ISBN: 0-314-07342-6
- *Arguments to the United States Supreme Court Video* ISBN: 0-314-07070-2
- **Court TV Videos**—West Legal Studies is pleased to offer the following videos from Court TV for a minimal fee:
  - *New York v. Ferguson—Murder on the 5:33: The trial of Colin Ferguson* ISBN: 0-7668-1098-4
  - *Ohio v. Alfieri* ISBN: 0-7668-1099-2
  - *Flynn v. Goldman Sachs—Fired on Wall Street: A case of Sex Discrimination?* ISBN: 0-7668-1096-8
  - *Dodd v. Dodd—Religion and Child Custody in Conflict* ISBN: 0-7668-1094-1
  - *In Re Custody of Baby Girl Clausen—Child of Mine: The fight for Baby Jessica* ISBN: 0-7668-1097-6
  - *Fentress v. Eli Lilly & Co., et al.—Prozac on Trial* ISBN: 0-7668-1095-x
  - *Garcia v. Garcia—Fighting over Jerry's Money* ISBN: 0-7668-0264-7
  - *Hall v. Hall—Irretrievable Broken—A Divorce Lawyer Goes to Court* ISBN: 0-7668-0867-x
  - *Maglica v. Maglica—Broken Hearts, Broken Commitments* ISBN: 0-7668-0867-x
  - *Northside Partners v. Page and New Kids on the Block—New kids in Court: Is Their Hit Song a Copy?* ISBN: 0-7668-9426-7

ACKNOWLEDGMENTS

Acknowledgments are due Linda Selfridge and Deborah Reinhardt who prepared the manuscript and to the following individuals for their fine efforts in reviewing the third edition of the text.

Hank Arnold
Aiken Technical College
Aiken, SC

Chelsea Campbell
Lehman College
Bronx, NY

Robert Diotalevi
Florida Gulf Coast
   University
Fort Myers, FL

David Hallett
Pioneer Pacific College
Wilsonville, OR

Luci Hoover
Rockford Business College
Rockford, IL

Toni Marsh
Georgetown University
Washington, DC

Please note the internet resources are of a time-sensitive nature
and URL addresses may often change or be deleted.
Contact us at *www.westlegalstudies.com.*

Table of Exhibits

Introduction to the Law of Real Property

"For 'tis the only thing in the world that lasts. 'Tis the only thing worth working for, fighting for, dying for."

—Margaret Mitchell, Gone with the Wind

OBJECTIVES

After reading this chapter you should be able to:

- Distinguish between real and personal property
- Understand the legal concept of property ownership
- Identify the modern estates of ownership for real property
- Understand and be able to explain the legal concept of adverse possession
- Identify various ways of becoming an owner of real property

Scarlett O'Hara's father's sentiments about Tara are shared by millions of homeowners throughout the world. Home ownership ranks high on most people's wish list, and a home is considered the most valuable asset in many households. The real estate industry, with all its many facets, such as development, construction, sales, leasing, and finance, generates vast concentrations of wealth and creates millions of jobs. Real estate is a valuable commodity, and almost every aspect of its use, sale, and development is regulated by law. These laws are steeped in history and tempered with logic and practicality. Representation of real estate clients is a major area of practice for many law firms, and the opportunities for the trained real estate legal assistant are numerous. Preparation for this work begins with an introduction to the basic principles of real property law.

REAL PROPERTY LAW

What law governs real property transactions? The law of the United States comprises two separate systems of law: federal law and state law. Federal law applies uniformly throughout the country, whereas state law, because of differences in local history and conditions, varies from state to state. The law of real property in general is governed by state law and, therefore, is somewhat different in each of the various states. The law of the state in which the real property is located usually governs. For example, if a New York couple owns a beach house on Cape Cod, the laws of the Commonwealth of Massachusetts control the couple's ownership rights to the property and the form and content of the various legal documents and procedures involved in the sale, leasing, financing, inheritance, and so on of the property.

There are, however, basic legal principles that govern real estate transactions, and the approach of this text is to describe these principles and to mention the more important instances in which the states do not agree.

What is real property? The law recognizes two classifications of property: real and personal. Real property relates to land and those things that are more or less permanently attached to the land, such as homes, office buildings, and trees. Personal property refers to all other things, such as automobiles, furniture, stocks, and bonds. John E. Cribbet, former dean of the

University of Illinois College of Law, in his treatise *Principles of the Law of Real Property*, points out that "the terminology makes no semantic sense because a car is just as 'real' as a farm and the family mansion is more 'personal' to the owner than shares of stock. The explanation lies not in the history of property, but in the history of procedure. In early common law a real action, so called because it led to the return of the thing itself, was used when land was wrongfully detained by another; a personal action, which gave only a money claim against the wrongdoer, was proper when things other than land were involved. Thus, the thing took the name of the action, and we have, to this day, real property and personal property."

Real property is more than just earth and things that are attached to the earth. Real property includes everything beneath the surface of the earth and in the air space above. Early lawyers used the ancient maxim *"cujus est solum, ejus est usque ad coelum et ad infernos,"* which means that land, in its legal signification, extends from the surface downward to the center of the earth and upward indefinitely to the stars.

An owner of real property usually owns all the minerals beneath the surface of the land. These minerals, such as oil, gas, or coal, often are more valuable than the land's surface. The owner can sell the minerals separate from the surface or lease them to a company with the technology to extract the minerals, retaining a royalty or percentage of the profits from the minerals. Conversely, the surface of the land can be sold, and the owner can retain the rights to the minerals beneath the surface.

The owner of real property also owns the air space above the surface of the land. This air space can be quite valuable, such as in a crowded city like New York, where the air space can be used for building purposes. Air space also can be valuable in less populous areas to preserve a scenic view of a mountain or a shoreline. The advent of solar energy also has increased the value of air space, and most states provide for solar easements that create the right to purchase adjoining air space to permit the sun to shine on solar heating or cooling units of a building.

Trees, plants, and other things that grow in the soil may be considered real property. Trees, perennial bushes, grasses, and so on that do not require annual cultivation are considered real property. Annual crops produced by labor, such as wheat, corn, and soybeans, are considered personal property.

An owner of real property has certain ownership rights to use water that is located on the surface or beneath the surface of the land. The users of water are diverse, such as farmers, manufacturers, and consumers. Water pollution and changes in weather patterns that are responsible for below-average rainfall have combined to drastically reduce the amount of usable water available in many sections of the nation and have heightened competition among the users of water. Many states, in an effort to resolve this conflict, have enacted laws regulating the transfer, ownership, and use of water rights.

The source of water governs, to a great extent, a landowner's rights to own and use the water. The categories of water sources are (a) groundwater, such as an underground stream or spring; (b) surface water, which accumulates on the surface of the land from rain; and (c) water that accumulates in a river, stream, or natural lake.

Groundwater is water beneath the surface of the land. It is created by underground streams or by rain that soaks through the soil. A landowner's right to use an underground stream is governed by the same rules that govern rivers and streams on the surface of the land, which are hereinafter discussed. Groundwater that has been created by rain soaking through the soil is deemed to belong to the owner of the land on which the groundwater is found. The landowner has the right to use the groundwater in any way he or she chooses as long as the landowner does not use or divert the water in such a way as to intentionally harm an adjoining property owner.

A landowner can use *surface water* in any way he or she chooses as long as the use does not harm an adjoining property owner. The diversion of surface water by a landowner onto a neighbor's land may be a problem, especially when the terrain is hilly. For example, a property owner owns land that is at or near the bottom of a hill. Because of the natural flow of surface water, the property floods during rainy periods. The property owner decides to build a dam on the property to keep the surface water from flooding the land. The dam protects the property from flooding by diverting the water uphill onto a neighbor's property, causing the neighbor's property to flood. The flooding of the neighbor's property is unnatural because the flooding is caused by the artificial dam. The owner of the dam in this situation is liable to the neighbor for damages caused by the flooding because the dam altered the natural flow of the water. A property owner does not have the right to alter the natural flow of surface water.

Water located within a river, stream, or natural lake is owned by the state or federal government and not by the individual property owners whose properties adjoin the river, stream, or natural lake. Although an adjoining property owner to a river, stream, or natural lake does not have ownership rights of the water, in most states, the owner has a right to the beneficial use of the water. The right to the beneficial use of the water is governed by one of two areas of water law known as riparian rights and appropriation. **Riparian rights,** derived from the Latin word *ripa,* for river, are based on an ancient doctrine that all owners of riparian lands must share equally in the use of the water for domestic purposes. Riparian lands are those that border a stream, river, or natural lake. Under the riparian rights doctrine, an owner of riparian land has the right to use the water equally with other owners of riparian lands. This equal ownership means that a riparian owner does not have a right to interfere with the natural flow of the water in the river, stream, or lake. For example, an owner of riparian land could not create a dam across the river so that the water would cease to flow to other owners of riparian land. In addition, the riparian owner would not be able to channel the water from the river into a reservoir located on his or her property. Both the dam and the reservoir would alter the natural flow of the water and violate other owners' riparian rights to beneficial use of the water.

Appropriation, sometimes referred to as prior appropriation, is found in western states where water is scarce. This doctrine was developed in the nineteenth century to regulate the conflicts of water usage between settlers of the western states, predominantly miners, farmers, and ranchers. Under the appropriation or prior appropriation water rights doctrine, the right to use the water is given to the landowner who uses the water first. The date of appropriation determines the user's priority to use water, with the earliest user having the superior right. If the water is insufficient to meet all needs, those earlier in time or first in time obtain all the allotted water and those who appropriate later receive only some or none of the water. The first in time, or first-right appropriation, concept contrasts sharply with the riparian tradition of prorating the entitlement to water among all users during times of scarcity.

Under the appropriation theory of water rights, it is required that a landowner show valid appropriation. The elements of valid appropriation are (a) intent to apply water to a beneficial use, (b) an actual diversion of water from a natural source, and (c) application of the water to a beneficial use within a reasonable time.

A beneficial use that will support an appropriation must have a specific stated purpose. In general, water may be appropriated for any use the state deems beneficial.

All states that follow the appropriation theory of water rights usage have established administrative agencies to issue water permits in connection with water usage. The chief purpose of the administrative procedures is to provide an orderly method for appropriating water and regulating established water rights. Water rights under the appropriation theory are transferable from one property owner to another. It is possible to transfer water rights without a transfer of land and to transfer land without a transfer of water rights. Each state has its own regulatory system and requirements for the transfer of water rights.[1]

What are fixtures? It usually is easy to tell if an item is personal property or real property, but in some situations the determination may be difficult. Take, for example, a stove and a refrigerator that are located in the kitchen of a house. Are these items real property or personal property? The answer to this question is governed by the law of fixtures.

A **fixture** is an article of personal property, such as an air-conditioning unit or a dishwasher, that has been installed in or attached to land or a building and, on attachment, is regarded by the law as part of the real property. A number of judicial tests exist to determine if an article is a fixture. For example, some courts examine the manner in which the article is attached to the real property. The more permanent the attachment, the more likely the court will determine that the item is a fixture. Other courts examine the character of the article and its adaptation to the real property. If it is clear that the item has been specifically constructed or fitted with a view to its location and use in a particular building, such as a jacuzzi on the deck of a house, then the item is more likely to be a fixture. Other courts pay strict attention to the intention of

riparian rights
Rights of the owners of lands adjoining streams, rivers, and lakes relating to the water and its use.

appropriation
In regard to water law, doctrine stating that water belongs to the person who first makes beneficial use of it.

fixture
Item of personal property that becomes real property because of its attachment to the land or a building.

---

[1]David H. Getches, *Water Law in a Nutshell,* 2nd Ed., St. Paul: West Publishing Company, 1990.

the parties. If it is clear from the circumstances surrounding the attachment of the item to the building that the parties intended for it to be a fixture and part of the real property, this will be given weight by the court. In addition, if the parties have indicated in writing an intention that an item shall be a fixture or shall not be a fixture, a court will enforce this written intention.

The classification of an item as a fixture is important because if the item is a fixture, it is part of the real property and will be transferred with the real property unless there clearly is an intent for it not to be transferred. This means that if a person buys a building, he or she also will obtain all the fixtures within the building. Classification also is important in a loan transaction because if a person pledges real property as security for a debt, not only will the real property be pledged, but also any items deemed to be fixtures located on the real property.

Failure to identify an item as a fixture may send a person to jail, as shown by the case of *Ex Parte Brown*.

Ownership of Real Property

The legal profession, including legal assistants, spends time and clients' money worrying about the ownership of real property. The basic principle that only the owner of real property can sell or pledge it as security for a debt means that on any typical sale or loan transaction, title examinations and other efforts are made by legal counsel for the purchaser or lender to determine the extent of the seller's or borrower's ownership of the real property.

The chief legal rights accorded an owner of real property are possession, use, and power of disposition. An owner of real property has the right to possess the property and the term "possession" refers to control or mastery over the land. **Possession** is occupation of the land evidenced by visible acts such as an enclosure, cultivation, the construction of improvements, and the occupancy of existing improvements. Possession gives the property owner the right to exclude others from the land. Occupancy of land by someone without the permission of the owner is a trespass. The owner may evict the trespasser from the land and/or sue the trespasser for money damages.

A landowner has the right to use the land for profit or pleasure. Absolute freedom to use land has never existed, and the modern owner is faced with a number of limitations on the use of land arising from public demands of health, safety, and public welfare as well as the rights of neighbors to the safety and enjoyment of their property. The law, however, does favor the free use of land, and doubts will be resolved in favor of the owner.

An owner of property has the right to dispose of that ownership. The power of disposition may take place at the owner's death by inheritance or will, or it may take place during the owner's lifetime by contract, deed, or lease. The law favors the free right to transfer ownership, and any restraint on this right will not be upheld unless the restraint supports some important public purpose or private right.

Private property rights are subject to the right of sovereignty exercised by federal, state, and local governments. Therefore, private ownership is subject to the powers to tax; to regulate the use of private property in the interest of public safety, health, and the general welfare; and to take private property for public use. A government's power to regulate, tax, and take private property for public use is discussed in Chapter 3.

METHODS OF ACQUIRING OWNERSHIP TO REAL PROPERTY

The main methods of acquiring ownership to real property are inheritance, devise, gift, sale, and adverse possession.

Inheritance and Devise

The first two methods, inheritance and devise, are ownership transfers that take place on the death of the previous owner. **Inheritance,** or descent, as it also is known, is the passage of title and ownership of real property from one who dies intestate (without a will) to people whom the law designates, because of blood or marriage, as the owner's heirs. Each state has its own descent statute, and the statutes vary slightly from state to state. The law of the state in which the property is located will decide who is to inherit.

---

possession
Occupation of land evidenced by visible acts such as an enclosure, cultivation, the construction of improvements, or the occupancy of existing improvements.

inheritance
Ability to acquire ownership to real property because of one's kinship to a deceased property owner.

CASE

WRIGHT, Presiding Judge.

Ruby and Louis Brown were divorced by decree of the Lauderdale County Circuit Court in November 1983. As part of this decree, the husband was awarded the family home, "including all fixtures and realty appurtenant thereto." The wife was awarded all furniture in the home with the exception of the master bedroom suite, the dining room furniture, kitchen appliances and one-half of all silver, silverware and other kitchenware, which was awarded to the husband. The wife was to remove all of the furniture and personal property awarded to her prior to relinquishing possession of the home. In February 1984, the husband filed a petition with the circuit court asking that the wife be found to be in contempt for violating the property settlement provisions of the divorce decree. In May 1985, the court issued an order which specifically stated:

"The evidence shows that under the decree of divorce the Plaintiff [husband] was awarded certain items of personal property which the Defendant [wife] removed from the Plaintiff's home. A microwave of the value of $400.00 and a refrigerator of the value of $500.00. Further, the Plaintiff was awarded the family home and there was attached thereto a bookcase and china cabinets of the value of $2,000.00 which the Defendant removed from the home. Therefore, the Plaintiff was deprived of real and personal property of the value of $2,900.00 and the Defendant's action in removing these items is [a] violation of the decree and a contempt of the Court."

For her contempt, the court ordered the wife to serve ten days in the county jail, allowing, however, that she could purge herself of the contempt by making a payment of $2,900 to the Clerk of the Circuit Court of Lauderdale County. Thereafter, the wife filed this petition for certiorari asking that we review this finding of contempt.

* * *

We are perplexed by the wife's first argument for reversal. She admits that she acted in contempt of the court's order when she removed the microwave and refrigerator from the home, but argues that the bookcase and china cabinets were not fixtures appurtenant to the home and thus could be removed by her as furniture. She does not argue that the ten-day jail sentence was excessive, *see Williams v. Stumpe*, 439 So.2d 1297 (Ala.Civ.App.1983), nor that she is unable to pay the $2,900 necessary to purge herself of this contempt, *see Zeigler v. Butler*, 410 So.2d 93 (Ala.Civ.App.1982). Instead, the real issue she wishes this "court to address is whether the $2,900 is an accurate" assessment of the damage caused the husband by her contempt.

[1] It is settled that a trial court can assess damages in favor of an aggrieved party in civil contempt proceedings.

Lightsey v. Kensington Mortgage & Finance Corp., 294 Ala. 281, 315 So.2d 431 (1975); *Smith v. Smith*, 365 So.2d 88 (Ala.Civ.App.1978). It is also settled that "a party who has been found in contempt and who has been assessed compensatory damages should seek review of the finding of contempt by means of extraordinary writ (certiorari or habeas corpus), and should seek review of the question of the assessed amount of compensatory damages by appeal." *Smith, supra*. The wife has not appealed the $2,900 award. However, out of deference to the parties, we note that even if the wife had not admitted her contempt, there is ample evidence in the record to support the trial judge's determination that the bookcase and china cabinets were fixtures appurtenant to the house.

"A 'fixture' is an article that was once a chattel, but which, by being physically annexed or affixed to realty, has become assessory to it and 'part and parcel of it.' " *Milford v. Tennessee River Pulp and Paper Company*, 355 So.2d 687 (Ala.1978). Whether an article is a fixture is a determination that must be made on the particular circumstances of each case. *Id.* The supreme court has articulated the criteria to be used in making this determination as follows:

"(1) Actual annexation to the realty or to something appurtenant thereto; (2) Appropriateness to the use or purposes of that part of the realty with which it is connected; (3) The intention of the party making the annexation of making permanent attachment to the freehold. This intention of the party making the annexation is inferred; (a) From the nature of the articles annexed; (b) The relation of the party making the annexation; (c) The structure and mode of annexation; (d) The purposes and uses for which the annexation has been made."

Id. (quoting *Langston v. State*, 96 Ala. 44, 11 So. 334 (1891)).

In her own testimony, the wife revealed that the articles had all been custom-built for the express purpose of being used with the family house, not just to be used in any house. All of the articles were anchored to the walls, and Under our limited scope of review, we cannot say that this testimony does not support a finding that the articles were intended to be fixtures, "part and parcel" of the house.

* * *

We are of the opinion that the trial court has not committed error in finding that the wife acted in contempt of the divorce decree. Further, her sentence of ten days in jail, with the opportunity to purge her contempt by paying to the clerk $2,900, is not unconstitutional. The decision of the trial court is affirmed.

AFFIRMED.

BRADLEY and HOLMES, JJ., concur.

EXHIBIT 1–1
Schedule of Kinship Relationship to a Decedent

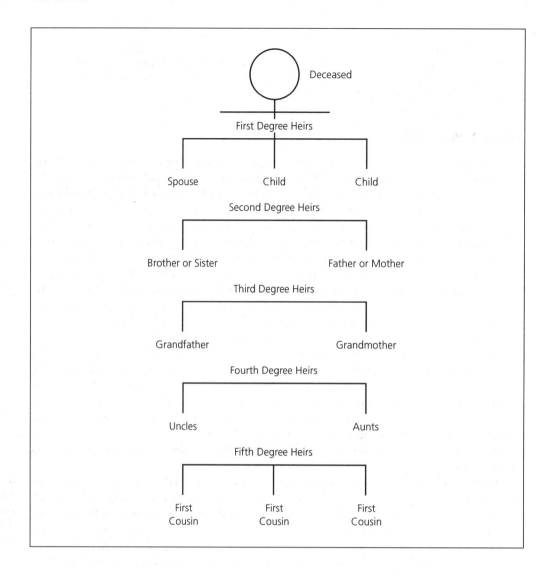

An example of a schedule of kinship relationship to a decedent based on typical descent statute is shown in Exhibit 1–1. The closest group of heirs to the deceased property owner will inherit all the property. For example, in Exhibit 1–1, if the deceased property owner is survived by a spouse and children, the spouse and children will inherit all the property. If the deceased property owner is not survived by a spouse or children, the deceased property owner's surviving parents and siblings, if any, will inherit the property.

The acquisition of ownership by **devise** is the passage of title of real property from one who dies *with* a will. A **will** is a legal document prepared during the property owner's lifetime that indicates where and how the owner's property is to be disposed of at the owner's death. The **conveyance** of real property in a will is referred to as a devise. The will must comply with the state law governing wills. Again, the state law where the real property is located will control.

Gift

Ownership to real property also can be obtained by a gift. Once the gift is complete—and with real property this would be on the proper execution and delivery of a deed to the property—the gift is irrevocable. The promise to make a gift, however, usually is revocable. An exception to the revocation of gifts rule is in the event that the recipient of the gift has detrimentally relied on the belief that the gift would be made. The injured party may recover costs for the detrimental reliance. For example, you purchase insurance for a home based on someone's promise to give you that home. If the gift is not made, you would be able to recover the costs of the insurance.

devise
Conveyance of real property by means of a last will and testament.

will
Legal document by which a person disposes of his or her property. A will takes effect on the death of the property owner.

conveyance
Act of transferring ownership from one person to another.

Contract and Sale

Property ownership can be obtained by buying the property. This is the transaction that involves most real estate legal assistants and attorneys. A complete discussion of contracts and the sale of property is found in Chapter 4.

Adverse Possession

Possession of real property is given substantial legal protection. Even a party in unlawful possession of the real property has the right to exclude anyone else from possession except for the true owner. Possession, in and of itself, also engenders, through time, the inference that the possession began lawfully. The longer the continued possession, the stronger this inference. If possession is maintained long enough, it is possible that the person in possession becomes the owner through a process known as **adverse possession.** Adverse possession operates as a statute of limitations in the sense that it precludes all others from contesting the title of the possessor.

adverse possession
Method of acquiring ownership to real property by possession for a statutory time period.

The rules on adverse possession vary from state to state. Typically, the possessor must possess the property for a period of time ranging from seven to twenty years. The possession also must be adverse, which means without the consent or permission of the true owner. In some states it is necessary that an adverse possessor actually have knowledge that he is in adverse possession of the property. An example of how this works follows.

Assume that property owners Andy and Maria are neighbors, and that Andy has built a fence on what Andy believes to be the property line, but in fact the fence encroaches one foot onto Maria's property. Andy is unaware of this encroachment. Andy maintains the fence for twenty years. In a state that requires Andy to have knowledge that he is an adverse possessor, Andy, even though he has satisfied the statute of limitations for adverse possession, would not become the owner of this additional one foot of Maria's property.

In addition to the possession being adverse, it must be public, continuous, peaceful, exclusive, and uninterrupted.

Tacking of possession is permitted if there is some contractual or blood relationship between the two adverse possessors. Tacking is the adding of possession periods by different adverse possessors. For example, adverse possessor Bill enters into possession of the property, keeps it for seven years, and then sells it to adverse possessor Mary. Adverse possessor Mary, in a state that requires twenty years of adverse possession, could tack or add onto adverse possessor Bill's period of possession because of the contractual relationship between the two. Then Mary would have to stay in possession only thirteen years to obtain ownership.

tacking
Combinations of possession periods by different adverse possessors.

The meaning of possession varies from state to state. Possession, in a strict sense, means occupancy and use of the property. Some states, however, require that the adverse possessor pay taxes on the real property during the period of possession.

Even though ownership to real property can be obtained through adverse possession, there is not any written documentation or proof of this ownership. If the adverse possessor attempts to sell the real property, chances are he or she will have a difficult time establishing title. One means of establishing ownership through adverse possession is by bringing what is known as a "quiet title" action. In a quiet title action the adverse possessor sues the entire world and challenges anyone to step forward and object to the adverse possessor's claim of ownership. In the suit the adverse possessor would then bring proof through affidavits or witnesses as to the adverse possessor's necessary period of possession and the nature of that possession. If the court finds that the adverse possessor is now the owner, it will issue a judgment adjudicating the adverse possessor's ownership. This judgment could then be used to establish ownership for purposes of future sales.

HISTORY OF AMERICAN REAL PROPERTY LAW _____

The early settlers who came to America from Europe brought with them the laws of their native land, including the laws concerning land ownership. Except for Louisiana, Texas, and portions of the Southwest, where the civil laws of France and Spain have substantial influence, most modern real property law is the product of English feudal law.

Feudalism grew out of the chaos of the Dark Ages. Because of the collapse of all central law and order, people banded together for security and stability, with usually the strongest member of the group taking command. The stronger members became known as lords, and the weaker members became known as tenants or vassals of the lord. For the lord to keep the allegiance of the vassals, it became necessary to compensate them for their services. Because almost all the wealth of the lords at that time was in the form of land, the land was parceled out to the vassals for services. Tenures or rights to possession were created. The early tenures were of four main types: (1) *knight tenure,* land given in return for pledged armed services; (2) *serjeantry tenure,* land given in return for performance of ceremonial services for the lord (later this evolved into ordinary domestic services such as cook and butler); (3) *frankalmoin tenure,* land given for religious purposes to priests and other religious bodies; and (4) *socage tenure,* land given to farmers. These early field tenures evolved into the concept of estates (derived from the latin word *status*), which became the primary basis of classification of interests in land. The word "estate" is still used today to express the degree, quantity, nature, duration, or extent of an owner's interest in real property.

Modern-Day Estates in Real Property

There are six types of modern-day estates in real property: (1) fee simple or fee simple absolute, (2) fee simple determinable, (3) fee simple on condition subsequent, (4) life estate, (5) estate for years, and (6) estate at will.

Fee Simple or Fee Simple Absolute

fee simple absolute
Estate of real property with infinite duration and no restrictions on use.

Fee simple or **fee simple absolute** is the highest and best kind of estate an owner can have. It is one in which the owner is entitled to the entire estate, with unconditional powers of disposition during the owner's lifetime and the power to transfer the property to heirs and legal representatives on the owner's death. Fee simple or fee simple absolute is maximum legal ownership and of a potential infinite duration and unrestricted inheritability. In most states no special language is needed to create a fee simple absolute. The presumption is that a fee simple estate is created at every conveyance unless a lesser estate is mentioned and limited in the conveyance. Most homes and commercial properties are owned in fee simple.

Fee Simple Determinable

fee simple determinable
Estate of real property with potential infinite duration. The ownership of a fee simple determinable is subject to a condition, the breach of which can result in termination of the estate. A fee simple determinable automatically expires on the nonoccurrence or occurrence of a condition.

A **fee simple determinable** is an ownership in real property limited to expire automatically on the happening or nonhappening of an event that is stated in the deed of conveyance or the will creating the estate. For example, Aaron conveys to Bill "to have and to hold to Bill so long as the land is used for residential purposes. When the land is no longer used for residential purposes, it shall revert to Aaron." This language in a deed or will creates a fee simple determinable. The estate granted is a fee, and like the fee simple absolute, it can be inherited and may last forever so long as the condition is not broken. Yet it is a determinable fee because there is a condition. The estate will automatically expire on the nonoccurrence or occurrence of the event—for example, the use of the land for nonresidential purposes. The estate conveyed to Bill will automatically end if and when the land is used for nonresidential purposes, and Aaron will again own the estate in fee simple absolute. During the existence of Bill's ownership of the fee simple determinable, Aaron retains a future interest in the land called a possibility or right of reverter. Aaron's possibility of reverter can be passed on to Aaron's heirs at Aaron's death. Aaron's possibility of reverter also may be transferred to a third party at the time of the conveyance to Bill. For example, Aaron to Bill to "have and to hold so long as the land is used for residential purposes, then to Carol. If the land is not used for residential purposes, it will go to Carol, Aaron's possibility of reverter having been transferred to Carol."

Fee Simple on Condition Subsequent

fee simple on condition subsequent
Estate of real property with a potential infinite duration. The ownership of a fee simple on condition subsequent is subject to a condition, the breach of which can result in termination of the estate. A fee simple on condition subsequent continues in existence until an action is brought to recover the property.

A **fee simple on condition subsequent** exists when a fee simple is subject to a power in the grantor (person who conveyed the fee) to recover the conveyed estate on the happening of a specified event. "Aaron transfers to Bill on the express condition that the land shall not be used for nonresidential purposes, and if it is, Aaron shall have the right to reenter and possess the land." Bill has a fee simple on condition subsequent, and Aaron has the right of entry or power of termination. On the happening of the stated event, the granted estate will continue in existence until Aaron effectively exercises the option to terminate by making entry or bringing an action to recover the property. A breach of the condition does not cause an automatic termination of the fee simple on condition subsequent estate. The basic difference, therefore, between the fee simple determinable and the fee simple on condition subsequent is that the former automatically expires on violation of the specified condition contained in the instrument creating the estate, whereas the latter continues until it is terminated by the exercise of the grantor's power to terminate. Aaron's right to reenter can be transferred to a third party in the same manner as the possibility of reverter in a fee simple determinable.

Creation of a fee simple determinable or fee simple on condition subsequent gives a property owner the means of controlling the use of the property after the transfer or after the property owner's death. This element of control may be important to the property owner for a number of reasons. For example, a farmer owns a farm that has been in the family for generations. The farmer has three children. Two of the children have left the farm and live in the city. The third child has expressed an interest in staying on the farm and taking it over on the farmer's retirement or death. The farmer may be able to satisfy his objectives by transferring the family farm to the child who desires to continue farming in fee simple on condition subsequent or fee simple determinable, on the condition that the land always be used as a farm.

Another example of when a conditional fee is used is in transfers of property to a charity. Often a property owner is willing to transfer valuable land to a charity provided that it is used for specific charitable purposes. For example, a property owner is willing to convey land to her college provided that the land be used to expand the college's law school. The property owner could accomplish this by transferring a conditional fee to the college on the condition that the land be used for the expansion of the law school. The property owner may want to give the possibility of reverter or right of reentry to the property owner's family.

Fee simple determinable or fee simple on condition subsequent ownership, owing to the threat that ownership will terminate in the event the condition is breached, makes this form of ownership difficult to sell. In addition, most lending institutions who lend money on the security of real property will not make a loan or receive conditional fee title as security for a loan. These reasons have made the fee simple determinable and fee simple on condition subsequent somewhat uncommon forms of ownership.

Life Estate

A **life estate** has its duration measured by the life or lives of one or more persons.

An estate for life may either be for the life of the owner or the life of some other person or people ("measuring life"). Life estates may be created by deed, will, or an express agreement of the parties. For example, an elderly woman owns a duplex home. Her daughter, to provide her mother with money, wants to buy the duplex. The daughter is willing to give to the mother a life estate in the side of the duplex that the mother has been living in for the past several years. Therefore, the mother will continue living in her portion of the duplex during her lifetime, and on her death the daughter would have full fee simple title to all of the duplex.

At the time of the creation of a life estate there also is retained or created a reversion or remainder interest. For example, Aaron transfers to Bill a life estate for the life of Bill. As part of this transfer, a reversion right to Aaron is implicitly created. This means that on Bill's death, the property will revert back to Aaron. Aaron's reversion right is not contingent on Aaron's surviving Bill, and Aaron's reversion right can be transferred by Aaron during Aaron's lifetime, or it may be inherited by Aaron's heirs at his death. This reversion right also can be transferred by Aaron to a third party, and this transfer could take place at the time of the transfer of the life estate to Bill. For example, Aaron transfers to Bill a life estate for the life of Bill and then to Carol. This means that on Bill's death, the property will go to Carol. Carol has what is known as a vested remainder in fee simple. Carol's right to own the property in fee simple on Bill's death is not dependent on Carol's surviving Bill. If Carol dies before Bill, Carol's vested remainder in fee simple will pass to Carol's heirs or the devisees under her will. Carol's heirs or the devisees under the will will receive the property on Bill's death. The difference between a reversion and a remainder is illustrated in the following life estate, timeline diagram (Exhibit 1–2)

life estate
Estate of real property, the duration of which is measured by the life or lives of one or more persons.

EXHIBIT 1–2
Difference between a Reversion and a Remainder

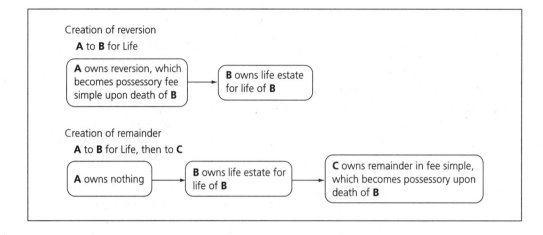

The owner of a life estate is entitled to the full use and enjoyment of the real property so long as the owner exercises ordinary care and prudence for the preservation and protection of the real property and commits no acts intending to cause permanent injury to the person entitled to own the real property after the termination of the life estate. If the life estate owner of the real property does not take care of the real property, the owner will be deemed to commit **waste** and the life estate will terminate, even though the measuring life is still alive. Failure to make needed repairs or improvements, the cutting of timber for sale, or the mining of minerals have all been held to be acts of waste. Because forfeiture of ownership is the penalty for waste, most courts are reluctant to find waste, and the decisions vary from state to state as to what acts of a life estate owner constitute waste.

As a general rule, the life estate owner is entitled to all income generated from the real property, and is entitled to possession of the real property during the ownership of the life estate. Life estates are transferable, although the life estate owner can transfer only what he or she has, which is a life estate for the measuring life. A life estate owner usually has the obligation to pay taxes on the real property, keep the real property adequately insured, and pay any debts secured by the real property. Because death terminates the life estate and death is so uncertain an event, a life estate ownership is difficult to sell or pledge as security for a loan.

Estate for Years

An **estate for years** is limited in its duration to a fixed period. For example, "Aaron to Bill for twenty years" would create an estate for years in Bill. The estate for years would continue until the period of ownership terminates. Next to the fee simple estate, the estate for years is the most common form of ownership. An estate for years may be a lease, but not all leases are estates for years. For a lease to be an estate for years, it must be clear that ownership to the real property is conveyed and not mere rights to possession.

Estate at Will

An **estate at will** is an estate with no fixed term that is created by the express or implied agreements of the parties. An estate at will can be terminated at any time by either party; however, under modern law, there may be some notice requirement (thirty- or sixty-day notice) before termination. An estate at will may be created by implication. For example, Aaron transfers to Bill an estate for years for twenty years. At the expiration of the twenty years, Bill remains in possession of the real property and continues to pay rental to Aaron, which Aaron accepts. Once the estate for years has expired (i.e., the twenty years), Bill is not in possession as an owner of an estate for years, so the law usually will imply that Bill now has an estate at will, that is, Bill is in possession with the consent of Aaron. Aaron can terminate Bill's possession and ownership rights immediately or on any statutory notice if required in the state where the real property is located.

---

waste
Action or nonaction that causes a loss of value to real property.

estate for years
Estate of real property, the duration of which is for a definite period.

estate at will
Estate of real property, the duration of which is for an indefinite period. An estate at will can be terminated at the will of the parties.

RESEARCH MATERIALS FOR REAL PROPERTY LAW

The law of real property is generally governed by state law, and it is the law of the state in which the real property is located that controls. State law is generally divided into two classifications: statutes and judicial decisions. Statutes are laws passed by the state's elected legislature. These statutes are usually codified into a code. Most codes are available in law libraries managed by law firms, law schools, courthouses, and even public libraries.

Decisions rendered by a state court such as a court of appeals or supreme court are published and bound together in the form of a reporter for each state. Reporters are generally found in the same law libraries as statutes.

Decisions of trial courts are generally not recorded or published. These decisions are generally not considered precedent for future decisions but can be helpful in understanding a particular trial court's interpretation of the law. Trial court decisions are unofficial and can only be obtained by going and reviewing the courthouse files regarding the case in which the decision was issued.

Most state bar associations or local publishers publish practice books on areas of real property law. Since most states require attorneys to continue education in order to maintain a license to practice law, these continuing education programs often publish very valuable materials concerning both the law and practical aspects of real estate transactions. Many of these continuing education program books can be purchased through the sponsors of the programs, and many law firms purchase and keep continuing education books within their libraries.

Treatises, or short comprehensive summaries on areas of law, are also published by many local state law publishers. These treatises may be written by a law professor or practicing attorney in the area in which the treatise is focused. Most law libraries will maintain the major treatises published within the state.

Access to the state statutes, judicial decisions, treatises, and other source information on real property law can be obtained through computerized database programs. These programs, such as Westlaw, provide a user (for a fee) the ability to access a wide range of legal source materials via the computer.

 E T H I C S : Introduction

Ethics, the service to others performed in a moral and honest manner, is the cornerstone of a professional practice. It is essential that the system for establishing and dispensing justice be developed and maintained in such a way that the public shall have absolute confidence in the integrity and impartiality of its administration. Such a system cannot exist unless the conduct and motives of the members of the legal profession merit the approval of all just and honest citizens. Not only is the future of this country and its justice system dependent on the ethical conduct of those who are licensed to administer justice, but the future of the legal profession depends on its members acting in an ethical manner. Lawyers are asked daily to deal with the most intimate and serious problems that affect clients. Only a profession made up of members with the highest ethical considerations can continue to deliver the service and confidence demanded by the public.

Attorneys are governed by two sets of ethical rules: the American Bar Association's Model Rules of Professional Conduct and Model Code of Professional Responsibility and the ethical codes and rules of professional responsibility promulgated by state bar associations. A violation of these rules can result in disciplinary action being brought against the errant attorney, including such drastic penalties as the loss of a license to practice law.

It is not clear that legal assistants are bound and covered by the various ethical codes and rules of professional conduct applicable to attorneys. Because legal assistants are not licensed, there is no removal of license sanction that could be imposed against a legal assistant for violation of ethical codes or rules of professional conduct. *Attorneys, however, who are responsible for and supervise the activities of the legal assistant can be sanctioned and disciplined for the actions of the legal assistant under the attorney's control and supervision.* It is in the best interest of the legal profession that legal assistants adhere to the ethical codes and rules of professional responsibility applicable to attorneys.

The Internet also contains a large amount of both free and paid for information concerning real property law. The Real Property, Probate, and Trust Law Section of the American Bar Association maintains free information on a Web site at http://www.abanet.org/rppt/home.html and a Web site known as Dirt, http://cctr.umkc.edu/dept/dirt/index.html, provides worthwhile information for a fee.

ROLE OF LEGAL ASSISTANT IN REAL ESTATE LEGAL PRACTICE

Legal assistants participate in all aspects of a real estate practice. The skills used by legal assistants in a real estate practice include preparation of legal documents, examination and review of real property titles, preparation of land descriptions, preparation and review of leases, and fact-finding investigation required to represent purchasers, sellers, and lenders in connection with real estate transactions. Real estate legal assistants are employed in private law firms, corporate legal departments, and government agencies. Real estate is a "bread-and-butter" practice of many law firms, from sole practitioners to the largest national firms. Many corporations have as a major part of their business an involvement with real estate. These corporations include not only development and construction corporations, but also corporations that involve retail operations, such as Wal-Mart, Sears, and Gap. Banks and life insurance companies are major lenders of money for real estate projects, and many have in-house legal departments that supervise the company's real estate lending activities. Gas, telephone, and electric utility companies have corporate legal departments that deal with real estate. Government agencies, such as public housing authorities and rapid transportation authorities, are responsible for the regulation and development of real estate. Many of these law firms, corporations, banks, life insurance companies, utilities, and government agencies employ legal assistants. The opportunities for the real estate legal assistant are plentiful and diversified.

SUMMARY

Most legal assistants employed by law firms or corporations are used to assist in the transfer of ownership to real property, the development and leasing of real property, and the closing of loans secured by real property. At any sale, lease, or loan transaction it is important to determine who owns the real property in question and what estate is held by the owner. It is important in each transaction that the estate owned be sufficient to satisfy all the parties' expectations to the transaction. A fee simple absolute estate usually would be satisfactory under all circumstances. The other estates may not be satisfactory, and a legal assistant must be conscious of the limitations that each of the lesser estates impose on the ownership and use of the real property.

Under many circumstances the ownership of the real property is not vested in a single person. For example, it is common for husbands and wives to own homes together and for investment partners to collectively own commercial real property. A discussion of the legal issues involving co-ownership of real property follows in Chapter 2.

KEY TERMS

adverse possession	fee simple absolute	possession
appropriation	fee simple determinable	riparian rights
conveyance	fee simple on condition subsequent	tacking
devise	fixture	waste
estate at will	inheritance	will
estate for years	life estate	

SELF-STUDY EXAMINATION _____

(Answers provided in Appendix)

1. T or F. The law of real property in general is governed by the law of the state in which the real property is located.

2. T or F. A fixture is classified as personal property.

3. T or F. An estate for years is the highest and best kind of estate in real property an owner can own.

4. T or F. A life estate may be for the life of a person other than the owner.

5. T or F. A life estate is transferable during the lifetime of the owner.

6. T or F. A promise to make a gift is not revocable.

7. T or F. Inheritance is the transfer of ownership of real property when a person dies with a will.

8. T or F. An owner of real property usually owns all the minerals beneath the surface of the land.

9. T or F. An heir must always be a relative of the decedent.

10. T or F. An owner cannot separate ownership of the minerals from ownership of the surface of the land.

11. What are the two categories into which all property is classified?

12. What are the basic rights that go with ownership of real property?

13. What are the physical components of real property?

14. Name the various ways a person can become an owner of real property.

15. What is the concept of waste and how is it applicable to a life estate?

16. Aaron transfers to Bob a life estate in a house with the remainder to Carol, and Carol dies before Bob. On Bob's death, will the property go to Aaron, or to Carol's heirs?

17. What is required to become an owner by adverse possession?

18. What test does a court use to determine if an item is a fixture?

19. What is a "reversion" interest in real property?

20. How is an estate for years different from a fee simple absolute estate?

21. Briefly list the categories of water sources.

22. Briefly describe the riparian rights water doctrine.

23. Briefly describe the appropriation water doctrine.

24. The elements of valid appropriation are:

25. What is the difference between inheritance and devise?

Concurrent Ownership

"Two live as one
One live as two
Two live as three
Under the bam
Under the boo
Under the bamboo tree"

—Sweeney Agonistes—T. S. Eliot

OBJECTIVES

After reading this chapter you should be able to:

- Distinguish and explain the four types of concurrent ownership
- Identify the rights, duties, and liabilities of common owners
- Understand the difference between individual and community property

joint tenancy with right of survivorship
Ownership of real property by two or more persons. Joint tenants with the right of survivorship hold equal interest in the real property, and on the death of any owner, the deceased owner's interest in the real property will pass to the surviving owner.

tenancy in common
Co-ownership of real property by two or more persons. Each owner's interest in the property is capable of inheritance.

tenancy by the entirety
Ownership of real property by a husband and wife. The husband and wife are treated as a single owner, and neither the husband nor the wife can transfer the property without the other's consent.

community property law
Rule of law in states following the civil law of Spain and France, which provides that real property acquired during marriage is owned equally by the husband and wife.

Real property may be owned by a single owner or by a group of owners. When a single owner owns real property, this is known as ownership in severalty. A single owner has all the attributes of ownership, that is, the sole exclusive right to possess and use the property, the right to transfer the property, and the responsibility for all expenses and other charges in connection with the property.

Real property often is owned by more than one person. The combinations are endless: married couples own homes together, family members inherit real property together, partners join together in commercial investment. Ownership of real property by more than one person provokes some interesting questions. Can one owner sell his or her interest without the consent of the other owners? Will the debts of an owner attach to the real property as a whole, thereby affecting the interests of the other owners? How are the expenses and income of the real property divided among the owners? What happens if an owner does not pay his or her share of the expenses? Can the owners terminate the group ownership and divide the real property among themselves? These and other questions are faced daily by attorneys and legal assistants when dealing with real property that is owned by more than one person.

To decide what rights group owners and third parties who deal with these owners have in the real property, it is necessary to determine how the concurrent ownership is held.

TYPES OF CONCURRENT OWNERSHIP

Four types of concurrent ownership exist: (1) **joint tenancy with the right of survivorship,** (2) **tenancy in common,** (3) **tenancy by the entirety,** and (4) **community property.** The law of the state in which the real property is located will determine how the concurrent ownership is held. For example, owners who reside in South Carolina but own property in California will be bound by California concurrent ownership law.

The old common law term of "tenant" or "tenancy," which is synonymous with the modern use of the word "owner" or "ownership," is still used to describe some of the types of concurrent ownership.

Joint Tenancy with Right of Survivorship

A joint tenancy with the right of survivorship is recognized in most states. It can be created by a deed or a will. It usually occurs when real property is transferred to two or more persons with express language that they are to take the real property as "joint tenants with the right of survivorship," or similar language. Thus, when a joint tenancy is desired, most instruments use boilerplate: "to A and B as joint tenants with rights of survivorship, not as tenants in common."

Under a joint tenancy with right of survivorship each owner owns an equal and undivided interest in the whole of the real property. Each owner has the right to use and possess the entire real property; this right to use or possession is held in common with the other owners.

The existence of a single ownership as a unit rather than as separate interests in the individual units is the essence of joint tenancy with the right of survivorship. This emphasis on the estate as a unit led to the common law requirements that four items—interest, title, time, and possession—be present for the creation of a joint tenancy with the right of survivorship. In other words, each owner's interest must constitute an identical interest (e.g., fee simple or life estate), must accrue by the same conveyance (deed or will), must commence at the same time, and must be held in the same undivided possession. If any of the four items or "unities" is lacking in a conveyance, the estate is not a joint tenancy with right of survivorship, but is instead a tenancy in common.

The outstanding feature of the joint tenancy with right of survivorship is the right of survivorship. The right of survivorship provides that if one of the joint owners dies, the real property is passed on to the surviving joint owners. This process will continue until the sole survivor of the joint owners owns all the real property. For example, Aaron, Bob, and Carlos are joint tenants with right of survivorship. Aaron dies and wills his property to Donna. Donna will actually receive nothing. Bob and Carlos will be joint owners with the right of survivorship, each owning one-half interest in the real property. Later Bob dies and wills his property to Elena. Again, Elena will receive nothing. At this point Carlos will be the sole owner of the property. This survivorship feature is illustrated in Exhibit 2–1.

A severance of the joint tenancy means that the survivorship feature no longer takes effect. A joint tenancy with right of survivorship can easily be severed in most states. The sale of a joint tenant's interest in the real property will create a severance of the joint tenancy. In many states a contract to sell or even the granting of a mortgage on the real property will sever the joint tenancy. An example of how this severance might work is as follows: Aaron, Bob, and Carlos

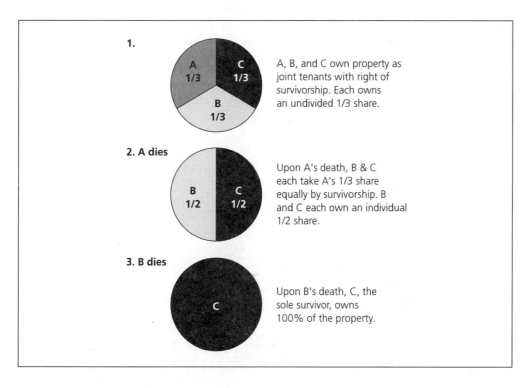

EXHIBIT 2–1
Right of Survivorship

1.

A, B, and C own property as joint tenants with right of survivorship. Each owns an undivided 1/3 share.

2. A dies

Upon A's death, B & C each take A's 1/3 share equally by survivorship. B and C each own an individual 1/2 share.

3. B dies

Upon B's death, C, the sole survivor, owns 100% of the property.

are joint tenants with the right of survivorship. Aaron, during the lifetime of Aaron, Bob, and Carlos, conveys an undivided one-third interest to Donna. This conveyance will sever the joint tenancy as to the interest being conveyed to Donna, and Donna will be a tenant in common with Bob and Carlos, who are still joint tenants with the right of survivorship. When Donna dies, Donna's interest will pass by will or by inheritance to Donna's heirs. When Bob dies, Bob's interest will pass to Carlos. At such time Donna (if living) and Carlos would become tenants in common. Donna would own one-third and Carlos, two-thirds.

Under a joint tenancy with right of survivorship each owner owns an equal and undivided interest in the whole of the real property. Each owner has the right to use and possess the entire real property; this right to use or possession is held in common with the other owners.

For example, Aaron and Bob own a twenty-acre farm as joint tenants with the right of survivorship. Aaron and Bob would each own an undivided 50 percent interest in the farm. Assume that a third party, Carlos, would want to buy five acres of the farm. Neither Aaron nor Bob could sell to Carlos the five acres, since each of them individually owns only an undivided 50 percent of the five acres. Carlos, therefore, would have to purchase the five acres from both Aaron and Bob.

Tenancy in Common

Tenancy in common is a form of co-ownership in which two or more persons are each entitled to possession of the same real property. A tenancy in common may be created voluntarily by grant, lease, devise, or bequest, or involuntarily by descent to heirs. Title does not have to arise at the same time or by the same instrument. Unlike a joint tenancy with right of survivorship, there is no right to survivorship in a tenancy in common. Each common owner's interest in the real property will pass by will or by inheritance on the common owner's death. In addition, under a tenancy in common, the owners may hold unequal shares, if so provided in the conveyance. For example, Aaron's deed conveys real property to Bob (an undivided one-quarter interest) and to Carlos (an undivided three-quarters interest). Most states prefer a tenancy in common over a joint tenancy with right of survivorship. This means that if real property is conveyed to two or more persons and the deed or will does not indicate how the ownership is to be held, the ownership will be deemed a tenancy in common.

Rights, Duties, and Liabilities of the Common Owners

Each common owner, whether it be a joint tenancy with right of survivorship or a tenancy in common, has a right to enter on the common real property and take possession of the whole property, subject only to the equal rights of the other common owners to do the same thing. Subject to the rights of the other common owners, a common owner of real property may use and enjoy the property as though he were the sole owner. A common owner may occupy and utilize every portion of the real property at all times and in all circumstances. The right to use and possess, however, is not exclusive, and each of the common owners has the same right. A common owner has been held to have a right to extract minerals, drill for oil, or cut timber from the common land. Any income produced from these activities that exceeds the common owner's proportionate share is to be distributed to the other common owners. A common owner is held to a standard of reasonable care, and must take care of the real property as a prudent person would take care of his or her own property.

A common owner is entitled to his or her fractional proportionate share of any rent or income produced from the real property. For example, a common owner with a 15 percent interest in the real property would be entitled to 15 percent of the income or rent from the real property. Any common owner who has received money from a third party for the use of the common real property is a trustee of the amount collected for purposes of distribution to the other common owners for all sums over and above the common owner's share.

contribution
Right for a co-owner of real property to receive reimbursement from other co-owners for their share of expenses that are common to the real property.

In a similar manner to rents and income, a common owner is responsible for expenses, such as taxes and repairs, in proportion to his or her respective interest in the real property. Any common owner who pays more than his or her share of the common expenses is entitled to have the other common owners refund to him or her their proportionate shares of the amount paid. This right to reimbursement is known as the right of **contribution.** It is clear in most states (Alabama, Arkansas, California, Colorado, Delaware, Georgia, Idaho, Illinois, Indiana, Iowa, Kentucky, Maryland, Massachusetts, Michigan, Minnesota, Mississippi, Missouri, Nebraska, Nevada, New Hampshire, New Jersey, New York, North Carolina, Ohio, Oregon, Tennessee, Texas, Virginia, Washington, West Virginia, and Wisconsin) that payment of taxes or repairs made to preserve the property entitle a common owner to a right of contribution against the other common owners for their share of the taxes or repairs. It is not clear whether a co-owner is entitled to any contribution for the cost of an improvement if he or she has improved the real property without the consent of the other common owners. Some states (Illinois, Indiana, Kentucky, Michigan, Missouri, Texas, Virginia, and West Virginia) permit a common owner who improves real property in good faith to recover by contribution from the other common owners their share of the lesser of (a) the cost of the improvement or (b) the increase in value to the common property by the improvement. For example, a common owner builds a garage onto a home that is held in equal shares by three common owners. The cost of the garage is $15,000, but the garage increases the value of the property only by $9,000. Therefore, the improving common owner can recover only $3,000 from each of the other common owners, since the increase in value is less than the cost of the improvement.

Repairs usually are defined as expenditures for the purposes of keeping property in ordinary and efficient operating condition. Repairs do not add to the value of the property or appreciably prolong the property's life. Improvements, on the other hand, are defined as replacements, alterations, or additions to the property that prolong the life of the property, increase its value, or make it adaptable to a different use.

A common owner may enforce his or her right of contribution against other common owners by way of a lien on the other common owners' interests in the real property. This lien, if not voluntarily paid, can be enforced by a sale of the real property.

As to each common owner's undivided interest in the real property, he or she has a free right without the consent of the other common owners to sell, lease, or mortgage his or her undivided real property interest. A common owner, however, cannot convey a greater interest than he or she owns. Any deed executed by a common owner will be treated as conveying only his or her undivided interest in the real property, even though the deed may, on its face, purport to convey the entire real property. A single common owner does not have the power to rent the common property, grant an easement across the property, sell the property, or mortgage the property without the consent of the other common owners. Common owners usually are not considered agents for one another, and one common owner cannot bind the other common owners to any agreement regarding the common property. The debts of a single common owner will bind his or her interest in the property but will not affect the common property. For example, a property is owned in common by Aaron, Bob, and Carol in equal shares. Aaron has substantial debts and judgments attached against him. Aaron's judgments will attach only to his undivided one-third interest in the property and will in no manner affect or attach to Bob's and Carol's interest in the common property. Common owners are, however, 100 percent responsible for injuries to a third person by reason of a dangerous condition on the common property.

Partition

The common owners may divide the common property into separate ownerships. This process is called **partition.** The partition may be by voluntary agreement of the common owners or by court action. The parties can voluntarily agree to a partition by executing an agreement allocating separate tracts to each owner or by exchanging deeds executed by all the common owners. Any division by agreement or deed should be accompanied by a survey or plat showing the new agreed-on boundaries. No new consideration is necessary to support a written division.

If the common owners cannot agree on a voluntary division, the law in most states provides the judicial machinery for partitioning real property between common owners or selling it and dividing the proceeds. A suit to partition commonly owned real property can be brought by any owner of an undivided interest in the real property. The defendants to the petition are each of the other people who own an interest in the real property. Holders of any mortgages or other debt on the real property usually are joined in the partition. Notice of the partition normally is given personally to each owner.

partition
Method by which co-owners of real property can divide the common property into separate ownerships. Partition may be by voluntary agreement of the co-owners or by court action.

The court usually divides the real property into parcels with a market value equivalent to each owner's undivided interest in the real property. For example, as tenants in common, Aaron owns 25 percent, Bob 25 percent, and Carol 50 percent. The court, on partition, will divide the property into parcels, of which Aaron's parcel will be equivalent to 25 percent of the value of all parcels, Bob's parcel will be equivalent to 25 percent of the value of all parcels, and Carol's parcel will be equivalent to 50 percent of the value of all parcels. The court usually has the authority to hire surveyors to describe the parcels and appraisers to establish values of each parcel. If the common owners do not want the real property divided or the real property is not capable of division, such as a single-family home, then the court will order the real property sold and the proceeds divided according to each owner's undivided interest in the real property.

Tenancy by the Entirety

A tenancy by the entirety is an estate held by husband and wife as a unit. Tenancy by the entirety is based on an old English common law view that a husband and wife are one person for the purpose of owning property. The married couple were treated as a single person, and the couple, both husband and wife, owned the property as a single unit. In this situation neither the husband nor wife, so long as they were married, had an interest in the real property that could be sold, leased, or mortgaged. For example, the individual debt of a husband would not attach to the real property owned by the husband and wife as tenants by the entirety. Neither spouse could dispose of any interest in the tenancy by the entirety, and both spouses had to join in any sale, lease, or mortgage of the real property.

Several states recognize tenancy by the entirety (Arkansas, Delaware, Illinois, Indiana, Kentucky, Maine, Maryland, New Hampshire, New Jersey, New York, North Carolina, Oregon, Pennsylvania, Tennessee, Vermont, Virginia, and Wisconsin). In a state that recognizes tenancy by the entirety a conveyance to husband and wife automatically creates a tenancy by the entirety, unless the deed or will provides otherwise. A divorce will convert a tenancy by the entirety to a tenancy in common, with each party owning a half interest in the real property.

A tenancy by the entirety contains a right of survivorship. On the death of one spouse the surviving spouse owns the real property as a whole. Owners by the entirety have no individual interest that they can convey so as to break the unities of title and defeat survivorship. Thus, neither spouse can in any manner affect the right of survivorship with the other during their joint lives. For example, a husband and wife own a piece of property as tenancy by the entirety. The husband dies and wills all his property to his daughter by a first marriage. The daughter will not take an interest in the tenancy by the entirety property, since the wife will, by the survival feature, own the entire interest in the real property.

Community Property

Tenancy by the entirety, joint tenancy with the right of survivorship, and tenancy in common are all English common law concepts. The rules of community property, however, are borrowed from the civil laws of Spain and France, and currently are found in the states that were founded by the Spanish or French (Arizona, California, Idaho, Louisiana, Nevada, New Mexico, Texas, and Washington). The system is entirely statutory and varies from state to state. A few general propositions will give some notion of the differences between the common law and the community property forms of ownership.

The community property system creates a form of common ownership of property by the husband and wife similar to that of a partnership. During marriage all property individually or jointly acquired by the husband or wife, other than by gift, bequest, devise, or descent, is held by them as a community property. The property may consist of the earnings of both spouses, borrowings, land or buildings purchased by them, or the rents and profits received from these land and buildings.

States that follow community property law have a concept of separate property and community property. Property that is not part of the community property is termed separate property. It consists of all property owned by either spouse before marriage or acquired by one spouse during marriage by gift, inheritance, bequest, or devise. Income from separate property also is separate property in most states. Property acquired during marriage with funds derived from separate property usually will retain the separate property classification. If both community and separate funds are used, the property will be apportioned between the two spouses according to their respective contributions from each classification. For example, a husband and wife purchase a building during marriage. The husband contributes 50 percent of the purchase price from the sale of separate property. The other 50 percent is contributed through the joint earnings of husband and wife. The property will be deemed to be 50 percent separate property belonging to the husband and 50 percent community property, with the husband and wife each owning one half interest. In other words, the husband will have a 75 percent interest in the new real property and the wife, 25 percent interest.

Property that is deemed to be community property is owned equally by both husband and wife, and neither can convey the whole without the other's consent. On divorce the property typically is divided equally and is held to be owned by the husband and wife as tenants in common, or the real property is partitioned, if partition is possible.

There are presumptions of law that exist in community property states. Property acquired during marriage and owned at the dissolution of marriage is presumed to be community property. When community property and separate property become so commingled as to make it impossible to identify the separate property, a presumption will render the property community property. It is important for husbands and wives in a community property state to keep accurate records of how the property was obtained to overcome presumptions of community property.[1]

One main difference between community property and the English forms of concurrent ownership (tenancy by the entirety, joint tenants with right of survivorship, and tenancy in common) is that community property is created by operation of law and not by operation of conveyance. A conveyance in a community property state could be to an individual person. If the person is married, and the property is community property, however, an unnamed spouse will be deemed to be a one-half owner of the property. For example, Harold and Maude are married. Juan conveys community property to Harold. The deed from Juan is to Harold only. Because the property is community property, Maude will own one-half interest in the property, even though Maude is not mentioned in the deed.

Community Property and Prenuptial Agreements

Although not a romantic idea, some husbands and wives in both community property states and non-community property states may enter into agreements before marriage concerning the ownership of real property by the married couple or by the individual spouses. In community property states the spouses may enter into an agreement that will set forth in detail what property is deemed to be separate property owned by the individual spouses and what property is deemed to be community property. This type of agreement resolves disputes of property ownership at the time of divorce or on sale of the property.

Some married couples in non-community property states may enter into **prenuptial agreements** regarding the division and ownership of property in the event of a separation or divorce. It is common under these agreements for one spouse to renounce, waive, or give up any claims to property owned by the other spouse.

prenuptial agreement
Agreement entered into by a married couple that, among other things, outlines an agreement between the couple regarding the division and ownership of property in the event of separation or divorce.

Dower and Curtesy

A **dower** is an interest in real property of the husband that the law in some states gives to the widow to provide the widow with a means of support after the husband's death. A dower interest is either a life estate or a fee simple interest and some undivided fraction (usually one-third or one-quarter) of the real property that the husband owned during the marriage. The requirements for a dower interest are (a) a valid marriage, (b) the husband owned the real property during the marriage, and (c) the husband dies before the wife.

dower
Widow's interest in real property of her husband that provides a means of support after the husband's death.

---

[1] Richard H. Chused, *A Modern Approach to Property* (New York: Matthew Bender & Co., 1985), 223, 225, 316–17, 330–36. Copyright 1985 by Matthew Bender & Co., Inc. Reprinted by permission of Matthew Bender & Co. and Richard H. Chused.

Although the dower right does not become a present interest until the husband dies, it is created at the time of the marriage. It is necessary in a state that recognizes dower that all conveyances of property owned by the husband be consented to by the wife to release the dower interest in the conveyed property.

Many states provide to a husband a right similar to dower in the wife's property. This right is called **curtesy.** The requirements for a curtesy interest are (a) a valid marriage, (b) the wife owned real property during the marriage, and (c) the wife dies before the husband.

Dower and curtesy rights have been substantially altered or abolished in many states. It is necessary in dealing with dower or curtesy to check a particular state's law before proceeding.

Elective Share

Many states in which dower exists give to the widow at her husband's death the right to elect between her dower and some fee simple ownership share of property owned by her husband. Depending on the state, this fee simple ownership is either one-fourth or one-third interest in the property owned by the husband. The widow's share in some states (e.g., Alaska, Colorado, Connecticut, Georgia, Mississippi, New York, North Dakota, Oklahoma, Oregon, South Dakota, and Wyoming) may be limited to property that the husband owned at his death, which would mean that the widow would have no claim on property conveyed by the husband during his lifetime without her signature.

In other states (e.g., Florida, Indiana, Iowa, Kansas, Maine, Maryland, Minnesota, Missouri, Nebraska, Pennsylvania, and Utah) the widow receives an ownership share in lieu of dower in all property owned during the lifetime of the husband. In these states the wife's signature is necessary on any deed, mortgage, or contract of sale given by the husband.

Most states also provide for the husband a similar **elective share** in property owned by the wife.

Practice Note: Any time a transaction, such as a lease, sale, or loan, involves all the common real property, it will be necessary for each and every common owner of the property to sign all the legal documents involved. If the transaction involves property in a community property state or in a state that recognizes dower, it is necessary for both the owner of the property and the owner's spouse to sign all deeds, leases, sales, mortgages, contracts, or other legal documents involving the property. The safest approach is to treat all real property owned by a married person in a community property state as community property and to require both the husband and the wife to execute all the legal documents. A table summarizing the various types of co-ownerships and the rights of each individual co-owner under each co-ownership is set forth as Exhibit 2–2.

curtesy
Interest in real property of the wife that the law in some states gives to the surviving husband at the time of the wife's death.

elective share
Right given to a widow in many states to elect, at her husband's death, to receive either dower or some ownership (fee simple) share of her husband's real property.

EXHIBIT 2–2
Co-Ownership

FORM OF CO-OWNERSHIP	JOINT TENANCY WITH SURVIVORSHIP	TENANCY IN COMMON	TENANCY BY ENTIRETY	COMMUNITY PROPERTY
Creation	By conveyance • Deed • Will	By conveyance • Deed • Will • Inheritance	By conveyance • Deed • Will	Operation of law
Identity of owner	Two or more persons indentified in conveyance	Two or more persons identified in conveyance	Husband and wife identified in conveyance	Husband and wife by operation of law
Quantity of interest in property	Equal shares	Shares as set forth in conveyance may not be equal	Husband and wife as a unit own property, individuals own nothing	Equal shares

(continued)

EXHIBIT 2-2
Co-Ownership (continued)

Nature of interest	Undivided	Undivided	Undivided	Undivided
Responsibility for expenses of ownership (taxes, mortgages, and insurance)	Equal responsibility	Responsibility according to percentage of ownership	Equal responsibility	Equal responsibility
Right of survivorship	Yes	No	Yes	No
Right of partition	Yes in some states; no in some states	Yes	No, except in event of divorce	No, except in event of divorce
Right to sell co-owner's interest in common property	Yes	Yes	No	No
Debts of individual co-owner attach to co-owner's interest in property	Yes	Yes	No	Yes
Debts of individual co-owner attach to common property as a whole	No	No	No	No

SUMMARY

Real property may be owned by a single owner or by a group of owners. The ownership of real property by more than one owner creates a number of legal issues concerning the use, possession, and responsibility of the property among the co-owners, as well as a number of legal issues involving the sale, mortgage, or lease of the real property to a person or party outside the ownership group. A legal assistant who is working on a transaction involving real property owned by more than one owner must be able to identify what form of co-ownership exists in regard to the property and must understand how that form of co-ownership will affect the transaction.

KEY TERMS

community property law
contribution
curtesy
dower

elective share
joint tenancy with right of
   survivorship
partition

prenuptial agreement
tenancy by the entirety
tenancy in common

E T H I C S : Unauthorized Practice of Law

You are a legal assistant with a law firm that represents a bank. Your main responsibility is to assist the attorneys of the firm in the closing of real estate loans. Through these activities, you have become good friends with a number of loan officers at the bank. These loan officers often call you directly with questions or comments on the various files you are working on. One afternoon, one of these loan officers calls to inform you that she and her husband are buying a home. They intend to buy the home as joint tenants with the right of survivorship because they heard on a radio talk show that this form of ownership does away with the necessity of having a will and avoids all probate proceedings. She asks that you advise her as to whether she and her husband need a will. You believe that you know the answer to her question and can advise her of the proper way to proceed. Do you give the advice, or do you refer her to one of the attorneys in the firm? What is the ethical consideration of your choice?

The practice of law is defined in many states to include conveyancing, preparing legal documents, rendering opinions as to the validity or invalidity of titles to real or personal property, and giving legal advice. Most ethical codes of conduct prohibit a lawyer from aiding a nonlawyer in the unauthorized practice of law. Because legal assistants are not licensed to practice law, the use of a legal assistant in the areas referenced above could result in a breach of ethics on the part of the attorney. A legal assistant, on the other hand, is actively involved in many aspects of the actions referenced above, which constitute the practice of law. This apparent conflict is resolved in most states by permitting the legal assistant to be involved in these activities, provided the lawyer maintains a direct relationship with the client involved, supervises and directs the work delegated to the legal assistant, and assumes complete and ultimate responsibility for the work product produced by the legal assistant. Supervision of the legal assistant's work by the attorney must be direct and constant to avoid any charges of aiding the unauthorized practice of law. Therefore, although it may be improper in many states for a legal assistant to actually close a real estate transaction without the assistance or supervision of an attorney, it is not improper for the legal assistant to prepare the closing documents and to arrange for other aspects of the closing, provided the legal assistant's work is closely supervised by the attorney.

The legal assistant in this example should refer the loan officer to an attorney at the firm for an answer to the question regarding the will. The answer involves the giving of legal advice which, if given by the legal assistant, would constitute an unauthorized practice of law.

SELF-STUDY EXAMINATION

(Answers provided in Appendix)

1. T or F. A joint tenancy with the right of survivorship can be created by a deed or a will.

2. T or F. A survivorship feature of a joint tenancy with right of survivorship can never be terminated by the parties.

3. T or F. It is mandatory that tenants in common have equal shares.

4. T or F. An owner of a tenancy in common can sell or mortgage his or her interest in the common property without the other common owners' consent.

5. T or F. The debts of a single common owner will bind his or her interest in the property but will not affect the common property.

6. T or F. Tenants by the entirety must always be married to each other.

7. T or F. The division of common property into separate ownerships is called contribution.

8. T or F. A common owner cannot waive his or her right to partition.

9. T or F. Property owned by a spouse before marriage in a community property state is separate property.

10. T or F. Property acquired by a spouse by gift in a community property state is community property.

11. What are the four unities required for a joint tenancy with the right of survivorship?

12. How is a tenancy in common different from a joint tenancy with right of survivorship?

13. What is the difference between a tenancy by the entirety and community property?

14. What is dower?

15. What is the right of contribution, and why is it important to a co-owner of real property?

16. What are the advantages of a prenuptial agreement and a community/separate property agreement?

17. Aaron conveys by deed a parcel of real property to Juan, Jane, and Susan as joint tenants with the right of sur-

vivorship. Juan, during the lifetime of all the joint owners, transfers his interest in the property to Carol. After Juan's transfer to Carol, Jane dies and wills her interest in the property to Barbara. After Jane's death, Susan dies and wills her interest in the property to Stewart. Who are the owners of the property, and in what proportion?

18. You are reviewing a deed. The deed indicates that the ownership of property has been transferred from Ajax Realty Company to David Farris, Mary Farris, and John Farris. What form of co-ownership do David, Mary, and John own in the real property?

19. You are a legal assistant working with a law firm that is representing a purchaser of a parcel of real property. The purchaser desires to purchase 100 percent of the property and has entered into a contract with Samuel Seller. The title examination of the property reveals that Samuel Seller owns the property together with Susan Seller and Sarah Seller. What additional precautions or safeguards must you take to protect the purchaser in this transaction?

20. You are a legal assistant in a law firm that represents a creditor who has made a loan to Robert Black. You discover that Robert Black owns a parcel of real property together with his wife, Margo Black. Will the creditor be able to sell Robert Black's interest in the home for purposes of satisfying the debt? What factors are important in answering this question?

21. Explain how the survivorship feature of a joint tenancy with the right of survivorship works.

22. A common owner in a tenancy in common is entitled to what share of rent or income produced from the real property?

23. How can common property be partitioned?

24. What is community property and how is it created?

25. What property in a community property state is considered not to be community property?

Encumbrances, Easements, and Licenses

"Trespass not on my heart; license is granted thee to dwell."

—Anonymous

OBJECTIVES

After reading this chapter you should be able to:

* Understand the public restrictions on the use of real property such as zoning, building codes, eminent domain, and subdivision restrictions
* Identify the various private encumbrances
* Understand the uses of an easement
* Identify the various kinds of easements and their methods of creation and termination
* Explain the purpose of a license and distinguish it from an easement

I deally, a person who owns real property wants the use of the property to be unrestricted and the title to be debt-free. In real life it is unusual for real property, especially urban real property, to be totally free of restrictions or debts. Most ownership of real property is burdened with encumbrances. An **encumbrance** is defined by *Black's Law Dictionary* as "any claim, lien, charge, or liability attached to and binding real property which may exist in another person to the diminishment of the land's value or interfere with the unrestricted use of the land by the owner." Encumbrances usually include such things as zoning restrictions, restrictive covenants, money judgments against the owner, taxes, mortgages, easements, and licenses. Although some encumbrances, such as zoning restrictions or easements, may have a positive effect on the ownership of the property, an encumbrance usually is viewed as an unwanted item. Encumbrances are discovered by title examinations, which are discussed later in this book, and it often is the legal assistant's responsibility to review encumbrances that pose problems for the client. The legal assistant normally works with an attorney to advise the client as to the acceptability of any encumbrance. This chapter discusses the many types of public and private encumbrances that can affect real property.

encumbrance
Claim, lien, charge, or liability attached to and binding real property that may exist in another person to the diminishment of the value of the real property or that interferes with the use of the real property by the owner.

PUBLIC ENCUMBRANCES

Federal, state, and local governments are vested with power to restrict or take private property for the purpose of promoting the health and welfare of the general public. This power to protect and promote the "public welfare" gives to governmental authorities the power to impose on private real property such things as zoning regulations, building codes, subdivision regulations, environmental protection laws, the power of eminent domain, and taxation.

Zoning

The power to regulate land use is within the legitimate police powers of a government, and it is not unusual for city and county governments to issue **zoning** regulations that restrict private land use. The main objective of zoning is to improve living and working conditions in congested areas by preventing the liberties of one property owner from interfering with the rights of another. For example, you can imagine how irate you would be as a property owner if you purchased a beautiful home in a quiet residential neighborhood and then discovered that your neighbor has sold his or her property to a company that intends to build a twenty-four-hour diner on the property.

zoning
Legitimate police power of government to regulate the use of real property.

Zoning is considered constitutional as long as the zoning regulation bears some reasonable relationship to the public welfare. If a zoning regulation is unreasonable, it may amount to the "taking" of the real property, and the owner may be entitled to compensation or to having the zoning regulation voided.

Zoning consists of (a) dividing the city or county into districts; (b) prescribing within each district the types of structures and architectural designs for buildings to be located there; and (c) prescribing the uses for the buildings within each district.

For example, a city council may divide the city into four districts. One district may be reserved for single-family residential use; another district may be reserved for multifamily use, such as apartments, condominiums, and town houses; a third district may be retail commercial, in which there can be stores and offices; and the fourth district may be industrial, in which there could be manufacturing plants.

Zoning is a political process; it usually is considered a legislative function of a governmental authority. Zoning requires procedural due process. This means that notice must be given and a hearing held before a zoning regulation can be passed. The notice usually is by means of a sign on the property or a notice in the newspaper. It is not required that landowners be given personal notice of any intentions to change the zoning on their property. All zoning hearings are public. Landowners, with or without counsel, have an opportunity to speak at these hearings. The governmental authorities must present evidence to support the zoning classifications. A property owner does have a right to appeal a zoning decision or classification to a court of law. The court, however, in reviewing the zoning decision, will not overturn the governmental authorities' decision unless it finds that there is a clear case of abuse by the government.

Real property that has been used for a particular purpose but is later changed by the zoning regulations is deemed to be a preexisting or nonconforming use. These uses are permitted to continue, provided they are not expanded. Some zoning statutes provide a phase-out of nonconforming uses over a period of years. For example, you are the owner of a small neighborhood grocery in a residential neighborhood. The city decides to zone the entire neighborhood residential, making your retail grocery store a nonconforming use. You may continue to operate the grocery store as you have in the past under the nonconforming use protection. You would not, however, be able to change the grocery store into a restaurant or other use, nor would you be able to expand the existing facilities. *Shackford & Gooch v. The Town of Kennebunk*, 486 A.2d 102, illustrates the problems a property owner has in expanding or altering a nonconforming use.

Zoning is enforced through injunction by the public authorities. For example, a property owner decides to operate a business from her home. The property is zoned single-family residential, and the operation of the business is in violation of the zoning ordinance. The government could obtain an injunction that would order the property owner to stop operating the business. If the property owner continues to operate the business, she could be held in contempt of court and face both fines and imprisonment. The issuance of building permits is another way to enforce a zoning ordinance. A building permit will be refused unless the proposed improvement and its intended use comply with zoning.

GLASSMAN, Justice.

Shackford & Gooch, Inc. *et al.*, opponents to the issuance of a building permit to B. & B. Coastal Enterprises, Inc., appeal from a judgment of the Superior Court, York County, ordering the Kennebunk Zoning Board of Appeals to issue a permit to B. & B. Coastal Enterprises to build and use a deck on the roof of its restaurant. B. & B. Coastal Enterprises cross-appeals, challenging that portion of the judgment holding that the Zoning Board of Appeals was not estopped from enforcing its ordinance. We grant the appeal and deny the cross-appeal.

I.

B. & B. Coastal Enterprises, Inc. operates Bartley's Dockside Restaurant (Dockside) in a building that is nonconforming because its setbacks do not meet the requirements of the Kennebunk Zoning Ordinance. In March 1982, Dockside applied to the Kennebunk building inspector for a permit to build stairs on the outside of the restaurant. The inspector granted the permit, at the same time giving Dockside verbal authorization to build a deck on the flat roof of the restaurant, assuring Dockside that a building permit for the deck was not necessary. When Dockside began construction of the deck, Shackford & Gooch, Inc., owner of an abutting fish market, petitioned the building inspector to stop the work on the grounds that a building permit was necessary, and that the deck violated local zoning ordinances.

The controversy eventually came before the Kennebunk Zoning Board of Appeals (Board), which decided in June 1982 that, based on an estoppel theory, Dockside could retain and use the roof deck, subject to a restricted number of seats. On review of this decision, the Superior Court ruled that the Board's finding of estoppel was incorrect as a matter of law. The court vacated the decision of the Board and remanded the case for the Board to determine initially whether the deck met the requirements of the Kennebunk Zoning Ordinance and, if not, whether Dockside was entitled to a variance.

After a hearing in September 1983, the Board found that Dockside's deck constituted an expansion of a nonconforming structure and did not comply with the setback requirements of the ordinance. The Board denied Dockside's request for the necessary variances. On review of the Board's decision, the Superior Court held as a matter of law that the deck as a vertical addition to the building did not extend the non-conforming horizontal setbacks of Dockside. The court further held the deck created no increase in Dockside's seating capacity that would necessitate a parking variance. Declining to reconsider the Superior Court's earlier ruling on estoppel, the court ordered the Board to issue a permit to Dockside to build and

use its deck in accordance with the seating restriction established in the June 1982 hearing.

· · ·

When the Superior Court acts as an appellate court reviewing an action of an administrative board, we directly examine the record developed before the board. *See Driscoll v. Gheewalla*, 441 A.2d 1023, 1026 (Me.1982); *see also Nancy W. Bayley, Inc. v. Maine Employment Security Commission*, 472 A.2d 1374, 1377 (Me.1984). On review of an action taken by a zoning board of appeals, we may not make factual findings independent of those of the board, nor may we substitute our judgment for that of the board. *Mack v. Municipal Officers of the Town of Cape Elizabeth*, 463 A.2d 717, 719–20 (Me.1983); *Driscoll*, 441 A.2d at 1026. Our role is to determine whether the board abused its discretion, committed an error of law, or made findings not supported by substantial evidence in the record. *Mack*, 463 A.2d at 719; *Driscoll*, 441 A.2d at 1026.

The Board found in its remand hearing that Dockside's roof deck was not in compliance with the side yard, rear yard, or shoreland zoning setback requirements of the Kennebunk ordinance. The Board thus considered the deck to be an expansion of a nonconforming structure requiring a variance. The ordinance provides:

> No lawfully non-conforming use of buildings or land shall be changed, extended, or enlarged in any manner for any purpose not permitted under this Ordinance, except as may be permitted as a variance, not, as an exception.

Kennebunk, Me., Zoning Ordinance § 1.4(B) (1963). The section on variance appeals provides:

> The Board may allow a relaxation, in a moderate degree, of the lot area, lot width, yard depth, or percentage of lot covered requirements of this Ordinance. Such a relaxation may be granted only when the Board determines that, by reason of physical conditions [sic] peculiar to the land or building under appeal (conditions virtually unique to that property and not arising or applying as to other land and building(s) adjoining or nearby within the same zoning district), unusual difficulty or particular hardship would be caused by literal application and rigorous enforcement of the terms of the Kennebunk Zoning Ordinance. The Board may also permit modest expansion of any lawfully non-conforming building or use of land, but only on land occupied by such use at the time the use became lawfully non-conforming and not onto any additional lot adjoining.

Id. at § 7.6(C)(2).

[4–6] We agree with the Board that the addition of a roof deck, or indeed, any significant alteration of a nonconforming structure is an extension or expansion. *See* 1 R. Anderson, *American Law of Zoning* 2d § 6.43 at 455 (2d ed. 1976). Dockside argues that because the roof deck does not encroach any further into the nonconforming setbacks than do the lawfully nonconforming walls of the restaurant, it does not constitute an expansion of the nonconformity. To permit such an addition to a nonconforming structure without a variance, however, would offend the policy of zoning, which is to "gradually or eventually eliminate nonconforming uses as speedily as justice will permit." *See Keith v. Saco River Corridor Commission,* 464 A.2d 150, 154 (Me.1983). When an ordinance prohibits enlargement of a nonconforming building, a landowner cannot as a matter of right alter the structure, even if the alteration does not increase the nonconformity.

· · ·

Judgment vacated;

Remanded for entry of judgment as follows: appeal denied; decision of Zoning Board of Appeals affirmed.

All concurring.

Building Codes and Subdivision Regulations

Building code regulations also are a legitimate use of a city's or county's police power to protect the health and welfare of its citizens. For example, most cities have codes that regulate the electrical wiring and plumbing of homes and buildings. **Building codes** regulate methods and materials to be used in construction of improvements. Most cities and counties do not permit a building to be constructed and occupied without a permit and a final inspection by the building department.

Most city and county governments can create and enforce subdivision laws. State and federal governments can create and enforce environmental protection laws. Subdivision laws require that streets and sewers be approved in advance by the government. The streets and sewers are not accepted for public maintenance by the government without a satisfactory inspection.

building codes
Public laws that regulate methods and materials to be used in the construction of improvements.

Environmental Protection Laws

Fifty years ago "environmental law" was not a commonly used term in either legal literature or the common popular vernacular. During the 1960s various conservation societies such as the Sierra Club, through their spirited crusades, prompted a deeper study of the ecology of nature and created a public awareness that we only enjoy the natural resources of earth as trustees for future generations and that we must protect them against pollution and exploitation. The result has been the creation of a wide body of both federal and state law designed to protect the quality of our earth, water, and air.

Water is one of the earth's most precious commodities. Without water, no life would exist. The quality of water is regulated by federal environmental laws such as the Clean Water Act, 33 U.S.C. § 1251-1387. The Clean Water Act empowers the federal government with enforcement powers to ensure the quality of water, as well as monetary fines for people who would contaminate or pollute our water sources.

Another aspect concerning water is the preservation of marshlands or wetlands. Research has shown the importance of these areas as breeding and feeding grounds for migratory birds and as natural oxygen producers. It is believed that the entire ecological chain which leads from the microscopic life forms to our own life form is dependent upon the preservation of adequate marshlands or wetlands. Both federal and state laws protect the use and development of wetlands. This protection is generally in the form of denying a developer a permit or ability to develop property identified as wetlands and of monetary fines or injunctive relief for those developers who do disturb wetland properties. Generally, the identification of wetlands is determined by the United States Army Corps of Engineers. It is not uncommon for a developer who is attempting a project that may include wetlands to have a surveyor or other trained person to carefully study Army Corps of Engineers maps to determine if any wetland properties are located within the project boundaries.

Air, like water, goes with the land but is not confined to it, and the landowner has a transient right to use the air as it flows over his boundaries. A landowner has a right to receive air in a reasonably clean and pure state from his neighbors and must let it pass over his property without adding pollution or debris. Air quality standards are established by the federal government under the Clean Air Act, 42 U.S.C. § 7401-7671. Many states have similar statutes that regulate the quality of air. Clean air acts are generally enforced through injunctions or monetary fines against violators. Excessive noise may also be regarded as a form of air pollution and is subject to similar controls by both federal and state legislation.

The problems of closed or abandoned disposal sites of hazardous waste is handled by the Environmental Protection Agency (EPA) under the **Comprehensive Environmental Response, Compensation and Liability Act (CERCLA)** passed in 1980, 42.U.S.C. § 9601 et seq. CERCLA, also known as Superfund, for the trust fund designed by the act to finance the activities of the EPA under the act, puts vigor and teeth into environmental law enforcement. CERCLA gave the EPA the authority to take notice of release of hazardous substances and to recover the cleanup costs from the responsible parties. In addition, CERCLA provides private parties with the ability both to sue responsible parties for hazardous waste cleanup and to claim government help if the government has ordered them to perform a cleanup and the responsible party has failed to do so.

Under CERCLA are four classes of parties potentially liable for the cleanup of hazardous substances: first, the present owners and operators of facilities that generate or create hazardous substances; second, owners and operators who in the past have created hazardous waste or disposed of hazardous waste; third, those who arrange for the treatment and transport of disposable hazardous waste; and finally, those parties who accept hazardous waste for treatment, transport, or disposal.

CERCLA creates strict joint and several liability among the responsible parties for the cost of cleaning up hazardous waste sites. The EPA has a variety of strong enforcement weapons to accomplish the cleanup responsibilities. The EPA may seek a court injunction ordering the responsible party to clean up the hazardous waste. In addition, the EPA can clean up the hazardous waste and assess the costs against the responsible party, including placing a lien on the property to secure payment of the cost. A responsible party who fails to comply with any order from the EPA to clean up hazardous waste may be subject to treble damages and penalties.

The EPA expects that there are thousands of contaminated sites throughout the United States. The average cost of cleaning up a Superfund contaminated site is now estimated to be in excess of $25 million.

It is easy to see why contaminated property could become an expensive liability for its owner. In many cases the cost of cleaning up the property would exceed the value of the property. CERCLA has an "innocent purchaser" defense to protect an innocent purchaser or lender who makes a loan on contaminated property. This innocent purchaser defense provides an exception to the strict joint and several liability for cleanup costs under the Superfund law. It provides that anyone who purchases or makes a loan on contaminated property who at the time of the acquisition or making of the loan was not aware that the property was contaminated will not be liable for the cost of cleanup of the contamination.

To avail itself of the innocent party defense, a person must (1) have no actual knowledge of the contamination at the time of the purchase or making of the loan, and (2) have undertaken at the time of acquisition or making of the loan all appropriate inquiry into the previous ownership and uses of the property consistent with good commercial or customary practice. Generally, then, a buyer or lender, at the time of acquisition or making of the loan, must have the property correctly investigated for the likelihood of subsurface contamination. This inquiry is generally done by hiring an environmental engineer to prepare a review of the property for possible contamination. This review is generally referred to as a **Phase I** environmental examination. Most Phase I environmental examinations are performed in accordance with the American Society of Testing and Materials (ASTM) standards for environmental assessments. The use of the ASTM standards is voluntary, but most environmental engineers adhere to them.

The ASTM standards generally require the environmental engineer to review a survey or site plan of the site to be examined and determine its exact boundaries. As a part of this review, the environmental engineer must determine the upgradient direction for the possible flow of contamination. Because contamination generally flows in a gravity direction, an upgradient of property would be property with a higher elevation to that of the property being examined. The environmental engineer also during the Phase I review will look at regulatory data concerning

Comprehensive Environmental Response, Compensation and Liability Act (CERCLA)
Also known as Superfund, is federal legislation which created a trust fund designed to finance the activities of the Environmental Protection Agency and gave the Environmental Protection Agency the authority to recover cleanup costs for contaminated properties from the responsible parties for the contamination.

Phase I
An examination of real property to determine if it contains environmental contamination.

the property and the surrounding area of the property. The regulatory data usually include any state or county lists of hazardous waste generators and an examination of the public records to determine if environmental liens have been filed. The review also requires a search of the United States EPA database for a list of hazardous waste generators, transporters, and storage and treatment facilities. The environmental engineer will also look to see if there are any underground storage tanks either on the property or within a reasonable vicinity of the property which might leak and contaminate the property. The environmental engineer will inspect the property, looking for any evidence of toxic materials, including their storage, handling, and disposal. Many times this review will involve looking at vegetation on the property to see if it is discolored or dying, which might indicate some subsurface contamination. If requested, the environmental engineer may, during the site inspection, also review the property for other contaminants such as asbestos, lead-base paint, and polychlorinate biphenyls (PCBs) which can be contained in hydraulic oils and found in electrical transformers. Another source of potential subsurface contamination is the cleaning fluids and solvents used for dry-cleaning plants. These solvents are highly toxic and quite capable of contaminating the underground water supply.

After all the historical data and government databases have been reviewed, including the site review, the engineer will then write a Phase I environmental assessment indicating the likelihood of contamination on the property. The Phase I environmental assessment, depending on the type of project being assessed, can cost several thousand dollars. The Phase I report may indicate that there is some concern regarding contamination of the property which may require additional testing. The additional testing is generally referred to as the **Phase II** environmental assessment. The Phase II environmental assessment involves the environmental engineer obtaining soil and water samples from the property. These soil and water samples are then analyzed in a laboratory to determine if they contain elements of contamination in excess of the limits considered normal by federal and state government standards. Phase II environmental assessments are generally more intensive than Phase I and can be quite expensive.

Phase II
A more intensive environmental examination of property usually including the testing of soil and water for evidence of contamination.

Since an examination is necessary for a purchaser or lender to avail themselves of the innocent party defense under CERCLA, Phase I environmental examinations have become almost an absolute requirement in connection with the purchase or making of a loan on a commercial property. Many purchasers and lenders, in addition to the Phase I environmental assessment, will also require the seller or borrower to provide them with an environmental indemnity.

Underground Storage Tanks

Underground storage tanks containing gasoline, petroleum products, or other fluids are generally not regulated directly by CERCLA. Underground storage tanks containing petroleum are generally regulated by state law. These state laws usually impose liability for the owner of an underground storage tank for leaks that cause contamination to soil or water sources. Many states require an owner of property to remove, or to fill with sand, tanks not in use. Many states have trust funds that provide money for the purpose of remediating or cleaning up sites which have been contaminated by leaking underground storage tanks. The money to fund the trust fund is collected from owners of underground storage tanks through taxes or other assessments. Most owners of gasoline stations are required to pay a tax to the state for each gallon of gasoline sold, which is deposited into a fund for remediation of all leaking underground storage tanks within the state. By participating in the fund, the owner, in the event his tanks leak, will be eligible to receive monies from the fund for the purpose of remediation.

Radon and Lead-Based Paint

Other areas of environmental concern often found in residential transactions are radon and lead-based paint. Radon, which is a product of decaying uranium, is a tasteless, colorless, odorless gas that is typically found in areas with deposits of granite, phosphate, shale, and uranium ore. It is believed that exposure to high levels of radon gas may pose a threat to health, including the cause of cancer. It is prudent in states where radon may be prevalent for purchasers to have investigations or assessments of the property to determine if radon does exist. In addition, many states have required sellers of homes known to have radon to make full disclosure to a purchaser concerning the radon levels in the home.

Lead-based paint is also an environmental concern in many residences. Lead poisoning generally does not result in death, but can result in brain damage and other serious health side effects. The highest risk is for children growing up in homes with lead-based paint who may, as a result of exposure to the paint, not develop properly and suffer brain damage or other health problems as adults. Lead-based paint was commonly used in homes built prior to 1978. The federal government banned the sale of this type of paint in 1977. Federal government regulations require the owners of housing built before 1978 to notify buyers and tenants that the property was built before 1978 and may contain lead-based paint. The notice must also disclose the hazards of such paint and the symptoms and treatment of its poisoning. In addition, the notice must prescribe precautions that can be taken to avoid lead-based paint poisoning. The owners must give this notice to a prospective buyer or tenant before they purchase or rent the property. All contracts of sale, leases, or management agreements for such pre-1978 housing must include provisions insuring that buyers and tenants received the required notices. In addition to these federal regulations, some states have similar regulations concerning the disclosure and sale of residential properties containing lead-based paint. Inspections can be made by qualified inspectors to determine if a property contains lead-based paint.

Power of Eminent Domain

eminent domain
Power of government to take private property for public use.

Federal, state, and local governments have the right to take private property for public use. Thus, private ownership of all real property is held subject to a perpetual repurchase option in favor of the United States; the various states; the county, city, and other numerous government agencies; and, in some cases, even privately owned public utilities. Because the taking of private property for public use can have a harsh and disastrous effect on the private owner, constitutional safeguards have been set up to protect the owner against any arbitrary or unreasonable use of **eminent domain** power. The government cannot exercise its right of power of eminent domain without first establishing that the private property is needed for a public use and paying the private owner adequate compensation for the property.

A property owner is provided with a number of procedural safeguards with any exercise of the power of eminent domain. The property owner is entitled to due notice and a hearing before the time the private property can be taken. The property owner, at the hearing, has an opportunity to be represented by counsel and to prove that the taking is not necessary for public use or that the compensation being offered is unreasonable. The government has a wide range of public uses that support the exercise of the power of eminent domain, such as the taking of private property for the purpose of constructing public streets, sewer facilities, airports, government buildings, slum clearance or redevelopment projects, forest reserves, and even recreational areas, such as parks and wildlife preserves. Because of the wide range of public uses that support the exercise of the power of eminent domain, the main issue in most condemnation proceedings is that of compensation. A property owner is entitled to the fair market value of the property being taken.

Taxation

ad valorem taxes
Taxes assessed against real property usually measured by the value of the real property being taxed.

Governmental bodies have the right to tax real property that is located within their jurisdictional boundaries. It is not unusual to find real property taxed at both the city and the county levels. Sometimes real property taxes are called **ad valorem taxes.** This definition comes from the fact that the taxes are measured on the value of the real property being taxed.

The city or county tax authorities have the power not only to value the real property for purposes of taxation, but also to establish a millage rate for purposes of computing the tax. For example, if you have real property that had a tax assessment value of $51,900 and a millage rate of .0112500, you would multiply the millage rate by the assessed value, and the tax would be $583.87.

lien
Money debt attached to real property. The holder of the lien can sell the real property to pay the debt.

Most governmental bodies have a tax year, which may be the calendar year or some other period of time. The taxes become a **lien** or debt charged against the real property on the first day of the tax year. For example, if the tax year is the calendar year, then on January 1 the taxes for that year would become a lien, even though the taxes may not be due and payable until sometime later in the year. Tax liens have a super priority over any mortgage or other property interest in connection with the real property and must be paid before all other debts, liens, or claims. Tax liens can be enforced by foreclosure and sale of the real property by the public authority.

Governmental authorities also have the right to levy special assessments against real property owners for the costs of such things as grading, curbing, paving, and establishing sewer and water lines or sidewalks, which benefit a person's real property. Special assessments are enforceable by foreclosure and public sale of the real property.

PRIVATE ENCUMBRANCES

Private encumbrances are voluntarily created by private parties who deal with the real property and consist of judgment liens, mechanics' and materialmen's liens, mortgages and trust deeds, restrictive covenants, easements, and licenses.

Judgment Liens

A **judgment lien** is a money debt attached to real property. It is created when the property owner has been sued for a sum of money and has lost. For example, a property owner is involved in an automobile accident. The property owner is sued for negligence and has assessed against him by a court of law a $50,000 judgment.

Judgment liens do not become liens on real property until they have been recorded in a special book, called the Judgment Book or General Execution Docket, in the county where the real property is located.

A judgment lien remains a lien on real property until it has been paid, or expires by passage of time. Most states have laws that limit the duration of a judgment lien. These laws provide that a judgment lien, if not paid, will expire within seven to fourteen years after becoming a lien on real property.

judgment
Money debt resulting from a lawsuit. Judgments are liens on real property owned by the judgment debtor.

Mechanics' and Materialmen's Liens

A **mechanics' or materialmen's lien** is imposed by law on real property to secure payment for work performed or materials furnished for the construction, repair, or alteration of improvements on the real property. Each state has its own laws for the creation of these liens. Claimants under most mechanics' or materialmen's lien statutes include contractors, laborers, subcontractors, material suppliers, lessors of equipment and machinery, architects, professional engineers, and land surveyors.

Most privately owned real property is subject to mechanics' or materialmen's liens. The lien attaches to all real property, including improvements, and all real property contiguous to the improved real property. Public real property is not subject to mechanics' or materialmen's liens.

mechanics' or materialmen's lien
Lien imposed by law on real property to secure payment for work performed or materials furnished for the construction, repair, or alteration of improvements on the real property.

Special Mechanics' and Materialmen's Lien Situations

Sometimes special situations exist that prompt the creation of mechanics' and materialmen's liens.

Landlord and Tenant Work performed for a tenant of real property only attaches to the tenant's interest in the real property unless the landlord of the real property consents to the work and agrees to pay for the work.

Contract Seller and Purchaser Work performed for a purchaser of real property before the contract closes only attaches to the purchaser's interest unless the seller has consented to the work.

Husband and Wife Work performed at the request of one spouse is not a lien on the other spouse's real property interest unless the other spouse has consented or agreed to pay for the work.

Joint Tenants A lien binds only the interest in the real property of the joint tenant who ordered the work. A joint tenant is not an agent for the other tenants, and unless the other tenants have consented or agreed to pay for the work, their interests in the real property are not liened.

Other Mechanics' and Materialmen's Lien Considerations

The amount of the lien depends on whether the state in which the construction takes place follows the "New York" or the "Pennsylvania" theory of lien claim. Under the New York theory, the amount of the mechanics' and materialmen's lien is limited to the contract price between the owner and the general contractor. Payment of the contract price by the owner is a defense to a mechanics' or materialmen's lien claim by a subcontractor or material supplier. Under the Pennsylvania theory, the original contract between the owner and the general contractor does not limit the amount of lien claims that can be filed by subcontractors and material suppliers. Payment of the contract price, under the Pennsylvania theory, is not a defense to subcontractor or material supplier lien claims.

For example, an owner of real property enters into a contract with a general contractor to build a home. The contract price for the construction is $100,000. A general contractor hires a number of subcontractors to build the home. The owner pays to the general contractor $80,000 of the $100,000 contract price. After having paid the $80,000, the owner discovers that a number of lien claims are filed against the home by subcontractors and material suppliers. The subcontractor and material supplier lien claims total $50,000. Under the New York theory, the owner would be responsible to the subcontractors and material suppliers only for $20,000 (the difference between the $100,000 contract price and the $80,000 previously paid to the general contractor). Under the Pennsylvania theory, the owner would be responsible to the subcontractors and material suppliers for the full amount of their claims, or $50,000.

The right to a mechanics' or materialmen's lien usually exists once the work is performed or the material is furnished. The lien right must be perfected by filing a notice or claim of lien in the public records where the real property is located. Most states require that this notice or claim of lien be recorded within a reasonable period of time after completion of the work (60 to 120 days). A claim or notice of lien requires the following information: (a) the amount of the claim, (b) the name of the lien claimant, (c) the name of the owner, (d) a description of real property to be liened, and (e) the notarized signature of the lien claimant.

The priority of a lien claim dates from the time the first work is performed or the material is furnished. It does not attach from the date the claim of lien is filed, except for architects, engineers, and land surveyors.

For example, a material supplier provides materials for the construction of a home on March 1. The material supplier is not paid, and finally files a claim of lien on May 1 for the unpaid materials. The material supplier's lien claim dates from March 1, the date the materials were furnished. This also means that the material supplier is ahead in terms of priority, and will be paid ahead of any other lien claims that date after March 1.

A mechanics' or materialmen's lien is enforced through a foreclosure suit or sale of the real property. States also impose time limits for filing the foreclosure suit. The most common time limit is one year from the date the claim is due.

A mechanics' and materialmen's lien can be waived and terminated by a written waiver or release of lien. Most states require that lien waivers or releases of lien be signed by the lien claimant and be witnessed or notarized.

Mortgages and Trust Deeds

Real property can be pledged as security to pay debts of the owner. Mortgages and trust deeds are fully discussed in Chapter 6.

Restrictive Covenants

It is possible for real property owners to restrict the use of the real property. These restrictive covenants may be in the form of restrictions or covenants found in deeds of conveyance to the real property or in restrictions that are recorded against the real property. It is not unusual for real property that has been subdivided, such as single-family home subdivisions, industrial parks, or condominiums, to have restrictions regarding the use of the property by future real property owners. Private restrictive covenants often perform the same function as public zoning regulations. The private restrictions attempt to regulate the development of the real property in such a manner as to enhance the value of each individual owner's lot or share of the real property. For example, restrictive covenants found in residential subdivisions usually restrict the size of the homes that can be built on the lots, subject the homes to architectural review committees, regulate the height of the homes, and require that certain portions of the property be left vacant for purposes of creating front, rear, and side yards. All these restrictions are designed to create a nice residential environment that will enhance the value of each individual owner's home.

Restrictive covenants are enforced by injunction or suit for damages. Enforcement may be brought by any person who bought real property with notice of the restrictions and in reliance on the restrictions. Therefore, any homeowner in a single-family subdivision can enforce the restrictive covenants against other homeowners.

EASEMENTS

An easement, although an encumbrance, may be a benefit to real property. For example, Aaron and Carol each own neighboring lots of lakefront property. They are both constructing a vacation cottage on their respective lots. They discover during the construction process that it would be in their best interest to construct a driveway that would be located one-half on Aaron's property and one-half on Carol's property. Through the use of an easement, a joint driveway can be created for the benefit of Aaron and Carol. Aaron will give Carol an easement for the use of that portion of the driveway located on Aaron's property, and Carol will grant to Aaron an easement for the use of that portion of the driveway located on Carol's property. Aaron and Carol also could agree to share the costs of maintaining the driveway. Although the joint driveway easement restricts the use of both Aaron's and Carol's property, the restriction of use is minimal compared with the benefit that each owner receives through the use of the driveway.

An **easement** is a right to use the real property of another owner for a specific purpose. It is considered an encumbrance on the real property on which the easement is located. Some common examples of easements are utility easements and access easements. *Utility easements* are rights given to utility companies, such as the gas, electric, and telephone companies, that permit them to install transmission lines over real property. *Access easements* give a party the right to travel over or across real property to a public street. A sample of a utility easement appears at the end of this chapter (Exhibit 3–4).

Easements are divided into two categories: **appurtenant easements** and **easements in gross.** An appurtenant easement is an easement created for the benefit of a particular tract of land. An example is shown in Exhibit 3–1.

easement
Right granted to a nonowner of real property to use the real property for a specific purpose; for example, a right given to an electric utility company to locate an electric line on real property.

appurtenant easement
Easement created to benefit a particular parcel of real property. The easement transfers automatically with a transfer of the ownership of the real property benefited by the easement.

easement in gross
Easement granting the owner of the easement the right to use real property for a particular purpose. The easement does not benefit a parcel of real property owned by the owner of the easement.

EXHIBIT 3–1
Appurtenant Easement

An easement is created over Parcel A to provide access for Parcel B to the public street. Parcel B is known as the **dominant tenement,** the parcel of land benefited by the easement, and Parcel A is known as the **servient tenement,** the land on which the easement is located. This easement would be an encumbrance on Parcel A and a benefit to Parcel B.

Appurtenant easements are regarded as being so closely connected to the dominant tenement that on the sale of the dominant tenement, the easement passes automatically, even if the deed does not mention the easement. In other words, a sale of Parcel B, even with a deed that does not mention the easement over Parcel A, conveys Parcel B and the easement over Parcel A to the new owner.

An easement in gross does not benefit a particular parcel of land. Utility easements are easements in gross. For example, an electric power company acquires an easement to locate a high-tension electric power line across several owners' properties. The easement benefits the power company but does not benefit any particular parcel of real property.

dominant tenement
Parcel of land benefited by an appurtenant easement.

servient tenement
Parcel of land on which an appurtenant easement is located.

Creation of Easements

An easement may be created by (a) express grant, (b) implication, (c) prescription, or (d) necessity.

Express Grant

An easement can be created by an express grant. The grant of an easement is prepared with the same formality of requirements as a deed. The easement is in writing and describes the use of the easement and the real property on or over which the easement is located. It also is signed by the grantor of the easement, witnessed, notarized, and delivered to the grantee of the easement.

The grantor of the easement must be the owner of the real property on which the easement is located. The grantor cannot convey an easement for any longer term than the grantor's ownership of the real property. For example, a grantor who owns a life estate in a parcel of real property can grant an easement only for the period of the life estate and no longer. A title examination of the grantor's real property is conducted to determine what rights the grantor of the easement has to the real property. In addition, encumbrances on the real property, such as a mortgage or a deed of trust, can create problems for the holder of the easement. A mortgage or a trust deed on the easement property that is recorded before the express grant of the easement has priority over the easement, and if the mortgage or the deed of trust goes into default and is foreclosed, the foreclosure terminates the easement. If an easement is granted over real property that is encumbered by a mortgage or a trust deed, the grantee of the easement may obtain the consent of the mortgagee or subordination of the mortgage or trust deed to the easement.

The grantee of an appurtenant easement is the owner of the real property being benefited by the easement. The grantee of an easement in gross is the party to whom the special use is being granted, such as a utility company. Easements in gross in some states are not assignable unless the express grant of easement provides so.

Implied Easement

An easement may be created by implication. An **implied easement** can only be made in connection with a conveyance of the real property being served by the easement. Implied easements are based on a theory that when real property is conveyed, the conveyance contains whatever is necessary for the beneficial use and enjoyment of the real property or retains whatever is necessary for the beneficial use and enjoyment of real property retained by the grantor. In creating an implied easement the law is attempting to arrive at the intent of the parties to the conveyance as shown by all the facts and circumstances under which the conveyance was made.

For example, Luther received ownership to real property that is described as being bounded by a private street or right-of-way. Luther receives an implied easement of access over the street. This easement is created provided that the seller of the real property owns the private street or road. In addition, a conveyance of real property by use of a platted description in which the plat describes certain rights-of-way and other easement rights benefiting the conveyed real property shall grant to the new owner an implied easement to these rights or other uses.

implied easement
Easement created by the conduct of the parties to the easement, not by written agreement.

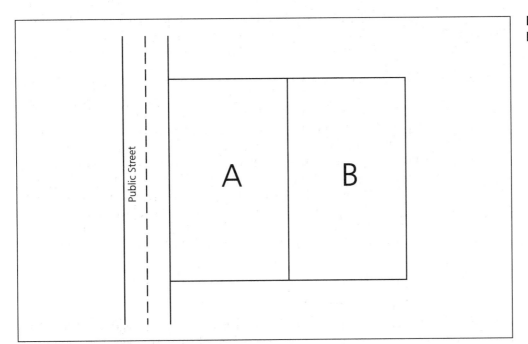

EXHIBIT 3–2
Implied Easement

Another situation in which an implied easement is created is when the owner of two tracts of land sells one of the tracts without any mention of an easement in the deed, and the result of the transaction is to cause the parcel sold to become landlocked. The courts in such a situation imply that there is an easement created over the remaining tract of land to benefit the land sold.

In the example shown in Exhibit 3–2 a single owner owns tracts A and B and sells tract B without any reference to an easement. The law implies that there is an easement over tract A for the benefit of tract B to gain access to the public street.

The reverse situation, however, does not always create a reserved right of implied easement. For example, a single owner owns tracts A and B and sells tract A without any reference to a reservation of easement for the benefit of tract B. In this situation the law is not uniform in granting the owner of tract B a reserved implied easement over tract A to benefit tract B. The law in some states grants the easement; the law in others denies the easement.

Prescriptive Easement

An easement may be acquired by prescription. **Prescriptive easements** are created when a person uses property without the permission of the owner for a period of time. A prescriptive easement is similar to the concept of adverse possession discussed in Chapter 1. A person who acquires a prescriptive easement, however, does not exercise such dominion and control over the real property in question as to become an owner of the real property through adverse possession. Instead, the owner of a prescriptive easement has used the real property only for a particular purpose, and therefore acquires rights to continue to use the real property for that purpose. A prescriptive easement can be obtained over any private real property but cannot be acquired in real property belonging to the United States or any other governmental authority. A prescriptive easement requires that the prescriptive use take place for a period of time. This period of time varies from state to state, but periods of ten to twenty years are common.

An important element of a prescriptive easement is that the use made of the easement must be adverse and hostile to the owner of the real property over which the use is being made. Adverse use means without the owner's permission or consent. An owner's permission to the use before the time the prescriptive easement ripens (i.e., before the expiration of the term of years required in order to obtain a prescriptive easement) causes the prescriptive easement to terminate. Therefore, an owner can prevent prescriptive rights from being made to his or her real property by granting consent to the use. This consent can be given on conditions favorable to the owner of the real property. For example, a landowner notices that his neighbor is using a corner

prescriptive easement
Easement created when a person uses real property for a period of time without the owner's permission.

EXHIBIT 3–3
Prescriptive Easement

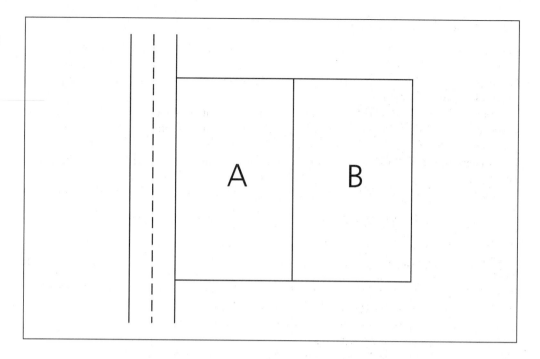

of his property as a right-of-way to a public street. The landowner grants the neighbor an express easement to use the corner of his property for a right-of-way. The express easement provides that the landowner can terminate the easement on thirty days' notice. The express grant of permission to the neighbor prevents the neighbor from obtaining perpetual prescriptive rights, and the landowner still maintains, with the thirty-day cancellation option, total control over his property.

In addition to the prescriptive use being adverse, the holder of the prescriptive easement must use and enjoy the easement on a continuous and uninterrupted basis. If at any time before the expiration of the term required to create a prescriptive easement the prescriptive use is interrupted by the owner of the land or is voluntarily abandoned by the party claiming the easement, the prescriptive easement is not created. The erection of gates and barriers as well as suits for trespass have all been held to be sufficient interruption by the landowner to defeat a claim of prescriptive use.

Prescriptive use also must be open, visible, and notorious. The use must be apparent enough to give the owner of the land knowledge or full opportunity to assert his or her rights to interrupt the prescriptive use.

In the example of prescriptive use shown in Exhibit 3–3, B does not have access to the public highway but starts driving across A's property. B drives across A's property for the necessary prescriptive period but without A's consent and without being interrupted by A. B will acquire the right to continue driving across A's property.

Prescriptive easements, once created, are perpetual. They also are appurtenant easements and are transferred with the dominant tenement. In the example shown in Exhibit 3–3, the sale of tract B will transfer the prescriptive easement over tract A.

Easement by Necessity

Many states provide a landowner who does not have access to a public road or street the right to apply for the grant of a private way or an easement over adjacent lands in order to gain access. This is an **easement by necessity.** It grants to a landowner a quasi-private right to condemn an adjoining owner's land for purposes of acquiring an access easement to a public street or road. An easement by necessity requires that fair compensation be paid to the landowner of the condemned easement. Easements by necessity are created by statutory procedures. These statutes limit the width of the right-of-way as well as provide for a method to determine fair compensation. Because there are strict requirements concerning easements by necessity, it is important to check a particular state's requirements before proceeding.

easement by necessity
Easement for access to a public street that is necessary for the use and enjoyment of the property benefited by the easement.

Termination of Easements

An easement, once granted, continues to exist until terminated by the operation of some rule of law or by the terms of the express grant. An easement may be terminated by (a) expiration of express term, (b) abandonment, (c) merger, (d) foreclosure of prior servient liens, or (e) express release or termination.

As previously mentioned, an easement by express grant can be made for any duration, or it can be terminated on the happening of a certain event. For example, a private road easement may be terminated on the dedication of the road to public use.

An easement may be terminated by abandonment. Abandonment is a matter of the intention of the grantee of the easement as evidenced by the acts of the grantee and surrounding circumstances. Abandonment is nonuse with the intent to never use again. Evidence of abandonment may be the permanent removal of physical installations, such as rails or bridges, that permit the use of the easement, or actions that permit others to maintain obstructions to prevent the exercise of the easement. For example, a railroad has an easement for a spur/side track. After a number of years the railroad stops using the spur/side track and even removes the rails and ties. A strong argument could be made that the railroad has abandoned the easement and that the easement has terminated. Although easements usually cannot be lost by nonuse alone, nonuse is evidence of an intent to abandon.

An easement may be lost by the merger of the dominant and the servient tenement. For example, Aaron grants to Luis the right to cross over Aaron's property to the public road. The right-of-way over Aaron's property is an appurtenant easement to Luis's property. Later Luis acquires the fee simple title to Aaron's property over which the easement travels. Luis now owns both the fee title and the easement over the former property of Aaron. This ownership of the dominant and servient tenements causes a merger, and the easement is terminated, since Luis no longer needs the easement to travel over Luis's own property.

An easement also may be lost by the foreclosure of a mortgage or a deed of trust that was on the servient property before the time the easement was created. Easements in some states are terminated by a tax foreclosure sale of the servient estate.

An easement can be terminated by an express written release or termination given by the easement owner to the owner of the servient estate. Written releases of easements should be drafted with the same formality as the easement and be recorded in the public records of the county in which the easement is located.

LICENSES

Black's Law Dictionary defines a **license** as "the authority to do a particular act or series of acts upon another's land, without possession of any estate therein." For example, an owner of a farm that has a lake located on it gives a neighbor permission to fish in the lake. The permission to fish in the lake includes permission to walk across the farm fields to reach the lake. It is understood that the permission to fish in the lake can be terminated at any time by the farmer and that the neighbor acquires no rights in the farmer's land. A license is distinguished from an easement in that an easement is a property interest and a license is mere permission to perform a certain act.

A license can be created orally or in writing, or it can be implied from the conduct of the parties. An oral license without any consideration being paid for the license is revocable at the will of the person granting the license. On the other hand, a license in writing for which compensation and consideration has been paid usually is irrevocable. An implied license may come about from custom or from acts constituting an invitation, such as signs and advertisements. For example, the owner of a retail store extends a license to the customers of the store to enter on the land where the store is located, shop, buy merchandise, and so on. An implied license is revocable at any time, and once revoked, if the licensee does not leave the property, the licensee becomes a trespasser.

The terms of a license are strictly interpreted, and a licensee cannot extend or vary the terms. Third persons who interfere with the licensing or unlawful exercise of the license may be liable to the licensee in damages.

license
Authority or permission to do a particular act or series of acts on another person's land.

E T H I C S :   False Witness

Your supervising attorney has just had a difficult closing. The closing has lasted a day and has occupied a couple of conference rooms. It is near the end of the day, and the attorney brings you a stack of documents. The attorney asks you to witness a number of signatures on the documents. You indicate that you have not seen these people sign. The attorney apologizes but states that the people have already gone home and that the signatures must be witnessed. To avoid a confrontation, you witness the documents. Was this the proper thing to do?

It is unethical for an attorney or legal assistant to give false witness or commit perjury on behalf of a client. Few attorneys or legal assistants intentionally lie or misrepresent the facts involving a real estate transaction. These same honest attorneys and legal assistants, however, may routinely witness or notarize the unseen signature of parties to various legal documents.

Most legal documents, such as deed and mortgages, require a witness for the document to be recorded or be valid. They also require that the witness actually see the person sign the document. Witnessing a document in which the witness has not seen the party sign the document is a misrepresentation of fact and a breach of legal ethics. The notarization of a signature without having seen the party sign is even a more serious matter. When notarizing a signature, a notary is swearing under the notarial oath that she or he has seen the person sign the document. A notarization of the signature is, therefore, a witness under oath, and if the notary has not seen the person sign the document, the notary is committing perjury.

It is advisable that a legal assistant in the beginning of an employment situation confer with his or her supervising attorney concerning what procedures will be followed in the witness or notarization of legal documents. The legal assistant should strongly stress that he or she will not witness or notarize documents unless he or she has seen the signing of the documents.

SUMMARY

Although an encumbrance may be beneficial to a property owner, encumbrances usually are considered unwanted items in connection with real property. Encumbrances are discovered by an examination of the record title or by a physical inspection of the real property.

Easements are common encumbrances. Easements may be essential in the use and enjoyment of a parcel of real property. A legal assistant will encounter easements in almost all urban real property transactions and in many rural transactions. A legal assistant actively involved in real estate transactions will, with the supervision of an attorney, review easements and advise clients as to the restrictions and benefits of easements and prepare easements.

KEY TERMS

ad valorem taxes	easement in gross	mechanics' or materialmen's lien
appurtenant easement	eminent domain	Phase I
building codes	encumbrance	Phase II
CERCLA	implied easement	prescriptive easement
dominant tenement	judgment	servient tenement
easement	license	zoning
easement by necessity	lien	

SELF-STUDY EXAMINATION

(Answers provided in Appendix)

1. T or F. Zoning is a judicial process and usually involves court proceedings.

2. T or F. State governments have the right to take private property for public use.

3. T or F. Private restrictions on the use of real property are enforceable.

4. T or F. Subcontractors are not entitled to a mechanics' lien.

5. T or F. Zoning is enforced through injunction.

6. T or F. Property benefited by an easement is known as the servient tenement.

7. T or F. Appurtenant easements are transferable.

8. T or F. An easement can be terminated by abandonment of use.

9. T or F. Land on which an easement is located is known as the dominant tenement.

10. T or F. A license must always be written.

11. List and briefly discuss various types of government regulation of private property.

12. What is the general rule for the priority of a mechanics' or materialmen's lien claim, and why is this priority important?

13. What are the main legal issues involved in an eminent domain proceeding?

14. How are private restrictive covenants enforced?

15. What is a judgment lien, and why should a real property owner be concerned about it?

16. Name four ways an easement can be created.

17. The owner of parcel A gives the owner of parcel B an easement to use a driveway located on parcel A. Which parcel is the dominant tenement, and which parcel is the servient tenement?

18. What is an easement by necessity, and how does it differ from a prescriptive easement?

19. Is there any written proof of a prescriptive or implied easement?

20. You are a legal assistant in a law firm that represents a real estate developer. The developer has obtained a necessary driveway easement to her property. After the easement was obtained, it was discovered that the property over which the driveway is located had been earlier pledged as security for a debt to the First Bank and Trust. It also has been discovered that the First Bank and Trust debt is in default and that the First Bank and Trust is having a public foreclosure auction of the property to pay the debt. Should the real estate developer be concerned? If so, what steps can be taken to protect the developer?

21. Is an encumbrance generally viewed as a positive or a negative thing for a property owner?

22. What is the main objective of zoning?

23. What is the theory behind the creation of implied easements?

24. List the ways in which an easement can be terminated.

25. How is a license different from an easement?

26. How does a Phase I environmental examination differ from a Phase II environmental examination?

27. Briefly explain the "innocent purchaser defense," which is available under CERCLA.

ADDENDUM

Exhibit 3–4   Utility Right-of-Way Easement

**EXHIBIT 3–4
Utility Right-of-Way
Easement**

STATE OF_____ , _____ COUNTY.

    In consideration of the sum of _____ , ($_____) Dollars in hand paid by The American Power Company, hereinafter called the Company, the receipt and sufficiency whereof is hereby acknowledged, the undersigned, _____ , whose Post Office Address is _____ , _____ , does hereby grant and convey to said Company, its successors and assigns, the right, privilege and easement to go in, upon and along the tract of land owned by the undersigned to Land Lot _____ , of the _____ District of _____ County, known as No. _____ in or near the City or Town of _____ , _____ , together with the right to construct, operate and maintain upon said land its lines for transmitting electric current, erected on one line of poles, with wire and other necessary apparatus, fixtures and appliances; with the right to permit the attachment of the wires and appliances of any other company, or person, to said poles; together with the right at all times to enter upon said premises for the purpose of inspecting the lines, making repairs, removals, alterations and extensions thereon, thereto or therefrom; also the right to cut away or trim and keep clear of said lines all trees, limbs of trees and other obstructions that may interfere or be likely to interfere with the proper operation of said lines; also the right of ingress and egress over said lines to and from said lines.

    The undersigned does not convey any land, but merely grants the hereinabove described rights, privileges and easements.

    Said Company shall not be liable for, or bound by, any statement or agreement or understanding not herein expressed.

    IN WITNESS WHEREOF, the said _____ , has hereinto set _____ hand_____ and seal_____ , this _____ day of _____ , 20_____ .

                                  _____ (SEAL)

                          By: _____ (SEAL)

                          Title: _____ (SEAL)

Grantors
Signed, sealed and delivered in the presence of:

Witness

Notary Public
My Commission Expires:

    This document to be signed in the presence of two (2) witnesses, one of whom should be a Notary Public.

Contracts

"But having passed his word, more or less, he stuck to it, and they went out behind the barn and made their bargain. Jabez Stone had to prick his finger to sign, and the stranger lent him a silver pen. The wound healed clean, but it left a little white scar."

—The Devil and Daniel Webster—Stephen Vincent Benet

OBJECTIVES

After reading this chapter you should be able to:

- Explain the requirements of a valid real estate contract
- Identify the remedies for default of a real estate contract
- Understand the role of a real estate agent in the procurement of a real estate contract
- Review a real estate contract for the sale and purchase of a home and understand its contents
- Prepare a real estate contract for the sale and purchase of a home
- Review a real estate contract for the sale and purchase of commercial real property and understand its contents
- Prepare a real estate contract for the sale and purchase of commercial real property

One of the main areas of a legal assistant's involvement in real estate is the assistance in representing a purchaser or seller in the sale and purchase of real property. When ownership to real property is acquired through purchase and sale, the transaction requires the negotiation and preparation of a contract before the actual transfer of ownership to the real property. The contract sets forth the terms for the purchase and sale. A legal assistant who participates in a real estate contract transaction should be aware of the general legal rules governing the validity of a contract, as well as the remedies available for an injured party in the event of default under a contract.

REQUIREMENTS OF A VALID CONTRACT

A **contract** is an agreement between two or more persons consisting of a promise or mutual promises that the law will enforce or the performance of which the law will in some way recognize as a duty. For a valid real estate contract to exist and the promises therein to be enforceable, a number of legal requirements exist. These requirements are (a) legal capacity of the parties, (b) mutual agreements (c) consideration, (d) lawful purpose, and (e) written agreement. All the requirements must be present or the contract is invalid and the promises unenforceable.

Legal Capacity to Contract

Legal capacity means that the people entering into the contract are responsible in such a way that the law will make them bound by their promises. In this section we examine how this concept relates to minors, mental incompetents, corporations, partnerships, limited liability companies, executors, trustees, and agents.

contract
Agreement between two or more persons consisting of a promise, or mutual promises that the law will enforce or the performance of which the law recognizes as a duty.

Minors or Infants

The law protects a minor or an infant from his or her contractual promises. A minor is deemed to be a person under a certain age (eighteen years in most states). A minor's contract is voidable at the election of the minor. The minor can void or fail to perform the contract if the minor so desires, but if the minor performs, the other party is bound. For example, an adult enters into a contract to purchase a car from a sixteen-year-old. If the sixteen-year-old decides not to sell the car, the adult has no legal recourse. On the other hand, if the adult decides not to buy the car, the sixteen-year-old can legally enforce the contract and require the adult to buy the car or pay damages.

Mental Incompetents

Mental incompetents are protected from their promises in most states. In other words, a mental incompetent is someone who does not understand the essence of the contract. A mental incompetent does not understand that he or she owns property or does not understand the value of the property or the value of what the purchaser is offering. A mental incompetent may be a person who does not understand that by signing the contract, he or she is obligated to perform some task, such as to sell or purchase property. The test for mental incompetence is a high standard. The lack of knowledge or inability or failure to read a contract does not make one a mental incompetent. Illiteracy is not mental incompetence.

Corporations

A contract entered into by a corporation presents special legal capacity problems. A corporation is created by state statute and only has the power granted to it by state corporate law or by its corporate charter. Most business corporations have the authority to buy and sell real property, and therefore capacity is not a problem. Many nonprofit corporations, on the other hand, have limited powers. A nonprofit corporation's corporate charter should be examined to determine if the corporation has the legal authority to buy and sell real property.

Even though the corporation probably has the authority to enter into a contract, human representatives of the corporation negotiate and sign the contract. Do these representatives truly represent the corporation, and do they have the authority to make the contract binding on the corporation? These questions of authority and capacity should be carefully examined by the legal assistant. A corporate officer's authority is set forth in a resolution passed by the board of directors of the corporation. These board resolutions or corporate resolutions are obtained at the time the contract is signed.

Partnerships

General partnerships and limited partnerships also create special authorization problems. A general partnership formed under the Uniform Partnership Act has the power to enter into contracts for the sale and purchase of real property. Unless the partnership agreement designates a managing partner, all partners must consent to any contracts entered into by the partnership. A review of the partnership agreement is necessary to determine what authority the partners have if less than all the partners are negotiating and signing the contract.

Limited partnerships formed under the Uniform Limited Partnership Act authorize the general partners to act on behalf of the partnership and to buy and sell partnership real property. The consent or agreement of the limited partners is not required. The powers of the general partners, however, can be limited by the partnership agreement, and a review of the agreement is necessary to determine what authority the general partners have to sign contracts binding on the limited partnership. In addition, general partners do not have the authority, without limited partners' consent, to sell all the assets of the limited partnership. Often a real property limited partnership may have only one asset, such as an apartment project or a shopping center. A careful examination of the affairs of the limited partnership as well as the agreement is necessary in these situations.

Limited Liability Companies

A limited liability company is a relatively new form of legal entity which has become attractive for owners and investors of real property. The limited liability company has the taxation features of a partnership, and thus is not a separate taxable entity. Income earned by the limited liability company will not be taxed at the company level, but instead will be passed through to the members of the company and taxed on their individual returns. A limited liability company also contains the limitation of liability features of a corporation; thus, the members of the limited liability company are not personally responsible for the debts of the company, nor are they responsible for contracts entered into by the company.

A limited liability company consists of members of the company who either collectively act on behalf of the company or appoint managers or managing members to act on behalf of the company. Generally any contract entered into by a limited liability company will need the consent or agreement of all members evidenced either by their signatures on the contract or by giving authority to a manager or group of members to sign the contract. A careful examination of the limited liability company articles of organization and operating agreement is necessary to determine which members have authority to sign contracts on behalf of the company.

Executors and Administrators

An executor of an estate has limited power to enter into contracts to buy and sell real property on behalf of the estate. An executor only has the power given by state law and under the will. An executor cannot act in violation of the will without a court order. Therefore, when reviewing contracts entered into with estates of deceased people, it is necessary to review not only state law regarding executor's powers, but also the actual will that appoints the executor.

An administrator of an intestate estate (one in which the deceased died without a will) has limited power to buy and sell property. In many states an administrator cannot enter into a contract to sell estate property without a court order or without consent from all the heirs who would be entitled to inherit the property.

Trustees

Trustees of a trust have problems similar to those of executors and administrators. A trustee only has the authority given by state law and by the actual trust instrument. A contract entered into with a trust requires that the trust document be carefully reviewed to see if the trustee has the authority to bind the trust to the contract.

Trustees also have a fiduciary responsibility to the beneficiaries of the trust. This means that the trustee cannot deal with trust property in such a way as to be detrimental to the beneficiaries. For example, a trustee could not enter into a contract to sell trust property to herself, her relatives, or any other entity in which the trustee has a financial interest. This would be self-dealing, and a breach of the fiduciary duty. In addition, a trustee cannot enter into a contract to sell trust property if the trustee intends to use the proceeds for purposes other than to benefit the beneficiaries. In any situation where a trustee is breaching his or her fiduciary duty the trustee does not have the authority to act and can act only if all the beneficiaries consent to the action. Beneficiaries who are under legal age cannot give their consent without the appointment of a guardian.

Agents

Occasionally a person appoints an agent or an attorney-in-fact to sign contracts on his or her behalf. These agency appointments are called *powers of attorney*. A person who appoints an agent is called a **principal** under the **power of attorney.** An attorney-in-fact only has the power granted to it by the express written agency appointment.

In reviewing contracts signed by an attorney-in-fact, it is necessary to review the power of attorney carefully to make sure the attorney-in-fact is acting within the scope of authority. Powers of attorney cannot be expanded on, nor can any powers be implied.

principal
A person who hires an agent to act on his or her behalf. A principal is generally responsible for the acts of the agent.

power of attorney
Written document authorizing another person to act as one's agent.

The language must be carefully drawn to provide the attorney with the power to act. For example, a power of attorney that gives the attorney the authority to sell property does not give the attorney the authority to purchase property.

When dealing with real property contracts, it is necessary that the agency appointment or power of attorney be written and have the same formality as the contract. For example, if the contract is under seal (usually designated by the word seal at the end of the signature lines), the power of attorney must likewise have the same formality and be under seal.

A power of attorney can be revoked at any time by the person appointing the agent. In addition, powers of attorney are automatically revoked by death or insanity of the principal or by the appointment of a new agent for the same purpose. It is essential to establish, as best one can, that the power of attorney has not been revoked at the time the agent signs the contract.

Mutual Agreement

A valid contract requires that an agreement and bargain be struck between the parties to the contract. The parties must agree on the same thing, on the same terms, and at the same time. This is referred to as "meeting of the minds." This mutual consent may be manifested by an offer on the part of one party and an acceptance of the offer on the part of the other party. The acceptance must be on the same terms as the offer. For example, Juan offers to sell a house to Bill for $100,000. Bill responds with an offer to buy the house for $95,000. At this stage of negotiations Juan has offered to sell for $100,000 and Bill has offered to buy for $95,000. Bill's offer to buy for $95,000 is a counteroffer to Juan's offer to sell for $100,000. Bill's counteroffer revokes Juan's original offer. The only offer that can be accepted or rejected is Bill's offer to buy for $95,000. Until such time as Juan and Bill agree on the same price, there is no mutual agreement and no contract.

Consideration

consideration
Something of value given to make the promises in a contract enforceable.

A contract must state the consideration flowing from one party to the other or from each to both. **Consideration** may be money, something of value, or, in many states, just a recital of the agreement of the parties to buy and sell.

Lawful Purpose

A contract must be for a lawful purpose to be enforceable. Contracts to commit crimes or contracts that are against public policy are unenforceable. Almost all real estate contracts are for a lawful purpose.

Written Agreements

Not every contract must be in writing to be enforceable. However, early in the development of contract law it was observed that oral agreements were subject to much abuse. Consequently, in 1677, the Statute of Frauds was enacted in England. Its purpose was to prevent any fraudulent practices as were commonly upheld by perjury in the law courts. The Statute of Frauds, which has been adopted in almost every state, basically provides that certain contracts are not enforceable unless there exists some written memorandum or agreement that is signed by the party to be charged with the obligation. The Statute of Frauds requires various categories of contracts to be in writing. These categories are (a) a contract to answer for the debt of another person (guaranty or surety contract); (b) an agreement made on consideration of marriage; (c) any agreement that is not to be performed within one year from the date thereof; and (d) any contract for the sale of land or any interest in land.

A written real estate contract should contain at least the following essential details: (a) the names of the parties (seller and buyer); (b) the stated agreement to buy and sell; (c) description of the real property to be bought and sold; (d) purchase price; (e) terms of payment; (f) amount and disposition of the earnest money paid by the purchaser; (g) date of closing (when the transfer of ownership is to actually take place); (h) statement that "time is of the essence"; (i) if the parties so desire, a list of any conditions before the sale; and (j) signature of the parties.

PROFILES

CHRISTINE A. HANSEN

What do you like best about your work?

One of the benefits of working in the real estate field is that it offers several specializations, which include, but are not limited to, lease administration, mortgage lending, and purchase and sales in commercial real estate. A paralegal can utilize each specialization separately or combined. At Fulbright & Jaworski LLP, I was fortunate to be able to specialize in commercial mortgage lending closings, from the initial document preparation to the final closing process; and in reviewing commercial office space leases and preparation of lease summaries for various clients. Having the experiences in the specializations of mortgage lending and lease administration in a New York City firm has prepared me to utilize and draw on those specializations to function in all aspects of commercial mortgage lending and facilitate loan closings, work on problem loans, sale of real estate properties, resolve various loan servicing requests that may arise, and prepare and negotiate Subordination and Non-Disturbance Attornment Agreements at ING Investment Management LLC.

What is the greatest challenge that you face in your area of work?

Although specializing in various areas of real estate law is a benefit, it is also one of the greatest challenges I face on a daily basis, because it is a substantial amount of information to obtain. In the past I have only had to be knowledgeable of New York Real Estate Law, but after moving to Georgia, New York Real Estate Law was no longer my boundary for mortgage lending law and lease law. I have had to quickly obtain information on Georgia Real Estate Law, and with being a paralegal at ING Investment Management LLC, which concentrates on all states, I have had to adapt and research various jurisdictions. I do believe that my training in the preparation of mortgage and transfer and lease documents in New York has broadened my analytical skills so that I am able to perform well in any jurisdiction and has taught me to use various resources, such as legal research and Internet research of various jurisdictions, in order to obtain the information required to facilitate a real estate transaction. As long as a paralegal has the basic knowledge of real estate law practices and concepts, he or she will be able to utilize the resources out there to obtain the laws of other jurisdictions.

What advice do you have for would-be paralegals in your area of work?

The best advice I could give to a would-be paralegal is to acclimate oneself with several specializations of commercial real estate law, because as previously mentioned, one could utilize this knowledge of specializations for several types of transactions. Not only does the knowledge of several specializations benefit a paralegal's self-gratification but it also makes a paralegal more valuable professionally, which can lead to more opportunities within real estate departments of law firms, corporations, lending institutions, and governmental authorities. It is also very helpful to be knowledgeable of the various business entities, because the majority of all commercial lending and lease transactions are between various types of business entities.

What are some tips for success as a paralegal in your area of work?

To be successful as a paralegal in my area of work or any other area is to be able to work indepen-dently with little attorney supervision, but, on the other hand, be able to work on a transaction as a team player to seek the end result—a lease executed or a loan closed. Real estate transactions usually involve several parties, so people skills will be very beneficial to facilitate a transaction and see it through. Take pride in your work to produce high-quality work and the end result will be self-gratification and professional recognition.

Christine Hansen is a commercial real estate paralegal with ING Investment Management LLC, where she works on servicing matters, problem loans, sale of real estate, and closing transactions for commercial real estate. Christine began her paralegal career at Cullen & Dykman, one of the oldest law firms in the country, as a Real Estate Closing Coordinator for various lenders. She chose to obtain commercial real estate experience at one of the top firms in the country, Fulbright & Jaworski LLP, where she specialized in lease review and engaged in all aspects of a commercial closing. Christine has taken various continuing education courses, such as Georgia Commercial Real Estate, Office and Commercial Leases, Negotiating Leases, and Drafting Contract Agreements. She received a Bachelor of Arts in political science with a concentration in law and government from Stony Brook University in 1996 and graduated with honors from Hofstra University's Paralegal Studies Program in 1998.

REMEDIES FOR BREACH OF A REAL ESTATE CONTRACT _____

In the event one of the parties to a contract for the purchase and sale of real estate breaches the contract and fails to perform the obligations under the contract, the injured party is entitled to one of the following remedies: (a) specific performance, (b) money damages, (c) rescission, or (d) liquidated damages.

Specific Performance

specific performance
Remedy for breach of real estate contract that requires a defaulting party to perform the promises under the contract.

The remedy of **specific performance** follows a theory that real property is unique; therefore, when a party defaults under a contract, that party should be required to perform the obligations under the contract. Under the remedy of specific performance, the party in default is ordered by the court to perform. For example, if a seller defaults on a contract, the court orders the seller to sell the real property to the purchaser pursuant to the terms of the contract. This is an ideal remedy for the purchaser, since he or she receives what was originally bargained for—the real property at the agreed-to purchase price. Specific performance also can be awarded to a seller against a defaulting purchaser. In this case the court orders the purchaser to pay the contract price to the seller and receive title to the real property.

One limitation on the use of specific performance is the ability of the defaulting party to perform. For example, a person who does not own a parcel of real property contracts to sell the real property to a purchaser. The seller then, because of lack of title, fails to perform. The court cannot order specific performance, since performance is impossible; therefore, the injured party is left with money damages or rescission.

Money Damages

The theory for money damages is that the injured party is to be placed in the same situation he or she would be in if the contract had been performed, insofar as money can do it. The amount of money damage is the difference between the contract price and the market value of the real property at the time and place of default. For example, a seller can only recover damages for the purchaser's default if the fair market value of the real property is less than the contract price at the time of default. It is only in this circumstance that the seller has lost money as a result of the sale not closing. On the other hand, a purchaser can only recover from a seller for money damages if the fair market value of the real property is more than the purchase price at the time of the default. It is only under this circumstance that the purchaser has lost money as a result of the sale not going through. The determination of fair market value usually is done by expert witnesses such as appraisers.

Rescission

rescission
Remedy for default of a real estate contract wherein the contract is terminated and the defaulting party must reimburse the injured party for expenses incurred in connection with the contract.

Rescission operates under a different theory than money damages or specific performance. Here, instead of trying to put the injured party in the position he or she would have been in had the contract been performed, the law attempts to place the injured party in the position he or she would have been in had the contract not been entered into. That is, restore the "status" to the time before entering into the contract. The remedy of rescission provides that the contract is to be terminated and the injured party reimbursed for any expenses incurred in preparation for the performance of the contract. For example, the seller breaches the obligation to sell property to a purchaser. The purchaser, in preparation of performance of the contract, has hired an attorney to do a title examination and prepare the contract, and a surveyor to survey the property. The purchaser has bills totaling $2,000, so if the purchaser is awarded rescission, the contract is terminated and the seller is ordered to pay the purchaser $2,000 as reimbursement for expenses.

It is easy to see that money damages, specific performance, and rescission are inconsistent remedies. It is impossible to require a party to perform and collect money damages at the same time. A party cannot rescind or terminate the contract and also have the court order the performance under the contract. Because these remedies are inconsistent, the injured party is entitled to only one of the remedies. However, at the time of suit, to enforce the contract the party need not "elect" a certain remedy but instead may ask the court to award in the alternative all three forms of relief. The courts then will decide, after all the evidence is presented, which remedy will be awarded. For example, if the seller does not own the real property, or the real property has serious title defects that cannot be corrected, then performance is not granted. Instead, the purchaser is left with the remedy of either money damages or rescission. In the same example, if it turns out that the fair market value of the real property and the contract price are the same, then the purchaser cannot recover money damages but is left with rescission as the only remedy.

Liquidated Damages

Sometimes the parties do not want to rely on money damages, specific performance, or rescission as a remedy for breach of contract and instead agree within the contract that a certain sum of money is to be paid in the event of default. This agreed-upon sum, called **liquidated damages,** is enforceable, provided it does not result in a penalty. The amount agreed on must be reasonably close to what actual money damages would be in the event of default. When liquidated damages are included within a contract, they typically are the exclusive remedy. The parties can only collect liquidated damages, unless for some reason the provision is enforceable. It is not unusual for contracts to provide that the purchaser will forfeit earnest money as liquidated damages in the event of the purchaser's default.

liquidated damages
Amount of money agreed on by the parties to a contract to be the damages in the event of a default of the contract.

REAL ESTATE BROKER _____

Although real estate may be sold without the services of a real estate broker, many sale transactions are arranged by a real estate broker, who earns a commission in matching a buyer and seller.

A real estate broker is subject to license by various state agencies to protect the public from unscrupulous practices and to establish professional standards of conduct. Most licensing criteria require the real estate broker to demonstrate a certain degree of competence in the area of real property law and that the broker maintain continuing education credits. Generally, a real estate license authority may deny a license to a person applying to be a broker if the person does not have a good reputation for honesty, trustworthiness, and integrity, or has been convicted of certain enumerated crimes, or has been sanctioned by any regulatory agency for violating a law regulating the sale of real estate. A broker who does not have a license or whose license has been suspended is not entitled to receive a real estate commission.

Agency Relationship

The relationship between a real estate broker and his or her client is known as an agency relationship. An agency relationship is one based upon trust and confidence of the parties and is a fiduciary relationship. The client who can either be a seller or buyer of real property is known as the principal in the relationship and the real estate broker is the agent. The broker is also a fiduciary. A **fiduciary** is defined as a person who holds a special relationship of confidence and trust to a principal and owes to the principal a duty to exercise all of the affairs of the principal in good faith and with loyalty. An agent or fiduciary also has the obligation to do what is best for the principal and to not self-deal or seek any benefit from a transaction that would be a detriment to the principal. For example, an agent who is hired by a principal to seek out and identify commercial properties for which the principal would be interested in buying cannot, while in the employment of the principal, find such commercial property and then, as an agent, invest in such properties on his or her own behalf. This type of self-dealing would be a breach of the fiduciary obligation that the agent owed to the principal.

Generally, an agent owes certain other duties or responsibilities to a principal. In most states these duties are (1) a duty to follow the instructions of the principal, (2) a duty to exercise reasonable care and skill in the performance of the agent's duties, (3) a duty to fully

fiduciary
A person who holds a special relationship of confidence and trust to a principal and owes to the principal a duty to exercise all of the affairs of the principal in good faith and with loyalty.

disclose all matters that the agent becomes aware of relating to the agency relationship, and (4) a duty to account for any money belonging to the principal which comes into the agent's possession.

An agency relationship is a bilateral relationship, and a principal owes certain duties and obligations to the agent. Generally these duties are (1) a duty to compensate the agent for his or her work, (2) a duty to reimburse the agent for any expenditures that the agent has reasonably incurred in connection with the performance of the agency, and (3) a duty to indemnify the agent against any third-party claims that may be made against the agent due to his or her performance under the agency agreement.

An agent may also have the power and authority to bind the principal to agreements entered into or actions taken by the agent on behalf of a principal. The authority of an agent to bind a principal may be divided into both express authority and implied authority. **Express authority** is authority that has clearly been given by the principal to the agent. This authority generally is in written form such as a listing agreement or property management agreement. For example, it is not unusual for owners of apartments to hire a property manager to manage the leasing and maintenance of the apartment units. Generally, the owner will enter into a property management agreement with the agent, outlining the terms under which the agent may lease apartments to prospective tenants. The actual leasing and in many cases the execution of the leases will be done by the agent. Although the agent signs the leases, it will be the principal who is responsible to the tenant for the lease terms.

Implied authority, on the other hand, is not authority expressly given to an agent by the principal. Instead, **implied authority** is authority that is implied by law to be those things necessary and proper for the agent to carry out the duties of the agency. For example, an agent or property manager hired by a property owner to lease apartments may also have the implied authority to advertise the rental of such apartments in newspapers and also have the authority to contract for office supplies and other materials necessary to enable them to lease the apartments. Since the principal is responsible for all acts of the agent including acts exercised by implied authority, the principal would be responsible to pay the cost for the advertising as well as honor the contract for the office supplies and other materials.

Traditionally, real estate brokers represented owners of properties who were interested in selling their property. These brokers would find a purchaser to buy the property and would collect a commission from the seller. The broker, although he or she spent most of his or her time with respective purchasers for the property, was really an agent for the seller, and it is the seller to whom the agent has a fiduciary obligation.

Recently there has been a growth of real estate brokers who specialize in representing purchasers. These brokers will work with persons who are interested in purchasing property, and the services may involve the identity of properties to purchase as well as negotiating the terms of the purchase. A purchaser's agent may be paid a commission from the owner of the property once the sale is completed, or may receive a commission from the purchaser.

Many states also recognize dual agents. A dual agent is a broker who simultaneously has a client relationship with both the seller and purchaser in the same real estate transaction. Although a dual agency may be legal, it is easy to see how it is difficult for a dual agent to perform fiduciary obligations to two principals who do not have a mutual interest in the transaction. A dual agent trying to get the best price for a property on behalf of the seller and at the same time get a fair price for the purchaser may find his or her duties of loyalty and good faith strained. Generally, a broker may only act as a dual agent after a full disclosure of the relationship and with the written consent of both buyer and seller.

Services Provided by a Real Estate Broker

A real estate broker can provide a number of useful services, which can assist an owner in the sale of real property. A broker may specialize in a particular type of property such as high-priced homes or commercial shopping centers or in certain geographic areas of the community. This specialization enables a broker to assist an owner in determining a correct price for the property, as well as identify potential purchasers who might be interested in the property.

---

express authority
Authority that has clearly been given by a principal to an agent.

implied authority
Authority that is implied by law to be those things necessary and proper for an agent to carry out the duties of an agency.

Pricing property for sale is a very important aspect of the transaction and one in which a broker can provide a valuable service. Ideally, the owner wants the best price that he or she can receive from the sale of the property, however, one must be realistic concerning this price. Property that is placed on the market at too high a price may not sell for a long period of time, or until the price is reduced. Both the delay in sale and a future reduction in price are unpleasant for the owner. On the other hand, if a property is priced too low, even though a sale might quickly take place, the owner may be unhappy because of money that was lost in pricing the property. A real estate broker generally has access to what similar properties have sold for in the community. This ability to use a database that shows comparison pricing, as well as new listings and sales, enables a broker to provide an owner with pricing information to accomplish the owner's objectives of a quick sale and a fair price.

A real estate broker can also help an owner prepare a property for sale. A homeowner who has lived in a home for several years cannot see it with the same eyes as a harried househunter. A skilled real estate broker can quickly take in the scene and suggest ways to improve the property's appearance for sale. For example, new paint will brighten up the exterior of the house or the interior walls and make it more attractive. Removal of clutter from the home will make it appear more spacious. A broker can also compile a sale booklet for prospective purchasers containing information about taxes, utility rates, nearby schools and parks, and available transportation.

A broker can assist an owner in advertising a property for sale and hold "open house" tours of the property. Generally during these "open house" tours, the owner of the home is not present. A broker will generally prefer to work without the owner so that the broker can, in an objective and professional manner, present the home for sale.

A real estate broker's main service to an owner is to find a purchaser. A good broker who is constantly working with a group of potential purchasers will become familiar with their needs or wants with respect to property. For example, a residential broker may work with a young couple who is looking for their first home. The broker may have shown the couple a number of houses that did not meet their tastes, requirements, or financial budget. Over a period of time spent with the couple, the broker will learn what types of properties they are interested in, what they do not like, and what they can afford. Once a property comes on the market, which seems to satisfy all of the couple's requirements, the broker can quickly identify the property and hopefully assist in the consummation of the sale.

Although real estate brokers are not attorneys, they often do many things that resemble the practice of law. It is not unusual for many states to permit real estate brokers to prepare contracts for the sale of real property. A broker may also act as an escrow agent for the purpose of holding earnest money deposits or other payments in connection with the contract. Real estate brokers are very experienced in closings of sales for real estate and often assist both sellers and purchasers in preparing for the closing. It is not unusual for a real estate broker to arrange for the preparation of title examinations, surveys, insurance, inspection reports, and other matters that must be attended to in order for the sale to take place.

A broker or an agent earns a real estate commission if the broker or agent produces a person who is ready, willing, and able to purchase the real property at the price and on the terms required by the seller in the **listing agreement.** The broker or agent must be the procuring cause of the sale. This means that the broker or agent must find a purchaser within the time agreed in the listing, and the purchaser's offer must meet the terms of the listing unless modifications are agreed to by the real property owner. The term "able to buy" means that the purchaser has the financial ability as well as the legal and mental capacity to enter into an enforceable contract to purchase the real property. The broker or agent earns the commission once a purchaser who meets the terms of the seller's offer to sell the property is presented to the seller. The commission is earned even if the seller refuses the purchaser's offer, or if the seller and purchaser go to contract but the contract does not close.

listing agreement
Agreement entered into between an owner and a real estate broker retaining the real estate broker to assist the owner in selling real property.

Although the commission is earned at the time the purchaser and seller contract, it typically is not paid until the contract closes and the purchase money is received by the seller. The real estate commission typically is a percentage of the sale price and is paid by the seller. The real estate contract usually outlines the commission rights of a broker or an agent, and the broker or agent is made a party to the contract for the purpose of enforcing the commission rights.

Some states provide for a broker to have a lien on the property being sold in the event the broker's commission is not paid. Generally, real estate broker lien laws apply only to the sale of commercial property and not to the sale of condominiums and homes. A broker, in order to perfect a lien for a commission, must file a written notice of lien upon the property providing information concerning the amount of the unpaid commission and other factual information regarding the claim of lien. Once the lien is recorded, it becomes a monetary charge against the property and cannot be removed until either payment of the commission or a settlement with the broker. The broker has the right to require the liened property to be sold to pay the commission.

Real Estate Brokers and the Internet

Real estate brokers have embraced the Internet for purposes of advertising properties for sale. Through the use of digital photography a broker is capable of providing to a prospective purchaser a virtual tour of any home listed with the broker for sale. A prospective purchaser, by use of the Internet, can review both the exterior and the interior of a number of homes in a very short period of time. Homes that appear attractive on the Internet can then be viewed in person at a later time.

Recently there has been an increasing number of low-cost Internet realtors who operate entire brokerage companies on the Internet. These Internet brokers may acquire listings for placement on the Internet or may contract with other more traditional brokers for listings, with an agreement that if the home sells through the Internet broker the traditional broker will receive a share of the commission. While most buyers use on-line listings essentially for background information, the use of the Internet to facilitate the sale of a property is a growth industry, and as both buyers and sellers become more familiar with its use, the Internet may become a major factor in the method of selling real property.

INTRODUCTION TO THE PREPARATION AND REVIEW OF A REAL ESTATE CONTRACT

Legal assistants prepare real estate contracts for an attorney's final review or assist the attorney in a review of contracts prepared by other counsel. During the process of preparing or reviewing a contract, one should remember that the contract is the primary controlling document in a real estate sale transaction. It follows the negotiations of the parties and, it is hoped, captures their agreements in writing. It dictates the rights and responsibilities of the parties, and in most instances its effect goes well beyond the consummation of the transaction it contemplates. A legal assistant must pay close attention to the contents of the real estate contract because of its vital importance to the transaction.

ELEMENTS IN A REAL ESTATE CONTRACT

The Parties

Obviously the contract will have a seller and a purchaser. Other parties may join in the execution of the contract—for example, a real estate broker or an escrow agent. All parties signing the contract should be clearly and distinctly identified by name and capacity (i.e., seller, buyer, and agent). In addition, it is helpful to put the parties' addresses and telephone numbers on the contract. In the event that a party to a contract is not a natural person, such as a corporation or a partnership, the authority of the representative to sign should be revealed in the contract. For example, in a corporate contract the corporation should be made a party to the contract, but the officer signing on behalf of the corporation should be identified as well as the office he or she holds with the corporation.

A seller should be identified in the contract exactly the way the seller holds title to the real property. Purchasers should be identified the way in which they desire to take title. The name

Residential
Neighborhood

of each person signing the contract should be typed underneath the signature line (Examples 4–1 and 4–20).

EXAMPLE 4–1

THIS AGREEMENT OF PURCHASE AND SALE (the "Agreement" is made and entered into as of the Effective Date, as hereafter defined, by and between JOANNE SELLER, ALICE SELLER LONGWORTH, AND WARREN SELLER (hereinafter collectively "Seller"); and PURCHASER, INC., a Colorado corporation (hereinafter "Purchaser") and AMERICAN REALTY COMPANY, a Colorado corporation (hereinafter "Broker").

Consideration

A contract must state the consideration flowing from one party to the other or from each to both (Example 4–2). Consideration may be money or something of value. In many states a recital of the agreement of the parties to buy and sell is sufficient.

EXAMPLE 4–2

That for and in consideration of the mutual promises and covenants herein contained and the mutual advantages accruing to Seller and Purchaser hereunder and the sum of $10.00 and other good and valuable considerations paid by Purchaser to Seller, receipt of which is hereby acknowledged by Seller, it is mutually covenanted and agreed by the parties hereto as follows:

The Agreement

At a minimum, a contract should contain statements whereby the seller agrees to sell and the buyer agrees to buy the property. Typically, the contract also contains other agreements between the parties, but without an agreement to buy and sell, the sales contract is not valid.

The Property

A contract should adequately describe the real property being bought and sold. A true and correct description of the real property prepared from a survey is preferable, but the minimum requirement in most states is that the real property be clearly and distinctively identified (Example 4–3). Does the description of the property point to a particular parcel of identifiable property? If so, the description is adequate. If anything other than unimproved real property is the subject matter of a contract, it should so indicate. Any personal property to be included with the purchase should be accurately described. Although fixtures are included as part of the realty by operation of law, if there is any question as to whether an item is a fixture, the contract should cover the questioned item with certainty. It is better practice to clearly list all items included in the sale than to rely on items being included as fixtures by the operation of law. Likewise, if some items are to be excluded from the contract, they should be expressly excluded rather than relying on the operation of law to exclude them. If personal property items are to be excluded from the sale, the contract should discuss the method and time of removal and the means for repair to the real property if such repairs are required as a result of the removal of the excluded personal property.

EXAMPLE 4–3

Property. Seller hereby agrees to sell and convey to Purchaser and Purchaser hereby agrees to purchase from Seller, subject to the terms and conditions hereinafter set forth, the property located in Land Lot 99, 17th District, Colorado Springs, Elk County, Colorado, described on *Exhibit A* attached hereto and made a part hereof containing approximately 2.544 acres (the "Land") as shown on that certain survey of the Land prepared by D. W. Transit, Colorado Registered Land Surveyor No. 1845, for JoAnne Seller et al., dated July 25, 20_____, last revised December 17, 20_____ (the "Existing Survey"), together with the following:

(a) *Improvements.* All improvements on the Land owned by Seller, including, without limitation, a two-story retail shopping center containing approximately 54,520 net rentable square feet more commonly known as the "Mountains Square" and together with drives, sidewalks, drainage, sewerage and utility facilities, and surface parking areas (collectively the "Improvements");

(b) *Tangible Personal Property.* All fixtures, equipment, machinery, building supplies, tools, furniture, and other personal property, if any, and all replacements thereof, located on or about the Land and Improvements and used exclusively in the operation and maintenance thereof (the "Tangible Personal Property"), but expressly excluding any and all property owned by tenants occupying the Improvements;

(c) *Intangible Property.* Any and all of the Seller's rights and interests in and to all intangible property pertaining to the Land, the Improvements or the Tangible Property or the use thereof, including without limitation, any trade names used in connection therewith, the landlord's interest in all leases regarding the Property to the extent assignable, and all other licenses, franchises, permits, tenant security deposits (unless Purchaser receives a credit for same), contract rights, agreements, transferable business licenses, tenant lists, correspondence with tenants and suppliers, booklets, manuals, advertising materials, transferable utility contracts, and transferable telephone exchange numbers (the "Intangible Property");

(d) *Easements.* Any and all of Seller's rights in and to all easements, if any, benefiting the Land or the Improvements; and

(e) *Rights and Appurtenances.* All rights and appurtenances pertaining to the foregoing, including any right, title, and interest of Seller in and to adjacent streets, alleys, or rights-of-way. All of the property described in Subsections (a), (b), (c), (d), and (e) of this Section, together with the Land, are hereinafter sometimes collectively referred to as the "Property."

The Price

A contract should state the purchase price of the real property or provide for an exact method by which the purchase price can be computed (Example 4–4). The easiest approach is to always have a fixed price for the real property, but that may not always be appropriate for the transaction. In dealing with commercial real property or undeveloped acreage, the price often is expressed in terms of dollars per acre, square foot, or feet of road frontage. If such is the case, the contract needs to speak to the following questions: (a) What method will be used to determine the area or frontage (a survey)? (b) Does either party have the right to question the accuracy of such a method? (c) Are all areas within the boundary of the survey to be used in the computation, or are certain areas (e.g., flood plains, easements, and public or private rights-of-way) excludable? (d) Is the seller warranting a minimum area or amount of frontage that is acceptable to the purchaser?

The Method of Payment[1]

Closely related to the price is the way in which the price will be paid and received. A contract should provide for an exact method of payment and the medium (e.g., cash, certified funds, notes, or personal checks). The most common methods of payment are (a) cash; (b) the seller accepting a note, usually secured by the real property; (c) the purchaser assuming preexisting encumbrances or debts against the real property or taking title subject thereto; and (d) the seller accepting other property, either real or personal, in exchange for the real property that is the subject matter of the contract. Many transactions involve a combination of these methods (Example 4–4).

EXAMPLE 4-4

(a) *Purchase Price.* The Purchase Price (the "Purchase Price") to be paid for the Property shall be Seven Million Three Hundred Thousand and No/100 Dollars ($7,300,000.00) to be paid in the following manner:

(i) Purchaser shall take subject to a first mortgage loan on the Property held by Wearever Life Assurance Company in the original Principal amount of Five Million Five Hundred Thousand Dollars ($5,500,000.00), which mortgage loan currently bears interest at the rate of ten percent per annum (10%) and is due and payable in full on January 1, 20 _____. Seller agrees to pay one-half of any and all transfer, assumption, or other fees assessed by the holder of the mortgage loan in connection with the transfer of the Property subject to the mortgage loan; and

(ii) Purchaser shall deliver to Seller a purchase money note ("Note") in the amount of Six Hundred Fifty Four Thousand Dollars ($654,000.00). Said Note shall bear interest at ten percent per annum (10%) and shall be payable interest only quarterly with a final payment of all unpaid principal and accrued and unpaid interest being due and payable two years from the Closing Date (hereinafter defined). The Note shall provide that it can be prepaid in whole or in part at any time without premium or penalty. The Note shall provide that the holder of the Note shall give the Maker of the Note at least twenty (20) days written notice of default prior to any acceleration of the Note for default or exercise of any other remedies that the holder may have to collect the indebtedness evidenced by the Note; provided, however, the Note shall be cross-defaulted with the Wearever Life Assurance Company loan ("Wearever Loan") and defaults under the Wearever Loan are to be governed by the notice and cure periods provided for in the Wearever Loan. The Note shall be secured by a second priority Deed of Trust ("Deed") on the Property. The Deed shall provide that insurance and condemnation proceeds shall be used for restoration of the Property; shall provide for twenty (20) days written notice of default prior to any exercise of remedies thereunder; shall not provide for any tax or insurance escrows; shall not have any restrictions on the transfer of the Property or upon any further financing or encumbrancing of the Property. The Note and Deed shall be nonrecourse to Purchaser and shall contain no personal guaranty whatsoever. The Note shall be in the form of the Note attached hereto as Exhibit "_____" and the Deed shall be in the form of the Deed of Trust attached hereto as Exhibit "_____".

(iii) The balance of the Purchase Price in the approximate amount of One Million One Hundred Forty-Six Thousand Dollars ($1,146,000.00) shall be payable in cash or by bank check drawn on a Federal Reserve Bank of Denver or by wire transfer or good funds on the Closing Date (hereinafter defined). Upon request by Purchaser prior to closing, Seller shall designate the account of Seller into which the net proceeds of the sale are to be deposited.

---

[1]From Donald Lee Mize, *The Sales Contract: Real Estate Practice and Procedure Program Materials,* Institute of Continuing Legal Education, Athens, Georgia, 1985. Used by permission of the Institute of Continuing Legal Education.

Cash

The simplest situation is one in which the purchaser is paying all cash for the real property. Although drafting and reviewing an all-cash contract requires less attention to the method of payment, there are some points that require thought. Do the parties in fact mean cash, or do they mean cash or its equivalent? It is unusual for purchasers to bring hundred-dollar bills to a closing. Cash equivalents often are the method of payment. Cash equivalents can be certified funds or a cashier's or treasurer's check. A **certified check** is a personal check in which the bank certifies that the funds are in the account and that the check will be honored on presentment for payment. A **cashier's** or treasurer's **check** is a check issued by a bank. Either mode of alternative payment usually is acceptable.

Seller Financing

The seller financing method of payment requires a great deal of skill and thought on the part of the legal assistant in drafting or reviewing the contract. It involves a continuation of rights and obligations between the parties subsequent to the closing of the purchase and sale. The contract should carefully detail each aspect of the financing instruments that will be executed at closing and, if possible, attach copies of these instruments as exhibits to the contract. At a minimum, a contract should touch on the following aspects of seller financing: (a) the security for the note (usually this is the real property being sold); (b) the priority of the lien created (is it a first mortgage lien or a junior lien?); (c) when installment payments are due under the note; (d) late penalties for payments not timely made; (e) prepayment penalties or privileges; (f) will the obligation be due on the subsequent sale by the purchaser of the property? (g) interest rates payable; (h) if the transaction so dictates, release provisions if the purchaser should desire to have a portion of the real property released from the lien before payment of the full loan; (i) maintenance of insurance on the real property for benefit of the seller; (j) personal liability to purchaser under the note and security instrument; and (k) the amount of the note and the exact method by which the amount of the note will be determined at closing.

Preexisting Obligations

The term *loan assumption* often is used to cover both the situation in which the purchaser is in fact assuming liability under some preexisting debt and the situation in which a purchaser is taking title to the property subject to a preexisting debt. The difference is one of liability for the purchaser. A purchaser who "assumes" a preexisting debt is personally obligated to pay the debt. A purchaser who takes "subject to" a preexisting debt is not personally responsible for payment. The maximum risk to a purchaser who takes "subject to" a preexisting obligation is the loss of the real property through foreclosure in the event the obligation is not paid. A thorough discussion of the differences between "assumption" and "subject to" appears in Chapter 6. A contract should clearly identify the preexisting obligation by giving the name of the holder thereof, the amounts and due dates of payments, the interest rates, the account or loan number (if any), and the loan balances as of a given date. Also, information concerning the assumability of the loan should be included in the contract. Certain representations concerning the preexisting obligation should be required from the seller, such as representation that the loan is not in default, that the seller will comply with all the terms and conditions of the financing documents in the normal course before closing, and of the existence or lack of any condition that the holder of such loan may impose on the purchaser.

Exchanges

An exchange of one parcel of real property for another parcel of real property is done for tax purposes to postpone the occurrence of a taxable event (e.g., the recognition of gain on the sale of appreciated real property). Contracts that contemplate a tax-free exchange should be carefully drafted and reviewed from both a tax and a real property law perspective. Legal assistants are seldom involved in the drafting or negotiation of tax-free exchange contracts.

---

certified check
Personal check in which the bank certifies that the funds are in the account and that the check will be honored on presentment for payment.

cashier's check
Check issued by a bank, the payment of which is guaranteed by the full faith and credit of the bank.

Quality of Title

A contract should contain a description of the quality of title the seller is obligated to convey and the purchaser is obligated to accept at the time of closing (Example 4–5). The terms usually used in contracts are "marketable title" and "insurable title." A purchaser can agree to accept some lesser quality of title. In drafting or reviewing a contract, the inclusion of catch words such as marketable title and insurable title without a clear definition can create problems. Marketable title usually means title that a prudent purchaser with full knowledge of all the facts would accept. Insurable title means title that is insurable by a title insurance company as being marketable. Real property may be "marketable" for a particular purpose even though numerous liens and encumbrances exist against the title; and title to any property is insurable, provided the owner is willing to pay a sufficient premium or accept insurance that excepts to any and every defect in title.

EXAMPLE 4–5

(a) Seller shall sell, convey, and assign to Purchaser at Closing good and marketable fee simple title to the Property subject only to the Permitted Title Exceptions as defined and set forth on *Exhibit B* attached hereto.

(b) Within thirty (30) days after the effective date of this contract, Purchaser shall cause title to the Property to be examined and shall furnish Seller with a written statement of any and all title matters, other than the Permitted Title Exceptions to which Purchaser objects. Purchaser shall also have the right to examine, or cause to be examined, title to the Property at any time or times after such initial title examination and prior to Closing and to furnish Seller with a written statement or statements of any and all additional matters, other than the Permitted Title Exceptions that affect the title to the Property or the use thereof and that arise, or first appear on record from and after the date of the initial title examination hereunder and to which Purchaser objects. Seller shall cooperate with Purchaser after receipt of any such written statement to correct, cure, or remove all matters described in such statement, and covenants to exercise diligent and good faith efforts to do so. Notwithstanding the above or the terms of this Section, in the event that any such matter results from any affirmative action taken by Seller subsequent to the date hereof, Seller covenants to expend such money and to take such other actions as may be necessary to correct, cure, or remove same. The Closing Date shall be postponed automatically for thirty (30) days, if necessary, to permit Seller to cure. If Seller shall fail to correct, cure, or remove all such matters within the time allowed by this Section, then Purchaser, at its option exercised by written notice, may:

(i) decline to purchase the Property; or

(ii) waive such matter and proceed to close the purchase and sale of the Property without a reduction in the Purchase Price and allow Seller to convey title to the Property in accordance with the terms hereof; or

(iii) in the event the matter results from affirmative action of Seller subsequent to the effective date of this contract, require Seller by action of specific performance or otherwise to exercise diligent and good faith efforts to correct, cure, or remove such matters and convey the Property in accordance with the terms of this Agreement, in which case the Closing Date shall be postponed until such correction, cure, or removal by Seller has been completed (provided, however, that at any time during such period Purchaser may exercise its options as set forth in Section (b)(i) or Section (b) (ii) above).

Should Purchaser accept, by written waiver, its interest in the Property subject to matters in addition to the Permitted Title Exceptions, such acceptable matters shall be added to the list now set forth in *Exhibit B* and shall thereafter be deemed to be Permitted Title Exceptions except that, in the event any of such matters results from any affirmative action taken by Seller subsequent to the date hereof, such acceptance shall be without prejudice to Purchaser's thereafter seeking monetary damages from Seller for any such matter. If Purchaser shall decline to accept the Seller's interest in the Property subject to such matters, pursuant to Section (b) above, then Escrowee shall refund to Purchaser the Deposit and the parties hereto shall have no further rights, obligations, duties, or liabilities hereunder whatsoever, except for those rights, obligations, duties, and liabilities that, by the express terms hereof, survive any termination hereof and except for Purchaser's right to seek monetary damages from Seller for any matter which Seller shall have failed so to correct and which shall have resulted from any affirmative action taken by Seller after the date hereof.

(c) Purchaser may, at its expense, elect to obtain a standard ALTA Form 1992 owner's policy of title insurance pursuant to which fee simple title to the Property shall be insured. Seller covenants to Purchaser that title to the Property shall at Closing not only be good and marketable, but, in the event Purchaser elects so to purchase such an owner's policy of title insurance, shall be insurable by an ALTA title insurer or other title insurance company reasonably acceptable to Purchaser at its regular rates, without exceptions or reservations to coverage of any type or kind, other than the Permitted Title Exceptions.

The contract should clearly set forth exceptions to title that the purchaser is willing to accept. All permitted exceptions should be specifically stated in the contract. Most purchasers are unwilling to accept title "subject to utility easements and other restrictions of record." Such a broad statement could include many title exceptions that are unacceptable or that would be detrimental to the real property. Be especially careful of standard permitted title exceptions, which often appear in preprinted forms. These preprinted form exceptions include (a) utility easements of record serving the real property, (b) zoning ordinances that affect the property, (c) subdivision restrictions of record, and (d) leases. The real property may be so heavily burdened by utility easements as to prevent any improvements from being constructed thereon. Zoning ordinances may preclude a purchaser from using the real property in the way he or she desires. Subdivision restrictions may place financial burdens on the purchaser or may require approval of owners' associations before the consummation of the transaction. Finally, agreeing to accept title subject to leases without first reviewing the leases can create serious problems.

A contract should require the purchaser to notify the seller of any unacceptable title exceptions disclosed as a result of an examination of the public records and afford the seller the opportunity to cure these defects. A contract should provide either a reasonable time to search title and reasonable time to cure defects, or a stated period of time for the purchaser to examine title and a stated period of time required for curative action by the seller. The contract should contain provisions dealing with the failure of the parties to meet their obligations with reference to the title.

A contract should provide that the seller shall not alter or encumber the title to the property after the date of the contract without the written consent of the purchaser.

Possession of the Property

A definite date and time for the purchaser to take possession of the property should be included in every contract. Ideally, the time of possession should follow immediately after the closing. In many situations, however, sellers may have legitimate business or personal reasons for remaining in possession for a few days after closing. For example, in a home sale it is not unusual for the seller to remain in possession for a few days after the sale, to remove his or her personal effects from the property. If possession is delayed until after closing, the contract should address the issues of maintenance, insurance, loss through fire or other casualty, and rent for the period of the seller's possession after closing.

The Closing

closing
Date set forth in a real estate contract on which the parties agree to perform all the promises of the contract. The date on which ownership of the real property is transferred from seller to purchaser and the purchaser pays the seller the purchase price for the real property.

The **closing** of a contract is the date on which the parties agree to perform all their promises under the contract. It is the time when the purchaser is required to pay the purchase price and the seller is required to transfer title and ownership to the purchaser. The date, time, and, if possible, the place for the closing should be established in the contract (Example 4–6). If the closing date is omitted from the contract, the courts will impose on the parties a reasonable time and place to close the transaction.

EXAMPLE 4–6

Closing Date. Unless this Agreement is terminated by Purchaser pursuant to the terms of this Agreement, the Closing shall take place at the offices of Purchaser's attorneys, or such location as is mutually agreeable to Purchaser and Seller, beginning at 10:00 A.M. on a business day (in Colorado Springs, Colorado) selected by Purchaser on or before November 11, 20_____. The date of Closing shall hereinafter be referred to as the "Closing Date." Purchaser shall give Seller notice of the Closing Date at least five (5) business days prior thereto; provided, however, if Purchaser gives Seller no such notice of the Closing Date, then the Closing Date shall be November 11, 20_____.

Closing Documents

A contract should list the documents that the parties will be expected to sign at closing (Example 4–7). Because, in most cases, a comprehensive list is not available before the closing itself, the parties should be obligated to execute such other documents as are reasonably necessary to carry out the purpose and intent of the contract. Closing documents usually include affidavits of title, settlement statements, deeds of conveyance, bills of sale, and assignments of warranty; notes, security instruments, and assignments of leases also may be included. Ideally, all closing forms would be identified and attached as exhibits to the contract; however, time and cost requirements and the fact that most of these documents have taken on a relative standard format have made that somewhat unnecessary. The contract should, however, identify the type of deed that will be executed at closing to convey title to the real property. The deed usually is a general warranty deed, wherein the seller warrants to the purchaser that the title to the real property is free from liens and claims by any parties other than those listed therein and the seller covenants to defend the title represented against any claims. If a contract is silent regarding the form of deed, a general warranty deed will be required. A lesser type of deed, however, can be contracted for.

EXAMPLE 4–7

Seller's Obligations. At Closing, Seller shall:

(a) Execute, acknowledge, and deliver to Purchaser a general warranty deed in recordable form, the form of which is attached hereto as *Exhibit* _____ conveying the Property to Purchaser subject only to (i) taxes for the years subsequent to the year of Closing; (ii) the zoning classification as of the Effective Date; and (iii) the Permitted Exceptions;

(b) Execute and deliver to Purchaser the following additional conveyance documents: (A) an Affidavit reciting Seller's non-foreign status within the meaning of Section 1445(f)(3) of the Internal Revenue Code of 1986; (B) an Assignment and Assumption of Leases assigning to Purchaser lessor's interest in the Leases, a form of which is attached hereto as *Exhibit* _____; (C) an Assignment of Contracts, Other Rights, and Intangible Property assigning to Purchaser the Intangible Property, the form of which is attached hereto as *Exhibit* _____; (D) Lender Estoppel Letter from the holder of the Mortgage Loan, a proposed form of which is attached hereto as *Exhibit* _____; and (E) Subordination, Attornment, and Non-Disturbance Agreements satisfactory to Lender signed by tenants leasing at least eighty-five percent (85%) of the net rentable square footage of the Property, a proposed form of which is attached hereto as *Exhibit* _____;

(c) Execute and deliver to Purchaser a Closing Statement setting forth the adjustments and prorations to closing as well as the costs pursuant to this Agreement as elsewhere specifically provided herein (the "Closing Statement");

(d) Deliver to Purchaser a certified and updated rent roll reflecting all the tenants under Leases to the Property as of the Closing Date and indicating thereon any delinquencies with respect to rent due;

(e) Deliver to Purchaser all Permits, certificates of occupancy, and licenses issued by Governmental Authorities or utility companies in connection with the occupancy and use of the Improvements as are in the possession of Seller;

(f) Deliver to Purchaser a form letter to all tenants under Leases stating that Purchaser has acquired the Property from Seller, that future rents should be paid as specified by Purchaser, and that Purchaser will be responsible for all tenants' security deposits, if any;

(g) A certificate of Seller stating (A) that Seller has no knowledge of any pending or threatened condemnation proceedings or any taking by any Governmental Authority that in any way affects the Property, (B) that there are no Leases (other than Leases approved by Purchaser), no Service Contracts (whether written or oral), no employees, no insurance policy endorsements or claims, and no other notices from any Governmental Authority regarding any violations of any Requirements of Law affecting the Property except as heretofore provided to Purchaser as required elsewhere in this Agreement;

(h) The plans and specifications for the Improvements, including all amendments thereto, as are in the possession of Seller;

(i) The originals of all Leases, including all amendments thereto;

(j) All information and materials required for full compliance under the Foreign Investors in Real Property Tax Act;

(k) All keys to the Improvements in Seller's possession and a list of all other persons who, to the best of Seller's knowledge, are in possession of keys to the Improvements, other than keys to tenant space in the possession of tenants;

(l) Such other documents, instruments, and agreements as Purchaser may reasonably require to effect and complete the transactions contemplated herein and to obtain an owner's title insurance policy insuring the interest of Purchaser, as owner, in the amount of $7,300,000.00, free and clear of all excepts except the Permitted Exceptions, for a premium calculated at standard rates, including, without limitation, a Seller's Affidavit of Title in the form attached hereto as *Exhibit* _____ and a Bill of Sale in the form attached hereto as *Exhibit* _____.

Purchaser's Obligations at Closing. On the Closing Date, subject to the terms, conditions, and provisions hereof, Purchaser shall:

(a) Execute and deliver to Seller an assumption agreement whereby Purchaser assumes all liabilities and agrees to perform all obligations of Seller under all the Leases, the form of which is contained in *Exhibit* _____, and the Service Contracts and all employee contracts assumed by Purchaser pursuant hereto, the form of which is contained in *Exhibit* _____. Said assumption agreements shall contain an indemnification by Purchaser of Seller and an agreement to hold Seller harmless from and against any and all claims, debts, liabilities, and the like affecting or relating to the Property, or any part thereof, and the Leases after the Closing Date. Likewise, said assumption agreements shall contain an agreement to hold Purchaser harmless from and against any and all claims, debts, liabilities, and the like affecting or relating to the Property, or any part thereof, and the Leases prior to and including the Closing Date.

(b) Execute and deliver to Seller a copy of the Closing Statement.

Proration, Closing Costs, and Financial Adjustments

Any item that will be prorated between the parties at the time of sale should be listed in the contract, along with the date of such proration (Example 4–8). These items usually include insurance premiums; property taxes for the current year; rents; interest on any loans against the real property that the purchaser is assuming; special assessments, such as sanitation fees, which are liens against the real property; utility charges; and mandatory owners' association fees. The contract should provide for the handling of any items that will be credits to either party and debits to the other, such as fees for utility deposits. Furthermore, a contract should designate which party will pay the costs involved in closing the transaction. These costs include document recording, taxes on transfer, title examination charges, legal fees for each party, survey, title insurance, intangible tax, assumption fees, and loan costs. Closing costs usually are negotiable, and the allocation of these costs will be whatever the parties agree to.

EXAMPLE 4-8

Closing Costs. In connection with Closing, Seller shall pay the Colorado real estate transfer tax and all costs relating to the satisfaction, cure, and removal of all title defects (except the Permitted Exceptions) undertaken by Seller as herein required and the payment of one-half (1/2) of all transfer, assumption, or other fees due the holder of the Mortgage Loan to obtain the consent to the transfer of the Property to the Purchaser and the consent to the Note and Deed of Trust. Purchaser shall pay the costs of the premiums payable or costs incurred in connection with the issuance of the owner's title insurance commitment and the owner's title insurance policy in favor of Purchaser and all costs of recording the general warranty deed. The Purchaser shall be solely responsible for the new survey costs. Each party shall pay its own attorney's fees.

Prorations. The following items shall be apportioned and prorated (based on a 30-day month, unless otherwise indicated) between the Seller and the Purchaser as of the Closing Date so that credits and charges for all days prior to the Closing Date shall be allocated to the Seller and credits and charges for the Closing Date and for all days thereafter shall be allocated to the Purchaser:

(a) *Taxes.* At the Closing, all *ad valorem* property taxes, water and sewer charges and assessments of any kind on the Property for the year of the Closing shall be prorated between Purchaser and Seller as of 12:01 a.m. on the Closing Date. Such proration shall be based upon the latest *ad valorem* property tax, water, sewer charge, and assessment bills available. If, upon receipt of the actual *ad valorem* property tax, water, sewer, and assessment bills for the Property, such proration is incorrect, then either Purchaser or Seller shall be entitled, upon demand, to receive such amounts from the other as may be necessary to correct such malapportionment. This obligation so to correct such malapportionment shall survive the Closing and not be merged into any documents delivered pursuant to the Closing.

(b) *Rents.* Purchaser shall receive a credit for all amounts due under the Leases in effect at Closing, hereinafter referred to as the "Rent," collected by Seller prior to Closing and allocable in whole or in part to any period following the Closing Date. Seller shall deliver to Purchaser any Rent received after Closing. Purchaser shall deliver to Seller any Rents received after Closing that relate to periods prior to and through the Closing Date; provided, however, that any such Rents collected by Purchaser after the Closing shall be applied first toward Rents due which shall have accrued after the Closing Date and then toward Rents that accrued prior to the Closing Date. Purchaser shall use its best efforts (short of incurring legal fees and expenses or taking other action that would not be in its best interest as owner of the Property) to collect all such delinquent Rents.

In the event that Purchaser is unable to collect delinquent Rents due Seller within thirty (30) days after the Closing Date, then Seller may pursue collection of such delinquent Rents from the respective Tenants in accordance with its rights under Colorado law; provided, however, Seller shall have no right to collect Rents in any manner that would result in an interference with the Tenant's rights of possession under its lease or in any way interfere with the landlord/tenant relationship between Purchaser and the Tenant. (For example, Seller shall have no rights to dispossess Tenant in an effort to collect delinquent Rents.)

(c) *Other Expense Prorations.* All other reasonable expenses normal to the operation and maintenance of the Property that require payments either in advance or in arrears for periods that begin prior to the Closing Date and end thereafter. Without limiting the generality of the foregoing, such expenses shall include water; electric; telephone and all other utility and fuel charges; fuel on hand (at cost plus sales tax); any deposits with utility companies; employee wages, salaries, benefits and pension, health and welfare insurance, social security, and such other contributions; and charges under employee contracts and/or Service Contracts.

(d) *Security Deposits.* Purchaser shall receive a credit for the security deposits paid under the Leases in existence and in effect on the Closing Date.

(e) *Leasing Commissions.* Seller warrants and represents that there are no leasing commissions due and owing or to become due and owing under any of the Leases or any renewals and extensions thereof, as of the Closing Date. Seller agrees to hold harmless from and to indemnify and defend Purchaser from and against any and all such leasing commissions and all other fees, charges, and compensation whatsoever due any person or entity in connection with the procuring of any Lease together with all extensions and renewals thereof or otherwise relating to any Lease. This provision shall survive the Closing and the consummation of the transactions contemplated herein.

Condition of the Property and Risk of Loss

Most contracts provide that the real property will be in substantially the same condition at the time of closing as at the time of contract, natural wear and tear excepted. It is suggested that this warranty be extended to the time of possession, if possession should occur after closing. In addition, contracts usually provide that heating, plumbing, and electrical systems will be in normal working order at the time of closing and further provide that the purchaser has the right and obligation to make inspection of these systems before closing. Many contracts provide the purchaser with a right of inspection before closing and require the seller to repair any items found in need of repair as a result of that inspection. Sellers often limit in the contract their responsibility to make repairs to the expenditure of a fixed sum of money, and the contract provides that if the repairs exceed the fixed sum of money, the purchaser does not have to purchase the real property.

A contract also should indicate which party bears the risk of loss by fire or other casualty to the real property during the contract period (Example 4–9). In most states the purchaser bears the risk of loss unless the contract provides otherwise. Most purchasers are unaware of this rule, and many do not buy insurance until the day before closing. The contract should allocate the risk of loss during the contract period to the seller. The contract should indicate whether options are available to the purchaser if the real property should be partially damaged or totally destroyed before closing. These options might include consummating the transaction and receiving the proceeds of any insurance settlement resulting from the loss or requiring the seller to restore the real property with insurance proceeds or termination of the contract.

EXAMPLE 4–9

Risk of Loss. Risk of loss or damage to the Property or any part thereof by condemnation, eminent domain, or similar proceedings, or by deed in lieu or under threat thereof (collectively, a "Taking"), or by fire, flood, or other casualty from the effective date of the contract until delivery of the limited warranty deed will be on Seller and after the delivery of the limited warranty deed will be on Purchaser. In the event of any such loss or damage to all or to a material part of the Property or any part of the Improvements prior to the delivery of the general warranty deed, this Agreement may, at the option of Purchaser to be exercised by written notice to Seller, be declared null and void and Purchaser shall be returned the Deposit and both parties hereto shall be released from any further rights and duties hereunder, or this Agreement shall remain in full force and effect and Seller shall transfer to Purchaser on the Closing Date all insurance proceeds or condemnation awards received by Seller because of such casualty or Taking and all of Seller's rights, title, and interest in and to any recovery or claims under any insurance policies or condemnation awards relating to the Property.

Upon the happening of one of the events in the preceding paragraph, subsequent to the Inspection Deadline and prior to delivery of the general warranty deed, if the cost of repair or replacement or, in the event of a Taking, if the reduction in the value of the project is TWENTY-FIVE THOUSAND DOLLARS ($25,000.00) or less, Purchaser shall close and take the Property as diminished by such events and Seller shall transfer to Purchaser on the Closing Date all insurance proceeds or condemnation awards received by Seller because of such casualty or Taking and all of Seller's right, title, and interest in and to any recovery or claim under any insurance policies or condemnation awards relating to the Property together with a credit to Purchaser for the amount of any deductibles contained in any insurance policy.

Earnest Money

earnest money
Money paid by the purchaser at the time the real estate contract is signed. The money may be used as a down payment on the purchase price or may be retained by the seller for damages in the event the purchaser defaults on the contract.

Earnest money is money paid by the purchaser at the time the contract is signed. It is not easy to describe what role in the contract the earnest money plays. Earnest money is not consideration for the contract unless the contract specifically provides so. Earnest money is not a partial payment of the purchase price unless so designated and delivered to the seller. Earnest money is not a prepaid penalty unless so provided in the contract. At best, earnest money seems to be a token deposit made to evidence the purchaser's intent to be bound by the terms of the contract (i.e., a showing of good faith). The contract should provide for the disposition of the earnest money in every possible situation (e.g., consummation of the transaction, default by seller, default by purchaser, failure of a contingency, exercise of an election to void the contract granted to either party, mutual termination of the contract) (Example 4–10). In addition, if real estate brokers are involved, a contract should take into account what claims, if any, the brokers may have on the earnest money deposit in all such events. Earnest money often is placed in a trust interest-bearing account. Contracts should provide what quality of account it is to be invested in—for example, FDIC-insured deposits. In addition, the contract should make it clear who is to get the interest. The party who is entitled to the interest should provide the holder of the escrow deposit with their federal tax identification number.

EXAMPLE 4-10

Earnest Money Deposits. Purchaser shall deliver his or her earnest money deposit to Colorado Title Company (the "Escrowee") upon Purchaser's execution of this Agreement in the form of a cashier's check (drawn on a Colorado financial institution) in the sum of SEVENTY-FIVE THOUSAND DOLLARS ($75,000.00) (the "Earnest Money"), made payable to Escrowee in trust (said Earnest Money together with any interest earned thereon shall hereinafter be referred to as the "Deposit"). The Deposit shall be held and disbursed by Escrowee as provided in this Agreement.

The Escrowee is directed to hold the Deposit as escrowed funds in an FDIC-insured, interest-bearing account, at The Second National Bank in Colorado Springs, Colorado. Purchaser represents that its U.S. federal tax identification number is 86-11314. Purchaser's tax identification number shall be credited with any interest earned on the Earnest Money prior to its being disbursed by Escrowee. Purchaser shall complete and execute a Payer's Request for Taxpayer Identification Number (Form W-9). Seller and Purchaser hereby agree to hold Escrowee harmless from any loss of escrowed funds, including the Deposit, for any reason whatsoever except for Escrowee's fraud or gross negligence or for loss of interest caused by any delay in the deposit or early withdrawal of the Deposit, from the interest-bearing account. This Agreement shall serve as escrow instructions and an executed copy of this Agreement shall be deposited by Purchaser with Escrowee. At Closing, the Deposit shall be delivered to Seller and applied against the Purchase Price. In the event of a termination of this Agreement or a default under this Agreement, the Deposit shall be delivered or disbursed by the Escrowee as provided in this Agreement. If any dispute or difference arises between the Purchaser and Seller or if any conflicting demands be made upon the Escrowee, the Escrowee shall not be required to determine the same or to take any action thereon. Rather, the Escrowee may await settlement of the controversy or deposit the Deposit into the Registry of the Superior Court of Elk County, Colorado, in an interpleader action or otherwise for the purpose of having the respective rights of the parties adjudicated. Upon making such deposit or upon institution of such interpleader action or other actions, the Escrowee shall be fully relieved and discharged from all further obligations hereunder with respect to the sums so deposited.

Should any party terminate this Agreement, as permitted herein, or declare the other party in default of its obligations hereunder, and demand payment of the Deposit to it, then Escrowee shall pay to it the Deposit, provided that declaring party provides evidence of the other party's receiving its demand notice, and within seven (7) business days following the other party's receipt of same, the nondeclaring party has not delivered written objection to Escrowee's disbursing the Deposit. If any dispute arises that is not resolved within thirty (30) days after such written objection, Escrowee shall deposit the Deposit into the Registry of the Superior Court of Elk County, Colorado, whereupon Escrowee's obligations and liabilities hereunder shall cease and terminate.

Brokers

If a real estate broker is involved, the contract should provide for the rights of the broker to a commission and the obligations incumbent on the broker under the contract (Example 4–11). It is not unusual for contracts to provide that the commission will be payable only on the closing of the transaction and in accordance with the terms of the contract. In addition, if the seller should not receive full proceeds at closing, the payment of the commission might be tied to subsequent receipt of such proceeds. This usually is done by requiring the broker to accept a note from the seller as part payment of the commission. The note requires a payment in the same ratio and at the same time the seller receives payment from the purchaser and conditions the seller's obligations to pay on purchaser's receipt of buyer's payments. For example, if the sale price is being paid in four equal annual installments, the contract may provide that the real estate commission will be paid by the seller to the broker in four equal annual installment payments at the same time the seller receives payment from the purchaser.

EXAMPLE 4–11

Brokerage Commissions. Each party further represents to the other that except for American Realty Company ("Broker"), no broker has been involved in this transaction. Seller shall be solely responsible for paying any commission due to the Broker in connection with this transaction. Seller shall pay in cash or good funds at Closing brokerage commissions of one percent (1%) to Broker. No commission shall be due and owing Broker should the sale and purchase of the Property fail to close for any reason whatsoever, including, without limitation, the breach of this Agreement by Seller or Purchaser. Under no circumstances whatsoever shall Broker be entitled to retain any portion of the Deposit. In the event any other claims for brokerage commissions or fees are ever made against the Seller or the Purchaser in connection with this transaction, all such claims shall be handled and paid by the party whose actions or alleged commitments form the basis of such claim. Seller further agrees to indemnify and hold harmless the Purchaser from and against any and all such claims or demands with respect to any brokerage fees or agent's commissions or other compensation asserted by any person, firm, or corporation in connection with this Agreement or the transactions contemplated hereby arising from actions or alleged commitments of the Seller. Purchaser further agrees to indemnify and hold harmless the Seller from and against any and all such claims or demands with respect to any brokerage fees or agent's commissions or other compensation asserted by any person, firm, or corporation in connection with this Agreement or the transaction contemplated hereby arising from actions or alleged commitments of the Purchaser. This provision shall survive Closing and the conveyance of the Property by Seller to Purchaser.

Many preprinted contract forms used by realty or broker associations provide that the commission will be payable to the broker in full at closing. They also provide that a default of either purchaser or seller will enable the broker to enforce commission rights against the defaulting party, usually by application of the earnest money. In addition, the contract may include statements to the effect that neither party has relied on warranties or representations made by the broker, but rather only those made by the other parties; that the broker is acting for the accommodation of the parties in holding earnest money and is therefore indemnified by each against any claims in connection therewith; and that the broker is the procuring cause of the contract. A broker should be made a party of the contract to enforce commission rights.

If no broker is involved in the transaction, a contract should so indicate, and have the parties mutually indemnify each other against the possible claims of brokers resulting from the actions of each.

Survival

The law in many states provides that all the promises, conditions, and covenants contained in a contract are merged into the deed of conveyance at the time of closing and do not survive the closing of the sale. This rule can be circumvented by providing in the contract that all provisions shall survive closing, or by having the parties sign at closing an agreement for the survival of warranties, representations, and obligations of the parties contained in the contract (Example 4–12).

EXAMPLE 4–12

Survival. The provisions of this Agreement shall survive Closing and the execution and delivery of the deed and instruments conveying the Property.

Assignment of Contract

The general rule is that contracts are freely assignable by the purchaser and seller unless assignment is prohibited in the contract. Most sellers never agree to the unlimited assignability of the contract by the purchaser. This is particularly true when a unique relationship exists between the parties that is, at least in part, the reason the seller has entered into the contract—for example, when the seller is extending credit for a portion of the price and is relying on the financial strength of the purchaser, or when the seller is giving preferential price or terms to a friend or relative. It is, therefore, not uncommon for a contract to contain a provision requiring the seller's written consent before the assignment of the purchaser's interest. The giving of consent to assignment can be conditioned on, among other things, the proposed assignees' agreeing to assume all obligations binding on the assignor under the contract and being bound by all terms of the contract as if an original party. In addition, a seller may require the original purchaser to agree to remain liable for damages if the assignee should default under the contract. If, at the time of contracting, there exists a possibility that the purchaser may desire to close the sale in some name other than that in which the contract is executed—for example, a general or limited partnership or a corporation not yet in existence—the contract also should provide for the seller's consent (Example 4–13).

EXAMPLE 4–13

Assignability. Purchaser shall not have the right to assign this Agreement to any person(s), partnership, or corporation, including a partnership or corporation to be formed hereafter, without the consent of Seller. In the event of such assignment, the assignee shall assume the obligations of Purchaser under this Agreement, and Purchaser shall have no further obligation or liability under this Agreement. Seller may assign its rights but shall remain bound under the terms of this Agreement and the representations, warranties, and covenants contained herein.

Time Is of the Essence

time is of the essence
Provision contained in a contract that requires strict performance of the contract by the date or dates provided therein.

The general rule is that time limits set forth in a contract are not strictly enforceable unless **time is of the essence.** If time is not of the essence, then a date for performance is not an exact critical date. The courts will permit performance to take place within a reasonable period of time after the date specified in the contract. For example, if the closing date is August 15 and time is not of the essence, the courts will permit the parties to close within a reasonable period of time after August 15. Most sellers and purchasers do not want to operate within the nebulous realm of reasonable time, and so desire that dates set forth in a contract be critical and strictly enforceable. Therefore, every contract should contain a provision that time is of the essence for the contract and for each and every obligation of the purchaser and seller (Example 4–14). The phrase most often used is simply "time is of the essence."

EXAMPLE 4–14

Time. Time is of the essence of this Agreement and of each of its provisions.

Warranties of the Parties

Any warranty, statements, or representations made by either the seller or the purchaser that were relied on by the other in deciding to enter the contract for purchase and sale of the property should be affirmatively set out in the contract (Example 4–15). Warranties commonly required of a seller include the following: (a) that the seller holds title to the real property of equal quality to that which the seller is required to convey; (b) that the seller will perform all duties and obligations of the contract; (c) that the seller has the right and full authority to enter into the contract; (d) that no other party is expressing any claim to any portion of the real property and the seller will take no action before closing that would diminish the quality of title; (e) that the seller will make no change in the zoning of the real property; (f) that the seller is aware of no pending governmental action that will affect the real property or burden it with additional assessments; (g) that utilities are available to the real property; (h) that the real property is accessible by way of public roads; and (i) that the real property contains a minimum number of acres or square feet or has a minimum amount of frontage on a public street.

EXAMPLE 4–15

(a) *Seller's Covenants and Representations.*

(i) Seller has obtained all consents, approvals, or authorizations necessary to execute this Agreement and to consummate the transaction contemplated hereby, and all documents referred to herein will be validly executed and delivered and binding upon Seller.

(ii) Seller has no knowledge of any material defect in the Improvements or any part thereof and has no knowledge of and has received no notice from any Governmental Authority (as defined below) of any violation of any Requirement of Law (as defined below) relating to the Property or any part thereof;

(iii) Seller has no knowledge of and has received no notice from any insurance company or board of fire underwriters or similar agency that there exists any condition or circumstances on the Property or any part thereof, which must be corrected in order to maintain the effectiveness, or as a condition precedent to the issuance of, any insurance policy affecting the Property or any part thereof or which is in violation of any applicable fire code or similar rule, regulation, or order for such board of fire underwriters or similar agency;

(iv) Seller has no knowledge of and has received no notice of any litigation, claim, or suit that is pending or threatened that could adversely affect the Property or any part thereof or title thereto (exclusive of any litigation, claim, or suit brought against a tenant of the Property after the effective date of the contract wherein Seller is not named a defendant or a third party defendant and wherein no counterclaims are alleged against Seller, provided, however, that Seller will give Purchaser prompt notice of all such litigation, claims, and suits);

(v) Neither Seller nor, to the best of Seller's knowledge, any previous owner of the Property or any part thereof has used, generated, stored, or disposed of any Hazardous Materials (as defined below) in or on the Property or any part thereof; or has used or disposed of any Hazardous Materials in connection with the use, operation, construction, or repair of the Property or any part thereof. Seller shall hold Purchaser harmless and shall indemnify and defend Purchaser from and against any and all losses, damages, claims, and liabilities whatsoever in any way relating to or arising out of any breach of the foregoing representation. This provision shall survive Closing and the consummation of the transactions contemplated hereby;

(vi) Seller owns good and unencumbered title to the Tangible Personal Property and Intangible Personal Property, and Seller has done nothing to encumber same during Seller's ownership thereof other than those certain Loan Documents listed on *Exhibit B* attached hereto;

(vii) Seller has not operated the Property within the past five (5) years under any other name or trade name of which Seller has not notified Purchaser;

(viii) Seller shall not cause or permit to exist (A) any mortgage, deed to secure debt, security deed, security agreement, assignment, or other similar instrument or agreement or any lien or encumbrance whatsoever (other than the Permitted Exceptions or those listed on *Exhibit C.*) to attach to or affect title to the Property or any part thereof from and after the Effective date except for the Leases approved by Purchaser; or (B) any matters not shown on the new survey;

(ix) Seller represents, to the best of its knowledge, that the mechanical, electrical, plumbing, HVAC, roofing, drainage, sanitary sewerage, and utility equipment facilities and systems servicing the Property and the improvements thereon are in operational order and shall be so maintained through and including the Closing Date. Seller represents that it is aware of no defects in any of said systems;

(x) Seller covenants that it shall not enter into any leases pertaining to the Property after the Effective Date without prior written approval of Purchaser. Purchaser shall approve leases containing reasonable business terms, including base rentals of at least $16.00 per square foot and $1.75 of C.A.Ms. Seller covenants and represents that it shall incur no brokerage commissions pertaining to leases entered into prior to the Closing Date on any leases negotiated in any respect by Seller prior to the Closing Date;

(xi) Seller represents that it has no notice of and is not aware of any violation of the Property and improvements of any applicable zoning laws, ordinances, or regulations including, without limitation, all parking requirements and building setback requirements (except as shown on the existing survey, which Purchaser has the right to consider during the inspection period);

(xii) Seller shall continue to operate, manage, and maintain the Property in good condition and in a good businesslike manner, such operation and maintenance to include the undertaking of any reasonably necessary capital improvements or repairs, through and including the Closing Date. Such continuous operation and maintenance shall also be a condition precedent to Closing and

(b) *Purchaser's Covenants and Representations.* Purchaser hereby represents and warrants to Seller that Purchaser has obtained all consents, approvals, or authorizations necessary to execute this Agreement and to consummate the transaction contemplated hereby, and all documents referred to herein will be validly executed and delivered and binding upon Purchaser.

Warranties commonly asked for from a purchaser are (a) that the purchaser has the right and authority to enter into the agreement; (b) that the purchaser has financial resources to meet the financial obligations required under the contract; (c) that the purchaser will perform its duties in accordance with the agreement; (d) that no parties have initiated or threatened any action that might affect the purchaser's ability to perform; and (e) that the purchaser will take no action that would diminish the quality of the seller's title before closing.

It is a good idea to have the parties reaffirm the warranties and representations at closing by separate instrument. The contract should provide that the parties will sign such a separate instrument at closing. Contracts also usually provide for the rights and obligations of the parties in the event that any warranty proves untrue. Specifically, the contract will provide that in the event a warranty proves untrue, a party can either terminate the contract or treat such failure as a default under the contract and exercise all its remedies for default.

Contingencies

condition precedent
Condition in a contract that must be satisfied in accordance with the terms of the contract before one or both of the parties are required to perform their contractual obligations.

A **condition precedent** in a contract is a situation that must be resolved in accordance with the terms of the contract before one or both of the parties are required to perform their contractual obligations. These elements are called conditional clauses of the contract, or contingencies. A contract can be made conditional on virtually anything. Some of the more common contingencies include financing, rezoning, sale of other property, purchase of adjacent property, engineering reports, issuance of building or use permits, and review of documents affecting title to the property. In drafting conditional clauses, exact standards by which the parties can determine when and if the condition has been met must be provided. In addition, the contract should require the parties to use due diligence and good faith in attempting to meet the contingency. A failure to meet a condition precedent would make a contract unenforceable. Most contracts provide for repercussions in the event a contingency fails with regard not only to the contract as a whole, but to any earnest money as well. The contract also should indicate for whose benefit the condition applies and provide if either party has a right to waive the conditions.

Definitions

Although most terms and phrases used in a contract take on their ordinary meanings, many contracts include a definitions section that carefully and clearly defines key words and phrases. This is particularly important when the parties are not from the same geographical area, and the possibility exists for misunderstanding as to the exact meaning of certain terms.

Default

A contract should provide the exact rights and obligations of the parties in the event that one party fails to perform in accordance with the terms of the contract. The contract also should list the events that constitute a default.

Notice

Because most contracts provide that parties need to notify each other of different events, such as title objections, date for closing, and results of inspection reports, there should be a paragraph that outlines when and how notices are to be given (Example 4–16). Most notice provisions deal with personal delivery and certified mail, although, under modern practice, contracts should consider overnight express carriers as well as telephone facsimile transmissions. If one of the parties is a partnership or corporation, the contract should specify an individual to receive notice.

EXAMPLE 4–16

Notification. Any notice or demand under which the terms of this Agreement or under any statute must or may be given or made by the parties hereto shall be made in writing and shall be deemed to have been delivered when hand delivered; as of the date sent by an overnight courier; or as of the date of postmark affixed by the U.S. Postal Service, by mailing the same by certified mail return receipt requested addressed to the respective parties at the following addresses:

To Purchaser:

Purchaser, Inc.
535 East Paces Ferry Road
Denver, Colorado
Attn: George Purchaser

To Seller:

c/o JoAnne Seller
2970 Crabtree Road, N.W.
Suite 500
Colorado Springs, Colorado

Such addresses may be changed by the giving of written notice as provided in this paragraph; provided, however, that any mailed notice of changed address shall not be effective until the fifth (5th) day after the date of postmark by the U.S. Postal Service.

Entire Agreement

The **parol evidence rule** that is applicable in most states provides that a written agreement is the best and only evidence of the agreement between the parties, and that the parties are not permitted to bring in oral testimony regarding other agreements concerning the transaction. The law in many states, however, requires that the contract contain a clause that indicates that it is the entire agreement and that no other written or oral agreements affecting the transaction exist (Example 4–17). Typically, the clause states that "the contract contains the entire agreement of the parties thereto concerning the subject matter thereof and that representations, inducements, promises, or agreements oral or otherwise not expressly set forth therein shall not be of any force or effect."

parol evidence rule
Rule of evidence that provides that a written agreement is the best and only evidence of the agreement between the parties and that the parties are not permitted to bring in oral testimony regarding other agreements concerning the transaction.

EXAMPLE 4–17

Entire Agreement. No agreements, representations, or warranties unless expressly incorporated or set forth in this Agreement shall be binding upon any of the parties.

In addition, the contract should provide that it cannot be amended or modified unless in writing and executed by all parties thereto.

Applicable Law

The general rule in most states is that a contract for the sale and purchase of real property will be governed by the law of the state in which the real property is located. Despite this general rule, most contracts do specify the law of the state that will govern the construction and enforcement of the contract (Example 4–18).

EXAMPLE 4–18

This Agreement shall be construed and interpreted under the Laws of the State of Colorado.

Additional Provisions

It is not unusual, when using a preprinted form, to find additional provisions added to the contract by way of addendum or exhibit. It is important that there be a provision in the contract that provides that if conflict between the preprinted portion of the contract and the special stipulations contained in the addendum or exhibit should arise, the special stipulations will control.

Offer and Acceptance

Because most contracts are not signed at the same time by both seller and purchaser, but are prepared by the seller or the purchaser and presented to the other party for consideration, it is important that the contract contain a clause that addresses the issue of when and how the offer is to be accepted and converted into a contract. This usually is done by a provision that indicates that the contract represents an offer that must be accepted by the signature of the other party to the contract on or before a certain date (Example 4–19).

EXAMPLE 4–19

This instrument shall be regarded as an offer by the Purchaser or Seller who first signs to the other and is open for acceptance by the other until _____ o'clock _____ .m., on this _____ day of _____, 20_____, by which time written acceptance of such offer must have been actually received. The above offer is hereby accepted, _____ o'clock _____ .m. on this _____ day of _____; 20_____.

In addition, it is preferable to make the date of the contract a certain date, especially if other dates, such as the date for doing a title examination or inspection of the property, are calculated from the date of the contract. For example, the purchaser must examine title and present objections to the seller not later than thirty days from the date of contract.

Execution

execution
Signature of a party to a legal document. The act of signing a legal document.

The seller, purchaser, and other parties to a contract should **execute** the contract properly and in accordance with their authority (Example 4–20). It is not necessary for real estate contracts to be witnessed and notarized, and real estate contracts usually are not recorded. From the seller's perspective, recording of the contract is not advisable because if the contract is not closed, the record of the contract might represent a cloud on the property title, thus creating future problems for the seller.

EXAMPLE 4–20

IN WITNESS WHEREOF, the parties hereto have set their hands and seals as of the Effective Date.

PURCHASER:
PURCHASER, INC., a Colorado corporation
By: _____ (SEAL)
　　　George W. Purchaser,
　　　President
Date Executed: _____

SELLER:
_____ (SEAL)
JoAnne Seller
_____ (SEAL)
Alice Seller Longworth
_____ (SEAL)
Warren Seller
Date Executed: _____

The undersigned as Escrowee hereby acknowledges receipt of a copy of this Agreement and of the initial Earnest Money deposit by check $_____ drawn on _____, subject to collection, and agrees to hold said funds pursuant to the terms of this Agreement.

COLORADO TITLE COMPANY

Dated:_____   By: _____
　　　　　　　　　　　　　　　　　　　Charles B. Jares, as
　　　　　　　　　　　　　　　　　　　Executive Vice President

The preceding is by no means an exhaustive list of all possible areas of concern in preparing or reviewing a real estate sales contract. The outline does touch on the major issues that a legal assistant can expect a real estate contract to address. A legal assistant should remember that each contract is unique and should reflect the agreement between the parties to that particular transaction. Drafting and reviewing a comprehensive sales contract requires time and careful attention to detail but should ultimately reduce the possibility of later misunderstanding between the parties.

OPTIONS

Buyers and sellers of real property occasionally use an option initially instead of entering into a contract for the purchase and sale of the property. An **option** is a contract by which an owner of property, usually called the optionor, agrees with another person, usually called the optionee, that the optionee shall have the right to buy the owner's real property at a fixed price within a certain time on agreed terms and conditions. The effect of an option is to bind an owner of real property to an agreement to sell the property to the optionee in the event the optionee elects to purchase the property at the fixed price and on the terms set forth in the option. The decision to enter into the contract to purchase the property is entirely at the discretion of the optionee. An option usually is based on valuable consideration and is an irrevocable offer to sell by the owner of the real property. Option agreements must be in writing and be supported by something of value, usually money paid as an option price. An option form is shown as Exhibit 4–3 at the end of this chapter.

option
A contract by which an owner of property, usually called the optionor, agrees with another person, usually called the optionee, that the optionee shall have the right to buy the owner's real property at a fixed price within a certain time on agreed terms and conditions.

SUMMARY

A purchaser and seller of real property each has a number of issues and concerns that must be addressed and agreed to in the contract for purchase and sale. A legal assistant who participates in the preparation and review of a real estate contract must not only be aware of the general is-

---

 E T H I C S :   Illegal or Fraudulent Activity

A legal assistant is employed with a law firm. A client of the firm is a real estate developer who builds and sells single-family homes. The developer is generally honest but is having trouble selling one of its homes. The developer finally has a purchaser who is willing to buy the home, but the purchaser does not have any money. The developer wants to prepare a contract that will show that the purchaser is making a down payment of 20 percent of the purchase price, which should enable the purchaser to go to a lending institution and get a loan for the other 80 percent. The developer, however, will not actually receive the 20 percent down payment. The developer instead will take a note from the purchaser for the 20 percent, which will be paid out over a period of time. This means that the purchaser actually will not have any money invested in the property at the time of the sale. This activity on the part of the developer and purchaser constitutes a fraud on the lending institution that will be making a loan to the purchaser.

The developer has explained all of this to an attorney who works at the firm. The attorney has decided that he will go ahead and prepare a contract that will show that a down payment of 20 percent has been made and received by the developer. The attorney has asked a legal assistant at the firm to assist in the preparation of the contract. Does the preparation of the contract, which shows that a down payment of 20 percent has been made when in fact it has not, constitute a breach of ethics on the part of the attorney as well as the legal assistant?

An attorney or a legal assistant should never assist a client in conduct that is illegal or fraudulent. Assisting a client to commit fraud can result in a loss of license to practice law on the part of the attorney and could subject both the attorney and the legal assistant to civil and criminal penalties. The participation by the attorney and legal assistant in the preparation of the contract to assist the developer in perpetrating a fraud on the lending institution is a serious breach of ethics.

sues and concerns of purchasers and sellers of real property, but also ask the client about any special issues or concerns. The contract is the agreement that outlines responsibilities and duties of the respective seller and purchaser, and is the blueprint that will be followed at the time of the closing of the sale and purchase. Careful thought and attention to detail must be given to the preparation and review of real estate contracts.

The real estate contract is the mutual promise of both purchaser and seller of the future transfer of ownership to real property. The contract does not transfer ownership, but merely promises to do so at some future date and time. At the time that ownership is to be transferred, the transfer is accomplished by a separate legal document known as a deed.

KEY TERMS

cashier's check	execution	parol evidence rule
certified check	express authority	power of attorney
closing	fiduciary	principal
condition precedent	implied authority	rescission
consideration	liquidated damages	specific performance
contract	listing agreement	time is of the essence
earnest money	option	

SELF STUDY EXAMINATION

(Answers provided in Appendix)

1. T or F. A contract entered into between an adult and a minor is unenforceable by both parties.

2. T or F. A person being appointed to act under a power of attorney must be a lawyer.

3. T or F. A real estate contract must be in writing to be enforceable.

4. T or F. A real estate agent or broker, to earn a commission, must be the procuring cause of the sale.

5. T or F. A liquidated damage provision in a contract is enforceable, provided it does not result in a penalty.

6. T or F. It is not necessary for a contract to state the purchase price of the property.

7. T or F. The date on which the parties agree to perform all their promises under the contract is known as the closing date.

8. T or F. A purchaser usually takes possession of the property at the time the contract is signed.

9. T or F. Contracts are freely assignable by purchaser and seller.

10. T or F. Property taxes for the current year are prorated under a contract.

11. What is the Statute of Frauds, and what effect does it have on the validity of contracts?

12. Explain the three remedies available for the breach of a real estate contract.

13. When is a real estate broker entitled to a commission?

14. Seller and purchaser enter into a contract for the purchase and sale of real property for the price of $90,000. The property has a value of $100,000. The purchaser fails to perform. What is the amount of money damages to be awarded to the seller?

15. Sam Seller offers to sell his home to Pat Purchaser for the sum of $75,000. Pat Purchaser responds that she will only purchase the home for $65,000. Sam Seller rejects Pat Purchaser's offer to purchase for $65,000; Pat Purchaser then offers $75,000 for Sam Seller's home. Is there a contract between Sam Seller and Pat Purchaser for the sale and purchase of the home at $75,000?

16. Why is careful attention to detail required in the preparation of a real estate contract?

17. What does the "time is of the essence" phrase mean in a real estate contract?

18. If, under a real estate contract, the Seller is to provide financing to the purchaser, what issues should be discussed concerning seller financing?

19. What items are prorated in a real estate contract?

20. The following is a list of contract provisions. Do these provisions favor the seller or the purchaser?

a. Seller is to convey insurable title to the real property at closing.

b. Seller is to convey title to the real property subject to utility easements and other restrictions of record.

c. Seller shall not alter or encumber the title to the property after the date of the contract without the prior written consent of purchaser.

d. The real estate contract is freely assignable.

e. The contract is silent as to risk of loss between date of contract and date of closing.

21. What is meant by legal capacity to contract?

22. What are the necessary elements in order to have mutual agreement?

23. What is a listing agreement?

24. What is a closing?

25. When does the risk of loss shift from seller to buyer in a real estate contract?

26. What duties are owed by an agent to a principal?

27. What duties are owed by a principal to an agent?

ADDENDUM

The exhibits referred to in the contracts are not included in the materials presented.

EXHIBIT 4-1
Contract for Purchase and Sale of a Home

PURCHASE AND SALE AGREEMENT

Date:_____, 20_____

2002 Printing

1. <u>Purchase and Sale.</u> The undersigned buyer ("Buyer") agrees to buy and the undersigned seller ("Seller") agrees to sell all that tract or parcel of land, with such improvements as are located thereon, described as follows: All that tract of land lying and being in Land Lot _____ of the _____ District, _____ Section of _____ County, Georgia, and being known as Address _____, City_____, Georgia Zip Code _____, according to the present system of numbering in and around this area, being more particularly described as Lot _____, Block _____, Unit _____, Phase/Section _____of _____Subdivision, as recorded in Plat Book _____, Page _____, _____ County, Georgia records together with all fixtures, landscaping, improvements, and appurtenances, all being hereinafter collectively referred to as the "Property." The full legal description of the Property is the same as is recorded with the Clerk of the Superior Court of the county in which the Property is located and is made a part of this Agreement by reference.

2. <u>Purchase Price and Method of Payment.</u> Buyer warrants that Buyer will have sufficient cash at closing, which when combined with the loan(s), if any, referenced herein, will allow Buyer to complete the purchase of the Property. Buyer does not need to sell or lease other real property in order to complete the purchase of the Property. The purchase price of the Property to be paid by Buyer at closing is: _____ U.S. Dollars, $_____ subject to the following: *[Select sections A, B, C, and/or D below. The sections not marked are not a part of this Agreement.]*

   ☐ **A.** **All Cash At Closing:** Buyer shall pay the purchase price to Seller in cash, or its equivalent. Buyer's obligation to close shall not be subject to any financial contingency. Buyer shall pay all closing costs.

   ☐ **B.** **Loan To Be Assumed:** See Exhibit "_____."

   ☐ **C.** **New Loan To Be Obtained:** This Agreement is made conditioned upon Buyer's ability to obtain a loan (except if the loan is denied because Buyer lacks sufficient cash to close excluding the amount of the loan and/or because Buyer has not sold or leased other real property) in the principal amount of _____% of the purchase price listed above, with an interest rate at par of not more than _____% per annum on the unpaid balance, to be secured by a first lien security deed on the Property; the loan to be paid in consecutive monthly installments of principal and interest over a term of not less than _____ years. "Ability to obtain" as used herein means that Buyer is qualified to receive the loan described herein based upon lender's customary and standard underwriting criteria. The loan shall be of the type selected below: *[The sections not marked are not a part of this Agreement.]*

   (1) **Loan Type:** ☐ **Conventional;** ☐ **FHA** (see attached exhibit); ☐ **VA** (see attached exhibit) ; ☐ **Other** (see attached exhibit)

   (2) **Rate Type:** ☐ **Fixed Rate Mortgage Loan;** ☐ **Adjustable Rate Mortgage ("ARM") Loan;**

   (3) **Closing Costs and Discount Points:** Seller shall, at the time of closing, contribute a sum not to exceed $_____ to be used by Buyer to pay for: (a) preparation of the warranty deed and owner's affidavit by the closing attorney; (b) at Buyer's discretion, closing costs, loan discount points, survey costs, and insurance premiums (including flood insurance, if applicable) relating to the Property and/or loan; and (c) at Buyer's discretion, other costs to close including escrow establishment charges and prepaid items, if allowed by lender. Buyer shall pay all other costs, fees, and amounts for the above referenced items and to fulfill lender requirements to otherwise close this transaction.

   (4) **Closing Attorney:** This transaction shall be closed by the law firm of_____ _____, provided the firm is approved to close loans for Buyer's lender.

   (5) **Loan Obligations:** Buyer agrees to: (a) make application for the loan within _____ days from the Binding Agreement Date; (b) immediately notify Seller of having applied for the loan and the name of the lender; and (c) pursue qualification for and approval of the loan diligently and in good faith. Should Buyer not timely apply for the loan, Seller may terminate the Agreement if Buyer does not, within five days after receiving written notice thereof, cure the default by providing Seller with written evidence of loan application. Buyer agrees that a loan with terms consistent with those described herein shall satisfy this loan contingency. Buyer may also apply for a loan with different terms and conditions and close the transaction provided all other terms and conditions of this Agreement are fulfilled, and the new loan does not increase the costs charged to the Seller. Buyer shall be obligated to close this transaction if Buyer has the ability to obtain a loan with terms as described herein and/or any other loan for which Buyer has applied and been approved. From the Binding Agreement Date until closing, Buyer shall not intentionally make any material changes in Buyer's financial condition which would adversely affect Buyer's ability to obtain a loan. In the event any application of Buyer for a loan is denied, Buyer shall promptly provide Seller with a letter from the lender denying the loan stating the basis for the loan denial.

   ☐ **D. Second Loan to be Obtained,** see Exhibit "_____."

3. <u>Earnest Money.</u> Buyer has paid to _____ ("Holder") earnest money of $_____ check, OR $_____ cash, which has been received by Holder. The earnest money shall be deposited in Holder's escrow/trust account (with Holder retaining the interest if the account is interest bearing) within five banking days from the

F20, Purchase and Sale Agreement, Page 1 of 5 01/01/02

(continued)

EXHIBIT 4-1
Contract for Purchase and Sale of a Home (continued)

Binding Agreement Date and shall be applied toward the purchase price of the Property at the time of closing. In the event any earnest money check is not honored, for any reason, by the bank upon which it is drawn, Holder shall promptly notify Buyer and Seller. Buyer shall have three banking days after notice to deliver good funds to Holder. In the event Buyer does not timely deliver good funds, the Seller shall have the right to terminate this Agreement upon written notice to the Buyer. Holder shall disburse earnest money only as follows: (a) upon the failure of the parties to enter into a binding agreement; (b) at closing; (c) upon a subsequent written agreement signed by all parties having an interest in the funds; (d) upon order of a court or arbitrator having jurisdiction over any dispute involving the earnest money; or (e) upon a reasonable interpretation of this Agreement by Holder. Prior to disbursing earnest money pursuant to a reasonable interpretation of this Agreement, Holder shall give all parties fifteen days notice, stating to whom the disbursement will be made. Any party may object in writing to the disbursement, provided the objection is received by Holder prior to the end of the fifteen-day notice period. All objections not raised in a timely manner shall be waived. In the event a timely objection is made, Holder shall consider the objection and shall do one or more of the following: (a) hold the earnest money for a reasonable period of time to give the parties an opportunity to resolve the dispute; (b) disburse the earnest money and so notify all parties; and/or (c) interplead the earnest money into a court of competent jurisdiction. Holder shall be reimbursed for and may deduct from any funds interpleaded its costs and expenses, including reasonable attorneys' fees. The prevailing party in the interpleader action shall be entitled to collect from the other party the costs and expenses reimbursed to Holder. No party shall seek damages from Holder (nor shall Holder be liable for the same) for any matter arising out of or related to the performance of Holder's duties under this earnest money paragraph. If Buyer breaches Buyer's obligations or warranties herein, holder may pay the earnest money to Seller by check, which if accepted and deposited by Seller, shall constitute liquidated damages in full settlement of all claims of Seller. It is agreed to by the parties that such liquidated damages are not a penalty and are a good faith estimate of Seller's actual damages, which damages are difficult to ascertain.

4. **Closing and Possession.**
   A. **Property Condition:** Seller warrants that at the time of closing or upon the granting of possession if at a time other than at closing, the Property will be in substantially the same condition as it was on Binding Agreement Date, except for normal wear and tear, and changes made to the condition of the Property pursuant to the written agreement of Buyer and Seller. Seller shall deliver Property clean and free of debris at time of possession. If the Property is destroyed or substantially damaged prior to closing, Seller shall promptly notify Buyer of the amount of insurance proceeds available to repair the damage and whether Seller will complete repairs prior to closing. Buyer may terminate this Agreement not later than five days after receiving such notice by giving written notice to Seller. If Buyer does not terminate this Agreement, Buyer shall receive at closing such insurance proceeds as are paid on the claim which are not spent to repair the damage.
   B. **Taxes:** Real estate taxes on said Property for the calendar year in which the sale is closed shall be prorated as of the date of closing. Seller shall pay State of Georgia property transfer tax.
   C. **Timing of Closing and Possession:** This transaction shall be closed on _____, 20____ or on such other date as may be agreed to by the parties in writing, provided, however, that: (1) in the event the loan described herein is unable to be closed on or before said date; or (2) Seller fails to satisfy valid title objections, Buyer or Seller may, by notice to the other party (which notice must be received on or before the closing date), extend this Agreement's closing date and the date for surrender of occupancy if later than the closing date, up to seven days from the above-stated closing date. Buyer agrees to allow Seller to retain possession of the Property through: *[Select sections A, B, or C below. The sections not marked are not a part of this Agreement.]*
      ☐ A. the closing; or ☐ B. _____ hours after the closing; or ☐ C. _____ days after the closing at _____ m. o'clock
   D. **Warranties Transfer:** Seller agrees to transfer to Buyer, at closing, subject to Buyer's acceptance thereof, Seller's interest in any manufacturer's warranties, service contracts, termite bond or treatment guarantee and/or other similar warranties which, by their terms, may be transferable to Buyer.
   E. **Prorations:** Seller and Buyer agree to prorate all utility bills between themselves, as of the date of closing (or the day of possession of the Property by the Buyer, whichever is the later) which are issued after closing and include service for any period of time the Property was owned/occupied by Seller or any other person prior to Buyer.
   F. **Closing Certifications:** Buyer and Seller shall execute and deliver such certifications, affidavits, and statements as are required at closing to meet the requirements of the lender and of federal and state law.

5. **Title.**
   A. **Warranty:** Seller warrants that, at the time of closing, Seller will convey good and marketable title to said Property by general warranty deed subject only to: (1) zoning; (2) general utility, sewer, and drainage easements of record on the Acceptance Date upon which the improvements do not encroach; (3) subdivision and/or condominium declarations, covenants, restrictions, and easements of record on the Acceptance Date; and (4) leases and other encumbrances specified in this Agreement. Buyer agrees to assume Seller's responsibilities in any leases specified in this Agreement.
   B. **Examination:** Buyer may, prior to closing, examine title and furnish Seller with a written statement of objections affecting the marketability of said title. If Seller fails to satisfy valid title objections prior to closing or any extension thereof, then Buyer may terminate the Agreement upon written notice to Seller, in which case Buyer's earnest money shall be returned. Good and marketable title as used herein shall mean title which a title insurance company licensed to do business in Georgia will insure at its regular rates, subject only to standard exceptions.
   C. **Survey:** Any survey of the Property attached hereto by agreement of the parties prior to the Binding Agreement Date shall be a part of this Agreement. Buyer shall have the right to terminate this Agreement upon written notice to Seller if a new survey performed by a surveyor licensed in Georgia is obtained which is materially different from any attached survey with respect to the Property, in which case Buyer's earnest money shall be returned. The term "materially different" shall not apply to any improvements constructed by Seller in their agreed-upon locations subsequent to Binding Date Agreement. Matters revealed in said survey shall not relieve the warranty of title obligations of Seller referenced above.

6. **Seller's Property Disclosure.** Seller's Property Disclosure Statement is attached hereto and incorporated herein. Seller warrants that to the best of Seller's knowledge and belief, the information contained therein is accurate and complete as of the Binding Agreement Date.

F20, Purchase and Sale Agreement, Page 2 of 5 01/01/02

(continued)

EXHIBIT 4–1
Contract for Purchase and Sale of a Home (continued)

7. <u>Termite Letter</u>. An official Georgia Wood Infestation Report ("Report") prepared by a licensed pest control operator, covering each dwelling and garage on the Property and dated within one hundred eighty days of the acceptance date is ☐, **OR,** is not ☐ attached to this Agreement as an exhibit. If the Report is not attached, Seller shall provide such a Report to Buyer within seven days from the Binding Agreement Date. Buyer shall have the right to terminate this Agreement within ten days from the Binding Agreement Date if either of the following events occur: (a) the Report is not timely provided to Buyer; or (b) the Report provided after the Binding Agreement Date indicates present infestation of, or damage to, the Property from termites or other wood destroying organisms. If Buyer does not timely give Seller notice of Buyer's decision to terminate this Agreement, Buyer's right to terminate the Agreement pursuant to this paragraph shall be waived. Notwithstanding the above, Buyer shall continue to have whatever other rights to terminate this Agreement, if any, that exist elsewhere in this Agreement. Unless otherwise noted on the Seller's Property Disclosure Statement, to the best of Seller's knowledge, the information contained in any attached or later provided Report is accurate and complete, and no other termite inspections have been performed or reports issued, the findings of which are inconsistent with the Report attached hereto. Prior to closing, Seller shall treat active infestation of termites and other wood destroying organisms, if any. At closing, Seller shall provide Buyer with a Report prepared by a licensed pest control operator dated within thirty days of the closing, stating that each dwelling and garage has been found to be free from active infestation of termites and other wood destroying organisms. This paragraph shall not limit Buyer's right to request that Seller repair and/or replace defects resulting from termites and other wood destroying organisms if the Property is sold with the right to request repairs in accordance with the Inspection Paragraph herein.

8. <u>Inspection</u>. Buyer and/or Buyer's representatives shall have the right to enter the Property at Buyer's expense and at reasonable times (including immediately prior to closing) to thoroughly inspect, examine, test and survey the Property. This shall include the right to inspect and test for lead-based paint and lead-based paint hazards for not less than ten days from the Binding Agreement Date. Seller shall cause all utility services and any pool, spa, and similar items to be operational so that Buyer may complete all inspections under this Agreement. The Buyer agrees to hold the Seller and all Brokers harmless from all claims, injuries, and damages arising out of or related to the exercise of these rights.

[Select section A or B below. The section not marked shall not be part of this Agreement.]

Buyer(s)
Initials
☐   **A. Property Sold With Right to Request Repairs.**
(1) Buyer shall have the right to request that Seller repair and/or replace only defects in the Property identified by Buyer's representative(s) by providing Seller, within _____ days from Binding Agreement Date, with a copy of inspection report(s) and a signed written amendment to this Agreement setting forth the defects noted in the report which Buyer requests be repaired and/or replaced. The term "defects" shall mean any portion of or item in the Property which: (a) is not in good working order and repair (normal wear and tear excepted); (b) constitutes a violation of applicable laws, governmental codes or regulations and is not otherwise grandfathered; or (c) is in a condition which represents a significant health risk or an unreasonable risk of injury or damage to persons or property. If Buyer does not timely present the written amendment and inspection report, Buyer shall be deemed to have accepted the Property "as is" in accordance with paragraph B below.
(2) If Buyer timely submits the inspection report and the written amendment, Buyer and Seller shall have _____ days (hereinafter "Defect Resolution Period") from the Binding Agreement Date to negotiate through written offers and counteroffers the defects to be repaired and/or replaced by Seller.
(3) Neither party may terminate this Agreement prior to the end of the Defect Resolution Period due to the failure to agree on the repair and/or replacement of defects without the written consent of the other party.
(4) If Seller at any time during the Defect Resolution Period notifies Buyer that Seller will repair and/or replace all of the defects listed in the initial amendment submitted by Buyer, an agreement on the repair and/or replacement of defects shall be deemed to have been reached and all parties shall execute an amendment to that effect.
(5) If Buyer and Seller have not within the Defect Resolution Period agreed on the defects to be repaired and/or replaced by signing a written amendment to this Agreement, Buyer may either accept the last unexpired counteroffer of Seller or accept the Property "as is" in accordance with paragraph B below, by giving notice to Seller within three days after the end of the Defect Resolution Period. If Buyer fails to timely give this notice, this Agreement shall terminate immediately, and Buyer's earnest money shall be returned in accordance with the Earnest Money paragraph above. All agreed-upon repairs and replacements shall be completed in a good and workmanlike manner prior to closing.

Buyer(s)
Initials
☐
OR

B. Property Sold "As Is." All parties agree that the Property is being sold "as is," with all faults including but not limited to lead-based paint and lead-based paint hazards and damage from termites and other wood destroying organisms. The Seller shall have no obligation to make repairs to the Property.

9. <u>Other Provisions</u>.
   A. **Binding Effect, Entire Agreement, Modification, Assignment:** This Agreement shall be for the benefit of, and be binding upon, Buyer and Seller, their heirs, successors, legal representatives and permitted assigns. This Agreement constitutes the sole and entire agreement between the parties hereto and no modification or assignment of this Agreement shall be binding unless signed by all parties to this Agreement. No representation, promise, or inducement not included in this Agreement shall be binding upon any party hereto. Any assignee shall fulfill all the terms and conditions of this Agreement.
   B. **Survival of Agreement:** All conditions or stipulations not fulfilled at time of closing shall survive the closing until such time as the conditions or stipulations are fulfilled.
   C. **Governing Law:** This Agreement may be signed in multiple counterparts, is intended as a contract for the purchase and sale of real property and shall be interpreted in accordance with the laws of the State of Georgia.

F20. Purchase and Sale Agreement, Page 3 of 5 01/01/02

(continued)

EXHIBIT 4-1
Contract for Purchase and Sale of a Home (continued)

D. **Time of Essence:** Time is of the essence of this Agreement.

E. **Terminology:** As the context may require in this Agreement: (1) the singular shall mean the plural and vice versa; and (2) all pronouns shall mean and include the person, entity, firm, or corporation to which they relate.

F. **Responsibility to Cooperate:** All parties agree to timely take such actions and produce, execute, and/or deliver such information and documentation as is reasonably necessary to carry out the responsibilities and obligations of this Agreement.

G. **Notices.** Except as otherwise provided herein, all notices, including offers, counteroffers, acceptances, amendments and demands, required or permitted hereunder shall be in writing, signed by the party giving the notice and delivered either: (1) in person, (2) by an overnight delivery service, prepaid, (3) by facsimile transmission (FAX) (provided that an original of the notice shall be promptly sent thereafter if so requested by the party receiving the same) or (4) by the United States Postal Service, postage prepaid, registered or certified return receipt requested. The parties agree that a faxed signature of a party constitutes an original signature binding upon that party. Notice shall be deemed to have been given as of the date and time it is actually received. Notwithstanding the above, notice by FAX shall be deemed to have been given as of the date and time it is transmitted if the sending FAX produces a written confirmation with the date, time and telephone number to which the notice was sent. Receipt of notice by the Broker representing a party as a client shall be deemed to be notice to that party for all purposes herein, except in transactions where the Broker is practicing designated agency, in which case, receipt of notice by the designated agent representing a party as a client shall be required to constitute notice. All notice requirements referenced herein shall be strictly construed.

10. **Disclaimer.** Buyer and Seller acknowledge that they have not relied upon any advice, representations or statements of Brokers and waive and shall not assert any claims against Brokers involving the same. Buyer and Seller agree that Brokers shall not be responsible to advise Buyer and Seller on any matter including but not limited to the following: any matter which could have been revealed through a survey, title search or inspection of the Property; the condition of the Property, any portion thereof, or any item therein; building products and construction techniques; the necessity or cost of any repairs to the Property; hazardous or toxic materials or substances; termites and other wood destroying organisms; the tax or legal consequences of this transaction; the availability and cost of utilities or community amenities; the appraised or future value of the Property; any condition(s) existing off the Property which may affect the Property; the terms, conditions and availability of financing; and the uses and zoning of the Property whether permitted or proposed. Buyer and Seller acknowledge that Brokers are not experts with respect to the above matters and that, if any of these matters or any other matters are of concern to them, they should seek independent expert advice relative thereto. Buyer further acknowledges that in every neighborhood there are conditions which different buyers may find objectionable. Buyer shall therefore be responsible to become fully acquainted with neighborhood and other off site conditions which could affect the Property.

11. **Agency and Brokerage.**
   A. **Agency.**
   (1) In this Agreement, the term "Broker" shall mean a licensed Georgia real estate broker or brokerage firm and where the context would indicate the broker's affiliated licensees. No Broker in this transaction shall owe any duty to Buyer or Seller greater than what is set forth in their brokerage engagements and the Brokerage Relationships in Real Estate Transactions Act, O.C.G.A. § 10-6A-1 et .seq.;
   (2) Seller and Buyer acknowledge that if they are not represented by a Broker they are each solely responsible for protecting their own interests, and that Broker's role is limited to performing ministerial acts for that party.
   (3) The Broker, if any, working with the Seller is identified on the signature page as the "Listing Broker"; and said Broker is ☐, **OR,** is **NOT** ☐ representing the Seller;
   (4) The Broker, if any, working with the Buyer is identified on the signature page as the "Selling Broker", and said Broker is ☐, **OR,** is **NOT** ☐ representing the Buyer; and
   (5) If Buyer and Seller are both being represented by the same Broker, a relationship of either designated agency ☐, **OR,** dual agency ☐ shall exist.
      (a) **Dual Agency Disclosure.** [*Applicable only if dual agency has been selected above*] Seller and Buyer are aware that Broker is acting as a dual agent in this transaction and consent to the same. Seller and Buyer have been advised that:
         1 - In serving as a dual agent the Broker is representing two clients whose interests are or at times could be different or even adverse;
         2 - The Broker will disclose all adverse, material facts relevant to the transaction and actually known to the dual agent to all parties in the transaction except for information made confidential by request or instructions from another client which is not otherwise required to be disclosed by law;
         3 - The Buyer and Seller do not have to consent to dual agency; and
         4 - The consent of the Buyer and Seller to dual agency has been given voluntarily and the parties have read and understood their brokerage engagement agreements.
         5 - Notwithstanding any provision to the contrary contained herein, Seller and Buyer each hereby direct Broker, while acting as a dual agent, to keep confidential and not reveal to the other party any information which could materially and adversely affect their negotiating position.
      (b) **Designated Agency Assignment.** [*Applicable only if the designated agency has been selected above*] The Broker has assigned _____ to work exclusively with Buyer as Buyer's designated agent and _____ to work exclusively with Seller as Seller's designated agent. Each designated agent shall exclusively represent the party to whom each has been assigned as a client and shall not represent in this transaction the client assigned to the other designated agent.

(continued)

EXHIBIT 4–1
Contract for Purchase and Sale of a Home (continued)

    (c)   **Material Relationship Disclosure.** The Broker and/or affiliated licensees have no material relationship with either client except as follows:_____.
        (A material relationship means one actually known of a personal, familial or business nature between the Broker and affiliated licensees and a client which would impair their ability to exercise fair judgment relative to another client.)

B. **Brokerage.** The Broker(s) identified herein have performed valuable brokerage services and are to be paid a commission pursuant to a separate agreement or agreements. Unless otherwise provided for herein, the Listing Broker will be paid a commission by the Seller, and the Selling Broker will receive a portion of the Listing Broker's commission pursuant to a cooperative brokerage agreement. The closing attorney is directed to pay the commission of the Broker(s) at closing out of the proceeds of the sale. If the sale proceeds are insufficient to pay the full commission, the party owing the commission will pay any shortfall at closing. If more than one Broker is involved in the transaction, the closing attorney is directed to pay each Broker their respective portion of said commission. In the event the sale is not closed because of Buyer's and/or Seller's failure or refusal to perform any of their obligations herein, the non-performing party shall immediately pay the Broker(s) the full commission the Broker(s) would have received had the sale closed, and the Selling Broker and Listing Broker may jointly or independently pursue the non-performing party for their portion of the commission.

12. <u>Time Limit of Offer.</u> This instrument shall be open for acceptance until_____ o'clock _____M. on the _____ day of _____, 20_____.

13. <u>Exhibits and Addenda.</u> All exhibits and/or addenda attached hereto, listed below, or referenced herein are made a part of this Agreement. If any such exhibit or addendum conflicts with any preceding paragraph, said exhibit or addendum shall control:

SPECIAL STIPULATIONS: The following Special Stipulations, if conflicting with any exhibit, addendum, or preceding paragraph, shall control.

☐ **(Mark box if additional pages are attached.)**

_____ (_____)
Selling Broker   MLS Office Code

By: _____
    Broker or Broker's Affiliated Licensee

Print or Type Name:_____

Bus. Phone:_____ FAX #_____

Multiple Listing #_____

_____ (_____)
Listing Broker   MLS Office Code

By: _____
    Broker or Broker's Affiliated Licensee

Print or Type Name: _____

Bus. Phone:_____FAX# _____

_____
Buyer's Signature: SS/FEI#

Print or Type Name:_____

_____
Buyer's Signature: SS/FEI#

Print or Type Name:_____

_____
Seller's Signature: SS/FEI#

Print or Type Name:_____

_____
Seller's Signature: SS/FEI#

Print or Type Name:_____

<u>Acceptance Date</u>
The above proposition is hereby accepted, _____ o'clock_____ m. on the_____ day of _____, 20____.

<u>Binding Agreement Date</u>
This instrument shall become a binding agreement on the date ("Binding Agreement Date") when notice of the acceptance of this Agreement has been received by offeror. The offeror shall promptly notify offeree when acceptance has been received.

     F20, Purchase and Sale Agreement, Page 5 of 5 01/01/02

EXHIBIT 4–2
Contract for Purchase
and Sale of Retail
Shopping Center

AGREEMENT OF PURCHASE AND SALE

THIS AGREEMENT OF PURCHASE AND SALE (the "Agreement" is made and entered into as of the Effective Date, as hereafter defined, by and between _____

_____

_____ (hereinafter collectively "Seller");

and _____, a corporation (hereinafter "Purchaser").

WITNESSETH:

That for and in consideration of the mutual promises and covenants herein contained and the mutual advantages accruing to Seller and Purchaser hereunder and the sum of $10.00 and other good and valuable considerations paid by Purchaser to Seller, receipt of which is hereby acknowledged by Seller, it is mutually covenanted and agreed by the parties hereto as follows:

1. Property.

Seller hereby agrees to sell and convey to Purchaser and Purchaser hereby agrees to purchase from Seller, subject to the terms and conditions hereinafter set forth, the property located in Land Lot _____, _____ District, My Town, Great County, State described on *Exhibit A* attached hereto and made a part hereof containing approximately 2.544 acres (the "Land") as shown on that certain survey of the Land prepared by ___, Registered Land Surveyor No. 1845, for _____, dated July 25, 20___, last revised December 17, 20___ (the "Existing Survey"), together with the following:

(a) *Improvements.* All improvements on the Land owned by Seller, including, without limitation, a two-story retail shopping center containing approximately 54,520 net rentable square feet more commonly known as the "Village Square" and together with drives, sidewalks, drainage, sewerage and utility facilities, and surface parking areas (collectively the "Improvements");

(b) *Tangible Personal Property.* All fixtures, equipment, machinery, building supplies, tools, furniture and other personal property, if any, and all replacements thereof, located on or about the Land and Improvements and used exclusively in the operation and maintenance thereof (the "Tangible Personal Property"), but expressly excluding any and all property owned by tenants occupying the Improvements;

(c) *Intangible Property.* Any and all of the Seller's rights and interests in and to all intangible property pertaining to the Land, the Improvements or the Tangible Property or the use thereof, including without limitation any trade names used in connection therewith, the Landlord's interest in all leases regarding the Property to the extent assignable, and all other licenses, franchises, permits, tenant security deposits (unless Purchaser, receives a credit for same), contract rights, agreements, transferable business licenses, tenant lists, correspondence with tenants and suppliers, booklets, manuals, advertising materials, transferable utility contracts, and transferable telephone exchange numbers (the "Intangible Property");

(d) *Easements.* Any and all of Seller's rights in and to all easements, if any, benefiting the Land or the Improvements; and

(e) *Rights and Appurtenances.* All rights and appurtenances pertaining to the foregoing, including any right, title and interest of Seller in and to adjacent streets, alleys or right-of-way.

All of the property described in Subsections (a), (b), (c), (d), and (e) of this Section 1 together with the Land are hereinafter sometimes collectively referred to as the "Property."

2. Purchase Price and Earnest Money Deposits.

(a) *Purchase Price.* The Purchase Price (the "Purchase Price") to be paid for the Property shall be Seven Million Three Hundred Thousand and No/100 Dollars ($7,300,000.00) to be paid in the following manner:

(i) Purchaser shall take subject to a first mortgage loan on the Property held by Wearever Life Assurance Company in the original principal amount of Five Million Five Hundred Thousand Dollars ($5,500,000.00), which mortgage loan currently bears interest at the rate of ten percent per annum

(continued)

EXHIBIT 4-2
Contract for Purchase
and Sale of Retail
Shopping Center
(continued)

(10 percent) and is due and payable in full on January 1, 20___. Seller agrees to pay one-half of any and all transfer, assumption, or other fees assessed by the holder of the mortgage loan in connection with the transfer of the Property subject to the mortgage loan; and

(ii) Purchaser shall deliver to Seller a purchase money note ("Note") in the amount of Six Hundred Fifty Four Thousand Dollars ($654,000.00). Said Note shall bear interest at ten percent per annum (10 percent) and shall be payable interest only quarterly with a final payment of all unpaid principal and accrued and unpaid interest being due and payable two years from the Closing Date (hereinafter defined). The Note shall provide that it can be prepaid in whole or in part at any time without premium or penalty. The Note shall provide that the holder of the Note shall give the Maker of the Note at least twenty (20) days written notice of default prior to any acceleration of the Note for default or exercise of any other remedies which the holder may have to collect the indebtedness evidenced by the Note; provided, however, the Note shall be cross-defaulted with the Wearever Life Assurance Company loan ("WLA Loan") and defaults under the WLA Loan are to be governed by the notice and cure periods provided for in the WLA Loan. The Note shall be secured by a second priority Deed to Secure Debt ("Deed") on the Property. The Deed shall provide that insurance and condemnation proceeds shall be used for restoration of the property; shall provide for twenty (20) days written notice of default prior to any exercise of remedies thereunder; shall not provide for any tax or insurance escrows; shall not have any restrictions on the transfer of the Property or upon any further financing or encumbrancing of the Property. The Note and Deed shall be nonrecourse to Purchaser and shall contain no personal guaranty whatsoever. The Note shall be in the form of the Note attached hereto as Exhibit "L" and the Deed shall be in the form of the Deed to Secure Debt attached hereto as Exhibit "L-1".

(iii) The balance of the Purchase Price in the approximate amount of One Million One Hundred Forty-Six Thousand Dollars ($1,146,000.00) shall be payable in cash or by bank check drawn on a Federal Reserve Bank or by wire transfer or good funds on the Closing Date (hereinafter defined). Upon request by Purchaser prior to closing, Seller shall designate the account of Seller into which the net proceeds of the sale are to be deposited.

(b) *Earnest Money Deposits.* Purchaser shall deliver its earnest money deposit to Ajax Realty, Inc. (the "Escrowee") upon Purchaser's execution of this Agreement in the form of a cashier's check (drawn on a State financial institution) in the sum of SEVENTY FIVE THOUSAND DOLLARS ($75,000.00) (the "Earnest Money"), made payable to Escrowee in trust (said Earnest Money together with any interest earned thereon shall hereinafter be referred to as the "Deposit"). The Deposit shall be held and disbursed by escrowee as provided in this Agreement.

The Escrowee is directed to hold the Deposit as escrowed funds in an FDIC insured, interest-bearing account, at The Bank in My Town, State. Purchaser represents that his U.S. federal tax identification number is _____. Purchaser's tax identification number shall be credited with any interest earned on the Earnest Money prior to its being disbursed by Escrowee. Purchaser shall complete and execute a Payer's Request for Taxpayer Identification Number (Form W-9). Seller and Purchaser hereby agree to hold Escrowee harmless from any loss of escrowed funds, including the Deposit, for any reason whatsoever except for Escrowee's fraud or gross negligence or for loss of interest caused by any delay in the deposit or early withdrawal of the Deposit, from the interest-bearing account. This Agreement shall serve as escrow instructions and an executed copy of this Agreement shall be deposited by Purchaser with Escrowee. At Closing, the Deposit shall be delivered to Seller and applied against the Purchase Price. In the event of a termination of this Agreement or a default under this Agreement, the Deposit shall be delivered or disbursed by the Escrowee as provided in this Agreement. If any dispute or difference arises between the Purchaser and Seller or if any conflicting demands be made upon the Escrowee, the Escrowee shall not be required to determine the same or to take any action thereon. Rather, the Escrowee may await settlement of the controversy or deposit the Deposit into the Registry of the Superior Court of Great County, State, in an interpleader action or otherwise for the purpose of having the respective rights of the parties adjudicated. Upon making such deposit or upon institution of such interpleader action or other actions, the Escrowee shall be fully relieved and discharged from all further obligations hereunder with respect to the sums so deposited.

(c) Should any party terminate this Agreement, as permitted herein, or declare the other party in default of its obligations hereunder, and demand payment of the Deposit to it, then Escrowee shall pay to it the Deposit provided that declaring party provides evidence of the other party's receiving its demand notice, and within seven (7) business days following the other party's receipt of same, the nondeclaring party has not delivered written objection to Escrowee's disbursing the Deposit. If any dispute arises that is not resolved within thirty (30) days after such written objection, Escrowee shall deposit the Deposit into the Registry of the Superior Court of Great County, State, whereupon Escrowee's obligations and liabilities hereunder shall cease and terminate.

3. Inspection Period.

Purchaser shall have until 11:59 p.m. of August 26, 20____; (the "Final Inspection Date") within which to make an inspection of: the Property; all of Seller's operating financial records of the Property for the period of Seller's ownership of the Property (including the current year) pertaining to the Property and all items required to be delivered by Seller pursuant to this Agreement. All such records and items shall be made available to Purchaser at the office of the Seller in My Town, State. Purchaser shall have the right to enter upon the Property and make a complete inspection of the Property. Purchaser shall upon reasonable notice to Seller have the right to talk with all tenants, lenders' representatives (if any) and all service personnel involved with or connected with the Property. If for any reason the results of Purchaser's inspection are not deemed by Purchaser to be satisfactory for any reason whatsoever, in its sole discretion, then Purchaser may elect to terminate this Agreement by written notice of such election to Seller no later than the Final Inspection Date, in which event neither Purchaser nor Seller shall have any further rights or obligations hereunder, and Escrowee shall return to Purchaser the Deposit together with accrued interest and thereafter this Agreement shall be deemed terminated and of no further force or effect. If Purchaser fails to make such election to terminate this Agreement as aforesaid by the Final Inspection Date, then Purchaser shall be deemed to have waived its right to terminate this Agreement pursuant to this Section.

4. Title of the Property.

(a) Seller shall sell, convey and assign to Purchaser at Closing good and marketable fee simple title to the Property subject only to the Permitted Title Exceptions as defined and set forth on *Exhibit B* attached hereto.

(b) Within thirty (30) days following the Effective Date, Purchaser shall cause title to the Property to be examined and shall furnish Seller with a written statement of any and all title matters, other than the Permitted Title Exceptions to which Purchaser objects. Purchaser shall also have the right to examine, or cause to be examined, title to the Property at any time or times after such initial title examination and prior to Closing and to furnish Seller with a written statement or statements of any and all additional matters, other than the Permitted Title Exceptions which affect the title to the Property or the use thereof and which arise, or first appear of record from and after the date of the initial title examination hereunder and to which Purchaser objects. Seller shall cooperate with Purchaser after receipt of any such written statement to correct, cure or remove all matters described in such statement, and covenants to exercise diligent and good faith efforts to do so. Notwithstanding the above or the terms of this Section 4(b), in the event that any such matter results from any affirmative action taken by Seller subsequent to the date hereof, Seller covenants to expend such money and to take such other actions as may be necessary to correct, cure or remove same. The Closing Date shall be postponed automatically for thirty (30) days, if necessary, to permit Seller to cure. If Seller shall fail to correct, cure or remove all such matters within the time allowed by this Section 4(b), then Purchaser, at its option exercised by written notice, may:

(i) decline to purchase the Property; or

(ii) waive such matter and proceed to close the purchase and sale of the Property without a reduction in the Purchase Price and allow Seller to convey title to the Property in accordance with the terms hereof; or

(iii) in the event the matter results from affirmative action of Seller subsequent to the Effective Date, require Seller by action of specific performance or otherwise to exercise diligent and good faith efforts to correct, cure or remove such matters and convey the Property in accordance with the terms of this Agreement in which case the Closing Date shall be postponed until such correction, cure or removal by Seller has been completed (provided, however, that at any time during such period Purchaser may exercise its options as set forth in Section 4(b)(i) or Section 4(b)(ii) above).

Should Purchaser accept, by written waiver, its interest in the Property subject to matters in addition to the Permitted Title Exceptions, such acceptable matters shall be added to the list now set forth in *Exhibit B* and shall thereafter be deemed to be Permitted Title Exceptions except that, in the event any of such matters results from any affirmative action taken by Seller subsequent to the date hereof, such acceptance shall be without prejudice to Purchaser's thereafter seeking monetary damages from Seller for any such matter. If Purchaser shall decline to accept the Seller's interest in the Property subject to such matters, pursuant to Section 4(b) above, then Escrowee shall refund to Purchaser the Deposit and the parties hereto shall have no further rights, obligations, duties or liabilities hereunder whatsoever, except for those rights, obligations, duties and liabilities which, that, by the express terms hereof, survive any termination hereof and except for Purchaser's right to seek monetary damages from Seller for any matter which Seller shall have failed so to correct and which shall have resulted from any affirmative action taken by Seller after the date hereof.

(c) Purchaser may, at its expense, elect to obtain a standard A.L.T.A. Form 1992 owner's policy of title insurance pursuant to which fee simple title to the Property shall be insured. Seller covenants to Purchaser that title to the Property shall at Closing not only be good and marketable, but, in the event Purchaser elects so to purchase such an owner's policy of title insurance, shall be insurable by Ticor Title Insurance Company of California or by Chicago Title Insurance Company or other title insurance company reasonably acceptable to Purchaser at its regular rates, without exceptions or reservations to coverage of any type or kind, other than the Permitted Title Exceptions.

5. Survey.

(a) Purchaser shall have within thirty (30) days from the Effective Date the option to obtain a current accurate as-built survey of the Premises (the "New Survey") and such New Survey discloses any matter which is not set forth on the Existing Survey to which Purchaser objects (any such matter being herein referred to as "New Survey Objections"), then Purchaser shall give Seller notice of such New Survey Objections. Purchaser shall be entitled to make its best efforts to cure said New Survey Objections and Seller covenants that it shall cooperate with Purchaser to the extent necessary to effectuate said cures.

(b) If Seller shall have failed to correct, cure or remove all such New Survey Objections prior to time set for closing, then Purchaser, at its option, exercised by written notice, may:

(i) decline to purchase the Property; or

(ii) waive such matter and proceed to close the purchase and sale of the Property without a reduction in the Purchase Price and allow Seller to convey title to the Property in accordance with the terms hereof; or

(iii) or, if such New Survey Objection should arise by affirmative action of Seller after the Execution Date, require Seller by action of specific performance or otherwise to exercise diligent and good faith efforts to correct, cure or remove such New Survey Objections and convey the Property in accordance with the terms of this Agreement in which case the Closing Date shall be postponed until such correction, cure or removal by Seller has been completed (provided, however, that at any time during such period Purchaser may exercise its options as set forth in Section 5(b)(i) or Section 5(b)(ii) above).

Should Purchaser accept, by written waiver, its interest in the Property subject to New Survey Objections, such acceptable matters shall be added to the list now set forth in *Exhibit B* and shall thereafter be deemed to be Permitted Title Exceptions except that, in the event any of such matters results from any affirmative action taken by Seller subsequent to the date hereof, such acceptance shall be without prejudice to Purchaser's thereafter seeking monetary damages from Seller for any such matter. If Purchaser shall decline to accept the Seller's interest in the Property subject to such matters, pursuant to Section 5(b)(i) above, then Escrowee shall refund to Purchaser the Deposit and the parties hereto shall have no further rights, obligations, duties or liabilities hereunder whatsoever, except for those rights, obligations, duties and liabilities which, that, by the express terms hereof, survive any termination hereof and except for Purchaser's right to seek monetary damages from Seller for any matter which Seller shall have failed so to correct and which shall have resulted from any affirmative action taken by Seller after the date hereof.

(continued)

6. Seller's Deliveries.

(a) Seller shall deliver to Purchaser or Purchaser's designee the following items, in possession of Seller or any entity related to Seller, as soon as reasonably possible after the Effective Date, but in any event within five (5) days after the Effective Date, unless another time period is otherwise indicated below:

(i) True, correct, and complete copies of all leases of space on the Property together with any amendments thereto and all brokerage commission agreements relating thereto and together with all lease abstracts, tenant correspondence files, and other relevant information, all necessary information and documentation necessary to establish the base index, such as the consumer price index for the base year of such lease, for any escalation clause in any lease, and copies of all written correspondence to or received from any lessee regarding such additional rental charges or rental escalation provisions (all leases of space on the Property together with any amendments thereto and such brokerage commission agreements and other documents described hereinabove are hereinafter collectively referred to as the "Leases", and each lease of space on the Property together with any amendments thereto and such brokerage commission agreements is hereinafter individually referred to as a "Lease");

(ii) A true, correct, and complete rent roll concerning all Leases as of the Effective Date or a more current date, indicating thereon any delinquencies with respect to rent due and owing and indicating all brokerage commissions and similar fees owing and relating to the Leases;

(iii) True, correct, and complete copies of all contracts other than Leases, if any, pertaining to the Property (the "Service Contracts") in existence as of the Effective Date or a more current date, including but not limited to all management contracts, maintenance contracts, contracts or agreements relating to any unfinished improvements to the Property, service leases, and contracts for parking on a monthly or yearly basis, together with a list of those contracts which cannot be unilaterally terminated by Purchaser as of the Closing Date without further payment;

(iv) A true, correct, and complete inventory of all the Tangible Personal Property as of the Effective Date or a more current date;

(v) [INTENTIONALLY DELETED]

(vi) True, correct, and complete copies of the latest personal property and real estate tax bills for the Property and all tax bills, notices, assessments and communications relating to the Property, or any part thereof, promptly upon receipt of same by Seller;

(vii) True, correct, and complete copies of the most recent title insurance policy relating to the Land, if any, in the possession of Seller; together with true, correct and complete copies of all exceptions listed on Schedule B thereof which are not inchoate liens or surveys exceptions;

(viii) True, correct, and complete copies of all matters listed on *Exhibit B* attached hereto which are not inchoate liens or survey exceptions (to the extent that such copies are not furnished to Purchaser pursuant to Section 6(a)(vii) above);

(ix) True, correct, and complete copies of all inspection reports and tests and studies relating to the Property, including, without limitation, engineering studies, environmental assessments or reports, and maintenance schedules;

(x) A true, correct, and complete copy of any offering circular, private placement memorandum, registration statement or other similar information or materials relating to the Property, which is in the possession of the Seller;

(xi) True, correct, and complete copies of all existing insurance policies relating to the Property (or if the Property is insured pursuant to a master policy, then true, correct, and complete copies of all certificates (issued pursuant to such master policies) which evidence the insurance coverages relating to the Property) and true, correct, and complete copies of all records and communications concerning all claims, losses and demands made under any insurance policy relating to the Property since Seller acquired the Property and otherwise in possession of Seller, together with a listing of the names, addresses and account representatives of all insurance companies which issued policies relating to the Property since Seller acquired the Property and otherwise in the possession of Seller;

(xii) A memorandum, which Seller shall prepare if presently not in Seller's possession, describing all oral contracts and agreements pertaining to the Property, if any, which memorandum shall

(continued)

include, without limitation, the names, address and telephone numbers of all persons or entities which are parties to such contracts or agreements together with a description of the terms, conditions and provisions of such contracts and agreements;

(xiii) True, complete, and correct copies of all documents, including, but not limited to, plans, specifications, contracts, budgets, schedules, and certificates pertaining to the current construction, renovation, paving, and all other improvement to the Property;

(xiv) On or before November 1, 20_____, tenant estoppel letters subsequentially in the form attached hereto as *Exhibit C* (the "Tenant Estoppels") each dated no earlier than October 1, 20_____, duly executed by all tenants of the Property or in such form as required by Lender. Seller shall use its best efforts to obtain the Tenant Estoppels from all tenants. If Seller is unable to obtain Tenant Estoppels from tenants occupying at least eighty-five percent (85%) of the net rented square footage of the Improvements under leases existing as of October 1, 20_____, as required above, then Purchaser may either (A) accept those Tenant Estoppels obtained by Seller and close the subject transaction otherwise in accordance with the terms of the Agreement; or (B) decline to purchase the Property. If Purchaser elects to close the subject transaction pursuant to its option set forth in Section 6(a)(xiv)(A) above, then with respect to all those Leases for which a tenant estoppel letter is not obtained and delivered to Purchaser at or before Closing, Seller shall deliver to Purchaser at Closing a certificate setting forth the status of each such Lease and providing the information set forth in the tenant estoppel letters;

(xv) True, correct, and complete copies of all Permits (as defined below), certificates of occupancy and licenses issued by any Governmental Authority (as defined below) or utility company in connection with the occupancy and use of the Improvements as are in the possession of Seller;

(xvi) True, correct, and complete copies, if any, of all notes and other unrecorded documents, agreements and instruments relating to indebtedness secured by the Property or any part thereof; and

(b) In the event any event of circumstances shall occur which renders any documents, materials or other information provided by Seller to Purchaser pursuant to Section 6(a) no longer true, correct, and complete, Seller shall immediately deliver to Purchaser all documentation, material and information necessary to supplement the same so as to render such documents, material and information true, correct and complete. Purchaser shall have seven (7) business days in which to review such supplemental material and, in the event that such supplemental materials differ materially and adversely in Purchaser's sole opinion, from the information and materials previously furnished or made available to Purchaser and are not deemed by Purchaser to be satisfactory, then Purchaser may elect to terminate this Agreement by delivering written notice of such election to Seller no later than seven (7) business days after the receipt by Purchaser of such necessary material, to permit the running of such period of seven (7) business days. If, however, any such documents, materials, or other information provided by Seller to Purchaser pursuant to Section 6(a) is untrue, incorrect or incomplete as of the date provided pursuant to Section 6(a), Seller shall be deemed to have breached this Agreement, and Purchaser shall be entitled to all remedies provided in Section 20 of this Agreement.

7. Legal Description.

In the event that the legal description of the Land as set forth in the New Survey differs from the legal description of the Land as set forth in the Existing Survey, Seller shall convey at Closing to Purchaser by quitclaim deed all Seller's right, title, and interest in and to the Land as described in the New Survey, together with all Property relating thereto or existing therein; provided, however, that nothing in the preceding sentence shall limit Purchaser's right to deem any such material differences as a New Survey Objection, thereby entitling Purchaser to the rights and remedies set forth in Section 5 above. In any event, Seller must convey by a legal description for which Purchaser may obtain standard title insurance through Chicago Title Insurance Company, Ticor Title Insurance Company of California or Lawyers Title Insurance Company, at standard rates.

8. Purchaser's Access to the Property and Seller's Records.

At any time prior to Closing (unless this Agreement is terminated as herein provided), the Purchaser, its agents, employees and contractors, shall have the right to enter upon the Property after reasonable notice to Seller for purposes of surveying, inspecting and testing the Property; provided, however, that in the event this Agreement fails to close for any reason, Purchaser shall (on or

(continued)

before the scheduled Closing Date) restore the Property to its original condition and further provided that Purchaser shall use its best efforts not to disrupt the ordinary course of business of Seller or any of the tenants under Leases. Purchaser agrees to indemnify and hold Seller harmless against any property damage or personal injury or claim of lien against the Property resulting from the activities permitted by this Section (including, without limitation, reasonable attorneys fees and expenses paid or incurred by the Seller during litigation and appeals thereof, if any). All inspections, tests, investigations and other activities carried on by Purchaser pertaining to the Property, shall be at Purchaser's sole cost and expense. In addition to and not in limitation of Purchaser's rights elsewhere set forth herein. Purchaser shall have the right upon three (3) business days prior written notice to Seller to inspect all property, books, leases and records of Seller pertaining directly to the operation of the Property, for the period of Seller's ownership of the Property, provided that the cost of copying such items shall be borne by Purchaser and such items shall be made available to Purchaser by Seller at the Office of Seller in My Town, State or such other location in My Town, State where said items are normally stored.

9. Covenants and Representations.

(a) *Seller's Covenants and Representations.*

(i) Seller has obtained all consents, approvals, or authorizations necessary to execute this Agreement and to consummate the transaction contemplated hereby, and all documents referred to herein will be validly executed and delivered and binding upon Seller;

(ii) Seller has no knowledge of any material defect in the Improvements or any part thereof and has no knowledge of and has received no notice from any Governmental Authority (as defined below) of any violation of any Requirement of Law (as defined below) relating to the Property or any part thereof;

(iii) Seller has no knowledge of and has received no notice from any insurance company or board of fire underwriters or similar agency that there exists any condition or circumstances on the Property or any part thereof, which must be corrected in order to maintain the effectiveness, or as a condition precedent to the issuance of, any insurance policy affecting the Property or any part thereof or which is in violation of, any applicable fire code or similar rule, regulation or order for such board of fire underwriters or similar agency;

(iv) Seller has no knowledge of and has received no notice of any litigation, claim, or suit which is pending or threatened which could adversely affect the Property or any part thereof or title thereto (exclusive of any litigation, claim or suit brought against a tenant of the Property after the Effective Date wherein Seller is not named a defendant or a third party defendant and wherein no counterclaims are alleged against Seller, provided, however, that Seller will give Purchaser prompt notice of all such litigation, claims and suits);

(v) Neither Seller, nor, to the best of Seller's knowledge, any previous owner of the Property or any part thereof has used, generated, stored or disposed of any Hazardous Materials (as defined below) in or on the Property or any part thereof; or has used or disposed of any Hazardous Materials in connection with the use, operation, construction or repair of the Property or any part thereof. Seller shall hold Purchaser harmless and shall indemnify and defend Purchaser from and against any and all losses, damages, claims and liabilities whatsoever in any way relating to or arising out of any breach of the foregoing representation. This provision shall survive Closing and the consummation of the transactions contemplated hereby;

(vi) Seller owns good and unencumbered title to the Tangible Personal Property and Intangible Personal Property, and Seller has done nothing to encumber same during Seller's ownership thereof other than those certain Loan Documents listed on *Exhibit K* attached hereto;

(vii) Seller has not operated the Property within the past five (5) years under any other name or trade name of which it has not notified Purchaser;

(viii) All documents, materials, and information delivered to Purchaser pursuant to Section 6(a), as supplemented by such documents, materials, and information delivered to Purchaser pursuant to Section 6(b), are true, correct and complete;

(ix) Seller shall not cause or permit to exist (A) any mortgage, deed to secure debt, security deed, security agreement, assignment or other similar instrument or agreement or any lien or encumbrance whatsoever (other than the Permitted Exceptions or those listed on *Exhibit K*) to attach to or

(continued)

affect title to the Property or any part thereof from and after the Effective Date except for the Leases approved by Purchaser; or (B) any matters not shown on the New Survey;

(x) Seller represents, to the best of its knowledge, that the mechanical, electrical, plumbing, HVAC, roofing, drainage, sanitary sewerage, and utility equipment facilities and systems servicing the Property and the improvements thereon are in operational order and shall be so maintained through and including the Closing Date. Seller represents that it is aware of no defects in any of said systems;

(xi) Seller covenants that it shall not enter into any leases pertaining to the Property after the Effective Date without prior written approval of Purchaser. Purchaser shall approve leases containing reasonable business terms, including base rentals of at least $16.00 per square foot and $1.75 of C.A.Ms. Seller covenants and represents that it shall incur no brokerage commissions pertaining to leases entered into prior to the Closing Date on any leases negotiated in any respect by Seller prior to the Closing Date;

(xii) Seller represents that it has no notice of and is not aware of any violation of the Property and improvements of any applicable zoning laws, ordinances or regulations including, without limitation, all parking requirements and building set back requirements (except as shown on the Existing Survey which Purchaser has the right to consider during the Inspection Period);

(xiii) [INTENTIONALLY DELETED]

(xiv) Seller shall continue to operate, manage, and maintain the Property in good condition and in a good business like manner, such operation and maintenance to include the undertaking of any reasonably necessary capital improvements or repairs, through and including the Closing Date. Such continuous operation and maintenance shall also be a condition precedent to Closing; and

(b) *Purchaser's Covenants and Representations.* Purchaser hereby represents and warrants to Seller that Purchaser has obtained all consents, approvals, or authorizations necessary to execute this Agreement and to consummate the transaction contemplated hereby, and all documents referred to herein will be validly executed and delivered and binding upon Purchaser.

10. Additional Conditions Precedent.

(a) This Agreement is contingent upon Purchaser being able to Purchase the Property subject to the current mortgage loan in the original principal amount of FIVE MILLION FIVE HUNDRED THOUSAND AND NO/100 DOLLARS ($5,500,000.00) held by Wearever Life Assurance Company (the "Mortgage Loan") being evidenced by (a) certain Real Estate Note, dated December 17, 20____, from Seller to Wearever Life Assurance Company, (b) Deed to Secure Debt and Security Agreement by and between the same parties dated December 17, 20____, recorded at Deed Book 11234, Page 137, Great County, State Records, and (c) an Assignment of Leases and Rents by and between the same parties dated December 17, 20____, recorded at Deed Book 11234, Page 162, Great County, State Records (hereinafter referred to as the "Mortgage Loan Documents"). One-half ($^1/_2$) of all costs, assumption fees, transfer fees, paid to the holder of the Mortgage Loan to obtain permission to transfer the Property to Purchaser shall be paid by Seller and the other one-half ($^1/_2$) by Purchaser. The tax and insurance provisions contained in the Mortgage Loan Documents are to be waived upon the same terms and conditions they are presently being waived for Seller. The terms of the Mortgage Loan, including but not limited to, the rate of interest, the amount of the monthly installments, the Maturity Date, are to remain unchanged. Seller shall provide Purchaser with an Estoppel Agreement from the holder of the Mortgage Loan in substantially the same form as that attached hereto as *Exhibit "I"*. Purchaser agrees to provide the holder of the Mortgage Loan with any financial information necessary to enable the holder of the Mortgage Loan to approve the transfer of the Property from Seller to Purchaser. This Agreement shall remain contingent upon the ability of Purchaser to obtain the Property subject to the Mortgage Loan and the consent by the holder of the Mortgage Loan to the Note and Deed.

If the Seller has not obtained the permission from the holder of the Mortgage Loan to transfer the Property to Purchaser subject to the Mortgage Loan and upon the terms set forth therein and the consent to the Note and Deed on or before September 26, 20___, then Purchaser may by written notice to Seller notify Seller of its election to terminate this Agreement, whereupon this Agreement shall terminate and the Deposit together with accrued interest thereon, shall be returned to Purchaser, and thereafter the parties hereto shall have no further rights, duties, obligations or liabilities hereunder.

(continued)

(b) Seller shall continuously operate and maintain the Property in good condition and continue business like management through and including the Closing Date.

11. Closing Date.

Unless this Agreement is terminated by Purchaser pursuant to the terms of this Agreement, the Closing shall take place at the offices of Purchaser's attorneys, Winkom, Blinkholm and Nodd, 1400 Crabtree Place Tower, My Town, State, or such location as is mutually agreeable to Purchaser and Seller, beginning at 10:00 a.m. on a business day (in My Town, State) selected by Purchaser on or before November 11, 20____. The date of Closing shall hereinafter be referred to as the "Closing Date". Purchaser shall give Seller notice of the Closing Date at least five (5) business days prior thereto; provided, however, if Purchaser gives Seller no such notice of the Closing Date, then the Closing Date shall be November 11, 20____.

12. Seller's Obligations.

At Closing, Seller shall:

(a) Execute, acknowledge and deliver to Purchaser a limited warranty deed in recordable form, the form of which is attached hereto as *Exhibit D* conveying the Property to Purchaser subject only to: (i) taxes for the years subsequent to the year of Closing; (ii) the zoning classification as of the Effective Date; and (iii) the Permitted Exceptions;

(b) Execute and deliver to Purchaser the following additional conveyance documents: (A) an Affidavit reciting Seller's non-foreign status within the meaning of Section 1445(f)(3) of the Internal Revenue Code of 1986; (B) an Assignment and Assumption of Leases assigning to Purchaser lessor's interest in the Leases, a form of which is attached hereto as *Exhibit E*; and (C) an Assignment of Contracts, Other Rights and Intangible Property assigning to Purchaser the Intangible Property, the form of which is attached hereto as *Exhibit F*; and (D) Lender Estoppel Letter from the holder of the Mortgage Loan, a proposed form of which is attached hereto as *Exhibit "I"*; (E) Subordination, Attornment and Non-Disturbance Agreements satisfactory to Lender signed by tenants leasing at least eighty-five percent (85%) of the net rentable square footage of the Property, a proposed form of which is attached hereto as *Exhibit J*; and (F) a certificate that Seller knows of no defects in the system referred to in Sections 9(a)(x) and (xi) of this Agreement as of the Closing Date;

(c) Execute and deliver to Purchaser a Closing Statement setting forth the adjustments and prorations to closing as well as the costs pursuant to this Agreement as elsewhere specifically provided herein (the "Closing Statement");

(d) Deliver to Purchaser a certified and updated rent roll reflecting all the tenants under Leases to the Property as of the Closing Date and indicating thereon any delinquencies with respect to rent due;

(e) Deliver to Purchaser all Permits, certificates of occupancy, and licenses issued by an Governmental Authorities or utility companies in connection with the occupancy and use of the Improvements as are in the possession of Seller;

(f) Deliver to Purchaser a form letter to all tenants under Leases stating that Purchaser has acquired the Property from Seller, that future rents should be paid as specified by Purchaser, and that Purchaser will be responsible for all tenants' security deposits, if any;

(g) A certificate of Seller stating (A) that Seller has no knowledge of any pending or threatened condemnation proceedings or any taking by any Governmental Authority which in any way affects the Property, (B) that there are no Leases (other than Leases approved by Purchaser), no Service Contracts (whether written or oral), no employees, no insurance policy endorsements or claims, no other notices from any Governmental Authority regarding any violations of any Requirements of Law affecting the Property except as heretofore provided to Purchaser as required under Section 6 above and elsewhere in this Agreement;

(h) The plans and specifications for the Improvements, including all amendments thereto, as are in the possession of Seller;

(i) The originals of all Leases including all amendments thereto;

(j) All information and materials required for full compliance under the Foreign Investors in Real Property Tax Act;

(k) All keys to the Improvements in Seller's possession and a list of all other persons which, to the best of Seller's knowledge are in possession of keys to the Improvements, other than keys to tenant space in the possession of tenants;

(l) Such other documents, instruments, and agreements as Purchaser may reasonably require to effect and complete the transactions contemplated herein and to obtain an owner's title insurance policy insuring the interest of Purchaser, as owner, in the amount of $7,300,000.00, free and clear of all exceptions except the Permitted Exceptions, for a premium calculated at standard rates, including, without limitation, a Seller's Affidavit of Title in the form attached hereto as *Exhibit G* and a Bill of Sale in the form attached hereto as *Exhibit H*; and

(m) Seller's estoppel certificates to the extent required by Section 6(a)(xiv) above.

13. Purchaser's Obligations at Closing.

On the Closing Date, subject to the terms, conditions, and provisions hereof, Purchaser shall:

(a) Execute and deliver to Seller an assumption agreement whereby Purchaser assumes all liabilities and agrees to perform all obligations of Seller under all the Leases, the form of which is contained in *Exhibit E,* and the Service Contracts and all employee contracts assumed by Purchaser pursuant hereto, the form of which is contained in *Exhibit F.* Said assumption agreements shall contain an indemnification by Purchaser of Seller and an agreement to hold Seller harmless from and against any and all claims, debts, liabilities and the like affecting or relating to the Property, or any part thereof, and the Leases after the Closing Date. Likewise, said assumption agreements shall contain an agreement to hold Purchaser harmless from and against any and all claims, debts, liabilities and the like affecting or relating to the Property, or any part thereof, and the Leases prior to and including the Closing Date.

(b) Execute and deliver to Seller a copy of the Closing Statement.

(c) Deliver to Seller pursuant to the terms of Section 2 herein the Note and Deed and pursuant to Section 2 herein, the sums required to be paid hereunder, and Purchaser shall execute such other documents, instruments, affidavits and agreements as may be required to close the transaction contemplated herein.

14. Closing Costs.

In connection with Closing, Seller shall pay the State real estate transfer tax and all costs relating to the satisfaction, cure and removal of all title defects (except the Permitted Exceptions) undertaken by Seller as herein required and the payment of one-half ($^1/_2$) all transfer, assumption or other fees due the holder of the Mortgage Loan to obtain the consent to the transfer the Property to the Purchaser and the consent to the Note and Deed. Purchaser shall pay the costs of the premiums payable or costs incurred in connection with the issuance of the owner's title insurance commitment and the owner's title insurance policy in favor of Purchaser and all costs of recording the limited warranty deed. The Purchaser shall be solely responsible for the New Survey costs. Each party shall pay its own attorney's fees.

15. Prorations.

The following items shall be apportioned and prorated (based on a 30-day month, unless otherwise indicated) between the Seller and the Purchaser as of the Closing Date so that credits and charges for all days prior to the Closing Date shall be allocated to the Seller and credits and charges for the Closing Date and for all days thereafter shall be allocated to the Purchaser:

(a) *Taxes.* At the Closing, all ad valorem property taxes, water and sewer charges and assessments of any kind on the Property for the year of the Closing shall be prorated between Purchaser and Seller as of 12:01 a.m. on the Closing Date. Such proration shall be based upon the latest ad valorem property tax, water, sewer charge and assessment bills available. If, upon receipt of the actual ad valorem property tax, water, sewer and assessment bills for the Property, such proration is incorrect, then either Purchaser or Seller shall be entitled, upon demand, to receive such amounts from the other as may be necessary to correct such mal-apportionment. This obligation so to correct such mal-apportionment shall survive the Closing and not be merged into any documents delivered pursuant to the Closing.

(b) *Rents*. Purchaser shall receive a credit for all amounts due under the Leases in effect at Closing, hereinafter referred to as the "Rent", collected by Seller prior to Closing and allocable in whole or in part to any period following the Closing Date. Seller shall deliver to Purchaser any Rent received after Closing. Purchaser shall deliver to Seller any Rents received after Closing which relate to periods prior to and through the Closing Date; provided, however, that any such Rents collected by Purchaser after the Closing shall be applied first toward Rents due which shall have accrued after the Closing Date and then towards Rents which accrued prior to the Closing Date. Purchaser shall use its best efforts (short of incurring legal fees and expenses or taking other action which would not be in its best interest as owner of the Property) to collect all such delinquent Rents.

In the event that Purchaser is unable to collect delinquent Rents due Seller within thirty (30) days after the Closing Date, then Seller may pursue collection of such delinquent Rents from the respective Tenants in accordance with its rights under Georgia law; provided, however, Seller shall have no right to collect Rents in any manner which would result in an interference with the Tenant's rights of possession under its lease or in any way interfere with the landlord/tenant relationship between Purchaser and the Tenant (for example, Seller shall have no rights to dispossess Tenant in an effort to collect delinquent Rents.)

(c) *Other Expense Prorations*. All other reasonable expenses normal to the operation and maintenance of the Property that require payments either in advance or in arrears for periods which begin prior to the Closing Date and end thereafter. Without limiting the generality of the foregoing, such expenses shall include: water, electric; telephone and all other utility and fuel charges; fuel on hand (at cost plus sales tax) any deposits with utility companies; employee wages, salaries, benefits and pension, health and welfare insurance, social security and such other contributions; and charges under employee contracts and/or Service Contracts.

(d) *Security Deposits*. Purchaser shall receive a credit for the security deposits paid under the Leases in existence and in effect on the Closing Date.

(e) *Leasing Commissions*. Seller warrants and represents that there are no leasing commissions due and owing or to become due and owing under any of the Leases or any renewals and extensions thereof, as of the Closing Date. Seller agrees to hold harmless from and to indemnify and defend Purchaser from and against any and all such leasing commissions and all other fees, charges and compensation whatsoever due any person or entity in connection with the procuring of any Lease together with all extensions and renewals thereof or otherwise relating to any Lease. This provision shall survive the Closing and the consummation of the transactions contemplated herein.

16. Employees and Service Contracts.

Seller represents and warrants that there are no employees or employment contracts relating to the Property which cannot be terminated on or prior to Closing because of contractual terms or applicable law. From and after the Effective Date, Seller will not enter into or extend or renew any contracts relating to the Property which cannot by their express terms terminate with thirty (30) days notice, without the prior written approval of Purchaser. With respect to all other employees and contracts relating to the Property, Purchaser shall not be obligated to continue the employment of all such employees and to continue all such contracts and to assume all obligations therefor as of the Closing Date, unless Purchaser notifies Seller of its intention to continue the employment of employees under any or all of such employee agreements and/or contracts prior to Closing, in which event Seller shall be responsible for terminating the employment of such personnel and such contracts capable of being terminated and designated for termination by Purchaser's notice. With respect to any leasing brokerage agreements in connection with the Property, Seller shall terminate and obtain release of same prior to or on the Closing Date.

17. Brokerage Commissions.

Each party further represents to the other that except for_____

(collectively "Brokers"), no broker has been involved in this transaction. Seller shall be solely responsible for paying any commission due to the Brokers in connection with this transaction. Seller shall pay in cash or good funds at Closing brokerage commissions of one percent (1%) to

EXHIBIT 4–2
Contract for Purchase and Sale of Retail Shopping Center (continued)

_____ and one percent (1%) of the Purchase Price to_____. No commission shall be due and owing Brokers should the sale and purchase of the Property fail to close for any reason whatsoever, including, without limitation, the breach of this Agreement by Seller or Purchaser. Under no circumstances whatsoever shall Brokers be entitled to retain any portion of the Deposit. In the event any other claims for brokerage commissions or fees are ever made against the Seller or the Purchaser in connection with this transaction, all such claims shall be handled and paid by the party whose actions or alleged commitments form the basis of such claim. Seller further agrees to indemnify and hold harmless the Purchaser from and against any and all such claims or demands with respect to any brokerage fees or agent's commissions or other compensation asserted by any person, firm, or corporation in connection with this Agreement or the transactions contemplated hereby arising from actions or alleged commitments of the Seller. Purchaser further agrees to indemnify and hold harmless the Seller from and against any and all such claims or demands with respect to any brokerage fees or agent's commissions or other compensation asserted by any person, firm or corporation in connection with this Agreement or the transaction contemplated hereby arising from actions or alleged commitments of the Purchaser. This provision shall survive Closing and the conveyance of the Property by Seller to Purchaser.

18. Risk of Loss.

Risk of loss or damage to the Property or any part thereof by condemnation, eminent domain, or similar proceedings, or by deed in lieu or under threat thereof (collectively, a "Taking"), or by fire, flood, or other casualty from the Effective Date until delivery of the limited warranty deed will be on Seller and after the delivery of the limited warranty deed will be on Purchaser. In the event of any such loss or damage to all or to a material part of the Property or any part of the Improvements prior to the delivery of the limited warranty deed, this Agreement may, at the option of Purchaser to be exercised by written notice to Seller, be declared null and void and Purchaser shall be returned the Deposit and both parties hereto shall be released from any further rights and duties hereunder, or this Agreement shall remain in full force and effect and Seller shall transfer to Purchaser on the Closing Date all insurance proceeds or condemnation awards received by Seller because of such casualty or Taking and all of Seller's rights, title and interest in and to any recovery or claims under any insurance policies or condemnation awards relating to the Property.

Upon the happening of one of the events in the preceding paragraph, subsequent to the Inspection Deadline and prior to delivery of the limited warranty deed, if the cost of repair or replacement or, in the event of a Taking, if the reduction in the value of the project is TWENTY–FIVE THOUSAND DOLLARS ($25,000.00) or less, Purchaser shall close and take the Property as diminished by such events and Seller shall transfer to Purchaser on the Closing Date all insurance proceeds or condemnation awards received by Seller because of such casualty or Taking and all of Seller's right, title, and interest in and to any recovery or claim under any insurance policies or condemnation awards relating to the Property together with a credit to Purchaser for the amount of any deductibles contained in any insurance policy.

19. Purchaser's Default.

In the event the transaction contemplated hereby is not closed because of Purchaser's default, the Deposit shall be paid to Seller as full liquidated damages for such failure to close, the parties acknowledging the difficulty of ascertaining Seller's damages in such circumstances, whereupon neither party hereto shall have any further rights, claims or liabilities under this Agreement except for the provisions which are made to survive the termination or cancellation of this Agreement. Said liquidated damages shall be Seller's sole and exclusive remedy, and Seller shall expressly not have the right to seek specific performance.

20. Seller's Default.

If the Seller fails to perform any of the covenants of this Agreement, or if Seller otherwise defaults hereunder, the Purchaser shall have the right, in addition to all rights and remedies herein provided, to pursue any right or remedy it may have against Seller at law or in equity for such breach and/or default, including, without limitation, the right of specific performance of all provisions of this Agreement. Purchaser's monetary damages in the event of such breach and/or default by Seller shall be limited to $100,000.00. The parties hereto acknowledge the difficulty of ascertaining Purchaser's monetary damages in such event.

21. Assignability.

Purchaser shall have the right to assign this Agreement to any person(s), partnership or corporation, including a partnership or corporation to be formed hereafter, with notice to but without the consent of Seller, and the transaction contemplated by this Agreement shall be consummated in the name of such assignee. In the event of such assignment, the assignee shall assume the obligations of Purchaser under this Agreement, and Purchaser shall have no further obligation or liability under this Agreement. Seller shall have the right to assign its interest in this Agreement, only with the written consent of Purchaser, except insofar as such assignment is made to effectuate a tax free exchange. In the latter instance, Seller may assign its rights but shall remain bound under the terms of this Agreement and the representations, warranties, and covenants contained herein.

Seller is entering into this contract with the intention of disposing of the Property through alike kind exchange of properties, pursuant to Section 1031 of the Internal Revenue Code of 1954, as amended. Purchaser agrees that, upon request of Seller, Purchaser will convey or cause to be conveyed to Seller at closing other like kind property acceptable to Seller in lieu of paying cash to Seller, or will pay the purchase price for the property to a third party, who will convey like kind property to Seller. At the election of Seller, Seller may convey the Property to a third party prior to closing as part of a like kind exchange of properties with such third party, provided that such third party agrees to be bound by all of the terms and provisions of this contract, and provided further that no such conveyance to any third party shall relieve Seller of any of its obligations hereunder. Anything contained herein to the contrary notwithstanding, Purchaser shall not be obligated to incur any additional liability or expense in connection with any exchange of properties by Seller. Furthermore, Seller shall indemnify Purchaser for any liability or expense incurred in any respect in connection with its cooperation with Seller in effectuating a tax-free exchange. Subject to the foregoing, this Agreement shall inure to the benefit of and shall be binding upon Seller and Purchaser and their respective successors and assigns.

22. Entire Agreement.

No agreements, representations, or warranties unless expressly incorporated or set forth in this Agreement shall be binding upon any of the parties.

23. Notification.

Any notice or demand under which the terms of this Agreement or under any statute must or may be given or made by the parties hereto shall be made in writing and shall be deemed to have been delivered when hand delivered; as of the date sent by an overnight courier; or as of the date of postmark affixed by the U.S. Postal Service, by mailing the same by certified mail return receipt requested addressed to the respective parties at the following addresses:

To Purchaser:

With Copies to:

To Seller:

With Copy to:

Such addresses may be changed by the giving of written notice as provided in this paragraph; provided, however that any mailed notice of changed address shall be not be effective until the fifth (5th) day after the date of postmark by the U.S. Postal Service.

(continued)

24. Time.

Time is of the essence of this Agreement and of each of its provisions.

25. Survival and Last Execution Date.

The provisions of this Agreement shall survive Closing and the execution and delivery of the deed and instruments conveying the Property. If this Agreement is not executed by all parties hereto on or before 5:00 P.M. on August 17, 20____, this Agreement shall be null and void.

26. Headings.

Descriptive headings are for convenience only and shall not control or affect the meaning or construction of any provision of this Agreement.

27. Binding Effect.

This Agreement shall be binding upon and shall inure to the benefit of the parties hereto and their successors and assigns subject to the provisions of Section 21 above.

28. Severability.

In case any one or more of the provisions contained in this Agreement shall for any reason be held to be invalid, illegal or unenforceable in any respect, such invalidity, illegality, or unenforceability shall not affect any other provision hereof, and this Agreement shall be construed as if such invalid, illegal, or unenforceable provision had never been contained herein.

29. Effective Date of this Agreement.

The Effective Date of this Agreement shall be the last date upon which either the Purchaser or Seller shall have executed this Agreement, as demonstrated by the date(s) below their respective signatures on the signature page to this Agreement.

30. Business Day.

If the Closing is to occur on a holiday or other non-business day, or if any period of time set forth in this Agreement expires on a holiday or other non-business day, then the Closing or the expiration date of such period shall be the next business day. For purposes of this Agreement, the term "business day" shall mean any day which is not a Saturday, Sunday or other day on which banks in My Town, State are not open for business during regular business hours.

31. Certain Definitions.

As used herein, the following terms are defined as follows:

(a) *Governmental Authority* means any nation or government, any state, municipal or other political subdivision thereof, and any entity exercising executive, legislative, judicial, regulatory or administrative functions of or pertaining to government.

(b) *Hazardous Materials* means all hazardous wastes, polychlorinated biphenyl (commonly known as "PCBs"), toxic substance and similar substances including, without limitation, substances defined as "hazardous substances" or "toxic substances" in the Comprehensive Environmental Response and Liability Act of 1980, as amended, 42 U.S.C. § 9601 et seq., the Hazardous Materials Transportation Act, and Recovery Act, as amended, 42 U.S.C. § 6901 et seq.

(c) *Permits* means all consents, certificates, authorizations, licenses, approvals and permits required for the removal, alteration or demolition of any structure or improvement, or any part thereof, on the Land or for construction, completion, use, occupancy and operation of the Existing Improvements or the Improvements in accordance with all Requirements of Law affecting the Property, including, without limiting the generality of the foregoing, demolition permits, building permits, drainage permits, curb cut, access and traffic permits and approvals, sewerage, waste and drainage permits and environmental approvals and permits.

(d) *Requirements of Law* means any person or entity, the certificate of incorporation and by-laws or partnership agreement or limited partnership agreement or other organizational or governing documents of such person or entity, and any law, treaty, rule or regulation, or determination, judgment or order of an arbitrator or a court or other Governmental Authority, in each case applicable to or binding upon such person or entity or any of its property or to which such person or entity or any of its property is subject; and, as to the Real Property, any applicable environmental, zoning or building, land use laws, requirements, standards and regulations of the fire marshall and similar agencies, ordinances, rules or regulations of any governmental authority or agency, and any applicable covenants and restrictions.

32. Possession.

Seller shall deliver actual possession of the Property to Purchaser at Closing.

33. Seller's Guaranty of Income.

At closing, Seller will execute and deliver to Purchaser a Guaranty ("Guaranty") which guarantees the gross rental income from the Property as hereinafter set forth. For a period commencing with the Closing Date and ending one year from the Closing Date, Seller shall guarantee that the gross rental income from the Property shall not be less than Eight Hundred Fifty Thousand and No/100 Dollars ($850,000.00). Seller agrees to pay to Purchaser a sum equal to the difference of Eight Hundred Fifty Thousand Dollars ($850,000.00) and the actual gross rental income received from the Property during the one year period. Seller agrees to pay Purchaser the income shortfall on a quarterly basis. For example, during the first calendar quarter following the Closing Date if gross rental income from the Property does not equal $212,500.00, Seller shall pay to Purchaser on the last day of the quarter the difference between $212,500.00 and the gross rental income actually received during that period of time. The Seller's obligation to pay Purchaser for rental income shortfall pursuant to this paragraph shall not exceed $100,000.00 during the year succeeding the Closing Date. Purchaser shall provide Seller with a written itemized statement of all rentals received certified to be true and correct by Purchaser. Seller shall further agree that in the event that Seller does not pay Purchaser any rental deficit on a quarterly basis, Purchaser shall have the right to set off said amount due from Seller against the payments under the Note.

Commencing one year from the Closing Date and ending on the same day which is two years from the Closing Date, Seller guarantees that the gross rental income from the Property shall be Eight Hundred Seventy Five Thousand and No/100 Dollars ($875,000.00). Seller agrees to pay to Purchaser a sum equal to the difference between Eight Hundred Seventy Five Thousand Dollars ($875,000.00) and the actual gross rental income received from the Property during that period. Seller agrees to pay Purchaser the income shortfall on a quarterly basis. For example, during the first calendar quarter of the second year following the Closing Date if gross rental income from the Property does not equal $218,750.00, Seller shall pay to Purchaser on the last day of said quarter the difference between $218,750.00 and the gross rental income actually received during that period of time. The Seller's obligation to pay Purchaser for rental income shortfall pursuant to this paragraph shall not exceed $100,000.00 during the second year from Closing Date. Purchaser shall provide Seller with a written itemized statement of all rentals received certified to be true and correct by Purchaser. Seller shall further agree that in the event that Seller does not pay Purchaser any rental deficit on a quarterly basis, Purchaser shall have the right to set off said amount due from Seller against the payments under the Note.

Seller's obligation to pay Purchaser for the rental income shortfall shall be adjusted annually and in the event the rental income shortfall is less than the sum of the quarterly payments Purchaser has received from Seller, then Purchaser shall refund the difference between the annual rental income shortfall and the amount of rental guaranty payments received from Seller. The annual adjustment shall take place within thirty days from a date which is one year from Closing Date, and a second annual adjustment shall take place within thirty days from a date which is two years from Closing Date.

During the rental guaranty period as set forth herein, Purchaser shall make every effort to lease existing vacant spaces, including but not limited to, paying full commissions to outside brokers, market the Property in a quality manner and maintain the Property in a neat and professional manner. If Purchaser relocates any of the existing tenants in Village Square to another property owned by or affiliated with Purchaser, then the tenant's rental income based on the rental being paid by the tenant prior to relocation which would have been received by Purchaser had tenant not been relocated shall be credited against the annual gross rental income guaranteed by Seller (i.e. against the $850,000.00 during year one or the $875,000.00 during year two).

(continued)

Any new space that is leased on the Property during the two year guaranty period will be created toward the income guaranty (i.e. toward the $850,000.00 during year one or the $875,000.00 during year two). Also, the credit will be the greater of $15.00 per square foot of annual gross rental or the actual gross rental amount received under the lease. Credit for new leases against Seller's income guaranty will commence the earlier of when rental payments begin or six months following occupancy by the tenant.

If Purchaser elects to terminate or not to renew any of the existing leases whereby the tenant wants to stay at the Property and is willing to pay the lesser of tenants present rent or fair market rent, then Seller shall receive a credit against the guaranteed income amounts of the amount of the lost rental. (i.e. against the $850,000.00 during year one or the $875,000.00 during year two).

34. Additional Provisions.

(a) In the event that Lender requires a form of Tenant Estoppel different from the form attached hereto as *Exhibit C* or in the event that Lender requires a form of Subordination, Attornment and Non-Disturbance Agreement difference from the form attached hereto as *Exhibit J*, then Purchaser shall deliver such different form(s) to Seller on or before October 1, 20____.

(b) In the event that the sale and purchase of the Property does not close for any reason other than Seller's default, Purchaser will provide Seller with copies of all surveys, reports, tests, and other materials relating to the Property obtained by Purchaser pursuant to the terms of this Agreement.

35. Miscellaneous.

(a) This Agreement shall be construed and interpreted under the Laws of the State.

(b) No failure of Purchaser or Seller to exercise any power given either party hereunder or to insist upon strict compliance by either party of its obligations hereunder, and no custom or practice of the parties at variance with the terms hereof shall constitute a waiver of either party's right to demand exact compliance with the terms hereof. Any condition, contingency or right of termination or recision granted by this Agreement to either Purchaser or Seller may be waived in writing by the party for whose benefit such condition or right was granted.

(c) This Agreement may be signed in number of counterparts. Each counterpart shall be an original but all such counterparts shall constitute one agreement. It shall be fully executed when each party whose signature is required has signed at least one counterpart even though no one counterpart contains the signatures of all the parties.

IN WITNESS WHEREOF, the parties hereto have set their hands and seals as of the Effective Date.

PURCHASER:
    Date Executed: _____

SELLER:
    Date Executed: _____

The undersigned as Escrowee hereby acknowledges receipt of a copy of this Agreement and of the initial Earnest Money deposit by check $_____ drawn on _____, subject to collection, and agrees to hold said funds pursuant to the terms of this Agreement. The undersigned as Broker hereby agrees to the terms of Section 17 of this Agreement.

Dated: _____

EXHIBIT 4-3
Option to Purchase

STATE OF _____)
)   SS:
COUNTY OF _____)

OPTION TO PURCHASE

IN CONSIDERATION OF ONE HUNDRED AND NO/100 DOLLARS ($100.00) (herein called "Option Consideration") in hand paid, the receipt and sufficiency of which are hereby acknowledged, the undersigned FARRIS DEVELOPMENT CORPORATION, a _____ corporation (hereinafter referred to as "Optionor") hereby grants, conveys and extends to JAMES B. MILLER and ALICE C. MILLER (hereinafter collectively called "Optionee"), the exclusive right and option to purchase upon the terms and conditions set forth herein, all that tract or parcel of land lying and being in Land Lots 31 and 32 of the 13th District, _____ County, _____(state)_____ and being known as the Birch Hill Apartments, a 284 unit apartment complex, and being more particularly described on Exhibit "A" attached hereto and made a part hereof, together with all improvements situated thereon and appurtenances thereto (hereinafter called "Property").

1. Option Term. This Option shall begin on September 1, 20___ and terminate at 11:30 P.M. on December 15, 20___.

2. Exercise of Option. This Option may be exercised by Optionee any time prior to the expiration of the Option, by the execution and delivery to Optionor of that certain Real Estate Contract attached hereto as Exhibit "B" and made a part hereof. Upon the exercise of the Real Estate Contract by Optionee and submission to Optionor, Optionor shall sign the Agreement and it shall become a binding Agreement between the parties hereto. The executed Real Estate Contract is to be sent to Optionor at the following address:

    604 Clairemont Avenue
    _____(city)_____, _____(state)_____ 30060

3. Purchase Price. The Purchase Price for the sale of the Property shall be ONE MILLION FIVE HUNDRED THOUSAND AND NO/100 DOLLARS ($1,500,000.00) and shall be paid pursuant to the terms set forth in the Real Estate Contract attached hereto as Exhibit "B" and made a part hereof.

4. No Assignment. This Option is personal to the Optionee and is not assignable.

5. Miscellaneous. This agreement constitutes the entire agreement between the parties hereto and it is understood and agreed that all undertakings and agreements heretofore had between the parties have merged herein. No representation, promise, inducement not included herein shall be binding upon any party hereto.

IN WITNESS WHEREOF, the parties have hereunto set their hands and seals this _____ day of _____, 20___.

OPTIONOR:
FARRIS DEVELOPMENT CORPORATION
By: _____
David H. Farris, President
OPTIONEE:
_____ (SEAL)
JAMES B. MILLER
_____ (SEAL)
ALICE C. MILLER

EXHIBIT 4–4
Exclusive Seller Listing Agreement

EXCLUSIVE SELLER LISTING AGREEMENT
(ALSO REFERRED TO AS EXCLUSIVE SELLER BROKERAGE AGREEMENT)

2002 Printing

State law prohibits Broker from representing Seller as a client without first entering into a written agreement with Seller under O.C.G.A. § 10-6A-1 et. seq.

For and in consideration of the mutual promises contained herein and other good and valuable consideration, _____ as seller (hereinafter referred to as "Seller"), and _____ as broker and its licensees (hereinafter collectively referred to as "Broker") do hereby enter into this Agreement, this ____ day of _____, 20_____.

1. **Exclusive Listing Agreement.** Seller hereby grants to Broker the exclusive right and privilege as the Agent of the Seller to show and offer for sale the following described property as the real estate broker for Seller: All that tract of land lying and being in Land Lot _____ of the _____ District, _____ Section of _____ County, Georgia, and being known as Address _____, _____ City, Georgia Zip Code _____, according to the present system of numbering in and around this area, being more particularly described as Lot ___, Block _____, Unit _____, Phase/Section _____ of _____ subdivision, as recorded in Plat Book _____, Page _____, _____ County, Georgia records together with all fixtures, landscaping, improvements, and appurtenances, all being hereinafter collectively referred to as the "Property." The full legal description of the Property is the same as is recorded with the Clerk of the Superior Court of the county in which the Property is located and is made a part of this Agreement by reference. The term of this Agreement shall begin on _____, 20_____ and shall continue through _____, 20_____ (hereinafter referred to as "Listing Period").

2. **Broker's Duties To Seller.** Broker's sole duties to Seller shall be to: (a) use Broker's best efforts to procure a buyer ready, willing, and able to purchase the Property at a sales price of at least $_____ (including commission) or any other price acceptable to Seller; (b) assist to the extent requested by Seller, in negotiating the terms of and filling out a pre-printed real estate purchase and sale agreement; and (c) comply with all applicable laws in performing its duties hereunder including the Brokerage Relationships in Real Estate Transaction Act, O.C.G.A. § 10-6A-1 et. seq.

3. **Seller's Duties.** Seller represents that Seller: (a) presently has title to the Property or has full authority to enter into this Agreement; (b) will cooperate with Broker to sell the Property to prospective buyers and will refer all inquiries concerning the sale of the Property to the Broker during the terms of this agreement; (c) will make the Property available for showing at reasonable times as requested by Broker; and (d) will provide Broker with accurate information regarding the Property (including information concerning all adverse material facts pertaining to the physical condition of the Property).

4. **Marketing.**
   A. **Advertisements:** Broker may advertise the Property for sale in all media and may photograph and/or videotape and use the photographs and/or videotapes in connection with Broker's marketing efforts. Seller agrees not to place any advertisements on the property or to advertise the property for sale in any media except with the prior written consent of Broker. Broker is also hereby authorized to place Broker's "For Sale" sign on the Property. Broker is authorized to procure buyers to purchase the Property in cooperation with other real estate brokers and their affiliated licensees. Broker may distribute listing and sales information (including the sales price) to them and other members of the multiple listing service(s), and said cooperating brokers and their licensees may republish such information on their Internet web sites. Broker and other real estate brokers and their affiliated licensees may show the Property without first notifying the Seller.
   B. **Lockboxes:** A lockbox may be used in connection with the marketing of the Property. There have been isolated instances of reported burglaries of homes on which lockboxes have been placed and for which the lockbox has been alleged to have been used to access the home. In order to minimize the risk of misuse of the lockbox, Broker recommends against the use of lockboxes on door handles that can be unscrewed from the outside or on other parts of the home from which the lockbox can be easily removed. Since others will have access to the Property, Seller agrees to either remove all valuables or put them in a secure place.
   C. **Multiple Listing Service(s):** Seller acknowledges that Broker is a member of the following multiple listing service(s): _____("Service(s)"). Broker agrees that Broker will file this listing with said Service(s) within forty eight hours after Seller signs the same (excepting weekends, federal holidays and postal holidays).

   Seller acknowledges that the Service(s) is/are not a party to this Agreement and is/are not responsible for errors or omissions on the part of Seller or of Broker. Seller agrees to indemnify the Service(s) from and against any and all claims, liabilities, damages or losses arising out of or related to the listing and sale of the Property.

5. **Commission.** Seller agrees to pay Broker no later than at closing a real estate commission of _____ percent (_____%) of the purchase price of the Property or $_____ in the event that during the term of this Agreement, (1) Broker procures a buyer

F1, Exclusive Seller Listing Agreement, Page 1 of 3 01/01/02

(continued)

EXHIBIT 4-4
Exclusive Seller Listing Agreement (continued)

ready, willing, and able to purchase the Property at the price described above; or (2) Seller enters into an enforceable contract for the sale or exchange of the Property with any buyer, whether through the efforts of Broker or any other person, including Seller. Broker shall share this commission with a cooperating broker, if any, who procures the buyer of the Property by paying such cooperating broker _____ % of Broker's commission or $ _____. Cooperating brokers are expressly intended to be third-party beneficiaries under this Agreement. In the event that Seller sells or contracts to sell the Property to any buyer introduced to the Property by Broker within _____ days after the expiration of the Listing Period, then Seller shall pay the commission referenced above to Broker at the closing of the sale or exchange of the Property. Notwithstanding the above, in the event that the Property is sold to the prospective buyer by or through another licensed broker with whom Seller has signed an exclusive right to sell listing agreement, then no commission shall be owed to Broker by virtue of this Agreement. The commission obligations set forth herein shall survive the termination of this Agreement.

6. <u>Limits on Broker's Authority and Responsibility</u>. Seller acknowledges and agrees that Broker: (a) may show other properties to prospective buyers who are interested in Seller's Property; (b) is not an expert with regard to matters that could be revealed through a survey, title search, or inspection; the condition of property; the necessity or cost of repairs; hazardous or toxic materials; the availability and cost of utilities or community amenities; conditions existing off the property that may affect the property; uses and zoning of the property; the appraised or future value of the property; termites and wood-destroying organisms; building products and construction techniques; the tax or legal consequences of a contemplated transaction; or matters relating to financing (and if these matters are of concern to Seller, Seller is hereby advised to seek independent expert advice on any of these matters of concern to Seller); (c) shall owe no duties to Seller nor have any authority to act on behalf of Seller other than what is set forth in this Agreement; (d) may make all disclosures required by law; (e) may disclose all information about the Property to others; and (f) shall, under no circumstances, have any liability greater than the amount of the real estate commission paid hereunder to Broker (excluding any commission amount paid to a cooperating real estate broker, if any).

Seller agrees to hold Broker harmless from any and all claims, causes of action, or damages arising out of or relating to: (a) Seller providing Broker incomplete and/or inaccurate information; (b) the handling of earnest money by anyone other than Broker; or (c) any injury to persons on the Property and/or loss of or damage to the Property or anything contained therein.

7. <u>Extension</u>. If during the term of this Agreement, Seller and a prospective buyer enter into a real estate sales contract which is not consummated for any reason whatsoever, then the original expiration date of this Agreement shall be extended for the number of days that the Property was under contract.

8. <u>Seller's Property Disclosure Statement and Official Georgia Wood Infestation Report</u>. Within ____ days of the date of this Agreement , Seller agrees to provide Broker with a current, fully executed Seller's Property Disclosure Statement. Additionally, within ____ days of the date of this Agreement, Seller agrees to provide Broker with an Official Georgia Wood Infestation Report dated not more than one hundred eighty days prior to the date of this Agreement. Broker is hereby authorized to distribute the same to prospective buyers interested in the Property.

9. <u>Required State Law Disclosures</u>. (a) Broker agrees to keep all information which Seller asks to be kept confidential by express request or instruction unless the Seller permits such disclosure by subsequent word or conduct or such disclosure is required by law. (b) Broker may not knowingly give customers false information. (c) In the event of a conflict between Broker's duty not to give customers false information and the duty to keep the confidences of Seller, the duty not to give customers false information shall prevail. (d) Unless specified below, Broker has no other known agency relationships with other parties which would conflict with any interests of Seller (except that Broker may represent other buyers, sellers, landlords, and tenants in buying, selling or leasing property).

10. <u>Broker's Policy on Agency</u>. Unless Broker indicates below that Broker is not offering a specific agency relationship, the types of agency relationships offered by Broker are: seller agency, buyer agency, designated agency, dual agency, landlord agency, and tenant agency.

The agency relationship(s), if any, **NOT** offered by Broker is/are the following:_____

<u>Dual Agency Disclosure:</u> *[Applicable only if Broker's agency policy is to practice dual agency]* Seller does hereby consent to Broker acting in a dual agency capacity in transactions in which Broker is representing as clients both the Buyer and Seller and Broker is not acting in a designated agency capacity. By entering this Agreement, Seller acknowledges that Seller understands that Seller does not have to consent to dual agency, is doing so voluntarily, and that this brokerage engagement has been read and understood. In serving as a dual agent, Broker is representing two parties as clients whose interests are or at times could be different or even adverse. As a dual agent, Broker will disclose to both parties all adverse material facts relevant to the transaction actually known to the dual agent except for information made confidential by request or instructions from client and which is not required to be disclosed by law. Seller hereby directs Broker, while acting as a dual agent to keep confidential and not reveal to the Buyer any information which would materially and adversely affect the Seller's negotiating position. Broker or Broker's affiliated licensees will timely disclose to each client the nature of any material relationship the broker and the broker's affiliated licensees have with the other client or clients, other than that incidental to the transaction. A material relationship shall mean any actually known personal, familial, or business relationship between Broker and a client which would impair the ability of Broker to exercise fair and independent judgment relative to another client. The other party whom Broker may represent in the event of dual agency may or may not be identified at the time Seller enters into this Agreement. If any party is identified after the Agreement and has a material relationship with Broker, then Broker shall timely provide to Seller a disclosure of the nature of such relationship.

F1, Exclusive Seller Listing Agreement, Page 2 of 3 01/01/02

(continued)

EXHIBIT 4–4
Exclusive Seller Listing Agreement (continued)

11. <u>Entire Agreement</u>. This Agreement constitutes the sole and entire agreement between the parties hereto, and no modification of this Agreement shall be binding unless signed by all parties. No representation, promise, or inducement not included in this Agreement shall be binding upon any party hereto.

12. <u>Governing Law</u>. This Agreement shall be governed by and interpreted pursuant to the laws of the State of Georgia.

SPECIAL STIPULATIONS: The following Special Stipulations, if conflicting with any preceding paragraph, shall control.

☐ (Mark box if additional pages are attached.)

BY SIGNING THIS AGREEMENT, SELLER ACKNOWLEDGES THAT: (1) SELLER HAS READ ALL PROVISIONS AND DISCLOSURES MADE HEREIN; (2) SELLER UNDERSTANDS ALL SUCH PROVISIONS AND DISCLOSURES AND HAS ENTERED INTO THIS AGREEMENT VOLUNTARILY; AND (3) SELLER IS NOT SUBJECT TO A CURRENT LISTING AGREEMENT WITH ANY OTHER BROKER.

RECEIPT OF A COPY OF THIS AGREEMENT IS HEREBY ACKNOWLEDGED BY SELLER.

The above proposition is hereby accepted, _____ o'clock _____ M., on the _____ day of _____, 20_____.

Company _____

By: _____
    Broker or Broker's Affiliated Licensee

Print/Type Name: _____

Phone #: _____

Fax #: _____

Seller _____ SS/FEI# _____

Seller _____ SS/FEI# _____

Print/Type Name(s): _____

Phone #: _____

Fax #: _____

Address: _____

_____

    F1, Exclusive Seller Listing Agreement, Page 3 of 3 01/01/02

Deeds

"We were born on it, and we got killed on it, died on it. Even if it's no good, it's still ours. That's what makes it ours—being born on it, working it, dying on it. That makes ownership, not a paper with numbers on it."

—The Grapes of Wrath—John Steinbeck

OBJECTIVES

After reading this chapter you should be able to:

- Identify the type of deeds used in modern real estate practice
- Explain the basic requirements of a valid deed
- Prepare a deed

Adeed is a written document that transfers ownership of real property from one person to the next. In most law firms legal assistants prepare **deeds.** For this reason this chapter discusses the general law involving deeds and offers practical suggestions for the preparation of deeds and samples of deed forms.

deed
Written document that transfers ownership of real property from one person to another.

TYPES OF DEEDS

Three types of deeds commonly are used in the United States: (1) general warranty deed, (2) limited (special) warranty deed, and (3) quitclaim deed.

General Warranty Deed

Caveat emptor ("Let the buyer beware") applies to the law of real property transfers. In the absence of some express covenant for title, the full risk of title failure falls on the purchaser of real property. Therefore, the prudent purchaser will ask for and obtain certain covenants of title. These covenants usually are found in a deed known as a **general warranty deed.** The form of a general warranty deed varies from state to state. Some states require the warranties to be expressly set forth in the deed; in other states the warranties may be included merely with the use of such words as "grant," "bargain and sell," or "warrant."

A general warranty deed contains six **covenants** or **warranties:** (1) covenant of seisin, (2) covenant of right to convey, (3) covenant against encumbrances, (4) covenant for further assurance, (5) covenant for quiet enjoyment, and (6) covenant for warranty. The covenants are made by the **grantor,** the person who is transferring ownership of the land.

general warranty deed
Deed containing full warranty of title.

warranty or covenant
Promise that a fact is true or that an event will take place.

grantor
Transferor of real property by deed.

Covenant of Seisin

Seisin has its roots in the feudal law of England. There is a great deal of argument among legal scholars as to the exact meaning of seisin. Practically speaking, seisin means the right to possession of property. The grantor (the seller) under a general warranty deed will warrant that the grantor has possession of the land being transferred, or has a right to the possession of the land. The covenant of seisin also warrants that the grantor has ownership or title to the land.

Covenant of Right to Convey

The covenant of the right to convey is a promise made on behalf of the grantor of the deed that the grantor owns the land and has the right to transfer ownership of the land. An interest in the land held by a person other than the grantor would cause a breach of this covenant.

Covenant against Encumbrances

The covenant against encumbrances is a promise or warranty by the grantor that the land is unencumbered; that is, the land is free and clear from mortgages, liens, taxes, leases, easements, or any other restrictions that might restrict the use of the land or be a debt on the land.

Covenant of Further Assurance

conveyance
Transfer of title or ownership to real property from one person to another by deed. The terms may be used to include assignment, lease, mortgage, or encumbrance of real property.

The covenant of further assurance is a promise by a grantor that in the future, the grantor will make any **conveyance** necessary to vest in the grantee of the deed the title intended to be conveyed. For example, if the grantor intends to convey fee simple absolute title by the deed but later discovers that he has only a conditional fee, through the covenant of further assurance he agrees to satisfy or remove the conditions so the title to the land conveyed is fee simple absolute.

Covenants of Quiet Enjoyment and Warranty

grantee
Person in whom real property has been transferred by deed.

The covenants of quiet enjoyment and warranty usually are the same, and involve a warranty that the **grantee** of the deed will be able to quietly enjoy the land without fear of eviction and without fear of any third party assertions of adverse claims.

Present versus Future Covenants

The covenants of seisin, right to convey, and against encumbrances are called *present covenants* because if they are breached, it is at the time the deed is delivered. The immediate grantee (original purchaser or recipient of the land) is the only person who can sue for breach of a present covenant. Present covenants are not transferable when the land is subsequently sold.

The covenants of further assurance, quiet enjoyment, and warranty are called *future covenants* because they may be breached at some time in the future. Future covenants are transferable, and run with the land. Any owner of the land has standing to sue for breach of a future covenant contained in a general warranty deed.

The following example illustrates the distinction between present and future covenants. Juan transfers land by general warranty deed to Bob. Bob transfers the same land by general warranty deed to Carol. Carol later transfers the same land again by general warranty deed to Theo. Each deed is a general warranty deed with all the six covenants. After the transfers have been made, Theo, the current owner of the land, discovers that there is a mortgage on the land that had been created by Juan at the time Juan owned the property. The mortgage, at the time of its discovery, is a breach of the covenant against encumbrances. Because the covenant against encumbrances is a present covenant, Theo can only recover losses as a result of the mortgage from Carol for the breach. If the holder of the mortgage attempts to foreclose and to evict Theo from possession of the land, the foreclosure and attempted eviction will become a breach of the covenant of quiet enjoyment (a future covenant). Theo, on breach of the future covenant, will have the right to recover from Carol, Bob, and Juan, since the covenant of quiet enjoyment is a future covenant that runs with the land and is transferable. A claim under a future covenant can be asserted by any owner of the land against any person who has given a general warranty deed in the chain of title. Exhibit 5–1 illustrates the difference between present and future covenants. A breach of a covenant in a warranty deed may be sued on by the grantee of the deed, even though the grantee was aware of, or should have been aware of, the defect at the time the grantee received the deed. This principle of law is illustrated in *Lunsford v. King*, 209 S.E.2d 27.

EXHIBIT 5–1
Present versus Future
Covenants

Present Covenants	*Future Covenants*
Can only be enforced by the immediate grantee of a deed	Can be enforced by any owner of the property against the grantor of the deed
• Covenant of Seisin	• Covenant of Further Assurance
• Covenant of Right to Convey	• Covenant of Quiet Enjoyment
• Covenants against Encumbrances	• Covenant of Warranty

C A S E

Lunsford v. King
209 S.E.2d 27 (Ga. 1974)

STOLZ, Judge.

Plaintiff Lunsford, vendee of a certain tract of land in Fulton County, Georgia, described in a contract of sale by metes and bounds, brought an action against Fulton County, Mrs. King (his vendor), and the vendor's predecessors in title, seeking to enjoin the county from taking or interfering with, without condemnation, the plaintiff's use of a strip of said tract which one of the defendant predecessors in title had dedicated to the defendant county for road-widening purposes, but which had been included in all of the legal descriptions in all of the subsequent warranty deeds, including the plaintiff's. The complaint prayed alternatively, if it be judicially determined that the county could legally proceed under its right-of-way deed, for damages from the remaining defendants, his predecessors in title, jointly and severally, for breach of warranty in the amount of $2,475. The plaintiff appeals from the grant of the summary judgment in favor of the defendant vendor and defendant King-Williams Land Co., Inc., now King Williams Realty & Mortgage, Inc. (the vendor's immediate predecessor in title). The plaintiff's appeal from the trial court's judgment denying the injunctive relief against Fulton County had been dismissed previously for lack of a certificate for immediate review. *Lunsford v. Fulton County,* 227 Ga. 547, 181 S.E.2d 865, *Held:*

"Where, as here, a certain tract of land is described in a contract of sale by definite boundaries, and it later appears that the vendor has no title to a portion of the tract contained within the described boundaries, this is a defect in the vendor's title as contemplated by Code § 29-202 rather than a deficiency in quantity as contemplated by Code § 29-201." *Lawton v. Byck,* 217 Ga. 676(2), 124 S.E.2d 369. The plaintiff's right to recovery of damages under Code § 29-202, is not defeated by his constructive knowledge of the prior recorded deed to the county. "A general warranty of title in a deed against the claims of all persons covers defects in the title though known to the purchaser at the time of taking the deed." Code § 29-304.

Accordingly, the plaintiff is entitled to prove his case before a jury, including the amount of the unliquidated damages for the "reduction of the price according to the relative value of the land so lost." Code § 29-202. Therefore, the trial judge erred in granting the summary judgment in favor of the defendant vendor, Mrs. King, and defendant King-Williams Land Co., Inc., now King Williams Realty & Mortgage, Inc.

Judgment reversed.

Limited (Special) Warranty Deed

A **limited** or **special warranty deed** is a warranty deed in which the grantor covenants only against the lawful claims of people claiming by, through, or under the grantor. For example, a grantor of a limited warranty deed would be liable only if the ownership of the land by the grantee of the deed is disturbed by some claim arising from some act of the grantor. For example, if the grantor has placed an easement on the property and warrants in the limited warranty deed an express covenant against encumbrances, then the grantor of the limited warranty deed would be responsible and could be sued for the easement. If the easement already existed on the land at the time the grantor of the limited warranty deed received title to the land, and the easement was created by some person prior in title to the grantor, the grantor, by giving a limited warranty deed, would not be responsible for the easement. Remember that in this same example, if the grantor had given a general warranty deed, which is an absolute warranty against encumbrances, the grantor would have been responsible for the easement, regardless of whether the grantor was the cause or creation of the easement or the easement was created by a predecessor in title.

limited or special warranty deed
Deed wherein the grantor covenants and warrants only against the lawful claims of people claiming by, through, or under the grantor.

Quitclaim Deed

A **quitclaim deed** transfers only the interest the grantor has in the land and not the land itself. If the grantor of a quitclaim deed has complete ownership at the time of the execution of the deed, a quitclaim deed will pass complete ownership to the grantee. A quitclaim deed contains no covenants or warranties of title. If a grantor of a quitclaim deed conveys land that is encumbered or land not owned by the grantor, the grantee usually, absent some evidence of fraud, is without claim against the grantor. Quitclaim deeds often are found in other forms of deeds, such as foreclosure deeds (deeds received from foreclosures of property by mortgage or tax foreclosures), executor's deeds (deeds executed by the executor of an estate), administrator's deeds (deeds executed by an administrator of an intestate estate), and trustee's deeds (deeds executed by the trustee of a trust). Independent investigation of the title to the land is essential in a transaction that involves a quitclaim deed.

Generally speaking, purchasers of land will want the best kind of deed, the general warranty deed. The type of deed typically is negotiated within the contract for sale of the land, and every effort is made to obtain the best deed.

BASIC REQUIREMENTS OF A VALID DEED

The basic requirements of a valid deed are (a) written instrument, (b) competent grantor, (c) identity of the grantee, (d) words of conveyance, (e) adequate description of land, (f) consideration, (g) signature of grantor, (h) witnesses, and (i) delivery of the completed deed to the grantee.

Written Instrument

A deed must be in writing, but no generally prescribed form is essential to the validity of a deed. Even a letter in most states could constitute a valid deed provided all the requirements are met.

Some states—for example, New York—by statute prescribe the form of a deed and the specific language that must be used in order for the deed to be valid. The law of the state in which the real property to be transferred is located will control as to the form required for the deed. Legal assistants should review the appropriate law before a deed is prepared.

Competent Grantor

The deed must be signed by a party who is competent. Deeds executed by minors (people under the age of eighteen years) are voidable, and deeds executed by mentally incompetent people usually are void. Partnership deeds should be executed by all the partners, and corporate deeds should have proper corporate authority from the board of directors. The grantor also must be the owner or have an ownership interest in the land conveyed by the deed.

Identity of the Grantee

A deed must identify with certainty the grantee. A deed to a nonexistent grantee is thought to be void. Every effort should be made to correctly identify the name of the grantee for both individual and corporate deeds. For corporations, the correct name is obtained from the corporate records' division of the secretary of state's office in the state of incorporation.

Words of Conveyance

A deed must contain words of conveyance that indicate the grantor's intent to make a present conveyance of the land by the instrument. No special words are needed, but words such as "grant, convey, assign, setover, transfer, and give" have all been held to express the intent to pass title and are sufficient to make an instrument a deed.

Description of the Property

The deed must describe the land being conveyed with specificity. A platted description, government rectangular survey description, or a metes and bounds description based on a registered land surveyor's survey should be used. A deed conveys only the land described in the deed. The deed will convey all improvements, buildings, air rights, mineral rights, and other appurtenances that belong to the owner of the land unless excluded by express reference.

Consideration

A deed must have consideration to be valid. **Consideration** is defined as something of value given for the deed. This value is the purchase price of the land being conveyed, although gift deeds for love and affection are recognized in all states. A recital of consideration is sufficient. A typical recital of consideration may be "for Ten Dollars and other good and valuable consideration."

consideration
Something of value given to make the promises of a contract enforceable. Consideration also is something of value given for a deed.

Signed by the Grantor

The grantor is the only person required to sign the deed. Deeds are not signed by the grantee. Some states, however, require that the grantee sign if the grantee is assuming the payment of a mortgage on the land or is purchasing a condominium and intends to be bound by the covenants and restrictions of the condominium. Although a few states dictate where the deed must be signed, deeds typically are signed in the lower right-hand corner.

Witnessing of Deeds

The requirement for the witnessing, attestation, or acknowledgment of the grantor's signature to a deed varies from state to state. Some states require that deeds be witnessed only to permit the deed to be recorded. In these states a deed is valid between the parties without recordation, and therefore valid without witnessing. Other states require that the grantor's signature must be witnessed for the deed to be valid. Therefore, within these states all deeds must be witnessed. Each state has its own witnessing requirements in terms of number and who may be a witness to a deed. A witness may be a notary public or other disinterested person. An interested witness, such as the grantee, cannot witness the grantor's signature to a deed. The usual number of required witnesses is two.

Delivery to Grantee

The deed does not transfer title to land until the deed is delivered to the grantee or someone on the grantee's behalf. A deed is delivered when the grantor places the deed in the possession of the grantee with the intention that the deed passes present title of the land to the grantee and the grantee accepts this delivery. There are many presumptions regarding the delivery or nondelivery of a deed. Possession of the deed by the grantee is a presumption of delivery. Possession of the deed by the grantor is presumption of nondelivery. Recordation of a deed in the public records is presumption of delivery. All these presumptions are rebuttable if facts can be shown to the contrary.

PREPARATION OF A VALID DEED

Real property law is local law, and the law of deeds is no exception. The law of the state in which the land to be conveyed by the deed is located controls the form as well as the formal requirements of the deed. It is important to check local and state law before preparing a deed.

The preparation of a valid deed is a simple process. It is advisable to use the forms that are available from state bar associations, title companies, or law firms.

Most deed forms have the following formal parts: caption, premises or preamble, granting clause, description, habendum, warranty clause, and testimonium. The location of each of the formal parts of the deed is keyed by number on the sample deed form shown in Exhibit 5–2.

EXHIBIT 5-2
Formal Parts of a Deed
(1) caption,
(2) premises or preamble,
(3) granting clause,
(4) description,
(5) habendum,
(6) warranty clause, and
(7) testimonium.

WARRANTY DEED

1

STATE OF   COUNTY OF

THIS INDENTURE, Made the   day of   , in the year
two thousand   , between

2

of the County of   , and State of Georgia, as party or parties of the
first part, hereinafter called Grantor, and

as party or parties of the second part, hereinafter called Grantee (the words "Grantor" and
"Grantee" to include their respective heirs, successors and assigns where the context requires or
permits).

WITNESSETH that: Grantor, for and in consideration of the sum of
(   ) DOLLARS
in hand paid at and before the sealing and delivery of these presents, the receipt whereof is hereby
acknowledged, has granted, bargained, sold, aliened, conveyed and confirmed, and by these presents
does grant, bargain, sell, alien, convey and confirm unto the said Grantee,

3

4

TO HAVE AND TO HOLD the said tract or parcel of land, with all and singular the rights,
members and appurtenances thereof, to the same being, belonging, or in anywise appertaining, to the
only proper use, benefit and behoof of the said Grantee forever in FEE SIMPLE.   **5**

AND THE SAID Grantor will warrant and forever defend the right and title to the above
described property unto the said Grantee against the claims of all persons whomsoever.   **6**

IN WITNESS WHEREOF, the Grantor has signed and sealed this deed, the day and year above
written.   **7**

Signed, sealed and delivered in presence of:

_____   _____ (Seal)

_____   _____ (Seal)

_____   _____ (Seal)

Caption

The **caption** or heading of a deed is designed to show the place of execution of the deed. The caption indicates the county and state in which the deed was signed by the grantor. The caption does *not* refer to the county and state in which the land is located.

Premises or Preamble

The premises or **preamble** to a deed is the section that sets forth the parties to the deed and the date of the deed. A deed is valid without a date, but most deeds are dated. The date should be the date of execution by the grantor. The parties to the deed are the grantor and grantee. Every effort should be made to use the correct name for both the grantor and the grantee. Titles such as Mr. and Mrs., and Ms. are seldom used.

Granting Clause

The granting clause contains the language indicating that the instrument is a deed and that the land is being granted or conveyed. Few states require any particular words, and therefore any words indicating a present intent to transfer the land are sufficient. The granting clause in many deeds also contains a recital of consideration.

Description

The main portion of any deed is the description of the land to be conveyed. It is important to use the best description available, which usually is a description prepared by a registered land surveyor or a description prepared from a registered land survey.

Habendum Clause

The **habendum** clause indicates what estate is being transferred, such as life estate or fee simple.

Warranty Clause

The warranty clause usually contains words of warranty or, in the case of quitclaim deeds, a lack thereof of warranty words.

Testimonium

The **testimonium** is the execution portion of the deed. Most deeds are signed under hand and seal and are witnessed. A recital of this action is found in the testimonium.

Completing Sections of a Deed

The following are examples for completing the sections of a deed.

Preamble

The grantor and grantee designations, which appear in the preamble of a deed, may be completed as follows:

If the grantor is an individual, the preamble may read as follows:

Joseph R. Snead, an individual

If the grantors are husband and wife, the preamble may read as follows:

Joseph R. Snead and Mary T. Snead, husband and wife

If the grantor is an unmarried individual in a community property state, the preamble may read as follows:

Joseph R. Snead, an unmarried individual

If the grantor is a corporation, the preamble may read as follows:

The Farris Corporation, an Ohio corporation

If the grantor is a general partnership, the preamble may read as follows:

Farris Associates, a North Carolina general partnership

If the grantor is a limited partnership, the preamble may read as follows:

Farris Associates, Ltd., a North Carolina limited partnership

If the grantor is the trustee of a Trust, the preamble may read as follows:

David H. Farris, Trustee of Trust created by Joseph R. Snead for the benefit of Mary T. Snead, pursuant to Trust Agreement dated July 26, 2003

If the grantor is the executor of an estate, the preamble may read as follows:

David H. Farris, Executor under the Last Will and Testament of Joseph R. Snead, deceased, of Richland County, Illinois

If the grantor is the administrator of the estate of a person who has died without a will, the preamble may read as follows:

David H. Farris, Administrator of the intestate estate of Joseph R. Snead, deceased, of Richland County, Illinois

If the grantee of a deed is an individual, married couple, corporation, partnership, trustee, executor, or administrator, the same language as that used above may be used to describe the grantee.

If the grantees of a deed are husband and wife and the property conveyed by the deed is located in a state that recognizes the tenancy by entirety form of ownership, the preamble for the grantee may read as follows:

Joseph R. Snead and Mary T. Snead, husband and wife and as tenants by the entirety

If the grantees of a deed want to hold title as joint tenants with the right of survivorship, the grantee preamble may read as follows:

Joseph R. Snead and Mary T. Snead, as joint tenants with the right of survivorship

If the grantees of a deed want to hold title as tenants in common, the grantee preamble may read as follows:

Joseph R. Snead and Mary T. Snead, as tenants in common

If the grantees of a deed are tenants in common and want to own unequal shares of the property, the grantee preamble may read as follows:

Joseph R. Snead (an undivided seventy-five percent) and Mary T. Snead (an undivided twenty-five percent), as tenants in common

Granting Clause

An example of a recital of nominal consideration in the granting clause is as follows:

Ten and No/100 Dollars ($10.00) and other good and valuable consideration

A deed of gift contains a recital of consideration such as the following:

For love and affection

Description

The legal description of the land conveyed by the deed should be described with full certainty on the face of the deed. If the description is too long to fit on the first page of the deed, it must be attached as an exhibit to the deed. A deed that uses an exhibit description should refer to the exhibit on the face of the deed. This reference can be as follows:

All that tract or parcel of land lying and being in Land Lot 75 of the 5th District of Hall County, Georgia, and being more particularly described on Exhibit "A" attached hereto and by reference incorporated herein

A general warranty deed warrants that the land is unencumbered. Often the land is encumbered, and exceptions to the warranty must be created. These exceptions often are stated in the description portion of the deed. The exceptions may be shown as follows:

This conveyance is subject to the following title exceptions:

(a) Taxes for the year 2000 and subsequent years.

(b) Easement from The Farris Corporation to Alabama Power Company; dated August 12, 2000, and recorded August 18, 2000, at Deed Book 35, Page 749, Montgomery County, Alabama.

Title exceptions to a general warranty deed also may be shown on an exhibit to the deed.

This conveyance is subject to the title exceptions shown on Exhibit "A" attached hereto and by reference incorporated herein.

It is the custom in some states to refer to title exceptions in general terms, such as:

This conveyance is subject to all easements, restrictions, and encumbrances of record.

If the land conveyed in a deed is encumbered by a mortgage, and the purchaser-grantee is willing to accept the land with the mortgage but not willing to assume personal responsibility for payment of the mortgage, the mortgage is described in the deed as follows:

This conveyance is subject to a Mortgage from The Farris Corporation to First Bank and Trust, dated April 12, 2000, recorded April 22, 2000, at Mortgage Book 632, Page 58, Carl County, North Dakota, securing the original principal indebtedness of $76,500.00.

If the purchaser-grantee is willing to assume personal responsibility for payment of the mortgage, the following language may be used in the deed:

This conveyance is subject to a Mortgage from The Farris Corporation to First Bank and Trust, dated April 12, 2000, recorded April 12, 2002, at Mortgage Book 632, Page 58, Carl County, North Dakota, securing the original principal indebtedness of $76,500.00, and the Grantee by the acceptance of this deed assumes and agrees to pay the outstanding indebtedness according to its terms and assumes and agrees to be bound by all other terms and covenants contained in the Mortgage.

Testimonium

If the grantor is an individual, the deed may be prepared for signature as follows:

_____ (SEAL)

DAVID F. FARRIS

Deeds executed by partnerships are executed by all the partners.

D & F REALTY COMPANY, a
Georgia general partnership

By: _____ (SEAL)

DAVID F. FARRIS
General Partner

By: _____ (SEAL)

FRANCIS F. FARRIS
General Partner

A deed executed by a limited partnership is signed by all the general partners.

D & F Realty Company, Ltd., a New Jersey limited
partnership by all the general partners:

By: _____ (SEAL)
DAVID F. FARRIS
General Partner

By: _____ (SEAL)
FRANCIS F. FARRIS
General Partner

Corporate deeds are executed by duly authorized officers on behalf of the corporation.

D & F REALTY COMPANY, INC., a Georgia corporation

By: _____ (SEAL)
DAVID F. FARRIS
President

Attest: _____ (SEAL)
FRANCIS F. FARRIS
Secretary

[CORPORATE SEAL]

It is a good idea with corporate deeds to identify the names and titles of the officers who are signing the deeds and to affix the corporate seal to the deed.

A deed from a trust is executed by the trustee. The execution usually identifies the trustee and the trust instrument under which the trustee operates.

By: _____ (SEAL)
DAVID F. FARRIS, Trustee under agreement with JANE FARRIS dated June 1, 2002, for the benefit of MARY S. FARRIS

Deeds executed by estates are done by the executor in the case of a testate estate and by the administrator in the case of an intestate estate. Again, the execution usually identifies the estate under which the deed is being signed.

(Testate estate)

_____ (SEAL)
DAVID F. FARRIS, Executor under the Will of SUSAN F. FARRIS, Deceased, duly probated and recorded

(Intestate estate)

_____ (SEAL)
DAVID F. FARRIS, Administrator of the Estate of SUSAN F. FARRIS, who died intestate under Letters of Administration issued August 15, 2002

Exercises in Deed Preparation

Experience teaches competence in the preparation of deeds. It is helpful for a legal assistant who is first starting to prepare deeds to review deeds that have been used in other transactions.

In the deed shown in Exhibit 5–3 Alice Miller and David Miller are transferring ownership of their home to Susan Dickson and William Dickson. The home is encumbered by (a) an easement from Acme Land and Development Co. to Georgia Power and Light, dated June 8, 1998, recorded June 12, 1998, at Book 418, Page 292, Morris County, Georgia; and (b) unpaid real estate taxes for the current year. The land is described as follows:

EXHIBIT 5-3
Miller–Dickson Deed

WARRANTY DEED

STATE OF   COUNTY OF

THIS INDENTURE, Made the   day of   , in the year two thousand   , between

         Alice Miller and David Miller

of the County of   , and State of Georgia, as party or parties of the first part, hereinafter called Grantor, and

         Susan Dickson and William Dickson

as party or parties of the second part, hereinafter called Grantee (the words "Grantor" and "Grantee" to include their respective heirs, successors and assigns where the context requires or permits).

     WITNESSETH that: Grantor, for and in consideration of the sum of Ten Dollars and other good and valuable consideration   ($10.00   ) DOLLARS in hand paid at and before the sealing and delivery of these presents, the receipt whereof is hereby acknowledged, has granted, bargained, sold, aliened, conveyed and confirmed, and by these presents does grant, bargain, sell, alien, convey and confirm unto the said Grantee,

     ALL THAT TRACT or parcel of land lying and being in Land Lot 341 of the 8th Land District of Morris County, Georgia being more particularly described as Lot 6, Block C of The Oaks Subdivision as per plat recorded at Plat Book 6, Page 23, Morris County, Georgia Plat Records, which Plat is incorporated herein and made a part of this description by reference.

     THIS CONVEYANCE IS SUBJECT TO THE FOLLOWING TITLE EXCEPTIONS:

(a)   Real estate taxes for the current year and subsequent years,
(b)   An easement from ACME Land & Development Co., to Georgia Power and Light, dated June 8, 1998, recorded June 12, 1998 at Deed Book 418, Page 292 Morris County, Georgia Records.

     TO HAVE AND TO HOLD the said tract or parcel of land, with all and singular the rights, members and appurtenances thereof, to the same being, belonging, or in anywise appertaining, to the only proper use, benefit and behoof of the said Grantee forever in FEE SIMPLE.

     AND THE SAID Grantor will warrant and forever defend the right and title to the above described property unto the said Grantee against the claims of all persons whomsoever.

     IN WITNESS WHEREOF, the Grantor has signed and sealed this deed, the day and year above written.

Signed, sealed and delivered in presence of:

_____   _____ (Seal)
Witness   Alice Miller

_____ -   _____ (Seal)
Notary Public   David Miller

My Commission Expires: _____ (Seal)

     [NOTARIAL SEAL]

ALL THAT TRACT or parcel of land lying and being in Land Lot 341 of the 8th Land District of Morris County, Georgia, and being more particularly described as Lot 6, Block C of The Oaks Subdivision, as per plat recorded at Plat Book 6, Page 23, Morris County, Georgia Plat Records, which Plat is incorporated herein and made a part of this description by reference.

Exhibit 5–4 is an example of a deed to transfer ownership of land from the Knox Land Development Company, an Illinois corporation, to Carole S. Jackson. The land is encumbered by (a) unpaid real estate taxes for the current year and (b) a mortgage from Knox Land Development Company to First National Bank of Salem, dated October 14, 2000, recorded October 14, 2000, at Mortgage Book 21, Page 466, Knox County, Illinois. The mortgage secures an original principal indebtedness of $84,000.00. Carole Jackson is willing to assume the mortgage.

EXHIBIT 5–4
Knox–Jackson Deed

Associated – Champaign Office ● Chicago Title Insurance Company
201 North Neil – Champaign, Illinois 61820 – Phone 356-0501

DOCUMENT NO. _____

WARRANTY DEED

For Recorder's Certificate Only

THE GRANTOR__, _____

Knox Land Development Company, an Illinois corporation

_____

of the _____ of _____, in the County

of __Knox_____, and State of _____Illinois_____,

for and in consideration of Ten Dollars ($10.00) and other good and

valuable consideration in hand paid, **CONVEY__ AND WARRANT__** to

the **GRANTEE__**, _____

Carole S. Jackson

of the _____ of _____, County of __Knox_____, and State

of __Illinois_____, the following described real estate:

ALL THAT TRACT or parcel of land lying and being in the Northwest quarter of Section 27, Township 24 South, Range 35 East, Knox County, Illinois and being more particularly described on Exhibit "A" attached hereto and by reference incorporated herein.

THIS CONVEYANCE IS SUBJECT TO THE FOLLOWING TITLE EXCEPTIONS:

(a)   Mortgage from Knox Land Development Company to First National Bank of Salem, dated October 14, 2000, recorded October 14, 2000 at Mortgage Book 21, Page 466, Knox County, Illinois, securing the original principal indebtedness of $84,000.00. The Grantee by the acceptance of this deed assumes and agrees to pay the outstanding indebtedness according to its terms and assumes and agrees to be bound by all other terms and covenants contained in the Mortgage.

Subject to: (1) Real estate taxes for the year 20 ____ and subsequent years;
            (2) Covenants, conditions, restrictions and easements apparent or of record
            (3) All applicable zoning laws and ordinances;

Dated this _____ day of _____, 20____.

Knox Land Development Company, an
Illinois corporation

By: _____ (SEAL)

Attest: _____, Its President
           Its Secretary (SEAL)

STATE OF ILLINOIS)
) SS
CHAMPAIGN COUNTY)

I, the undersigned, a Notary Public in and for said County and State aforesaid, **DO HEREBY CERTIFY**, that

[CORPORATE SEAL]

personally known to me to be the same person__ whose name__ _____ subscribed to the foregoing instrument, appeared before me this day in person and acknowledged that __h____ signed, sealed and delivered the said instrument as _____ free and voluntary act, for the uses and purposes therein set forth, including the waiver of the right of homestead.

(SEAL)

Given under my hand and Notarial Seal, this _____

day of _____, A.D. 20____.

_____
Notary Public

Deed Prepared By: _____

Send Tax Bill To:

____ _____

_____

Exempt under provisions of Paragraph _____ Section 4, Real Estate Transfer Tax Act.

Date _____ Signature _____
                                          Buyer, Seller or Representative

The land is described as property lying and being in the northwest quarter of Section 27, Township 24 South, Range 35 East, Knox County, Illinois. The description is too long to be included on the first page of the deed.

Using the deed shown in Exhibit 5–5 as a guide, practice preparing deeds for the following hypothetical transfer situations.

EXHIBIT 5–5
Warranty Deed

WARRANTY DEED

STATE OF   COUNTY OF

THIS INDENTURE, Made the   day of   , in the year
two thousand   , between

of the County of   , and State of Georgia, as party or parties of the
first part, hereinafter called Grantor, and

as party or parties of the second part, hereinafter called Grantee (the words "Grantor" and "Grantee" to include their respective heirs, successors and assigns where the context requires or permits).

WITNESSETH that: Grantor, for and in consideration of the sum of
(   ) DOLLARS
in hand paid at and before the sealing and delivery of these presents, the receipt whereof is hereby acknowledged, has granted, bargained, sold, aliened, conveyed and confirmed, and by these presents does grant, bargain, sell, alien, convey and confirm unto the said Grantee,

TO HAVE AND TO HOLD the said tract or parcel of land, with all and singular the rights, members and appurtenances thereof, to the same being, belonging, or in anywise appertaining, to the only proper use, benefit and behoof of the said Grantee forever in FEE SIMPLE.

AND THE SAID Grantor will warrant and forever defend the right and title to the above described property unto the said Grantee against the claims of all persons whomsoever.

IN WITNESS WHEREOF, the Grantor has signed and sealed this deed, the day and year above written.

Signed, sealed and delivered in presence of:

_____   _____ (Seal)

_____   _____ (Seal)

_____   _____ (Seal)

Practice Deed No. 1

Hodges Development Co., Inc., a South Carolina corporation, is purchasing land from Mills Brothers Associates, a South Carolina general partnership, with Edward S. Mills and Thomas C. Mills as the general partners. The land is encumbered by (a) unpaid real estate taxes for the current year; (b) an easement from Harrison Maddox to South Carolina Power & Light, dated January 14, 2000, recorded January 26, 2000, at Book 253, Page 4, Spring County, South Carolina Records; and (c) restrictive covenants created by Declaration of Restrictive Covenants from Mills Brothers Associates, dated March 23, 2001, recorded at Book 261, Page 419, Spring County, South Carolina Records. The land is described as follows:

> ALL THAT TRACT or parcel of land lying and being in Land Lots 14, 15, and 16 of the 4th Land District of Spring County, South Carolina, and being more particularly described as Lots 21, 22, 23, and 24, Block C, Lots 15, 16, 19, and 22, Block D, and Lots 3, 4, 5, 8, 10, and 14, Block E, of The Mills Plantation Subdivision as per plat recorded at Plat Book 10, Page 103, Spring County, South Carolina Plat Records, which plat is incorporated herein and made a part of this description by reference.

Practice Deed No. 2

Charles D. Hoover and Martha L. Hoover are transferring ownership of their home to James C. Brooks and Doris L. Brooks. James and Doris want to take the property as joint tenants with the right of survivorship. The home is encumbered by (a) unpaid real estate taxes for the current year and (b) a mortgage from Charles D. Hoover and Martha L. Hoover to First Federal Savings and Loan Association securing the original principal indebtedness of $78,325, dated August 15, 2000, recorded August 16, 2000, at Mortgage Book 212, Page 82, Todd County, Wisconsin. The purchasers are willing to assume the mortgage. The land is described as follows:

> ALL THAT TRACT or parcel of land lying and being in the Southeast Quarter of Township 14 North, Section 3, Range 15 West, Todd County, Wisconsin, and being more particularly described as Lot 14, Block A, of The Blue Springs Subdivision as per Plat recorded at Plat Book 3, Page 47, Todd County, Wisconsin Plat Records, which Plat is incorporated herein and made a part of this description by reference.

CORRECTION OF DEEDS

Although every attempt should be made to avoid mistakes, mistakes do happen, and many times deeds must be corrected. The customary method of correcting an error in a deed is for the grantor to execute and deliver to the grantee a corrective deed. A corrective deed is valid without any additional consideration. Acceptance by the grantee is admission of the error found in the original deed.

Reformation and Cancellation of Deed

If a mutual mistake of fact is involved in the preparation, execution, and delivery of a deed, equity will reform the deed to its correct status. If there is some unilateral mistake of fact (only one party is mistaken) or fraud involved in the execution and delivery of a deed, the deed can be rescinded by the party who is mistaken or on whom the fraud was perpetrated.

Destruction of a deed does not return legal title to the grantor, nor does the return of a deed by the grantee to the grantor deliver title to the grantor. If it is desired for some reason that the grantee return the land to the grantor, the proper method is for the grantee to prepare, sign, and deliver a new deed to the grantor.

Practice Deed No. 3

The deed shown in Exhibit 5–6 was prepared for the following described transaction and contains mistakes. Please review the deed, list all the mistakes, and prepare a corrective deed.

Pine Tree Development Company, Inc., is transferring title to Jacob Willson and Alice Willson. The property is unencumbered, and described as follows:

ALL THAT TRACT or parcel of land lying and being in Land Lot 48 of the 14th District of Fulton County, Georgia, and being more particularly described as follows:

COMMENCING on the north side of Ponce de Leon Avenue 653.5 feet east from the northeast corner of Ponce de Leon Avenue and Bedford Place (formerly Fort Street), running east along the north side of Ponce de Leon Avenue, 90 feet; run thence north 365 feet; running thence west 89.5 feet; run thence south 381.9 feet to the POINT OF BEGINNING on Ponce de Leon Avenue and being improved property known as 638 Ponce de Leon Avenue, N.E., in the City of Atlanta, Georgia.

EXHIBIT 5-6
Deed Containing Mistakes

WARRANTY DEED

STATE OF GEORGIA   COUNTY OF FULTON

THIS INDENTURE, Made the 11th   day of   December   , in the year two thousand   , between

PINETREE DEVELOPMENT COMPANY, INC.

of the County of Fulton   , and State of Georgia, as party or parties of the first part, hereinafter called Grantor, and

JACOB WILSON and ALICE WILSON

as party or parties of the second part, hereinafter called Grantee (the words "Grantor" and "Grantee" to include their respective heirs, successors and assigns where the context requires or permits).

WITNESSETH that: Grantor, for and in consideration of the sum of TEN AND NO/100 and other good and valuable consideration   ($10.00   ) DOLLARS in hand paid at and before the sealing and delivery of these presents, the receipt whereof is hereby acknowledged, has granted, bargained, sold, aliened, conveyed and confirmed, and by these presents does grant, bargain, sell, alien, convey and confirm unto the said Grantee, all that tract or parcel of land lying and being in Land Lot 48 of the 14th District of Fulton County, Georgia, and being more particularly described as follows:

COMMENCING on the north side of Ponce de Leon Avenue, 653.5 feet east from the northeast corner of Ponce de Leon Avenue and Bedford Place (formerly Fort Street), running thence east along the north side of Ponce de Leon Avenue, 90 feet; running thence north 356 feet; running thence west 89.5 feet; running thence south 381.9 feet to the POINT OF BEGINNING on Ponce de Leon Avenue, and being improved property known as 368 Ponce de Leon Avenue, N.E., in the City of Atlanta, Georgia.

TO HAVE AND TO HOLD the said tract or parcel of land, with all and singular the rights, members and appurtenances thereof, to the same being, belonging, or in anywise appertaining, to the only proper use, benefit and behoof of the said Grantee forever in FEE SIMPLE.

AND THE SAID Grantor will warrant and forever defend the right and title to the above described property unto the said Grantee against the claims of all persons whomsoever.

IN WITNESS WHEREOF, the Grantor has signed and sealed this deed, the day and year above written.

PINETREE DEVELOPMENT CO., INC.

Signed, sealed and delivered in presence of:

By: _____ (Seal)
_____   Carol Tree, President
Unofficial Witness   _____ (Seal)

_____   Attest: _____ (Seal)
Notary Public   Susan Pine, Secretary

(Corporate Seal)

E T H I C S :   Falsification of Documents

A legal assistant is helping an attorney represent a client in the transfer of ownership to real property. The transfer is taking place on October 2. During the closing of the transfer of ownership, the seller, a corporation, informs the attorney and legal assistant that its tax year ended on September 30 and that it had intended for this transfer of ownership to take place during its past tax year. The seller requested that the deed be backdated to September 30 so that the sale and transfer of ownership would appear to take place during the past tax year. Should the attorney and legal assistant backdate the deed?

The American Bar Association's Code of Professional Responsibility prohibits an attorney from falsifying a document for any reason. Likewise, a legal assistant should not, under any circumstances, falsify a document for a client. Changing the date of a deed to reflect a different time for transfer of ownership, especially one that may affect the taxable consequences of the transfer, would be a violation of ethics. The attorney and legal assistant in this situation should inform the client that they cannot falsify the document.

 C H E C K L I S T

Preparation of a Deed

❑ I. Research before Preparation
  ❑ A. Review the contract or other agreement covering the transfer of ownership to the property.
  ❑ B. Review the title examination to make sure of the correct name of the title owner to the property.
  ❑ C. Confirm the correct spellings of all names of the grantor and grantee.
  ❑ D. Carefully review the title examination and determine what title exceptions should be identified in the deed.
  ❑ E. Confirm if prospective purchasers have any special requirements for taking title, such as joint tenancy with the right of survivorship and tenancy in common in a tenancy by entirety state or unequal shares.
  ❑ F. Review survey legal description with description in grantor's current deed to make sure no difference exists between the two descriptions.
❑ II. Preparing the Deed
  ❑ A. Draft the caption.
    1 Indicate the county and state in which the deed is signed.
    2. Date the deed with the date of execution and delivery.
    3. Indicate the correct name of the grantor, who should be the record titleholder of the property.
    4. Indicate the correct name of the grantee or grantees, indicating any special forms of ownership, such as joint tenancy, right of survivorship, and unequal shares.
  ❑ B. Draft the consideration. In most instances use a nominal recital of consideration.
  ❑ C. Draft the legal description.
    1. Use the correct legal description verified by survey and title examination.
    2. If the legal description is too long to be included on the face of the deed, use an exhibit and identify the exhibit on the face of the deed.
    3. List all title exceptions that are being transferred with the property.
  ❑ D. Draft signature blanks.
    1. The grantor is the only person who signs the deed.
    2. Correctly identify the grantor's name and confirm that it is the same as that shown in the caption of the deed.
    3. Type all names underneath the signature lines.
    4. The deed must be signed and sealed.
    5. Make certain the deed contains the proper number of witnesses and the notary designation is correct.

SUMMARY

Ownership to real property is transferred by deed. Legal assistants prepare and review deeds. A checklist to help in the preparation of a deed follows this section. Deed forms vary from state to state, and a legal assistant should be familiar with the forms used in the state in which he or she works.

Every transaction that involves the sale and purchase of real property requires a deed. Most sales and purchases of real property also require that the purchaser borrow a portion of the purchase price. A number of financial institutions engage in the lending of funds for the purchase of real property. These financial institutions usually secure their loans by a mortgage or trust deed on the real property. The law regarding mortgages and trust deeds is discussed in Chapter 6.

KEY TERMS

caption	grantee	quitclaim deed
consideration	grantor	testimonium
conveyance	habendum	warranty or covenant
deed	limited or special warranty deed	
general warranty deed	preamble	

SELF-STUDY EXAMINATION

(Answers provided in Appendix)

1. T or F. In the absence of an express covenant for title, the full risk of title failure falls on the purchaser of real property.

2. T or F. A covenant of quiet enjoyment is a future covenant.

3. T or F. A deed that covenants against the lawful claims of people claiming by, through, or under the grantor is known as a quitclaim deed.

4. T or F. The grantee of a deed is a competent witness to the grantor's signature of a deed.

5. T or F. A deed must be in writing.

6. T or F. Deeds are signed only by the grantor.

7. T or F. Deeds for love and affection with no monetary consideration are not valid.

8. T or F. Possession of the deed by the grantor is presumption of delivery.

9. T or F. The execution portion of a deed is known as the testimonium.

10. T or F. The law of the state in which the land to be conveyed is located controls the formal requirements of a deed.

11. What warranties does a quitclaim deed contain?

12. Do both the grantor and the grantee sign a deed?

13. What are the general requirements for witnesses in regard to a deed?

14. The law of which state controls the form as well as the formal requirements of a deed?

15. Must the grantee of a deed be competent?

16. What is the difference between a general warranty deed and a limited warranty deed?

17. What are the basic requirements of a valid deed?

18. Does a quitclaim deed convey marketable title?

19. List the six covenants or warranties included in a general warranty deed.

20. Samuel Adams is selling his Boston townhouse to Harrison Stone. Who is required to sign the deed in connection with the transfer of ownership?

21. List and briefly describe the formal parts of a deed.

22. You are a legal assistant involved in a closing of a purchase of real property. The real property is owned by Ruth White. The purchasers of the property are Albert Greene and Aretha Greene. You have prepared the deed for Ruth White's signature and you are in a state that requires two witnesses to Ruth White's signature. Can Timothy White, Ruth White's husband, witness her signature on the deed? Can Aretha Greene witness Ruth White's signature on the deed? Can you witness Ruth White's signature on the deed?

23. What is the difference between a present covenant and a future covenant?

24. If you are a purchaser of real property, which type of deed would you prefer to receive? Why?

25. Briefly describe three presumptions regarding delivery of deeds.

Legal Aspects of Real Estate Finance

"Worm or beetle—drought or tempest—on a farmer's land may fall, Each is loaded full o' ruin, but a mortgage beats em all."

—The Tramp's Story—William McKendree [Will] Carleton

OBJECTIVES

After reading this chapter you should be able to:

- Prepare a promissory note
- Prepare a guaranty
- Understand the basic provisions contained in a promissory note
- Understand the basic provisions contained in a guaranty
- List the legal requirements for a mortgage, deed of trust, or security deed
- Understand the risks inherent in a second mortgage
- Identify the various legal remedies available to both the borrower and the lender in the event of a default on a mortgage loan

R eal estate mortgage loans involve large sums of money and numerous risks for both the borrower and the lender. The borrower may be unable to pay the debt, and may lose the real property pledged as security for the debt. The lender may not be repaid as promised, and may resort to the real property security or other measures to collect on the debt. Over the years a number of legal documents have been created to evidence and secure mortgage loan transactions. Legal assistants are actively involved in the preparation of these documents, and need to be familiar with the different legal documents required to make a loan secured by real property. The main legal documents are a promissory note and a security instrument, which, depending on the location of the real property, may be a mortgage, a deed of trust, or a security deed. A promissory note is the written promise made by a property owner to repay the money borrowed from a lender or creditor; the security instrument (mortgage, deed of trust, or security deed) is the instrument conveying real property as security for the repayment of the money.

promissory note
Legal document that contains a promise by one party to pay money to another party.

maker / payor
Party to a promissory note who promises to pay money.

payee
Party to a promissory note to whom a promise to pay money has been made.

holder
Person who is the owner of a promissory note.

endorsement
Method of transferring ownership of a promissory note.

PROMISSORY NOTE

A **promissory note** is a promise by one party to pay money to another party. The parties in a promissory note are referred to as payor or **maker** (the party who promises to pay) and **payee** (the party to whom the promise is made). A promissory note should be written and signed by the maker and contain an unconditional promise to pay a sum certain of money on demand or at a definite time.

Notes commonly are transferred by the payees. The person receiving a transfer of a note from the original payee is referred to as a **holder.** A note is transferred and sold by **endorsement.** An endorsement is simply a direction, usually printed on the back of the note or attached to the note, ordering that the money be paid to the order of the new owner of the note.

A maker's promise on a note is unconditional, and the maker is not released by the sale of the security securing the note. For example, a homeowner signs a note promising to pay $100,000 secured by her home. The homeowner later sells the home. The sale of the home does not release the homeowner from the promise to pay the $100,000 on the note.

In some situations, there are more than one maker on a note, such as in the case of a husband and wife signing a note for the purpose of purchasing a home. In such an event, each maker of the note, referred to as a co-maker, is fully responsible for the payment of the note. The note can be collected from each of the co-makers in full. This is known as joint and several liability. For example, Stanley White and Maria White purchase a home. As part of the purchase, they borrow $100,000 from First Bank and Trust and sign a note promising to pay the $100,000. The bank can collect the $100,000 in full from either Stanley White or Maria White.

A note cannot be prepaid before the date established in the note for payment. If the maker of the note wants the privilege to prepay, this privilege must be provided for in the note. It is not unusual for a lender to condition prepayment on the payment of an additional premium or penalty.

Most states have statutes that establish a ceiling or maximum rate of interest to be charged on a loan. These statutes are called **usury** statutes. The penalty for usury varies from state to state. It usually is the loss of all interest on the loan, but it can be as extreme as the forfeiture of the entire loan amount. Lenders, therefore, are careful to establish an interest rate that does not violate the usury laws.

usury
Interest rates that are determined to be in excess of the maximum permitted by law.

The note is signed by the maker, but the signature is not witnessed or notorized. The note usually is not recorded, but in some states, such as Louisiana, a copy of the note is attached as an exhibit to the deed of trust and recorded.

Practice Suggestions

A note is an important legal document, and the original of the note is the best evidence of the note at the time of collection. Special care should be taken in preparing a note to make sure it correctly reflects the terms of the loan and the repayment of the money. Corrections on notes should be avoided. If an error on a note is corrected by whiting it out or using some other typing correction technique, the correction should be initialed by the maker. For notes that are more than one page long, the maker should initial each page of the note.

Three note forms are included at the end of this chapter (Exhibit 6–1, FNMA Residential Fixed Rate Note; Exhibit 6–2, FNMA Residential Adjustable Rate Note; and Exhibit 6–3, Commercial Loan Note). The following is a checklist to assist in the preparation of a note.

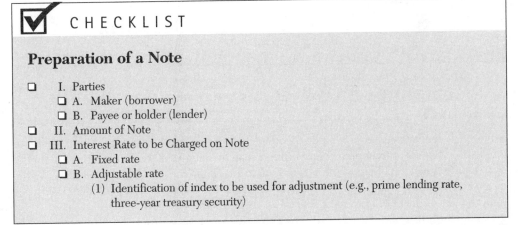

☑ CHECKLIST

Preparation of a Note

❑ I. Parties
    ❑ A. Maker (borrower)
    ❑ B. Payee or holder (lender)
❑ II. Amount of Note
❑ III. Interest Rate to be Charged on Note
    ❑ A. Fixed rate
    ❑ B. Adjustable rate
        (1) Identification of index to be used for adjustment (e.g., prime lending rate, three-year treasury security)

(continued)

(2) Intervals of adjustment (e.g., daily, monthly, annually)

(3) Indication of any minimum or maximum interest rates

❏ IV. Payments

    ❏ A. Time and place of payments

    ❏ B. Amount of payments

❏ V. Maker's Right to Prepay

    ❏ A. May prepay in whole or in part at any time

    ❏ B. May prepay in whole at any time after reasonable notice

    ❏ C. No prepayment allowed

    ❏ D. No prepayment allowed for a certain period of time

    ❏ E. Prepayment allowed but on payment of prepayment fee

    ❏ F. No prepayment allowed for a certain period of time and after that period of time prepayment allowed only on payment of prepayment fee

❏ VI. Maker's Failure to Pay as Required

    ❏ A. Late charge for overdue payment

        (1) Time for late charge to commence (e.g., 10 days, 15 days after due date)

    ❏ B. Amount of late charge (e.g., 4 percent of late payment)

    ❏ C. Default for failure to pay

        (1) Grace period

        (2) Notice of default and period of time to cure default

        (3) Acceleration of loan on default

            a. Optional acceleration

        (4) Payment of holder's cost and expenses for collection of note

            a. Attorney's fees

            b. Court costs and other reasonable expenses

    Default interest rate is higher during periods of default than normal note rate.

❏ VII. Identify Security Given for Note

    ❏ A. Mortgage or deed of trust

    ❏ B. Assignment of leases and rents

    ❏ C. Security agreement

    ❏ D. Other documents

❏ VIII. Usury Savings Clause

❏ IX. Choice of Applicable Law

❏ X. Waiver of Homestead Exemption or Other Debtor's Rights

❏ XI. Joint and Several Liability

❏ XII. Waiver of Notice of Default, Presentment of Notice of Dishonor

❏ XIII. Signatures

    ❏ A. Only maker signs note

        (1) Corporate maker

            a. Identify name of corporation

            b. Identify the officers of the corporation signing the note by name and by title

            c. Affix corporate seal

    ❏ B. Partnership maker

        (1) Identify partnership by name

        (2) Identify all partners signing the note by name

    ❏ C. Names of all people signing the note should be typed underneath the signature line

    ❏ D. Notes are not witnessed or notarized

GUARANTY

guaranty

Legal document that obligates the maker of the document to pay the debt of another person.

guarantor

Person who signs a guaranty promising to pay the debt of another person.

A mortgage lender may require a person other than the debtor to guarantee the payment of the debtor's note. For example, when making a loan to a corporate debtor, a mortgage lender may require the shareholders of the corporation to guarantee the loan. This **guaranty** gives the mortgage lender the right to sue the shareholders for payment of the note and, if necessary, the right to recover the debt from the personal assets of the shareholders.

A guaranty of a note must be written. The written guaranty form is closely interpreted by the courts, and the guarantor's liability is not extended by implication or interpretation. A guaranty may be a "payment guaranty" or a "collection guaranty." The **guarantor** who signs a payment guaranty unconditionally guarantees to pay the note when due without resort to any other party, including the maker of the note. The holder of a note may go directly to a payment guarantor for payment once the note becomes due and payable.

The guarantor who signs a collection guaranty promises to pay the note only after the holder of the note has sued the original maker of the note, has reduced the claim to a judgment, and has attempted to collect against the assets of the maker. A guarantor who signs a collection guaranty will be required to pay the note only in the event the maker of the note is insolvent or otherwise lacks assets sufficient to pay the note.

Under the terms of both the payment guaranty and a collection guaranty, a change in the terms of the note being guaranteed without the guarantor's consent releases the guarantor. Therefore, anytime the note is modified or amended in any way, it is necessary that all guarantors consent to the modification and amendment.

A form of a payment guaranty is shown in Exhibit 6–4 at the end of the chapter.

Conessed Judgment Note (handwritten margin note)

MORTGAGES, DEEDS OF TRUST, AND SECURITY DEEDS

The companion legal document to a promissory note secured by real estate is the security instrument. Depending on the state in which the real property is located, the security instrument may be a mortgage, a deed of trust, or a security deed. Regardless of the form of security instrument being used, its main purpose is to convey real property as security for the repayment of the debt evidenced by the note.

The three basic types of security instruments are (1) mortgage, (2) deed of trust, and (3) security deed. Mortgage, deed of trust, and security deed forms are included at the end of this chapter (Exhibit 6–5, Florida Mortgage; Exhibit 6–6, North Carolina Deed of Trust; Exhibit 6–7, FNMA Residential Mortgage; and Exhibit 6–8, Georgia Commercial Deed to Secure Debt).

Mortgage

Historically, the first real estate security instrument used was a mortgage. A **mortgage** created an encumbrance on the real property but left legal title to the property with the owner. Mortgages are still used in a number of states.

mortgage
Legal document that creates an encumbrance on real property to secure a debt.

Deed of Trust

Several states use a deed of trust form for real estate loans. A **deed of trust** is a document wherein the owner of the real property conveys title to the real property to a third party, known as a trustee. The trustee then holds the title in trust for the benefit of the lender. If the debt being secured by the deed of trust is not paid, the trustee has the power to sell the title to the real property and to use the proceeds from the sale to pay the debt owed to the lender.

deed of trust
Legal document that conveys title to real property to a trustee who holds the title as security for a debt to a lender.

Security Deed

A security deed or **deed to secure debt** is a security instrument wherein the owner of the real property conveys legal title directly to the lender as security for the repayment of the debt. The lender is given the power to sell the real property in the event the debt is not paid.

Regardless of which security instrument is used, the owner stays in possession of the real property and can use and enjoy the real property so long as the debt is being paid.

For simplicity of reference, all three security instruments are referred to as a mortgage throughout this chapter. Please keep in mind that, depending on the state in which the real property is located, the security instrument may be a mortgage, a deed of trust, or a security deed.

deed to secure debt
Legal document that conveys title to real property to a lender to secure a debt.

Requirements of a Mortgage

A mortgage must meet all the requirements of a deed, together with a description of the debt being secured. These requirements are (a) names of the parties, (b) words of conveyance or grant, (c) valid description of the property conveyed, (d) proper execution and attestation, and (e) effective delivery to the lender.

The mortgage may contain a power of sale as well as numerous other provisions designed to protect the lender in every conceivable situation.

Parties to a Mortgage

mortgagor
Person who signs a mortgage pledging real property to secure a debt.

mortgagee
Person who receives a mortgage.

A mortgage is entered into by two parties, the **mortgagor** and the **mortgagee.** The mortgagor is the owner of the property (the debtor), or borrower, and the mortgagee is the lender, or creditor. A mortgage is given by the owner to the lender. In the case of a deed of trust, the instrument may be entered into by three parties, with the addition of the trustee.

Because it is a fundamental rule that only the owner of real property can pledge the real property as security for a loan, it is important that the title to the real property be examined to determine the correct owner and that the owner be made the mortgagor. If the mortgagor is a corporation, proper corporate authority must be presented not only to authorize the loan and the pledge of real property as security, but also to authorize the corporate officers to sign the mortgage. A mortgage signed by a partnership requires that all partners sign the mortgage. Mortgages given by co-owners of property require the signatures of all owners.

Secured Debt

A valid debt must exist to have a valid mortgage. A mortgage must describe in words and figures the debt secured. The date of the final maturity of the debt also is identified.

open-end or dragnet clause
Mortgage provision that provides that the mortgage will secure any and all debt between the mortgagor and the mortgagee, including past debt, present debt, and even future debt incurred after the mortgage is signed.

A mortgage may be given to secure any and all debt between the mortgagor and the mortgagee, including past debt, present debt, and even future debt incurred after the mortgage is in place. These mortgages are called **open-end** or **dragnet** because of the unlimited amount of debt that can be secured.

For example, on March 15 a borrower enters into a mortgage loan transaction with a lender wherein the borrower borrows $100,000 to buy a parcel of land. The mortgage given to the lender contains an open-end or dragnet provision that makes the mortgage secure any and all debts between the borrower and the lender. At the time the loan is entered on March 15, the borrower only owes $100,000 to the lender, and therefore the mortgage only secures $100,000. On August 10 of the same year the borrower goes to the lender and obtains another loan for an unrelated purpose in the amount of $25,000. The borrower signs a note to evidence the debt, but there is no discussion regarding the mortgage or any amendments to the mortgage. Despite the fact that the note does not refer to the mortgage and that there are no amendments to the mortgage, the dragnet or open-end effect of the mortgage causes the mortgage to secure the additional $25,000, for a total of $125,000. Furthermore, any future loans the borrower receives from the lender will be secured by the mortgage.

An open-end or dragnet mortgage can create a problem for the borrower because a default under any of the separate loans secured by the mortgage can give the lender the right to foreclose and have the real property sold. In addition, at the time the mortgage is to be paid and satisfied, the lender can require that all the debt between the borrower and the lender be paid in full before the mortgage is released.

Example 6–1 shows an open-end or dragnet clause.

EXAMPLE 6–1

This mortgage is made and intended to secure all indebtedness now or hereafter owing by Mortgagor to Mortgagee, however or whenever created, incurred, arising or evidenced, whether direct or indirect, joint or several, absolute or contingent, or due or to become due, and any and all renewal or renewals, extension or extensions, modification or modifications or any substitution or substitutions for said indebtedness, either in whole or in part.

Secured Property

Any land or interest in land that can be conveyed by ordinary deed may be conveyed by a mortgage. Real property in a mortgage is described with the same degree of accuracy as in a deed, with the description usually being prepared from a land survey. Real property can be added to the mortgage by amendment or modification. The priority of the mortgage with respect to the added real property is determined as of the date of the addition and *not* as of the date of the original mortgage.

For example, a mortgage is given on Tract A on March 15. The priority of the mortgage as to Tract A is determined as of March 15. This means that the mortgage is subject to any outstanding property interests, such as other mortgages or easements, that occur before March 15, but it is superior and senior to any property interests created after March 15. On October 10 Tract B is added by amendment to the mortgage. Even though the mortgage is originally dated March 15, it only has priority, as to Tract B, from October 10. Any easements, mortgages, or other property interests that are created or exist against the Tract B project before October 10 have priority over the mortgage.

Assignment of Mortgage

Mortgages are freely assignable and often are. A person who buys a mortgage may exercise any and all powers contained in the mortgage. A transfer of mortgage conveys the real property and the secured debt, even though both may not be mentioned in the transfer. A transfer of the note usually includes a transfer of the mortgage, and a transfer of the mortgage includes a transfer of the note.

Most mortgages are assigned either by the inclusion of transfer or assignment language on the mortgage or by a separate assignment that is executed by the assigning lender and recorded. An example of an assignment is shown in Example 6–2.

EXAMPLE 6–2

TRANSFER AND ASSIGNMENT

FOR VALUE RECEIVED, the undersigned hereby transfers, assigns, and conveys unto _____

_____

all of its right, title, interest, powers and options in, to, and under the within and foregoing Mortgage as well as the Premises described therein and the Indebtedness (without recourse) secured thereby.

IN WITNESS WHEREOF the undersigned has caused this transfer and assignment to be executed by its officer and its seal affixed hereto this _____ day of _____ , 20_____ .

Signed, sealed and
delivered in the
presence of:

_____   By: _____
Unofficial Witness   Title: _____

_____   Attest: _____
Notary Public   Title: _____
                                                      (Seal)

Transfer of Property Encumbered by a Mortgage

The fact that real property is mortgaged does not in itself prohibit the owner from selling the real property. However, close attention should be paid to the actual mortgage document. A provision known as **due on sale** is commonly found in mortgages. This provision prohibits the sale of real property without the mortgagee's consent. A sale in violation of this provision is a default of the mortgage and could result in a foreclosure of the real property.

Example 6–3 shows a mortgage "due on sale" provision.

EXAMPLE 6–3

If all or any part of the property or any interest in it is sold or transferred without mortgagee's prior written consent, mortgagee may, at its option, require immediate payment in full of all sums secured by this mortgage.

due on sale clause
Clause found in a mortgage that prohibits the sale of the real property described in the mortgage without the lender's consent. A sale in violation of this provision is a default of the mortgage.

When the borrower is not a natural person, such as a corporation or a partnership, a lender may have a broadened definition of what constitutes a sale. An example of this type of mortgage "due on sale" provision is shown in Example 6–4.

EXAMPLE 6–4

Unless the written consent of mortgagee is first obtained, mortgagee shall have the right, at its option, to declare all sums secured hereby immediately due and payable if (a) mortgagor (by deed or contract of sale or otherwise) sells, conveys, transfers, or further encumbers the mortgaged property or any part thereof; or (b) mortgagor suffers its title or interest therein to be divested, whether voluntarily or involuntarily; or (c) mortgagor changes or permits to be changed the character or use of the mortgaged property; or (d) if mortgagor is a partnership and any of the general partner's interests are transferred or assigned, whether voluntarily or involuntarily, to an entity that the general partner of the mortgagor is not also a general partner therein; or (e) if mortgagor is a corporation with fewer than 100 stockholders at the date of execution of this mortgage and more than 10% of the capital stock thereof is sold, transferred, or assigned during a twelve (12)-month period. If any of the events numerated in (a) through (e) above, inclusive, occurs, and if mortgagee consents to the same or fails to exercise its right to declare all sums secured hereby to be due and payable, such consent or failure shall not be deemed or construed as a waiver, and the consent of mortgagee shall be required on all successive occurrences.

Subject to Versus Assumption

Real property may be sold "subject to" or with an "assumption of" an existing mortgage. A purchaser who buys the real property "subject to" a mortgage does not have personal liability for payment of the debt. The new owner will make the loan payments to protect the real property from foreclosure, but the owner cannot be personally sued to recover on the debt. A lender in a "subject to" sale can foreclose and sell the real property in the event the debt is not paid, and the lender can sue the original mortgagor for payment of the debt, since a sale of the real property does not release the original mortgagor.

A purchaser who buys real property and "assumes" the mortgage becomes personally liable for the debt. If the loan is in default, the lender can (a) foreclose on the real property; (b) sue the new owner of the real property who has assumed the debt; and (c) sue the original mortgagor. The express words used in the transfer from the original mortgagor to the new owner are determinative of whether the real property has been sold "subject to" or "assumption of" the mortgage. If the words "assume and agree to pay" appear in the deed or any other document that has been signed in connection with the deed, then there is an assumption, and the new owner becomes personally liable.

The original mortgagor who sells the real property is not released from the obligation to pay the debt, and will not be released unless a separate, written release from the mortgagee lender is obtained.

If the original mortgagor pays the mortgage in a "subject to" transaction, the mortgagor can recover only against the real property. The original mortgagor is substituted or subrogated in place of the lender, and has the right to foreclose on the real property to recover on the debt. If the original mortgagor pays the lender in a "loan assumption" transaction, the original mortgagor can recover the payments by foreclosing against the real property, suing the current owner personally for recovery on the debt, or both, until payment is received in full.

Selling real property subject to a mortgage or with an assumption of mortgage is a matter of negotiation between the purchaser and the seller. Purchasing real property subject to a mortgage is to the advantage of the purchaser, and purchasing property with a loan assumption is to the advantage of the seller. A lender benefits if the mortgage is assumed because an additional person is obligated on the debt. If the mortgage contains a due on sale provision and the lender's consent to the sale is necessary, it is not unusual for the lender to require that the purchaser assume the mortgage.

Cancellation or Satisfaction of Mortgage

A mortgage is automatically released by full payment of the debt. Full payment of the debt, however, does not release the mortgage of record, and the mortgagee has a duty to file a cancellation or satisfaction of mortgage in the deed records where the mortgage has been recorded. In many states failure to satisfy or cancel the mortgage of record can impose a fine of money on the mortgagee lender. Example 6–5 shows mortgage cancellation or satisfaction.

EXAMPLE 6–5

Satisfaction

The indebtedness which this instrument was given to secure having been paid in full or other arrangements for payment of the indebtedness having been made to the satisfaction of mortgagee, this instrument is hereby cancelled and the Clerk of the Superior Court of _____ County, _____ is hereby authorized and directed to mark it satisfied of record.

This _____ day of _____ , 20_____

By: _____

Title: _____

Second-Mortgage Loans

A borrower, unless prohibited by the express terms of the mortgage, can mortgage the real property more than once. In fact, a person can mortgage the real property as many times as a lender is willing to take the real property as security for a loan. Under the current economic environment, it is not unusual for some home and commercial properties to have more than one mortgage.

A lender who makes a second-mortgage loan assumes some risk. The main risk is that the first mortgage (first in time on the real property and superior to the second mortgage) will be paid. If the first mortgage is not paid, goes into default, and is foreclosed, the second mortgage will be terminated at the foreclosure sale. It is, therefore, not unusual for second-mortgage lenders to receive estoppel certificates from the first-mortgage lender concerning the nature of the outstanding debt. The estoppel certificate provides that the first-mortgage lender will not foreclose the loan without first giving a notice of default to the second-mortgage lender and providing the second-mortgage lender with time to cure the default. A form of estoppel certificate is shown in Example 6–6.

EXAMPLE 6–6

STATE OF _____
COUNTY OF _____

Estoppel Certificate

The undersigned hereby certifies as of the date of execution hereof as follows:

(a) That the undersigned (the "Lender") is the holder of a certain Promissory Note dated _____ from _____ in the original principal amount of $ _____ (the "Note").

(b) The Note is secured by a Mortgage from _____ to Lender dated _____ and recorded in Deed Book _____ , Page _____ , _____ County, _____ located in _____ County, _____ (the "Property") more particularly described on Exhibit "A" attached hereto and made a part hereof;

(c) True and correct copies of the Note and Mortgage are attached hereto as Exhibits "B" and "C";

(d) That the Note and Mortgage are in full force and effect and there have been no events of default in connection therewith;

(e) That all payments of interest and principal under the Note and Mortgage are current; that as of this date, the outstanding principal balance due on the Note is $_____, that the last payment received on the Note was on the _____ day of _____, 20_____; and that the next payment is due on _____.

(f) Lender understands that _____ is pledging as security the Property to _____ to secure loans in the collective amount of $_____ (the "Security Conveyance"). The Security Conveyance is hereby consented to and approved and shall not constitute an event of default in connection with the Note or the Mortgage;

(g) That there is no failure of compliance, breach, default, or event of default that has occurred in the Note or the Mortgage as of this date;

(h) Lender agrees to provide to _____ , notice of any default under the Note or the Mortgage and to permit _____ thirty (30) days to cure any default under the Note or Mortgage, prior to Lender's acceleration of the Note. _____, at its option, shall have the right to purchase the Note and Mortgage in the event the default cannot be cured.

The undersigned acknowledges that _____ is relying on this certificate.

WITNESS my hand and seal this _____ day of _____, 20_____.

_____ (SEAL)

Signed, sealed and delivered _____ (SEAL)
in the presence of:

_____

Witness

_____

Notary Public
Sworn to before me this
_____ day of _____ , 20_____ .
My Commission Expires:

_____

A second-mortgage lender also wants to provide in the mortgage that a default under any prior mortgage shall constitute an event of default under the second mortgage. The second-mortgage lender wants the right to cure any defaults under a prior mortgage and add the cost of curing the defaults to the debt secured by the second mortgage. The lender of a second mortgage takes the assignment of any excess proceeds that may be generated from the foreclosure and sale of a prior mortgage. An example of a mortgage provision providing these safeguards is shown in Example 6–7.

EXAMPLE 6–7

This Mortgage is subject to a prior mortgage held by _____ (hereinafter called the "Prior Mortgage"). Mortgagor covenants and agrees that it will at all times fully perform and comply with all agreements, covenants, terms, and conditions imposed on the Mortgagor under the Prior Mortgage, and if Mortgagor fails to do so, Mortgagee may (but shall not be obligated to) declare such failure to be an event of default hereunder and or may take any action Mortgagee deems necessary or desirable to prevent or to cure any default by Mortgagor and the performance and compliance with any of Mortgagor's covenants or obligations under the Prior Mortgage. Any sums of money advanced by Mortgagee to cure Mortgagor's defaults under the Prior Mortgage shall be added to the Indebtedness secured hereby. Mortgagor shall immediately on receiving any knowledge or notice of any default under the Prior Mortgage give written notice to Mortgagee. Mortgagor assigns any proceeds that may belong to Mortgagor resulting from the foreclosure sale of the property by the holder of the Prior Mortgage.

Uniform Commercial Code and Financing Statement

The method for securing a loan with personal property, including fixtures, is provided by Article 9 of the UCC, a standardized law that has been passed in all states. Under Article 9 of the UCC, a loan secured by personal property, including fixtures, is secured by having the debtor sign a security agreement and by filing a UCC-1 financing statement. A security agreement is a written agreement conveying a security interest in personal property for purposes of securing a debt. Most mortgage forms include additional language that makes the mortgage a security agreement.

A recent revision to the UCC mandates a national UCC financing statement form. A copy of the national form of a UCC-1 financing statement is shown as Exhibit 6–9. The debtor's signature is not required on the new national form financing statement. A secured party may file the financing statement as long as it is authorized by the debtor to do so. This authorization may be in the security agreement or in the case of fixtures, the mortgage entered into between the debtor and the secured party. The financing statement may be filed either electronically or by paper filing. The filing officer who maintains the records for financing statements can dictate which medium of filing is required.

EXHIBIT 6-9
UCC Financing Statement

UCC FINANCING STATEMENT
FOLLOW INSTRUCTIONS (front and back) CAREFULLY

A. NAME & PHONE OF CONTACT AT FILER [optional]

B. SEND ACKNOWLEDGMENT TO: (Name and Address)

THE ABOVE SPACE IS FOR FILING OFFICE USE ONLY

1. DEBTOR'S EXACT FULL LEGAL NAME - insert only one debtor name (1a or 1b) - do not abbreviate or combine names

1a. ORGANIZATION'S NAME			
OR 1b. INDIVIDUAL'S LAST NAME	FIRST NAME	MIDDLE NAME	SUFFIX
1c. MAILING ADDRESS	CITY	STATE / POSTAL CODE	COUNTRY

1d. TAX ID #: SSN OR EIN	ADD'L INFO RE ORGANIZATION DEBTOR	1e. TYPE OF ORGANIZATION	1f. JURISDICTION OF ORGANIZATION	1g. ORGANIZATIONAL ID #, if any	NONE

2. ADDITIONAL DEBTOR'S EXACT FULL LEGAL NAME - insert only one debtor name (2a or 2b) - do not abbreviate or combine names

2a. ORGANIZATION'S NAME			
OR 2b. INDIVIDUAL'S LAST NAME	FIRST NAME	MIDDLE NAME	SUFFIX
2c. MAILING ADDRESS	CITY	STATE / POSTAL CODE	COUNTRY

2d. TAX ID #: SSN OR EIN	ADD'L INFO RE ORGANIZATION DEBTOR	2e. TYPE OF ORGANIZATION	2f. JURISDICTION OF ORGANIZATION	2g. ORGANIZATIONAL ID #, if any	NONE

3. SECURED PARTY'S NAME (or NAME of TOTAL ASSIGNEE of ASSIGNOR S/P) - insert only one secured party name (3a or 3b)

3a. ORGANIZATION'S NAME			
OR 3b. INDIVIDUAL'S LAST NAME	FIRST NAME	MIDDLE NAME	SUFFIX
3c. MAILING ADDRESS	CITY	STATE / POSTAL CODE	COUNTRY

4. This FINANCING STATEMENT covers the following collateral:

5. ALTERNATIVE DESIGNATION [if applicable]	LESSEE/LESSOR	CONSIGNEE/CONSIGNOR	BAILEE/BAILOR	SELLER/BUYER	AG. LIEN	NON-UCC FILING

6. This FINANCING STATEMENT is to be filed [for record] (or recorded) in the REAL ESTATE RECORDS Attach Addendum [if applicable]	7. Check to REQUEST SEARCH REPORT(S) on Debtor(s) [ADDITIONAL FEE] [optional]	All Debtors	Debtor 1	Debtor 2

8. OPTIONAL FILER REFERENCE DATA

FILING OFFICE COPY — NATIONAL UCC FINANCING STATEMENT (FORM UCC1) (REV. 07/29/98)

A financing statement perfecting a security interest in fixtures must be filed in the county where the real property is located. A financing statement perfecting security interests in collateral other than a fixture, has as a proper place for filing the debtor's location. For corporations, registered limited partnerships, or limited liability companies, the debtor's location will be the state in which the company was incorporated or registered. For other organizations, the debtor's location will be the organization's principal place of business, if it has only one place of business, or its chief executive office, if it has more than one place of business. Individual debtors are considered located in the state of their principal residence. A general filing in the state of the debtor's location will be with the secretary of state, but a state may designate another filing office for the statements.

The information required on a UCC-1 financing statement includes a debtor's name and address, secured party (creditor's) name and address, description of the personal property, and a description of the real property on which the personal property is located. The property must be described with specificity so that it can be identified. The debtor must be correctly identified on the financing statement. If the debtor is a registered organization, such as a corporation, a limited liability company, a limited partnership, etc., the debtor must be shown on the financing statement in exactly the same name as is shown in the organization's registration with the secretary of state.

FORECLOSURE AND OTHER MORTGAGEE REMEDIES

Mortgage documents would be unnecessary if all borrowers voluntarily paid debts on time. It is only in the situation where the borrower fails or is unable to pay the debt that the mortgage lender and its attorneys begin to carefully examine the mortgage documentation to see what rights and remedies the lender has. A holder of a mortgage on real property has a number of rights against the property and the borrower in the event the debt is not paid.

Foreclosure

foreclosure
Sale brought by a holder of a mortgage, deed of trust, or security deed of the real property conveyed in the instrument for the purposes of paying the debt secured by the real property.

Foreclosure is the big remedy that a mortgage holder has against the debtor property owner. Foreclosure is the legal means of requiring that the real property conveyed in the mortgage be sold and the sale proceeds used to pay the debt.

Grounds for Foreclosure

A holder of a mortgage does not have rights to foreclose or exercise other remedies unless the landowner (borrower) is in default under the mortgage. In addition to failure to pay the debt as it becomes due, most mortgages contain other provisions, the violation of which will result in default. These provisions include failure to pay taxes on the property, failure to insure the property, selling the property without the permission of the mortgagee, and failure to keep the property in good repair. The breach of any mortgage covenant gives the holder of the mortgage the right to foreclose or exercise its remedies.

Types of Foreclosure

Foreclosures take place either judicially or through a power of sale contained in the mortgage. The state in which the real property is located will determine which type of foreclosure will be used. States that use mortgages usually require judicial foreclosure. States that use deeds of trust or security deeds to secure a debt commonly use the power of sale foreclosure.

Judicial Foreclosure   A judicial foreclosure is a lawsuit. The mortgage holder will file a complaint against the debtor alleging there is a debt owed; the debt is in default; and the debt is secured by real property given in a mortgage. The creditor will then ask the court to grant relief by ordering the real property sold to pay the debt. The debtor is given an opportunity to answer and a hearing is held on the merits to decide if foreclosure should occur. If the court agrees the creditor has a right to foreclose, the court will then order the real property sold, usually by a public official such as a sheriff. The sale will be a public sale and will be held after proper notice has been given in the newspaper. Once a sale is held, the sale will then be reported back to the court for approval and, upon the court's approval, the sale will be final.

A judicial foreclosure is time-consuming but does afford the debtor numerous opportunities to avoid foreclosure by refinancing and paying the debt or defending in the event the foreclosure is wrongfully filed.

Power of Sale Foreclosure   A power of sale foreclosure is a nonjudicial foreclosure right which is given to the mortgage holder in the mortgage. Under a power of sale procedure, the mortgage lender or its agent will conduct a nonjudicial but public sale of the real property. Generally, there are strict procedures in a state governing power of sale foreclosures. These procedures usually set forth the time of day the property can be sold in a public sale and, perhaps, even the day of the month. Also, it requires that a published notice of the sale be placed in a newspaper some three to six weeks before the sale. The lender, as well as the debtor, may purchase at the sale.

Effect of a Valid Foreclosure Sale

A valid foreclosure sale, whether judicial or nonjudicial, has the effect of extinguishing all ownership rights of the debtor in and to the real property. It also has the effect of divesting all junior encumbrances on the real property. Any encumbrance, mortgage, easements, etc., which has been created after the date of the mortgage which is being foreclosed will be terminated at the foreclosure sale. For example, a parcel of real property is encumbered by a mortgage dated December 10, 1996, to First Bank and Trust Company and a mortgage dated March 15, 1997, to Second Bank and Trust. A foreclosure sale of the mortgage held by First Bank and Trust will terminate the mortgage on the real property held by Second Bank and Trust.

In most states, the debtor's rights to pay off the debt and redeem the real property are terminated at foreclosure. Some states do provide for **redemption** after sale. The redemption price is the price of the real property brought at the sale plus an interest or penalty charge. This redemption right may extend for one to two years from the sale date. This means that even though the real property has been sold, a debtor can, by paying the debt or the amount paid at the sale, whichever is greater, recover the real property. Postsale redemptions do have the effect of interfering with the marketability of the real property, and only a few states recognize postsale redemption.

A foreclosure sale does not automatically terminate a federal tax lien that is filed against the real property. Federal tax liens that are filed after the date of the mortgage being foreclosed are not terminated at the time of the foreclosure sale unless the Internal Revenue Service receives a written notice of the foreclosure sale twenty-five days before the date of the sale. If the required twenty-five days' notice is given to the Internal Revenue Service, then the tax lien is terminated at the time of sale. The Internal Revenue Service has a 120-day right of redemption to redeem the property after the date of the sale. The redemption price is the purchase price at the sale together with an interest penalty. Failure to give the required twenty-five days' notice permits the Internal Revenue Service tax lien to survive the foreclosure of the sale, and the purchaser at the sale takes the property subject to the tax lien.

Distribution of Money in a Foreclosure Sale

The money received at a foreclosure sale is used to pay the expenses of the sale and the debt. If there is excess money, this money belongs either to the debtor or the holders of junior mortgages. Most mortgage lenders interplead the money into court to avoid liability. The **interpleader** proceeding is a means by which the money is paid into the court, and the debtor and all junior mortgage holders who may have an interest in the money are notified of the proceeding. The debtor and junior mortgage holders will then go into court and try to convince the court that they are worthy to receive the money. The interpleader has the effect of releasing the lender from any liability in making the decision as to where the excess money should go.

Remedies Other Than Foreclosure

A lender, on an event of default under a mortgage, may exercise certain remedies other than foreclosure. These remedies usually are taking possession of the mortgaged real property or having a receiver appointed to take possession of the property.

redemption
Right of a property owner to buy back his property after a foreclosure.

interpleader
Judicial proceeding in which money is paid into the court and all parties who claim an interest in the money are allowed to process their claims to the money in the court proceeding.

Mortgagee (Lender) in Possession

Most mortgages grant the mortgage holder the right to seize possession of the real property in the event of a default. This right to seize possession may become important if the real property is income-producing, such as an apartment project, because it gives the mortgage holder a chance to collect the rents from the tenants. A mortgagee in possession is an agent of the mortgagor, and income collected from the real property must be used to pay the debt. Mortgagees usually are permitted to deduct reasonable expenses of management and maintenance of the real property from income.

Appointment of a Receiver

receiver
Third party appointed by a court to take possession of real property in the event of a mortgage default. A receiver acts as a caretaker for the property.

A **receiver** is a third party appointed by a court to take possession of the real property in the event of a mortgage default. A receiver acts similar to a mortgagee in possession in that the receiver is responsible to take care of the real property, collect rents and income from the real property, and make sure this money is properly applied to the debt or to the expenses of the upkeep of the real property. Most mortgages give a mortgagee the right to have a receiver appointed. The appointment of a receiver is a court action, and the mortgagee will have to prove that the mortgage is in default and the mortgagee has a right under the mortgage for the appointment of a receiver.

Waiver of Default

If the mortgagee, on notice that there has been a default under the mortgage, does not act promptly to exercise its remedies or acts in such a manner as to indicate to the landowner that being in default is acceptable, the holder of the mortgage may, by these actions, waive the default and not be entitled to exercise its remedies. A good example of this is acceptance of late payments by the mortgage holder. Acceptance of late payments estops the mortgage lender from declaring a default unless ample notice is given to the landowner of the intention to require prompt payments in the future.

DEBTOR'S REMEDIES OR DEFENSE TO FORECLOSURE _____

The debtor's remedies or defense to foreclose include injunction, suit for conversion, and bankruptcy.

Injunction

If a debtor believes a foreclosure is not justified, the debtor has a right to seek an injunction to stop the sale. Grounds for injunctive relief are, for example, invalidity of debt, absence of default, payment of debt, and improperly conducted sale.

The debtor also may void a sale that has already been held on the same grounds as injunctive relief. In some states a foreclosure sale can be voided if the property brought an inadequate price at the sale.

Suit for Conversion

conversion
Act of taking a person's property without a legal right to do so.

Foreclosing on real property without the legal right to do so is the tort of **conversion.** A debtor can sue for conversion and recover not only actual damages, but also punitive damages from the foreclosing lender.

Bankruptcy

Bankruptcy is the debtor's main defense to a foreclosure, since the filing of a bankruptcy petition has the effect of an automatic injunction stopping the foreclosure sale.

Bankruptcy law is federal law designed to protect debtors and to give debtors a fresh start. Bankruptcy petitions can be filed voluntarily or involuntarily. Once the bankruptcy petition is filed, the act of filing the petition operates as an automatic injunction of all litigation against the debtor and efforts to collect claims or enforce liens against the debtor's property, including foreclosure sales. This automatic injunction remains in force throughout the bankruptcy proceeding and is not terminated until the case is either closed or dismissed, or the debtor's discharge is granted or denied. A creditor, such as a mortgage lender, who wants to seek relief from the automatic stay can bring an action in the bankruptcy court requesting that the court remove the injunction so that the mortgage lender can foreclose the real property. The grounds for lifting the automatic stay in a bankruptcy proceeding are as follows:

- The mortgage holder is not being "adequately protected" within the bankruptcy proceeding. Loosely defined, this term means that the mortgage security is declining in value in the bankruptcy proceeding. Adequate protection can be achieved by requiring the debtor to maintain the property or make payments on the mortgage loan, keep the property insured, and so on.
- The debtor has no equity interest in the real property (the value of the property is equal to or less than the amount of the debt).
- The real property is not necessary to an effective reorganization or liquidation of the debtor's estate.

The burden of proof is on the debtor to prove that the stay should remain in full force and effect. The issue of whether the debtor's real property is equal to or less than the value of the debt is an evidentiary burden of the creditor.

Rejection of Executory Contracts and Unexpired Leases

A debtor's bankruptcy also may involve contracts to buy real property or leases on real property. For example, an owner of a shopping center may be seriously in default on its loan to a bank. The shopping center is partially leased but contains a number of vacancies. The owner is desperately trying to sell the shopping center and has a contract for its sale, but a closing is several months away. The bank begins foreclosure proceedings against the shopping center. The owner of the shopping center, to defend against the foreclosure proceedings, files bankruptcy. The bankruptcy stops the bank from foreclosing but raises a number of interesting questions concerning the shopping center leases and the contract to purchase the shopping center.

A debtor's bankruptcy confers on the bankruptcy trustee, or the bankrupt debtor in some bankruptcy proceedings, the right to reject unexpired leases and executory contracts for the sale of real property.

A bankruptcy trustee in a Chapter 7 bankruptcy or the bankrupt debtor in a Chapter 11 bankruptcy has the power to reject unexpired leases and executory contracts for the lease or sale of real property. An unexpired lease is a lease that has a term remaining at the time the bankruptcy petition is filed. An executory contract is a contract that has not been fully performed at the time the bankruptcy petition has been filed. The trustee or debtor has sixty days after the bankruptcy petition has been filed to either reject contracts and leases or assume them. If nothing is done within the sixty-day period, the contract and leases are deemed automatically rejected.

If a contract or lease is to be assumed, which means that the lease or contract remains in full force and effect during the bankruptcy proceeding, all current defaults under the lease or the contract must be cured and adequate assurance of future performance must be provided.

If an unexpired lease is rejected and the bankrupt debtor is the tenant, this gives the landlord (non-bankrupt party) the right to have the lease immediately terminated, and the tenant must leave the premises. The landlord has a right to file a claim in the tenant's bankrupt estate for the damages caused by the rejection. Damages usually are limited to one year's rental. If a lease is rejected and the bankrupt debtor is the landlord, the tenant (non-bankrupt party) under the lease is given the option of treating the lease as terminated and may leave, or the tenant may remain in possession for the balance of the lease term. If the tenant decides to remain in possession for the balance of the lease term, the tenant is required to perform all duties under the lease, including those of the bankrupt landlord. The tenant may, however, set off against any rent that is due the landlord the costs of nonperformance caused by the landlord's bankruptcy.

If an executory contract to sell real property is rejected and the bankrupt party is the seller, and the purchaser is in possession of the real property at the time the bankruptcy petition is filed,

ETHICS: Confidentiality of Client Information

The firm that employs you represents a high-profile real estate developer. The attorney you work for has just informed you that the developer has serious financial problems and has asked you to assist in the attempted restructure of a number of bank loans. That evening your spouse asks you if anything interesting happened at the office. Do you tell about the developer's financial problems, or do you discuss the upcoming firm's spring picnic?

The practice of law often involves the resolution of a client's most intimate personal problems. The client expects his or her attorney to be a trusted confidant. Without this trust, the client would be reluctant or unwilling to disclose to the attorney all the facts necessary for the attorney to evaluate the client's problem and give legal advice. Ethical considerations, therefore, require an attorney and a legal assistant to keep all client information and correspondence confidential. When working on a real estate transaction, the legal assistant should not discuss any aspects of the transaction with anyone except other members of the legal assistant's law firm.

Sometimes a legal assistant will be requested by another party in a real estate transaction to disclose confidential information received from a client. For example, a real estate developer client has had a parcel of property under contract for sale for a number of months. The contract has not closed, and the developer considers the contract to be null and void. The developer has applied for a loan on the property. An attorney or legal assistant representing the bank mentions to you that he has heard that the property is under contract for sale and that there may be a lawsuit concerning the contract. They ask you to confirm or deny this rumor. In a situation such as this, it is important to remember that only the client can give permission for the release or disclosure of confidential information. When a request for disclosure is made, the legal assistant should not make any disclosures until the matter has been discussed with the supervising attorney. It should be the responsibility of the supervising attorney to contact the client and respond to the request for confidential information.

The keeping of a client's confidence requires not only that the legal assistant not discuss confidential matters with third parties, but also that the legal assistant keep copies of all confidential letters and other documents out of the sight or view of third parties. It is not wise to bring files home from the office and leave them on tables and countertops in full view of neighbors, friends, and visitors.

---

the purchaser has the option of treating the contract as terminated, or remaining in possession and tendering the full purchase price to the trustee and receiving title to the real property. If the purchaser elects to treat the contract as terminated, he or she may file a damage claim in the bankruptcy proceedings that is the difference between the fair market value of the real property and the contract price at the time of rejection. If the purchaser is not in possession of the real property, he or she has only a damage claim in the bankruptcy. If a purchaser of real property has already given a downpayment or paid earnest money to the bankrupt seller, the purchaser has a lien against the property for the amount of the purchase money paid.

If an executory contract in which the bankrupt debtor is the purchaser of the property is rejected, the contract is deemed terminated, and the seller has the right to file a damage claim in the purchaser's bankruptcy proceeding. The amount of the damage claim is the difference between the fair market value and the contract price of the real property at the time of rejection.

SUMMARY

Although the legal concepts behind a note and security instrument to evidence and secure a mortgage loan are simple, the forms are complex, and vary in format from state to state. Legal assistants prepare mortgage loan documents and assist in the mortgage loan closing process. It is important that the legal assistant be familiar with the different forms that are used in the state in which he or she practices and that he or she be aware of the many provisions that can be included in these forms.

KEY TERMS

conversion	deed to secure debt	endorsement
deed of trust	due on sale clause	foreclosure

guarantor
guaranty
holder
interpleader
maker

mortgage
mortgagee
mortgagor
open-end or dragnet clause
payee

promissory note
receiver
redemption
usury

SELF-STUDY EXAMINATION

(Answers provided in Appendix)

1. T or F. The method of transferring a note is by endorsement.

2. T or F. Each co-maker of a note is fully responsible for the payment of the note.

3. T or F. The maker of a note is released by the sale of the security securing the note.

4. T or F. A valid debt must exist to have a valid mortgage.

5. T or F. The mortgagor of a mortgage is the lender or creditor.

6. T or F. A foreclosure of a first mortgage will terminate a second mortgage lien on the secured property.

7. T or F. A property sold with a mortgage assumption means that the purchaser does not have personal liability to pay the debt.

8. T or F. Foreclosures may take place either judicially or nonjudicially.

9. T or F. A mortgage cannot be given to secure a future debt.

10. T or F. A debtor always has the right to pay off the debt and redeem the real property from foreclosure before the sale.

11. What is an open-end or dragnet mortgage?

12. What is the difference between purchasing real property subject to a mortgage and assuming a mortgage?

13. What risks are inherent in second-mortgage loans?

14. Why is bankruptcy a good debtor's defense to a foreclosure?

15. You are assisting in the representation of a lending institution as the holder of a promissory note from the Good Earth Land Company. The note is personally guaranteed by the principal shareholder of Good Earth Land Company, Gooden Earth. The note currently is being modified to extend the final term for repayment for an additional five years. Is there any documentation in regard to this extension in addition to the note you should receive from Gooden Earth?

16. You are assisting a mortgage lender who specializes in making second-mortgage loans to homemakers. You have been requested to prepare an estoppel certificate to be signed by the first mortgagee on the home. What types of things would you include in the estoppel certificate to be signed by the first mortgagee?

17. You are a legal assistant in a law firm that handles foreclosures for mortgage lenders. You are attending a power of sale foreclosure. The bidder at the sale bids and buys the property for $100,000 more than the debt owed to the foreclosing lender. As you are standing there with the $100,000 in hand, a person approaches you. The person tells you that he has a second mortgage on the property in the amount of $50,000 and that he is entitled to that amount of the excess proceeds. Should you give this person the money? What should you do with the excess money?

18. What are the requirements for a valid mortgage?

19. What is the effect of a valid foreclosure sale?

20. What is the difference between a promissory note and a guaranty?

21. Name the parties to a promissory note.

22. Must a guaranty of a note be written?

23. List the three basic security instruments given to secure a note in connection with a loan secured by real property.

24. List the parties to a deed of trust.

25. When is interpleader used in connection with a foreclosure sale?

26. What is the importance of filing a UCC Financing Statement?

27. What information is required on the UCC-1 Financing Statement?

ADDENDUM

Exhibit 6–1   FNMA Residential Fixed Rate Note
Exhibit 6–2   FNMA Residential Adjustable Rate Note
Exhibit 6–3   Commercial Loan Note
Exhibit 6–4   Payment Guaranty

Exhibit 6–5   Florida Mortgage
Exhibit 6–6   North Carolina Deed of Trust
Exhibit 6–7   FNMA Residential Mortgage
Exhibit 6–8   Georgia Commercial Deed to Secure Debt

EXHIBIT 6-1
FNMA Residential Fixed Rate Note

NOTE

_____, _____   _____, _____
            [Date]   [City]   [State]

_____
                              [Property Address]

1.   BORROWER'S PROMISE TO PAY

In return for a loan that I have received, I promise to pay U.S. $_____ (this amount is called "Principal"), plus interest, to the order of the Lender. The Lender is _____
_____. I will make all payments under this Note in the form of cash, check or money order.

I understand that the Lender may transfer this Note. The Lender or anyone who takes this Note by transfer and who is entitled to receive payments under this Note is called the "Note Holder."

2.   INTEREST

Interest will be charged on unpaid principal until the full amount of Principal has been paid. I will pay interest at a yearly rate of _____%.

The interest rate required by this Section 2 is the rate I will pay both before and after any default described in Section 6(B) of this Note.

3.   PAYMENTS

(A) Time and Place of Payments

I will pay principal and interest by making a payment every month.

I will make my monthly payment on the _____ day of each month beginning on _____, _____. I will make these payments every month until I have paid all of the principal and interest and any other charges described below that I may owe under this Note. Each monthly payment will be applied as of its scheduled due date and will be applied to interest before Principal. If, on _____, 20_____, I still owe amounts under this Note, I will pay those amounts in full on that date, which is called the "Maturity Date."

I will make my monthly payments at _____
_____ or at a different place if required by the Note Holder.

(B) Amount of Monthly Payments

My monthly payment will be in the amount of U.S. $_____.

4.   BORROWER'S RIGHT TO PREPAY

I have the right to make payments of Principal at any time before they are due. A payment of Principal only is known as a "Prepayment." When I make a Prepayment, I will tell the Note Holder in writing that I am doing so. I may not designate a payment as a Prepayment if I have not made all the monthly payments due under the Note.

I may make a full Prepayment or partial Prepayments without paying a Prepayment charge. The Note Holder will use my Prepayments to reduce the amount of Principal that I owe under this Note. However, the Note Holder may apply my Prepayment to the accrued and unpaid interest on the Prepayment amount, before applying my Prepayment to reduce the Principal amount of the Note. If I make a partial Prepayment, there will be no changes in the due date or in the amount of my monthly payment unless the Note Holder agrees in writing to those changes.

5.   LOAN CHARGES

If a law, which applies to this loan and which sets maximum loan charges, is finally interpreted so that the interest or other loan charges collected or to be collected in connection with this loan exceed the permitted limits, then: (a) any such loan charge shall be reduced by the amount necessary to reduce the charge to the permitted limit; and (b) any sums already collected from me which exceeded permitted limits will be refunded to me. The Note Holder may choose to make this refund by reducing the Principal I owe under this Note or by making a direct payment to me. If a refund reduces Principal, the reduction will be treated as a partial Prepayment.

EXHIBIT 6–1
FNMA Residential Fixed Rate Note (continued)

6. BORROWER'S FAILURE TO PAY AS REQUIRED

(A) Late Charge for Overdue Payments

If the Note Holder has not received the full amount of any monthly payment by the end of _____ calendar days after the date it is due, I will pay a late charge to the Note Holder. The amount of the charge will be _____% of my overdue payment of principal and interest. I will pay this late charge promptly but only once on each late payment.

(B) Default

If I do not pay the full amount of each monthly payment on the date it is due, I will be in default.

(C) Notice of Default

If I am in default, the Note Holder may send me a written notice telling me that if I do not pay the overdue amount by a certain date, the Note Holder may require me to pay immediately the full amount of Principal which has not been paid and all the interest that I owe on that amount. That date must be at least 30 days after the date on which the notice is mailed to me or delivered by other means.

(D) No Waiver By Note Holder

Even if, at a time when I am in default, the Note Holder does not require me to pay immediately in full as described above, the Note Holder will still have the right to do so if I am in default at a later time.

(E) Payment of Note Holder's Costs and Expenses

If the Note Holder has required me to pay immediately in full as described above, the Note Holder will have the right to be paid back by me for all of its costs and expenses in enforcing this Note to the extent not prohibited by applicable law. Those expenses include, for example, reasonable attorneys' fees.

7. GIVING OF NOTICES

Unless applicable law requires a different method, any notice that must be given to me under this Note will be given by delivering it or by mailing it by first class mail to me at the Property Address above or at a different address if I give the Note Holder a notice of my different address.

Any notice that must be given to the Note Holder under this Note will be given by delivering it or by mailing it by first class mail to the Note Holder at the address stated in Section 3(A) above or at a different address if I am given a notice of that different address.

8. OBLIGATIONS OF PERSONS UNDER THIS NOTE

If more than one person signs this Note, each person is fully and personally obligated to keep all of the promises made in this Note, including the promise to pay the full amount owed. Any person who is a guarantor, surety or endorser of this Note is also obligated to do these things. Any person who takes over these obligations, including the obligations of a guarantor, surety or endorser of this Note, is also obligated to keep all of the promises made in this Note. The Note Holder may enforce its rights under this Note against each person individually or against all of us together. This means that any one of us may be required to pay all of the amounts owed under this Note.

9. WAIVERS

I and any other person who has obligations under this Note waive the rights of Presentment and Notice of Dishonor. "Presentment" means the right to require the Note Holder to demand payment of amounts due. "Notice of Dishonor" means the right to require the Note Holder to give notice to other persons that amounts due have not been paid.

10. UNIFORM SECURED NOTE

This Note is a uniform instrument with limited variations in some jurisdictions. In addition to the protections given to the Note Holder under this Note, a Mortgage, Deed of Trust, or Security Deed (the "Security Instrument"), dated the same date as this Note, protects the Note Holder from possible losses which might result if I do not keep the promises which I make in this Note. That Security Instrument describes how and under what conditions I may be required to make immediate payment in full of all amounts I owe under this Note. Some of those conditions are described as follows:

> If all or any part of the Property or any Interest in the Property is sold or transferred (or if Borrower is not a natural person and a beneficial interest in Borrower is sold or transferred) without Lender's prior written consent, Lender may require immediate payment in full of all sums secured by this Security Instrument. However, this option shall not be exercised by Lender if such exercise is prohibited by Applicable Law.

EXHIBIT 6-1
FNMA Residential Fixed Rate Note (continued)

       If Lender exercises this option, Lender shall give Borrower notice of acceleration. The notice shall provide a period of not less than 30 days from the date the notice is given in accordance with Section 15 within which Borrower must pay all sums secured by this Security Instrument. If Borrower fails to pay these sums prior to the expiration of this period, Lender may invoke any remedies permitted by this Security Instrument without further notice or demand on Borrower.

WITNESS THE HAND(S) AND SEAL(S) OF THE UNDERSIGNED

_____ (Seal)
                                                   Borrower

_____ (Seal)
                                                - Borrower

_____ (Seal)
                                                - Borrower

[Sign Original Only]

MULTISTATE FIXED RATE NOTE—Single Family—Fannie Mae/Freddie Mac **UNIFORM INSTRUMENT**   **Form 3200**   1/01 *(page 3 of 3 pages)*

EXHIBIT 6-2
FNMA Residential Adjustable Rate Note

ADJUSTABLE RATE NOTE
(1 Year Treasury Index -- Rate Caps)

THIS NOTE CONTAINS PROVISIONS ALLOWING FOR CHANGES IN MY INTEREST RATE AND MY MONTHLY PAYMENT. THIS NOTE LIMITS THE AMOUNT MY INTEREST RATE CAN CHANGE AT ANY ONE TIME AND THE MAXIMUM RATE I MUST PAY.

_____, _____   _____, _____

[Date]   [City]   [State]

_____

[Property Address]

1. BORROWER'S PROMISE TO PAY

In return for a loan that I have received, I promise to pay U.S. $_____ (this amount is called "Principal"), plus interest, to the order of the Lender. The Lender is _____ _____. I will make all payments under this Note in the form of cash, check or money order.

I understand that the Lender may transfer this Note. The Lender or anyone who takes this Note by transfer and who is entitled to receive payments under this Note is called the "Note Holder."

2. INTEREST

Interest will be charged on unpaid principal until the full amount of Principal has been paid. I will pay interest at a yearly rate of _____%. The interest rate I will pay will change in accordance with Section 4 of this Note.

The interest rate required by this Section 2 and Section 4 of this Note is the rate I will pay both before and after any default described in Section 7(B) of this Note.

3. PAYMENTS

(A) Time and Place of Payments

I will pay principal and interest by making a payment every month.

I will make my monthly payment on the first day of each month beginning on _____, _____. I will make these payments every month until I have paid all of the principal and interest and any other charges described below that I may owe under this Note. Each monthly payment will be applied as of its scheduled due date and will be applied to interest before Principal. If, on _____, 20____, I still owe amounts under this Note, I will pay those amounts in full on that date, which is called the "Maturity Date."

I will make my monthly payments at _____ _____ or at a different place if required by the Note Holder.

(B) Amount of My Initial Monthly Payments

Each of my initial monthly payments will be in the amount of U.S. $_____. This amount may change.

(C) Monthly Payment Changes

Changes in my monthly payment will reflect changes in the unpaid principal of my loan and in the interest rate that I must pay. The Note Holder will determine my new interest rate and the changed amount of my monthly payment in accordance with Section 4 of this Note.

4. INTEREST RATE AND MONTHLY PAYMENT CHANGES

(A) Change Dates

The interest rate I will pay may change on the first day of _____, _____, and on that day every 12th month thereafter. Each date on which my interest rate could change is called a "Change Date."

(B) The Index

Beginning with the first Change Date, my interest rate will be based on an Index. The "Index" is the weekly average yield on United States Treasury securities adjusted to a constant maturity of one year, as made available by the Federal Reserve Board. The most recent Index figure available as of the date 45 days before each Change Date is called the "Current Index."

If the Index is no longer available, the Note Holder will choose a new index which is based upon comparable information. The Note Holder will give me notice of this choice.

EXHIBIT 6-2
FNMA Residential Adjustable Rate Note (continued)

(C) Calculation of Changes

Before each Change Date, the Note Holder will calculate my new interest rate by adding _____ _____ percentage points (_____%) to the Current Index. The Note Holder will then round the result of this addition to the nearest one-eighth of one percentage point (0.125%). Subject to the limits stated in Section 4(D) below, this rounded amount will be my new interest rate until the next Change Date.

The Note Holder will then determine the amount of the monthly payment that would be sufficient to repay the unpaid principal that I am expected to owe at the Change Date in full on the Maturity Date at my new interest rate in substantially equal payments. The result of this calculation will be the new amount of my monthly payment.

(D) Limits on Interest Rate Changes

The interest rate I am required to pay at the first Change Date will not be greater than _____% or less than _____%. Thereafter, my interest rate will never be increased or decreased on any single Change Date by more than one percentage point (1.0%) from the rate of interest I have been paying for the preceding 12 months. My interest rate will never be greater than _____%.

(E) Effective Date of Changes

My new interest rate will become effective on each Change Date. I will pay the amount of my new monthly payment beginning on the first monthly payment date after the Change Date until the amount of my monthly payment changes again.

(F) Notice of Changes

The Note Holder will deliver or mail to me a notice of any changes in my interest rate and the amount of my monthly payment before the effective date of any change. The notice will include information required by law to be given to me and also the title and telephone number of a person who will answer any question I may have regarding the notice.

5. BORROWER'S RIGHT TO PREPAY

I have the right to make payments of Principal at any time before they are due. A payment of Principal only is known as a "Prepayment." When I make a Prepayment, I will tell the Note Holder in writing that I am doing so. I may not designate a payment as a Prepayment if I have not made all the monthly payments due under the Note.

I may make a full Prepayment or partial Prepayments without paying a Prepayment charge. The Note Holder will use my Prepayments to reduce the amount of Principal that I owe under this Note. However, the Note Holder may apply my Prepayment to the accrued and unpaid interest on the Prepayment amount, before applying my Prepayment to reduce the Principal amount of the Note. If I make a partial Prepayment, there will be no changes in the due dates of my monthly payment unless the Note Holder agrees in writing to those changes. My partial Prepayment may reduce the amount of my monthly payments after the first Change Date following my partial Prepayment. However, any reduction due to my partial Prepayment may be offset by an interest rate increase.

6. LOAN CHARGES

If a law, which applies to this loan and which sets maximum loan charges, is finally interpreted so that the interest or other loan charges collected or to be collected in connection with this loan exceed the permitted limits, then: (a) any such loan charge shall be reduced by the amount necessary to reduce the charge to the permitted limit; and (b) any sums already collected from me which exceeded permitted limits will be refunded to me. The Note Holder may choose to make this refund by reducing the Principal I owe under this Note or by making a direct payment to me. If a refund reduces Principal, the reduction will be treated as a partial Prepayment.

7. BORROWER'S FAILURE TO PAY AS REQUIRED

(A) Late Charges for Overdue Payments

If the Note Holder has not received the full amount of any monthly payment by the end of _____ calendar days after the date it is due, I will pay a late charge to the Note Holder. The amount of the charge will be _____% of my overdue payment of principal and interest. I will pay this late charge promptly but only once on each late payment.

(B) Default

If I do not pay the full amount of each monthly payment on the date it is due, I will be in default.

(C) Notice of Default

If I am in default, the Note Holder may send me a written notice telling me that if I do not pay the overdue amount by a certain date, the Note Holder may require me to pay immediately the full amount of Principal which has not been paid and all the interest that I owe on that amount. That date must be at least 30 days after the date on which the notice is mailed to me or delivered by other means.

(D) No Waiver By Note Holder

Even if, at a time when I am in default, the Note Holder does not require me to pay immediately in full as described above, the Note Holder will still have the right to do so if I am in default at a later time.

(E) Payment of Note Holder's Costs and Expenses

If the Note Holder has required me to pay immediately in full as described above, the Note Holder will have the right

EXHIBIT 6-2
FNMA Residential Adjustable Rate Note (continued)

to be paid back by me for all of its costs and expenses in enforcing this Note to the extent not prohibited by applicable law. Those expenses include, for example, reasonable attorneys' fees.

8. GIVING OF NOTICES

Unless applicable law requires a different method, any notice that must be given to me under this Note will be given by delivering it or by mailing it by first class mail to me at the Property Address above or at a different address if I give the Note Holder a notice of my different address.

Any notice that must be given to the Note Holder under this Note will be given by delivering it or by mailing it by first class mail to the Note Holder at the address stated in Section 3(A) above or at a different address if I am given a notice of that different address.

9. OBLIGATIONS OF PERSONS UNDER THIS NOTE

If more than one person signs this Note, each person is fully and personally obligated to keep all of the promises made in this Note, including the promise to pay the full amount owed. Any person who is a guarantor, surety or endorser of this Note is also obligated to do these things. Any person who takes over these obligations, including the obligations of a guarantor, surety or endorser of this Note, is also obligated to keep all of the promises made in this Note. The Note Holder may enforce its rights under this Note against each person individually or against all of us together. This means that any one of us may be required to pay all of the amounts owed under this Note.

10. WAIVERS

I and any other person who has obligations under this Note waive the rights of Presentment and Notice of Dishonor. "Presentment" means the right to require the Note Holder to demand payment of amounts due. "Notice of Dishonor" means the right to require the Note Holder to give notice to other persons that amounts due have not been paid.

11. UNIFORM SECURED NOTE

This Note is a uniform instrument with limited variations in some jurisdictions. In addition to the protections given to the Note Holder under this Note, a Mortgage, Deed of Trust, or Security Deed (the "Security Instrument"), dated the same date as this Note, protects the Note Holder from possible losses which might result if I do not keep the promises which I make in this Note. That Security Instrument describes how and under what conditions I may be required to make immediate payment in full of all amounts I owe under this Note. Some of those conditions are described as follows:

If all or any part of the Property or any Interest in the Property is sold or transferred (or if Borrower is not a natural person and a beneficial interest in Borrower is sold or transferred) without Lender's prior written consent, Lender may require immediate payment in full of all sums secured by this Security Instrument. However, this option shall not be exercised by Lender if such exercise is prohibited by Applicable Law. Lender also shall not exercise this option if: (a) Borrower causes to be submitted to Lender information required by Lender to evaluate the intended transferee as if a new loan were being made to the transferee; and (b) Lender reasonably determines that Lender's security will not be impaired by the loan assumption and that the risk of a breach of any covenant or agreement in this Security Instrument is acceptable to Lender.

To the extent permitted by Applicable Law, Lender may charge a reasonable fee as a condition to Lender's consent to the loan assumption. Lender may also require the transferee to sign an assumption agreement that is acceptable to Lender and that obligates the transferee to keep all the promises and agreements made in the Note and in this Security Instrument. Borrower will continue to be obligated under the Note and this Security Instrument unless Lender releases Borrower in writing.

EXHIBIT 6-2
FNMA Residential Adjustable Rate Note (continued)

If Lender exercises the option to require immediate payment in full, Lender shall give Borrower notice of acceleration. The notice shall provide a period of not less than 30 days from the date the notice is given in accordance with Section 15 within which Borrower must pay all sums secured by this Security Instrument. If Borrower fails to pay these sums prior to the expiration of this period, Lender may invoke any remedies permitted by this Security Instrument without further notice or demand on Borrower.

WITNESS THE HAND(S) AND SEAL(S) OF THE UNDERSIGNED.

_____ (Seal)
                                                              -Borrower

_____ (Seal)
                                                              -Borrower

_____ (Seal)
                                                              -Borrower

[Sign Original Only]

MULTISTATE ADJUSTABLE RATE NOTE--ARM 5-1--Single Family--Fannie Mae/Freddie Mac UNIFORM INSTRUMENT   Form 3501 1/01 *(page 4 of 4 pages)*

EXHIBIT 6-3
Commercial Loan Note

$1,600,000.00   (City), (State)

September 14, 20____

REAL ESTATE NOTE

FOR VALUE RECEIVED, the undersigned, HARRIS OFFICE PARK LIMITED PARTNERSHIP, an Ohio limited partnership, hereinafter referred to as "Borrower," promises to pay to the order of WHEREVER INSURANCE COMPANY, an Ohio corporation, hereinafter referred to as "Payee," at the main office of Payee located at

_____

_____, or at such other place as Payee shall designate in writing, in lawful money of the United States of America which shall at the time of payment be legal tender for payment of all debts, public and private, the principal sum of ONE MILLION SIX HUNDRED THOUSAND AND NO/100 DOLLARS ($1,600,000.00), together with interest thereon at the rate of ten and one-half percent (10.50%) per annum in two-hundred seventy-six (276) consecutive monthly installments, installments 1 to 275 both inclusive, being for the sum of FIFTEEN THOUSAND THREE HUNDRED EIGHTY NINE AND 88/100 DOLLARS ($15,389.88) each, and installment number 276 being for the balance of the principal and interest then owing.

Interest only on the outstanding principal balance of the indebtedness shall be due and payable on October 1, 20____ and the first of said monthly amortized installments of principal and interest shall be due and payable on November 1, 20____, and continue to be due and payable on the first day of each month thereafter, with the final installment of all unpaid principal and unpaid and accrued interest, unless sooner paid, being due and payable on the 1st day of October, 20 ____. Each such amortized installment of principal and interest, when paid, shall be applied first to the payment of interest accrued on the unpaid principal balance and the residue thereof shall be applied toward the payment of principal.

Notwithstanding anything contained in this note to the contrary, Payee shall have the right, at its sole option and discretion, to declare the entire outstanding principal balance of this note and all accrued and unpaid interest thereon to be due and payable in full at the end of the seventh (7th), twelfth (12th), seventeenth (17th), or twenty-second (22nd) Loan Years (hereinafter defined) and each date is hereinafter referred to as a ("Call Date"). Payee shall give notice of the exercise of such option to Borrower at least six (6) months in advance. In the event Payee shall elect to so declare this note due, then this note shall be and become due and payable in full on the due date of the eighty-fourth (84th), one-hundred forty-fourth (144th), two-hundred fourth (204th), or two-hundred sixty-fourth (264th) installment of principal and interest due hereunder, depending upon whether or not Payee elects to declare this note due, and upon which Call Date Payee exercises the option to declare this Note due. No prepayment premium as hereinafter described shall be due and payable if this Note is prepaid because of Payee's exercise of its rights to declare the Note due pursuant to this paragraph.

Late Charge. Borrower shall pay a late charge of four percent (4%) of any payment of principal and interest which is not paid within fifteen (15) days of the due date thereof. The collection of any such late charge by Payee shall not be deemed a waiver by Payee of any of its rights hereunder or under any document or instrument given to secure this note. During the entire term of this note, Borrower shall pay all costs of collection, including reasonable attorney's fees not to exceed fifteen percent (15%) of the principal and interest due, if collected by or through an attorney-at-law.

Prepayment Privilege. This note may not be prepaid in whole or in part except as herein specifically provided. No prepayment of the principal of this note shall be permitted or allowed prior to the end of the third (3rd) Loan Year, as hereinafter defined. After the end of the third (3rd) Loan Year, this note may be prepaid in whole, but not in part, upon any principal and interest payment date as provided herein, provided that (a) no later than sixty (60) days prior to the date of such prepayment, Borrower delivers written notice to Payee, that Borrower intends to prepay the note in full on the date specified in the notice; and (b) Borrower pays to Payee at the time of such prepayment, a percentage of the prepaid principal amount of the indebtedness as a prepayment premium. The amount of the prepayment premium shall be the product obtained by multiplying the prepaid principal amount of the indebtedness by the product of the following: (i) the amount obtained by subtracting the annualized yield on a United States Treasury Bill, Note, or Bond with a maturity date which occurs closest to the next applicable Call Date of this note, as such annualized yield is reported by *The*

EXHIBIT 6-3
Commercial Loan
Note (continued)

Wall Street Journal, on the business day preceding the date of prepayment, from 10.50% multiplied by: (ii) the number of years and any fraction thereof remaining between the date of prepayment and the next applicable Call Date of this note.

Notwithstanding the foregoing, however, in the event of acceleration of this note at any time, including the period of time prior to the end of the third (3rd) Loan Year, and subsequent involuntary or voluntary prepayment, the prepayment premium as calculated above shall be payable, however, in no event shall it exceed an amount equal to the excess, if any, of (i) interest calculated at the highest applicable rate permitted by applicable law, as construed by courts having jurisdiction thereof, on the principal balance of the indebtedness evidenced by this note from time to time outstanding from the date hereof to the date of such acceleration; over (ii) interest theretofore paid and accrued on this note. Any prepaid amounts specified in any notice shall become due and payable at the time provided in such notice. Under no circumstances shall the prepayment premium ever be less than zero. The amount of prepayment shall never be less than the full amount of the then outstanding principal indebtedness and accrued interest thereon.

A Loan Year for the purposes of this note shall mean each successive twelve (12) month period, beginning with the date of the first installment payment of principal and interest hereunder, provided, however, that the first (1st) Loan Year shall include the period from the date of this note to the date of such first installment payment of principal and interest.

Borrower further agrees to pay, in addition to the above-described prepayment premium, a reinvestment fee of one-half of one (1/2%) percent of the outstanding prepaid principal indebtedness evidenced by this note to Payee. Borrower agrees that the reinvestment fee together with the prepayment premium shall be due and payable regardless of whether the prepayment is made involuntarily or voluntarily.

Collateral. This note is secured by, among other instruments, (i) a Deed of Trust of even date herewith executed by Borrower in favor of Payee (the "Security Deed"), conveying and covering certain real property lying and being in Land Lot 50 of the 17th District, of Simkin County, Ohio, as the same is more particularly described in the Security Deed (the "Premises"), (ii) Security Agreement of even date herewith executed by Borrower in favor of Payee (the "Security Agreement"), conveying a security interest in certain personal property as more particularly described in the Security Agreement, (iii) Assignment of Leases and Rents of even date herewith executed by Borrower in favor of Payee (the "Rent Assignment") covering the Premises.

Default. If Borrower fails to pay when due any amount payable under this note or if Borrower shall be in default under the Security Deed, Security Agreement, or Rent Assignment, then Borrower shall be in default under this note. In the event Borrower shall be in default under this note, at the option of Payee and without further demand or further notice of any kind, the entire unpaid principal balance of this note, together with accrued interest thereon, may be declared and thereupon immediately shall become due and payable, and the principal portion of such sum shall bear interest at the rate of two percent (2%) per annum in excess of the highest rate of interest then being charged under this note from the date of default until paid, and Payee, at the option of Payee and without demand or notice of any kind, may exercise any and all rights and remedies provided for or allowed by the Security Deed, Security Agreement, Rent Assignment, or provided for or allowed by law or inequity. Any acceleration of payment of the indebtedness evidenced by this note pursuant to the terms hereof or pursuant to the terms of the Security Deed shall be considered prepayment of such indebtedness authorizing Payee, upon any such acceleration, and in addition to the balance of principal and interest accrued thereon and all other amounts due under this note and the Security Deed, to the extent permitted by applicable law, to recover any amount equal to the prepayment premium provided for hereinabove as if such indebtedness has been prepaid otherwise.

Time. Time is of the essence of this note.

Waiver. Demand, presentment, notice, protest, and notice of dishonor are hereby waived by Borrower and by each and every co-maker, endorser, guarantor, surety, and other person or entity primarily or secondarily liable on this note. Borrower and each and every co-maker, endorser, guarantor, surety, and other person or entity primarily or secondarily liable on this note: (i) severally waives, each for himself and family, any and all homestead and exemption rights by which any of them or the family of any of them may have under or by virtue of the Constitution or laws of the United States of America or of any state as against this note or any and all renewals, extensions, or modifications of,

EXHIBIT 6-3
Commercial Loan
Note (continued)

or substitutions for, this note; (ii) hereby transfers, conveys, and assigns to Payee a sufficient amount of such homestead or exemption as may be allowed, including such homestead or exemption as may be set apart in bankruptcy, to pay the indebtedness evidenced by this note in full, with all costs of collection; (iii) does hereby direct any trustee in bankruptcy having possession of such homestead or exemption to deliver to Payee a sufficient amount of property or money set apart as exempt to pay the indebtedness evidenced by this note, and any and all renewals, extensions, and modifications of, and substitutions for, this note; and (iv) does hereby appoint Payee attorney in-fact to claim any and all homestead exemptions allowed by law.

Third Party Liability. With the consent of Payee, this note may be extended or renewed, in whole or in part, without notice to or consent of any co-maker, endorser, guarantor, surety or other person or entity primarily or secondarily liable on this note and without affecting or lessening the liability of any such person or entity, and each such person or entity hereby waives any right to notice of or consent to such extensions and renewals. Failure of Payee to exercise any rights under this note shall not affect the liability of any co-maker, endorser, guarantor, surety or other person or entity primarily or secondarily liable on this note.

Forbearance. Payee shall not be deemed to waive any of Payee's rights or remedies under this note unless such waiver be express, in writing and signed by or on behalf of Payee. No delay, omission, or forbearance by Payee in exercising any of Payee's rights or remedies shall operate as a waiver of such rights or remedies. A waiver in writing on one occasion shall not be construed as a waiver of any right or remedy on any future occasion.

Governing Law and Severability. This note shall be governed by, construed under, and interpreted and enforced in accordance with the laws of the State of Ohio. Wherever possible, each provision of this note shall be interpreted in such manner as to be effective and valid under applicable law, but if any provision of this note shall be prohibited by or invalid under the applicable law, such provision shall be ineffective only to the extent of such prohibition or invalidity, without invalidating the remainder of such provision or the remaining provisions of this note.

This note and all provisions hereof and of all documents securing this note conform in all respects to the laws of the State of Ohio so that no payment of interest or other sum construed to be interest or charges in the nature of interest shall exceed the highest lawful contract rate permissible under the laws of the State of Ohio as applicable to this transaction. Therefore, this note and all agreements between Borrower and Payee are limited so that in no contingency or event whatsoever, whether acceleration of maturity of the indebtedness or otherwise, shall the amount paid or agree to be paid to the Payee of the use, forbearance, or detention of the money advanced by or to be advanced hereunder exceed the highest lawful rate permissible under the laws of the State of Ohio as applicable to this transaction. In determining whether or not the rate of interest exceeds the highest lawful rate, the Borrower and Payee intend that all sums paid hereunder which are deemed interest for the purposes of determining usury be prorated, allocated, or spread in equal parts over the longest period of time permitted under the applicable laws of the State of Ohio. If, under any circumstances whatsoever, fulfillment of any provision hereof, or of any other instrument evidencing or securing this Indebtedness, at the time performance of such provisions shall be due, shall involve the payment of interest in excess of that authorized by law, the obligation to be fulfilled shall be reduced to the limit so authorized by law, and if under any circumstances Payee shall ever receive as interest an amount which would exceed the highest lawful rate, the amount which would be excessive shall be either applied to the reduction of the unpaid principal balance of the Indebtedness, without payment of any prepayment fee (and not to the payment of interest), or refunded to the Borrower, and Payee shall not be subject to any penalty provided for the contracting for, charging, or receiving interest in excess of the maximum lawful rate regardless of when or the circumstances under which said refund or application was made.

Notices. All notices, requests, demands, and other communications of this note shall be in writing and shall be deemed to have been duly given if given in accordance with the provisions of the Security Deed.

Terms. The word "Borrower" as used herein shall include the legal representatives, successors, and assigns of Borrower as if so specified at length throughout this note, all of which shall be liable for all indebtedness and liabilities of Borrower. The word "Borrower" as used herein shall also include all makers of this note, and each of them, who shall be jointly and severally liable under this note, should more than one maker execute this note; and shall include all endorsers, guarantors, sureties,

EXHIBIT 6–3
Commercial Loan
Note (continued)

and other persons or entities primarily or secondarily liable on this note, and each of them; and shall include the masculine and feminine genders, regardless of the sex of Borrower or any of them; and shall include partnerships, corporations, and other legal entities, should such an entity be or become primarily or secondarily liable on this note. The word "Payee" as used herein shall include the transferees, legal representatives, successors, and assigns of Payee, as if so specified at length throughout this note, and all rights of Payee under this note shall inure to the successors and assigns of Payee.

IN WITNESS WHEREOF, Borrower by its duly authorized general partner has executed this note under seal and has delivered this note to Payee, this _____ day of September, 20_____.

BORROWER:

HARRIS OFFICE PARK LIMITED
PARTNERSHIP, an Ohio limited
partnership

General Partner:

_____ (SEAL)
Veronica F. Harris

EXHIBIT 6–4
Payment Guaranty

GUARANTY

_____ 20_____

(City)_____, (State)_____

FOR VALUE RECEIVED, the sufficiency of which is hereby acknowledged, and in consideration of any loan or other financial accommodation heretofore or hereafter at any time made or granted to _____ (hereinafter called the "Debtor") by _____ (hereinafter, together with its successors and assigns, called the "Bank"), the undersigned hereby unconditionally guarantee(s) the full and prompt payment when due, whether by declaration or otherwise, and at all times hereafter, of all obligations of the Debtor to the Bank, however and whenever incurred or evidenced, whether direct of indirect, absolute or contingent, or due or to become due (collectively called "Liabilities"), and the undersigned further agree(s) to pay the following (herein called "Expenses"): (a) all expenses paid or incurred by the Bank in endeavoring to collect the Liabilities or any part thereof from the Debtor, including attorney's fees of 15% of the total amount sought to be collected if the Bank endeavors to collect from the Debtor by law or through an attorney at law; and (b) all expenses paid or incurred by the Bank in collecting this guaranty, including attorney's fees of 15% of the total amount sought to be collected if this guaranty is collected by law or through an attorney at law. The right of recovery against the undersigned is, however, limited to _____ Dollars ($_____) of the principal amount of the Liabilities plus the interest on such amount and plus the Expenses as applicable thereto and as applicable to this guaranty.

Undersigned hereby represents that loans or other financial accommodations by the Bank to the Debtor will be to the direct interest and advantage of the undersigned.

Undersigned hereby transfers and conveys to the Bank any and all balances, credits, deposits, accounts, items, and monies of the undersigned now or hereafter with the Bank, and the Bank is hereby given a lien upon security title to and a security interest in all property of the undersigned of every kind and description now or hereafter in the possession or control of the Bank for any reason, including all dividends and distributions on or other rights in connection therewith.

EXHIBIT 6–4
Payment Guaranty
(continued)

In the event of the death, incompetency, dissolution or insolvency (as defined by the Uniform Commercial Code as in effect at the time in Georgia) of the Debtor, or if a petition in bankruptcy be filed by or against the Debtor, of if a receiver be appointed for any part of the property or assets of the Debtor, or if any judgment be entered against the Debtor, or if the Bank shall feel insecure with respect to Liabilities and if any such event should occur at a time when any of the Liabilities may not then be due and payable, the undersigned agrees to pay to the Bank upon demand the full amount which would be payable hereunder by the undersigned if all Liabilities were then due and payable.

Bank may, without demand or notice of any kind, at any time when any amount shall be due and payable hereunder by any of the undersigned, appropriate and apply toward the payment of such amount, and in such order of application as the Bank may from time to time elect, any property, balances, credits, deposits, accounts, items, or monies of such undersigned in the possession or control of the Bank for any purpose.

This guaranty shall be continuing, absolute and unconditional, and shall remain in full force and effect as to the undersigned, subject to discontinuance of this guaranty as to any of the undersigned (including, without limitation, any undersigned who shall become deceased, incompetent or dissolved) only as follows: Any of the undersigned, and any person duly authorized and acting on behalf of any of the undersigned, may given written notice to the Bank of discontinuance of this guaranty as to the undersigned by whom or on whose behalf such notice is given, but no such notice shall be effective in any respect until it is actually received by the Bank and no such notice shall affect or impair the obligations hereunder of the undersigned by whom or on whose behalf such notice is given with respect to any Liabilities existing at the date of receipt of such notice by the Bank, any interest thereon or any expenses paid or incurred by the Bank in endeavoring to collect such Liabilities, or any part thereof, and in enforcing this guaranty against such undersigned. Any such notice of discontinuance by or on behalf of any of the undersigned shall not affect or impair the obligations hereunder of any other of the undersigned.

The Bank may, from time to time, without notice to the undersigned (or any of them), (a) retain or obtain a security interest in any property to secure any of the Liabilities or any obligation hereunder, (b) retain or obtain the primary or secondary liability of any party or parties, in addition to the undersigned, with respect to any of the Liabilities, (c) extend or renew for any period (whether or not longer than the original period), alter or exchange any of the Liabilities, (d) release or compromise any liability of any of the undersigned hereunder or any liability of any other party or parties primarily or secondarily liable on any of the Liabilities, (e) release its security interest, if any, in all or any property securing any of the Liabilities or any obligation hereunder and permit any substitution or exchange for any such property, and (f) resort to the undersigned (or any of them) for payment of any of the Liabilities, whether or not the Bank shall have resorted to any property securing any of the Liabilities or any obligation hereunder or shall have proceeded against any other of the undersigned or any other party primarily or secondarily liable on any of the Liabilities.

Any amount received by the Bank from whatever source and applied by it toward the payment of the Liabilities shall be applied in such order of application as the Bank may from time to time elect.

The undersigned hereby expressly waive(s): (a) Notice of the acceptance of this guaranty, (b) notice of the existence or creation of all or any of the Liabilities, (c) presentment, demand, notice of dishonor, protest, and all other notices whatsoever, and (d) all diligence in collection or protection of or realization upon the Liabilities or any thereof, any obligation hereunder, or any security for any of the foregoing.

The creation or existence from time to time of Liabilities in excess of the amount to which the right of recovery under this guaranty is limited is hereby authorized, without notice to the undersigned (or any of them), and shall in no way affect or impair this guaranty.

The Bank may, without notice of any kind, sell, assign or transfer all or any of the Liabilities, and in such event each and every immediate and successive assignee, transferee, or holder of all or any of the Liabilities, shall have the right to enforce this guaranty, by suit or otherwise, for the benefit of such assignee, transferee, or holder, as fully as if such assignee, transferee, or holder were herein by name specifically given such rights, powers, and benefits, but the Bank shall have an unimpaired right, prior and superior to that of any such assignee, transferee or holder, to enforce this guaranty for the benefit of the Bank, as to so much of the Liabilities as it has not sold, assigned, or transferred.

EXHIBIT 6–4
Payment Guaranty
(continued)

No delay or failure on the part of the Bank in the exercise of any right or remedy shall operate as a waiver thereof, and no single or partial exercise by the Bank of any right or remedy shall preclude other or further exercise thereof or the exercise of any other right or remedy. No action of the Bank permitted hereunder shall in any way impair or affect this guaranty. For the purpose of this guaranty, Liabilities shall include all obligations of the Debtor to the Bank, notwithstanding any right or power of the Debtor or anyone else to assert any claim or defense, as to the invalidity or unenforceability of any such obligation, and no such claim or defense shall impair or affect the obligations of the undersigned hereunder.

This guaranty is cumulative of and shall not effect, modify or limit any other guaranty executed by the undersigned with respect to any Liabilities.

This guaranty shall be binding upon the undersigned, and upon the heirs, legal representatives, successors, and assigns of the undersigned. If more than one party shall execute this guaranty, the term "undersigned" shall mean all parties executing this guaranty, and all such parties shall be jointly and severally obligated hereunder.

This guaranty has been made and delivered in the State of Georgia, and shall be governed by the laws of that state. Wherever possible each provision of this guaranty shall be interpreted in such manner as to be effective and valid under applicable law, but if any provision of this guaranty shall be prohibited by or invalid under such law, such provision shall be ineffective to the extent of such prohibition or invalidity, without invalidating the remainder of such provision or the remaining provisions of this guaranty.

IN WITNESS WHEREOF the undersigned have hereunto set their hands and affix their seals the day and year above written.

_____ (SEAL)

_____ (SEAL)

_____ (SEAL)

EXHIBIT 6–5
Florida Mortgage

THIS INDENTURE, made this _____ day of _____ in the year of our Lord two-thousand and _____, by and between _____ _____ _____ of the _____, County of _____, and State of Florida, hereinafter called the Mortgagor; and _____; hereinafter called the Mortgagee:

Whereas the said Mortgagor is justly indebted to the said Mortgagee in the principal sum of _____ _____ Dollars, as evidenced by a certain promissory note of even date herewith, executed by _____ _____ and payable to the order of the Mortgagee, with interest and upon terms as provided therein.

Said note provides that all installments of principal and interest are payable in lawful money of the United States of America, which shall be legal tender for public and private debts at the time of payment, at the office of _____, or at such other place as the holder thereof may from time to time designate in writing. Said note also provides that the final installment of principal and interest shall be due and payable on the _____ day of _____, 20____.

Said note provides that each maker and endorser, jointly and severally, shall pay all costs of collection, including a reasonable attorney's fee, on failure to pay any principal and interest when due

EXHIBIT 6-5
Florida Mortgage
(continued)

thereon, and that all principal due thereunder shall bear interest at the maximum permissible rate per annum from due date until paid.

Said note further provides that if any instalment of principal and/or interest shall not be paid when due, then the entire principal sum and accrued interest shall become due and payable at once, at the option of the holder thereof.

NOW THIS INDENTURE WITNESSETH that the said Mortgagor, to secure said indebtedness and interest thereon, and also for and in consideration of the sum of One Dollar paid by Mortgagee, at or before the ensealing and delivery of these presents, the receipt whereof is hereby acknowledged, has granted, bargained, sold and conveyed and by these presents does grant, bargain, sell, and convey unto the Mortgagee all that certain lot, parcel, or piece of land lying and being in the County of _____ and State of Florida, more particularly described as _____

ALSO TOGETHER WITH all buildings and improvements thereon situate or which may hereafter be erected or placed thereon and all and singular the tenements, hereditaments, appurtenances and easements thereunto belonging or in anywise appertaining, and the rents, issues and profits thereof, and together with all heating, ventilating, and air conditioning equipment, all plumbing apparatus, fixtures, hot water heaters, water and sprinkler systems and pumps, all lighting fixtures and all screens, awnings, venetian blinds, built-in equipment, and built-in furniture (whether or not affixed to land or building) now or hereafter located in or on said premises, including all renewals, replacements, and additions thereto.

TO HAVE AND TO HOLD the above granted and described premises unto the said Mortgagee; its successors or assigns, forever.

And the said Mortgagor hereby covenants with the Mortgagee that the said Mortgagor is indefeasibly seized of said land in fee simple; that the said Mortgagor has full power and lawful right to convey the same in fee simple as aforesaid; that it shall be lawful for the Mortgagee at all times peaceably and quietly to enter upon, hold, occupy, and enjoy said land and every part thereof; that the land is free from all encumbrances, except as aforesaid; that said Mortgagor will make such further assurances to prove the fee simple title to said land in said Mortgagee as may be reasonably required; and that said Mortgagor does hereby fully warrant the title to said land and every part thereof and will defend the same against the lawful claims of all persons whomsoever.

PROVIDED ALWAYS, and these presents are on this express condition, that if said Mortgagor shall well and truly pay said indebtedness unto the said Mortgagee, and any renewals or extensions thereof, and the interest thereon, together with all costs, charges, and expenses, including a reasonable attorney's fee, which the said Mortgagee may incur or be put to in collecting the same by foreclosure, or otherwise, and shall perform and comply with all other terms, conditions, and covenants contained in said promissory note and this mortgage, then these presents and the estate hereby granted shall cease, determine, and be null and void.

And the said Mortgagor hereby jointly and severally covenants and agrees to and with the said Mortgagee as follows:

1. To pay all and singular the principal and interest and the various and sundry sums of money payable by virtue of said promissory note and this mortgage, each and every, promptly on the days respectively the same severally become due.

2. To pay all and singular the taxes, assessments, levies, liabilities, obligations, and encumbrances of every nature and kind now on said described property, and/or that hereafter may be imposed, suffered, placed, levied or assessed thereupon and/or that hereafter may be levied or assessed upon this mortgage and/or the indebtedness secured hereby, each and every, before they become delinquent, and in so far as any thereof is of record the same shall be promptly satisfied and discharged of record and the original official document (such as, for instance, the tax receipt or the satisfaction paper officially endorsed or certified) shall be placed in the hands of said Mortgagee within ten days next after payment.

3. To keep the buildings now or hereafter situate on said land and all personal property used in the operation thereof continuously insured against loss by fire and such other hazards as may from time to time be requested by Mortgagee, in companies and in amounts in each company as may be approved by and acceptable to Mortgagee; and all insurance policies shall contain the usual standard mortgagee clause making the loss under said policies payable, without contribution, to said

EXHIBIT 6–5
Florida Mortgage
(continued)

Mortgagee as its interest may appear, and each and every such policy shall be promptly delivered to and held by said Mortgagee; and, not less than ten (10) days in advance of the expiration of each policy, to deliver to said Mortgagee a renewal thereof, together with a receipt for the premium of such renewal. Any insurance proceeds, or any part thereof, may be applied by Mortgagee, at its option, either to the indebtedness hereby secured or to the restoration or repair of the property damaged.

4. To keep said land and the buildings and improvements now or hereafter situate thereon in good order and repair, and to permit, commit or suffer no waste, impairment or deterioration of said property or any part thereof.

5. To comply, as far as they affect the mortgaged property, with all statutes, laws, ordinances, decrees, and orders of the United States, the State of Florida, and of any political subdivision thereof.

6. In case Mortgagor shall fail to promptly discharge any obligation or covenant as provided herein, the Mortgagee shall have the option, but no obligation, to perform on behalf of the Mortgagor any act to be performed by Mortgagor in discharging such obligation or covenant, and any amount which Mortgagee may expend in performing such act, or in connection therewith, with interest thereon at the rate of ten (10) percent per annum and together with all expenses, including reasonable attorney's fees, incurred by Mortgagee shall be immediately payable by Mortgagor and shall be secured by this mortgage; and Mortgagee shall be subrogated to any rights, equities, and liens so discharged.

7. That if the principal or interest on the note herein described or any part of the indebtedness secured by this mortgage or interest thereon, be not paid within ten (10) days after they are due, or if default be made in the full and prompt performance of any covenant or agreement herein contained, or if any proceeding be instituted to abate any nuisance on the mortgaged property, or if any proceeding be instituted which might result to the detriment of the use and enjoyment of the said property or upon the rendering by any court of last resort of a decision that an undertaking by the Mortgagor as herein provided to pay any tax, assessment, levy, liability, obligation, or encumbrance is legally inoperative or cannot be enforced, or in the event of the passage of any law changing in any way or respect the laws now in force for the taxation of mortgages or debts secured thereby for any purpose, or the manner of collection of any such tax, so as to affect this mortgage or the debt secured hereby; or if the Mortgagor shall make an assignment for the benefit of creditors, or if a receiver be appointed for the Mortgagor or any part of the mortgaged property, or if Mortgagor files a petition in bankruptcy, or is adjudicated a bankrupt or files any petition or institutes any proceedings under the National Bankruptcy Act, then on the happening of any one or more of these events, this conveyance shall become absolute and the whole indebtedness secured hereby shall immediately become due and payable, at the option of the Mortgagee, and this mortgage may thereupon be foreclosed for the whole of said money, interest and costs; or Mortgagee may foreclose only as to the sum past due, without injury to this mortgage or the displacement or impairment of the remainder of the lien thereof, and at such foreclosure sale the property shall be sold subject to all remaining items of indebtedness; and Mortgagee may again foreclose, in the same manner, as often as there may be any sum past due.

8. Except during such period or periods as the Mortgagee may from time to time designate in writing, the Mortgagor will pay to the Mortgagee on the first day of each month throughout the existence of this mortgage a sum equal to the Mortgagee's estimate of the taxes and assessments next due on the mortgaged property and premiums next payable on or for policies of fire and other hazard insurance thereon, less any sums already paid the Mortgagee with respect thereto, divided by the number of months to elapse before one month prior to the date when such taxes, assessments, and premiums become due and payable, such sums to be held by the Mortgagee, without interest, to pay such items. If at any time the estimated sum is insufficient to pay an item when due, the Mortgagor shall forthwith upon demand pay the deficiency to the Mortgagee. The arrangement provided for in this paragraph is solely for the added protection of the Mortgagee and entails no responsibility on the Mortgagee's part beyond the allowing of due credit, without interest, for sums actually received by it. Upon the occurrence of a default under this mortgage, the Mortgagee may apply all or any part of the accumulated funds then held, upon any obligation secured hereby. Upon assignment of this mortgage, any funds on hand shall be turned over to the assignee and any responsibility of the assignor with respect thereto shall terminate. Each transfer of the mortgaged

EXHIBIT 6-5
Florida Mortgage
(continued)

property shall automatically transfer to the grantee all right of the grantor with respect to any funds accumulated hereunder.

9. That in case of default or the happening of any event which would enable the Mortgagee to declare the whole indebtedness secured hereby immediately due and payable, the Mortgagee shall be entitled to the appointment of a receiver of all the rents, issues, and profits, regardless of the value of the mortgaged property and the solvency or insolvency of the Mortgagor and other persons liable to pay said indebtedness.

10. That the Mortgagee may collect a "late charge" not to exceed four cents (4¢) for each dollar of each payment due hereunder made more than fifteen (15) days in arrears to cover the extra expense involved in handling delinquent payments.

11. That the words "Mortgagor" and "Mortgagee" when used herein shall be taken to include singular and plural number and masculine, feminine, or neuter gender, as may fit the case, and shall also include the heirs, administrators, executors, successors, and assigns of the parties hereto. Each and all of the terms and provisions hereof shall extend to and be a part of any renewal or extension of this mortgage.

12. That this mortgage and the note secured hereby constitute a Florida contract and shall be construed according to the laws of that state.

IN WITNESS WHEREOF, the said Mortgagor has hereunto set his hand and seal the day and year first above written.

EXHIBIT 6-6
North Carolina Deed
of Trust

SATISFACTION: The debt secured by the within Deed of Trust together with the note(s) secured thereby has been satisfied in full.

This the .... day of ...., 20 ....

Signed: ....

....

....

Mail after recording to:

....

....

....

This instrument prepared by:

.... | Recording: Time, Book and Page

NORTH CAROLINA DEED OF TRUST

THIS DEED of TRUST made this   day of   , 20   , by and between:

GRANTOR	TRUSTEE	BENEFICIARY
		SOUTHERN NATIONAL BANK OF NORTH CAROLINA, a national banking association

Enter in appropriate block for each party: name, address, and, if appropriate, character of entity, e.g. corporation or partnership.

The designation Grantor, Trustee, and Beneficiary as used herein shall include said parties, their heirs, successors, and assigns, and shall include singular, plural, masculine, feminine or neuter as required by context.

WITNESSETH: The Grantor is indebted to the Beneficiary in the sum of _____

_____ DOLLARS ($ ....)
(the "Debt") for money loaned, as evidenced by promissory Note(s) of even date herewith, the terms of which are incorporated herein by reference.

NOW, THEREFORE, as security for the Debt, together with interest thereon, and as security for all renewals, extensions, deferments, amortizations and re-amortizations thereof, in whole or in part, together with interest thereon whether at the same or different rates, and for a valuable consideration, receipt of which is hereby acknowledged, the Grantor has bargained, sold, granted and conveyed and does by these presents bargain, sell, grant and convey to the Trustee, his heirs, or

successors, and assigns, the real property situated in the City of _____ , _____ Township, _____
County, State of North Carolina, particularly described as follows:

DESCRIPTION SET FORTH HEREINBELOW AND ON SCHEDULE "A", IF ANY, ATTACHED HERETO AND MADE A PART HEREOF

EXHIBIT 6–6
North Carolina Deed of Trust (continued)

TO HAVE AND TO HOLD said real property, including all buildings, improvements and fixtures now or hereafter located thereon, with all the rights, privileges and appurtenances thereunto belonging, to the Trustee, his heirs, or successors, and assigns forever, upon the trusts, terms and conditions, and for the uses hereinafter set forth.

If the Grantor shall pay the Debt secured hereby in accordance with the terms of the note(s) evidencing the same, and all renewals, extensions, deferments, amortizations and reamortizations thereof, in whole or in part, together with interest thereon, and shall comply with all the covenants, terms and conditions of the deed of trust, then this conveyance shall be null and void and may be cancelled of record at the request of the Grantor. If, however, there shall be any default in any of the covenants, terms, or conditions of the Note(s) secured hereby, or any failure or neglect to comply with the covenants, terms, or conditions contained in this deed of trust, then and in any of such events, if the default is not made good within (15) days, the Note(s) shall, at the option of the Beneficiary, at once become due and payable without notice, and it shall be lawful for and the duty of the Trustee, upon request of the Beneficiary, to sell the land herein conveyed at public auction for cash, after having first given such notice of hearing as to commencement of foreclosure proceedings and obtaining such findings or leave of court as may be then required by law and giving such notice and advertising the time and place of such sale in such manner as may be then provided by law, and upon such and any resales and upon compliance with the then law relating to foreclosure proceedings to convey title to the purchaser in fee simple.

The proceeds of the Sale shall, after the Trustee retains his commission, be applied to the costs of sale, the amount due on the Note(s) hereby secured and otherwise as required by the then existing law relating to foreclosures. The Trustee's commission shall be five per cent of the gross proceeds of the sale or the minimum sum of $ ...., whichever is greater, for a completed foreclosure. In the event foreclosure is commenced, but not completed, the Grantor shall pay all expenses incurred by Trustee and a partial commission computed on five per cent of the outstanding indebtedness or the above stated minimum sum, whichever is greater, in accordance with the following schedule, to wit: one-fourth thereof before the Trustee issues a notice of hearing on the right to foreclose; one-half thereof after issuance of said notice; three-fourths thereof after such hearing; and the greater of the full commission or minimum after the initial sale.

And the said Grantor does hereby covenant and agree with the Trustee and the Beneficiary as follows:

1. INSURANCE. Grantor shall keep all improvements on said land, now or hereafter erected constantly insured for the benefit of the Beneficiary against loss by fire, windstorm and such other casualties and contingencies, in such manner and in such companies and for such amounts as may be satisfactory to or required by the Beneficiary. Grantor shall purchase such insurance, pay all premiums therefor, and shall deliver to Beneficiary such policies along with evidence of premium payment as long as the Note(s) secured hereby remains unpaid. If Grantor fails to purchase such insurance, pay the premiums therefor or deliver said policies with mortgagee clause satisfactory to Beneficiary attached thereto, along with evidence of payment of premiums thereon, then Beneficiary, at his option, may purchase such insurance. Such amounts paid by Beneficiary shall be added to the Note(s) secured by this Deed of Trust, and shall be due and payable upon demand by Grantor to Beneficiary.

2. TAXES, ASSESSMENTS, CHARGES. Grantor shall pay all taxes, assessments and charges as may be lawfully levied against said premises within thirty (30) days after the same shall become due. In the event that Grantor fails to so pay all taxes, assessments and charges as herein required, then Beneficiary, at his option, may pay the same and the amounts so paid shall be added to the Note(s), secured by this Deed of Trust, and shall be due and payable upon demand by Grantor to Beneficiary.

3. PARTIAL RELEASE. Grantor shall not be entitled to the partial release of any of the above described property unless a specific provision providing therefor is included in this Deed of Trust. In the event a partial release provision is included in this Deed of Trust, Grantor must strictly comply with the terms thereof. Notwithstanding anything herein contained, Grantor shall not be entitled to any release of property unless Grantor is not in default and is in full compliance with all of the terms and provisions of the Note(s), this Deed of Trust, and any other instrument that may be securing said Note(s).

4. WASTE. The Grantor covenants that he will keep the premises herein conveyed in as good order, repair and condition as they are now, reasonable wear and tear excepted, and that he will not commit or permit any waste.

5. WARRANTIES. Grantor covenants with Trustee and Beneficiary that he is seized of the premises in fee simple, has the right to convey the same in fee simple, that title is marketable and free and clear of all encumbrances, and that he will warrant and defend the title against the lawful claims of all persons whomsoever, except for the exceptions hereinafter stated. Title to the property hereinabove described is subject to the following exceptions:

6. CONVEYANCE; ACCELERATION: If Grantor sells, conveys, transfers, assigns or disposes of the hereinabove-described real property or any part thereof or interest therein, by any means or method, whether voluntary or involuntary, without the written consent of Beneficiary, then at the option of Beneficiary and without notice to Grantor, all sums of money secured hereby, both principal and interest, shall immediately become due and payable and in default, notwithstanding anything herein or in the Note(s) secured hereby to the contrary.

7. SUBSTITUTION OF TRUSTEE. Grantor and Trustee covenant and agree to and with Beneficiary that in case the said Trustee, or any successor trustee, shall die, become incapable of acting, renounce his trust, or for other similar or dissimilar reason become unacceptable to the holder of the Note(s), then the holder of the Note(s) may appoint, in writing, a trustee to take the place of the Trustee; and upon the probate and registration of the same, the trustee thus appointed shall succeed to all the rights, powers, and duties of the Trustee.

8. CIVIL ACTION. In the event that the Trustee is named as a party to any civil action as Trustee in this Deed of Trust, the Trustee shall be entitled to employ an attorney at law, including himself if he is a licensed attorney, to represent him in said action and the reasonable attorney's fees of the Trustee in such action shall be paid by Beneficiary and charged to the Note(s) and secured by this Deed of Trust.

9. PRIOR LIENS. Default under the terms of any instrument secured by a lien to which this deed of trust is subordinate shall consitute default hereunder.

IN WITNESS WHEREOF, the Grantor has hereunto set his hand and seal, or if corporate, has caused this instrument to be signed in its corporate name by its duly authorized officers and its seal to be hereunto affixed by authority of its Board of Directors, the day and year first above written.

(Corporate Name)

.... (SEAL)

By: ....

.... President

.... (SEAL)

ATTEST:

.... (SEAL)

.... Secretary (Corporate Seal)

.... (SEAL)

USE BLACK INK ONLY

SEAL-STAMP   Use Black Ink

STATE OF NORTH CAROLINA, COUNTY OF ....

I, ..., a notary public of said county do hereby certify that .... Grantor, personally appeared before me this day and acknowledged the execution of the foregoing instrument. Witness my hand and official stamp or seal, this .... day of ...., 20 ....

My commission expires: .... Notary Public

SEAL-STAMP   Use Black Ink

STATE OF NORTH CAROLINA, COUNTY OF ....

I, ..., a Notary Public of the County and State aforesaid, certify that ...., personally came before me this day and acknowledged that .... he is .... Secretary of .... a North Carolina corporation, and that by authority duly given and as the act of the corporation, the foregoing instrument was signed in its name by its .... President, sealed with its corporate seal and attested by .... as its .... Secretary.

Witness my hand and official stamp or seal, this .... day of ...., 20 ....

My commission expires: .... Notary Public

The foregoing Certificate (s) of ....

is/are certified to be correct. This instrument and this certificate are duly registered at the date and time and in the Book and Page shown on the first page hereof.

.... REGISTER OF DEEDS FOR .... COUNTY

By .... Deputy/Assistant - Register of Deeds

EXHIBIT 6-7
FNMA Residential Mortgage

After Recording Return To:

_____

_____

_____

_____

_____ [Space Above This Line For Recording Data] _____

MORTGAGE

DEFINITIONS

Words used in multiple sections of this document are defined below and other words are defined in Sections 3, 11, 13, 18, 20 and 21. Certain rules regarding the usage of words used in this document are also provided in Section 16.

(A) "Security Instrument" means this document, which is dated _____, _____, together with all Riders to this document.

(B) "Borrower" is _____. Borrower is the mortgagor under this Security Instrument.

(C) "Lender" is _____. Lender is a _____ organized and existing under the laws of _____. Lender's address is _____ _____. Lender is the mortgagee under this Security Instrument.

(D) "Note" means the promissory note signed by Borrower and dated _____, _____. The Note states that Borrower owes Lender _____ Dollars (U.S. $_____) plus interest. Borrower has promised to pay this debt in regular Periodic Payments and to pay the debt in full not later than _____.

(E) "Property" means the property that is described below under the heading "Transfer of Rights in the Property."

(F) "Loan" means the debt evidenced by the Note, plus interest, any prepayment charges and late charges due under the Note, and all sums due under this Security Instrument, plus interest.

(G) "Riders" means all Riders to this Security Instrument that are executed by Borrower. The following Riders are to be executed by Borrower [check box as applicable]:

☐ Adjustable Rate Rider	☐ Condominium Rider	☐ Second Home Rider
☐ Balloon Rider	☐ Planned Unit Development Rider	☐ Other(s) [specify] _____
☐ 1-4 Family Rider	☐ Biweekly Payment Rider	

IOWA--Single Family--Fannie Mae/Freddie Mac UNIFORM INSTRUMENT   Form 3016 1/01 *(page 1 of 16 pages)*

EXHIBIT 6–7
FNMA Residential Mortgage (continued)

(H) **"Applicable Law"** means all controlling applicable federal, state and local statutes, regulations, ordinances and administrative rules and orders (that have the effect of law) as well as all applicable final, non-appealable judicial opinions.

(I) **"Community Association Dues, Fees, and Assessments"** means all dues, fees, assessments and other charges that are imposed on Borrower or the Property by a condominium association, homeowners association or similar organization.

(J) **"Electronic Funds Transfer"** means any transfer of funds, other than a transaction originated by check, draft, or similar paper instrument, which is initiated through an electronic terminal, telephonic instrument, computer, or magnetic tape so as to order, instruct, or authorize a financial institution to debit or credit an account. Such term includes, but is not limited to, point-of-sale transfers, automated teller machine transactions, transfers initiated by telephone, wire transfers, and automated clearinghouse transfers.

(K) **"Escrow Items"** means those items that are described in Section 3.

(L) **"Miscellaneous Proceeds"** means any compensation, settlement, award of damages, or proceeds paid by any third party (other than insurance proceeds paid under the coverages described in Section 5) for: (i) damage to, or destruction of, the Property; (ii) condemnation or other taking of all or any part of the Property; (iii) conveyance in lieu of condemnation; or (iv) misrepresentations of, or omissions as to, the value and/or condition of the Property.

(M) **"Mortgage Insurance"** means insurance protecting Lender against the nonpayment of, or default on, the Loan.

(N) **"Periodic Payment"** means the regularly scheduled amount due for (i) principal and interest under the Note, plus (ii) any amounts under Section 3 of this Security Instrument.

(O) **"RESPA"** means the Real Estate Settlement Procedures Act (12 U.S.C. §2601 et seq.) and its implementing regulation, Regulation X (24 C.F.R. Part 3500), as they might be amended from time to time, or any additional or successor legislation or regulation that governs the same subject matter. As used in this Security Instrument, "RESPA" refers to all requirements and restrictions that are imposed in regard to a "federally related mortgage loan" even if the Loan does not qualify as a "federally related mortgage loan" under RESPA.

(P) **"Successor in Interest of Borrower"** means any party that has taken title to the Property, whether or not that party has assumed Borrower's obligations under the Note and/or this Security Instrument.

TRANSFER OF RIGHTS IN THE PROPERTY

This Security Instrument secures to Lender: (i) the repayment of the Loan, and all renewals, extensions and modifications of the Note; and (ii) the performance of Borrower's covenants and agreements under this Security Instrument and the Note. For this purpose, Borrower irrevocably

EXHIBIT 6-7
FNMA Residential Mortgage (continued)

mortgages, grants and conveys to Lender, with power of sale, the following described property located in the _____ of _____:

[Type of Recording Jurisdiction]   [Name of Recording Jurisdiction]

which currently has the address of _____

[Street]

_____, Iowa _____("Property Address"):

[City]   [Zip Code]

TOGETHER WITH all the improvements now or hereafter erected on the property, and all easements, appurtenances, and fixtures now or hereafter a part of the property. All replacements and additions shall also be covered by this Security Instrument. All of the foregoing is referred to in this Security Instrument as the "Property."

BORROWER COVENANTS that Borrower is lawfully seised of the estate hereby conveyed and has the right to grant and convey the Property and that the Property is unencumbered, except for encumbrances of record. Borrower warrants and will defend generally the title to the Property against all claims and demands, subject to any encumbrances of record.

THIS SECURITY INSTRUMENT combines uniform covenants for national use and non-uniform covenants with limited variations by jurisdiction to constitute a uniform security instrument covering real property.

UNIFORM COVENANTS. Borrower and Lender covenant and agree as follows:

1. **Payment of Principal, Interest, Escrow Items, Prepayment Charges, and Late Charges.** Borrower shall pay when due the principal of, and interest on, the debt evidenced by the Note and any prepayment charges and late charges due under the Note. Borrower shall also pay funds for Escrow Items pursuant to Section 3. Payments due under the Note and this Security Instrument shall be made in U.S. currency. However, if any check or other instrument received by Lender as payment under the Note or this Security Instrument is returned to Lender unpaid, Lender may require that any or all subsequent payments due under the Note and this Security Instrument be made in one or more of the following forms, as selected by Lender: (a) cash; (b) money order; (c) certified check, bank check, treasurer's check or cashier's check, provided any such check is drawn upon an institution whose deposits are insured by a federal agency, instrumentality, or entity; or (d) Electronic Funds Transfer.

EXHIBIT 6-7
FNMA Residential Mortgage (continued)

Payments are deemed received by Lender when received at the location designated in the Note or at such other location as may be designated by Lender in accordance with the notice provisions in Section 15. Lender may return any payment or partial payment if the payment or partial payments are insufficient to bring the Loan current. Lender may accept any payment or partial payment insufficient to bring the Loan current, without waiver of any rights hereunder or prejudice to its rights to refuse such payment or partial payments in the future, but Lender is not obligated to apply such payments at the time such payments are accepted. If each Periodic Payment is applied as of its scheduled due date, then Lender need not pay interest on unapplied funds. Lender may hold such unapplied funds until Borrower makes payment to bring the Loan current. If Borrower does not do so within a reasonable period of time, Lender shall either apply such funds or return them to Borrower. If not applied earlier, such funds will be applied to the outstanding principal balance under the Note immediately prior to foreclosure. No offset or claim which Borrower might have now or in the future against Lender shall relieve Borrower from making payments due under the Note and this Security Instrument or performing the covenants and agreements secured by this Security Instrument.

2. **Application of Payments or Proceeds.** Except as otherwise described in this Section 2, all payments accepted and applied by Lender shall be applied in the following order of priority: (a) interest due under the Note; (b) principal due under the Note; (c) amounts due under Section 3. Such payments shall be applied to each Periodic Payment in the order in which it became due. Any remaining amounts shall be applied first to late charges, second to any other amounts due under this Security Instrument, and then to reduce the principal balance of the Note.

If Lender receives a payment from Borrower for a delinquent Periodic Payment which includes a sufficient amount to pay any late charge due, the payment may be applied to the delinquent payment and the late charge. If more than one Periodic Payment is outstanding, Lender may apply any payment received from Borrower to the repayment of the Periodic Payments if, and to the extent that, each payment can be paid in full. To the extent that any excess exists after the payment is applied to the full payment of one or more Periodic Payments, such excess may be applied to any late charges due. Voluntary prepayments shall be applied first to any prepayment charges and then as described in the Note.

Any application of payments, insurance proceeds, or Miscellaneous Proceeds to principal due under the Note shall not extend or postpone the due date, or change the amount, of the Periodic Payments.

3. **Funds for Escrow Items.** Borrower shall pay to Lender on the day Periodic Payments are due under the Note, until the Note is paid in full, a sum (the "Funds") to provide for payment of amounts due for: (a) taxes and assessments and other items which can attain priority over this Security Instrument as a lien or encumbrance on the Property; (b) leasehold payments or ground rents on the Property, if any; (c) premiums for any and all insurance required by Lender under Section 5; and (d) Mortgage Insurance premiums, if any, or any sums payable by Borrower to Lender in lieu of the payment of Mortgage Insurance premiums in accordance with the provisions of Section 10. These items are called "Escrow Items." At origination or at any time during the term of the Loan, Lender may require that Community Association Dues, Fees, and Assessments, if any, be escrowed by Borrower, and such dues, fees and assessments shall be an Escrow Item. Borrower shall promptly furnish to Lender all notices of amounts to be paid under this Section. Borrower shall pay Lender the Funds for Escrow Items unless Lender waives Borrower's obligation to pay the

EXHIBIT 6-7
FNMA Residential Mortgage (continued)

Funds for any or all Escrow Items. Lender may waive Borrower's obligation to pay to Lender Funds for any or all Escrow Items at any time. Any such waiver may only be in writing. In the event of such waiver, Borrower shall pay directly, when and where payable, the amounts due for any Escrow Items for which payment of Funds has been waived by Lender and, if Lender requires, shall furnish to Lender receipts evidencing such payment within such time period as Lender may require. Borrower's obligation to make such payments and to provide receipts shall for all purposes be deemed to be a covenant and agreement contained in this Security Instrument, as the phrase "covenant and agreement" is used in Section 9. If Borrower is obligated to pay Escrow Items directly, pursuant to a waiver, and Borrower fails to pay the amount due for an Escrow Item, Lender may exercise its rights under Section 9 and pay such amount and Borrower shall then be obligated under Section 9 to repay to Lender any such amount. Lender may revoke the waiver as to any or all Escrow Items at any time by a notice given in accordance with Section 15 and, upon such revocation, Borrower shall pay to Lender all Funds, and in such amounts, that are then required under this Section 3.

Lender may, at any time, collect and hold Funds in an amount (a) sufficient to permit Lender to apply the Funds at the time specified under RESPA, and (b) not to exceed the maximum amount a lender can require under RESPA. Lender shall estimate the amount of Funds due on the basis of current data and reasonable estimates of expenditures of future Escrow Items or otherwise in accordance with Applicable Law.

The Funds shall be held in an institution whose deposits are insured by a federal agency, instrumentality, or entity (including Lender, if Lender is an institution whose deposits are so insured) or in any Federal Home Loan Bank. Lender shall apply the Funds to pay the Escrow Items no later than the time specified under RESPA. Lender shall not charge Borrower for holding and applying the Funds, annually analyzing the escrow account, or verifying the Escrow Items, unless Lender pays Borrower interest on the Funds and Applicable Law permits Lender to make such a charge. Unless an agreement is made in writing or Applicable Law requires interest to be paid on the Funds, Lender shall not be required to pay Borrower any interest or earnings on the Funds. Borrower and Lender can agree in writing, however, that interest shall be paid on the Funds. Lender shall give to Borrower, without charge, an annual accounting of the Funds as required by RESPA.

If there is a surplus of Funds held in escrow, as defined under RESPA, Lender shall account to Borrower for the excess funds in accordance with RESPA. If there is a shortage of Funds held in escrow, as defined under RESPA, Lender shall notify Borrower as required by RESPA, and Borrower shall pay to Lender the amount necessary to make up the shortage in accordance with RESPA, but in no more than 12 monthly payments. If there is a deficiency of Funds held in escrow, as defined under RESPA, Lender shall notify Borrower as required by RESPA, and Borrower shall pay to Lender the amount necessary to make up the deficiency in accordance with RESPA, but in no more than 12 monthly payments.

Upon payment in full of all sums secured by this Security Instrument, Lender shall promptly refund to Borrower any Funds held by Lender.

4. **Charges; Liens.** Borrower shall pay all taxes, assessments, charges, fines, and impositions attributable to the Property which can attain priority over this Security Instrument, leasehold payments or ground rents on the Property, if any, and Community Association Dues, Fees, and Assessments, if any. To the extent that these items are Escrow Items, Borrower shall pay them in the manner provided in Section 3.

EXHIBIT 6–7
FNMA Residential Mortgage (continued)

Borrower shall promptly discharge any lien which has priority over this Security Instrument unless Borrower: (a) agrees in writing to the payment of the obligation secured by the lien in a manner acceptable to Lender, but only so long as Borrower is performing such agreement; (b) contests the lien in good faith by, or defends against enforcement of the lien in, legal proceedings which in Lender's opinion operate to prevent the enforcement of the lien while those proceedings are pending, but only until such proceedings are concluded; or (c) secures from the holder of the lien an agreement satisfactory to Lender subordinating the lien to this Security Instrument. If Lender determines that any part of the Property is subject to a lien which can attain priority over this Security Instrument, Lender may give Borrower a notice identifying the lien. Within 10 days of the date on which that notice is given, Borrower shall satisfy the lien or take one or more of the actions set forth above in this Section 4.

Lender may require Borrower to pay a one-time charge for a real estate tax verification and/or reporting service used by Lender in connection with this Loan.

5. Property Insurance. Borrower shall keep the improvements now existing or hereafter erected on the Property insured against loss by fire, hazards included within the term "extended coverage," and any other hazards including, but not limited to, earthquakes and floods, for which Lender requires insurance. This insurance shall be maintained in the amounts (including deductible levels) and for the periods that Lender requires. What Lender requires pursuant to the preceding sentences can change during the term of the Loan. The insurance carrier providing the insurance shall be chosen by Borrower subject to Lender's right to disapprove Borrower's choice, which right shall not be exercised unreasonably. Lender may require Borrower to pay, in connection with this Loan, either: (a) a one-time charge for flood zone determination, certification and tracking services; or (b) a one-time charge for flood zone determination and certification services and subsequent charges each time remappings or similar changes occur which reasonably might affect such determination or certification. Borrower shall also be responsible for the payment of any fees imposed by the Federal Emergency Management Agency in connection with the review of any flood zone determination resulting from an objection by Borrower.

If Borrower fails to maintain any of the coverages described above, Lender may obtain insurance coverage, at Lender's option and Borrower's expense. Lender is under no obligation to purchase any particular type or amount of coverage. Therefore, such coverage shall cover Lender, but might or might not protect Borrower, Borrower's equity in the Property, or the contents of the Property, against any risk, hazard or liability and might provide greater or lesser coverage than was previously in effect. Borrower acknowledges that the cost of the insurance coverage so obtained might significantly exceed the cost of insurance that Borrower could have obtained. Any amounts disbursed by Lender under this Section 5 shall become additional debt of Borrower secured by this Security Instrument. These amounts shall bear interest at the Note rate from the date of disbursement and shall be payable, with such interest, upon notice from Lender to Borrower requesting payment.

All insurance policies required by Lender and renewals of such policies shall be subject to Lender's right to disapprove such policies, shall include a standard mortgage clause, and shall name Lender as mortgagee and/or as an additional loss payee. Lender shall have the right to hold the policies and renewal certificates. If Lender requires, Borrower shall promptly give to Lender all receipts of paid premiums and renewal notices. If Borrower obtains any form of insurance coverage, not otherwise required by Lender, for damage to, or destruction of, the Property, such policy shall

EXHIBIT 6-7
FNMA Residential Mortgage (continued)

include a standard mortgage clause and shall name Lender as mortgagee and/or as an additional loss payee.

In the event of loss, Borrower shall give prompt notice to the insurance carrier and Lender. Lender may make proof of loss if not made promptly by Borrower. Unless Lender and Borrower otherwise agree in writing, any insurance proceeds, whether or not the underlying insurance was required by Lender, shall be applied to restoration or repair of the Property, if the restoration or repair is economically feasible and Lender's security is not lessened. During such repair and restoration period, Lender shall have the right to hold such insurance proceeds until Lender has had an opportunity to inspect such Property to ensure the work has been completed to Lender's satisfaction, provided that such inspection shall be undertaken promptly. Lender may disburse proceeds for the repairs and restoration in a single payment or in a series of progress payments as the work is completed. Unless an agreement is made in writing or Applicable Law requires interest to be paid on such insurance proceeds, Lender shall not be required to pay Borrower any interest or earnings on such proceeds. Fees for public adjusters, or other third parties, retained by Borrower shall not be paid out of the insurance proceeds and shall be the sole obligation of Borrower. If the restoration or repair is not economically feasible or Lender's security would be lessened, the insurance proceeds shall be applied to the sums secured by this Security Instrument, whether or not then due, with the excess, if any, paid to Borrower. Such insurance proceeds shall be applied in the order provided for in Section 2.

If Borrower abandons the Property, Lender may file, negotiate and settle any available insurance claim and related matters. If Borrower does not respond within 30 days to a notice from Lender that the insurance carrier has offered to settle a claim, then Lender may negotiate and settle the claim. The 30-day period will begin when the notice is given. In either event, or if Lender acquires the Property under Section 22 or otherwise, Borrower hereby assigns to Lender (a) Borrower's rights to any insurance proceeds in an amount not to exceed the amounts unpaid under the Note or this Security Instrument, and (b) any other of Borrower's rights (other than the right to any refund of unearned premiums paid by Borrower) under all insurance policies covering the Property, insofar as such rights are applicable to the coverage of the Property. Lender may use the insurance proceeds either to repair or restore the Property or to pay amounts unpaid under the Note or this Security Instrument, whether or not then due.

6. Occupancy. Borrower shall occupy, establish, and use the Property as Borrower's principal residence within 60 days after the execution of this Security Instrument and shall continue to occupy the Property as Borrower's principal residence for at least one year after the date of occupancy, unless Lender otherwise agrees in writing, which consent shall not be unreasonably withheld, or unless extenuating circumstances exist which are beyond Borrower's control.

7. Preservation, Maintenance and Protection of the Property; Inspections. Borrower shall not destroy, damage or impair the Property, allow the Property to deteriorate or commit waste on the Property. Whether or not Borrower is residing in the Property, Borrower shall maintain the Property in order to prevent the Property from deteriorating or decreasing in value due to its condition. Unless it is determined pursuant to Section 5 that repair or restoration is not economically feasible, Borrower shall promptly repair the Property if damaged to avoid further deterioration or damage. If insurance or condemnation proceeds are paid in connection with damage to, or the taking of, the Property, Borrower shall be responsible for repairing or restoring the Property only if Lender has released proceeds for such purposes. Lender may disburse proceeds for

EXHIBIT 6-7
FNMA Residential Mortgage (continued)

the repairs and restoration in a single payment or in a series of progress payments as the work is completed. If the insurance or condemnation proceeds are not sufficient to repair or restore the Property, Borrower is not relieved of Borrower's obligation for the completion of such repair or restoration.

Lender or its agent may make reasonable entries upon and inspections of the Property. If it has reasonable cause, Lender may inspect the interior of the improvements on the Property. Lender shall give Borrower notice at the time of or prior to such an interior inspection specifying such reasonable cause.

8. **Borrower's Loan Application.** Borrower shall be in default if, during the Loan application process, Borrower or any persons or entities acting at the direction of Borrower or with Borrower's knowledge or consent gave materially false, misleading, or inaccurate information or statements to Lender (or failed to provide Lender with material information) in connection with the Loan. Material representations include, but are not limited to, representations concerning Borrower's occupancy of the Property as Borrower's principal residence.

9. **Protection of Lender's Interest in the Property and Rights Under this Security Instrument.** If (a) Borrower fails to perform the covenants and agreements contained in this Security Instrument, (b) there is a legal proceeding that might significantly affect Lender's interest in the Property and/or rights under this Security Instrument (such as a proceeding in bankruptcy, probate, for condemnation or forfeiture, for enforcement of a lien which may attain priority over this Security Instrument or to enforce laws or regulations), or (c) Borrower has abandoned the Property, then Lender may do and pay for whatever is reasonable or appropriate to protect Lender's interest in the Property and rights under this Security Instrument, including protecting and/or assessing the value of the Property, and securing and/or repairing the Property. Lender's actions can include, but are not limited to: (a) paying any sums secured by a lien which has priority over this Security Instrument; (b) appearing in court; and (c) paying reasonable attorneys' fees to protect its interest in the Property and/or rights under this Security Instrument, including its secured position in a bankruptcy proceeding. Securing the Property includes, but is not limited to, entering the Property to make repairs, change locks, replace or board up doors and windows, drain water from pipes, eliminate building or other code violations or dangerous conditions, and have utilities turned on or off. Although Lender may take action under this Section 9, Lender does not have to do so and is not under any duty or obligation to do so. It is agreed that Lender incurs no liability for not taking any or all actions authorized under this Section 9.

Any amounts disbursed by Lender under this Section 9 shall become additional debt of Borrower secured by this Security Instrument. These amounts shall bear interest at the Note rate from the date of disbursement and shall be payable, with such interest, upon notice from Lender to Borrower requesting payment.

If this Security Instrument is on a leasehold, Borrower shall comply with all the provisions of the lease. If Borrower acquires fee title to the Property, the leasehold and the fee title shall not merge unless Lender agrees to the merger in writing.

10. **Mortgage Insurance.** If Lender required Mortgage Insurance as a condition of making the Loan, Borrower shall pay the premiums required to maintain the Mortgage Insurance in effect. If, for any reason, the Mortgage Insurance coverage required by Lender ceases to be available from the mortgage insurer that previously provided such insurance and Borrower was required to make separately designated payments toward the premiums for Mortgage Insurance, Borrower shall pay

EXHIBIT 6-7
FNMA Residential Mortgage (continued)

the premiums required to obtain coverage substantially equivalent to the Mortgage Insurance previously in effect, at a cost substantially equivalent to the cost to Borrower of the Mortgage Insurance previously in effect, from an alternate mortgage insurer selected by Lender. If substantially equivalent Mortgage Insurance coverage is not available, Borrower shall continue to pay to Lender the amount of the separately designated payments that were due when the insurance coverage ceased to be in effect. Lender will accept, use and retain these payments as a non-refundable loss reserve in lieu of Mortgage Insurance. Such loss reserve shall be non-refundable, notwithstanding the fact that the Loan is ultimately paid in full, and Lender shall not be required to pay Borrower any interest or earnings on such loss reserve. Lender can no longer require loss reserve payments if Mortgage Insurance coverage (in the amount and for the period that Lender requires) provided by an insurer selected by Lender again becomes available, is obtained, and Lender requires separately designated payments toward the premiums for Mortgage Insurance. If Lender required Mortgage Insurance as a condition of making the Loan and Borrower was required to make separately designated payments toward the premiums for Mortgage Insurance, Borrower shall pay the premiums required to maintain Mortgage Insurance in effect, or to provide a non-refundable loss reserve, until Lender's requirement for Mortgage Insurance ends in accordance with any written agreement between Borrower and Lender providing for such termination or until termination is required by Applicable Law. Nothing in this Section 10 affects Borrower's obligation to pay interest at the rate provided in the Note.

Mortgage Insurance reimburses Lender (or any entity that purchases the Note) for certain losses it may incur if Borrower does not repay the Loan as agreed. Borrower is not a party to the Mortgage Insurance.

Mortgage insurers evaluate their total risk on all such insurance in force from time to time, and may enter into agreements with other parties that share or modify their risk, or reduce losses. These agreements are on terms and conditions that are satisfactory to the mortgage insurer and the other party (or parties) to these agreements. These agreements may require the mortgage insurer to make payments using any source of funds that the mortgage insurer may have available (which may include funds obtained from Mortgage Insurance premiums).

As a result of these agreements, Lender, any purchaser of the Note, another insurer, any reinsurer, any other entity, or any affiliate of any of the foregoing, may receive (directly or indirectly) amounts that derive from (or might be characterized as) a portion of Borrower's payments for Mortgage Insurance, in exchange for sharing or modifying the mortgage insurer's risk, or reducing losses. If such agreement provides that an affiliate of Lender takes a share of the insurer's risk in exchange for a share of the premiums paid to the insurer, the arrangement is often termed "captive reinsurance." Further:

(a) Any such agreements will not affect the amounts that Borrower has agreed to pay for Mortgage Insurance, or any other terms of the Loan. Such agreements will not increase the amount Borrower will owe for Mortgage Insurance, and they will not entitle Borrower to any refund.

(b) Any such agreements will not affect the rights Borrower has – if any – with respect to the Mortgage Insurance under the Homeowners Protection Act of 1998 or any other law. These rights may include the right to receive certain disclosures, to request and obtain cancellation of the Mortgage Insurance, to have the Mortgage Insurance terminated

EXHIBIT 6-7
FNMA Residential Mortgage (continued)

automatically, and/or to receive a refund of any Mortgage Insurance premiums that were unearned at the time of such cancellation or termination.

      11. **Assignment of Miscellaneous Proceeds; Forfeiture.** All Miscellaneous Proceeds are hereby assigned to and shall be paid to Lender.

      If the Property is damaged, such Miscellaneous Proceeds shall be applied to restoration or repair of the Property, if the restoration or repair is economically feasible and Lender's security is not lessened. During such repair and restoration period, Lender shall have the right to hold such Miscellaneous Proceeds until Lender has had an opportunity to inspect such Property to ensure the work has been completed to Lender's satisfaction, provided that such inspection shall be undertaken promptly. Lender may pay for the repairs and restoration in a single disbursement or in a series of progress payments as the work is completed. Unless an agreement is made in writing or Applicable Law requires interest to be paid on such Miscellaneous Proceeds, Lender shall not be required to pay Borrower any interest or earnings on such Miscellaneous Proceeds. If the restoration or repair is not economically feasible or Lender's security would be lessened, the Miscellaneous Proceeds shall be applied to the sums secured by this Security Instrument, whether or not then due, with the excess, if any, paid to Borrower. Such Miscellaneous Proceeds shall be applied in the order provided for in Section 2.

      In the event of a total taking, destruction, or loss in value of the Property, the Miscellaneous Proceeds shall be applied to the sums secured by this Security Instrument, whether or not then due, with the excess, if any, paid to Borrower.

      In the event of a partial taking, destruction, or loss in value of the Property in which the fair market value of the Property immediately before the partial taking, destruction, or loss in value is equal to or greater than the amount of the sums secured by this Security Instrument immediately before the partial taking, destruction, or loss in value, unless Borrower and Lender otherwise agree in writing, the sums secured by this Security Instrument shall be reduced by the amount of the Miscellaneous Proceeds multiplied by the following fraction: (a) the total amount of the sums secured immediately before the partial taking, destruction, or loss in value divided by (b) the fair market value of the Property immediately before the partial taking, destruction, or loss in value. Any balance shall be paid to Borrower.

      In the event of a partial taking, destruction, or loss in value of the Property in which the fair market value of the Property immediately before the partial taking, destruction, or loss in value is less than the amount of the sums secured immediately before the partial taking, destruction, or loss in value, unless Borrower and Lender otherwise agree in writing, the Miscellaneous Proceeds shall be applied to the sums secured by this Security Instrument whether or not the sums are then due.

      If the Property is abandoned by Borrower, or if, after notice by Lender to Borrower that the Opposing Party (as defined in the next sentence) offers to make an award to settle a claim for damages, Borrower fails to respond to Lender within 30 days after the date the notice is given, Lender is authorized to collect and apply the Miscellaneous Proceeds either to restoration or repair of the Property or to the sums secured by this Security Instrument, whether or not then due. "Opposing Party" means the third party that owes Borrower Miscellaneous Proceeds or the party against whom Borrower has a right of action in regard to Miscellaneous Proceeds.

EXHIBIT 6-7
FNMA Residential Mortgage (continued)

Borrower shall be in default if any action or proceeding, whether civil or criminal, is begun that, in Lender's judgment, could result in forfeiture of the Property or other material impairment of Lender's interest in the Property or rights under this Security Instrument. Borrower can cure such a default and, if acceleration has occurred, reinstate as provided in Section 19, by causing the action or proceeding to be dismissed with a ruling that, in Lender's judgment, precludes forfeiture of the Property or other material impairment of Lender's interest in the Property or rights under this Security Instrument. The proceeds of any award or claim for damages that are attributable to the impairment of Lender's interest in the Property are hereby assigned and shall be paid to Lender.

All Miscellaneous Proceeds that are not applied to restoration or repair of the Property shall be applied in the order provided for in Section 2.

12. Borrower Not Released; Forbearance By Lender Not a Waiver. Extension of the time for payment or modification of amortization of the sums secured by this Security Instrument granted by Lender to Borrower or any Successor in Interest of Borrower shall not operate to release the liability of Borrower or any Successors in Interest of Borrower. Lender shall not be required to commence proceedings against any Successor in Interest of Borrower or to refuse to extend time for payment or otherwise modify amortization of the sums secured by this Security Instrument by reason of any demand made by the original Borrower or any Successors in Interest of Borrower. Any forbearance by Lender in exercising any right or remedy including, without limitation, Lender's acceptance of payments from third persons, entities or Successors in Interest of Borrower or in amounts less than the amount then due, shall not be a waiver of or preclude the exercise of any right or remedy.

13. Joint and Several Liability; Co-signers; Successors and Assigns Bound. Borrower covenants and agrees that Borrower's obligations and liability shall be joint and several. However, any Borrower who co-signs this Security Instrument but does not execute the Note (a "co-signer"): (a) is co-signing this Security Instrument only to mortgage, grant and convey the co-signer's interest in the Property under the terms of this Security Instrument; (b) is not personally obligated to pay the sums secured by this Security Instrument; and (c) agrees that Lender and any other Borrower can agree to extend, modify, forbear or make any accommodations with regard to the terms of this Security Instrument or the Note without the co-signer's consent.

Subject to the provisions of Section 18, any Successor in Interest of Borrower who assumes Borrower's obligations under this Security Instrument in writing, and is approved by Lender, shall obtain all of Borrower's rights and benefits under this Security Instrument. Borrower shall not be released from Borrower's obligations and liability under this Security Instrument unless Lender agrees to such release in writing. The covenants and agreements of this Security Instrument shall bind (except as provided in Section 20) and benefit the successors and assigns of Lender.

14. Loan Charges. Lender may charge Borrower fees for services performed in connection with Borrower's default, for the purpose of protecting Lender's interest in the Property and rights under this Security Instrument, including, but not limited to, attorneys' fees, property inspection and valuation fees. In regard to any other fees, the absence of express authority in this Security Instrument to charge a specific fee to Borrower shall not be construed as a prohibition on the charging of such fee. Lender may not charge fees that are expressly prohibited by this Security Instrument or by Applicable Law.

If the Loan is subject to a law which sets maximum loan charges, and that law is finally interpreted so that the interest or other loan charges collected or to be collected in connection with

EXHIBIT 6-7
FNMA Residential Mortgage (continued)

the Loan exceed the permitted limits, then: (a) any such loan charge shall be reduced by the amount necessary to reduce the charge to the permitted limit; and (b) any sums already collected from Borrower which exceeded permitted limits will be refunded to Borrower. Lender may choose to make this refund by reducing the principal owed under the Note or by making a direct payment to Borrower. If a refund reduces principal, the reduction will be treated as a partial prepayment without any prepayment charge (whether or not a prepayment charge is provided for under the Note). Borrower's acceptance of any such refund made by direct payment to Borrower will constitute a waiver of any right of action Borrower might have arising out of such overcharge.

15. **Notices.** All notices given by Borrower or Lender in connection with this Security Instrument must be in writing. Any notice to Borrower in connection with this Security Instrument shall be deemed to have been given to Borrower when mailed by first class mail or when actually delivered to Borrower's notice address if sent by other means. Notice to any one Borrower shall constitute notice to all Borrowers unless Applicable Law expressly requires otherwise. The notice address shall be the Property Address unless Borrower has designated a substitute notice address by notice to Lender. Borrower shall promptly notify Lender of Borrower's change of address. If Lender specifies a procedure for reporting Borrower's change of address, then Borrower shall only report a change of address through that specified procedure. There may be only one designated notice address under this Security Instrument at any one time. Any notice to Lender shall be given by delivering it or by mailing it by first class mail to Lender's address stated herein unless Lender has designated another address by notice to Borrower. Any notice in connection with this Security Instrument shall not be deemed to have been given to Lender until actually received by Lender. If any notice required by this Security Instrument is also required under Applicable Law, the Applicable Law requirement will satisfy the corresponding requirement under this Security Instrument.

16. **Governing Law; Severability; Rules of Construction.** This Security Instrument shall be governed by federal law and the law of the jurisdiction in which the Property is located. All rights and obligations contained in this Security Instrument are subject to any requirements and limitations of Applicable Law. Applicable Law might explicitly or implicitly allow the parties to agree by contract or it might be silent, but such silence shall not be construed as a prohibition against agreement by contract. In the event that any provision or clause of this Security Instrument or the Note conflicts with Applicable Law, such conflict shall not affect other provisions of this Security Instrument or the Note which can be given effect without the conflicting provision.

As used in this Security Instrument: (a) words of the masculine gender shall mean and include corresponding neuter words or words of the feminine gender; (b) words in the singular shall mean and include the plural and vice versa; and (c) the word "may" gives sole discretion without any obligation to take any action.

17. **Borrower's Copy.** Borrower shall be given one copy of the Note and of this Security Instrument.

18. **Transfer of the Property or a Beneficial Interest in Borrower.** As used in this Section 18, "Interest in the Property" means any legal or beneficial interest in the Property, including, but not limited to, those beneficial interests transferred in a bond for deed, contract for deed, installment sales contract or escrow agreement, the intent of which is the transfer of title by Borrower at a future date to a purchaser.

EXHIBIT 6-7
FNMA Residential Mortgage (continued)

If all or any part of the Property or any Interest in the Property is sold or transferred (or if Borrower is not a natural person and a beneficial interest in Borrower is sold or transferred) without Lender's prior written consent, Lender may require immediate payment in full of all sums secured by this Security Instrument. However, this option shall not be exercised by Lender if such exercise is prohibited by Applicable Law.

If Lender exercises this option, Lender shall give Borrower notice of acceleration. The notice shall provide a period of not less than 30 days from the date the notice is given in accordance with Section 15 within which Borrower must pay all sums secured by this Security Instrument. If Borrower fails to pay these sums prior to the expiration of this period, Lender may invoke any remedies permitted by this Security Instrument without further notice or demand on Borrower.

19. **Borrower's Right to Reinstate After Acceleration.** If Borrower meets certain conditions, Borrower shall have the right to have enforcement of this Security Instrument discontinued at any time prior to the earliest of: (a) five days before sale of the Property pursuant to any power of sale contained in this Security Instrument; (b) such other period as Applicable Law might specify for the termination of Borrower's right to reinstate; or (c) entry of a judgment enforcing this Security Instrument. Those conditions are that Borrower: (a) pays Lender all sums which then would be due under this Security Instrument and the Note as if no acceleration had occurred; (b) cures any default of any other covenants or agreements; (c) pays all expenses incurred in enforcing this Security Instrument, including, but not limited to, reasonable attorneys' fees, property inspection and valuation fees, and other fees incurred for the purpose of protecting Lender's interest in the Property and rights under this Security Instrument; and (d) takes such action as Lender may reasonably require to assure that Lender's interest in the Property and rights under this Security Instrument, and Borrower's obligation to pay the sums secured by this Security Instrument, shall continue unchanged. Lender may require that Borrower pay such reinstatement sums and expenses in one or more of the following forms, as selected by Lender: (a) cash; (b) money order; (c) certified check, bank check, treasurer's check or cashier's check, provided any such check is drawn upon an institution whose deposits are insured by a federal agency, instrumentality or entity; or (d) Electronic Funds Transfer. Upon reinstatement by Borrower, this Security Instrument and obligations secured hereby shall remain fully effective as if no acceleration had occurred. However, this right to reinstate shall not apply in the case of acceleration under Section 18.

20. **Sale of Note; Change of Loan Servicer; Notice of Grievance.** The Note or a partial interest in the Note (together with this Security Instrument) can be sold one or more times without prior notice to Borrower. A sale might result in a change in the entity (known as the "Loan Servicer") that collects Periodic Payments due under the Note and this Security Instrument and performs other mortgage loan servicing obligations under the Note, this Security Instrument, and Applicable Law. There also might be one or more changes of the Loan Servicer unrelated to a sale of the Note. If there is a change of the Loan Servicer, Borrower will be given written notice of the change which will state the name and address of the new Loan Servicer, the address to which payments should be made and any other information RESPA requires in connection with a notice of transfer of servicing. If the Note is sold and thereafter the Loan is serviced by a Loan Servicer other than the purchaser of the Note, the mortgage loan servicing obligations to Borrower will remain with the Loan Servicer or be transferred to a successor Loan Servicer and are not assumed by the Note purchaser unless otherwise provided by the Note purchaser.

IOWA--Single Family--Fannie Mae/Freddie Mac UNIFORM INSTRUMENT   Form 3016   1/01   *(page 13 of 16 pages)*

EXHIBIT 6-7
FNMA Residential Mortgage (continued)

Neither Borrower nor Lender may commence, join, or be joined to any judicial action (as either an individual litigant or the member of a class) that arises from the other party's actions pursuant to this Security Instrument or that alleges that the other party has breached any provision of, or any duty owed by reason of, this Security Instrument, until such Borrower or Lender has notified the other party (with such notice given in compliance with the requirements of Section 15) of such alleged breach and afforded the other party hereto a reasonable period after the giving of such notice to take corrective action. If Applicable Law provides a time period which must elapse before certain action can be taken, that time period will be deemed to be reasonable for purposes of this paragraph. The notice of acceleration and opportunity to cure given to Borrower pursuant to Section 22 and the notice of acceleration given to Borrower pursuant to Section 18 shall be deemed to satisfy the notice and opportunity to take corrective action provisions of this Section 20.

21. **Hazardous Substances.** As used in this Section 21: (a) "Hazardous Substances" are those substances defined as toxic or hazardous substances, pollutants, or wastes by Environmental Law and the following substances: gasoline, kerosene, other flammable or toxic petroleum products, toxic pesticides and herbicides, volatile solvents, materials containing asbestos or formaldehyde, and radioactive materials; (b) "Environmental Law" means federal laws and laws of the jurisdiction where the Property is located that relate to health, safety or environmental protection; (c) "Environmental Cleanup" includes any response action, remedial action, or removal action, as defined in Environmental Law; and (d) an "Environmental Condition" means a condition that can cause, contribute to, or otherwise trigger an Environmental Cleanup.

Borrower shall not cause or permit the presence, use, disposal, storage, or release of any Hazardous Substances, or threaten to release any Hazardous Substances, on or in the Property. Borrower shall not do, nor allow anyone else to do, anything affecting the Property (a) that is in violation of any Environmental Law, (b) which creates an Environmental Condition, or (c) which, due to the presence, use, or release of a Hazardous Substance, creates a condition that adversely affects the value of the Property. The preceding two sentences shall not apply to the presence, use, or storage on the Property of small quantities of Hazardous Substances that are generally recognized to be appropriate to normal residential uses and to maintenance of the Property (including, but not limited to, hazardous substances in consumer products).

Borrower shall promptly give Lender written notice of (a) any investigation, claim, demand, lawsuit or other action by any governmental or regulatory agency or private party involving the Property and any Hazardous Substance or Environmental Law of which Borrower has actual knowledge, (b) any Environmental Condition, including but not limited to, any spilling, leaking, discharge, release or threat of release of any Hazardous Substance, and (c) any condition caused by the presence, use or release of a Hazardous Substance which adversely affects the value of the Property. If Borrower learns, or is notified by any governmental or regulatory authority, or any private party, that any removal or other remediation of any Hazardous Substance affecting the Property is necessary, Borrower shall promptly take all necessary remedial actions in accordance with Environmental Law. Nothing herein shall create any obligation on Lender for an Environmental Cleanup.

EXHIBIT 6-7
FNMA Residential Mortgage (continued)

NON-UNIFORM COVENANTS. Borrower and Lender further covenant and agree as follows:

22. **Acceleration; Remedies.** Lender shall give notice to Borrower prior to acceleration following Borrower's breach of any covenant or agreement in this Security Instrument (but not prior to acceleration under Section 18 unless Applicable Law provides otherwise). The notice shall specify: (a) the default; (b) the action required to cure the default; (c) a date, not less than 30 days from the date the notice is given to Borrower, by which the default must be cured; and (d) that failure to cure the default on or before the date specified in the notice may result in acceleration of the sums secured by this Security Instrument, foreclosure by judicial proceeding and sale of the Property. The notice shall further inform Borrower of the right to reinstate after acceleration and the right to assert in the foreclosure proceeding the non-existence of a default or any other defense of Borrower to acceleration and foreclosure. If the default is not cured on or before the date specified in the notice, Lender at its option may require immediate payment in full of all sums secured by this Security Instrument without further demand and may foreclose this Security Instrument by judicial proceeding. Lender shall be entitled to collect all expenses incurred in pursuing the remedies provided in this Section 22, including, but not limited to, reasonable attorneys' fees and costs of title evidence.

23. **Release.** Upon payment of all sums secured by this Security Instrument, Lender shall release this Security Instrument. Lender may charge Borrower a fee for releasing this Security Instrument, but only if the fee is paid to a third party for services rendered and the charging of the fee is permitted under Applicable Law.

24. **Waivers.** Borrower relinquishes all right of dower and waives all right of homestead and distributive share in and to the Property. Borrower waives any right of exemption as to the Property.

25. **HOMESTEAD EXEMPTION WAIVER. I UNDERSTAND THAT HOMESTEAD PROPERTY IS IN MANY CASES PROTECTED FROM THE CLAIMS OF CREDITORS AND EXEMPT FROM JUDICIAL SALE; AND THAT BY SIGNING THIS MORTGAGE, I VOLUNTARILY GIVE UP MY RIGHT TO THIS PROTECTION FOR THIS MORTGAGED PROPERTY WITH RESPECT TO CLAIMS BASED UPON THIS MORTGAGE.**

_____   _____
                                                        [Date]

_____   _____
                                                        [Date]

26. **Redemption Period.** If the Property is less than 10 acres in size and Lender waives in any foreclosure proceeding any right to a deficiency judgment against Borrower, the period of redemption from judicial sale shall be reduced to 6 months. If the court finds that the Property has been abandoned by Borrower and Lender waives any right to a deficiency judgment against Borrower, the period of redemption from judicial sale shall be reduced to 60 days. The provisions of this Section 26 shall be construed to conform to the provisions of Sections 628.26 and 628.27 of the Code of Iowa.

IOWA--Single Family--Fannie Mae/Freddie Mac UNIFORM INSTRUMENT   Form 3016 1/01 *(page 15 of 16 pages)*

EXHIBIT 6–7
FNMA Residential Mortgage (continued)

IMPORTANT: READ BEFORE SIGNING. THE TERMS OF THIS AGREEMENT SHOULD BE READ CAREFULLY BECAUSE ONLY THOSE TERMS IN WRITING ARE ENFORCEABLE. NO OTHER TERMS OR ORAL PROMISES NOT CONTAINED IN THIS WRITTEN CONTRACT MAY BE LEGALLY ENFORCED. YOU MAY CHANGE THE TERMS OF THIS AGREEMENT ONLY BY ANOTHER WRITTEN AGREEMENT.

BY SIGNING BELOW, Borrower accepts and agrees to the terms and covenants contained in this Security Instrument and in any Rider executed by Borrower and recorded with it.

Witnesses:

_____   _____(Seal)
                                                                     - Borrower

_____   _____(Seal)
                                                                    - Borrower

_____ [Space Below This Line for Acknowledgment] _____

IOWA--Single Family--Fannie Mae/Freddie Mac UNIFORM INSTRUMENT   Form 3016   1/01 *(page 16 of 16 pages)*

EXHIBIT 6-8
Georgia Commercial
Deed to Secure Debt

STATE OF GEORGIA

COUNTY OF_____

SECURITY DEED AND AGREEMENT

THIS INDENTURE is made this _____ day of _____, by

and between _____,

party of the first part, hereinafter referred to as "Grantor"; and _____

_____ party of the second part, hereinafter referred to as "Grantee";

WITNESSETH:

FOR AND IN CONSIDERATION of the financial accommodations to Grantor by Grantee resulting in the obligation which is hereinafter more particularly described, and in order to secure that obligation, Grantor hereby grants, bargains, conveys, transfers, assigns and sells unto Grantee the following described land:

TOGETHER WITH ANY AND ALL of the following: (i) all buildings, structures and other improvements now or hereafter located thereon or on any part or parcel thereof and all fixtures affixed or attached, actually or constructively, thereto; (ii) all and singular the tenements, hereditaments, easements and appurtenances belonging thereunto or in any wise appertaining thereto and the reversion and reversions, remainder or remainders thereof; (iii) all rents, issues, income, revenues and profits accruing therefrom, whether now or hereafter due; (iv) all accounts and contract rights now or hereafter arising in connection with any part or parcel thereof or any buildings, structures or improvements now or hereafter located thereon, including without limitation all accounts and contract rights in and to all leases or undertakings to lease now or hereafter affecting the land or any buildings, structures, or improvements thereon; (v) all minerals, flowers, crops, trees, timber, shrubbery and other emblements now or hereafter located thereon or thereunder or on or under any part or parcel thereof; (vi) all estates, rights, title and interest therein, or in any part or parcel thereof; (vii) all equipment, machinery, apparatus, fittings, fixtures whether actually or constructively attached thereto and including all trade, domestic and ornamental fixtures, furniture, furnishings and all personal property of every kind or description whatsoever now or hereafter located thereon, or in or on the buildings, structures and other improvements thereon, and used in connection with the operation and maintenance thereof, and all additions thereto and replacements thereof; and (viii) all building materials, supplies, goods and equipment delivered thereto and placed thereon for the purpose of being affixed to or installed or incorporated or otherwise used in the buildings, structures or other improvements now or hereafter located thereon or any part or parcel thereof. All of the foregoing are hereinafter sometimes referred to collectively as the "Premises."

TO HAVE AND TO HOLD the Premises to the only proper use, benefit and behoof of Grantee, forever, in fee simple.

GRANTOR WARRANTS that Grantor has good title to the Premises, that Grantor is lawfully seized and possessed of the Premises, that Grantor has the right to convey the Premises, that the Premises are unencumbered except as may be herein expressly provided and that Grantor shall forever warrant and defend the title to the Premises unto Grantee against the claims of all persons whomsoever.

THIS INSTRUMENT IS A DEED passing legal title pursuant to the laws of the State of Georgia governing deeds to secure debt and a security agreement granting a security interest pursuant to the Uniform Commercial Code of the State of Georgia, and it is not a mortgage. This deed and security agreement is made and intended to secure: (i) an obligation of Grantor to Grantee evidenced as follows:

(ii) any and all renewal or renewals, extension or extensions, modification or modifications thereof, and substitution or substitutions therefor, either in whole or in part; and (iii) all indebtedness now or hereafter owing by Grantor to Grantee, however or whenever created, incurred, arising or evidenced, whether direct or indirect, joint or several, absolute or contingent, or due or to become due, and any and all renewal or renewals, extension or extensions, modification or modifications of and substitution or substitutions for, said indebtedness, either in whole or in part. The obligations which this deed and security agreement is given to secure are hereinafter sometimes referred to collectively as the "Indebtedness." This deed and security agreement is hereinafter sometimes referred to as this "Security Deed."

GRANTOR COVENANTS AND AGREES: (1) *Junior Encumbrances:* Grantor shall not create or permit to exist any liens or encumbrances on the Premises which are junior and inferior in terms of priority to this Security Deed. (2) *Payments by Grantor:* Grantor shall pay, when due and payable: (i) the Indebtedness in accordance with the terms and conditions of the instruments evidencing the same; (ii) all taxes, all assessments, general or special, and all other charges levied on or assessed or placed or made against the Premises, this Security Deed, the Indebtedness or any interest of Grantee in the Premises, this Security Deed or the Indebtedness; (iii) premiums on policies of fire and casualty insurance covering the Premises, as required by this Security Deed; (iv) premiums on all life insurance policies now or hereafter pledged as collateral for the Indebtedness or any part thereof; (v) premiums for all liability, rental, mortgage and flood insurance policies required by this Security Deed or now or hereafter required by Grantee in connection with the Premises or the Indebtedness or any part of either; and (vi) all ground rents, lease rentals and other payments respecting the Premises payable by Grantor. Grantor shall promptly deliver to Grantee, upon request by Grantee, receipts showing payment in full of all the foregoing items; provided, however, that Grantee shall not require a receipt showing payment in full of the Indebtedness. In the event any state, federal, municipal or other governmental law, order, rule or regulation becomes effective subsequent to the date hereof and in any manner changes or modifies the laws in force on the date hereof governing the taxation of the Indebtedness or the manner of collecting the taxes thereon so as to adversely affect Grantee by requiring that a payment or payments be made or other action be taken to protect Grantee's interest under this Security Deed or the Indebtedness, Grantor shall promptly pay any amounts required on or before the date the same are due or take any other action required on or before the date any such action must be taken. (3) *Grantee's Acts on Behalf of Grantor:* In the event Grantor shall either fail or refuse to pay or cause to be paid, as the same shall become due and payable, any item (including all items specified at Paragraph (2) immediately above) which Grantor is required to pay hereunder or which Grantor may pay to cure an event of default hereunder, or in the event Grantor shall either fail or refuse to do or perform any act which Grantor is obligated to do or perform hereunder or which Grantor may do or perform to cure an event of default hereunder, then Grantee, at Grantee's option, may make such payment or do or perform such act on behalf of Grantor. All such payments made by Grantee and all costs and expenses incurred by Grantee in doing or performing all such acts shall be and shall become part of the Indebtedness secured hereby and shall bear interest at the highest rate per annum then being charged with respect to any part of the Indebtedness secured hereby from the date paid or incurred by Grantee, and such interest thereon shall also be part of the Indebtedness secured hereby. (4) *Further Assurances:* Grantor shall, at any time and from time to time upon request by Grantee, make, execute and deliver, or cause to be made, executed and delivered, any and all other and further instruments, documents, certificates, agreements, letters, representations and other writings which may be necessary or desirable, in the opinion of Grantee, in order to effectuate, complete, correct, perfect or continue and preserve the obligations of Grantor under the Indebtedness and the lien and security interest of Grantee hereunder. Grantor shall upon request by Grantee certify in writing to Grantee, or to any proposed assignee of this Security Deed, the amount of principal and interest then owing on the Indebtedness and whether or not any set-offs or defenses exist against all or any part of the Indebtedness.

EXHIBIT 6–8
Georgia Commercial Deed to Secure Debt (continued)

(5) *Rents and Leases:* Grantor hereby transfers, assigns and conveys unto Grantee all of Grantor's right, title and interest in and to all leases or undertakings to lease now or hereafter existing or made, and all other agreements for use or occupancy, with respect to the Premises or any part thereof, and grants to Grantee a security interest in all rents, issues, income, revenues, profits, accounts and contract rights due or to become due thereunder or otherwise deriving from the use and occupancy of the Premises. Grantor shall faithfully perform the covenants of Grantor as lessor under all present and future leases of all or any portion of the Premises and shall not do, neglect to do, or permit to be done, anything which may cause the termination of such leases, or any of them, or which may diminish or impair their value or the rents provided for therein or the interest of Grantor or Grantee therein or thereunder. Grantor, without first obtaining the written consent of Grantee, shall not further assign the rents, issues, income, revenues, profits, accounts or contract rights from the Premises or any part thereof, shall not consent to the cancellation or surrender of any lease of the Premises or any part thereof now existing or hereafter to be made, shall not modify any such lease so as to shorten the unexpired term thereof or so as to decrease the amount of the rent payable thereunder and shall not collect rents from the Premises or any part thereof for more than one month in advance. Grantor shall procure and deliver to Grantee upon request estoppel letters or certificates from each lessee, tenant, occupant in possession and other user of the Premises or any part thereof, as required by and in form and substance satisfactory to Grantee, and shall deliver to Grantee a recordable assignment of all of Grantor's interest in all leases now or hereafter existing or made with respect to the Premises or any part thereof, which assignment shall be in form and substance satisfactory to Grantee, together with proof of due service of a copy of such assignment on each lessee, tenant, occupant in possession or other user of the Premises or any part thereof. (6) *Maintenance and Repair:* Grantor shall maintain the Premises in good condition and repair, shall not commit or suffer any waste to the Premises, and shall comply with, or cause to be complied with, all statutes, ordinances, rules, regulations and directives of any governmental authority relating to the Premises or any part thereof or the use or occupancy of the Premises or any part thereof. No part of the Premises, including but not limited to any buildings, structures, parking lots, driveways or other improvements now or hereafter constructed on the land which is part of the Premises, shall be removed, demolished or materially altered without the prior written consent of Grantee. If at any time during the continuance of the Indebtedness any addition, alteration, change, repair, reconstruction or other work on the Premises of any nature, structural or otherwise, becomes necessary or desirable because of damage to or destruction of the Premises or any part thereof, the entire expense thereof, regardless of when the same shall be incurred or become due, shall be the sole obligation and responsibility of Grantor, and Grantor shall pay the entire expense thereof promptly when due. (7) *Hazard and Liability Insurance:* Grantor shall keep the Premises insured against loss or damage by fire and such other casualties and risks as the Grantee may require from time to time, with such companies, in such amounts and under such forms of policies as Grantee may approve. Such policies shall insure Grantee's interest in the Premises, name Grantee as an insured party thereunder, provide that losses thereunder shall be payable to Grantee pursuant to such forms of loss payable clauses as Grantee may approve and provide that no cancellation or reduction in coverage shall be effective unless the insuror first gives Grantee thirty (30) days prior written notice. Irrespective of the insurance required and approved by Grantee, Grantor shall assign and deliver to Grantee, as additional collateral for the payment of the Indebtedness, all policies of insurance which insure against loss or damage to the Premises, and Grantor hereby grants to Grantee a security interest in the proceeds from any and all such policies. Grantor shall also procure and maintain public liability insurance coverage with such companies, in such amounts and under such forms of policies as Grantee may approve, naming Grantee as an additional insured thereunder and providing that no cancellation or reduction in coverage thereunder shall be effective unless the insuror first gives Grantee thirty (30) days prior written notice. Forthwith upon the issuance of all such policies, Grantor shall deliver the same to Grantee together with evidence satisfactory to Grantee that the premiums therefor have been paid. Within fifteen (15) days prior to the expiration date of each such policy, Grantor shall deliver to Grantee a renewal policy together with evidence satisfactory to Grantee that the premium therefor has been paid. In the event of a foreclosure and sale by Grantee of the Premises, the purchaser of the Premises shall succeed to all rights of Grantor in and to such policies, including the right to the refund of unearned premiums and to dividends thereunder, and Grantee may, at Grantee's election, assign and deliver the policies to such purchaser without any warranty or representation, express or implied, and without recourse. In the event of damage to or destruction of the Premises or any part thereof, Grantee may adjust, settle or compromise claims under such policies, and the proceeds therefrom shall be paid to Grantee. Grantee, at Grantee's option and in Grantee's sole discretion, may either (i) apply the proceeds or any part thereof to the Indebtedness or (ii) require Grantor to repair, replace or reconstruct the Premises or any part thereof and disburse the proceeds to Grantor to be applied against the costs and expenses thereof as incurred or paid by Grantor. (8) *Flood Insurance:* Grantor represents and has certified to Grantee that no part of the Premises lies within a "special flood hazard area" as defined and specified by the United States Department of Housing and Urban Development pursuant to the Flood Disaster Protection Act of 1973. In the event Grantee determines that the rules or regulations of the Federal Reserve Board, the Comptroller of the Currency or any other governing agency licensing or regulating the operations of Grantee require that flood insurance coverage be obtained for the Premises or any part thereof in order for Grantee to comply with such rules or regulations or with the Flood Disaster Protection Act of 1973 as then in effect, then Grantor, upon receiving written notice from Grantee of such determination: (i) shall promptly purchase and pay the premiums for such flood insurance policies as Grantee deems required by such agency or agencies so that Grantee shall be deemed in compliance with the rules and regulations of such agency or agencies and with the Flood Disaster Protection Act of 1973 as then in effect; and (ii) shall deliver such policies to Grantee together with evidence satisfactory to Grantee that the premiums therefor have been paid. Such policies of flood insurance shall be in a form satisfactory to Grantee, shall name Grantee as an insured thereunder, shall provide that losses thereunder be payable to Grantee pursuant to such forms of loss payable clause as Grantee may approve, shall be for an amount at least equal to the Indebtedness or the maximum limit of coverage made available with respect to the Premises under the National Flood Insurance Act of 1968, as amended, whichever is less, and shall be noncancellable as to Grantee except upon thirty (30) days prior written notice given by the insuror to Grantee. Within ten (10) days prior to the expiration date of each such flood insurance policy, Grantor shall deliver to Grantee a renewal policy or endorsement together with evidence satisfactory to Grantee that the premium therefor has been paid. (9) *Condemnation:* To the extent of the Indebtedness, Grantor grants to Grantee a security interest in any and all payments, awards, judgments or settlements, including interest thereon, to which Grantor may be or may become entitled or which Grantee may receive by reason of injury or damage to, or loss of, the Premises or any part thereof as a result of the exercise of the right of eminent domain. Notwithstanding any injury or damage to, or loss of, the Premises or any part thereof as a result of the exercise of the right of eminent domain, Grantor shall continue to pay the Indebtedness. All sums paid or payable to Grantor by reason of any injury or damage to, or loss of, the Premises or any part thereof as a result of the exercise of the right of eminent domain shall be delivered to Grantee and Grantee, at Grantee's option and at Grantee's sole discretion, may either (i) apply the sum or any part thereof to the Indebtedness or (ii) require Grantor to repair, replace or reconstruct the Premises or any part thereof and disburse such sums to Grantor to be applied against the costs and expenses thereof as incurred or paid by Grantor. (10) *Inspection:* Grantor shall permit any person designated by Grantee to visit and inspect the Premises, to examine the books of account and other records of Grantor with respect to the Premises, and to discuss the affairs, finances and accounts of Grantor with and to be advised as to the same by Grantor or a knowledgeable and duly authorized representative of Grantor, all at such reasonable times and intervals as Grantee may desire. (11) *Restriction on Transfer:* Unless Grantee gives its written consent thereto and such consent is recorded in the public deed records of the Clerk of the Superior Court of the county in which this Security Deed is recorded, Grantor shall not grant, bargain, convey, transfer, assign, exchange or sell all or any portion of Grantor's interest in the Premises prior to the satisfaction and release by Grantee of this Security Deed.

EVENTS OF DEFAULT hereunder shall be the occurrence of any one or more of the following: (1) *Payment of Indebtedness:* Failure of Grantor to pay the Indebtedness or any part thereof when and as the same shall become due and payable, whether at the due date thereof or at a date fixed for prepayment or at a date fixed by reason of acceleration of the due date thereof or otherwise; (2) *Other Payments and Terms:* Failure of Grantor to make any payment (other than on the Indebtedness) required hereunder or to observe, perform, or comply with any of the covenants, terms or conditions set forth herein, or in any other instrument, document, agreement, letter or other writing heretofore, concurrently herewith or in the future executed by Grantor in favor of Grantee in connection with any transaction which resulted in the Indebtedness or any part thereof; (3) *False Statements:* If any certificate, representation, warranty, statement or other writing made herein or heretofore, now or hereafter furnished to Grantee by or on behalf of Grantor in connection with any transaction which resulted in the Indebtedness or any part thereof be false, untrue, incomplete or misleading in any respect as of the date made; (4) *Waste:* If the Premises or any part thereof should be subject to actual or threatened waste, or any part thereof be removed, demolished, or materially damaged or altered as a result of which the value of the Premises shall be diminished; (5) *Seizure or Levy:* If the Premises or any part thereof be seized or levied upon under legal process or a receiver be appointed for the Premises or any part thereof or for Grantor; (6) *Liens:* If any Federal tax lien or any claim of lien for labor, material or architectural or engineering services furnished or alleged to have been furnished in the improvement of or with respect to the Premises is filed of record against Grantor or the Premises and is not removed from record by payment or bond within thirty (30) days from the date of such filing; (7) *Priority Claim:* If any person shall assert any claim of priority over this Security Deed in any legal or equitable proceeding, and such claim shall not have been dismissed with prejudice within sixty (60) days after the filing thereof; (8) *Insolvency or Bankruptcy:* If Grantor shall become insolvent or make an assignment for benefit of creditors; or if Grantor should file a petition for bankruptcy or an arrangement pursuant to the Federal Bankruptcy Act or any similar statute, or if Grantor be adjudicated a bankrupt or an insolvent; or if any proceeding is instituted against or on behalf of Grantor alleging that Grantor is insolvent or unable to pay Grantor's debts as they mature; or if a petition for the bankruptcy or arrangement of Grantor, pursuant to the Federal Bankruptcy Act or any similar statute is filed; (9) *Receiver:* If there should be appointed a receiver, liquidator or trustee for Grantor or for any property of Grantor; (10) *Judgments:* If any judgment is rendered against Grantor which is not paid in full and satisfied or is not appealed from within the time allowed for appeals and paid in full and satisfied when it becomes final; (11) *Liquidation or Dissolution:* Should Grantor, if a corporation, be liquidated or dissolved or its articles of incorporation expire or be revoked, or, if a partnership or business association, be dissolved or partitioned, or, if a trust, be terminated or expire.

- 2 -

EXHIBIT 6-8
Georgia Commercial
Deed to Secure Debt
(continued)

GRANTEE'S REMEDIES AND POWER OF SALE upon the occurrence of an event of default shall be that, at Grantee's option and election without notice to Grantor, Grantee may declare all or any portion of the Indebtedness to be immediately due and payable, whereupon the same shall be and shall become due and payable forthwith without presentment, demand, protest or notice of any kind, all of which are expressly waived by Grantor, and Grantee, at Grantee's option and election, may do any one or more of the following: (1) *Entry and Possession:* Grantee may enter upon the Premises or any part thereof and take possession thereof, excluding therefrom Grantor and all agents, employees and representatives of Grantor; employ a manager of the Premises or any part thereof; hold, store, use, operate, manage, control, maintain and lease the Premises or any part thereof; conduct business thereon; make all necessary and appropriate repairs, renewals, and replacements; keep the Premises insured; or carry out or enter into agreements of any kind with respect to the Premises. (2) *Collection of Rents:* Grantee may collect and receive all rents, issues, income, revenues, profits, accounts and contract rights from the Premises and apply the same to the Indebtedness, after deducting therefrom all costs, charges, and expenses of taking, holding, managing, and operating the Premises, including the fees and expenses of Grantee's attorneys, and agents. (3) *Payments:* Grantee may pay any sum or sums deemed necessary or appropriate by Grantee to protect the Premises or any part thereof or Grantee's interest therein. (4) *Other Remedies:* Grantee may exercise all rights and remedies contained in any other instrument, document, agreement or other writing, heretofore, concurrently herewith or in the future executed by Grantor in favor of Grantee in connection with the transactions resulting in the Indebtedness or any part thereof. (5) *Appointment of Receiver:* Grantee may make application to any court and be entitled to the appointment of a receiver to take charge of the Premises or any part thereof without alleging or proving, or having any consideration given to, the insolvency of Grantor, the value of the Premises as security for the Indebtedness or any other matter usually incident to the appointment of a receiver. (6) *U.C.C. Remedies:* With respect to the personal property in which a security interest is herein granted, Grantee may exercise any or all of the rights accruing to a secured party under this Security Deed, the Uniform Commercial Code (§§109A-9-101 *et. seq.* of the Ga. Code Annotated) and any other applicable law. Grantor shall, if Grantee requests, assemble all such personal property and make it available to Grantee at a place or places to be designated by Grantee, which shall be reasonably convenient to Grantor and Grantee. Any notice required to be given by Grantee of a public or private sale, lease or other disposition of the personal property or any other intended action by Grantee may be personally delivered to Grantor or may be deposited in the United States mail with postage prepaid duly addressed to Grantor at the address of Grantor last known to Grantee at least five (5) business days prior to such proposed action, and shall constitute reasonable and fair notice to Grantor of any such action. (7) *Power of Sale:* Grantee may sell the Premises, or any part thereof or any interest therein separately, at Grantee's discretion, with or without taking possession thereof, at public sale before the courthouse door of the county in which the Premises, or a part thereof, is located, to the highest bidder for cash, after first giving notice of the time, place and terms of such sale by advertisement published once a week for four weeks (without regard for the number of days) in a newspaper in which advertisements of sheriff's sales are published in such county. The advertisement so published shall be notice to Grantor, and Grantor hereby waives all other notices. Grantee may bid and purchase at any such sale, and Grantee may execute and deliver to the purchaser or purchasers at any such sale a sufficient conveyance of the Premises, or the part thereof or interest therein sold. Grantee's conveyance may contain recitals as to the occurrence of any event of default under this Security Deed, which recitals shall be presumptive evidence that all preliminary acts prerequisite to such sale and conveyance were in all things duly complied with. The recitals made by Grantee shall be binding and conclusive upon Grantor, and the sale and conveyance made by Grantee shall divest Grantor of all right, title, interest and equity that Grantor may have had in, to and under the Premises, or the part thereof or interest therein sold, and shall vest the same in the purchaser or purchasers at such sale. Grantee may hold one or more sales hereunder until the Indebtedness has been satisfied in full. Grantor hereby constitutes and appoints Grantee as Grantor's agent and attorney-in-fact to make such sale, to execute and deliver such conveyance and to make such recitals, and Grantor hereby ratifies and confirms all of the acts and doings of Grantee as Grantor's agent and attorney-in-fact hereunder. Grantee's agency and power as attorney-in-fact hereunder are coupled with an interest, cannot be revoked by insolvency, incompetency, death or otherwise, and shall not be exhausted until the Indebtedness has been satisfied in full. The proceeds of each sale by Grantee hereunder shall be applied first to the costs and expenses of the sale and of all proceedings in connection therewith, including attorney's fees if applicable, then to the payment of the Indebtedness, and the remainder, if any, shall be paid to Grantor. If the proceeds of any sale are not sufficient to pay the Indebtedness in full, Grantee shall determine, at Grantee's option and in Grantee's discretion, the portions of the Indebtedness to which the proceeds (after deducting therefrom the costs and expenses of the sale and all proceedings in connection therewith) shall be applied and in what order the proceeds shall be so applied. Grantor covenants and agrees that, in the event of any sale pursuant to the agency and power herein granted, Grantor shall be and become a tenant holding over and shall deliver possession of the Premises, or the part thereof or interest therein sold, to the purchaser or purchasers at the sale or be summarily dispossessed in accordance with the provisions of law applicable to tenants holding over.

All rights and remedies set forth above are cumulative and in addition to any right or remedy provided for by statute, or now or hereafter existing at law or in equity, including without limitation the right of Grantee to collect or enforce the Indebtedness with or without taking any action with respect to the Premises. Grantee may, at Grantee's election and at Grantee's discretion, exercise each and every such right and remedy concurrently or separately.

ADDITIONAL PROVISIONS of this Security Deed, constituting additional covenants and agreements by Grantor, are as follows: (1) *Applicable Law:* This Security Deed shall be governed by and construed, interpreted and enforced in accordance with the laws of the State of Georgia. (2) *Forbearance:* Grantee shall not be deemed to waive any of Grantee's rights or remedies hereunder unless such waiver be in writing and signed by or on behalf of Grantee. No delay, omission or forbearance by Grantee in exercising any of Grantee's rights or remedies shall operate as a waiver of such rights or remedies, and a waiver in writing on one occasion shall not be construed as a consent to or a waiver of any right or any remedy on any future occasion. (3) *Time:* Time is and shall be of the essence of this Security Deed and the covenants and agreements by Grantor. (4) *Captions:* Any captions or heading preceding the text of separate sections, paragraphs and sub-paragraphs hereof are solely for reference purposes and shall not affect the meaning, construction, interpretation or effect of the text. (5) *Notices:* All notices, requests, demands and other communications hereunder shall be in writing and shall be deemed to have been duly given to Grantor if personally delivered or if mailed in the United States mail, by certified mail with a return receipt requested and with postage prepaid, to Grantor's last address known to Grantee. (6) *Severability:* In the event that any of the terms, provisions or covenants of this Security Deed are held to be partially or wholly invalid or unenforceable for any reason whatsoever, such holding shall not affect, alter, modify or impair in any manner whatsoever any of the other terms, provisions or covenants hereof not held to be partially or wholly invalid or unenforceable. (7) *Definitions:* The word "Grantor" as used herein shall include the plural should more than one Grantor execute this document; the masculine and feminine gender, regardless of the sex of Grantor or any of them; individuals, partnerships, joint ventures, corporations and other legal entities should such an entity execute this document; and the heirs, legal representatives, successors and assigns of Grantor. If more than one party shall execute this Security Deed, the word "Grantor" shall mean all parties signing, and each of them, and each and every agreement and obligation of Grantor shall be and mean the joint and several undertaking of each of them. The word "Grantee" as used herein shall include the transferees, successors, legal representatives and assigns of Grantee, and all rights of Grantee hereunder shall inure to the benefit of its transferees, successors, legal representatives and assigns. (8) *Other Provisions:* The terms and conditions set forth in Exhibit "B", if any, attached hereto are incorporated herein and made a part hereof by reference.

GRANTOR EXPRESSLY WAIVES the following: (1) *Notice and Hearing:* Any right Grantor may have under the Constitution of the State of Georgia or the Constitution of the United States of America to notice or to a judicial hearing prior to the exercise of any right or remedy provided to Grantee by this Security Deed, and Grantor waives Grantor's rights, if any, to set aside or invalidate any sale under power duly consummated in accordance with the provisions of this Security Deed on the ground (if such be the case) that the sale was consummated without prior notice or judicial hearing or both; and (2) all homestead exemption rights, if any, which Grantor or Grantor's family may have pursuant to the Constitution and laws of the United States, the State of Georgia or any other State of the United States, in and to the Premises as against the collection of the Indebtedness, or any part thereof. All waivers by Grantor in this paragraph have been made voluntarily, intelligently and knowingly by Grantor, after Grantor has been afforded an opportunity to be informed by counsel of Grantor's choice as to possible alternative rights. Grantor's execution of this Security Deed shall be conclusive evidence of the making of such waivers and that such waivers have been voluntarily, intelligently and knowingly made.

IN WITNESS WHEREOF, this Security Deed has been executed and sealed by Grantor the day and year first above written.

Signed, sealed and delivered
in the presence of:

_____(SEAL)

_____
Unofficial Witness

_____(SEAL)

_____
Notary Public

_____(SEAL)

Commercial Loan Department

Security Deed Form No. _____

_____(SEAL)

First Priority Lien Position

(Second Priority By Attaching Exhibit "B")

Title Examinations

"Titles are shadows."

—Daniel Defoe

OBJECTIVES

After reading this chapter you should be able to:

- Recognize the importance of title examinations
- Explain the three types of recording statutes
- Understand the process and procedures involved in conducting a title examination
- Review a title examination report

One of the main responsibilities of a real estate attorney or legal assistant is to make certain that a client has good title of ownership to real property. A real estate attorney representing a purchaser will insist that the seller produce satisfactory evidence of good title before the purchase. A real estate attorney representing a lender will insist that the borrower produce satisfactory evidence of good title before the loan is made. Typically, this evidence of good title of ownership is provided by a **title examination** of the public real property records and the issuance of title insurance.

The role of the legal assistant in title examinations varies from state to state, and even among law firms within a given state. In some law firms a legal assistant conducts the title examination. A real estate closing legal assistant usually does not conduct the examination, but is responsible for ordering the title examination, reviewing it, and converting it into a title insurance commitment, as discussed in Chapter 8. Regardless of whether the legal assistant is performing, ordering, or reviewing the title examination, an understanding of the process and procedures involved is essential for the legal assistant to carry out his or her responsibilities.

BONA FIDE PURCHASER FOR VALUE RULE

Why examine the public records of real property to obtain proof of ownership of property? Why record real estate documents? Warranty deeds, contracts, leases, mortgages, and easements are all enforceable without recording. Real estate attorneys and legal assistants, however, spend substantial time preparing these documents and having them executed with the formality required to place the documents on public record. Why? The answer is the common law **bona fide purchaser for value** rule. This rule states that anyone who purchases property in good faith for valuable consideration and without notice of any claim to or interest in the property by any other party is a bona fide purchaser, and takes the property free and clear of any claims to or interests in the property by other parties.

For example, Sam Owner has pledged his farm to secure a debt owed to Aunt Owner. Sam Owner has executed and delivered to Aunt Owner a mortgage on the farm, but the mortgage was not recorded. Sam Owner sells the farm to Catherine Purchaser. At the time of the sale Catherine Purchaser is unaware of the unrecorded mortgage to Aunt Owner. Catherine Purchaser is a bona fide purchaser for value and purchases the farm free and clear of Aunt Owner's mortgage. Aunt Owner's mortgage is unenforceable against the farm after the sale to Catherine Purchaser.

---

title examination
Examination of the real property records to determine the ownership to a particular tract of real property.

bona fide purchaser for value
Person who purchases real property in good faith for valuable consideration without notice of any claim to or interest in the real property by any other party.

A bona fide purchaser must pay something of value for the property, although the consideration paid need not be equal to the market value of the property. The person taking title to property by inheritance or as a recipient of a gift has not given valuable consideration, and therefore is not protected as a bona fide purchaser. This means that a person who has inherited real property takes the real property subject to all valid claims against the real property, regardless of whether the person had notice of the claims or whether the claims were recorded.

The bona fide purchaser status provides special protection not only to the bona fide purchaser, but also to anyone purchasing from the bona fide purchaser. The protection is extended to the subsequent purchaser whether or not the subsequent purchaser has notice of any prior adverse claim or interest to the property. The rationale for the extended protection is to permit the bona fide purchaser to sell the property for full value.

A bona fide purchaser for value receives ownership to real property subject to any and all claims of which the bona fide purchaser has actual or constructive notice of at the time the property is acquired. **Actual notice** occurs when the purchaser has direct knowledge or information about title matters. Actual notice includes any facts that the purchaser can see with his or her own eyes, any facts that the purchaser learns about the property, or any information the circumstances of which should put the purchaser on duty to conduct an investigation that would lead to the finding of certain facts in regard to the property.

actual notice
Title matters that a purchaser has direct knowledge or information about.

Constructive notice is a presumption of law that charges a purchaser with the responsibility of learning about all title matters that would result from an inspection of the property or an examination of the public real property records. Possession of land is notice to the world of the possessor's rights therein. For possession to constitute notice, it must be open, notorious, and exclusive. For example, a purchaser of a supposedly vacant lot of real property visits the lot and finds an inhabited mobile home on the lot. The purchaser is placed on notice to inquire about the mobile home inhabitant's rights to the property. If the mobile home inhabitants have a fifty-year unrecorded lease of the property, the prospective purchaser would purchase the property subject to the fifty-year lease, and the inhabitants of the mobile home would be permitted to remain on the property until the lease terminated. A purchaser of real property has a duty to inquire as to a party in possession's rights to the property. If no inquiries are made, the purchaser takes the property subject to any rights the possessor may have. A prudent purchaser will satisfy the constructive notice requirements of inspection by either inspecting the property or obtaining a full survey of the property by a registered land surveyor, or both.

constructive notice
A presumption of law that charges a person with notice of all title matters that can be discovered from an inspection of the real property or an examination of public real property records.

The second form of constructive notice is in regard to matters that an inspection of the public real property records would reveal. All states maintain public real property records for the purpose of recording real estate documents and establishing ownership to real property. A prudent purchaser will satisfy the constructive notice requirements by examining the public records in which the documents are recorded.

Constructive notice is imparted to the purchaser only to the extent that recorded instruments are in the **chain of title.** A chain of title is the sequence of subsequent owners to a particular piece of property, beginning with the original owner and moving through all successive grantors and grantees to the current owner. The chain of title concept limits the number of records imparting constructive notice and the number of records that must be examined. Courts in the states of Massachusetts and New York have pronounced views on the definition of "chain of title." The laws in other states follow either the Massachusetts or the New York definition. Under the Massachusetts definition of chain of title a purchaser need only examine conveyances from the point at which each owner received the property and until that owner conveyed the property to another owner. All other transactions are considered to be outside the chain of title, and are held not to provide constructive notice to a purchaser. Under the New York definition of chain of title the purchaser must examine all instruments made by successive owners, and not merely the instruments made during the ownership.

chain of title
Historical sequence of all owners to a particular tract of real property beginning with the original owner and all successive owners who have derived their title from the original owner.

Constructive notice also is imparted to unrecorded instruments that are referred to in a recorded instrument. For example, a recorded deed may make reference to an unrecorded mortgage. The purchaser must exercise reasonable diligence and prudence to ascertain the contents of the unrecorded mortgage, as he or she may be responsible to pay the debt secured by the mortgage.

In summary, if a person obtains an interest in property by way of being a purchaser, a lender of a security deed or mortgage, the holder of an easement, or so on, the only way this property interest can be protected against subsequent purchasers is to record the deed, easement, mortgage, or instrument in the proper records. The act of recording the instrument in its proper place will place future purchasers on constructive notice. These future purchasers will purchase the property subject to the rights of the holder of the recorded instrument.

Recording an instrument is essential to impart constructive notice. The time and location for such recordings normally are expressed in what is known as a state's recording statute. It is not always clear when an instrument is deemed recorded so as to impart constructive notice. Some courts have held that merely depositing the instrument in the office of the recorder is sufficient to impart constructive notice. Other courts have held that to impart constructive notice, the instrument must actually be transcribed in a permanent record book.

There also is a split of authority as to notice when an error has occurred in transcribing the instrument into the permanent record book. Some courts have imposed a duty on the person recording the instrument to make sure that it is correctly recorded, and such person shall bear full risk of the failure of the registrar of deeds to correctly record the instrument. An examination of the title records after the instrument has been recorded is necessary to discharge the duty. The examination is for the purpose of confirming that the recorded document has been correctly recorded and is in the chain of title. Under this view, the registrar of deeds is deemed to be the agent of the recording party. According to this view, an incorrectly recorded instrument does not impart constructive notice.[1]

Other courts have held that when an instrument is filed, constructive notice is given, regardless of whether the instrument was correctly indexed or recorded, provided that the party recording the instrument has compiled with the state's recording statute and that the mistake was made by the clerk's or registrar's office.

RECORDING STATUTES

The common law bona fide purchaser for value rule has been modified in many states by **recording statutes.** Recording statutes (a) give the community notice of the changes in ownership of the property; (b) protect subsequent purchasers and encumbrancers of property from the same common grantor by giving them notice of information contained in the recorded documents; and (c) determine priority among conflicting claims to real property.

There are three types of recording statutes: race, notice, and race-notice. The first type is used by the least number of states. Under the race statute, priority between successive grantees of the same land from a common grantor is determined by who wins the race to the recording office. No notice is imparted to a subsequent purchaser or encumbrancer until the instrument is recorded in the prescribed manner. The first to record an instrument has priority of title, irrespective of whether he or she was a prior or subsequent purchaser. Moreover, a purchaser with actual knowledge of a prior, but unrecorded, instrument from a common grantor of the same property will have priority if such subsequent purchaser is the first to record his or her instrument. For example, Alice Owner conveys her home to Paul Purchaser by deed dated March 1. Paul Purchaser does not record the deed until March 4. Alice Owner on March 2 conveys the same home to Doris Purchaser. Doris receives the deed to the home on March 2 with full knowledge that a deed had been given by Alice Owner on the previous day to Paul Purchaser. Doris Purchaser records the deed to the home on March 3. Under a race recording statute, Doris Purchaser would be the owner of the property, since Doris Purchaser recorded the deed to the property before the recording of the deed by Paul Purchaser.

The notice type of recording statute relies on the notice given by the recording of the instrument or on the notice obtained through means other than recording. Under the notice statute the grantee of a deed is not required to record the deed to obtain the priority in title over some subsequent purchaser of the same property. The notice statute provides that an unrecorded instrument is valid to a subsequent purchaser when the purchaser paid value with a notice of the unrecorded instrument, and is invalid if the subsequent purchaser paid value

recording statutes
State statutes that regulate the recordation of real property documents.

[1] Robert S. Maxwell and David B. Summers, "Recording Statutes: Their Operation and Effect," *Washburn Law Journal* 17 (1978): pp. 615–637. By permission of *Washburn Law Journal.*

without notice of the unrecorded instrument. Therefore, actual knowledge by a subsequent purchaser of the existence of a prior unrecorded document serves as notice in the same manner as the proper recording of the document. For example, Aaron Owner conveys his property to Hans Purchaser by deed dated January 1. Hans Purchaser neglects to record the deed promptly. On February 1 Aaron conveys the same property to Cindy Buyer, who has full knowledge of the deed to Hans. Cindy's deed is recorded on February 2. Thereafter, Hans on March 1 records the deed from Aaron dated January 1. Hans has priority of title even though Hans has the later recorded deed. This is so because Cindy had actual knowledge of the conveyance from Aaron to Hans at the time Cindy received Aaron's deed from Aaron.

The race-notice recording statute is the most common type. It combines the theory and recording requirements of both the race recording statute and the notice recording statute. The race-notice statute combines the theory that knowledge of a prior unrecorded instrument serves as notice in the same manner as the proper recording of the instrument with the recording principle that the first party to record an instrument has priority of title, regardless of whether that person was a prior or subsequent purchaser. Thus, under a race-notice statute, a subsequent purchaser has priority over the holder of a prior, but unrecorded, instrument if such subsequent purchaser makes the purchase without notice of the prior unrecorded instrument and records the instrument before the recording of the prior instrument. This type of recording statute operates as a pure notice statute until a subsequent purchaser takes title from the common grantor as a bona fide purchaser without notice of the prior recorded instrument. On that occurrence the race-notice statute operates as a pure race statute in determining priority solely on the basis of which party records first.

The following is an example of the effect of the various recording statutes on the same factual course of events: Alice Owner conveys her home to Ajax Purchaser on March 1. Ajax Purchaser does not record the deed until March 3. On March 2 Alice Owner conveys the same home to Elena Purchaser, who purchases the home on March 2 with no knowledge of the March 1 deed from Alice Owner to Ajax Purchaser. Elena Purchaser does not record her deed until March 4. Under a race-notice statute Ajax would have priority of title and would be the owner of the home because Ajax purchased the home without notice of any other claims and was the first to record the deed to the home. Under a notice statute Elena would have priority of title and would be the owner of the home because Elena was a purchaser without notice of the prior unrecorded deed to Ajax, and the subsequent recording by Ajax does not divest the title and ownership existing in Elena. Under a race statute Ajax would have priority and be the owner of the home because Ajax was the first to record a deed.

City of Richland Hills v. Bertelsen discusses both the concept of bona fide purchaser for value and the policy issues behind recording statutes.

 **C A S E** | **City of Richland Hills v. Bertelsen**
724 S.W. 2d 428 (Texas 1987)

OPINION

BURDOCK, Justice.

Appellant, the City of Richland Hills, appeals the trial court's denial of its motion for summary judgment and entry of partial summary judgment for appellee. The summary judgment motions arose from appellee, Keith Bertelsen's action for a declaratory judgment seeking to invalidate the city's claim to property owned by him.

We affirm as modified.

Appellee purchased the real property described below from Frank C. Campbell, for $30,000 cash:

Lots A-L inclusive, Block 53, and Lots A-K inclusive, Block 44, Long Addition to the City of Richland Hills, Tarrant County, Texas, according to the revised Plat

recorded in Volume 388–68, Page 29, Deed Records of Tarrant County, Texas.

Subsequently, appellee requested that the recorded plat of the land be vacated by the city's Planning and Zoning Commission. Later the city informed appellee it claimed a public park and easement on Lots K and L in Block 53, and Lot K in Block 44 of the property, pursuant to an antecedent unrecorded plat given the city by appellee's grantor.

Appellant, the city, filed a motion for summary judgment, claiming as a matter of law there was a dedicated public park and drainage easement on the property. Appellee filed a motion for partial summary judgment and severance, solely contending that appellant had no valid claim to a public park on the property. The trial court granted appellee's motion for partial summary judgment and severance, removing the cloud placed on the property by appellant's claim to a public park.

In three of its points of error, appellant alleges the trial court erred in finding appellee was a bona fide purchaser of the property for value, and in failing to find Campbell, appellee's grantor, had dedicated the lots as a public park.

.   .   .

[1] Before considering any rights appellee may have in the land in dispute, we must first determine whether or not he was a bona fide purchaser. A person qualifies as a bona fide purchaser for value if he purchases property in good faith for valuable consideration without notice. *Neal v. Holt,* 69 S.W.2d 603, 609 (Tex.Civ.App—Texarkana 1934, writ ref'd). Since appellant does not allege appellee failed to pay valuable consideration or exhibited bad faith, we must only decide if appellee had notice of the city's claim.

It is elementary doctrine that, independent of valuable consideration and good faith, notice will destroy the character of a bona fide purchaser and defeat the protection otherwise given to him. *Id.* at 609.

Texas law has long favored the purpose of recording acts, which make land title information available to interested persons. *Leonard v. Benford Lumber Co.,* 110 Tex. 83, 216 S.W. 382, 383 (1919); *Hancock v. Tram Lumber Co.,* 65 Tex. 225, 232 (1885). In *Anderson v. Barnwell,* 52 S.W.2d 96, 101 (Tex.Civ.App.—Texarkana 1932), *affirmed,* 126 Tex. 182, 86 S.W.2d 41 (1935), the court stated:

> The intention of the recording acts is to compel every person receiving conveyances of real property to place such an instrument of record, not only that he may thereby protect his own rights, but also those of all others who may afterwards seek to acquire an interest in the same property.

Anderson, 52 S.W.2d at 101.

To be effectively recorded, an instrument relating to real property must be recorded in the public records in the county in which a part of the property is located. TEX.PROP.CODE ANN. sec. 11.001(a) (Vernon 1984). In addition, any conveyance of real property or an interest in real property is void as to a subsequent purchaser for valuable consideration without notice, unless the instrument has been acknowledged and filed for record as required by law. *See* TEX.PROP.CODE ANN. sec. 13.001(a) (Vernon 1984).

[2–4] Constructive notice is described as that notice one is charged with which is given by instruments of record, irrespective of any actual knowledge. 5 Lange, *Texas Land Titles,* sec. 811 (1961). Actual notice, on the other hand, exists when a person actually knows the facts charged to him, or should have known them if he had in-

quired about them, after learning of facts which put him on inquiry. *West v. Jennings,* 119 S.W.2d 685, 686 (Tex.Civ.App.—San Antonio 1938, no writ); 5 Lange, at see, 811. We find appellee purchased the property in good faith and for valuable consideration and without constructive notice of appellant's claim.

An examination of the pleadings here shows the only plat on file with the county clerk was a properly acknowledged plat, signed by appellee's grantor. The subsequent unsigned plat which the city relies on was incapable of being recorded, and would only be discovered if appellee had reason to search the city records. Appellee had a right to rely on the records properly recorded in the office of the Tarrant County Clerk. See *Lesley v. City of Rule,* 255 S.W.2d 312, 314 (Tex.Civ.App.—Eastland 1953, writ ref'd n.r.e.).

If the plat held by the city had been recorded, it would have been in appellee's chain of title and sufficiently put appellee on inquiry to inspect the city records. However, since nothing had been filed in the county records which constructively notified appellee of the existence of a dedicated park, we find he had no duty to search the city records. Without actual notice of the existence of a dedicated park, appellee takes the land free of the burden of a dedication to the city. *Pokorny v. Yudin,* 188 S.W.2d 185, 193 (Tex.Civ.App.—El Paso 1945, no writ).

In its third point of error, the city alleges the trial court erred in granting appellee's motion for summary judgment because appellant raised numerous fact issues. Most of appellant's complaints under this third point have already been discussed and overruled in our treatment of the first two points of error.

However, appellant raises one critical issue with its allegation that a fact issue existed regarding appellee's actual notice of the property's status as a city park. Ordinarily, actual notice is a fact question for the jury. *Goodwin v. Abilene State Bank,* 294 S.W. 883, 889 (Tex.Civ.App.—Eastland 1927, writ ref'd).

In support of its third point of error, the city relies in part on certain requests for admissions and their answers. A review of the record reveals that the city's requests for admissions and Bertelsen's answers are not included in the record on appeal pursuant to TEX.R.APP.P.51, 52. Therefore, they are not before the court.

Even if the requests and answers were properly before the court, appellant's third point of error could not be sustained. In response to appellant's requests for admissions, appellee denied he had either actual or constructive knowledge of the city's claim of a park at the time he purchased the property from Campbell. The pleadings and affidavits filed by appellant do not indicate appellee knew or should have known the property was a park.

.   .   .

Affirmed.

ORDERING A TITLE EXAMINATION _____

The primary purposes of a title examination, as discussed previously, are to ensure that a seller has the ability to convey good title to the purchaser at the time of the closing, or that a borrower has good title to the property being pledged as security for a loan. The purchaser's or lender's attorney or legal assistant usually orders or conducts the title examination. It is best to have the examination done as early as possible to allow time for dealing with unexpected complications. In addition, a title "check down" usually is done immediately before the closing of the sale or loan. This update ensures that no adverse interest has been recorded against the property between the date of the preliminary title examination and the closing of the transaction for which the examination was made.

Information Needed to Do an Examination

A title examiner should have as much accurate information as possible to perform the examination. The minimum information required is (a) a legal description of the property to be examined, (b) the name of the current owner, and (c) copies of all deeds, surveys, or any prior title examinations or title insurance policies that affect the property. If the examination is being prepared in connection with a sale, the sale's contract will have a description of the property to be purchased, and the seller of the property should be the current owner. If the examination is being prepared in connection with a mortgage loan, the loan application usually contains a description of the property, and the loan applicant, it is hoped, is the current owner of the property. The property owner should be contacted to see if he or she has information, such as prior title examinations, surveys, or deeds, concerning the property. It is a good idea to use a title order form on which pertinent information may be written. An example of a title order form is shown in Exhibit 7–1.

EXAMINING TITLE TO REAL PROPERTY _____

Place to Search

Title examinations usually are conducted in the courthouse of the county in which the property is located. If the property is located in more than one county, it may be necessary to conduct the examination in each county to have a full title examination. The public official who is responsible for keeping real property records varies from state to state, but usually he or she is the clerk of the court or a registrar of deeds. The real property records typically are kept in a record room located within the county courthouse.

Period of Examination

A title examination searches the owner's "chain of title" by starting at the present time and working backward to some predetermined point. The examination establishes a source of title for each owner in the chain. Title examinations are classified as either "full" or "limited" searches. The length of time for a full search differs from state to state, but usually requires that an owner's chain of title be established for a minimum of fifty to sixty years. Most potential defects in title, both recorded and unrecorded, will have no effect on the current ownership of the property after fifty or sixty years.

A limited search title examination is for a period less than that required for a full search. Limited searches often are performed for loan assumptions and second-mortgage closings. The theory supporting a limited search in these situations is an assumption that a full search was performed for the first security mortgage holder, and that all defects and objections were cured at that time. A title examination beginning from the recording date of the first mortgage should be sufficient to protect the interest of the parties. A limited search may be possible when the property is covered by a title insurance policy for which the full search was performed, or when the examiner can obtain a copy of a previous full title examination. Most title insurance companies

EXHIBIT 7–1
Abstract Order

ABSTRACT ORDER

Our File Number: _____ Date Ordered: _____ Need By: _____

Ordered by: _____ Date of Closing: _____

Present Owner/Seller: _____

Name of Purchaser: _____

RE Broker: _____

Brief Legal: _____

_____

Street Address: _____

Length of Search: _____

MISCELLANEOUS INFORMATION KNOWN:

Plat Information: _____

Back Title Policy: ( ) Yes ( ) No   Back Title Notes: ( ) Yes ( ) No

With Who: _____   _____

_____   _____

_____   _____

PLEASE PROVIDE US WITH ANY BANKRUPTCY INFORMATION: ( ) yes ( ) no

Other Information:

_____

In Addition, please provide the following:

( ) Copies of applicable Restrictive Covenants of record

( ) Copies of applicable easements of record

( ) Copies of any liens, executions, fi fa, etc. of record

( ) City, State and County Millage Rates (latest figures available)

( ) _____

---

issue title insurance based on a limited search from the date of an earlier title insurance policy. The client must be informed of the extent of the title examination in the title examiner's title opinion letter. The client also should be made aware that a limited search does not qualify as a full legal search and does not protect against title matters created before the starting date of the limited search.

What to Search

grantee index
Alphabetical index of the public real property records that lists the last name of all people who are grantees of real property interest during a given year within the county.

A title examination involves searching through a **grantee index** of the owner's chain of title backward in time to some predetermined point to establish a source of title for each owner in the chain. Then, for each grantor in the chain of title, the examiner searches the **grantor's index** from the date the grantor acquired title to the next grantor in the chain. Finally, the examiner searches other indices to determine whether there are any other recorded claims against the property, such as judgment liens, mechanics' liens, and tax liens.

Grantee–Grantor Indices

grantor index
Alphabetical index of the public real property records that lists the last name of all people who are grantors of real property interest during a given year within the county.

Most real property record rooms are indexed by the names of the grantees and the grantors of real property, and the interest recorded therein. Each entry referenced in the grantee or grantor index usually provides the following information:

- Name of grantor
- Name of grantee
- Date of instrument
- Date of recording of instrument
- Nature of the instrument (e.g., deed, mortgage, easement)
- Brief description of the property covered
- Place where the instrument can be found so that it can be examined and read (record book and page reference)

Grantee Index   The grantee index is an alphabetical index by last name of all people who are grantees of any property interest during a given year within the county. The index is maintained on a year-by-year basis from the beginning of time that the county maintained records. The grantee's property interest consists of purchasers, holders of mortgages and security deeds, easement holders, tenants, holders of liens, and so on.

The grantee index enables an examiner to build a chain of title from the present to the past. The first link in the chain of title is the conveyance to the current owner of the property. To find this first link, the examiner begins in the current year's grantee index and looks for the name of the current owner of the property. The examiner continues to search in each year's grantee index until the examiner finds the name of the current owner. Once this name is located, it is matched to the property in question. The examiner then looks to see who gave the property to the current owner (i.e., who was the grantor of the deed to the current owner); this person then becomes the next link in the chain of the title. The examiner searches the grantee index until this person's name is found. This process continues for fifty or sixty years in the grantee index, at which time the examiner should have a list of successive owners of the property, the dates they acquired ownership, and the dates they transferred ownership away for the fifty-or sixty-year history. Once this is done, the examiner uses the grantor index.

Grantor Index   A grantor index is an annual alphabetical index by last name of all people who are grantors of a real property interest within the county. Grantors of property are sellers, borrowers, mortgagors, grantors of easements, and so on. The examiner begins with the grantor index from the past and follows it to the present. The examiner starts with the last grantee that was found in the grantee index and then examines the grantor index until this person's name is found and there is a transfer of the property from them. For example, if the examiner, at the conclusion of the grantee index search, finds that in 1953 (for a fifty-year search beginning in 2003) Mary T. Sneed was the owner of the property, the examiner begins the grantor index searching for the name of Mary T. Sneed. He or she will begin in the 1953 index. The examiner continues the search in 1953, 1954, 1955, and so on until Mary T. Sneed's name is located as the grantor of a deed transferring ownership of the property. At this juncture the examiner searches for the name of the grantee of the deed from Mary T. Sneed, and this person becomes the next grantor to be located. The examiner stays with this person until they have conveyed away the property by deed. By reviewing the grantor index the examiner can discover any easements, mortgages, or other title exceptions to the property.

Plat Index

Most counties maintain a **plat index** and copies of all plats that have been recorded within the county. The index to the plats usually is based on one of the following criteria: (a) land lot and district (location designation), (b) name of owner designation, or (c) subdivision designation. For example, title is being examined to property in the Pine Tree Subdivision, which was developed by the Acme Realty Company and was located in Land Lot 100 of the 17th District of Salem County, Virginia. An index to a plat reference (a book and a page where a plat is recorded) for the subdivision can be found in one of three ways. First, there may be an entry under Land Lot 100 of the 17th District for Pine Tree. Second, there may be in the owner index a listing for Acme Realty Company and a list of all plats filed by Acme Realty Company, with a book and a page where the plats are located. Third, there may be a listing in the subdivision index for Pine Tree Subdivision. Once the plat has been found, it should be carefully examined. The plat contains a legal description of the property, and it should match the description being used for the examination. Any discrepancies in the description should be noted. Plats often have restrictive covenants printed on them that are binding on an owner of the property. Plats also show building setback lines, easements, and other matters. Most courthouses have photocopy equipment to enable the examiner to make a copy of the plat, and it is advisable to request that a copy be made for the legal assistant and the client.

plat index
Index of all plats that have been recorded within the county within a given year.

Reviewing the Various Instruments in the Chain of Title

A title examiner carefully examines each instrument's property description to make certain that it is the same as the property that is being examined. Title examiners should note any errors or discrepancies in the legal description. The legal description may change over the course of time, as a current parcel of property may have been included within larger tracts in the past history of the property. For example, a title examiner is examining record title to a residential subdivision lot. The lot is described by a plat book and page reference. The residential subdivision lot in its past history was part of a farm that was described by a metes and bounds legal description.

The examiner maps out each property conveyance, including the property conveyed and the property excluded from the conveyance, to determine that the property in question is being transferred each time and that the current legal description is a true description of the property vested in the current record owner. Subtle differences in property description that go undetected early can seriously impair the validity of the title examination.

When reviewing deeds, easements, or mortgages, an examiner usually does the following:

- Notes the identity of the parties to the instrument, the date the instrument was signed, and the date it was filed
- Examines the signature and witnessing requirements
- Makes a notation of what estate was being conveyed (fee simple life estate, etc.)
- Pays particular attention to any covenants or other requirements that may be set out in the instruments

Most title examiners make copies of all instruments in the chain of title that currently affect the property, and attach the copies as exhibits to the title examination report.

Other Things to Examine

In addition to searching the grantee-grantor indices and reviewing various documents contained therein, there are other potential title problems an examiner must look for. These items may change slightly from state to state, but usually they include the following.

Judgments

A money debt resulting from a lawsuit is called a judgment. A judgment may have been entered against an owner in the chain of title. Once a judgment has been recorded in the public records, it becomes a lien on all property of the judgment debtor. A docket or index for judgments can be found in the real property record room. The docket lists in alphabetical order the names of all people within the county within a given year against whom a judgment has been recorded. The index also refers to a book and page of a judgment book in which a copy of the judgment can be found. The index does not indicate the amount of the judgment or whether the judgment has been paid and satisfied. An examination of a copy of the judgment in the judgment book reveals the amount as well as whether or not the judgment has been satisfied. Most clerks print the word "Paid" or "Satisfied" on a judgment when it has been paid. Judgments in most states have only a five-to seven-year lifetime, but they can be renewed for an additional seven years. Because judgments attach at the time of recordation to all property then owned by the judgment debtor or to any property thereafter acquired by the judgment debtor, it is necessary for the examiner to examine the judgment index for the names of all people who have owned the property during the lifetime of a judgment (seven years). For example, Bryan Thompson, Martha Farris, and the Winston Company, Inc., have, by the grantee-grantor search, been found to be owners at one time or another, of the property during the last seven years. All these names should be searched in the judgment index.

Federal and State Tax Liens

The federal and state governments have the right to file a lien against the property of any delinquent taxpayer. A federal tax lien, once filed, becomes a lien on all property owned by the taxpayer at the time of filing as well as all future property acquired by the taxpayer until the lien has been paid in full. Most record rooms maintain a separate index for federal tax liens and a separate book in which the federal tax liens can be examined. The same considerations and procedures for examining judgments apply to federal and state tax liens, except that a federal tax lien has a life of ten years and a state tax lien may have an unlimited lifetime, and remains in full force and effect until it has been paid or satisfied.

Delinquent Taxes

All property is taxed by county or city governments, and may be separately assessed for sanitary, sewer, or other services. These tax liabilities and other assessments are liens on the property. Liens for assessments may be found in a tax assessor's or tax collector's office, which may be separate and apart from the real property record room. In many localities there are specialized tax services that examine tax and assessment records for a reasonable price. Most title examiners and law firms use these services, where they are available, to determine the tax obligations of a particular piece of property.

Uniform Commercial Code

Many real estate transactions involve both real and personal property. When personal property is involved, it is necessary for the examiner to search the Uniform Commercial Code (UCC) financing statement index to determine if any of the personal property has been pledged as security for a loan. This index is an alphabetical listing of the last name of all debtors who have pledged personal property as security for a loan. In states that also have central filing of UCC financing statements with the secretary of state's office, a state search must be conducted as well as a local search.

Lis Pendens

A lawsuit affecting title to real estate that has not been resolved and is still pending is not a cloud on the title to the property unless a **lis pendens** is filed in the real property records. A lis pendens charges third parties with notice that an action is pending against certain property, and that if they purchase the property or acquire a loan on the property, they will be bound by the subsequent judgment in the lawsuit. Both real and personal property are subject to a lis pendens. A lis pendens is inapplicable in a suit for a personal or money judgment. Lis pendens is applicable only in an action that directly affects title to property. For example, a lis pendens would be applicable to any suit that challenges the current ownership of the property. In addition, a lis pendens would be applicable in a suit for breach of contract against a current owner if the suit is asking for specific performance of the contract. An action for divorce does not ordinarily invoke a lis pendens, except when specific property is sought for either alimony purpose or a property settlement.

A lis pendens usually is a simple document that gives notice that a lawsuit has been filed, and information concerning the lawsuit, such as the court in which the lawsuit was filed, the parties involved, a civil action file number, and a brief description of the nature of the lawsuit. If a lis pendens is filed, the property in the lis pendens is subject to the outcome of the lawsuit, and a lis pendens is considered to be a cloud on the title. Most counties maintain separate records for the lis pendens. The lis pendens index is maintained alphabetically in the name of the property owner.

lis pendens
Notice recorded in the real property records that informs that a lawsuit affecting title to real property described in the notice has been filed and is pending.

Civil Suits

Technically, a pending civil suit, regardless of its nature, does not have any effect on title to real property unless a lis pendens notice has been recorded. Many title examiners, however, examine the civil dockets for informational purposes. For example, if a client is in the process of purchasing property from a seller and the examiner finds on the civil docket a number of lawsuits against the seller for breach of contract, the client should be advised to be cautious.

Probate Court Records

Property may pass through probate and estate proceedings because of the death of one of the owners. It may be necessary for the examiner to examine the probate court records to make sure that the will is properly probated and that the property has been distributed to the devisees under the will or the heirs at law, in the case of an intestate estate. In addition, if property has been sold by the executor of an estate, the title examiner searches the probate or estate records to ascertain if the proper authority for the sale had been obtained by the executor.

Mechanics' Liens

A mechanics' lien or lien given to a contractor, laborer, or material supplier who has contributed to the construction of improvements on real property may be found in the grantor index or in a separate index.

Preliminary Title Report

Once a title examination is completed, the examiner reports in writing the conclusion of the examination. If title insurance is being obtained, the examiner certifies title to the title insurance company, and an insurance commitment or binder is issued before the closing. At a minimum, the title report should reveal the following: (a) the name of the current **record title holder;** (b) legal description of captioned property; (c) existing unpaid loans or mortgages; (d) other lien holders; (e) status of taxes; (f) listing of all easements, covenants, and other restrictions, (g) any objections to marketability; (h) other matters that affect title; and (i) requirements for vesting marketable title in the purchaser.

The title examination should be reviewed as soon as it is received. Defects that may take time to cure should be addressed promptly to avoid a delay in closing.

Title Examination Example

An example of a title examination is shown in Example 7–1.

EXAMPLE 7–1 TITLE EXAMINATION

Property
ALL THAT TRACT or parcel of land lying and being in Land Lot 50 of the 3rd District, Fulton County, Georgia, Lot 3, Block A, Pines Subdivision, per plat recorded at Plat Book 10, page 64, Fulton County, Georgia Records.
Situation
Your firm represents a purchaser of the above-referenced property who has a contract with John Samson. You have been asked to examine title to the property to determine the title of John Samson. You have in your possession a title policy insuring title to the property under the name of the ABC Company, dated with an effective date of November 4, 1983. You have been asked to do a limited title examination from November 4, 1983, through the current date. The 1983 title policy revealed no exceptions to title.

The following is an example of the title notes taken from this limited title examination:
Grantee Index: (FIRST ENTRY): 3-1-2001, Samson, John–Sarah T. Davis–3-1-2001–WD–Lot 3, Block A, Pines Subdivision–DB 604, Page 91.

(SECOND ENTRY): 6-9-96–Davis, Sarah T.–George Farris–6-9-96–WD–Lot 3, Block A, Pines Subdivision–DB 496, Page 831.

(THIRD ENTRY): 2-7-87–Farris, George–ABC Co.-2-7-87–WD–Lot 3, Block A, Pines Subdivision–DB 291, Page 204.

(FOURTH ENTRY): 11-4-83–ABC Co.–Fred Smith–11-4-83–WD–20 Acres–Pines Subdivision–DB 283, Page 61.

Grantor Index: (FIRST ENTRY): 11-4-83–Smith, Fred-ABC Co.–11-4-83–WD–20 Acres–Pines Subdivision–DB 283, Page 61.

(SECOND ENTRY): 11-4-83–ABC Co.–First Bank–11-4-83–DSD–20 Acres–Pines Subdivision–DB 283, Page 63.

(THIRD ENTRY): 7-9-86–ABC Co.–Georgia Power–7-9-86–EASE–Pines Subdivision–DB 289, Page 150.

(FOURTH ENTRY): 2-7-87–ABC Co.–George Farris–2-7-87–WD–Lot 3, Block A Pines Subdivision–DB 291, Page 204.

(FIFTH ENTRY): 2-7-87–Farris, George–S.L. of Tucker–2-7-87–DSD–Lot 3, Block A, Pines Subdivision–DB 291, Page 205.

---

record title holder
Owner of real property as shown on the deed records from a title examination of the property.

(SIXTH ENTRY): 6-9-96–Farris, George–Sarah T. Davis–6-9-96–WD–Lot 3, Block A, Pines Subdivision–DB 496, Page 831.

(SEVENTH ENTRY): 3-1-2001–Davis, Sarah T.–John Samson–3-1-2001–WD–Lot 3, Block A, Pines Subdivision–DB 604, Page 91.

(EIGHTH ENTRY): 5-10-2001–Samson, John–Acme Finance–5-10-2001–DSD–Lot 3, Block A, Pines Subdivision–DB 608, Page 200.

Explanation of Title Notes

To prepare the title notes in Example 7–1, the title examination would have proceeded as follows:

Step 1. With a description of the property and the current owner's name, John Samson, the examiner goes to the Fulton County Courthouse.

Step 2. The examiner first examines the subdivision plat of Pines Subdivision. It is not necessary to use a plat index to locate the plat because a plat book and page number for the plat are part of the legal description. If the plat book or page number for the plat were not provided, it could have been obtained by looking in the subdivision name index under the Pines Subdivision.

Step 3. The plat shows the dimensions of Lot 3. The examiner notes any restrictive covenants, easements, or setback lines that affect Lot 3. The examiner makes a copy of the plat and attaches it to the title report.

Step 4. The examiner is now ready to start in the grantee index. The examiner looks in the current year's index under the "S's" for John Samson. Because John Samson may be a common name in the county, the examiner may find many entries for John Samson, but the examiner is only interested in the entry for John Samson that affects Lot 3, Block A, Pines Subdivision. According to the title notes, the examiner does not find any entries in the current year or any year until 2001. In the 2001 book, the examiner finds an entry dated March 1, 2001, from John Samson—Sarah T. Davis, a warranty deed affecting the property and recorded at Deed Book 604, Page 91. The examiner at this stage stops indexing and goes to Deed Book 604, Page 91, and looks at the deed to make sure that it is in fact the same parcel of property being examined. Once assured that it is the same parcel of property, the examiner returns to the grantee index for further indexing.

Step 5. The next person the examiner looks for in the grantee index is Sarah T. Davis. The examiner looks in the 2001 book for Davis because she may have acquired the property the day before she sold it to Brown. The examiner does not find Davis in the 2001 book and looks in the 2000, 1999, 1998, 1997, and 1996 books. In the 1996 book, the examiner finds an entry to Sarah T. Davis from George Farris, a warranty deed for the same property. Once this deed has been discovered, George Farris becomes the next person to look for in the grantee index. The examiner stays in the same period, 1996, and searches the "F's" for George Farris. The examiner then does the indices for 1995, 1994, 1993, 1992, 1991, 1990, 1989, 1988, and 1987. In the 1987 grantee index, the examiner finds an entry to George Farris from the ABC Co. for this property. ABC Co. then becomes the next grantee, and the examiner indexes ABC Co. all the way back to 1983, where the examiner finds an entry to ABC Co. from Fred Smith.

Step 6. Because the search is limited, this is the end of the grantee indexing. The grantee search gives the following information: ABC Co. owned the property from 11-4-83 to 2-7-87; George Farris owned the property from 2-7-87 to 6-9-96; Sarah T. Davis owned the property from 6-9-96 to 3-1-2001; and John Samson bought the property on 3-1-2001 from Sarah T. Davis. The examiner does not know if John Samson is still the owner of the property. This information cannot be determined except for a needle-in-the-haystack type of search from the grantee index. This information is more readily available in the grantor index.

Step 7. The examiner starts searching in the grantor index from the past to the present. The examiner starts in the grantor index for 1983 with the name Fred Smith and finds an entry from Fred Smith to ABC Co. on 11-4-83. The next grantor, then, is ABC Co., and the examiner stays with the name in the 1983 book. The examiner finds an entry on the same day to the First Bank. It is a DSD, which is an abbreviation for deed to secure debt.

The examiner stays with ABC Co. They have not transferred property but have only pledged the property as security for a loan to First Bank. The examiner runs the 1983, 1984, 1985, and 1986 books for ABC Co. In the 1986 grantor index, the examiner finds an entry from ABC Co. to Georgia Power, something called an EASE. This is an abbreviation for easement. (Many counties abbreviate all the identification of the instruments, and it may take a few days to learn all the abbreviations.) This entry to Georgia Power still does not divest ABC Co. of title to the property, and ABC Co. remains grantor. The examiner searches the 1987 index for ABC Co. and finds an entry of a warranty deed to George Farris. This entry does divest ABC Co. of title, and George Farris then becomes the next grantor. The examiner then switches to the 1987 index under the "F's" and finds an entry from George Farris to the S&L of Tucker. It is another deed to secure debt, which means that George Farris has pledged the property as security for a loan. The examiner stays with George Farris and looks in the 1987, 1988, 1989, 1990, 1991, 1992, 1993, 1994, 1995, and 1996 grantor index books for George Farris. In the 1996 grantor index, the examiner finds an entry from George Farris to Sarah T. Davis. It is a warranty deed entry, and Sarah T. Davis now becomes the next grantor. The examiner searches Davis for 1996, 1997, 1998, 1999, 2000, and 2001. In the 2001 book, there is an entry from Davis to John Samson, a warranty deed. John Samson now becomes the next grantor. The examiner searches Samson for 2001 and 2002, and in 2001 there is an entry from John Samson to Acme Finance, another deed to secure debt. The property has been pledged another time as security for a loan. The examiner continues to search John Samson forward to the most current date of the examination. Every attempt should be made to examine up to the date of the examination; however, some record rooms may be behind in indexing, and the search can only go as far as the record day. Most clerks post each day the "record date" of the system.

Once both the grantee and the grantor search are finished, the examiner can determine from the title notes the following: (a) John Samson owns the property and (b) the property is subject to a (i) deed to secure debt from ABC Co. to First Bank; (ii) an easement from ABC Co. to Georgia Power; (iii) a deed to secure debt from George Farris to S&L of Tucker; and (iv) a deed to secure debt from John Samson to Acme Finance.

It is now necessary for the examiner to review each and every document, including every deed in the chain of title. These documents are found by going to the deed book and pages that were discovered during the indexing. Satisfactions of deeds to secure debts or mortgages often are stamped in the book and are difficult to find through the indexing process.

Once all the deeds, security deeds, easements, and so on have been examined, the examiner does the other searches regarding judgments, tax liens, lis pendens, and so on.

Use of the Grantor–Grantee Indices to Locate Specific Documents

A legal assistant on occasion may be requested to go to a local courthouse's real property record room and to obtain a copy of a particular document or research a particular issue. For example, a client wishes to sell a parcel of property that he or she owns. The client, however, has lost the copy of his or her deed. It is important that a copy of the deed be obtained prior to the preparation of the contract for the sale of the property. A legal assistant given the assignment of locating a copy of the deed in the records may do so through the proper use of the grantor-grantee indices. First, the legal assistant should obtain from the client the approximate date of the client's purchase of the property. Assume the client believes that she purchased the property somewhere around 1990 and 1991, and the client's name is Cathy Howard. A legal assistant would know that Cathy Howard would be the grantee of a deed at the time that she purchased the property. A legal assistant would then go to the 1990 grantee index and look under "H" to see if there is a deed registered for Cathy Howard. The legal assistant would continue to look forward from 1990 in the grantee index until she found an entry for Cathy Howard. This entry would give the legal assistant the book and page where the deed can be found in the record room. The legal assistant then can go to that book and make a copy of the deed.

Another example might be a client who has a mortgage on his or her property. The client does not know the recording date of the mortgage but believes that the mortgage was placed on the property in 1997 and 1998. The client refinanced the mortgage about a year ago and does not recall receiving any recorded release or satisfaction of the mortgage. The client has asked the firm to determine through a search of the records if the mortgage has in fact been released. A legal assistant given this assignment would have to analyze the problem several different ways. Assuming that the client knows the name of the mortgage company, the legal assistant could grantee that company's name in the grantee index for the years 1997 and 1998 to locate the original recordation date of the mortgage. This, however, may not be practicable because the mortgage company might be a very popular one and there may be hundreds of entries for it in the grantee index. It would be easier for the legal assistant to grantor the client's name, since the client would have been the grantor of the mortgage in the years 1997 and 1998, and pick up the entry under the grantor index. Once this entry has been found, the legal assistant could then go to the book where the mortgage was recorded. Most mortgage satisfactions will be stamped or printed in the book, or there will be a reference in the book for another entry showing the satisfaction of the mortgage. It is easy to see that knowledge of the grantor-grantee system can be very helpful for a number of different situations other than a title examination.

ROLE OF A LEGAL ASSISTANT AND PRACTICE TIPS

A legal assistant may be utilized to perform a title examination, order a title examination, and/or review the results of a title examination. The results of an American Bar Association's utilization survey indicated that legal assistants were not utilized to any great extent in the performance of a title examination. The underutilization of legal assistants in this area may be the result of some states' unauthorized practice of law statutes which require that title examinations be performed by licensed attorneys. Several states, however, do not have such requirements, and it would appear that a title examination could be performed by a legal assistant. Although the principles involved in a title examination are somewhat simple, the examination process itself is difficult and would be best learned through an apprenticeship of the legal assistant with an experienced title examiner. Through this apprenticeship the legal assistant can, under the watchful eye of the examiner, learn the intricacies of title examination and the customs and usages of the various courthouse systems of how title records are organized and searches can be competently conducted. Attention to detail and organization are important requirements of any title examiner. Title examinations are considered from a legal malpractice viewpoint to be a high-risk area, as any items missed or misinterpreted in a title examination could be quite costly to the client.

The same American Bar Association utilization survey indicated that legal assistants were used to a great extent by attorneys to order title examinations and to review the results of such examinations. Practice tips on how to order title examinations can be found elsewhere in this chapter. A review of a title examination will involve studying the actual copies of all the items reported in the title examination as exceptions to title. These items generally will include liens, mortgages, restrictive covenants, and easements. A legal assistant will need to review each document carefully, including legal descriptions set forth in the document, to determine how these title exceptions affect the marketability and use of the property by the client. Easements will need to be carefully reviewed to determine the location of the easement and the use to which the owner of the easement has in regard to the property. Restrictive covenants need to be carefully reviewed to see what uses are permitted and restricted in regard to the property. In addition, the legal assistant should review carefully the enforcement remedies for restrictive covenants. Generally these enforcement remedies are injunctions or damages for breach of the covenants. Any restrictive covenant that provides for reversion of title in the event of a violation must be brought to the attention of the attorney and the client as a serious title matter. A legal assistant, when reviewing a title examination, should also pay attention to those matters described as title defects and problems, discussed previously in this chapter. Although practice varies from law firm to law firm, most legal assistants who are charged with the duty of reviewing a title examination will prepare a brief memorandum or summary of the title examination problems for presentation to the attorney and client.

The legal assistant should also review carefully the checklist at the end of this chapter for ordering or performing a title examination.

E T H I C S :   Document Falsification

A legal assistant works with a law firm in the real estate department. One of his duties is to receive title notes from the firm's title examiner and transcribe the notes into a title examination report that is then sent to the client. The legal assistant is overloaded with work and receives an extensive set of title notes from a title examiner. The supervisory attorney requests that a written title examination report be sent to the client by the end of the day. While the legal assistant is reviewing the title notes, he notices there are about eight utility easements affecting the property. A quick review of these easements leads him to believe that they do not materially affect the property. The legal assistant decides that to transcribe the notes into a written report to be sent to the client by the end of the day, he will delete four of the easements from the title examination report. Is this decision a correct one?

A legal assistant should never be involved in falsifying a document for any reason. Failure to list all the utility easements in the title examination report makes the report misrepresent record title to the property. It could be considered falsifying a title examination report. Even though the legal assistant believes the omitted easements do not materially affect the property, it is improper to omit the easements from the title examination report. An overload of work or time pressures to complete an assignment are not justifiable excuses for preparing a legal document that is false or incomplete.

RECORD ROOMS EMBRACE NEW TECHNOLOGY

Local governments are embracing the new computer technology in designing deed or title records. Title registry offices located in many metropolitan areas throughout the country have now automated all or a large portion of their title record systems. This automation involves new versions of the name-base indices and makes it more convenient for the users of the grantor-grantee system. Instead of searching through large books, which are updated on an annual basis, the title examiner today in many cities may simply run the grantor-grantee indices on a computer screen. In addition to the automation of the title records indices, many governments are also electronically filing documents that are recorded within the record room. By using an electronic database to store real property records, the record room need not expand in size with the increased activity within the county. It is possible to store a large volume of electronic records within a small physical area inside the courthouse or other government building.

This conversion from paper to electronic technology concerns many lawyers and other groups who rely on the accuracy of the county land records. They are concerned about computer glitches, viruses, or other problems that may destroy the electronic database or alter it. They are also concerned about public access to the record room. As record rooms become more electronic, the only way to access data is through computer terminals. Counties may incur additional costs to upgrade and maintain these terminals. Having to use terminals may also inhibit people who are not computer literate from using the record room. Although many recognize that using the new technology to preserve land records should be embraced, they also believe that paper records should be maintained. Several states have now passed laws requiring county governments that have committed to the use of electronic land title databases to also maintain a paper archive.

SUMMARY

This chapter has explained the importance of recording a deed, mortgage, easement, or other document conveying an interest in real property, and has introduced the student to the process of examining the public deed records to determine the ownership of real property. The procedures for examining the real property are quite detailed, and a number of title problems can be discovered from the examination. Although title examinations are mandatory on almost any type of real estate transaction that involves a transfer of ownership or a pledge of real property as security for a loan, the efforts by the legal profession to protect and ensure quality of title do not end with the title examination. Most transactions involve the issuance of title insurance.

☑ CHECKLIST

Ordering or Performing a Title Examination

- ❑ I. Purpose of Examination
  - ❑ A. Purchase and sale of property
  - ❑ B. Mortgage loan transaction
  - ❑ C. Acquisition of easement
  - ❑ D. Lease transaction
- ❑ II. Items Required for Examination
  - ❑ A. Current owner's name
    - 1. The seller in the contract for sale
    - 2. The borrower in the application for a loan
    - 3. The landlord of a lease
  - ❑ B. Legal description of property to be examined
  - ❑ C. Plats or survey of property to be examined
  - ❑ D. Prior title insurance policies on property to be examined
  - ❑ E. Prior title examinations or abstracts on property to be examined
- ❑ III. Period of Examination
  - ❑ A. Full examination (50–60 years)
  - ❑ B. Limited examination
    - 1. From date of prior title policy
    - 2. Date of prior mortgage
    - 3. From date of prior title examination
- ❑ IV. Indices to be Checked
  - ❑ A. Plat index
  - ❑ B. Grantee index
  - ❑ C. Grantor index
- ❑ V. Other Records to Be Searched
  - ❑ A. Judgment index and records
  - ❑ B. Federal and state tax lien index and records
  - ❑ C. Lis pendens
  - ❑ D. UCC financing index
  - ❑ E. Tax records
  - ❑ F. Special assessments (sanitary and water)
  - ❑ G. Probate records
  - ❑ H. Civil docket
- ❑ VI. Preliminary Title Examination
  - ❑ A. Certification to title company if title insurance is involved
  - ❑ B. Copies of all title exceptions

KEY TERMS

actual notice
bona fide purchaser for value
chain of title
constructive notice

grantee index
grantor index
lis pendens
plat index

recording statutes
record title holder
title examination

SELF-STUDY EXAMINATION

(Answers provided in Appendix)

1. T or F. A title examiner would search in the grantee index from the past to a present date.

2. T or F. A bona fide purchaser for value will receive ownership of property subject to all claims that the purchaser had actual or constructive notice of.

3. T or F. The most common recording statute is the notice recording statute.

4. T or F. The most common recording statute is the race recording statute.

5. T or F. Constructive notice is imparted to unrecorded instruments that are referred to in a recorded instrument.

6. T or F. A lis pendens gives notice of a federal tax lien against the property.

7. T or F. A person who acquires property by inheritance is not a bona fide purchaser for value.

8. T or F. Probate records should be examined when property is acquired or passes through an estate.

9. T or F. The grantor index enables an examiner to build a chain of title from the present to the past.

10. T or F. Once a judgment has been recorded in the public records, it becomes a lien on all property of the judgment debtor owned at the time of recording but not on any future property acquired by the debtor.

11. What is the difference between actual and constructive notice?

12. What are the three types of recording statutes, and how do they differ?

13. Explain the bona fide purchaser for value rule.

14. What is the difference between a grantor index and a grantee index?

15. Jose has been using a road over his neighbor Sam's property for the past twenty years. In the state where Jose and Sam live, the use by Jose of the road for twenty years gives Jose a prescriptive easement. There are no written documents evidencing the easement. The road is plainly visible from an inspection of the property. If Sam sells his property to Alice, does Alice have a right to stop Jose from using the road?

16. Mary owns a small apartment complex. At the time Mary purchased the apartment complex from Sam, she gave Sam a mortgage securing a debt for $100,000. The mortgage was mentioned in the recorded deed from Sam to Mary for the apartment complex, but the mortgage was not recorded. Mary sells the apartment complex to John. Mary does not tell John about the unrecorded mortgage to Sam. After the sale of the apartment complex from Mary to John, is the mortgage held by Sam enforceable against the apartment complex?

17. Would it be easier to find a recorded mortgage from Alice Owner to Sam Seller by looking under Alice Owner's name in the grantor index or by looking under Sam Seller's name in the grantee index?

18. You are assisting an attorney in the closing of a real estate transaction. You have in your possession a copy of the contract for the purchase and sale of the property. The contract contains the names of both the purchaser and the seller as well as a complete legal description of the property being bought and sold, and has been attached as an exhibit a survey of the property. You have been asked to order a title examination on behalf of your client. What information do you need to give to the title examiner?

19. Purchaser and Seller have entered into a contract for the sale of real property. Before closing, Seller has refused to honor the contract and decides to sell the property to a third party. Purchaser files suit against Seller for breach of contract. What else should Purchaser do to protect his or her rights against Seller and in the property?

20. What information is provided in a grantor or a grantee index entry?

21. Explain how an unrecorded document can be imparted as constructive notice to a bona fide purchaser for value.

22. Why is recording a real estate instrument important in connection with the bona fide purchaser for value rule?

23. Where are title examinations generally conducted?

24. When reviewing deeds and other instruments found in a title examination, the examiner usually will note what information concerning each instrument?

25. What is a lis pendens and why is it important in a title examination?

Title Insurance

"We shall make good our title. It is in the hands of my solicitor. My solicitor will be here presently to protect the property. Transportation or the gallows for anybody who shall touch the property!"

—Bleak House—Charles Dickens

OBJECTIVES

After reading this chapter you should be able to:

- Recognize the importance of title insurance
- Understand the coverage provided by the American Land Title Association owner's and mortgagee's title insurance policies
- Prepare a title insurance commitment
- Review a title insurance commitment and title insurance policy
- Identify title problems that are not insured by a title insurance policy
- Learn how to delete standard title insurance exceptions

One of the main responsibilities of a real estate attorney or legal assistant is to make certain that the client has good title to real property. This title assurance comes about by the use of three safeguards: (1) general warranty deed of conveyance to the property, (2) title examination before conveyance, and (3) title insurance.

General warranty deeds and title examinations are discussed in Chapters 5 and 7, respectively. Both of these methods for title assurance are highly recommended, and it would be imprudent to proceed without them; however, these methods do have certain limitations.

For example, liability on a warranty deed is difficult to enforce and collect. The grantor of the deed may have died or disappeared, or be insolvent. Even if the grantor is present and solvent, in most states liability under a warranty deed is limited to the original purchase price of the property and does not extend to the value of improvements that were erected on the property or the appreciated value of the property. In many states attorney's fees and other costs of enforcing a warranty deed are unrecoverable.

A title examination is only as good as the skill and solvency of the examiner. The title examiner may not have the financial ability to pay for any errors or mistakes in the examination. Although most title examiners carry malpractice insurance, the limits of this insurance may not be sufficient. In addition, there are some "remote risks" that are not covered by a competent title examination and, thus, not recoverable from the examiner in a malpractice action. Some of these remote risks are as follows:

- Impersonation of the real owner
- Forged signatures on deeds or releases
- Documents executed under a false power of attorney or a power of attorney that has expired
- Deeds delivered after the death of the grantor or without the consent of the grantor
- Undisclosed or missing heirs
- Wills that have not been probated
- Deeds, mortgages, or easements executed by minors or incompetents
- Mistakes made in the indexing of legal documents (documents are lost in records room)

- Falsification of public records
- Confusion arising from similarity of names
- Titles passing by improperly conducted foreclosure sales

Because of these limitations, American ingenuity came up with a product to fill the gap. The product is title insurance, and the main function of title insurance is to eliminate all risks and prevent any loss caused by defects in title to the property.

title insurance
Contract to indemnify the insured against loss through defects in the title to real property.

Title insurance is a contract to indemnify the insured against loss through defects in the insured title or against liens or encumbrances that may affect the insured title at the time the policy is issued.

The main economic justifications of title insurance are to cover the remote risks of title examinations and to add financial substance to the title examination and to the deed warranties. Most title companies have deep pockets of money reserves that are annually audited by state authorities. It is rare that a valid claim is not paid by a title company because the title company lacks the money to pay for the claim.

Title insurance, unlike other forms of insurance, such as life, health, and fire insurance, does not assume risk. The main role for title insurance is risk elimination. A title insurance company will not issue a policy of title insurance unless it has performed an extensive title search and believes that there are no problems to the title. Some practitioners joke that if a title insurance company is willing to issue title insurance, then you probably don't need it because the title is risk-free. Title insurance, therefore, is issued only after a title examination has been conducted. The payment for title insurance is a one-time premium and can range anywhere from $1 to $3 per each $1,000 of coverage.

There are many title insurance companies across the country; most of them belong to the American Land Title Association (ALTA), a private trade association of title insurance companies. The ALTA has prepared over the years a number of standard form title insurance policies that they request and, in some cases, require the member companies to use. These forms are referred to as ALTA Owner's Policy, or ALTA Mortgagee-Loan Forms. The standard forms enable lawyers to transact a real estate practice on a national basis with a title company that belongs to the ALTA. Because most title insurance is issued on ALTA forms, the remainder of this chapter is a discussion of the basic provisions of the ALTA forms.

OWNER'S POLICY

owner's policy
Policy of title insurance that insures an owner's title to real property.

The most commonly used **owner's policy** insurance form is the ALTA Owner's Policy Form. A copy of the policy form is included at the end of this chapter (Exhibit 8–1). The ALTA owner's form contains many standard printed provisions concerning, for example, notice of loss and claim provisions, and two basic parts known as Schedule A and Schedule B. Schedule A is an identification schedule that sets forth the date of the policy (which usually is the date the deed or other instrument that is insured is filed for record), the amount of insurance covered by the policy, the identity of the insured, the estate or interest covered (whether it is a fee simple, life estate, and so on), the identity of the parties in whom title is vested as shown by the deed records, and a full description of the property insured.

Schedule B of the policy contains a list of exceptions to coverage. Any item shown on the Schedule B is not insured against in the insurance policy. Schedule B typically contains some standard exceptions, such as matters of survey, implied easements, building line restrictions, and rights of persons in possession. These standard exceptions can be deleted by the use of proper **affidavits** and a survey. The title company, when issuing its Schedule B, lists all title exceptions found in the title examination of the property. Because Schedule B items are not insured against, it is important that in reviewing title insurance policies, copies of all the documents that represent Schedule B exceptions are obtained and carefully reviewed.

affidavit
Sworn statement of fact.

Insuring Provisions of an ALTA Owner's Policy

There are four basic insuring provisions of an ALTA owner's policy, and it is against loss or damage incurred as a result of these four covered risks that the policy insures. The covered risks are (1) insurance that title to the estate or interest described in Schedule A is vested in the insured; (2) insurance against any defect, lien, or encumbrance on such title; (3) insurance that the property has access to public road; and (4) insurance that the title is marketable. The ALTA Form "A" policy used in some states does not insure marketability.

Vesting of Title

This provision is straightforward insurance that the insured owns the real property set forth in the policy. This coverage is the basic undertaking in the policy and the undertaking from which other title insurance protections spring.

Defects, Liens, or Encumbrances on Title

Title insurance protects against loss or damage incurred by reason of any defect in or lien or encumbrance on the title to the insured property. This language is concise in its application to title defects, liens, or encumbrances that have attached to the title as of the date of the issuance of a policy of title insurance. Coverage is provided against three separate kinds of title flaws: defects, liens, or encumbrances, each being somewhat distinct from the other. A title defect is the want or absence of something necessary for completeness or perfection of title, or a lapse or absence of something essential to completeness of title. For example, the adjudicated incompetency of a prior grantor before the execution of a deed in a chain of title renders the title defective.

A lien is not an imperfection in the passage of title, but a claim or charge on the property as security for the payment of a debt or the fulfillment of an obligation. The broader term "encumbrance" includes liens, but extends to every right or interest in property existing in third parties that diminishes the value of the real property but is consistent with the passing of a fee title such as restrictive covenants, or easements.

Access to and from the Property

An owner's policy insures against loss incurred by the insured for reason of the lack of a right of access to and from the land. This extension of coverage recognizes the obvious, that landlocked property is of little use or value. It is through the operation of this clause that the insured is protected against loss resulting from the nonexistence of a legal enforceable right to get to and from the property. There is, however, no insurance that the access will be the most convenient or appropriate way to and from the property, that the access will be by way of the route expected by the insured, or that the legal enforceable access way will be one that can be easily used or is physically passable. Stated affirmatively, the right-of-access coverage means the right to go between the property and the public right-of-way without unreasonable restrictions. Title insurance coverage protects against record title defects in the right of access, but not against the physical difficulties that may be associated with getting to and from the property.

This concept that title insurance insures only against title defects and not the defects of the physical condition of the land is illustrated in *Title & Trust Company of Florida v. Barrows*.

 **C A S E**   **Title & Trust Company of Florida v. Barrows**
381 So. 2d 1088

McCORD, Acting Chief Judge.

This appeal is from a final judgment awarding money damages to appellees for breach of title insurance policy. We reverse.

Through a realtor, appellees purchased, for $12,500, a lot surrounded on three sides by land owned by others, all of which is a part of a beach subdivision. The fourth side of appellee's lot borders on a platted street called Viejo

Street, the right-of-way for which has been dedicated to and accepted by St. Johns County. The right-of-way line opposite appellees' lot abuts a Corps of Engineers' right-of-way in which there is a stone breakwater. The intracoastal waterway flows on the other side of the breakwater.

The realtor who sold the lot to appellees represented to them that the county would build a road in the right-of-way along Viejo Street when appellees began plans for building on their lot. There have been no street improvements in the dedicated right-of-way, and St. Johns County has no present plans for making any improvements. The "road" is merely a continuation of a sandy beach.

A year after purchasing the land appellees procured a survey which disclosed that the elevation of their lot is approximately one to three feet above the mean high water mark. They later discovered that their lot, along with the Viejo Street right-of-way abutting it, is covered by high tide water during the spring and fall of each year.

At the time appellees purchased their lot, they obtained title insurance coverage from appellant. The title policy covered:

"Any defect in or lien or encumbrance on the title to the estate or title covered hereby . . . or a lack of a right of access to and from the land; . . . ."

Appellees' complaint of lack of right of access was founded on the impassable condition of the platted street. After trial without a jury, the trial court entered final judgment finding that appellees did not have access to their property and, therefore, were entitled to recover $12,500 from appellant—the face amount of the policy.

[1–3] Appellant and Florida Land Title Association, appearing as amicus curiae, argue that appellant cannot be held liable on grounds of "lack of right of access to and from the land" since there is no defect shown by the public record as to their right of access; that the public record shows a dedicated and accepted public right-of-way abutting the lot. They contend that title insurance does not insure against defects in the physical condition of the land or against infirmities in legal right of access not shown by the public record. See *Pierson v. Bill*, 138 Fla. 104, 189 So. 679 (1939). They argue that defects in the physical condition of the land such as are involved here are not covered by title insurance. We agree. Title insurance only insures against title defects.

The Supreme Court of North Carolina in *Marriott Financial Services, Inc. v. Capitol Funds, Inc.*, 288 N.C. 122, 217 S.E.2d 551 (1975), construed "right of access" to mean the right to go to and from the public right-of-way without

unreasonable restrictions. Compare *Hocking v. Title Insurance & Trust Company*, 37 Cal.2d 644, 234 P.2d 625 (1951), where, in ruling that the plaintiff failed to state a cause of action in a suit brought under her title policy, the court said:

"She appears to possess fee simple title to the property for whatever it may be worth; if she has been damaged by false representations in respect to the condition and value of the land her remedy would seem to be against others than the insurers of the title she acquired."

In *Mafetone et al. v. Forest Manor Homes, Inc., et al.*, 34 A.D.2d 566, 310 N.Y.S.2d 17 (N.Y.1970), the plaintiff brought an action against a title insurance company for damages allegedly flowing from a change in the grade of a street. There the court said:

"The title company is not responsible to plaintiffs for the damages incurred by reason of the change in elevating the abutting street to its legal grade, since the provisions of the standard title insurance policy here in question are concerned with matters affecting *title* to property and do not concern themselves with physical conditions of the abutting property *absent* a specific request by the person ordering a title report and policy . . . ." (Emphasis supplied.)

In *McDaniel v. Lawyers' Title Guaranty Fund*, 327 So.2d 852 (Fla. 2 D.C.A.1976), our sister court of the Second District said:

"The man on the street buys a title insurance policy to insure against defects in the record title. The title insurance company is in the business of guaranteeing the insured's title to the extent it is affected by the public records."

In the case here before us, there is no dispute that the public record shows a legal right of access to appellant's property via the platted Viejo Street. The title insurance policy only insured against record title defects and not against physical infirmities of the platted street.

REVERSED.

If any particular form of access is required by the insured for the full enjoyment of the property, the insured would be well advised to have that access specifically insured by the title insurance policy. This can be accomplished by having additional easement parcels included in the legal description on Schedule A or by endorsing the policy to expressly insure access to the property by way of a described route.

Unmarketability of Title

marketable title
Title to real property that is free from doubt and enables the owner to hold the real property in peace; free from the hazard of litigation or adverse claims.

The concept of marketability of title is legal in nature, rather than economic. A **marketable title** is title free from doubt that enables the owner to hold the land in peace, free from the hazard of litigation or adverse claims. Through this coverage title insurance usually provides protection for those matters that would render the title unmarketable. Once again, the focus is on marketability of title as a legal concept and not sale marketability. The ability to sell the property is an economic concept. Defects that merely diminish the value of the property do not render the title unmarketable within the meaning of the title insurance coverage.

Exclusions from Coverage

The ALTA Owner's Policy contains several exclusions from coverage. These exclusions are not negotiable and cannot be deleted from the policy. The exclusions are (a) zoning and other governmental police power rights; (b) rights of eminent domain; (c) matters created, suffered, assumed, or agreed to by the insured; (d) title defects not known to the insurance company and not shown by public records, but known to the insured, either at the date of the policy or when the insured acquired the estate or interest, and not disclosed in writing to the insurance company before the date he became an insured; (e) matters resulting in no loss or damage to the insured; (f) title defects that are first attached or created after the effective date of the policy; (g) matters resulting in a loss or damage that would not have been sustained if the insured had paid value for the estate or interest insured; and (h) environmental matters.

Zoning and Other Governmental Regulations

This exclusion is primarily designed to indicate that matters of zoning are not insured against by the title policy. Beyond that the exclusion also relates to building and other use restrictions, as well as restrictions concerning the right of occupancy and any government regulations concerning further subdivision of the property. This exclusion reflects the fact that all ownership of property is ultimately subject to control and regulation by the government. It is important that zoning information be independently obtained and reviewed to see if it unreasonably interferes with the proposed use of the real property. It is possible in some states to obtain a zoning **endorsement** from the title insurance company that insures against loss if the zoning classification is other than stated in the endorsement. Another endorsement that is available in some situations protects an insured against loss if the land as currently improved violates zoning or other governmental regulations. A title insurance company will not insure against future changes of government regulations.

title endorsement
Amendment to a title insurance policy that generally modifies existing coverage or adds special coverage to the policy.

Eminent Domain and Police Power

This exclusion recognizes that ownership for private property is subject not only to government control, but also to a government taking of the property by eminent domain or regulation under police power. If a notice of the exercise of such rights appears in the public records as of the effective date of the policy, as, for example, would be the case in a condemnation action, then the title insurance must disclose that fact to the insured or insure against any loss for failure to disclose.

Matters Created, Suffered, Assumed, or Agreed to by the Insured

This policy language excludes from coverage defects, liens, encumbrances, adverse claims, or other matters created, suffered, assumed, or agreed to by the insured claimant. This clause has the effect of limiting the title company's liability when the insured has expressly or implicitly assumed or agreed to various defects, liens, or encumbrances in the course of dealing with the property, or when the defect, lien, or encumbrance resulted from the insured's misconduct or inequitable dealings. For example, Pat Purchaser is purchasing real property from Sam Seller. As part of the transaction Pat Purchaser is to give a mortgage to Sam Seller to secure part of the purchase price that will be paid to Sam Seller over a period of time. The mortgage would be an encumbrance on the property purchased by Pat Purchaser, but it is an encumbrance created by Pat Purchaser, and therefore not insured by Pat Purchaser's title insurance policy.

On the other hand, the clause will not operate to limit the insurance company's liability for title defects, liens, or encumbrances resulting from the insured's negligence. The theory is that the title problem must result from the insured's knowing or intentional affirmative act or the insured's intentional failure to prevent the attachment of the adverse item. The courts usually apply this exclusion to protect the insurance company from liability for a loss resulting from the insured's wrongful conduct.

Title Defects Not Known to the Insurance Company

This exclusion, known as the "secret defect" exclusion, covers title matters that are not recorded but that the insured claimant knew about and failed to tell the title insurance company at the time of the transaction. The insured claimant must give written disclosure of all "off record" matters that affect the insured property. This exclusion does not apply to record matters even if the insured knows of their existence. The insured claimant must know about the adverse matter for the exclusion to apply. Knowledge usually means actual knowledge, not constructive knowledge, or notice that may be imputed to an insured by reason of any public records.

If a matter fits into the requirements of this exclusion, the only prudent way for the insured to obtain title insurance protection over the item is to make written disclosure of the item to the title insurance company and cause the title company to provide affirmative insurance against the item.

Matters Resulting in No Loss or Damage to the Insured Claimant

This provision fits into the concept that title insurance is a contract of indemnity. Simply put, if there is no loss, there is nothing for the indemnification aspects of the insurance obligation to operate on.

Title Defects That Are First Attached or Created after the Effective Date of the Policy

Title insurance is a rather unique insurance product. For a single premium the insured obtains protection for so long as an interest in the insured property is retained. In general, however, title insurance covers only those risks that exist in the title at the time the insured interest is taken. The exclusion for defects, liens, encumbrances, adverse claims, or other matters attaching to or created subsequent to the date of the policy makes it clear that the title insurance policy is not prospective in operation and provides no protection for agreements, liens, or problems arising after the policy is issued. The insurance covers only the losses attributable to matters in existence on the date of the policy. Title insurance policies contain an effective date, which usually is the date of the recording of the deed or, in the event of a loan policy, the date of the recording of the mortgage.

Matters Resulting in a Loss or Damage That Would Not Have Been Sustained If the Insured Had Paid Value for the Estate or Interest Insured

This exclusion is an example of how title insurance provisions reflect the protection afforded by the various state recording laws. If the recording laws of a state do not protect a party who takes real property for no consideration against a prior interest in the same property, the title policy will not protect the insured as well. For example, if you are representing someone who is receiving property as a gift, it is necessary to obtain an endorsement to the title policy to delete this exclusion.

Schedule A

Schedule A is an identification schedule that localizes or customizes the title insurance to the transaction. An example of a Schedule A form is shown in Example 8–1.

EXAMPLE 8–1

Schedule A of Owner's Policy

OFFICE FILE NUMBER	POLICY NUMBER	DATE OF POLICY	AMOUNT OF INSURANCE
1	2	3	4 $

1. Name of Insured:

2. The estate or interest in the land which is covered by this Policy is:
   Fee Simple
3. Title to the estate or interest in the land is vested in the Insured.
4. The land herein described is encumbered by the following mortgage or trust deed, and assignments:

   and the mortgages or trust deeds, if any, shown in Schedule B hereof.
5. The land referred to in this Policy is described as follows:

Policy Date

The date of the policy is important because of the nature of title insurance. Unlike other insurance that covers the future occurrence of risk, title insurance, with some limited exceptions, insures against risks that have already occurred but that have not manifested themselves. The date of the policy is the cutoff for coverage. The policy date is the date the transaction documents, such as the deed or mortgage, are recorded.

Amount of Insurance

The dollar amount of insurance coverage is the maximum loss the title insurer will bear in the event of an occurrence of a covered risk. It also is the prime factor in determining the amount of policy premium. The insured must balance the need to obtain adequate insurance coverage against the cost of the coverage. The amount of title insurance usually is the purchase price of the insured property for an owner's policy and the amount of the loan secured by the insured property for a loan policy.

Occasionally, however, to save premiums, the insured may deliberately underinsure. The title insurance company is aware that the property is being underinsured and that the insured has self-insured a portion of the risk. This situation brings a co-insurance clause into account. Through this clause the insurer limits its liability to that proportion of the loss, damage, or defense cost that the policy amount bears to the market value of the insured property at the time of the loss. For example, a purchaser buys a $100,000 parcel of property but only insures for $60,000. Under the co-insurance rules, if there is a loss in the amount of $30,000 under the title policy, the title insurance company will only pay 60 percent of the loss ($60,000 versus $100,000), or $18,000.

On the other hand, an insured may want more coverage than would be indicated by the amount of the transaction. An owner may anticipate an increase in the property value caused by natural market forces or because the property will be improved. A lender may want more insurance than the original amount of a loan in situations where negative amortization will occur.

Most title insurance companies are willing to sell additional coverage on the demonstration of a reasonable basis for the requested coverage.

Even after a policy is issued, the insured may approach the insurance company to increase the policy amount. This can be done by an endorsement that either changes or does not change the effective date of the policy.

Some insureds do not want to leave the availability of this coverage to chance. Although they seek adequate insurance at the outset (i.e., insurance in the amount of the purchase price of the property), they want to save the payment of the premium for more insurance until the additional value is added to the property. Although the insurer may be willing to agree to give this insurance, the insurer wants the insured's agreement to purchase the insurance. This is accomplished through an endorsement that contains the insured's agreement to purchase more insurance and the title company's undertaking to increase the policy amount and change the effective date of the policy, subject, however, to exception of matters created, recorded, attaching, or coming to the insured's attention subsequent to the original policy's effective date.

An owner may seek additional coverage to protect against the effects of inflation. This is done through inflation protection increases in the policy amount over time. This inflation protection can easily be built into Schedule A of a policy of insurance insuring residential property so that the insured amount will automatically increase by 10 percent on each of the first five policy anniversary dates.

Inflation protection also can be obtained on commercial policies. This coverage is given by endorsement that raises the policy amount by some index rate, such as the Consumer Price Index. In both residential and commercial policies the inflated policy amount will not exceed 150 percent of the original amount of insurance.

The Insured

The insured should be correctly identified. It should be noticed that, by definition, the insured extends not only to the named insured, but also to those who succeed to the interest of the insured by operation of law, as distinguished from purchase, including, but not limited to, heirs, distributees, devisees, survivors, personal representatives, next of kin, or a corporate and fiduciary successor.

A successor insured is subject to the same rights or defenses that the title company had against a named insured.

Because title insurance policies are issued for a one-time premium, it is of economic necessity to the title insurance company that the insurance undertaking be definitionally limited to not extend to those who take by purchase. In other words, an owner's title insurance policy is not transferable to someone who purchases the property from the owner. If the purchaser desires insurance, the purchaser will need to purchase a new policy.

A loan policy of insurance, however, extends the insurance by defining the named insured as the owner of the indebtedness secured by the insured mortgage, each successor in ownership of the indebtedness, and any governmental agency or instrumentality that insures or guarantees the indebtedness. The title insurance industry is aware that mortgage loans are often transferred from one lender to another, and to accommodate this industry practice with a minimum of cost has provided that the holder of the insured mortgage will be the named insured under the loan policy.

Insured Property

The policy definition of real property is the real property expressly described in Schedule A and the improvements affixed to the real property. Title to personal property is not included in the coverage of a title insurance policy.

It is of primary importance that the legal description contained in Schedule A be the same real property that the insured is purchasing or using to secure a loan.

The insured property often is made up of several parcels or tracts of land. It is important that the policy description set forth a full description of the parcels that are insured. If these parcels are being consolidated into one parcel, the insured should request that the title insurance company issue an endorsement ensuring that the tracts or parcels are contiguous to one another and that no gaps exist between the parcels. In addition, if the insured property involves a fee parcel and an easement for access to the fee parcel, the insured should request the contiguity endorsement. This endorsement ensures that the land described in both parcels is contiguous and the areas can be served with no intervening adverse interest.

Schedule B

Schedule B of an owner's policy contains exceptions to the insurance coverage. These exceptions are divided into two categories: (1) standard exceptions and (2) exceptions found in the title examination of the insured property. An example of a Schedule B of an owner's policy is shown in Example 8–2.

EXAMPLE 8-2

Schedule B of Owner's Policy

SCHEDULE B

Policy Number: _____

Owners

EXCEPTIONS FROM COVERAGE

This policy does not insure against loss or damage (and the Company will not pay costs, attorneys' fees or expenses) which arise by reason of:

General Exceptions:

(1) Rights or claims of parties in possession not shown by the public records.

(2) Encroachments, overlaps, boundary line disputes, or other matters which would be disclosed by an accurate survey and inspection of the premises.

(3) Easements, or claims of easements, not shown by the public records.

(4) Any lien, or right to a lien, for services, labor, or material heretofore or hereafter furnished, imposed by law and not shown by the public records.

(5) Taxes or special assessments which are not shown as existing liens by the public records.

Special Exceptions: The mortgage, if any, referred to in Item 4 of Schedule A.

Countersigned _____

Authorized Signatory

The standard exceptions to an owner's policy are (a) rights or claims of parties in possession not shown by public records; (b) encroachments, overlaps, boundary line disputes, and any other matters that would be disclosed by an accurate survey and inspection of the premises; (c) easements or claims of easement not shown by the public records; (d) any lien, or right to a lien, for services, labor, or material heretofore or hereafter furnished, imposed by law, and not shown by the public records; (e) taxes or special assessments that are not shown as existing liens by the public records.

Rights of Parties in Possession

The first of the general exceptions provides that the policy does not insure against loss or damage incurred by reason of the rights or claims of parties in possession not shown by the public records. Through this exception the insurance company is relieved of liability when the defect is caused by a claim of a party in possession. For example, a small retail shopping center is leased to a number of tenants. The tenants' leases are not recorded. The tenants are in possession of the property and are parties in possession. A purchaser purchases the shopping center for $500,000. The purchaser receives a title insurance policy that contains an exception for the rights of parties in possession. It is later discovered that one of the tenants has an option to purchase the shopping center for $400,000. The title insurance company does not insure the purchaser against any loss that it may suffer should the tenant exercise its option to purchase the property.

There is a rational basis for the presence of this exception. Constructive notice of rights in real property comes from many sources. Two such sources are the property itself and the public records. A title insurance company makes its underwriting determination based on a review of the public records and does not usually visit the property to determine what can be learned by viewing it and talking to the parties in possession. The purchaser, on the other hand, inspects the property, perhaps several times, in making the purchase determination. The purchaser thus has the ability to uncover the rights that can be determined from this inspection by seeking information of the parties in possession. Therefore, under this exception, a title insurance company does not insure against anyone who claims title to the property by way of adverse possession, or any person who is a tenant with an unrecorded lease, or any person who exercises any unrecorded easement rights over the property.

This exception can be deleted from a title policy by obtaining a title affidavit from the owner of the property. In this affidavit the owner swears under oath that there are no other parties in possession of the property except for the owner. A form of title affidavit is included at the end of this chapter (Exhibit 8–2).

Survey Exception

The second general exception precludes title insurance liability for encroachments, overlaps, boundary line disputes, and any other matters that would be disclosed by an accurate survey or inspection of the premises. Through the use of this exception the title insurance company protects itself against liability for matters that are primarily shown by the view of the land itself, through either the untrained eye of the insured or the trained eye and technical expertise of the surveyor.

A simple example of the application of this exception can be found in a situation where the insured purchased property and began to erect an industrial building. The building was placed on the site so as to afford adequate clearance for trucks using the building's loading docks. The owner of the adjoining property erected a fence along the property line at a point some 3 feet inside the place that the insured believed the line to be, thus blocking the effective use of the loading docks. A lawsuit resulted. It developed that the adjoining owner's survey was right about the location of the property line and the insured's survey was incorrect. A court held in this situation that the survey exception protected the title insurance company from liability over this boundary line dispute.

A general survey exception can be removed by preparing a survey in compliance with title insurance standards and by providing the title insurance company with the survey. On the receipt of a survey prepared according to title standards, a title insurance company usually will remove the standard survey exception, but will add special exceptions for any matters that appear on the survey.

Unrecorded Easement Exception

Another general exception states that the policy does not insure against loss incurred by the insured by reason of easements or claims of easements not shown by the public records. This exception primarily applies to unrecorded easements or rights-of-way that can only be discovered by a physical inspection of the land.

For example, Jose is a neighbor of Sam. Jose has been using a road on Sam's property for access to and from Jose's property for more than twenty years. In the state where Jose and Sam live Jose has a prescriptive easement to use the road on Sam's property. Jose's prescriptive easement would be an easement or claim of easement not shown by the public records.

A legal assistant should pay close attention to such features as footpaths, driveways, water and power lines, and other like matters that appear on the survey of the insured property, as all these features could be evidence of implied or prescriptive easement rights.

The standard unrecorded easement exception can be removed from the policy by providing the title company with a survey showing no easements prepared according to title standards and an affidavit from the owner swearing that no implied or prescriptive easements affect the insured property.

Mechanics' Lien Exception

An owner's policy does not insure against loss by reason of any lien or right to a lien for services, labor, or materials heretofore or hereafter furnished imposed by law and not shown by the public records. Once again, the title insurance policy reflects the insurance of record matters, but not nonrecord matters. If a claim of lien has been filed in the public records, it will, as a general rule, be excepted as a special exception under Schedule B or covered by the policy's protection. If it is not reflected of record as of the date of policy, it is, by operation of this general exception, excluded from liability, regardless if the lien relates to work or materials furnished before or after the effective date of the policy.

The mechanics' lien exception may be removed from the title insurance policy. The title insurance company may require, as a condition precedent to the deletion, lien waivers from all contractors, materialmen, and laborers supplying labor or materials to the property, an affidavit that all bills have been paid, or an affidavit that no work has been performed within the period of time required for the filing of a lien.

Taxes and Special Assessments

This general exception states that the policy does not insure against loss or damage incurred by reason of "taxes or special assessments which are not shown as existing liens by the public records." This exception focuses on the public records on the day the policy is issued, and covers real estate tax and special assessment laws within the jurisdiction where the real property is located. A title insurance company's liability will preclude liability for special assessments for real estate tax liens that become liens after the effective date of the policy.

Schedule B Special Exceptions

In addition to the standard exceptions, Schedule B contains all defects, encumbrances, liens, covenants, restrictions, or other matters that affect the insured property that were revealed by the title examination to the property.

MORTGAGE OR LOAN POLICIES

A title insurance policy also can be obtained to insure the interest of the mortgagee or lender who has a mortgage loan secured by real property. The ALTA **loan policy** form is included at the end of this chapter (Exhibit 8–3). The ALTA loan policy contains a Schedule A, Schedule B, Part I, and Schedule B, Part II.

Schedule A of a loan policy contains much of the same information as Schedule A of an owner's policy: (a) the effective date of the policy; (b) the amount of coverage; (c) the named insured; (d) the fee simple owner of the property; (e) a description of the mortgage or loan deed being insured; and (f) a description of the real property conveyed in the mortgage or loan deed. An example of a Schedule A of a loan title insurance policy is shown in Example 8–3.

mortgagee or loan policy
Policy of title insurance that insures the interest of a mortgagee or lender to the title of real property.

EXAMPLE 8-3

Schedule A of Loan Policy

SCHEDULE A

OFFICE FILE NUMBER	POLICY NUMBER	DATE OF POLICY	AMOUNT OF INSURANCE
1	2	3	4 $

1. Name of Insured:

2. The estate or interest in the land which is encumbered by the insured mortgage is:
   Fee Simple
3. Title to the estate or interest in the land is vested in:

4. The insured mortgage and assignments thereof, if any, are described as follows:

5. The land referred to in this Policy is described as follows:

Schedule B, Part I, of a loan policy contains both standard exceptions and special exceptions resulting from a title examination of the insured property. The standard exceptions are the same as the exceptions in an owner's policy, and can be deleted from a loan policy in the same manner, that is, by the use of surveys and title affidavits. The special exceptions are the title matters reported in the title examination.

The Schedule B, Part II, items are exceptions to the title with a priority junior and inferior to the insured loan. An example of a Schedule B, Part II, exception would be tenants of a commercial property with leases that are expressly subordinate to any mortgage or loan deed on the property.

Insurance Provisions

The first four insurance provisions of a loan policy are the same as those of an owner's policy, to wit: (1) title is vested in the borrower or maker of the mortgage or loan deed; (2) the property is free and clear of title defects, liens and encumbrances, except those shown in Schedule B; (3) the property has access to a public road; and (4) borrower's title to the property is marketable. In addition to these four items, the following insurance provisions are provided in the loan policy: (a) the mortgage is valid and enforceable, and the lender shall have the right to foreclosure in the event the debt is not paid; (b) the priority of the mortgage; (c) the mortgage is insured against any claims that may be asserted by mechanics' or materialmen's liens; and (d) the policy insures the validity and enforceability of any assignment of the mortgage or loan deed.

Validity or Enforceability of the Lien

The ALTA loan policy insures against loss resulting from the invalidity or unenforceability of the lien of the insured mortgage on said estate or interest. This is the most basic form of protection to a lender, insuring that the lien in the mortgage or deed of trust is a valid and enforceable lien on the property described therein.

There are two exceptions that the title insurance company does not insure. Title insurance does not insure against the invalidity or unenforceability of the mortgage lien which arises out of the transaction evidenced by the insured mortgage and is based on (a) a claim of usury or (b) any consumer credit protection or truth-in-lending claim.

Priority

The next area of lender's coverage is the natural compliment to insurance of the validity and enforceability of the lien, and that is insurance against priority of any lien or encumbrance over the lien of the insured mortgage. Thus, through these two insurance clauses, the lender obtains coverage for the validity, enforceability, and priority of the insured mortgage. This insurance provision is important because most lenders are concerned that the lien be of a required priority to satisfy regulatory and contractual requirements, and that on foreclosure, the full value of the secured property is made available to the lender.

Mechanics' Liens

Although mechanics' liens usually appear as a special exception to coverage in an owner's policy, they are expressly insured against in a loan policy.

Validity or Enforceability of an Assignment

The last insurance clause is written in the context of an increasingly active secondary-mortgage market. It insures against loss caused by the invalidity or unenforceability of any assignment, shown in Schedule A of the insured mortgage, and the failure of said assignment to vest title to the insured mortgage in the named assignee free and clear of all liens. This insurance clause is written to anticipate the assignment of the mortgage into the secondary-mortgage market simultaneous with the mortgage origination. If the mortgage and assignment documents are recorded, Schedule A of the policy, when issued, will show the record identification of the insured mortgage and the insured assignment. If the assignment is not recorded at the time of the issuance of the loan policy, it will not be described in Schedule A and will not be insured under the insuring clause. Insurance of the assignment must then be obtained by way of endorsement.

A loan policy has the same exclusions to coverage as an owner's policy, with the addition of an exclusion against any unenforceability of the insured mortgage because of the lender's not being qualified to do business within the state in which the property is located.

Miscellaneous Provisions

A loan policy is transferable, and the owner of the mortgage or loan deed being insured will be the insured under the policy. A loan policy usually is for the amount of the loan, and decreases as the loan is repaid. This rule can create problems in transactions in which the insured mortgage secures a revolving line of credit loan, such as a home equity loan, or a business line of credit loan, which contemplates that monies secured by the mortgage will be borrowed and repaid, reborrowed and repaid, and so on. A revolving line of credit mortgage requires an endorsement to the title insurance policy providing that the amount of insurance will always be the outstanding balance of the loan, despite the fact that monies have been borrowed and repaid numerous times under the loan.

CLAIMS PROCEDURES UNDER TITLE INSURANCE POLICIES

Both an owner's and a lender's policy protect the insured against any title defects that are not excluded or excepted from the coverage of the policy and that are created or attached before the effective date of the policy. The company settles these title defects or pays in the form of reimbursement to the insured sums of money lost as a result of the title defect up to the amount of the total insurance provided under the policy. A title company also has the obligation to defend, at its own expense, any title defects that are insured against. The insured has an obligation to immediately notify the title company once the title defects are discovered, and to provide the title company with full information concerning the title defects.

COMMITMENTS FOR TITLE INSURANCE

title insurance commitment

Commitment or contract by a title insurance company to issue a title insurance policy.

An owner's title insurance policy cannot be issued until the owner in fact owns the property. That is, the title insurance is a postclosing item that comes after the transaction and sale have been completed. The same is true with a loan policy: a lender cannot be insured until it in fact becomes a lender, which means that the insurance follows the funding and closing of a loan. Because title insurance is essentially a postclosing item, it is necessary that before the closing, the attorney or legal assistant representing the proposed insured obtain a pro forma copy of the insurance. This is accomplished by means of the title company issuing a **title commitment** or title binder, a contract to issue insurance once the transaction is closed. (An example of a title commitment appears at the end of the chapter in Exhibit 8–4.) The commitment is, for the most part, an example of how the actual policy will appear once the transaction is closed. The commitment shows all title exceptions and exclusions that will appear in the policy, and contains information concerning the insurance provisions of the policy. The main purpose of the commitment is to assure the proposed purchaser or lender that if it complies with the terms of the commitment, closes the transaction, and pays the necessary insurance premium, the proposed insured will have a title insurance policy subject only to the exceptions that appear in the commitment, unless defects, liens, encumbrances, or other matters intervene between the date of the commitment and the date of the policy. It is important that the date of the title commitment be as close as possible to the date of the actual closing of the transaction. In many cases a marked binder or marked commitment that brings the effective date down to the exact minute the deed or mortgage is recorded is used at closing.

A commitment for title insurance consists of three basic parts: Schedule A, Schedule B-1, and Schedule B-2. Schedule A shows the effective date of the title commitment (which, in most cases, is the date of the title examination of the property), sets forth the amount of coverage and the type of policy (either a loan or an owner's policy) that will be issued, reflects the current record owner of the property and the type of interest he owns (e.g., fee simple, life estate), and fully describes the property to be covered by the policy.

Schedule B, Section 1, of the commitment sets forth the requirements that must be met before the transaction closes for the title insurance to be issued.

Schedule B, Section 2, is a list of exceptions that will appear in Schedule B of the policy and that will not be insured against.

PRACTICE TIPS FOR THE PREPARATION AND REVIEW OF A TITLE INSURANCE POLICY

A legal assistant employed by a law firm or title insurance company may be responsible for the preparation or review of the final title insurance policy.

A title insurance policy cannot be prepared or issued until the transaction for which the insurance is to be issued has been completed. This will mean that all the documents which have been recorded have been returned from the courthouse and can be examined by the legal assistant in connection with the preparation of the policy. In addition, a final title examination is generally conducted to verify that the documents have been recorded and properly indexed and that there have been no matters recorded immediately prior to the consummation of the transaction. Once the legal assistant has this final examination and copies or originals of the recorded documents, the legal assistant can then prepare the title insurance policy.

The preparation of Schedule A to the policy should proceed as follows:

Step 1. The effective date of the title insurance policy is the date the insured instrument, a deed to the owner for an owner's policy, or the mortgage for a loan policy is recorded. This recordation date should be stamped on the copy or original of the recorded deed or mortgage. Generally, the exact time of recordation—including the day, hour, and minute—

will be used as the effective date for the title insurance policy. For example, if a deed on an owner's policy was recorded on September 25, 2003, at 3:16 P.M., the effective date of the owner's policy would be September 25, 2003, at 3:16 P.M.

Step 2. The amount of the insurance policy will be the amount shown from the title commitment, or if the commitment was not issued, would be the purchase price in the event of an owner's policy and the loan amount in the event of a loan policy.

Step 3. The title number for the title insurance would be the policy number issued by the title insurance company. All policies are consecutively issued. Each policy has its own number.

Step 4. The name of the insured will be taken from the recorded documents. In the event of an owner's policy, the name of the insured would be the grantee of the insured deed, and it would appear exactly as it appears in the deed. The name of the insured for a loan policy would be the lender shown on the recorded mortgage, and it would appear exactly as it is shown in the mortgage.

Step 5. The estate or interest which is covered in the policy will generally be fee simple, but if some other estate such as an estate for years is being insured, then that estate would appear in that information blank.

Step 6. The legal description of the property being insured should be the exact description as shown in the recorded deed or recorded mortgage being insured.

Step 7. On loan policies the insured mortgage is identified in the title insurance policy. The insured mortgage would be identified exactly as it is recorded, identifying both the name of the grantor and the name of the grantee, which would be the insured lender; the date of the mortgage; the amount of the mortgage; and the book and page number or other reference number for the recordation of the mortgage. An example of how an insured mortgage could be shown on a title insurance policy is as follows: "That certain mortgage from Ajax Realty Company to ABC Life Insurance Company dated March 1, 2003, securing a loan in the amount of $1,000,000 and being recorded on March 1, 2003, at Deed Book 716, Page 643, Knox County, Indiana Records."

Step 8. The preparation of Schedule B is an important part of the title insurance policy because it identifies all title exceptions not being insured against. These title exceptions will be taken from the title commitment and the final title examination. The legal assistant must carefully verify that all general exceptions are set forth in the title policy on Schedule B unless proper documents have been given to the title company to delete the general exceptions. These documents generally would be affidavits and an approved survey. The general exception for matters of survey will be deleted upon the presentation of an approved survey; however, matters that appear on the survey will be shown as Schedule B matters. That is, if the survey reveals encroachments or other matters, these will be set forth in detail on Schedule B. Other Schedule B matters include the special exceptions shown in the title examination but not satisfied or deleted at the time of the closing.

A legal assistant, when reviewing a title insurance policy on behalf of a client, should have available at the time of the review a copy of the marked title commitment or pro forma policy and a copy of all recorded documents. The legal assistant would then review a title policy to verify that it is correct in regard to the identification of the insured, the effective date of the policy, the amount of insurance and the proper identification of the insured deed or mortgage, and the legal description of the property being insured. The legal assistant would also match carefully the Schedule B exceptions in the final title policy against the Schedule B exceptions that appeared in the final pro forma policy or marked title insurance binder. The exceptions in the policy should be identical to those agreed to by the title company in the final marked binder or pro forma policy.

If the policy contains endorsements to the coverage, the legal assistant needs to verify that all required and approved endorsements have been added to the final title insurance policy. The client should receive from the title insurance company the original final title insurance policy.

E T H I C S : Personal Conflict of Interest

The responsibilities of a legal assistant working for a title insurance agency are to review title examinations and prepare title insurance commitments and title insurance policies. While working on a title insurance policy for a real estate sale transaction, the legal assistant discovers that a judgment lien is outstanding against the owner/seller of the property. Pursuant to the laws of the state in which the transaction is taking place, the judgment, unless it is levied on or paid, will expire in six months. The seller of the property has requested that the title insurance company insure over the judgment rather than pay the judgment. The title insurance company has agreed to the request but has asked that an amount of money equal to the amount of the judgment plus interest and other costs be deposited with the title insurance company until such time as the judgment expires. The legal assistant is a personal friend of someone who works for the company that is the judgment creditor. After the transaction has closed, the legal assistant calls the friend at the creditor company and informs her that a sum of money is being held by the title insurance company to pay the judgment. Was this an ethical thing for the legal assistant to do?

Professional ethics mandate that an attorney or a paralegal shall avoid conflicts of interest that may arise from family relationships or personal or business interests. The legal assistant in this particular transaction is working for a title agency whose customer was the owner/seller of the property. This customer/client had requested the title insurance company to not pay the judgment but instead to insure over it and to escrow money in the event the judgment holder should come forth and demand payment. The legal assistant's conflict of interest through his or her friendship with an employee of the judgment creditor and the telephone call informing the judgment creditor of the escrowed money is a conflict of interest and a breach of ethics. The legal assistant had a duty of loyalty and responsibility to the customer, which is a greater duty than the friendship with the employee of the judgment creditor.

SUMMARY

Title insurance is useful in protecting a purchaser or lender from economic loss resulting from defects in the title to real property. It does not, however, give complete protection to the purchaser or lender. It is important in any real estate transaction to completely understand what title defects are not covered by the title insurance. It is equally important to understand what coverages are available from title insurance, and how the standard title exceptions can be removed from the insurance policy. Complete familiarity with title insurance is important for any legal assistant who assists in the real estate closing process.

ACKNOWLEDGMENT

Portions of this chapter have been excerpted from *The Basics of Title Insurance* by Raymond J. Werner, *Title Insurance: The Lawyer's Expanding Role*, pages 3–67 (1985) American Bar Association all rights reserved; reprinted by permission of the American Bar Association.

KEY TERMS

affidavit

marketable title

mortgagee or loan policy

owner's policy

title endorsement

title insurance

title insurance commitment

SELF-STUDY EXAMINATION

(Answers provided in Appendix)

1. T or F. An owner's policy of title insurance insures access to and from the land.

2. T or F. Schedule B of a title policy contains a list of exceptions to coverage.

3. T or F. A title examination can protect a purchaser against forged signatures on deeds.

4. T or F. An ideal effective date for an owner's title policy is the date of the signing of the deed.

5. T or F. The amount of insurance in a title insurance policy will appear on Schedule B.

6. T or F. An owner's title insurance policy insures marketability of title, which means it ensures that the owner can sell the property.

7. T or F. A title insurance policy does not insure against matters not of public record and not known to the title company.

8. T or F. An owner's title insurance policy is not transferable to a purchaser of the property.

9. T or F. A loan policy of title insurance is not transferable.

10. T or F. A title insurance commitment is a contract to issue insurance once the transaction has been closed.

11. Identify and discuss the three safeguards that ensure good title.

12. What risks are covered by an ALTA owner's policy?

13. How are exclusions from coverage on a title insurance policy different from exceptions to title?

14. Why is a review of Schedule B to a title policy so important?

15. What is a title commitment, and why is it important in a real estate transaction?

16. What is the effective date of a title insurance policy, and why is it important?

17. Kim Buyer is purchasing a home. The purchase price of the home is $125,000. Kim is obtaining a loan from Acme Loan Company for $105,000. What is the amount of title insurance that Kim can purchase? What is the amount of title insurance that Acme Loan Company can purchase?

18. T. Sawyer has purchased a home. T. Sawyer obtained an owner's title insurance policy that insured the home to be free and clear of any liens and encumbrances. T. Sawyer, after purchasing the home, sells the home to B. Thatcher. B. Thatcher does not buy title insurance. Later it is discovered that there is a mortgage on the property held by H. Finn that dates before the effective date of T. Sawyer's title insurance policy. Does B. Thatcher have any claim against the title insurance purchased by T. Sawyer? Will the result be different if B. Thatcher had inherited the property from T. Sawyer on T. Sawyer's death?

19. You are involved in a real estate transaction. The sale took place on December 26, but the deed was not recorded until January 5. When you receive the owner's title insurance policy, you note that the effective date of the policy is December 26. Is this the correct effective date?

20. You are reviewing a title commitment that contains a standard exception for parties in possession. Your client does not want the standard exception to be included in the title insurance policy. What steps can you take to have the title insurance company delete the parties in possession exception?

21. What information is generally found on a Schedule A to an ALTA owner's title insurance policy?

22. What information is generally found on a Schedule B to an ALTA owner's title insurance policy?

23. What are the standard title exceptions found on a Schedule B to an owner's policy?

24. Why does a title insurance policy make an exception for any rights or claims of parties in possession not shown by public records?

25. What is generally found on Schedule B, Section 1 to a title commitment?

ADDENDUM

Exhibit 8–1 Owner's Policy—ALTA	Exhibit 8–3 Loan Policy
Exhibit 8–2 Owner's Affidavit	Exhibit 8–4 Title Commitment

EXHIBIT 8-1
Owner's Policy—ALTA

AMERICAN LAND TITLE ASSOCIATION
OWNER'S POLICY
(10-17-92)

SUBJECT TO THE EXCLUSIONS FROM COVERAGE, THE EXCEPTIONS FROM COVERAGE CONTAINED IN SCHEDULE B AND THE CONDITIONS AND STIPULATIONS, , herein called the Company, insures, as of Date of Policy shown in Schedule A, against loss or damage, not exceeding the Amount of Insurance stated in Schedule A, sustained or incurred by the insured by reason of:

1. Title to the estate or interest described in Schedule A being vested other than as stated therein;

2. Any defect in or lien or encumbrance on the title;

3. Unmarketability of the title;

4. Lack of a right of access to and from the land.

The Company will also pay the costs, attorneys' fees and expenses incurred in defense of the title, as insured, but only to the extent provided in the Conditions and Stipulations.

In Witness Whereof, : has caused this policy to be signed and sealed as of Date of Policy shown in Schedule A, the policy to become valid when countersigned by an authorized signatory.

Issued by:

ALTA Owner's Policy (10-17-92)

EXHIBIT 8-1
Owner's Policy—ALTA
(continued)

EXCLUSIONS FROM COVERAGE

The following matters are expressly excluded from the coverage of this policy and the Company will not pay loss or damage, costs, attorneys' fees or expenses which arise by reason of:

1. (a) Any law, ordinance or governmental regulation (including but not limited to building and zoning laws, ordinances, or regulations) restricting, regulating, prohibiting or relating to (i) the occupancy, use, or enjoyment of the land; (ii) the character, dimensions or location of any improvement now or hereafter erected on the land; (iii) a separation in ownership or a change in the dimensions or area of the land or any parcel of which the land is or was a part; or (iv) environmental protection, or the effect of any violation of these laws, ordinances or governmental regulations, except to the extent that a notice of the enforcement thereof or a notice of a defect, lien or encumbrance resulting from a violation or alleged violation affecting the land has been recorded in the public records at Date of Policy.

   (b) Any governmental police power not excluded by (a) above, except to the extent that a notice of the exercise thereof or a notice of a defect, lien or encumbrance resulting from a violation or alleged violation affecting the land has been recorded in the public records at Date of Policy.

2. Rights of eminent domain unless notice of the exercise thereof has been recorded in the public records at Date of Policy, but not excluding from coverage any taking which has occurred prior to Date of Policy which would be binding on the rights of a purchaser for value without knowledge.

3. Defects, liens, encumbrances, adverse claims or other matters:

   (a) created, suffered, assumed or agreed to by the insured claimant;

   (b) not known to the Company, not recorded in the public records at Date of Policy, but known to the insured claimant and not disclosed in writing to the Company by the insured claimant prior to the date the insured claimant became an insured under this policy;

   (c) resulting in no loss or damage to the insured claimant;

   (d) attaching or created subsequent to Date of Policy; or

   (e) resulting in loss or damage which would not have been sustained if the insured claimant had paid value for the estate or interest insured by this policy.

4. Any claim, which arises out of the transaction vesting in the Insured the estate or interest insured by this policy, by reason of the operation of federal bankruptcy, state insolvency, or similar creditors' rights laws, that is based on:

   (i) the transaction creating the estate or interest insured by this policy being deemed a fraudulent conveyance or fraudulent transfer; or

   (ii) the transaction creating the estate or interest insured by this policy being deemed a preferential transfer except where the preferential transfer results from the failure:

      (a) to timely record the instrument of transfer; or

      (b) of such recordation to impart notice to a purchaser for value or a judgment or lien creditor.

EXHIBIT 8-1
Owner's Policy—ALTA (continued)

SCHEDULE A

OFFICE FILE NUMBER	POLICY NUMBER	DATE OF POLICY	AMOUNT OF INSURANCE
1	2	3	4 $

1. Name of Insured:

2. The estate or interest in the land which is covered by this Policy is:

    Fee Simple

3. Title to the estate or interest in the land is vested in the Insured.

4. The land herein described is encumbered by the following mortgage or trust deed, and assignments:

    and the mortgages or trust deeds, if any, shown in Schedule B hereof.

5. The land referred to in this Policy is described as follows:

This Policy valid only if Schedule B is attached.

EXHIBIT 8–1
Owner's Policy—ALTA (continued)

SCHEDULE B

Policy Number: _____
Owners

EXCEPTIONS FROM COVERAGE

This policy does not insure against loss or damage (and the Company will not pay costs, attorneys' fees or expenses) which arise by reason of:

General Exceptions:

(1)   Rights or claims of parties in possession not shown by the public records.

(2)   Encroachments, overlaps, boundary line disputes, or other matters which would be disclosed by an accurate survey and inspection of the premises.

(3)   Easements, or claims of easements, not shown by the public records.

(4)   Any lien, or right to a lien, for services, labor, or material heretofore or hereafter furnished, imposed by law and not shown by the public records.

(5)   Taxes or special assessments which are not shown as existing liens by the public records.

Special Exceptions: The mortgage, if any, referred to in Item 4 of Schedule A.

Countersigned

_____
Authorized Signatory

Schedule B of this Policy consists of   pages.

EXHIBIT 8-1
Owner's Policy—ALTA (continued)

CONDITIONS AND STIPULATIONS

1. DEFINITION OF TERMS

The following terms when used in this policy mean:

(a) "insured": the insured named in Schedule A, and, subject to any rights or defenses the Company would have had against the named insured, those who succeed to the interest of the named insured by operation of law as distinguished from purchase including, but not limited to, heirs, distributees, devisees, survivors, personal representatives, next of kin, or corporate or fiduciary successors.

(b) "insured claimant": an insured claiming loss or damage.

(c) "knowledge" or "known": actual knowledge, not constructive knowledge or notice which may be imputed to an insured by reason of the public records as defined in this policy or any other records which impart constructive notice of matters affecting the land.

(d) "land": the land described or referred to in Schedule A, and improvements affixed thereto which by law constitute real property. The term "land" does not include any property beyond the lines of the area described or referred to in Schedule A, nor any right, title, interest, estate or easement in abutting streets, roads, avenues, alleys, lanes, ways or waterways, but nothing herein shall modify or limit the extent to which a right of access to and from the land is insured by this policy.

(e) "mortgage": mortgage, deed of trust, trust deed, or other security instrument.

(f) "public records": records established under state statutes at Date of Policy for the purpose of imparting constructive notice of matters relating to real property to purchasers for value and without knowledge. With respect to Section 1(a)(iv) of the Exclusions From Coverage, "public records" shall also include environmental protection liens filed in the records of the clerk of the United States district court for the district in which the land is located.

(g) "unmarketability of the title": an alleged or apparent matter affecting the title to the land, not excluded or excepted from coverage, which would entitle a purchaser of the estate or interest described in Schedule A to be released from the obligation to purchase by virtue of a contractual condition requiring the delivery of marketable title.

2. CONTINUATION OF INSURANCE AFTER CONVEYANCE OF TITLE

The coverage of this policy shall continue in force as of Date of Policy in favor of an insured only so long as the insured retains an estate or interest in the land, or holds an indebtedness secured by a purchase money mortgage given by a purchaser from the insured, or only so long as the insured shall have liability by reason of covenants of warranty made by the insured in any transfer or conveyance of the estate or interest. This policy shall not continue in force in favor of any purchaser from the insured of either (i) an estate or interest in the land, or (ii) an indebtedness secured by a purchase money mortgage given to the insured.

3. NOTICE OF CLAIM TO BE GIVEN BY INSURED CLAIMANT

The insured shall notify the Company promptly in writing (i) in case of any litigation as set forth in Section 4(a) below, (ii) in case knowledge shall come to an insured hereunder of any claim of title or interest which is adverse to the title to the estate or interest, as insured, and which might cause loss or damage for which the Company may be liable by virtue of this policy, or (iii) if title to the estate or interest, as insured, is rejected as unmarketable. If prompt notice shall not be given to the Company, then as to the insured all liability of the Company shall terminate with regard to the matter or matters for which prompt notice is required; provided, however, that failure to notify the Company shall in no case prejudice the rights of any insured under this policy unless the Company shall be prejudiced by the failure and then only to the extent of the prejudice.

4. DEFENSE AND PROSECUTION OF ACTIONS; DUTY OF INSURED CLAIMANT TO COOPERATE

(a) Upon written request by the insured and subject to the options contained in Section 6 of these Conditions and Stipulations, the Company, at its own cost and without unreasonable delay, shall provide for the defense of an insured in litigation in which any third party asserts a claim adverse to the title or interest as insured, but only as to those stated causes of action alleging a defect, lien or encumbrance or other matter insured against by this policy. The Company shall have the right to select counsel of its choice (subject to the right of the insured to object for reasonable cause) to represent the insured as to those stated causes of action and shall not be liable for and will not pay the fees of any other counsel. The Company will not pay any fees, costs or expenses incurred by the insured in the defense of those causes of action which allege matters not insured against by this policy.

(b) The Company shall have the right, at its own cost, to institute and prosecute any action or proceeding or to do any other act which in its opinion may be necessary or desirable to establish the title to the estate or interest, as insured, or to prevent or reduce loss or damage to the insured. The Company may take any appropriate action under the terms of this policy, whether or not it shall be liable hereunder, and shall not thereby concede liability or waive any provision of this policy. If the Company shall exercise its rights under this paragraph. it shall do so diligently.

(c) Whenever the Company shall have brought an action or interposed a defense as required or permitted by the provisions of this policy, the Company may pursue any litigation to final determination by a court of competent jurisdiction and expressly reserves the right, in its sole discretion, to appeal from any adverse judgment or order.

(d) In all cases where this policy permits or requires the Company to prosecute or provide for the defense of any action or proceeding, the insured shall secure to the Company the right to so prosecute or provide defense in the action or proceeding, and all appeals therein, and permit the Company to use, at its option, the name of the insured for this purpose. Whenever requested by the Company, the insured, at the Company's expense, shall give the Company all reasonable aid (i) in any action or proceeding, securing evidence, obtaining witnesses, prosecuting or defending the action or proceeding, or effecting settlement, and (ii) in any other lawful act which in the opinion of the Company may be necessary or desirable to establish the title to the estate or interest as insured. If the Company is prejudiced by the failure of the insured to furnish the required cooperation, the Company's obligations to the insured under the policy shall terminate, including any liability or obligation to defend, prosecute, or continue any litigation, with regard to the matter or matters requiring such cooperation.

5. PROOF OF LOSS OR DAMAGE

In addition to and after the notices required under Section 3 of these Conditions and Stipulations have been provided the Company, a proof of loss or damage signed and sworn to by the insured claimant shall be furnished to the Company within 90 days after the insured claimant shall ascertain the facts giving rise to the loss or damage. The proof of loss or damage shall describe the defect in, or lien or encumbrance on the title, or other matter insured against by this policy which constitutes the basis of loss or damage and shall state, to the extent possible, the basis of calculating the amount of the loss or damage. If the Company is prejudiced by the failure of the insured claimant to provide the required proof of loss or damage, the Company's obligations to the insured under the policy shall terminate, including any liability or obligation to defend, prosecute, or continue any litigation, with regard to the matter or matters requiring such proof of loss or damage.

In addition, the insured claimant may reasonably be required to submit to examination under oath by any authorized representative of the Company and shall produce for examination, inspection and copying, at such reasonable times and places as may be designated by any authorized representative of the Company, all records, books, ledgers, checks, correspondence and memoranda, whether bearing a date before or after Date of Policy, which reasonably pertain to the loss or damage. Further, if requested by any authorized representative of the Company, the insured claimant shall grant its permission, in writing, for any authorized representative of the Company to examine, inspect and copy all records, books, ledgers, checks, correspondence and memoranda in the custody or control of a third party, which reasonably pertain to the loss or damage. All information designated as confidential by the insured claimant provided to the Company pursuant to this Section shall not be disclosed to others unless, in the reasonable judgment of the Company, it is necessary in the administration of the claim. Failure of the insured claimant to submit for examination under oath, produce other reasonably requested information or grant permission to secure reasonably necessary information from third parties as required in this paragraph shall terminate any liability of the Company under this policy as to that claim.

6. OPTIONS TO PAY OR OTHERWISE SETTLE CLAIMS; TERMINATION OF LIABILITY

In case of a claim under this policy, the Company shall have the following additional options:

(a) To Pay or Tender Payment of the Amount of Insurance.

To pay or tender payment of the amount of insurance under this policy together with any costs, attorneys' fees and expenses incurred by the insured claimant, which were authorized by the Company, up to the time of payment or tender of payment and which the Company is obligated to pay.

Upon the exercise by the Company of this option, all liability and obligations to the insured under this policy, other than to make the payment required, shall terminate, including any liability or obligation to defend, prosecute, or continue any litigation, and the policy shall be surrendered to the Company for cancellation.

(b) To Pay or Otherwise Settle With Parties Other than the Insured or With the Insured Claimant.

(i) to pay or otherwise settle with other parties for or in the name of an insured claimant any claim insured against under this policy, together with any costs, attorneys' fees and expenses incurred by the insured claimant which were authorized by the Company up to the time of payment and which the Company is obligated to pay; or

(ii) to pay or otherwise settle with the insured claimant the loss or damage provided for under this policy, together with any costs, attorneys' fees and expenses incurred by the insured claimant which were authorized by the Company up to the time of payment and which the Company is obligated to pay.

EXHIBIT 8–1
Owner's Policy—ALTA (continued)

Upon the exercise by the Company of either of the options provided for in paragraphs (b)(i) or (ii), the Company's obligations to the insured under this policy for the claimed loss or damage, other than the payments required to be made, shall terminate, including any liability or obligation to defend, prosecute or continue any litigation.

7. DETERMINATION, EXTENT OF LIABILITY AND COINSURANCE

This policy is a contract of indemnity against actual monetary loss or damage sustained or incurred by the insured claimant who has suffered loss or damage by reason of matters insured against by this policy and only to the extent herein described.

(a) The liability of the Company under this policy shall not exceed the least of:

(i) the Amount of Insurance stated in Schedule A; or,

(ii) the difference between the value of the insured estate or interest as insured and the value of the insured estate or interest subject to the defect, lien or encumbrance insured against by this policy.

(b) In the event the Amount of Insurance stated in Schedule A at the Date of Policy is less than 80 percent of the value of the insured estate or interest or the full consideration paid for the land, whichever is less, or if subsequent to the Date of Policy an improvement is erected on the land which increases the value of the insured estate or interest by at least 20 percent over the Amount of Insurance stated in Schedule A, then this Policy is subject to the following:

(i) where no subsequent improvement has been made, as to any partial loss, the Company shall only pay the loss pro rata in the proportion that the amount of insurance at Date of Policy bears to the total value of the insured estate or interest at Date of Policy; or

(ii) where a subsequent improvement has been made, as to any partial loss, the Company shall only pay the loss pro rata in the proportion that 120 percent of the Amount of Insurance stated in Schedule A bears to the sum of the Amount of Insurance stated in Schedule A and the amount expended for the improvement.

The provisions of this paragraph shall not apply to costs, attorneys' fees and expenses for which the Company is liable under this policy, and shall only apply to that portion of any loss which exceeds, in the aggregate, 10 percent of the Amount of Insurance stated in Schedule A.

(c) The Company will pay only those costs, attorneys' fees and expenses incurred in accordance with Section 4 of these Conditions and Stipulations.

8. APPORTIONMENT

If the land described in Schedule A consists of two or more parcels which are not used as a single site, and a loss is established affecting one or more of the parcels but not all, the loss shall be computed and settled on a pro rata basis as if the amount of insurance under this policy was divided pro rata as to the value on Date of Policy of each separate parcel to the whole, exclusive of any improvements made subsequent to Date of Policy, unless a liability or value has otherwise been agreed upon as to each parcel by the Company and the insured at the time of the issuance of this policy and shown by an express statement or by an endorsement attached to this policy.

9. LIMITATION OF LIABILITY

(a) If the Company establishes the title, or removes the alleged defect, lien or encumbrance, or cures the lack of a right of access to or from the land, or cures the claim of unmarketability of title, all as insured, in a reasonably diligent manner by any method, including litigation and the completion of any appeals therefrom, it shall have fully performed its obligations with respect to that matter and shall not be liable for any loss or damage caused thereby.

(b) In the event of any litigation, including litigation by the Company or with the Company's consent, the Company shall have no liability for loss or damage until there has been a final determination by a court of competent jurisdiction, and disposition of all appeals therefrom, adverse to the title as insured.

(c) The Company shall not be liable for loss or damage to any insured for liability voluntarily assumed by the insured in settling any claim or suit without the prior written consent of the Company.

10. REDUCTION OF INSURANCE; REDUCTION OR TERMINATION OF LIABILITY

All payments under this policy, except payments made for costs, attorneys' fees and expenses, shall reduce the amount of the insurance pro tanto.

11. LIABILITY NONCUMULATIVE

It is expressly understood that the amount of insurance under this policy shall be reduced by any amount the Company may pay under any policy insuring a mortgage to which exception is taken in Schedule B or to which the insured has agreed, assumed, or taken subject, or which is hereafter executed by an insured and which is a charge or lien on the estate or interest described or referred to in Schedule A, and the amount so paid shall be deemed a payment under this policy to the insured owner.

12. PAYMENT OF LOSS

(a) No payment shall be made without producing this policy for endorsement of the payment unless the policy has been lost or destroyed, in which case proof of loss or destruction shall be furnished to the satisfaction of the Company.

Reorder Form No. 8256 (Rev. 10-17-92)

(b) When liability and the extent of loss or damage has been definitely fixed in accordance with these Conditions and Stipulations, the loss or damage shall be payable within 30 days thereafter.

13. SUBROGATION UPON PAYMENT OR SETTLEMENT

(a) The Company's Right of Subrogation.

Whenever the Company shall have settled and paid a claim under this policy, all right of subrogation shall vest in the Company unaffected by any act of the insured claimant.

The Company shall be subrogated to and be entitled to all rights and remedies which the insured claimant would have had against any person or property in respect to the claim had this policy not been issued. If requested by the Company, the insured claimant shall transfer to the Company all rights and remedies against any person or property necessary in order to perfect this right of subrogation. The insured claimant shall permit the Company to sue, compromise or settle in the name of the insured claimant and to use the name of the insured claimant in any transaction or litigation involving these rights or remedies.

If a payment on account of a claim does not fully cover the loss of the insured claimant, the Company shall be subrogated to these rights and remedies in the proportion which the Company's payment bears to the whole amount of the loss.

If loss should result from any act of the insured claimant, as stated above, that act shall not void this policy, but the Company, in that event, shall be required to pay only that part of any losses insured against by this policy which shall exceed the amount, if any, lost to the Company by reason of the impairment by the insured claimant of the Company's right of subrogation.

(b) The Company's Rights Against Non-insured Obligors.

The Company's right of subrogation against non-insured obligors shall exist and shall include, without limitation, the rights of the insured to indemnities, guaranties, other policies of insurance or bonds, notwithstanding any terms or conditions contained in those instruments which provide for subrogation rights by reason of this policy.

14. ARBITRATION

Unless prohibited by applicable law, either the Company or the insured may demand arbitration pursuant to the Title Insurance Arbitration Rules of the American Arbitration Association. Arbitrable matters may include, but are not limited to, any controversy or claim between the Company and the insured arising out of or relating to this policy, any service of the Company in connection with its issuance or the breach of a policy provision or other obligation. All arbitrable matters when the Amount of Insurance is $1,000,000 or less shall be arbitrated at the option of either the Company or the insured. All arbitrable matters when the Amount of Insurance is in excess of $1,000,000 shall be arbitrated only when agreed to by both the Company and the insured. Arbitration pursuant to this policy and under the Rules in effect on the date the demand for arbitration is made or, at the option of the insured, the Rules in effect at Date of Policy shall be binding upon the parties. The award may include attorneys' fees only if the laws of the state in which the land is located permit a court to award attorneys' fees to a prevailing party. Judgment upon the award rendered by the Arbitrator(s) may be entered in any court having jurisdiction thereof.

The law of the situs of the land shall apply to an arbitration under the Title Insurance Arbitration Rules.

A copy of the Rules may be obtained from the Company upon request.

15. LIABILITY LIMITED TO THIS POLICY; POLICY ENTIRE CONTRACT

(a) This policy together with all endorsements, if any, attached hereto by the Company is the entire policy and contract between the insured and the Company. In interpreting any provision of this policy, this policy shall be construed as a whole.

(b) Any claim of loss or damage, whether or not based on negligence, and which arises out of the status of the title to the estate or interest covered hereby or by any action asserting such claim, shall be restricted to this policy.

(c) No amendment of or endorsement to this policy can be made except by a writing endorsed hereon or attached hereto signed by either the President, a Vice President, the Secretary, an Assistant Secretary, or validating officer or authorized signatory of the Company.

16. SEVERABILITY

In the event any provision of the policy is held invalid or unenforceable under applicable law, the policy shall be deemed not to include that provision and all other provisions shall remain in full force and effect.

17. NOTICES, WHERE SENT

All notices required to be given the Company and any statement in writing required to be furnished the Company shall include the number of this policy and shall be addressed to the Company at the issuing office or to:

EXHIBIT 8–2
Owner's Affidavit

STATE OF GEORGIA   )
)   ss:
COUNTY OF FULTON   )

The undersigned, being duly sworn, states:

That the undersigned is the President of MARKAM INDUSTRIES, INC., a Georgia corporation (the "Company"), and is duly authorized to execute this affidavit in his capacity on behalf of the Company as well as in his individual capacity;

That the principal place of business, principal office and chief executive office of the Company is located in Gwinnett County, Georgia and has been located in said County at all times since the formation of the Company;

That the Company is the fee simple title owner of the real property described on Exhibit "A" attached hereto and incorporated herein by reference (the "Property").

That the lines and corners of the Property are clearly marked and there are no disputes concerning the location of said lines and corners;

That no improvements or repairs have been made or contracted for by the Company on the Property during the three (3) months immediately preceding the date of this affidavit, for which there are outstanding bills for labor or services performed or rendered, or for material supplied or furnished, or incurred in connection with improvements or repairs on the Property, or for the services of architects, surveyors or engineers in connection with improvements or repairs on the Property;

That, except for the matters set forth on Exhibit "B" attached hereto and incorporated herein by reference, the Property is free and clear of all claims, liens and encumbrances, and there is no outstanding indebtedness for or liens against any equipment or fixtures attached to, installed on, incorporated in or located on, or otherwise used in connection with the operation or maintenance of, the Property or the improvements thereon;

That there are no persons or other parties in possession of the Property who have a right or claim to possession extending beyond the date hereof;

That there are no suits, proceedings, judgments, bankruptcies, liens, or executions against the Company which affect title to the Property, the improvements thereon or the fixtures attached thereto;

That the undersigned is making this affidavit with the knowledge that it will be relied upon by lenders, attorneys, and title insurance companies interested in the title to the Property.

Sworn to and subscribed before me this
_____ day of _____, 20_____.

_____   _____
Notary Public   JIM BAXTER

My Commission Expires:

_____

[Notarial Seal]

EXHIBIT 8-3
Loan Policy

AMERICAN LAND TITLE ASSOCIATION
LOAN POLICY
(10-17-92)

SUBJECT TO THE EXCLUSIONS FROM COVERAGE, THE EXCEPTIONS FROM COVERAGE
CONTAINED IN SCHEDULE B AND THE CONDITIONS AND STIPULATIONS,
herein called the Company, insures, as of Date of Policy shown
in Schedule A, against loss or damage, not exceeding the Amount of Insurance stated in Schedule A, sustained or
incurred by the insured by reason of:

1. Title to the estate or interest described in Schedule A being vested other than as stated therein;
2. Any defect in or lien or encumbrance on the title;
3. Unmarketability of the title;
4. Lack of a right of access to and from the land;
5. The invalidity or unenforceability of the lien of the insured mortgage upon the title;
6. The priority of any lien or encumbrance over the lien of the insured mortgage;
7. Lack of priority of the lien of the insured mortgage over any statutory lien for services, labor or material:
    (a) arising from an improvement or work related to the land which is contracted for or commenced
        prior to Date of Policy; or
    (b) arising from an improvement or work related to the land which is contracted for or commenced
        subsequent to Date of Policy and which is financed in whole or in part by proceeds of the
        indebtedness secured by the insured mortgage which at Date of Policy the insured has advanced or
        is obligated to advance;
8. The invalidity or unenforceability of any assignment of the insured mortgage, provided the assignment
    is shown in Schedule A, or the failure of the assignment shown in Schedule A to vest title to the insured
    mortgage in the named insured assignee free and clear of all liens.

The Company will also pay the costs, attorneys' fees and expenses incurred in defense of the title or the lien of the
insured mortgage, as insured, but only to the extent provided in the Conditions and Stipulations.

In Witness Whereof, ·   has caused this policy to be signed and sealed as
of Date of Policy shown in Schedule A, the policy to become valid when countersigned by an authorized signatory.

Issued by:

EXHIBIT 8–3
Loan Policy (continued)

EXCLUSIONS FROM COVERAGE

The following matters are expressly excluded from the coverage of this policy and the Company will not pay loss or damage, costs, attorneys' fees or expenses which arise by reason of:

1. (a) Any law, ordinance or governmental regulation (including but not limited to building and zoning laws, ordinances, or regulations) restricting, regulating, prohibiting or relating to (i) the occupancy, use, or enjoyment of the land; (ii) the character, dimensions or location of any improvement now or hereafter erected on the land; (iii) a separation in ownership or a change in the dimensions or area of the land or any parcel of which the land is or was a part; or (iv) environmental protection, or the effect of any violation of these laws, ordinances or governmental regulations, except to the extent that a notice of the enforcement thereof or a notice of a defect, lien or encumbrance resulting from a violation or alleged violation affecting the land has been recorded in the public records at Date of Policy.

   (b) Any governmental police power not excluded by (a) above, except to the extent that a notice of the exercise thereof or a notice of a defect, lien or encumbrance resulting from a violation or alleged violation affecting the land has been recorded in the public records at Date of Policy.

2. Rights of eminent domain unless notice of the exercise thereof has been recorded in the public records at Date of Policy, but not excluding from coverage any taking which has occurred prior to Date of Policy which would be binding on the rights of a purchaser for value without knowledge.

3. Defects, liens, encumbrances, adverse claims or other matters:

   (a) created, suffered, assumed or agreed to by the insured claimant;

   (b) not known to the Company, not recorded in the public records at Date of Policy, but known to the insured claimant and not disclosed in writing to the Company by the insured claimant prior to the date the insured claimant became an insured under this policy;

   (c) resulting in no loss or damage to the insured claimant;

   (d) attaching or created subsequent to Date of Policy (except to the extent that this policy insures the priority of the lien of the insured mortgage over any statutory lien for services, labor or material); or

   (e) resulting in loss or damage which would not have been sustained if the insured claimant had paid value for the insured mortgage.

4. Unenforceability of the lien of the insured mortgage because of the inability or failure of the insured at Date of Policy, or the inability or failure of any subsequent owner of the indebtedness, to comply with applicable doing business laws of the state in which the land is situated.

5. Invalidity or unenforceability of the lien of the insured mortgage, or claim thereof, which arises out of the transaction evidenced by the insured mortgage and is based upon usury or any consumer credit protection or truth in lending law.

6. Any statutory lien for services, labor or materials (or the claim of priority of any statutory lien for services, labor or materials over the lien of the insured mortgage) arising from an improvement or work related to the land which is contracted for and commenced subsequent to Date of Policy and is not financed in whole or in part by proceeds of the indebtedness secured by the insured mortgage which at Date of Policy the insured has advanced or is obligated to advance.

7. Any claim, which arises out of the transaction creating the interest of the mortgagee insured by this policy, by reason of the operation of federal bankruptcy, state insolvency, or similar creditors' rights laws, that is based on:

   (i) the transaction creating the interest of the insured mortgagee being deemed a fraudulent conveyance or fraudulent transfer; or

   (ii) the subordination of the interest of the insured mortgagee as a result of the application of the doctrine of equitable subordination; or

   (iii) the transaction creating the interest of the insured mortgagee being deemed a preferential transfer except where the preferential transfer results from the failure:

      (a) to timely record the instrument of transfer; or

      (b) of such recordation to impart notice to a purchaser for value or a judgment or lien creditor.

CONDITIONS AND STIPULATIONS

1. DEFINITION OF TERMS

The following terms when used in this policy mean:

(a) "insured": the insured named in Schedule A. The term "insured" also includes

(i) the owner of the indebtedness secured by the insured mortgage and each successor in ownership of the indebtedness except a successor who is an obligor under the provisions of Section 12(c) of these Conditions and Stipulations (reserving, however, all rights and defenses as to any successor that the Company would have had against any predecessor insured, unless the successor acquired the indebtedness as a purchaser for value without knowledge of the asserted defect, lien, encumbrance, adverse claim or other matter insured against by this policy as affecting title to the estate or interest in the land);

(ii) any governmental agency or governmental instrumentality which is an insurer or guarantor under an insurance contract or guaranty insuring or guaranteeing the indebtedness secured by the insured mortgage, or any part thereof, whether named as an insured herein or not;

(iii) the parties designated in Section 2(a) of these Conditions and Stipulations.

(b) "insured claimant": an insured claiming loss or damage.

(c) "knowledge" or "known": actual knowledge, not constructive knowledge or notice which may be imputed to an insured by reason of the public records as defined in this policy or any other records which impart constructive notice of matters affecting the land.

(d) "land": the land described or referred to in Schedule A, and improvements affixed thereto which by law constitute real property. The term "land" does not include any property beyond the lines of the area described or referred to in Schedule A, nor any right, title, interest, estate or easement in abutting streets, roads, avenues, alleys, lanes, ways or waterways, but nothing herein shall modify or limit the extent to which a right of access to and from the land is insured by this policy.

(e) "mortgage": mortgage, deed of trust, trust deed, or other security instrument.

(f) "public records": records established under state statutes at Date of Policy for the purpose of imparting constructive notice of matters relating to real property to purchasers for value and without knowledge. With respect to Section 1(a)(iv) of the Exclusions From Coverage, "public records" shall also include environmental protection liens filed in the records of the clerk of the United States district court for the district in which the land is located.

(g) "unmarketability of the title": an alleged or apparent matter affecting the title to the land, not excluded or excepted from coverage, which would entitle a purchaser of the estate or interest described in Schedule A or the insured mortgage to be released from the obligation to purchase by virtue of a contractual condition requiring the delivery of marketable title.

2. CONTINUATION OF INSURANCE

(a) After Acquisition of Title. The coverage of this policy shall continue in force as of Date of Policy in favor of (i) an insured who acquires all or any part of the estate or interest in the land by foreclosure, trustee's sale, conveyance in lieu of foreclosure, or other legal manner which discharges the lien of the insured mortgage; (ii) a transferee of the estate or interest so acquired from an insured corporation, provided the transferee is the parent or wholly-owned subsidiary of the insured corporation, and their corporate successors by operation of law and not by purchase, subject to any rights or defenses the Company may have against any predecessor insureds; and (iii) any governmental agency or governmental instrumentality which acquires all or any part of the estate or interest pursuant to a contract of insurance or guaranty insuring or guaranteeing the indebtedness secured by the insured mortgage.

(b) After Conveyance of Title. The coverage of this policy shall continue in force as of Date of Policy in favor of an insured only so long as the insured retains an estate or interest in the land, or holds an indebtedness secured by a purchase money mortgage given by a purchaser from the insured, or only so long as the insured shall have liability by reason of covenants of warranty made by the insured in any transfer or conveyance of the estate or interest. This policy shall not continue in force in favor of any purchaser from the insured of either (i) an estate or interest in the land, or (ii) an indebtedness secured by a purchase money mortgage given to the insured.

EXHIBIT 8−3
Loan Policy (continued)

SCHEDULE A

OFFICE FILE NUMBER	POLICY NUMBER	DATE OF POLICY	AMOUNT OF INSURANCE
1	2	3	4 $

1. Name of Insured:

2. The estate or interest in the land which is encumbered by the insured mortgage is:

   Fee Simple

3. Title to the estate or interest in the land is vested in:

4. The insured mortgage and assignments thereof, if any, are described as follows:

5. The land referred to in this Policy is described as follows:

This Policy valid only if Schedule B is attached.

EXHIBIT 8-3
Loan Policy (continued)

SCHEDULE B

Policy Number: _____

Loan

EXCEPTIONS FROM COVERAGE

This policy does not insure against loss or damage (and the Company will not pay costs, attorneys' fees or expenses) which arise by reason of:

Special Exceptions:

Countersigned

_____

Authorized Signatory

Schedule B of this Policy consists of   pages.

EXHIBIT 8-3
Loan Policy (continued)

(c) Amount of Insurance. The amount of insurance after the acquisition or after the conveyance shall in neither event exceed the least of:

(i) the Amount of Insurance stated in Schedule A;

(ii) the amount of the principal of the indebtedness secured by the insured mortgage as of Date of Policy, interest thereon, expenses of foreclosure, amounts advanced pursuant to the insured mortgage to assure compliance with laws or to protect the lien of the insured mortgage prior to the time of acquisition of the estate or interest in the land and secured thereby and reasonable amounts expended to prevent deterioration of improvements, but reduced by the amount of all payments made; or

(iii) the amount paid by any governmental agency or governmental instrumentality, if the agency or instrumentality is the insured claimant, in the acquisition of the estate or interest in satisfaction of its insurance contract or guaranty.

3. NOTICE OF CLAIM TO BE GIVEN BY INSURED CLAIMANT

The insured shall notify the Company promptly in writing (i) in case of any litigation as set forth in Section 4(a) below, (ii) in case knowledge shall come to an insured hereunder of any claim of title or interest which is adverse to the title to the estate or interest or the lien of the insured mortgage, as insured, and which might cause loss or damage for which the Company may be liable by virtue of this policy, or (iii) if title to the estate or interest or the lien of the insured mortgage, as insured, is rejected as unmarketable. If prompt notice shall not be given to the Company, then as to the insured all liability of the Company shall terminate with regard to the matter or matters for which prompt notice is required; provided, however, that failure to notify the Company shall in no case prejudice the rights of any insured under this policy unless the Company shall be prejudiced by the failure and then only to the extent of the prejudice.

4. DEFENSE AND PROSECUTION OF ACTIONS; DUTY OF INSURED CLAIMANT TO COOPERATE

(a) Upon written request by the insured and subject to the options contained in Section 6 of these Conditions and Stipulations, the Company, at its own cost and without unreasonable delay, shall provide for the defense of an insured in litigation in which any third party asserts a claim adverse to the title or interest as insured, but only as to those stated causes of action alleging a defect, lien or encumbrance or other matter insured against by this policy. The Company shall have the right to select counsel of its choice (subject to the right of the insured to object for reasonable cause) to represent the insured as to those stated causes of action and shall not be liable for and will not pay the fees of any other counsel. The Company will not pay any fees, costs or expenses incurred by the insured in the defense of those causes of action which allege matters not insured against by this policy.

(b) The Company shall have the right, at its own cost, to institute and prosecute any action or proceeding or to do any other act which in its opinion may be necessary or desirable to establish the title to the estate or interest or the lien of the insured mortgage, as insured, or to prevent or reduce loss or damage to the insured. The Company may take any appropriate action under the terms of this policy, whether or not it shall be liable hereunder, and shall not thereby concede liability or waive any provision of this policy. If the Company shall exercise its rights under this paragraph, it shall do so diligently.

(c) Whenever the Company shall have brought an action or interposed a defense as required or permitted by the provisions of this policy, the Company may pursue any litigation to final determination by a court of competent jurisdiction and expressly reserves the right, in its sole discretion, to appeal from any adverse judgment or order.

(d) In all cases where this policy permits or requires the Company to prosecute or provide for the defense of any action or proceeding, the insured shall secure to the Company the right to so prosecute or provide defense in the action or proceeding, and all appeals therein, and permit the Company to use, at its option, the name of the insured for this purpose. Whenever requested by the Company, the insured, at the Company's expense, shall give the Company all reasonable aid (i) in any action or proceeding, securing evidence, obtaining witnesses, prosecuting or defending the action or proceeding, or effecting settlement, and (ii) in any other lawful act which in the opinion of the Company may be necessary or desirable to establish the title to the estate or interest or the lien of the insured mortgage, as insured. If the Company is prejudiced by the failure of the insured to furnish the required cooperation, the Company's obligations to the insured under the policy shall terminate, including any liability or obligation to defend, prosecute, or continue any litigation, with regard to the matter or matters requiring such cooperation.

5. PROOF OF LOSS OR DAMAGE

In addition to and after the notices required under Section 3 of these Conditions and Stipulations have been provided the Company, a proof of loss or damage signed and sworn to by the insured claimant shall be furnished to the Company within 90 days after the insured claimant shall ascertain the facts giving rise to the loss or damage. The proof of loss or damage shall describe the defect in, or lien or encumbrance on the title, or other matter insured against by this policy which constitutes the basis of loss or damage and shall state, to the extent possible, the basis of calculating the amount of the loss or damage. If the Company is prejudiced by the failure of the insured claimant to

provide the required proof of loss or damage, the Company's obligations to the insured under the policy shall terminate, including any liability or obligation to defend, prosecute, or continue any litigation, with regard to the matter or matters requiring such proof of loss or damage.

In addition, the insured claimant may reasonably be required to submit to examination under oath by any authorized representative of the Company and shall produce for examination, inspection and copying, at such reasonable times and places as may be designated by any authorized representative of the Company, all records, books, ledgers, checks, correspondence and memoranda, whether bearing a date before or after Date of Policy, which reasonably pertain to the loss or damage. Further, if requested by any authorized representative of the Company, the insured claimant shall grant its permission, in writing, for any authorized representative of the Company to examine, inspect and copy all records, books, ledgers, checks, correspondence and memoranda in the custody or control of a third party, which reasonably pertain to the loss or damage. All information designated as confidential by the insured claimant provided to the Company pursuant to this Section shall not be disclosed to others unless, in the reasonable judgment of the Company, it is necessary in the administration of the claim. Failure of the insured claimant to submit for examination under oath, produce other reasonably requested information or grant permission to secure reasonably necessary information from third parties as required in this paragraph, unless prohibited by law or governmental regulation, shall terminate any liability of the Company under this policy as to that claim.

6. OPTIONS TO PAY OR OTHERWISE SETTLE CLAIMS; TERMINATION OF LIABILITY

In case of a claim under this policy, the Company shall have the following additional options:

(a) To Pay or Tender Payment of the Amount of Insurance or to Purchase the Indebtedness.

(i) to pay or tender payment of the amount of insurance under this policy together with any costs, attorneys' fees and expenses incurred by the insured claimant, which were authorized by the Company, up to the time of payment or tender of payment and which the Company is obligated to pay; or

(ii) to purchase the indebtedness secured by the insured mortgage for the amount owing thereon together with any costs, attorneys' fees and expenses incurred by the insured claimant which were authorized by the Company up to the time of purchase and which the Company is obligated to pay.

If the Company offers to purchase the indebtedness as herein provided, the owner of the indebtedness shall transfer, assign, and convey the indebtedness and the insured mortgage, together with any collateral security, to the Company upon payment therefor.

Upon the exercise by the Company of either of the options provided for in paragraphs a(i) or (ii), all liability and obligations to the insured under this policy, other than to make the payment required in those paragraphs, shall terminate, including any liability or obligation to defend, prosecute, or continue any litigation, and the policy shall be surrendered to the Company for cancellation.

(b) To Pay or Otherwise Settle With Parties Other than the Insured or With the Insured Claimant.

(i) to pay or otherwise settle with other parties for or in the name of an insured claimant any claim insured against under this policy, together with any costs, attorneys' fees and expenses incurred by the insured claimant which were authorized by the Company up to the time of payment and which the Company is obligated to pay; or

(ii) to pay or otherwise settle with the insured claimant the loss or damage provided for under this policy, together with any costs, attorneys' fees and expenses incurred by the insured claimant which were authorized by the Company up to the time of payment and which the Company is obligated to pay.

Upon the exercise by the Company of either of the options provided for in paragraphs (b)(i) or (ii), the Company's obligations to the insured under this policy for the claimed loss or damage, other than the payments required to be made, shall terminate, including any liability or obligation to defend, prosecute or continue any litigation.

7. DETERMINATION AND EXTENT OF LIABILITY

This policy is a contract of indemnity against actual monetary loss or damage sustained or incurred by the insured claimant who has suffered loss or damage by reason of matters insured against by this policy and only to the extent herein described.

(a) The liability of the Company under this policy shall not exceed the least of:

(i) the Amount of Insurance stated in Schedule A, or, if applicable, the amount of insurance as defined in Section 2 (c) of these Conditions and Stipulations;

(ii) the amount of the unpaid principal indebtedness secured by the insured mortgage as limited or provided under Section 8 of these Conditions and Stipulations or as reduced under Section 9 of these Conditions and Stipulations, at the time the loss or damage insured against by this policy occurs, together with interest thereon; or

EXHIBIT 8-3
Loan Policy (continued)

(iii) the difference between the value of the insured estate or interest as insured and the value of the insured estate or interest subject to the defect, lien or encumbrance insured against by this policy.

(b) In the event the insured has acquired the estate or interest in the manner described in Section 2(a) of these Conditions and Stipulations or has conveyed the title, then the liability of the Company shall continue as set forth in Section 7(a) of these Conditions and Stipulations.

(c) The Company will pay only those costs, attorneys' fees and expenses incurred in accordance with Section 4 of these Conditions and Stipulations.

8. LIMITATION OF LIABILITY

(a) If the Company establishes the title, or removes the alleged defect, lien or encumbrance, or cures the lack of a right of access to or from the land, or cures the claim of unmarketability of title, or otherwise establishes the lien of the insured mortgage, all as insured, in a reasonably diligent manner by any method, including litigation and the completion of any appeals therefrom, it shall have fully performed its obligations with respect to that matter and shall not be liable for any loss or damage caused thereby.

(b) In the event of any litigation, including litigation by the Company or with the Company's consent, the Company shall have no liability for loss or damage until there has been a final determination by a court of competent jurisdiction, and disposition of all appeals therefrom, adverse to the title or to the lien of the insured mortgage, as insured.

(c) The Company shall not be liable for loss or damage to any insured for liability voluntarily assumed by the insured in settling any claim or suit without the prior written consent of the Company.

(d) The Company shall not be liable for: (i) any indebtedness created subsequent to Date of Policy except for advances made to protect the lien of the insured mortgage and secured thereby and reasonable amounts expended to prevent deterioration of improvements; or (ii) construction loan advances made subsequent to Date of Policy, except construction loan advances made subsequent to Date of Policy for the purpose of financing in whole or in part the construction of an improvement to the land which at Date of Policy were secured by the insured mortgage and which the insured was and continued to be obligated to advance at and after Date of Policy.

9. REDUCTION OF INSURANCE; REDUCTION OR TERMINATION OF LIABILITY

(a) All payments under this policy, except payments made for costs, attorneys' fees and expenses, shall reduce the amount of the insurance pro tanto. However, any payments made prior to the acquisition of title to the estate or interest as provided in Section 2(a) of these Conditions and Stipulations shall not reduce pro tanto the amount of the insurance afforded under this policy except to the extent that the payments reduce the amount of the indebtedness secured by the insured mortgage.

(b) Payment in part by any person of the principal of the indebtedness, or any other obligation secured by the insured mortgage, or any voluntary partial satisfaction or release of the insured mortgage, to the extent of the payment, satisfaction or release, shall reduce the amount of insurance pro tanto. The amount of insurance may thereafter be increased by accruing interest and advances made to protect the lien of the insured mortgage and secured thereby, with interest thereon, provided in no event shall the amount of insurance be greater than the Amount of Insurance stated in Schedule A.

(c) Payment in full by any person or the voluntary satisfaction or release of the insured mortgage shall terminate all liability of the Company except as provided in Section 2(a) of these Conditions and Stipulations.

10. LIABILITY NONCUMULATIVE

If the insured acquires title to the estate or interest in satisfaction of the indebtedness secured by the insured mortgage, or any part thereof, it is expressly understood that the amount of insurance under this policy shall be reduced by any amount the Company may pay under any policy insuring a mortgage to which exception is taken in Schedule B or to which the insured has agreed, assumed, or taken subject, or which is hereafter executed by an insured and which is a charge or lien on the estate or interest described or referred to in Schedule A, and the amount so paid shall be deemed a payment under this policy.

11. PAYMENT OF LOSS

(a) No payment shall be made without producing this policy for endorsement of the payment unless the policy has been lost or destroyed, in which case proof of loss or destruction shall be furnished to the satisfaction of the Company.

(b) When liability and the extent of loss or damage has been definitely fixed in accordance with these Conditions and Stipulations, the loss or damage shall be payable within 30 days thereafter.

12. SUBROGATION UPON PAYMENT OR SETTLEMENT

(a) The Company's Right of Subrogation.

Whenever the Company shall have settled and paid a claim under this policy, all right of subrogation shall vest in the Company unaffected by any act of the insured claimant.

The Company shall be subrogated to and be entitled to all rights and remedies which the insured claimant would have had against any person or property in respect to the claim had this policy not been issued. If requested by the Company, the insured claimant shall transfer to the Company all rights and remedies against any person or property necessary in order to perfect this right of subrogation. The insured claimant shall permit the Company to sue, compromise or settle in the name of the insured claimant and to use the name of the insured claimant in any transaction or litigation involving these rights or remedies.

If a payment on account of a claim does not fully cover the loss of the insured claimant, the Company shall be subrogated to all rights and remedies of the insured claimant after the insured claimant shall have recovered its principal, interest, and costs of collection.

(b) The Insured's Rights and Limitations.

Notwithstanding the foregoing, the owner of the indebtedness secured by the insured mortgage, provided the priority of the lien of the insured mortgage or its enforceability is not affected, may release or substitute the personal liability of any debtor or guarantor, or extend or otherwise modify the terms of payment, or release a portion of the estate or interest from the lien of the insured mortgage, or release any collateral security for the indebtedness.

When the permitted acts of the insured claimant occur and the insured has knowledge of any claim of title or interest adverse to the title to the estate or interest or the priority or enforceability of the lien of the insured mortgage, as insured, the Company shall be required to pay only that part of any losses insured against by this policy which shall exceed the amount, if any, lost to the Company by reason of the impairment by the insured claimant of the Company's right of subrogation.

(c) The Company's Rights Against Non-insured Obligors.

The Company's right of subrogation against non-insured obligors shall exist and shall include, without limitation, the rights of the insured to indemnities, guaranties, other policies of insurance or bonds, notwithstanding any terms or conditions contained in those instruments which provide for subrogation rights by reason of this policy.

The Company's right of subrogation shall not be avoided by acquisition of the insured mortgage by an obligor (except an obligor described in Section 1(a)(ii) of these Conditions and Stipulations) who acquires the insured mortgage as a result of an indemnity, guarantee, other policy of insurance, or bond and the obligor will not be an insured under this policy, notwithstanding Section 1(a)(i) of these Conditions and Stipulations.

13. ARBITRATION

Unless prohibited by applicable law, either the Company or the insured may demand arbitration pursuant to the Title Insurance Arbitration Rules of the American Arbitration Association. Arbitrable matters may include, but are not limited to, any controversy or claim between the Company and the insured arising out of or relating to this policy, any service of the Company in connection with its issuance or the breach of a policy provision or other obligation. All arbitrable matters when the Amount of Insurance is $1,000,000 or less shall be arbitrated at the option of either the Company or the insured. All arbitrable matters when the Amount of Insurance is in excess of $1,000,000 shall be arbitrated only when agreed to by both the Company and the insured. Arbitration pursuant to this policy and under the Rules in effect on the date the demand for arbitration is made or, at the option of the insured, the Rules in effect at Date of Policy shall be binding upon the parties. The award may include attorneys' fees only if the laws of the state in which the land is located permit a court to award attorneys' fees to a prevailing party. Judgment upon the award rendered by the Arbitrator(s) may be entered in any court having jurisdiction thereof.

The law of the situs of the land shall apply to an arbitration under the Title Insurance Arbitration Rules.

A copy of the Rules may be obtained from the Company upon request.

14. LIABILITY LIMITED TO THIS POLICY; POLICY ENTIRE CONTRACT

(a) This policy together with all endorsements, if any, attached hereto by the Company is the entire policy and contract between the insured and the Company. In interpreting any provision of this policy, this policy shall be construed as a whole.

(b) Any claim of loss or damage, whether or not based on negligence, and which arises out of the status of the lien of the insured mortgage or of the title to the estate or interest covered hereby or by any action asserting such claim, shall be restricted to this policy.

(c) No amendment of or endorsement to this policy can be made except by a writing endorsed hereon or attached hereto signed by either the President, a Vice President, the Secretary, an Assistant Secretary, or validating officer or authorized signatory of the Company.

15. SEVERABILITY

In the event any provision of this policy is held invalid or unenforceable under applicable law, the policy shall be deemed not to include that provision and all other provisions shall remain in full force and effect.

16. NOTICES, WHERE SENT

All notices required to be given the Company and any statement in writing required to be furnished the Company shall include the number of this policy and shall be addressed to the Company at the issuing office or to:

EXHIBIT 8–4
Title Commitment

AMERICAN LAND TITLE ASSOCIATION COMMITMENT — 1996

COMMITMENT FOR TITLE INSURANCE

, herein called the Company, for a valuable consideration, hereby commits to issue its policy or policies of title insurance, as identified in Schedule A, in favor of the proposed Insured named in Schedule A, as owner or mortgagee of the estate or interest covered hereby in the land described or referred to in Schedule A, upon payment of the premiums and charges therefor; all subject to the provisions of Schedules A and B and to the Conditions and Stipulations hereof.

This Commitment shall be effective only when the identity of the proposed Insured and the amount of the policy or policies committed for have been inserted in Schedule A hereof by the Company, either at the time of the issuance of this Commitment or by subsequent endorsement.

This Commitment is preliminary to the issuance of such policy or policies of title insurance and all liability and obligations hereunder shall cease and terminate six months after the effective date hereof or when the policy or policies committed for shall issue, whichever first occurs, provided that the failure to issue such policy or policies is not the fault of the Company.

IN WITNESS WHEREOF, caused this Commitment to be signed and sealed as of the effective date of Commitment shown in Schedule A, the Commitment to become valid when countersigned by an authorized signatory.

By:

Issued by:

President.

ATTEST:

Secretary.

_____
Authorized Signatory

EXHIBIT 8-4
Title Commitment (continued)

COMMITMENT

SCHEDULE A

1 OFFICE FILE NUMBER	
2 COMMITMENT NUMBER	3 EFFECTIVE DATE	4 LOAN AMOUNT
		OWNERS AMOUNT

1. Policy or Policies to be issued:
   ALTA LOAN POLICY.
   Proposed Insured:

   ALTA OWNER'S POLICY, Form
   Proposed Insured:

2. The estate or interest in the land described or referred to in this Commitment and covered herein is a fee simple, and title thereto is at the effective date hereof vested in:

3. The Land is described as follows:

Note: This Commitment consists of insert pages labeled in Schedule A. Schedule B-Section 1, and Schedule B-Section 2. This Commitment is of no force and effect unless all schedules are included, along with any Rider pages incorporated by reference in the insert pages.

EXHIBIT 8-4
Title Commitment (continued)

COMMITMENT

SCHEDULE B—Section 1

Commitment Number

Requirements

The following are the requirements to be complied with:

1. Instrument(s) creating the estate or interest to be insured must be approved, executed and filed for record, to wit:

2. Payment of the full consideration to, or for the account of, the grantors or mortgagors.

3. Payment of all taxes, charges, assessments, levied and assessed against subject premises, which are due and payable.

4. Satisfactory evidence should be that improvements and/or repairs or alterations thereto are completed; that contractor, subcontractors, labor and materialmen are all paid.

EXHIBIT 8–4
Title Commitment (continued)

COMMITMENT

SCHEDULE B—Section 2

Commitment Number

Exceptions

Schedule B of the policy or policies to be issued will contain exceptions to the following matters unless the same are disposed of to the satisfaction of the Company.

1. Defects, liens, encumbrances, adverse claims or other matters, if any, created, first appearing in the public records or attaching subsequent to the effective date hereof but prior to the date the proposed Insured acquires for value of record the estate or interest or mortgage thereon covered by this Commitment.

2. Any owner's policy issued pursuant hereto will contain under Schedule B the standard exceptions set forth on the inside cover. Any loan policy will also contain under Schedule B thereof, the standard exceptions set forth on the inside cover of this Commitment relating to the owner's policy.

3. Standard Exceptions 2 and 3 may be removed from the policy when a satisfactory survey and inspection of the premises is made.

4. Taxes and assessments for the year   and subsequent years.

Note: On loan policies, junior and subordinate matters, if any, will not be reflected in Schedule B.

EXHIBIT 8-4
Title Commitment (continued)

STANDARD EXCEPTIONS FOR OWNER'S POLICY

The owner's policy will be subject to the mortgage, if any, noted under item one of Section 1 of Schedule B hereof and to the following exceptions: (1) rights or claims of parties in possession not shown by the public records; (2) encroachments, overlaps, boundary line disputes, and any matters which would be disclosed by an accurate survey and inspection of the premises; (3) easements, or claims of easements, not shown by the public records; (4) any lien, or right to a lien, for services, labor, or material heretofore or hereafter furnished, imposed by law and not shown by the public records; (5) taxes or special assessments which are not shown as existing liens by the public records.

CONDITIONS AND STIPULATIONS

1. The term "mortgage," when used herein, shall include deed of trust, trust deed, or other security instrument.

2. If the proposed Insured has or acquires actual knowledge of any defect, lien, encumbrance, adverse claim or other matter affecting the estate or interest or mortgage thereon covered by this Commitment other than those shown in Schedule B hereof, and shall fail to disclose such knowledge to the Company in writing, the Company shall be relieved from liability for any loss or damage resulting from any act of reliance hereon to the extent the Company is prejudiced by failure to so disclose such knowledge. If the proposed Insured shall disclose such knowledge to the Company, or if the Company otherwise acquires actual knowledge of any such defect, lien, encumbrance, adverse claim or other matter, the Company at its option may amend Schedule B of this Commitment accordingly, but such amendment shall not relieve the Company from liability previously incurred pursuant to paragraph 3 of these Conditions and Stipulations.

3. Liability of the Company under this Commitment shall be only to the named proposed Insured and such parties included under the definition of Insured in the form of policy or policies committed for and only for actual loss incurred in reliance hereon in undertaking in good faith (a) to comply with the requirements hereof, or (b) to eliminate exceptions shown in Schedule B, or (c) to acquire or create the estate or interest or mortgage thereon covered by this Commitment. In no event shall such liability exceed the amount stated in Schedule A for the policy or policies committed for and such liability is subject to the insuring provisions, the Exclusions from Coverage and the Conditions and Stipulations of the form of policy or policies committed for in favor of the proposed Insured which are hereby incorporated by reference and are made a part of this Commitment except as expressly modified herein.

4. Any action or actions or rights of action that the proposed Insured may have or may bring against the Company arising out of the status of the title to the estate or interest or the status of the mortgage thereon covered by this Commitment must be based on and are subject to the provisions of this Commitment.

Real Estate Closings

"Just know your lines and don't bump into the furniture."

—Spencer Tracy

OBJECTIVES

After reading this chapter you should be able to:

- Review a real estate contract and prepare a closing checklist for both the purchaser and the seller
- Review a mortgage loan commitment and prepare a closing checklist for the borrower and lender
- Understand the legal procedures required for the closing of a sale of real property
- Understand the legal procedures required for the closing of a mortgage loan

Y ou enter a large room. Windows dominate one side of the room, offering the occupants a beautiful view of a downtown skyline. Framed English hunting prints adorn the other three walls. The focal point of the room is a large Queen Anne conference table ringed with a dozen chairs. Two couples are seated across from each other at one end of the table. One couple appears nervous. They look at each other and smile. Although the other couple appears sophisticated and blasé to the events that are taking place, they too look uneasy. A middle-aged well-dressed person seated in the corner of the conference room is talking on the telephone. The telephone caller has an appointment book and appears to be transacting business, oblivious to the other occupants of the room. At the other end of the conference table there is a large stack of manila folders and papers, a yellow legal pad, and some kind of metal seal or stamp.

As you enter the room everyone except the telephone caller in the corner, who is still in phone oblivion, immediately looks in your direction. You have just entered that phenomenon known as the Real Estate Closing Zone.

closing
Consummation of a real estate purchase and sale transaction.

The consummation of a real estate transaction is called a **closing.** Closings may be simple, as in the purchase and sale of a home, or complicated, as in the closing of a purchase and sale of a major resort hotel. The consummation of a loan secured by a mortgage is also called a closing, or **loan closing.** Many transactions involve a simultaneous sale and loan closing.

loan closing
Consummation of a loan secured by real property.

The real estate legal assistant is actively involved in helping the attorney in a real estate closing. Although ethical considerations in many states prohibit a legal assistant from actually conducting the closing, all states permit the legal assistant to assist the attorney in all phases and aspects of the closing.

THE ENVIRONMENT

Residential real estate transactions do not close in a perfect, stress-free environment. Months may have passed since the contract has been signed; frustrations and delays have been encountered at every turn. Credit reports have been lost; appraisals have been difficult to schedule or have turned out to be insufficient and have had to be rescheduled. The sellers desperately need the proceeds check because they have purchased another home and cannot afford two mortgage payments. The purchasers' dream house that looked so pretty two months ago has been slightly tarnished over the passage of time. The rooms appear smaller. There are cracks in the plaster. Everyone is concerned about the rubber raft tied to the third step of the basement. The real estate brokers have spent their commission and desperately need the check to pay creditors. The loan officer is being paid a base salary plus a percentage of all loans closed, and is behind on her quota. Residential loan closings are not a high-fee item for law firms, and can only be profitable from a high volume. The real estate attorney often juggles more loan closings than the Karuchi Brothers juggle knives. Everything is done at hyper speed. It is not unusual for people to arrive in the reception area before the loan package arrives from the lender. The U.S. Postal Service is passed over for more efficient means of delivery, such as courier and telephone facsimile. Everything resembles the trading floor of a commodities exchange. Unfortunately, in this environment, the professional real estate legal assistant must maintain order and composure and produce a quality, error-free package. This requires training, discipline, organization, and a good sense of humor.

Closing a commercial transaction is similar to and yet very different from closing a residential transaction. Commercial transactions are easier because the people involved are not strangers to the transaction. They know what they want and what to expect, and they are not under the pressures of having a moving van full of household belongings circle the block waiting for the closing to be completed.

Although commercial closings involve more sophisticated parties, they also involve larger sums of money and larger risks. The legal techniques used for commercial closings are more sophisticated, and translating these techniques into documents that properly set forth, in plain, concise language, what everyone has agreed to and understands can be difficult. Until you have it right, patient communication is necessary.

Unlike residential transactions, in which most of the documentations are preprinted forms, commercial loan transactions use more negotiated and tailored documentation. Lenders usually start with the basic form, but the form will be negotiated over the course of the loan closing transaction or will be tailored to each particular transaction. Unlike most residential closings, in which purchaser and seller are not represented by counsel and do no more than quickly review the documentation, all parties to commercial transactions usually are represented by competent counsel and the documents are reviewed many times, negotiated, debated, and changed before or at closing.

Commercial closings offer the luxury of higher fees for a law firm, and therefore more time can be spent on a single file. This does not mean that commercial loan closings are easier than residential, but it does mean that the legal assistant's attention does not have to be divided among ten or fifteen files at the same time, but can be concentrated on perhaps two or three.

One of the advantages in closing commercial loans is the opportunity to work with skilled counsel and other skilled legal assistants. It is easier to close a transaction if all the participants have a high level of knowledge with regard to real estate law.

Both residential and commercial closings have advantages and disadvantages, and most legal assistants specialize in one or the other.

ANATOMY OF A REAL ESTATE CLOSING

The difference between success and failure in a real estate closing is determined by the amount of preparation that was done before the closing. A real estate closing can be broken down into six areas: (1) file creation, (2) information gathering, (3) document preparation, (4) the closing, (5) disbursement, recording, and transmittal of the closing package, and (6) final close out.

File Creation

The first step in a real estate closing is the organization of the file. Most law firms that specialize in real estate have as clients lending institutions, such as savings and loan associations, banks, and life insurance companies, that make loans secured by residential and commercial properties. The case is referred to the firm for closing by way of a transmittal package from one of the loan officers at the lending institution, or, if there is a rush to close, by telephone call. An initial closing package typically includes a copy of the sales contract and a copy of the lender's loan commitment. It is common practice in some areas of the country for the lender to send an entire package of loan documents to the law firm.

Once the case is referred and the package is received, the law firm opens a file for purposes of billing in the name of the client and cross references the other parties involved, such as the seller, purchaser, and any brokers. The firm monitors and reviews all the names involved in the closing to check for any conflicts of interest. If a firm already has as a client one of the other parties, the potential exists for ethical problems or conflicts of interest. If a conflict of interest exists, the firm either declines representation of all parties in connection with the closing or obtains written consent from all parties after full disclosure of the conflict.

Assuming that no conflicts of interest exist, the file is logged onto the firm's computer system for billing, and a file is opened. The file may consist of nothing more than a manila folder with a label indicating the names of the parties and a file number for purposes of billing and reference.

It is advisable for a legal assistant to maintain his or her own filing system separate and apart from the firm's own internal file keeping. The separate file provides a convenient source of information to verify what the legal assistant has done in respect to a particular transaction. The two files may be merged following the conclusion of the closing.

Information Gathering

Most law firms use legal assistants to gather information required to prepare the sale and loan documents and to close the transaction.

A starting point for gathering information is the closing package received by the firm, which usually contains a real estate sales contract and a lender's commitment letter. These two basic documents provide most of the clues for the type of information needed to close the transaction. It is advisable to review the contract and loan commitment promptly on receipt of the file, and to prepare a checklist of the items required for the sale and the loan closing. File folders should be prepared for each item shown on the checklist. As the items are received or prepared they can be placed in their own folders and easily reviewed or recalled when needed.

Reviewing the Real Estate Contract

The real estate contract sets forth the obligations of the purchaser and seller in regard to the sale transaction. It is the main document to review in order to prepare a sale closing checklist. The contract sets forth the names of the parties, (seller, purchaser, and broker), the legal description of the property, the purchase price of the property, the amount of the earnest money, the date for closing, and what documents the respective seller and purchaser must furnish to each other at the closing.

The names of the seller, purchaser, and broker should be contained in the real estate contract, along with their addresses and telephone numbers. If telephone numbers are not included in the contract, they should be obtained, since there will be numerous contacts with each party before closing. It is necessary to verify the correct spelling of each of the names, since the seller's and purchaser's names will appear in most of the closing documents.

It is important when reviewing a real estate contract to determine the anticipated date of closing. Most contracts provide a closing date; however, the parties may want to close earlier, or the closing date may have been extended by an amendment. Early verification of the closing date is essential to prioritize activity. For example, if the closing is two weeks away, then the closing does not become a high-priority item, and the information can be gathered in a regular, orderly manner. Title examination orders, survey orders, payoff letters, and other routine correspondence can be handled by mail, thereby obviating the need for courier or facsimile transmittals. On the other hand, if the closing is scheduled for the day after tomorrow, then the gathering of the information becomes a high-priority item and must be done in the quickest manner available. The closing date also needs to be verified with the lender's expiration date on its loan commitment. Because of the fluctuation of interest rates, loan commitments have short durations. Although the closing on the contract may not be for a couple of weeks, the loan commitment may be effective only for a week. Therefore, to close under the current terms of the loan, the sale needs to close early. Another problem encountered in residential and commercial transactions is the availability and convenience of the parties. The parties often have a conflict with the date of closing set forth in the contract, and therefore a different closing date must be scheduled. Although it is not rational, parties to a real estate contract may place other, personal events ahead of the closing. It is not unusual for real estate closings to be scheduled around vacation plans or work schedules. It is recommended that legal assistants obtain large calendars or appointment books to schedule all the closing activities for a given month.

The contract should contain a legal description of the property. The legal description is important, as it will be used on all the sale and loan closing documents as well as to order title examinations and surveys.

The real estate contract will probably describe in some detail the documents required by the seller and purchaser at the time of closing. These requirements need to be carefully reviewed, understood, and added to any checklist being prepared. It is not unusual for preprinted broker's contracts, often used on residential transactions, to be sketchy in regard to the documents required at closing. These contracts may refer only to the deed of the seller to the purchaser. On any real estate sale transaction, the seller is required to furnish, at minimum, the following documentation: (a) owner's or title affidavit; (b) corporate resolution, if the seller is a corporation; (c) warranty deed; (d) bill of sale for any personal property included in the transaction; (e) an assignment of all appliance or other manufacturer's warranties in connection with the property, such as roof warranty and furnace warranty; (f) foreign person affidavit; and (g) Form 1099-B. The Internal Revenue Service requires that on all real estate transactions that involve a foreign person, a percentage of the sales proceeds be withheld from the closing and remitted to the Internal Revenue Service. It is the purchaser's responsibility to withhold the funds and to remit them to the government. The purchaser can be relieved of this responsibility by obtaining an affidavit from the seller that the seller is not a foreign person. The purchaser is entitled to rely on the sworn affidavit. A copy of the foreign person affidavit is included in Chapter 10.

The Internal Revenue Service also requires that the closing agent, usually the law firm, report all sales of one- to four-family residences to the Internal Revenue Service. This report usually is done by preparing Form 1099-B with all the necessary sale information and having it signed by the seller. A copy of Form 1099-B is included in Chapter 10.

In addition to the above minimum requirements, a seller also may be required to provide such things as (a) termite clearance letters, (b) keys, (c) warranties, (d) assignment of leases and security deposits, (e) assignments of service contracts, and (f) estoppel letters from prior lenders and tenants.

A purchaser under a contract is required to provide money and proof of insurance at closing. The purchaser's checklist may be extended if the contract provides for seller financing, as the purchaser will provide a note and mortgage to the seller at the time of closing.

The following is a closing checklist prepared from the sample contract that is shown in Exhibit 9–1.

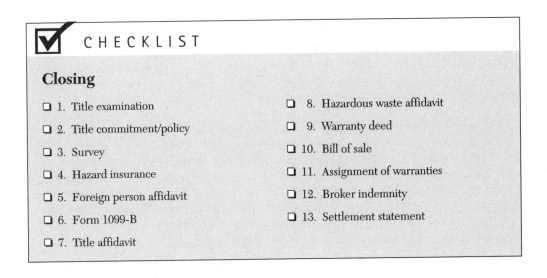

☑ CHECKLIST

Closing

❑ 1. Title examination

❑ 2. Title commitment/policy

❑ 3. Survey

❑ 4. Hazard insurance

❑ 5. Foreign person affidavit

❑ 6. Form 1099-B

❑ 7. Title affidavit

❑ 8. Hazardous waste affidavit

❑ 9. Warranty deed

❑ 10. Bill of sale

❑ 11. Assignment of warranties

❑ 12. Broker indemnity

❑ 13. Settlement statement

EXHIBIT 9–1
Real Estate Sales
Contract

This Contract is entered into this _____ day of January, 20____ by and between ACME, INC., as ("Purchaser"), I.M. SELLER ("Seller") and BROKER & ASSOCIATES, as ("Broker").

FOR VALUABLE CONSIDERATION RECEIVED, the receipt and sufficiency of which are hereby acknowledged, the parties hereby agree as follows:

1. Purchaser agrees to buy and Seller agrees to sell subject to the terms and conditions of this Contract as set forth herein ALL THAT TRACT OF PARCEL OF LAND with such improvements as are located thereon lying and being in Land Lot 1135, 2nd District, 2nd Section of _____ County, _____ , and being more particularly described on Exhibit "A" attached hereto and made a part hereof (hereinafter referred to as the "Property").

2. **Purchase Price.** The purchase price for the Property shall be SIX HUNDRED FIFTY THOUSAND AND NO/100 DOLLARS ($650,000.00), which shall be paid as follows: Purchaser shall pay to the Seller the sum of $650,000.00 in cash at closing.

3. **Earnest Money.** Purchaser has paid to Broker & Associates, a licensed broker acting on behalf of the Seller, FIVE THOUSAND AND NO/100 DOLLARS ($5,000.00) in the form of a check, the receipt whereof is hereby acknowledged by Broker & Associates as earnest money ("Earnest Money"), which Earnest Money shall be applied as part payment of the purchase price of said Property at the time the sale is consummated or paid to Seller or returned to Purchaser as otherwise provided herein.

4. **Warranties of Title.** Seller warrants that Seller presently has title to said Property and at the time the sale is consummated, agrees to convey good and marketable title to said Property to Purchaser by a general warranty deed subject only to such title exceptions as Purchaser shall agree to.

5. **Title.** Purchaser shall move promptly and in good faith after acceptance of this Contract by Seller to examine the title to said Property and to furnish Seller with a written statement of objections affecting the marketability of said title.

Seller shall have a reasonable time after receipt of said such objections to satisfy all valid objections specified by Purchaser and if Seller fails to satisfy such valid objections within a reasonable time, then Purchaser at Purchaser's option may cancel this Contract by giving Seller written notice of such cancellation and this Contract shall become null and void and Purchaser shall be entitled to a return of the Earnest Money. Marketability of title as used herein shall mean the quality of title which a title insurance Company licensed to do business in the State of _____ and a member of the American Land Title Association would insure at its regular rate without exception.

6. **Hazardous Waste Indemnity.** Purchaser's obligation to purchase the Property pursuant to this Contract is contingent upon there being no petroleum hydro carbons or contaminants contained in the soil, surface or subterranean water which are in violation of local, state, or federal statutes and regulations and that there be no other existence of any hazardous substances or waste located upon the Property. For purposes of this Agreement, the term "hazardous substances or wastes" shall mean petroleum, including crude oil or any fraction thereof, flammable explosives, radioactive materials, asbestos, any material containing polychlorinated biphenyls, and any of the substances defined as "hazardous substances" or "toxic substances" in the Comprehensive Environmental Response, Compensation and Liability Act of 1980, as amended, 42 U.S.C. Section 9601 *et seq.*, Hazardous Materials Transportation Act, 49 U.S.C. Section 1802 *et seq.*, the Resource Conservation and Recovery Act, 42 U.S.C. Section 6901 *et seq.*, and in the Toxic Substance Control Act of 1976, as amended, 15 U.S.C. Section 2601 *et seq.*, or any other federal, state, local or other governmental legislation, statute, law, code, rule, regulation or ordinance identified by its terms as pertaining to the disposal, storage, generation or presence of hazardous substances or waste (the "Environmental Laws"). Purchaser shall at Seller's expense have the Property inspected for purposes of discovering if hazardous substances or wastes exist. If upon inspection, hazardous wastes or substances do exist, Purchaser shall have the option of terminating his contract and receiving a refund of his $5,000.00 earnest money down payment. In the alternative, Seller shall have the right at its own expense to remove all hazardous substance or waste from the Property and to conclude the sale with Purchaser.

Seller warrants, represents, and agrees that (a) neither Seller nor any person has violated any of the applicable Environmental Laws as defined in the paragraph above relating to or affecting the Property; (b) the Property is presently in compliance with all Environmental Laws, and there are no facts or circumstances presently existing upon or under the Property or relating to the representations and warranties, which violate any of the applicable Environmental Laws, and there is not now pending nor threatened any action, suit, investigation or proceeding against Seller or the Property (or against any

(continued)

EXHIBIT 9–1
Real Estate Sales
Contract (continued)

other party related to the Property); (c) Seller has obtained all licenses, permits or other governmental regulatory approvals necessary to comply with Environmental Laws and Seller is in full compliance with the terms and provisions of all such licenses, permits or other governmental regulatory approvals; and (d) Seller has received no notice that any municipality or any governmental or quasi-governmental authorities are investigating or has determined that there are any violations of zoning, health, building, fire, pollution, environmental, or other statutes, ordinances, regulations affecting the Property.

7. **Inspection.** Purchaser, its agents and representatives, at Purchaser's expense and at reasonable times during normal business hours, shall have the right to enter upon the Property for purpose of inspection, examining, testing, surveying the Property. Purchaser assumes all responsibility for acts of itself, its agents, representatives, in exercising its rights under this paragraph and agrees to hold Seller harmless for any damages resulting therefrom.

8. **Condition of Improvements.** Seller warrants until the sale is consummated, that the Improvements located on the Property will be in the same condition as they are on the date this Contract is signed by the Seller, natural wear and tear excepted. Should the Improvements located on the Property be destroyed or substantially damaged before the Contract is consummated, then at the election of the Purchaser, (a) the Contract may be cancelled and Earnest Money refunded to Purchaser or (b) Purchaser may consummate the Contract and receive all insurance proceeds paid or due on the claim of loss.

This election is to be exercised within ten (10) days after the Purchaser has been notified in writing by Seller of the amount of the insurance proceeds, if any, Seller shall receive on the claim of loss; if Purchaser has not been notified within forty-five (45) days, subsequent to the occurrence of such damage or destruction, Purchaser may at its option cancel this Contract and receive a refund of its Earnest Money.

9. **Possession.** Seller shall deliver title and possession of the Property to Purchaser at closing free and clear of the claims of any and all tenants and all leases existing on the Property shall be cancelled and terminated by Seller at Seller's expense prior to closing.

10. **Closing.** Closing shall be held at the offices of attorney of Purchaser, _____ _____, 1400 Peachtree Place Tower, 999 Peachtree Street, N.E., _____, _____, or at such location as is agreeable to Purchaser and Seller, on a day selected by Purchaser not later than sixty (60) days from the date Seller can deliver title and possession of the Property free and clear of any and all leases or other rights of tenants in regard to the Property and a date not later than _____, 20____. Purchaser shall give Seller notice of the closing date at least five days prior thereto; provided, if Purchaser gives Seller no such notice of the closing date, then the closing date shall be _____, 20_____.

11. **Execution of Documents.** Seller shall execute and deliver to Purchaser a general warranty deed in recordable form conveying the Property to Purchaser as provided herein and shall execute and deliver to Purchaser all necessary affidavits in order for Purchaser to obtain a title insurance policy without exception and an affidavit indicating Seller's non-foreign status within the meaning of Section 1445(f)(3) of the Internal Revenue Code of 1986 and any and all other documents which may be required by Purchaser to carry out the terms of this Contract.

12. **Closing Costs.** In connection with the closing, Seller shall pay the real estate Transfer Tax and all costs for the satisfaction, cure and removal of all title exceptions undertaken by the Seller as herein required. All other closing costs incurred by Purchaser in connection with the sale shall be paid by Purchaser. Each party shall pay its own attorney's fees.

13. **Prorations.** At the closing all ad valorem property taxes, water and sewer charges and assessments of any kind on the Property for the year of the closing shall be prorated between Purchaser and Seller as of 12:01 a.m. on the closing date. Such proration shall be based upon the latest ad valorem property tax, water, sewer charge and assessment bills available. If, upon receipt of the actual ad valorem property tax, water, sewer and assessment bills for the Property, such proration is incorrect, then either Purchaser or Seller shall be entitled, upon demand, to receive such amounts from the other as may be necessary to correct such malapportionment. This obligation to correct such malapportionment shall survive the closing and not be merged into any documents delivered pursuant to the closing.

14. **Brokerage Commissions.** Upon consummation of the closing of the sale contemplated herein, a sales commission shall be paid by the Seller to Broker & Associates, Inc., Broker, which commission has been negotiated between Broker and Seller. Purchaser shall have no obligation

EXHIBIT 9–1
Real Estate Sales
Contract (continued)

whatsoever to Broker & Associates, Inc. for any real estate commission. Seller further agrees to indemnify and hold harmless the Purchaser from and by any and all claims or demands with respect to any brokerage fees or agent's commissions or other compensation asserted against any person, firm, or corporation in connection with this Contract or sale or the transactions contemplated hereby arising from actions or alleged commitments of the Seller. This provision shall survive closing and the conveyance of the Property by Seller to Purchaser.

15. **Purchaser Default.** In the event the transaction contemplated hereby is not closed because of Purchaser's default, the Earnest Money shall be paid to Seller as full liquidated damages for such failure to close, the parties acknowledging the difficulty of ascertaining Seller's damages in such circumstances, whereupon neither party hereto shall have any further rights, claims, or liabilities under this Agreement except for the provisions which were made to survive the termination or cancellation of this Agreement. Said liquidated damages shall be Seller's sole and exclusive remedy and Seller shall expressly not have the right to seek specific performance or other damages.

16. **Seller's Default.** If Seller shall be unable to deliver title in accordance with this Agreement, Seller's liability shall be limited to the return of the Earnest Money paid hereunder. In the event Seller fails to perform other covenants of this Agreement or if Seller otherwise defaults hereunder, the Purchaser shall have the right, in addition to all rights and remedies herein provided, to pursue any right or remedy it may have against Seller at law or in equity for such breach and/or default, including without limitation, the right of specific performance of all provisions of this Agreement. Purchaser's monetary damages in the event of such breach and/or default shall be limited to $25,000.00. The parties hereby acknowledge the difficulty of ascertaining Purchaser's monetary damages in such event.

17. **Assignability.** Purchaser shall have the right to assign this Agreement to any corporation or partnership of which Purchaser is a shareholder or partner without notice to and without consent of Seller, and the transaction contemplated by this Agreement shall be consummated in the name of such assignee. Purchaser shall not have the right to assign the Contract to any other party except as mentioned above without the prior written consent of Seller.

18. **Notification.** Any notice or demand under which the terms of this Agreement or under any statute must or may be given or made by the parties hereto shall be made in writing and shall be deemed to have been delivered when hand delivered; as of the date sent by an overnight courier; or as of the date of postmark affixed by the U.S. Postal Service, by mail of same by certified mail, return receipt requested, addressed to the respective parties at the following addresses:

TO PURCHASER:

TO SELLER:

TO BROKER:

19. **Time is of the Essence.** Time is of the essence of this Agreement and of each of its provisions. This instrument shall be regarded as an offer by the Purchaser or Seller who shall first sign this Contract to the other party and is open for acceptance by the other party until _____ : _____.m. on the _____ day of _____, 20_____.

The above proposition is hereby accepted this _____ day of _____, 20_____.

IN WITNESS WHEREOF, the undersigned parties hereinto set their hand and seal to this Contract.

PURCHASER:

_____ (SEAL)

SELLER:

_____ (SEAL)

_____ (SEAL)

BROKER
By: _____

CONTACT WITH SELLER, PURCHASER, AND BROKER _____

One of the first things the legal assistant needs to do is verify the correctness of the names that appear in the contract. The seller should be requested to provide any title information or surveys that the seller may have regarding the real property. If the seller is a corporation, copies of the articles of incorporation, bylaws, and a certificate of good standing with the secretary of state's office should be requested. A corporation should provide a corporate resolution with the names and titles of the people who will be signing on behalf of the corporation. The corporate seller should bring the corporate seal to closing. All the preceding items are required to ensure that the corporation has the authority to sell the real property.

If the seller is a partnership, a request should be made for copies of the partnership agreement and the names of all the partners who intend to be present at the closing to sign the closing documents. In the situation of a partnership, all partners must sign the documents unless the partnership agreement authorizes an individual partner or group of partners to sign. If less than all the partners intend to sign the closing documents, a partnership resolution should be obtained from all the partners giving their consent and authorizing the signature partners to consummate and close the transaction.

The seller should be questioned about loan numbers of any outstanding loans on the subject property. These computer loan numbers are necessary to obtain payoff information. Also discuss with the seller the approximate date of closing and any special instructions you might need to know in regard to the closing.

The purchaser should be contacted to verify the names that are to appear on the warranty deed and the name of their insurance agent, and to inquire about any special instructions. The purchaser should receive an explanation of the steps in a closing and assurance that closing money figures will be available at least on the day before the closing, to give the purchaser adequate time to obtain the necessary funds.

After the purchaser and seller are contacted, the real estate agents should be contacted to notify them of the approximate date of closing and to verify the amount of the real estate commissions due the agents.

Ordering the Title Examination

It is unusual for a closing legal assistant to examine the title to the property. Most title examinations are prepared by other members of the firm or by specialized firms that have a retainer relationship with the closing law firm. Title examinations may be handled by title insurance companies in some states. A title examination should be ordered quickly even though the closing may be several weeks away. The earlier the examination is received, the more time there will be to correct defects that may be revealed by the examination. The title examiner needs, at a minimum, the following information to conduct the examination: (a) the name of the current owner, which usually is the seller under the sale contract; (b) the legal description of the real property; and (c) any title information or surveys available.

The title examiner should be informed of the name of the title company issuing the title insurance, so that the title examiner's certification can be prepared and sent to the title company. The title examiner should be instructed to make copies of all exceptions to title. These copies should be provided to both the legal assistant and the title insurance company. The title examiner should establish a firm date for completion of the examination. This date should be recorded on a calendar or appointment book. It is a good idea to call the title examiner the day before the scheduled date of completion. This telephone call should be made not for the purpose of trying to obtain the title examination a day early, but to confirm that the title examination will be available on the date scheduled for completion. The title examiner's response to this preemptive telephone call may be that the title examination has already been completed and can be picked up on the day of the call, which means that the examination is delivered one day early. Or the preemptive telephone call may remind the title examiner of the date set for completion and will act as a further reminder to provide the title examination on time.

Ideally, a title examination order is given in writing by using a title examination form. A copy of such form is shown in Exhibit 9–2. Unfortunately, because of the fast-track nature of most residential closings, title examinations typically are ordered over the phone. Even if a

EXHIBIT 9–2
Title Examination Form

Abstract Order

Our File Number: _____   Date Ordered: _____   Need By: _____

Ordered by: _____   Date of Closing: _____

Present Owner/Seller: _____

Name of Purchaser: _____

RE Broker: _____

Brief Legal: _____

_____

Street Address: _____

Length of Search: _____

<u>MISCELLANEOUS INFORMATION KNOWN</u>:

Plat Information: _____

Back Title Policy: ( ) Yes   ( ) No   Back Title Notes: ( ) Yes   ( ) No

<u>With Who</u>: _____   _____

_____   _____

_____   _____

PLEASE PROVIDE US WITH ANY BANKRUPTCY INFORMATION: ( ) yes   ( ) no

Other Information:

_____

_____

_____

_____

_____

_____

_____

In addition, please provide the following:

( ) Copies of applicable Restrictive Covenants of record

( ) Copies of applicable easements of record

( ) Copies of any liens, executions, judgments, etc. of record

( ) City, State and County Millage Rates (latest figures available)

( ) _____

( ) _____

( ) _____

telephone request is made, it is a good idea to complete the written title examination form before making the call. This requires collecting the necessary information for the title examination and increases the efficiency of the telephone call. Ordering a title examination without completing the form could result in the examiner's receiving incomplete information. This will cause the title examination to be incomplete, or necessitate a second call to the examiner.

Ordering the Survey

Most law firms have a relationship with a surveying and engineering firm that can prepare surveys to satisfy title insurance company and lender client requirements. The names and telephone numbers of these surveyors will be provided to the legal assistant. Most surveys are ordered by telephone, and a surveyor will need, at minimum, the following information: (a) legal description of the property to be surveyed, (b) any information regarding previous surveys, (c) the correct names of the purchasers as they appear on the survey, (d) the correct name of the lending institution as it appears on the survey, and (e) any special lender requirements for a survey.

The surveyor will prepare an as-built survey locating the improvements and all easements, setback lines, and so forth on the survey. The surveyor will indicate if the property is located in a flood hazard zone. In some states the surveyor may prepare a title insurance company inspection report form. If so, the surveyor will need to know which title company is issuing the insurance so that the company's form can be used. At least six prints of the survey should be received, and the surveyor should be reminded to enclose the bill with the survey so that it can be paid at closing.

A firm date for the completion of the survey should be obtained from the surveyor. If possible, a survey should be received at least five business days before closing. The date for completion should be recorded on a calendar or appointment book, and a preemptive call made the day before the due date.

Ordering Hazard and Fire Insurance

Insurance against fire and other casualties is a requirement on all real estate closings that involve improved property. Often the insurance will be obtained by the purchaser or by one of the real estate agents in connection with the sale. An insurance company must receive the following information: (a) the name of the purchaser; (b) the correct address of the property; (c) the amount of the loan, since most lenders require that, at minimum, the insurance be for the amount of the loan; and (d) the name and address of the lender, as the lender will appear as a mortgagee on the insurance policy. This mortgagee endorsement contains both the name of the mortgagee and its address. If flood insurance is necessary, the agent should be given the finished flood elevation, which can be obtained from the surveyor. The insurance company should be given a date for delivery of the insurance.

Most lenders require the insurance premium to be paid one year in advance from date of closing, and the proof of such payment to be provided at closing. The insurance agent will provide a paid receipt for the insurance.

Most residential lenders require that the original policy be available at the time of closing. On commercial transactions commercial insurance policies are more difficult to obtain, and many lenders are willing to close on a binder or certificate of insurance. The policy will be provided after closing.

In the event the purchaser or real estate agent undertakes the task of obtaining the fire and casualty insurance, it is a good idea to receive from them the name of the agent and to verify with the agent all the necessary information that must appear in the policy. This direct communication with the insurance agent often reduces the number of mistakes in the final policy. Although most mistakes, such as misspelled names and incorrect property addresses, are not serious and usually will not hold up a closing, they do require corrective work after the closing.

Obtaining the Termite Clearance Letter or Bond

In many areas of the United States termites present special problems for real estate closings. It is not unusual in residential and even in commercial transactions that a termite clearance letter be required within the terms of the contract. These clearance letters or bonds are prepared by licensed pest control companies. The certificate reports that the pest control company has inspected the property in question and has either found no termites, powder-post beetles, or other wood-boring insects, or found such insects and treated the property. In addition, termite clearance letters report either that no damage was observed from past infestation of termites, powder-post beetles, or other wood-boring insects, or that past damage has been repaired.

Because of the serious nature of termite infestation, it is advisable that termite clearance letters be obtained before the date of closing. By obtaining the termite letter early, any termite infestation problem identified can be corrected by the closing date. Experience shows that a number of closings have been adjourned because termite letters that were delivered at the closing stated that the property had been damaged by infestation of termites. Receiving such a letter at the closing gives the closing attorney little time to react, and often the termite inspector who issued the report is not available to answer questions during the closing. The result is that the closing must be adjourned until more information can be received. Such adjournment wastes time, creates a major inconvenience, and potentially increases the interest rates and charges that the purchaser must pay if the loan commitment expires.

Reviewing the Title Examination

Once the title examination has been received, it should be carefully reviewed for any objections to title. All prior loans or debts on the property need to be paid at closing. It will be necessary to obtain from each lender or creditor a payment or satisfaction letter.

Satisfaction of Loans and Liens

Most lenders assign a computer number to each loan, and this number is needed to obtain a satisfaction amount for the loan. Some lenders will not give out information concerning any loan over the telephone or even by letter without the customer's consent and permission. It is a good idea to anticipate such problems and request the seller to contact their lender to obtain loan information or at least approve the legal assistant's obtaining such loan information. When requesting a payoff amount, it is necessary to give the lender a closing date and request a per diem interest charge if the sale does not close on the scheduled date. Ideally, any loan payoffs should be verified by written communication with the lender; however, because of the fast-track nature of residential loans, many loan payoffs are handled over the phone.

A sample loan payment request is shown in Exhibit 9–3. This form should be used even with a telephone request. It is advisable when receiving a telephone satisfaction amount that the name and telephone number of the person giving the information be obtained. A letter can then be sent from the firm to the lender verifying the telephone conversation and requesting to be notified immediately if the information contained in the letter is incorrect. A similar letter indicating that the check is being sent as payment in full pursuant to a telephone conversation of a certain date should be sent to the lender after closing. If a payoff letter was received, a copy of that letter should be enclosed with the letter accompanying the check.

The amount of unpaid taxes can be obtained by calling the tax collector's office. Most delinquent taxes accrue penalties and interest; thus a satisfaction amount as of the date of closing with a per diem charge is required.

The satisfaction of judgment liens or mechanics' liens requires a telephone call to the attorney representing the judgment creditor or lienor. The attorney's name and address usually appear somewhere on the recorded judgment or lien. It is advisable in obtaining satisfaction of liens and judgments that written information be provided. This is handled by making telephone contact and requiring the attorney representing the judgment creditor or lienor to provide a letter setting forth the amount needed for satisfaction. Arrangements also need to be made with judgment creditors and lienors to obtain a written satisfaction of the judgment or lien. This may require the attorney for the creditor or lien holder to attend the closing and tender the written satisfaction of lien or judgment in return for the payment check.

Satisfaction information for federal and state tax liens can be obtained through the Internal Revenue Service for federal tax liens and the state department of revenue for state tax liens. When speaking with the government authorities, full information concerning the lien, such as the date of the lien, the name of the taxpayer, and the place where the lien was filed and recorded, should be given. In addition, the closing date and a per diem interest charge should be provided.

EXHIBIT 9-3
Loan Payment Request

LOAN PAYMENT REQUEST

File # _____   Purchaser: _____
                        Phone: (H)_____(W)_____

( ) R.E. AGENTS:	Seller: (%) _____		Phone: _____
( )	Buyer: (%) _____		Phone: _____

( ) ABSTRACT: Date Ordered: _____   From: _____
                                                        ( ) collect at closing
                Date Received: _____   Cost: $ _____   ( ) included in fee

( ) SURVEY: Date Ordered: _____   From: _____
                                                        ( ) collect at closing
                Date Received: _____   Cost: $ _____   ( ) poc

( ) TERMITE   Date Ordered: _____   From: _____
LETTER   ( ) collect at closing
                Date Received: _____   Cost: $ _____   ( ) poc
                ( ) to be mailed   ( ) to be delivered at closing

( ) HAZARD INS: Date Ordered: _____   Date Received: _____
                 From: _____   Phone: _____
                 Address: _____   Agent: _____

                 Amt. of Coverage: $ _____   Eff. Date: _____
                                                  ( ) collect at closing
( ) new   *Yearly Premium: $ _____   ( ) poc
( ) exist.   ( ) collect at closing
( ) trans.   *Additional Prem. $ _____   ( ) poc

( ) FLOOD INS:: Date Ordered: _____   Date Received: _____
                 From: _____   Phone: _____
                 Address: _____   Agent: _____

                 Amt. of Coverage: $ _____   Eff. Date: _____
                                                  ( ) collect at closing
( ) new   *Yearly Premium: $ _____   ( ) poc
( ) exist.   ( ) collect at closing
( ) tran.   *Additional Prem: $ _____   ( ) poc

( ) PAYOFFS: Date Ordered: _____   Date Received: _____   Ordered by: _____

( ) 1st: To: _____   Deed Book: _____
                 Address: _____   Phone: _____
                 _____   Loan No.: _____
                                                  Attention: _____
                 *Payoff is: $ _____   as of: _____   Per Diem: $ _____

( ) 2nd: To: _____   Deed Book: _____
                 Address: _____   Phone: _____
                 _____   Loan No.: _____
                                                  Attention: _____
                 *Payoff is: $ _____   as of: _____   Per Diem: $ _____

( ) 3rd: To: _____   Deed Book: _____
                 Address: _____   Phone: _____
                 _____   Loan No.: _____
                                                  Attention: _____
                 *Payoff is: $ _____   as of: _____   Per Diem: $ _____

( ) OTHER CHARGES: Paid by:

(P/A/C/LT)

	( ) Attorneys Fees	$	Buyer Seller
	( ) Title Insurance	$	Buyer Seller
	( ) Toll Charges	$	Buyer Seller
( ) Loan	( ) Assignments	$	Buyer Seller
( ) Owners	( ) Power of Attorney	$	Buyer Seller
( ) S.I.	( ) Photocopies	$	Buyer Seller
( ) Const.	( ) Federal Express	$	Buyer Seller
	( )	$	Buyer Seller
	( )	$	Buyer Seller

PROFILES

JANE HEUSER

What do you like best about your work?

What I like best about my job is its diversity of responsibility. While our firm represents the lender, and my primary responsibility is to the lender's best interests, I take great pride in helping borrowers. I must coordinate information from the borrower, the title company, and the lender to facilitate timely, successful closings.

What is the greatest challenge that you face in your area of work?

The greatest challenge I face is organizing the voluminous amount of paperwork required for a closing while coordinating between fifty and seventy-five closings per week. Working in a dynamic, constantly changing environment and handling the divergent requirements of borrowers, lenders, and attorneys, requires patience and diplomacy while prioritizing responsibilities.

What advice do you have for would-be paralegals in your area of work?

The best advice I could give anyone contemplating a career as a real estate paralegal would be to always keep organized. Because of the extraordinary amount of information required to successfully handle each closing, keeping files organized and up-to-date is imperative so that items don't fall through the cracks.

What are some tips for success as a paralegal in your area of work?

An important tip for success is to always keep your priorities in order. Although there may be numerous issues that need to be addressed simultaneously, you must be able to determine which ones are most pressing and handle them accordingly. Keeping your head while being bombarded from all sides is a common occurrence that requires focusing on a predetermined goal and forging ahead! Even though we all may wish it to be different, there are only twenty-four hours in a day, so prioritizing is essential.

Jane Heuser is a paralegal Account Manager for Cullen & Dykman, Bleakley, Platt, LLP, a New York law firm founded over a half-century ago. Jane began her career twelve years ago with the firm as a Closing Coordinator and as a result of her attention to detail and the personal attention she gave to each borrower and lender, she became an Account Manager three years later. Jane received a B.B.A. in marketing from Hofstra University.

REVIEWING THE MORTGAGE LOAN COMMITMENT

loan commitment
Contract between a borrower and a lender to make and accept a mortgage loan secured by real property. The loan commitment sets forth the terms, requirements, and conditions for the mortgage loan.

The mortgage **loan commitment** provides a legal assistant with clues about what information and documents are required to close the transaction. A mortgage loan commitment is addressed to the borrower. It indicates the mortgage lender's approval of the borrower's loan application and the lender's commitment to loan the amount requested, provided the borrower agrees to comply with all the conditions listed in the commitment. It is the responsibility of the legal assistant to make certain that all the lender's requirements set forth in the loan commitment have been satisfied before or at the time of closing. The commitment is a binding legal agreement and will govern all future disputes between the borrower and the lender and the drafting of the formal loan documents.

The following is a discussion of the conditions and terms that can be found in a mortgage loan commitment. Some of these items can be found in any loan commitment, and others apply only to commercial loan transactions.

Parties

The parties to a loan commitment are the prospective borrower and the lender.

Loan Amount

The amount of the loan should be clearly indicated in every loan commitment. This amount is used throughout in the preparation of all the necessary loan documents, such as notes, mortgages, and assignment of rents and leases.

Interest Rate

The commitment should clearly specify the annual interest rate for the loan. The interest rate will be either fixed or a floating rate that adjusts pursuant to some index.

Term of Loan

The commitment should specify the exact number of years over which the loan must be repaid. The term should commence on the loan closing date or such other date as the loan funds are disbursed to the borrower.

Repayment Terms

The commitment should specify how the loan is to be repaid. It is customary to provide for monthly payments, but payments on any other basis may be agreed on.

Prepayment Terms

The loan commitment should indicate whether the loan can be prepaid before maturity. Most residential loans are prepayable in full or in part, provided the prepayments are made on a date otherwise scheduled for a regular payment of principal and interest. For example, if payments are made on the first day of each month, a prepayment must be made on the first day of each month as well.

Most institutional commercial lenders do not allow a voluntary prepayment of the loan in whole or in part during the first few years of the loan term. Thereafter, it is customary to provide for prepayment subject to the payment of a premium.

Security

A mortgage loan commitment indicates what security is required by the lender for the loan. As a general rule, the lender requires a valid and enforceable first lien on the real property being offered by the borrower, which in most situations is the real property being purchased with the proceeds of the loan. The lender typically requires that it receive fee simple title to the real property. Occasionally a commercial lender may make a loan based on an estate for years or leasehold interest. The commitment letter indicates what quality of title the lender is requiring as security for the loan.

Appraisal

Most loan commitments require that before closing, the lender be provided with a formal written appraisal of the value of the proposed real property security. This appraisal of value ensures that the lender is not lending more money than the real property security is worth or more money than a percentage of the total fair market value of such real property security versus loan amount.

Insurance

A mortgage loan commitment requires that at or before closing, the borrower deliver to the lender insurance policies indicating that the real property security is covered by the following types of coverages: (a) fire, with extended and additional extended insurance; (b) vandalism and malicious mischief; (c) sprinkler; (d) war (if available); (e) rent or business interruption; (f) public liability; (g) plate glass liability; (h) boiler liability; and (i) flood. The insurance company and the dollar limits of such coverage also are subject to the approval of the lender. With respect to the amount of fire coverage, the general rule is that the policy must be for at least the original amount of the loan or the full amount of the replacement value of the improvements on the real property as determined at regular intervals, whichever is less.

All policies must have a proper mortgagee clause or endorsement attached thereto insuring the lender as the first mortgagee. A lender also may require a carrier to provide that it will not cancel the policy for any reason without prior written notice to the lender. Thirty days is the time period often required for such notice.

With respect to the payment of insurance proceeds, most lenders require a standard **mortgagee loss payable** endorsement to a policy whereby the insured and carrier agree that any and all proceeds payable under the policy are to be paid by the carrier directly to the lender or to a mutually agreed on third party. Thereafter, the loan documents allow the lender to use such proceeds either as an offset of the borrower's outstanding indebtedness or for restoration of the real property security.

Escrow

A commitment may require that at closing, the borrower establishes with the lender an **escrow** account to assure the lender that all real estate taxes, special assessments, and insurance premiums relating to the security will be paid when due. The borrower is required to make monthly deposits to such account in the amount of one-twelfth of the annual taxes, assessments, and hazard insurance premiums as estimated by the lender. Thereafter, all tax, assessment, insurance premium payments are made by the lender, and a failure to make the requisite monthly deposits may be deemed a loan default by the borrower. No interest is paid on such deposits, and they are not held in trust, but may be commingled with the general assets of the lender.

Title Insurance

Most loan commitments require that the borrower obtain a mortgagee (loan) title insurance policy insuring that the proposed mortgage or deed of trust creates a valid first lien on the title to the real property security.

Survey

Most mortgage loan commitments require that an as-built survey of the real property be prepared. An as-built survey shows not only the perimeter lines of the subject property and all improvements located thereon, but also the location and path of any and all easements of record or those evident from an inspection of the property.

Compliance with Law

Most loan commitments require that the lender be provided with proof that all improvements on the real property (and their uses) comply fully with any and all applicable zoning and building laws, ordinances, and regulations and all other applicable federal, state, and municipal laws, rules, and regulations.

Financial Documents

Most loan commitments require that all financial information submitted by the borrower to the lender in connection with the mortgage loan application be recertified by the borrower at the time of closing. This typically is done by an affidavit of no adverse change wherein the borrower swears that all financial information previously submitted to the lender is true and correct, and that there has been no adverse material change in its financial condition since the application. A form of this affidavit can be found in Chapter 10.

Documents

The commitment specifies what loan documents are needed to close the loan. These documents include a note, a mortgage or deed of trust, and, in the case of a commercial loan, an assignment of leases and rents, a security agreement, and a Uniform Commercial Code

---

mortgagee loss payable clause
Endorsement to a policy of fire and hazard insurance whereby the owner of the insured property and the insurance company agree that any and all proceeds payable under the policy are to be paid directly to the lender who has a mortgage on the insured property.

escrow
Agreement that requires the deposit of a document or money into the possession of a third party to be held by that party until certain conditions are fulfilled.

Financing Statement. Construction mortgage loan commitments also may require a construction loan agreement and assignments of the construction contract and the architects' and engineers' contracts.

Defaults and Late Charges

A loan commitment provides that the loan documents include default provisions. Most default provisions are subject to reasonable notice and grace periods to cure before the various remedies available to the lender can be invoked. With respect to monetary defaults, such as failure to pay the debt or pay taxes or pay insurance premiums, a five- or ten-day right to cure is common. In the case of nonmonetary defaults, the borrower may be given twenty to thirty days to cure such default.

A loan commitment may specify a late fee for note payments not made on time. This fee reimburses the lender the cost of processing late payments. In addition to a late fee, the loan commitment may require that a default rate of interest be applied to the unamortized portion of the loan at the date of default. Default rates are substantially higher than the interest rate applicable to the loan when the borrower is not in default.

Commitment Fee

Most loan commitments require the borrower to deliver to the lender before closing a specified sum of money as consideration for the issuance of the commitment. This fee may be called a commitment fee deposit, standby fee, earnest money, or a similar name.

Loan Expenses

The commitment provides that all expenses, fees, and costs incurred with respect to the loan, including, but not limited to, lender's attorney fees, title insurance fees, survey costs, recording and filing fees, mortgage taxes or other taxes on the note and mortgage, cost of appraisals, and personal inspections, be paid by the borrower.

Closing and Commitment Expiration Date

A loan commitment indicates the date on which the loan closing is to be held and the lender is to disburse the loan proceeds. The closing is conditioned on the borrower's having complied with all conditions of the commitment to the satisfaction of the lender and its counsel.

In addition to the loan closing date, a commitment may set forth a commitment expiration date, which may or may not coincide with the closing date.

Disbursement of Loan Proceeds

A loan commitment specifies how the proceeds of the loan are to be disbursed on closing to the borrower, whether by cash, lender's check, check on federal funds, bank wire, or wire of federal funds. The lender may place good funds in the closing attorney's escrow account, and the closing attorney will disburse all checks from that account.

Acceptance of a Loan Commitment

A loan commitment is not effective or binding until it has been accepted by the borrower.

Assignability

A loan commitment is personal to the borrower and cannot be assigned without the lender's consent.

A review of the loan commitment provides the legal assistant with a checklist of items needed to close and fund the loan. A checklist of closing requirements compiled from an example of a loan commitment for a residential loan follows (Example 9–1).

EXAMPLE 9-1

Loan Commitment for Residential Loan

American Eagle Mortgage Company
March 7, 20_____

Ms. Helen Davis
849 Mentelle Drive, N.E.
Atlanta, Georgia 30308

Re: Mortgage Loan Commitment–$100,000.00 at 6% for thirty (30) years

Dear Ms. Davis:

American Eagle Mortgage Company (the "Company") is pleased to inform you that it has acted upon your application and has approved a loan to you, subject to all terms and conditions of this letter. The loan will be in the principal sum of $100,000.00 at an annual rate of 6%, to be repaid as follows:

In equal consecutive monthly installments of $599.51 per month for thirty (30) years.

Each installment, when paid, shall be applied first to the payment of accrued interest and then to the unpaid principal balance.

The holder may collect a "late charge" not to exceed an amount equal to four percent (4%) of any installment which is not paid within fifteen (15) days of the due date thereof, to cover the extra expenses involved in handling delinquent payments.

The loan proceeds shall be used for the acquisition of improved real estate (the "Property") located at 5167 Tilly Mill Road, Atlanta, Georgia.

The loan shall be secured by a first priority lien on the Property and on all improvements now or hereafter existing thereon. The Company's agreement to make the loan to you is subject to satisfaction of the following conditions, all at your sole cost and expense and in a manner acceptable to the Company.

1. The Company shall procure a standard form ALTA mortgagee's policy of title insurance insuring the loan as a first priority lien against the Property, showing there is to be no other encumbrances against the Property which render it unmarketable.

2. You shall provide the Company prior to closing with a recent plat of survey of the Property, together with a surveyor's certificate in form satisfactory to the Company's title insuror, depicting and certifying all improvements on the Property to be completely within the boundary lines of the Property and to be in compliance with all applicable building or setback line restrictions.

3. You shall provide the Company prior to closing with fire, lightning, and extended coverage insurance issued by a company or companies and upon terms acceptable to the Company in at least the sum of $100,000.00. Premiums for such insurance shall be paid by you for not less than one year in advance. All policies shall be issued with a mortgagee clause in favor of and acceptable to the Company and shall be non-cancellable without at least ten (10) days prior written notice to the Company.

4. The Company shall select an attorney to close the loan and to prepare all documents deemed necessary or appropriate by the Company to evidence the loan and to establish the Company's first priority lien against the Property and the Policy. All such loan documents will be in form and substance satisfactory to the Company's closing attorney.

5. All actual fees or expenses (including, without limitation, such closing attorney's fees, title insurance premiums, cost of title examination, abstract of title fee, document preparation fee, cost of survey, appraisal fee, recording fees, and intangibles or other taxes) incurred in connection with reviewing your loan application, or with closing, servicing, collecting, or cancelling the loan, shall be paid by you.

6. The loan may be assumed by a transferee of the Property, provided the Company gives prior written consent thereto; but any transfer of title to all or any part of the Property whatsoever, or any further encumbrance or other lien imposed against the Property without the Company's prior written consent, will authorize the Company to declare the loan immediately due and payable. Any such assumption, transfer, or encumbrance to which the Company shall consent shall be upon such terms and conditions as the Company shall determine and approve.

7. You shall pay a nonrefundable commitment fee of $1,000.00 to the Company upon your acceptance of this commitment letter.

8. You shall provide the Company with photographs of all buildings or other structural improvements on the Property prior to closing.

9. You shall pay an appraisal fee to the Company in the amount of $450.00.
10. The loan is to be escrowed for taxes and insurance premiums.

> Very truly yours,
> AMERICAN EAGLE MORTGAGE COMPANY
>
> By: _____
> J. Perry Drake
> Treasurer

✓ CHECKLIST

Loan Commitment for a Residential Loan

☐ 1. Title commitment/insurance   ☐ 5. Borrower's affidavit

☐ 2. Survey   ☐ 6. Note

☐ 3. Hazard insurance   ☐ 7. Mortgage

☐ 4. Truth-in-lending statement   ☐ 8. Settlement statement

THE CLOSING AND AFTERMATH

By the time the closing day arrives it is hoped that most of the requirements and all the loan and sale documents have been prepared. All the parties (seller, purchaser, and brokers) have been notified of the date, time, and place of the closing. The purchaser knows the exact amount of money to bring to the closing and has been instructed to bring good funds in the form of a certified or cashier's check.

Closings usually take place in a conference room of the law firm handling the closing. After the introduction of the parties to one another, the closing usually commences with the closing attorney explaining the sale documents to the seller and to the purchaser. Ideally, the seller and purchaser have received copies of all documents and have already reviewed and approved them. In many residential transactions this ideal is not met, and the parties may be seeing the documents for the first time at the closing table. Additional copies of each document should be prepared, so that each party will have its own copy to review while the documents are being explained. The item of prime interest is the closing statement, in which all the closing disbursements and costs have been outlined. The seller is interested in making certain that all payoffs and satisfaction of prior liens are correct according to his or her records and that brokerage commissions and other expenses he or she is required to pay are in the correct accounts. The agents are interested in determining that commission amounts are true and correct. It is not unusual for closing adjustments to be made at the time of closing. Unpaid charges, such as cleanup bills or other expenses that need to be reimbursed between the parties, may not be brought to the closing attorney's attention until the date of closing. Sums of money allocated to pay for termite protection, hazard insurance, and surveys may have already been paid and need to be deleted from the closing statement. Most seasoned closing attorneys review the closing statement first; if changes are to be made, they are taken care of while the closing is progressing. This results in a new and corrected closing statement at the end of the closing, which can then be signed.

The usual sequence of events for most closings is to handle the sale aspects first, with the seller signing all the transfer documents. Then the loan transaction takes place, with the purchaser signing all the loan documents. It may be desirable and prudent on some commercial transactions for the loan closing to take place before the sale. Many commercial borrowers do not want the seller to know what terms were arranged for financing the property. If this is desired by the parties, then two closings will be scheduled: first the loan closing and then the sale closing.

After all the documents have been signed, witnessed, and notarized, good funds have been verified from the purchaser and the lender, and all checks have been cut and disbursements made to those parties present at closing, the closing is finished. On many residential transactions the seller delivers keys to the purchaser, and the date for vacating and occupying the property is clearly understood between the parties. Purchaser and seller should receive copies of all closing documents signed by the seller and purchaser in connection with the closing. Most brokers require that only a copy of the closing statement be given to them.

Representatives of the lenders on residential closings seldom attend the closing. Representatives of the lender on a commercial closing may be present at the closing. This is important, since last-minute details in the loan often are negotiated at the closing table. Documents that are changed at closing should be either retyped or altered at the table. All alterations should be initialed by all parties affected by the alterations.

Disbursing, Recording, and Transmittal of Final Documents

After the purchaser, seller, and agent have gone home, the closing legal assistant still has much to do before the job is done. Checks have already been disbursed to the seller and real estate agents at closing. The next checks to disburse immediately after closing are the checks to pay off all prior mortgages, liens, or encumbrances against the real property. Before disbursing any moneys the legal assistant should be satisfied that the check received from the purchaser will be honored by the bank on which it is drawn, and satisfied that the check provided by the lender will be honored when it is presented. Because most firms disburse all moneys through their escrow accounts and all checks paid from closing will be firm checks, it is required that lenders, purchasers, or anyone supplying funds for the closing provide either cashier's or certified checks drawn on a federal reserve bank. If funds are to be wired into the firm's escrow account, they should be sent by federal wire. It is important when issuing checks that a ledger card be used to balance the funds received against the funds paid out.

All closing documents that are to be recorded should be recorded immediately after closing. This usually includes the deed of conveyance from seller to purchaser and the mortgage from purchaser or borrower to the lender. It also may include assignments for rents and leases, UCC financing statements, satisfaction of liens, or other matters that may be recorded in connection with a particular transaction. Most firms use couriers to deliver the recorded documents to the clerk's office. In some parts of the country rush recording is available for an additional fee. With rush recording the clerk's office can index, record, and copy the documents and return the originals the same day.

All monies to pay off liens or satisfactions should be sent by transmittal letter. The transmittal letter should include a statement that the money being sent constitutes payment in full of the debt and that the check is being cashed based on that assumption. It is a good idea to request that all satisfactions and releases of mortgages or liens be returned to the legal assistant. The legal assistant should provide a self-addressed, stamped envelope for the return. It also is advisable to call the person to whom satisfaction money has been sent to make sure that he or she has received it and that the sum is sufficient to pay off the debt.

Most lenders require that a loan document package consisting of all the original documents except those documents that have been sent to record be delivered to them the day after the closing. The transmittal package to the lender is important because it reveals the quality of the firm's work. There should be no errors, and all the lender's instructions should be followed to the letter. Making errors or not following instructions could lead to the law firm's being removed from the lender's approved list and could seriously affect the firm's economic viability.[1]

Final Close Out

After all deeds, mortgages, and other loan documents have been recorded and returned from the clerk's office and all cancellations and other satisfactions have been returned and recorded,

---

[1]Portions of this chapter have been excerpted from *The Residential Real Estate Closing* by Daniel J. Falligant, *Real Estate Practices and Procedures Program Materials* (pp. 5a. 1–5a.11: Institute of Continuing Legal Education of Georgia, 1985, Athens, Georgia). Used by permission of the publisher.

it is time to close out the file. Original recorded documents need to be sent to the parties entitled to receive them. The purchaser is entitled to receive the warranty deed, and the lender, the recorded mortgage, assignment of rents, UCC financing statements, and so on.

Another aspect of the close out is the issuance of the final title insurance policies. A final title examination is necessary to verify that the deed and loan documents have in fact been recorded and do properly appear in the index of the record room. A final title examination also searches for the recorded satisfactions on all prior liens and security deeds.

Most lenders will not accept title policies unless the general standard exceptions for parties in possession, matters of survey, unrecorded easements, and mechanics' liens are deleted. In addition, if any restrictions or covenants are set forth in Schedule B, most lenders require the inclusion of an affirmative provision in the policy stating that said restrictions have not been violated to date and that any future violation will not result in the forfeiture or reversion of title.

The title policy should follow the commitment exactly. The effective date of the owner's policy is the date of the recording of the deed, and the effective date of the loan policy is the date of the recording of the mortgage.

After the title policies have been prepared and sent to the lender with the recorded mortgage and to the purchaser with the recorded warranty deed, the file should be rechecked to make sure that everything has been taken care of and that all checks have been disbursed, ledger cards balanced, all documents recorded and delivered to the proper parties, and all liens and other debts satisfied and cancelled. The entire transaction is now completed and the file can be sent to storage.

It is not unusual for four to six weeks to elapse between the closing and the final completion of the file.

A real estate closing is a complicated procedure, and it is essential that the legal assistant be organized and pay attention to detail. The best method to achieve organization and to adhere to detail is to prepare a checklist for all the items required in a real estate closing. As previously discussed, each real estate closing is unique and will have its own checklist. The checklists that appear earlier in the chapter are examples of the types of things one would expect to find in a real estate closing. The checklist on page 236-238 is a general outline of all the aspects of a real estate closing.

NEW TECHNOLOGY FOR DOCUMENT PRODUCTION

The representation of a seller, purchaser, or lender in connection with a real estate closing involves the preparation of numerous legal documents. Computerized automated document preparation systems have been in existence for several years. These systems become more sophisticated each year as technology advances in the area. The automated document preparation systems generally in use today are either the traditional fill-in-the-blank search for the code document systems or the new intelligent document assembly systems. The older technology uses generic forms which have blanks for variable information such as the names of the parties, loan amounts, and legal descriptions. It is necessary for the user of this system to type in the variable information and then to identify on each form where this information is to be inserted by the computer. The computer would then print the forms with the variable information included. Residential closings using the standard FNMA forms and an automated database generally involve the traditional fill-in-the-blank software. This traditional automated system requires considerable manual input for it to work.

The document production software known as document assembly enables lawyers and legal assistants to develop their own set of standard forms. The software then permits these forms to be assembled and disassembled, rearranged, and used in any number of ways to create custom documents in the same period of time spent to create standard form documents. A document assembly program allows the legal assistant to create his or her own documents through the use of clause libraries. Once these clause libraries are established, the user can then select from the various clauses within the library to create custom forms. Most of the document assembly programs ask the user questions in order to assemble the necessary documents. A legal assistant using a document assembly program would answer the questions and input variables and therefore produce a highly complicated and sophisticated document for the lawyer's final review.

Document assembly software requires manual input and work to create the custom forms. Once these forms are created, however, the software permits the manipulation of this information and allows the lawyer or legal assistant to create sophisticated real estate documents efficiently.

Some of the closing software systems enable a legal assistant to prepare an HUDN-1 Settlement Statement, title insurance documents, and other transaction documents. Some programs will perform trust account balancing and will even enable a legal assistant to do check writing and any 1099 tax reporting that is required. Many of the programs permit the transfer of data to and from a lender or client database through a modem. Some closing programs are flexible enough that you can tailor a program for closing practices in any particular jurisdiction. For example, local recording fees and transfer tax formulas may be input into the system and the program will then automatically compute the amounts for each transaction.

In addition to software technology, most law firms also make use of the technological advances in computer hardware, including printers and scanners. Most law firms use a laser printer which can produce at high speed a quality print of a legal document. These laser printers may also print in color if required. Another useful hardware tool is the scanner or imaging system. A scanner is a piece of hardware that can scan (read) a written document and convert it into computer codes for one's database system. Through the use of a scanner the document then becomes a part of the permanent computer database and can be revised and printed from one's own computer system. Most scanners, although they can convert printed material into computer codes, generally do not make perfect copies and so the computer copy needs to be cleaned for mistakes or imperfections.

By using new computer technology—both hardware and software—attorneys are able to generate more documents efficiently and at a lower cost. This lower cost is often passed on to the client in the form of lower fees for the services performed, and some is retained by the firm to enhance its profits in maintaining a real estate closing practice.

It is critical that any legal assistant working in real estate have computer skills. Being able to type and being familiar with various computer software systems is as important as having real estate knowledge and other skills. Although many corporations and firms may have training programs for legal assistants who are not computer literate, many do not, and therefore the legal assistant is encouraged to obtain these computer skills through college education or other training sources.

 CHECKLIST

Real Estate Closing

☐ I. File Creation
    ☐ A. Open file
        1. Client name
        2. Client number
        3. Billing information
        4. Cross-reference and conflict check
☐ II. Information Gathering
    ☐ A. Review real estate contract
        1. Name of seller
        2. Name of purchaser
        3. Name of broker
        4. Description of real property

        5. Date of closing

        6. Requirements of seller

        7. Requirements of purchaser

  ❑ B. Prepare closing checklist from review of real estate contract

  ❑ C. Review loan commitment

        1. Name of lender

        2. Name of borrower

        3. Amount of loan

        4. Commitment expiration date

        5. Loan closing requirements

  ❑ D. Prepare a loan closing checklist

  ❑ E. Order title examination and title policy

        1. Description of real property

        2. Date when examination is required

        3. Name of title company

        4. Name of insured

        5. Insured amount

  ❑ F. Order survey

        1. Legal description of property

        2. Information regarding previous survey

        3. Name of purchaser and other names to appear on survey

        4. Name of lending institution to appear on survey

        5. Flood hazard certification

        6. Other special requirements for survey

        7. Date of completion for survey

  ❑ G. Order hazard and fire insurance

        1. Name of insured

        2. Proper address of property

        3. Amount of insurance

        4. Proof insurance premium has been paid one year in advance

        5. Name of lender for mortgagee clause

        6. Date for delivery of insurance policy

❑ III. Preclosing Procedures

  ❑ A. Review title examination and title policy

  ❑ B. Obtain copies of all title exceptions

  ❑ C. Request satisfaction amounts from any mortgages, liens, or encumbrances to be paid at closing

  ❑ D. Review survey

        1. Do improvements encroach over property line?

        2. Is survey in compliance with purchaser and lender requirements?

  ❑ E. Verify that all sale obligations have been met by both purchaser and seller

  ❑ F. Verify that all mortgage loan commitment requirements have been satisfied

❑ IV. Document Preparation

  ❑ A. Preparation of all purchase and sale documents

  ❑ B. Preparation of all loan documents

❑ V. Closing

  ❑ A. Inform all parties (purchaser, seller, broker, lender representatives) of the date, time, and place of closing

  ❑ B. Inform purchaser of proper amount of proceeds needed for closing and instruct purchaser to bring good funds

  ❑ C. Verify that lender has deposited loan proceeds with firm

  ❑ D. Reserve conference room

  ❑ E. Prepare closing packet of documents for purchaser and seller

❑ VI. Disbursing, Recording, and Transmittal of Final Documents

  ❑ A. Transmit deed, mortgage, and other documents to be recorded to courthouse for recording

  ❑ B. Transmit money necessary to pay prior liens, mortgages, and encumbrances to proper parties

  ❑ C. Prepare final package for purchaser and seller

  ❑ D. Prepare final loan package for lender

☐ VII. Final Close Out
  ☐ A. Obtain all deeds, mortgages, and other documents recorded from courthouse
  ☐ B. Obtain all satisfactions and cancellations for prior mortgages, liens, and encumbrances
  ☐ C. Order final title examination and verify proper recording and indexing of deed, mortgage, and other recorded documents
  ☐ D. Obtain and review title insurance policy
  ☐ E. Transmit recorded deed and title insurance policy to purchaser
  ☐ F. Transmit recorded mortgage and other loan documents and title insurance policy to lender
  ☐ G. Final review of file to verify that all closing procedures have been completed
  ☐ H. Close file and send to storage

ETHICS: Conflicts of Interest

You are a legal assistant with a firm that represents a bank. The bank makes a number of consumer home loans. You have received a new loan and have just contacted the purchasers for the purpose of going over the closing checklist. During your conversation, you realize that the purchasers think you represent them in the transaction. Should you keep quiet, or quickly inform the purchasers that you represent the bank and advise the purchasers to obtain their own legal representation?

Attorneys cannot accept employment in those situations in which the attorney's own interest might impair his or her independent professional judgment. This means that an attorney cannot represent a client in which the attorney has a financial interest or represent two clients in the same transaction. The residential real estate attorney daily faces these conflicts of interest. In many transactions that involve residential real estate, the attorney represents the lender but is the only attorney involved in the transaction. The seller and purchaser often look to this attorney for advice and even believe that the attorney is representing their interests in the transaction. It is necessary for the attorney and the legal assistant to be aware of this potential conflict of interest. Law firms and bar associations have different ways of resolving the conflict. Some law firms resolve the conflict by informing the parties early in the transaction as to the firm's representation. For example, a firm that represents the lender would notify, at the beginning of the transaction, both the seller and the purchaser that the attorney is representing the lender's interest. The attorney would invite both the seller and the purchaser to seek their own counsel in connection with the transaction. This early disclosure can help to resolve the conflicts of interest problem.

SUMMARY

The real estate closing is the main fee-generating transaction for most real estate attorneys. A real estate closing is a real-life event that requires the practical use of all the real estate attorney's or legal assistant's knowledge about title examinations, surveys, deeds, mortgages, and general real estate law. Although the accumulated knowledge of all real estate law is required to accomplish a successful closing, the closing process has its own identity with its own set of rules and procedures. The activities involved in a real estate closing can generally be divided into six areas: (1) file creation; (2) information gathering; (3) document preparation; (4) the closing; (5) disbursement, recording, and transmittal of the closing package; and (6) final close out. The legal assistant is generally actively involved in all six areas.

Information gathering or due diligence involves obtaining the necessary investigation and information to successfully close the transaction. A legal assistant will be actively involved in this area in ordering and reviewing title examinations, title insurance commitments, surveys, fire and casualty insurance, termite letters, and other documents required by the sale contract or loan commitment. A checklist of the due diligence items needed to close the transaction can generally be obtained by a careful reading of the real estate contract or loan commitment involved in connection with the transaction to be closed. Once all of the due diligence or information gathering has been completed, loan and sale documents will be prepared by the legal assistant. The legal assistant will use this information to prepare the required sale and loan documents. A checklist of the necessary documents will also be obtained by a careful review of the real estate contract and loan commitment. Once the transaction has been closed, the legal assistant will also be involved in disbursing the necessary sale and loan proceeds and recording the sale and transfer documents. A thorough knowledge of local customs concerning recording fees and expenses will be required by the legal assistant to competently perform these tasks. A legal assistant is also generally responsible for receiving all the necessary closing documents from the recorder's office and other places and transmitting these to the purchaser, seller, and lender involved in the transaction.

Examples of many of the legal forms used in a residential real estate closing follow in Chapter 10.

KEY TERMS

closing	loan closing	mortgagee loss payable clause
escrow	loan commitment	

SELF-STUDY EXAMINATION

(Answers provided in Appendix)

1. T or F. Most contracts contain a legal description of the property.

2. T or F. A title examination is the last thing to be ordered for a closing.

3. T or F. A loan can always be prepaid before its maturity.

4. T or F. Most mortgage loans are repaid semiannually.

5. T or F. Most loan commitments are not assignable by the borrower.

6. T or F. A penalty for late payment of a mortgage payment is known as a late charge.

7. T or F. A determination as to whether property is located in a flood hazard zone is made by the title examiner.

8. T or F. The main document to review to prepare a sale closing checklist is the real estate contract.

9. T or F. Most lenders require that a copy of the hazard insurance be provided to them at closing.

10. T or F. Most payments on mortgage loans are made in arrears.

11. What helpful information with respect to real estate closings can a legal assistant obtain from reviewing the real estate contract?

12. What helpful information with respect to real estate closings can a legal assistant obtain from reviewing the loan commitment?

13. What is the minimum documentation a seller must provide at a real estate closing?

14. What is the minimum documentation a purchaser must provide at a real estate closing?

15. What information does the surveyor need to prepare a survey?

16. What is the importance of hazard and fire insurance, and what is a mortgagee loss payable clause?

17. Why is it important for a legal assistant to prepare a checklist of documents and procedures to be followed in a real estate closing?

18. What is a prepayment fee or premium, and how is it different from a late charge?

19. Briefly describe the six steps of a real estate closing.

20. Explain some of the general differences between residential and commercial real estate closings.

Real Estate Closing Forms and Examples

"Practice is the best of all instructors."

—Maxim 439—Pubilius Syrus

OBJECTIVES

After reading this chapter you should be able to:

- Understand and prepare various kinds of affidavits
- Understand and prepare various real estate closing documents such as deeds, bills of sale, assignment of warranties, assignment of leases, and assignment of contracts
- Understand the importance and particular use of such real estate documents as corporate resolution, agreement regarding survival of loan commitment, indemnity of fees, attorney's opinions, and compliance agreements
- Prepare a HUD-1 Uniform Settlement Statement
- Understand the documentation involved in the closing of a residential sale and loan transaction

At a real estate closing ownership of real property is transferred from seller to purchaser. At a loan closing a loan is consummated between the lender and the borrower. The purchaser at a closing expects to receive good title to the real property that he or she has agreed to buy and to obtain whatever warranties and assurances the seller has made in the real estate sale contract. The seller at a closing expects to be paid the contract price for the real property and not obligate himself or herself to perform any duty not required under the contract. In the case of a loan closing the borrower expects to receive the loan proceeds from the lender, and the lender expects to receive good security for its loan as well as the satisfaction of all the borrower's promises and covenants contained in the loan commitment.

A real estate attorney uses a number of legal documents at the closing to accomplish and satisfy all the expectations of the parties involved. A real estate legal assistant prepares many of the legal documents required. These legal documents are numerous, and vary in form from state to state. The legal assistant should become familiar with the various legal forms used in the locality in which he or she works. This information can be obtained from the law firm that employs the legal assistant.

Some of the basic forms that are used in residential and commercial real estate closing transactions are discussed in this chapter. Many forms, such as deeds, notes, and mortgages, have already been discussed. References are made to the chapters in which these forms can be found.

AFFIDAVITS

affidavit
Written statement of fact that is sworn to by the person making the statement under oath as a true statement of facts.

An **affidavit** is a written statement of fact that is sworn to by the person making the statement (affiant) under oath as a true statement of facts. The person who administers the oath to the affiant is a notary public. The notary's signature usually appears on the affidavit as well as the notary seal. The penalty for a false affidavit is perjury. Perjury can result in both civil and criminal penalties.

Affidavits are used for many purposes in a real estate closing transaction. Some of the more common affidavits used by the real estate attorney or legal assistant are discussed in this section.

Title Affidavit

Most purchasers of real property require the seller to execute a title affidavit at the time of the sale. In addition, most lenders require the borrower to execute a title affidavit at the time the lender acquires a mortgage on the borrower's real property. The title affidavit is helpful in removing standard exceptions from title insurance policies. A title affidavit is a statement of facts swearing to the following: (a) the affiant owns the real property described in the affidavit; (b) the boundary lines of the real property are certain and not in dispute; (c) the affiant has a right to possession of the real property; (d) there are no liens, encumbrances, easements, or leases affecting the real property unless they are identified in the affidavit; (e) there are no judgments, bankruptcies, or other restrictions against the affiant owner of the real property; and (f) the affidavit is being made by the affiant with knowledge that it will be relied on by purchasers, lenders, and title insurance companies involved with the real property.

Exhibit 10–1 shows a title affidavit. Other title affidavits can be found in Chapter 8.

EXHIBIT 10–1
Affidavit of Title

STATE OF _____

COUNTY OF _____

AFFIDAVIT OF TITLE

The undersigned, _____ , being duly sworn, states:

That the undersigned is the fee simple title owner of the real property described on *Exhibit "A"* attached hereto and incorporated herein by reference (the "Property");

That the lines and corners of the Property are clearly marked and there are no disputes concerning the location of said lines and corners;

That no improvements or repairs have been made or contracted for on the Property during the three (3) months immediately preceding the date of this affidavit, for which there are outstanding bills for labor or services performed or rendered, or for materials supplied or furnished, or incurred in connection with improvements or repairs on the Property, or for the services of architects, surveyors, or engineers in connection with improvements or repairs on the Property;

That, except for the matters set forth on *Exhibit "B"* attached hereto and incorporated herein by reference, the Property is free and clear of all claims, liens, and encumbrances, and there is no outstanding indebtedness for or liens against any equipment or fixtures attached to, installed on, incorporated in or located on, or otherwise used in connection with the operation or maintenance of, the Property or the improvements thereon;

That there are no persons or other parties in possession of the Property who have a right or claim to possession extending beyond the date hereof, except for tenants under terms of written leases disclosed on *Exhibit "C"* attached hereto and incorporated herein by reference;

That there are no suits, proceedings, judgments, bankruptcies, liens, or executions against the undersigned which affect title to the Property, the improvements thereon, or the fixtures attached thereto;

That the undersigned is making this affidavit with the knowledge that it will be relied upon by lenders, attorneys, and title insurance companies interested in the title to the Property.

Sworn to and subscribed before

me this _____ day of _____ ,

20 ____ .

_____   _____ (SEAL)

Notary Public

My Commission Expires:

_____

[NOTARY SEAL]

Affidavit of No Change

It is not uncommon in loan transactions for several weeks to pass between the time the loan application is made and the time the loan is closed. Many lenders require the borrower, at the time of the loan closing, to sign an affidavit swearing that the borrower's financial condition has not materially changed from the date the loan application was made (Exhibit 10–2).

Same Name Affidavit

An owner of property may be referred to in the chain of title or in a transaction in a number of ways. For example, a person named William Clyde Smith may be referred to as W. C. Smith in some of the closing documents or the documents within the chain of title. It is important to make certain that W. C. Smith and William Clyde Smith are one and the same person. Often an affidavit to that effect is used (Exhibit 10–3).

Similar Name Affidavit

It is not unusual for a common name such as William Smith to appear on the judgment index during a title examination. The judgments may be against a person with the name of William Smith other than the borrower or seller of the real property involved in the real estate trans-action. To clear up the matter, most title companies will accept an affidavit signed by the real property owner indicating that the real property owner is not the same person mentioned in the judgments (Exhibit 10–4). On receipt of this affidavit the title company will insure the real property free and clear of the judgments.

EXHIBIT 10–2
Affidavit of No
Material Change

STATE OF _____)
) ss:
COUNTY OF _____)

AFFIDAVIT OF NO MATERIAL CHANGE

The undersigned, being duly sworn, state:

That the undersigned have received from SECOND FEDERAL SAVINGS AND LOAN ASSOCIATION a loan Commitment letter dated August 25, 20_____ , amended by letter dated December 13, 20_____ ("Commitment Letter"), to finance the construction of a 62,128 square-foot shopping center located in Gulfport, Mississippi;

That no adverse change has taken place in the undersigneds' business or financial condition or in connection with the property serving as collateral for the loan;

That the undersigned are making this affidavit with the knowledge that it will be relied upon by SECOND FEDERAL SAVINGS AND LOAN ASSOCIATION in making the loan set forth in the commitment letter.

_____ (SEAL)

_____ (SEAL)

Sworn to and subscribed before me this
_____ day of _____ , 20 _____ .

_____

Notary Public
My Commission Expires:

_____

Notarial Seal

EXHIBIT 10-3
Same Name Affidavit

SAME NAME AFFIDAVIT

STATE OF _____

COUNTY OF _____

    Before me came in person William Clyde Smith who, being duly sworn, on oath says:

    Deponent states that William Clyde Smith (s)he is one and the same person as W. C. Smith and is the same person as named in Warranty Deed dated November 14, 1998 and recorded at Deed Book 156, page 242, _____ County State of _____ .

_____

William Clyde Smith

Sworn to and subscribed before me this

_____ day of _____ , 20 _____ .

_____

Notary Public

EXHIBIT 10-4
Similar Name Affidavit

STATE OF _____

COUNTY OF _____

SIMILAR NAME AFFIDAVIT

    Before me, the undersigned attesting officer, came in person _____ , who, after having been first duly sworn, deposes and on oath says that deponent is not the _____ referred to in the following:

    That there are no judgments or executions of any kind or nature outstanding against deponent; and

    That this affidavit is made for the purpose of inducing _____ to make a loan secured by a loan deed on or to purchase property known as:

_____

_____

_____

Sworn to and subscribed before me this

_____ day of _____ , 20 _____ .

_____

Notary Public

Foreign Person Affidavit

The Internal Revenue Service requires that a purchaser of real property from a foreign person withhold 10 percent of the purchase price and pay it to the Internal Revenue Service. If the purchaser fails to withhold the 10 percent, the purchaser will be responsible for any tax assessed against the foreign person on account of the sale. The purchaser is not excused from this obligation unless the purchaser obtains an affidavit from the seller to the effect that the seller is not a foreign person (Exhibit 10–5). The foreign person affidavit has become standard on all real estate transactions.

EXHIBIT 10-5
Foreign Person
Affidavit

STATE OF _____
COUNTY OF _____

FOREIGN PERSON AFFIDAVIT

The undersigned, being duly sworn, deposes, certifies and states on oath as follows:

That the undersigned is not a "foreign person" as such term is defined in the United States Internal Revenue Code of 1986, as amended (the "Code") and regulations promulgated thereunder, and is not otherwise a "foreign person" as defined in Section 1445 of the Code;

That the undersigned's United States taxpayer identification number is; _____
_____;

That the undersigned is making this Affidavit pursuant to the provisions of Section 1445 of the Code in connection with the sale of the real property described on Exhibit "A" attached hereto and incorporated herein by reference, from the undersigned to   which sale constitutes the disposition of the undersigned of a United States real property interest, for the purpose of establishing that   is not required to withhold tax pursuant to Section 1445 of the Code in connection with such sale;

That the undersigned acknowledges that this Affidavit may be disclosed to the Internal Revenue Service by   , that this Affidavit is made under penalty of perjury, that any false statement made herein could be punished by fine, imprisonment, or both.

Under penalty of perjury, I declare that I have examined the foregoing Affidavit and hereby certify that it is true, correct, and complete.

Sworn to and subscribed before
me this _____ day of _____ ,
20 ____ .

_____   _____
Notary Public

SALE AND TRANSFER DOCUMENTS

The sale and transfer of real property requires the use of a number of legal documents. The type of real property being transferred often dictates what documents are required. For example, the sale of a home requires less documentation than the sale of a resort hotel. On most real estate transactions the sale and transfer at least requires the use of a deed, bill of sale, assignment of warranties, and, on commercial contracts, an assignment of leases and assignment of contracts.

Deed

A deed is a legal document that transfers ownership of real property from one person to another. A full discussion of deeds, together with several examples of different types of deeds, can be found in Chapter 5.

Bill of Sale

bill of sale
Legal document that transfers ownership to personal property.

A deed only transfers ownership to real property. If the real estate transaction involves both real and personal property, which is the case in most residential and commercial transactions, then a separate legal document must be used to transfer ownership of the personal property. The legal document that transfers ownership to personal property is a **bill of sale.** The bill of sale, similar to a deed, can either contain warranties of title or be a quitclaim bill of sale without warranties. A general warranty bill of sale usually contains warranties that (a) the seller lawfully owns and is possessed of the personal property being sold; (b) the seller has a right to sell, transfer, and convey the personal property to the purchaser; (c) the personal property is free and clear of any and all encumbrances or security interests; and (d) the seller will warrant and forever defend the title of the personal property against the claims of any and all people whom-

EXHIBIT 10–6
General Warranty Bill
of Sale

STATE OF _____

COUNTY OF _____

GENERAL WARRANTY BILL OF SALE

FOR AND IN CONSIDERATION of the sum of Ten and NO/100 Dollars ($10.00) and other good and valuable consideration in hand paid to _____ (hereinafter referred to as "Seller") by _____ (hereinafter referred to as "Purchaser"), Seller hereby sells and conveys to Purchaser, her successors and assigns, any and all existing fixtures, equipment, furniture, appliances, and other personal property owned by Seller and used in connection with and being situated on or within certain improved real estate of Seller located in _____ County, _____, and more particularly described on Exhibit "A" attached hereto and by this reference incorporated herein and made a part hereof.

Seller hereby covenants with and represents and warrants to Purchaser as follows:

1. That Seller is lawfully seized and possessed of said personal property;
2. That Seller has the right to sell, transfer, and convey the same;
3. That same is free and clear of any and all encumberances; and
4. That Seller warrants and will forever defend the title to same against all claims whatsoever.

IN WITNESS WHEREOF, Seller has hereunto caused its hand and seal to be applied this day of _____ 20__

Signed, sealed, and delivered this

day of _____ 20__ , in the

presence of:

_____

                                                    (Seal)

_____   _____

_____

Witness

_____

Notary Public

My Commission Expires:

_____

soever. The bill of sale usually is signed with the same formality as a deed, witnessed, and notarized. A bill of sale usually is not recorded. An example of a general warranty bill of sale appears as Exhibit 10–6.

Assignment of Leases

The sale of any commercial real property with tenants involves the transfer of the tenant leases from the seller to the purchaser. Most purchasers require that all leases be assigned to them together with all security deposits that must be returned to the tenant on the expiration of the leases. The purchaser also requires that the seller indemnify the purchaser against any claims that the tenants may have against the seller or the purchaser as a result of defaults under the leases that have happened before the date of the sale. Most sellers require that the purchaser indemnify the seller against all claims that may be made by the tenants against the seller because of defaults under the leases that occur after the date of the sale. An assignment of leases usually is signed by both purchaser and seller and their signatures are witnessed and notarized. The assignment of leases is not recorded unless the leases have been recorded. Exhibit 10–7 is an example of an assignment of leases.

Loan Documents

A real estate transaction that involves a loan secured by the real estate requires a number of loan documents. The basic loan documents are a note and a mortgage. On commercial properties the

EXHIBIT 10–7
Assignment of Leases
and Security Deposits

STATE OF _____)
)   ss:
COUNTY OF _____)

ASSIGNMENT OF LEASES
AND SECURITY DEPOSITS

    THIS INDENTURE, made and entered into this _____ day of _____ , 20 _____ , by and between _____ _____

(hereinafter referred to as "Assignor") and _____ _____ _____ ,

its successors and assigns, (hereinafter referred to as "Assignee").

W I T N E S S E T H :

    WHEREAS, Assignor has on even date herewith conveyed to Assignee certain improved real property located in _____ County, _____ (hereinafter referred to as the "Property"), more particularly described on Exhibit "A" attached hereto and made a part hereof, and in connection therewith Assignor desires to transfer and assign to Assignee the tenant leases and security deposits in existence with regard to the improvements located on the Property;

    NOW, THEREFORE, for and in consideration of the sum of TEN AND NO/100 ($10.00) DOLLARS and other good and valuable consideration, the receipt and sufficiency of which are hereby acknowledged, Assignor and Assignee covenant and agree as follows:

1. Assignment of Leases.

Assignor hereby transfers and assigns to Assignee all of Assignor's right, title, and interest as landlord or lessor in and to each of the leases described on Exhibit "B" attached hereto and made a part hereof (hereinafter referred to as the "Leases") affecting all or any part of the Property.

2. Indemnification of Assignee.

Assignor indemnifies, defends and holds Assignee, its successors and assigns, harmless from and against any claim against or liability of Assignee, its successors and assigns, arising out of the covenants and duties of the lessor/landlord under the Leases to be performed before the date hereof by Assignor.

3. Assignment of Security Deposit.

Assignor hereby transfers and conveys to Assignee all of Assignor's right, title, and interest in and to all security deposits collected by Assignor under the Leases, said security deposits being more particularly described on Exhibit "B" attached hereto and made a part hereof.

4. Indemnification of Assignor.

Assignee indemnifies, defends, and holds Assignor harmless from any and all claims against or liabilities of Assignor arising out of the covenants and duties of Assignor to return the security deposits and fees assigned herein and assumes the obligation of landlord or lessor and agrees to perform under the Leases pursuant to the conditions contained in the Leases.

5. Successors and Assigns.

This Assignment shall be binding upon and inure to the benefit of the Assignor and Assignee and their respective successors and assigns.

6. Governing Law.

This Assignment shall be governed and construed in accordance with the laws of the State of _____ .

    IN WITNESS WHEREOF, the undersigned parties have hereunto set their hands and seals, as of the day and year first above written.

EXHIBIT 10-7
**Assignment of Leases
and Security Deposits
(continued)**

```
                                  ASSIGNOR:
Signed, sealed, and delivered in the pres-   _____ (SEAL)
ence of:
_____
Witness

_____
Notary Public
My Commission Expires:
_____
Notarial Seal
                                  ASSIGNEE:
Signed, sealed, and delivered in the pres-   _____ (SEAL)
ence of:
_____
Witness

_____
Notary Public
My Commission Expires:
_____
Notarial Seal
```

note and mortgage may be supplemented by an assignment of leases and rents, a security agreement, and a Uniform Commercial Code financing statement. If the loan is a construction loan, a construction loan agreement and an assignment of construction and architect's contracts are required. A full explanation of loan documents and several examples of loan document forms are included in Chapter 6.

MISCELLANEOUS REAL ESTATE CLOSING DOCUMENTS _____

1099-B Report Form

The Internal Revenue Service requires that settlement agents report sales of real estate transactions to the Internal Revenue Service. The settlement agent, in most situations, is the real estate attorney. The failure to provide the informational form subjects the settlement agent to penalties. A 1099-B reporting form is shown as Exhibit 10–8.

Settlement or Closing Statement

A settlement or closing statement sets forth the financial terms of a sale or loan closing. The statement indicates all the money involved and to whom the funds have been disbursed. The settlement and closing statement forms vary, depending on the type of transaction involved. Law firms and even individual lawyers have their own favorite forms they like to use. The Real Estate Settlement Procedures Act of 1974 requires that on all federally related loans, which means residential consumer loans secured by one- to four-family residences, the HUD-1 form be used (Exhibit 10–9). Instructions on how to prepare the form follow.

Section A—Heading.   The heading of the closing statement that appears at the top of page 1 should be completed as follows.

Section A.   U.S. Department of Housing and Urban Development Settlement Statement

Section B.   Type of loan, file number, loan number, and mortgage insurance case number. The choices for type of loan are a Federal Housing Administration (FHA)-insured loan, a Veterans

EXHIBIT 10–8
Information for Real
Estate 1099–B Report
Filing as Required by
the Internal Revenue
Service

**INFORMATION FOR REAL ESTATE
1099–B REPORT FILING
AS REQUIRED
BY THE INTERNAL REVENUE SERVICE**

Section 6045 of the Internal Revenue Code, as amended by the Tax Reform Act of 1986, requires the reporting of certain information on every real estate transaction. From the information you provide below, a Form 1099-B will be produced, and a copy of it will be furnished to the I.R.S. and to you no later than January 31 of the next year. If you fail to furnish adequate information (in particular, a taxpayer ID number), then you will be subject to all I.R.S. Regulations, including the possible withholding of twenty percent (20%) of the current sales price.

FILE NUMBER: _____   FILE NAME: _____

SELLER'S NAME:

_____

_____

SELLER'S MAILING ADDRESS:

_____

_____

SOCIAL SECURITY NO.: _____

OR

FEDERAL TAX ID NO.: _____

CLOSING DATE: _____

PROPERTY ADDRESS: _____

_____

SALES PRICE: _____

WAS THIS YOUR PRINCIPAL RESIDENCE?:   Yes _____   No _____

 I (We) certify that the above information is correct and understand that it will appear on a Form 1099 that will be sent to me and to the Internal Revenue Service.

 DATE _____   _____

 SELLER'S SIGNATURE

 _____

 SELLER'S SIGNATURE

Administration (VA)-insured loan, a Farmers' Home Administration-insured loan, a conventional uninsured loan, and a conventional insured loan. In a conventional insured loan there is no government participation, but the payments of the loan are insured by a private mortgage insurance company. In a conventional uninsured loan there is no government participation, and the payments of the loan are not insured. The file number is the law firm's internal file number for the loan transaction. The loan number is the lender's loan number for the transaction. Most lenders give a loan number to a particular loan when they issue a commitment. The mortgage insurance case number is the file number for mortgage insurance, if mortgage insurance exists. Mortgage insurance referred to in paragraph B is the private mortgage insurance that insures the payments of the mortgage.

Section C.   Explanatory note printed on all HUD-1 statements. This note explains that the form is being furnished to give the borrower a statement of actual settlement costs. The amounts paid to and by the settlement agent are shown. The items marked (p.o.c.) were paid outside the closing. They are shown here for informational purposes and are not included in the total.

Section D.   Name and address of the borrower, who also is the purchaser of the property in a sale transaction. If the purchaser is buying the home to live in, the home address may be used as the address of the borrower.

EXHIBIT 10–9
Hud-1 Closing Statement

A. Settlement Statement

U.S. Department of Housing
and Urban Development

OMB No. 2502-0265

B. Type of Loan

1. ☐ FHA 2. ☐ FmHA 3. ☐ Conv. Unins.	6. File Number	7. Loan Number	8. Mortgage Insurance Case Number	
4. ☐ VA 5. ☐ Conv. Ins.				

C. Note: This form is furnished to give you a statement of actual settlement costs. Amounts paid to and by the settlement agent are shown. Items marked "(p.o.c.)" were paid outside the closing; they are shown here for information purposes and are not included in the totals.

D. Name and Address of Borrower	E. Name and Address of Seller	F. Name and Address of Lender

G. Property Location	H. Settlement Agent	
	Place of Settlement	I. Settlement Date

J. Summary of Borrower's Transaction		K. Summary of Seller's Transaction	
100. Gross Amount Due From Borrower		400. Gross Amount Due To Seller	
101. Contract sales price		401. Contract sales price	
102. Personal property		402. Personal property	
103. Settlement charges to borrower (line 1400)		403.	
104.		404.	
105.		405.	
Adjustments for items paid by seller in advance		Adjustments for items paid by seller in advance	
106. City/town taxes to		406. City/town taxes to	
107. County taxes to		407. County taxes to	
108. Assessments to		408. Assessments to	
109.		409.	
110.		410.	
111.		411.	
112.		412.	
120. Gross Amount Due From Borrower		420. Gross Amount Due To Seller	
200. Amounts Paid By or in Behalf of Borrower		500. Reductions in Amount Due To Seller	
201. Deposit or earnest money		501. Excess deposit (see instructions)	
202. Principal amount of new loan(s)		502. Settlement charges to seller (line 1400)	
203. Existing loan(s) taken subject to		503. Existing loan(s) taken subject to	
204.		504. Payoff of first mortgage loan	
205.		505. Payoff of second mortgage loan	
206.		506.	
207.		507.	
208.		508.	
209.		509.	
Adjustments for items unpaid by seller		Adjustments for items unpaid by seller	
210. City/town taxes to		510. City/town taxes to	
211. County taxes to		511. County taxes to	
212. Assessments to		512. Assessments to	
213.		513.	
214.		514.	
215.		515.	
216.		516.	
217.		517.	
218.		518.	
219.		519.	
220. Total Paid By/For Borrower		520. Total Reduction Amount Due Seller	
300. Cash At Settlement From/To Borrower		600. Cash At Settlement To/From Seller	
301. Gross Amount due from borrower (line 120)		601. Gross Amount due to Seller (line 420)	
302. Less amounts paid by/for borrower (line 220)	( )	602. Less reductions in amt. due seller (line 520)	( )
303. Cash ☐ From ☐ To Borrower		603. Cash ☐ To ☐ From Seller	

Previous Edition Is Obsolete
Great Lakes Business Forms, Inc.
Form No. 2384 (8702)

Great Lakes Business Forms, Inc.
To Order Call 1-800-530-9393 ☐ FAX 616-791-1131

HUD 1 13861
RESPA, HB 4305 2

(continued)

EXHIBIT 10-9
Hud-1 Closing Statement

L. Settlement Charges			Paid From Borrower's Funds at Settlement	Paid From Seller's Funds at Settlement
700. Total Sales/Broker's Commission based on price $ @ % =				
Division of Commission (line 700) as follows:				
701. $ to				
702. $ to				
703. Commission paid at Settlement				
704.				
800. Items Payable in Connection With Loan				
801. Loan Origination Fee %				
802. Loan Discount %				
803. Appraisal Fee to				
804. Credit Report to				
805. Lender's Inspection Fee				
806. Mortgage Insurance Application Fee to				
807. Assumption Fee				
808.				
809.				
810.				
811.				
900. Items Required By Lender To Be Paid in Advance				
901. Interest from to @$ /day				
902. Mortgage Insurance Premium for months to				
903. Hazard Insurance Premium for years to				
904. years to				
905.				
1000. Reserves Deposited With Lender				
1001. Hazard Insurance months @ $ per month				
1002. Mortgage Insurance months @ $ per month				
1003. City property taxes months @ $ per month				
1004. County property taxes months @ $ per month				
1005. Annual assessments months @ $ per month				
1006. months @ $ per month				
1007. months @ $ per month				
1008. months @ $ per month				
1100. Title Charges				
1101. Settlement or closing fee to				
1102. Abstract or title search to				
1103. Title examination to				
1104. Title Insurance binder to				
1105. Document preparation to				
1106. Notary fees to				
1107. Attorney's fees to				
(includes above items numbers:)				
1108. Title Insurance to				
(includes above items numbers:)				
1109. Lender's coverage $				
1110. Owner's coverage $				
1111.				
1112.				
1113.				
1200. Government Recording and Transfer Charges				
1201. Recording fees: Deed $;Mortgage $; Releases $				
1202. City/county tax/stamps: Deed $; Mortgage $				
1203. State tax/stamps: Deed $; Mortgage $				
1204.				
1205.				
1300. Additional Settlement Charges				
1301. Survey to				
1302. Pest inspection to				
1303.				
1304.				
1305.				
1400. Total Settlement Charges (enter on lines 103, Section J and 502, Section K)				

I have carefully reviewed the HUD-1 Settlement Statement and, to the best of my knowledge and belief, it is a true and accurate statement of all receipts and disbursements made on my account or by me in this transaction. I further certify that I have received a copy of HUD-1 Settlement Statement.

_____   _____

_____   _____

Borrowers   Sellers

The HUD-1 Settlement Statement which I have prepared is a true and accurate account of this transaction. I have caused or will cause the funds to be disbursed in accordance with this statement.

_____   _____

Settlement Agent   Date

WARNING: It is a crime to knowingly make false statements to the United States on this or any other similar form. Penalties upon conviction can include a fine or imprisonment. For details see: Title 18 U.S. Code Section 1001 and Section 1010.

(continued)

EXHIBIT 10-9
Hud-1 Closing Statement

ACKNOWLEDGMENT AND RECEIPT

DATED: _____

SELLER: _____

BORROWER: _____

LENDER _____

PROPERTY DESCRIPTION: _____

_____

_____

The Borrower and Seller this date have checked, reviewed, and approved figures appearing on the Disclosure/Settlement Statement (Statement of Actual Costs), consisting of 2 pages, and each acknowledges receipt of the payment of the loan proceeds in full, and Seller acknowledges payment in full of the proceeds due Seller from the Settlement.

The Borrower and Seller agree to adjust the tax prorations shown on the Settlement Statement when the actual ad valorem tax bill is rendered.

As part of the consideration of this sale, the contract between the parties is by reference incorporated herein, and made a part hereof; the terms and conditions contained therein shall survive the closing and shall not merge upon the delivery of the Warranty Deed.

MONTHLY PAYMENT: Payable to: _____

_____ .

PRINCIPAL AND INTEREST: $_____

HAZARD INSURANCE: $_____

STATE AND COUNTY TAX: $_____

CITY TAX: $_____

MORTGAGE INSURANCE: $_____

TOTAL: $_____

CERTIFICATION OF SETTLEMENT STATEMENT

I have carefully reviewed the HUD-1 Settlement Statement and to the best of my knowledge and belief, it is a true and accurate statement of all receipts and disbursements made on my account or by me in this transaction. I further certify that I have received a copy of the HUD-1 Settlement Statement.

_____   _____

SELLER(S)   BORROWER(S)

Seller's Federal Tax I.D. Number (Social Security Number) _____

The HUD-1 Settlement Statement which I have prepared is a true and accurate account of this transaction. I have caused the funds to be disbursed in accordance with this statement.

SETTLEMENT AGENT:

By: _____

Date: _____

WARNING: It is a crime to knowingly make false statements to the United States on this or any other similar form. Penalties upon conviction can include a fine and imprisonment. For details, see: Title 18 U.S. Code Section 1001 and Section 1010.

3497 e

Section E.   Name and address of the seller. The forwarding address for the seller should be used.

Section F.   Name and address of the lender.

Section G.   Description of the property. A street address is acceptable.

Section H.   Identification of the settlement agent and the place of settlement. This is the law firm and the law firm's address.

Section I.   Settlement date, which is the date of the closing.

Section J.   Summary of the borrower's (purchaser's) transaction. It is broken into three separate columns: 100 column, 200 column, and 300 column. The *100 column* is a summary of the gross amount of money due from the borrower (purchaser) in connection with the transaction. The *200 column* is a summary of all moneys previously paid either by the borrower (purchaser) or by other parties in connection with the transaction, or credits that the borrower (purchaser) is entitled to as part of the transaction. *Column 300* is a summary of columns 100 and 200, and determines whether the borrower (purchaser) gets cash from the closing or brings cash to the closing.

Instructions for the various line numbers within each column follow.

Line 101.   Contract sales price. This amount is determined from the contract.

Line 102.   Any money in addition to the contract sales price that is to be paid by the borrower for any personal property to be used in connection with the real property. If personal property is not being purchased or the personal property is included within the contract sales price, line 102 remains blank.

Line 103.   Total of all settlement charges to the borrower. The amount that appears on line 103 is the amount that appears on line 1400. Instructions for arriving at the amount for line 1400 follow.

Lines 106, 107, and 108.   Used to calculate the purchaser's portion of the real estate taxes, assessments, and sanitary taxes for the current year if the taxes have been paid in advance by the seller. These amounts are calculated by obtaining copies of the tax report and calling the sanitary tax office. The real property taxes are prorated by a formula that allocates to the seller the seller's portion of the tax year and to the purchaser the purchaser's portion of the tax year. The amount of the real estate taxes or sanitary taxes is divided by 365, the number of days in a year, to obtain a daily tax rate. The daily tax rate is then multiplied by the number of days in the tax year the purchaser or seller owned the property. These amounts are then entered on lines 106, 107, and 108. Lines 106, 107, and 108 are used only if the seller has already paid the taxes at the time of closing or if the taxes are due and payable at the time of closing and will be paid from the seller's funds at that time. For example, if the sale closes on October 15 of a given year and county taxes in the amount of $1,400 have already been paid by the seller, the purchaser's portion of the county tax bill is $291.84. This amount is entered on line 107 and is arrived at by the following computation: $1,400 ÷ 365 = $3.84 per day; October 16–December 31 = 76 days; $3.84 × 76 = $291.84.

Note that tax prorations are based on the tax year, and not the calendar year. For many taxing authorities the tax year is the calendar year, with the first day of the tax year being January 1 and the last day of the tax year being December 31. In the event the tax year is different, it will be necessary to know what the tax year is to arrive at the proration. For example, assume a tax year of March 1 to February 28. The closing takes place on October 15 and the seller has paid the taxes for the year. The purchaser's share of the taxes would be the number of days from October 16 (sale day usually being a seller's day) through February 28, or 135 days. The 135 days would then be multiplied by the daily tax rate to arrive at the purchaser's share of the tax bill.

Line 120.   Total of lines 101 through 112.

Line 201.   Amount of any earnest money or deposit that has already been paid by the purchaser. The real estate contract should indicate this amount.

Line 202.   Principal amount of any new loans that the purchaser is obtaining to buy the property. The loan commitment should indicate this amount.

Line 203.   Used only if the purchaser is buying the property and assuming an existing loan. An estoppel letter from the existing lender gives the amount needed for line 203.

Lines 201, 211, and 212.   Tax prorations. These are used if the taxes have not been paid in advance by the seller and are due and payable. The proration is the reverse of the proration used to obtain the numbers for lines 106, 107, and 108. For example, the closing takes place on April 15, and the county taxes are $1,400. The purchaser is entitled to a credit for the seller's portion of the year, January 1 through April 15, or 105 days. The purchaser's credit is $403.20. The computation to arrive at $403.20 is as follows: $1,400 \div 365 = 3.84; $3.84 \times 105 = 403.20.

Line 220.   Total of lines 201 through 219.

Line 301.   Repeat of line 120.

Line 302.   Repeat of line 220.

Line 303.   Line 301 usually is greater than line 302, and the difference is entered on *line 303* as cash required from the borrower at closing. If, for some reason, line 302 is greater than line 303, this indicates that the borrower will receive cash at closing.

Section K.   Summary of the seller's transaction. It consists of three columns: column 400, column 500, and column 600. *Column 400* is the gross amount of money due to the seller pursuant to the real estate contract. *Column 500* lists reductions in the amount of money due to the seller at closing. *Column 600* is a summary of columns 400 and 500, and indicates the amount of money the seller will take from the closing or, in some rare cases, the amount of money the seller will need to close. Instructions for the individual lines are as follows.

Line 401.   Contract sales price. This amount is taken from the sale contract.

Line 402.   Amount of money paid for any personal property in addition to the contract sale price.

Lines 406, 407, and 408.   Transfer of any amounts that appear on lines 106, 107, and 108.

Line 420.   Total of lines 401 through 412.

Line 501.   Amount of earnest money paid by the purchaser. Same amount as line 201.

Line 502.   All settlement charges due from the seller, which is the total that appears on line 1400. Instructions for obtaining this amount follows.

Line 503.   Amount of any loans that are being assumed by the purchaser at the time of closing. This line would be used only if the property is being sold subject to an existing loan that is not being paid at the time of closing. This amount is the same as that shown on 203, and is obtained in the same method.

Line 504.   Payoff of any existing first-mortgage loan on the property. This amount is obtained from a satisfaction letter from the mortgage lender.

Line 505.   Payoff of any second-mortgage loan on the property. This amount is obtained by a satisfaction letter from the mortgage lender.

Lines 506 through 509.   Payment of any other liens or matters that must be paid out of the seller's proceeds at the time of closing.

Lines 510, 511, and 512.   Repeat of the tax proration amounts that appear on lines 210, 211, and 212.

Line 520.   Total of lines 501 through 519.

Line 601.   Amount taken from line 420.

Line 602.   Amount taken from line 520.

Line 603.   Line 601 normally is greater than line 602, and the difference is shown on line 603 as cash to seller. If line 602 is greater than line 601, then 603 indicates the amount of money needed by the seller to close.

Section L.   Breakdown of all settlement charges or closing costs in connection with the sale and loan transaction. The section is divided into two columns: a borrower's column and a seller's column. The responsibility to pay for settlement costs usually is negotiated between the buyer and the seller in the real estate contract. It is not uncommon for a seller to agree to pay the real estate commissions and the loan and closing costs of a purchaser.

Line 700.   Amount of the real estate commission. This amount is taken from the real estate contract.

Lines 701 and 702.   Division of the real estate commission and the identity of the brokers receiving the money. These lines are used only when more than one broker is involved with the transaction. A listing broker often obtains from the seller the permission to place the property on the market, and a selling broker, a broker who found the purchaser, sells the property. These brokers may split the commission. The real estate contract should provide this information.

Line 703.   Total amount of commissions paid at closing. This is a seller-paid item.

800 Items.   Items payable in connection with the loan. These items can be obtained from the loan commitment letter or instruction letter from the lender. They consist of loan origination fees, loan discount fees, appraisal fees, credit reports, lender's inspection fees, mortgage insurance application fees, and any assumption fees or other charges that might be assessed by the lender. These items usually are paid by the borrower, but the contract should be checked to make sure that the seller has not agreed to pay them.

Column 900.   List of items required by the lender to be paid in advance at the time of closing.

Line 901.   Interest adjustment. The interest on most mortgage loans is paid in arrears. For example, a mortgage payment due on May 1 would pay interest for the month of April. Most lenders require that the payments start on the first day of the second month after the closing. For example, if a closing is on April 15, the first mortgage payment would not be until June 1. The June 1 payment would pay interest from May 1 through May 31, but would not pay the April interest. Therefore, it is necessary at the time of closing to collect interest for the month of closing, April 15 through April 30. A lender may give the per diem interest charge, and it is only necessary to multiply this per diem interest charge by the number of days left in the month, in this case sixteen. If the lender does not give a per diem interest charge, it can be calculated by multiplying the loan amount by the interest rate and dividing by 365 or 360. Some lenders calculate interest based on a 360-day year. The amount from said computation equals the per diem interest, which then can be multiplied by the number of days to be collected. For example, a loan in the amount of $80,000 at 10 percent interest closes on April 15. The amount of money needed to be collected from the borrower at closing for interest for the remaining part of April, April 15 through April 30 (sixteen days) is $355.52, and is calculated as follows: $80,000 × .10 = $8,000; $8,000 ÷ 360 = $22.22; $22.22 × 16 = $355.52.

Line 902. Used only when a private mortgage insurance company is insuring the payments on the loan. The amount to be entered on this line is given in the lender's instruction letter.

Line 903. Name of the insurance company issuing the fire insurance and the amount of the annual premium. If the borrower has already paid for the first year's insurance premium, then notation p.o.c. (paid outside of closing) is inserted. If the borrower has not paid for the insurance premium, then the amount of the insurance premium must be shown on this line.

Line 904. Flood insurance premiums that are due. This would be used only if the property is in a flood hazard zone.

Column 1000. Summary of all the insurance and tax reserves required by the lender at closing.

Column 1001. Amount of money necessary to establish an insurance escrow. This amount is arrived at by taking the annual premium for fire insurance and dividing it by 12 to get a monthly amount. Then how many of these monthly amounts are needed before the next due date on the insurance premium is calculated. The number of payments to be received monthly is subtracted from the amount needed, and that yields the amount to be collected and entered on line 1001. For example, a closing takes place on April 15, and insurance is paid for one year. The first payment under the loan is not due until June 1; therefore, one-twelfth of the hazard insurance premium will not be received by the lender until June 1. The lender then will receive one-twelfth on the first day of each month thereafter. The lender will receive eleven payments before the next year's April 15 premium due date. It would be necessary to collect at least one payment to have enough money on April 15 of the next year to pay the insurance premium. Lenders usually collect an escrow for insurance premiums for two months.

Line 1002. Computes the private mortgage insurance and is determined by multiplying the loan amount by the factor from a private mortgage insurance factor table. This number is given in the lender's instruction letter.

Lines 1003, 1004, and 1005. Escrows necessary to pay real estate taxes and assessments. The amounts to be entered on these lines are determined by first looking at the tax report to determine the annual taxes. It also is necessary to know when the tax bill becomes due. Then the tax bill is divided by 12 to arrive at a monthly tax amount. Then how many payments of these monthly tax amounts will be received before the due date of the tax bill is determined, and that amount is subtracted from the number of payments needed to pay the tax bill. For example, a loan closes on April 15, and the taxes are due October 1. The lender's first payment is due under the loan on June 1 and on the first day of each month thereafter. The lender receives in the due course of servicing the loan one-twelfth of the taxes on June 1, July 1, August 1, and September 1 before the October 1 due date. The lender will need eight monthly payments collected at closing to have an adequate amount of money in escrow to pay the taxes.

Column 1100. Attorneys' fees and title insurance charges in connection with the closing. This column usually is completed by filling in *line 1107* and indicating that this line includes items 1101 through 1106. The attorneys' fees are given by the firm closing the transaction.

Line 1108. Payment for the title insurance premium. This information is obtained from the title company. If the title insurance premium pays for both lender's and owner's coverages, the amount of the coverages should be indicated on lines 1109 and 1110. The lender's coverage is the amount of the loan, and the owner's coverage is the amount of the purchase price.

Column 1200. Summary of all government recording and transfer charges. These charges vary from state to state, and it is necessary to know the local charges in the place where the documents are to be recorded.

Column 1300. Any additional settlement charges that are not covered elsewhere. This column consists of such things as survey bills, pest inspection, and hazardous waste inspection. These amounts can be obtained from the service providers.

Line 1400. Summary of all total settlement charges and the amounts from line 1400 are entered on behalf of the purchaser on line 103, Section J, and on behalf of the seller on line 502, Section K.

RESIDENTIAL CLOSING EXAMPLE

This closing example involves a sale of a residence by a corporate seller, Markam Industries, Inc., to an individual, Helen Davis. Helen Davis is obtaining a loan from the American Eagle Mortgage Company for a portion of the purchase price. A review of the sales contract between Markam Industries, Inc., and Helen Davis (Exhibit 10–10 at the end of the chapter) and the loan commitment (Exhibit 10–11 at the end of the chapter) from American Eagle Mortgage Company to Helen Davis produces the following checklist.

✔ CHECKLIST

Residential Closing Example

❑ 1. Title examination

❑ 2. Title commitment and policy

❑ 3. Survey

❑ 4. Corporate resolution

❑ 5. Foreign person affidavit

❑ 6. 1099-B form

❑ 7. Owner's affidavit

❑ 8. Transfer tax certificate

❑ 9. Warranty deed

❑ 10. Bill of sale

❑ 11. Termite letter

❑ 12. Truth-in-lending disclosure statement

❑ 13. Borrower's affidavit

❑ 14. Promissory note

❑ 15. Deed to secure debt

❑ 16. Hazard and fire insurance

❑ 17. Settlement statement

After preparing the checklist a legal assistant would approach the checklist in the following manner.

Title Examination

The title examination should be ordered the same day the file is opened. The title examiner needs a legal description of the property and the current owner's name. In addition, the title examiner should be informed of the title company that will issue the insurance so that the examination can be certified in favor of the title company. The title examiner should be given a date for the completion of the examination. This date should be at least three to five business days before the closing date. The examination should be instructed to provide copies of all title exceptions and a copy of any plat involving the property. The seller's name and a description of the property can be taken from the real estate sales contract. The seller in this case is Markam Industries, Inc., and the property is Lot 12, Bassett Hall Subdivision, pursuant to plat recorded at Plat Book 68, Page 79, lying and being in Land Lot 359 of the 18th District of Fulton County, Georgia (Exhibit 10–12 at the end of the chapter).

Title Commitment

The title insurance company issuing the title commitment needs to be informed that a title examination is being prepared and will be delivered to it. The title company also needs to know the types of policies to be issued, the owners or lenders, the names of the insureds, and the amount of the insurance. The title company should be provided with the date for the issuance of the title commitment. In this case, assuming that both an owner's and a lender's policy will be issued, the title company should be instructed to issue a commitment for an $80,000 loan policy to American Eagle Mortgage Company and an owner's commitment for $100,000 to Helen Davis.

Survey

The survey should be ordered as soon as possible. The surveyor needs the legal description and the names of the parties to whom the survey should be certified. The survey typically is certified in the names of the purchaser and the lending institution. In this example these would be Helen Davis and American Eagle Mortgage Company. The surveyor also should indicate on the survey if the property is in a flood zone. The surveyor should provide the title company with a surveyor's inspection report form so that the title company can delete its standard survey exception. The date for completion of the survey, which should be three to five business days before the closing, should be given to the surveyor. The surveyor also should be instructed to provide the legal assistant with a minimum of six prints of the survey.

Corporate Resolution

Markam Industries, Inc., is a corporation, and a corporate seller of property requires a resolution of the board of directors authorizing the sale of the property and the signatures on the various documents (Exhibit 10–13 at the end of the chapter).

Foreign Person Affidavit

The Internal Revenue Service requires that the purchaser withhold 10 percent of the sale proceeds if the seller is a foreign corporation. An affidavit is used to indicate that the seller is not a foreign person or foreign corporation so that withholding is not required (Exhibit 10–14 at the end of the chapter).

Owner's Affidavit

The owner's affidavit is a title affidavit wherein the owner of the property, Markam Industries, Inc., swears that they own the property and that the property is free and clear of all liens and encumbrances except those shown on the exhibit attached (Exhibit 10–15 at the end of the chapter). The liens and encumbrances that appear on the exhibit are those that appear from the title examination.

Transfer Tax Certificate

The transfer tax certificate is unique to Georgia (Exhibit 10–16 at the end of the chapter). Georgia requires a transfer tax to be assessed on deeds. The tax is 10 cents for each $100 of consideration for the property being transferred. The certificate is filed in duplicate with the deed. Several other states have recording fees and requirements, and it is not unusual for some type of certificate to be provided to the clerk indicating the amount of tax due on the recordation of the deed.

Warranty Deed

The property is transferred by warranty deed, and in this case the deed is from Markam Industries, Inc., to Helen Davis (Exhibit 10–17 at the end of the chapter). The only title exceptions that will appear on the warranty deed are those title exceptions that survive closing: taxes for the current year and the two easements from the title examination.

Bill of Sale

The warranty deed transfers only title to real property. The personal property included in the sale is transferred by bill of sale (Exhibit 10–18 at the end of the chapter).

Termite Letter

In many states termites are a problem. This sales contract requires that a termite letter indicating that the property is free and clear of termites or that a termite bond be provided at closing.

Truth-in-Lending Disclosure Statement

Federal law requires on a residential loan that the borrower, Helen Davis, be informed of all the costs of the loan before the closing of the loan (Exhibit 10–19 at the end of the chapter).

Borrower's Affidavit

This is another title affidavit similar to the owner's affidavit signed by Markam Industries, Inc. (Exhibit 10–20 at the end of the chapter). This affidavit is signed by Helen Davis.

Promissory Note

This is the promise to pay money from Helen Davis to American Eagle Mortgage Company. The note should be prepared from the information found in the lender's commitment letter. Typically payments will begin on the first day of the second month following closing. Only one original note is signed at closing (Exhibit 10–21 at the end of the chapter).

Deed to Secure Debt

This is the security document conveying to American Eagle Mortgage Company the real property as security for the note. The grantor of the security deed will be Helen Davis and the grantee will be American Eagle Mortgage Company. All the necessary information to complete the form can be found from the contract for sale and the lender's commitment letter (Exhibit 10–22 at the end of the chapter).

Hazard Insurance

The lender requires that the real property be insured and that the lender, American Eagle Mortgage Company, appear as a mortgagee on the policy. The original insurance policy together with an endorsement showing American Eagle Mortgage Company as a mortgagee and a statement that the premium has been paid one year in advance must be made available at closing.

Settlement Statement

The settlement statement form is the HUD-1 required by the Real Estate Settlement Procedures Act. It is an outline and disclosure of all costs involved in the closing of the sale of the loan.

The form of HUD-1 used for the Helen Davis–Markam Industries, Inc., transaction is shown as Exhibit 10–23 at the end of the chapter. The following explanation is a line item-by-line item explanation of how the numbers that appear on the settlement statement were arrived at. The discussion begins with a computation of the settlement costs in Schedule L, which appears on the second page of the settlement statement.

Line 700 is used to compute the seller's broker commissions. These commissions are found in the contract of sale between the seller and buyer. The contract provides that the commission will be 7 percent of the sales price of $100,000, or $7,000. The commission is to be split in half between Ajax Realty Company and Northside Realty Co., Inc. Northside has received the $1,000 earnest money at closing and will retain the $1,000 as a credit against the commission owed to it. Therefore, total commissions paid at closing will be $7,000, less the $1,000 earnest money retained by Northside, or $6,000. The $6,000 is placed under the seller's column.

Line 800 items are payable in connection with the loan. These items are found in the lender's commitment letter. On this particular transaction, only the items shown on lines 801 and 803 are payable in connection with the loan, and they are payable by the borrower.

Line 900 items are required by the lender to be paid in advance at closing. This loan is closing on April 25, but the first payment is not due until June 1. The June 1 payment will pay interest in arrears from May 1 through May 31. It will, therefore, be necessary to collect, at closing, interest for the remainder of April. Interest will be collected from the date of closing through the end of April, or from April 25 to April 30—six days. A lender may in a commitment letter give a per diem interest charge. This loan amount has not been shown, and the method for calculating the charges is as follows:

Loan Amount: $88,000 × interest rate 8% = $6,400.

Divide the $6,400 by 365 (360 in some cases) to get $17.53.

Multiply $17.53 by the number of days (6) = $105.18.

The amount of $105.18 should be entered on line 901 under the borrower's column.

Line 1000 items are reserves deposited with the lender for taxes and insurance. To calculate the insurance reserve, take the total insurance bill for the year (see Example 10–1) and divide it by 12 ($480.00 divided by 12 equals $40.00 per month). Because the premium has been paid for one year in advance of the date of closing, the next premium on the insurance is not due until April 25 of the next year. The lender requires that one-twelfth of the insurance premium be paid each month, with the monthly payments beginning on June 1. Calculate the number of these payments from June 1 until April 25 of next year, and eleven payments will be made. The lender will need to collect at least one month's insurance to have enough to pay the bill. The lender can, under federal law, collect two months' insurance and usually does.

Lines 1003 and 1004 are the tax escrows. Tax bills can be obtained from the title report (Exhibit 10–12). Divide this tax bill by 12 to show a monthly amount. You will need to know when the tax bills are due to set up the escrow reserves. Tax bills in the example are due October 1, and the lender is going to receive one-twelfth of the taxes with each monthly payment— June, July, August, and September, or four payments. Therefore, it will be necessary to escrow at least eight payments to have enough money when the bills are due. The computation for this is as follows: city taxes $1,560.00 divided by 12 equals $130.00 per month times 8 equals $1,040.00; county taxes $1,850.00 divided by 12 equals $154.17 per month times 8 equals $1,233.36.

Line 1100 items are title charges and attorneys' fees. These are invoiced by the providers of the title charges. For this example, the charges are given on the expense sheet (Example 10–1).

Line 1200 items are recording and transfer charges. Recording fees vary from state to state. For this example, the recording fees are given on the expense sheet (Example 10–1).

EXAMPLE 10–1

FEES

Attorneys' Fees	$650.00
Title Insurance	400.00
Survey	350.00
Hazard Insurance Premium	480.00 per year
Recording Fees	$2.00 per page
	$1.00 per instrument
Transfer Tax–paid by seller	.10 per $100.00 of purchase price
Intangibles Tax–paid by purchaser	1.50 per $500.00 of loan amount
1st Mortgage Payoff	$82,460.00

Jim Baxter is President of Markam Industries, Inc.

Floyd Knox is Secretary of Markam Industries, Inc.

Settlement charges are always allocated between borrower and seller and totaled. The contract indicates which charges are assessed to the seller and which to the buyer.

Section J contains a summary of the borrower's transaction. Line 101 is the contract sales price, which can be found in the contract or, in this case, $100,000.

Paragraph 103 contains the settlement charges allocated to the borrower from line 1400—$5,612.54.

Paragraph 120 is a total of lines 101 and 103, or $105,612.54.

The *200 columns* are amounts paid by the borrower or on behalf of the borrower. These amounts reduce the borrower's cash requirements at closing.

Line 201 is any earnest money that has been paid. A review of the contract reveals an earnest money check of $1,000. This amount is entered on line 201.

Line 202 is the principal amount of any new loan, which in this case is the loan of $80,000 from American Eagle Mortgage Company. This amount is entered on line 202.

Lines 210 and 211 are prorations of city and county taxes between seller and buyer. The seller is responsible for the current year's taxes for the number of days the seller has owned the property. The computation is made by taking the tax bill for the entire year from the title examination and dividing the bill by 365. The amount received from that computation is then multiplied times the number of days the seller has owned the property to arrive at the appropriate credit amount for the borrower.

Annual tax bill for county Real Estate Taxes is $1,560 divided by 365 = $4.27 per day, multiplied by the number of days that the seller owned the property during the tax year, which is the number of days from January 1 through the closing April 25, for a total of 115 days = $491.05.

The calculation for the county tax bill of $1,850 divided by 365 = $5.07 per day. Multiply the $5.07 per day times the number of days, again using 115 days = $583.05.

Since the taxes have not been paid in the current year, the purchaser will receive a credit for these amounts in columns 210 and 211.

All 200 items are totaled and placed on line 220.

Line 300 is the summation of the borrower's transaction and discloses the amount of money needed from the borrower at closing. In this example, the borrower needs $23,538.44. The borrower should be made aware of this as early as possible and informed to bring a cashier's check made payable to the law firm.

Section K is a summary of the seller's transaction. Line 401 is the amount of the sales contract, or $100,000.

Section 500 is reductions from the amount of the sales price due to the seller.

Line 501 is the earnest money deposit of the purchaser.

Line 502 is the total of settlement charges due to the seller from line 1400, or $6,103.00.

Line 504 is a payoff of the existing first loan of $82,460 on the property. This amount is shown on the expense sheet (Example 10–1).

Lines 510 and 511 are the same prorations under lines 210 and 211.

All of the *500 items* are totaled, and the sum is entered on line 520.

The *600 column* is the settlement of the seller's transaction and reveals that the seller will leave the closing with $9,362.90.

After a settlement statement is prepared, it is necessary to do a cash reconciliation to make sure that cash in equals cash out. An example of the cash reconciliation for this transaction is shown in Example 10–2.

EXAMPLE 10–2

Cash In:

$ 80,000.00—American Eagle Mortgage Company
$ 23,538.44—Helen Davis
$103,538.44

Cash Out:

$ 82,460.00—Payment of first loan
$ 9,362.90—Payment to seller
$ 6,000.00—Real estate commission
$ 1,000.00—Commitment fee to American Eagle Mortgage Company
$ 500.00—Appraisal fee to American Eagle Mortgage Company
$ 105.18—Prepaid interest to American Eagle Mortgage Company
$ 80.00—Insurance reserves to American Eagle Mortgage Company

$ 1,040.00—Reserves for city property taxes to American Eagle Mortgage Company

$ 1,233.36—Reserves for county property taxes to American Eagle Mortgage Company

$ 650.00—Attorney's fees (law firm)

$ 400.00—Title premium (title company)

$ 17.00—Recording fees

$ 240.00—Intangible tax

$ 100.00—Transfer tax

$ 350.00—Survey

$ 103,538.44

Closing procedures and document preparation, like other aspects of business life, have been computerized. Software applications exist to assist the legal assistant in preparing a HUD-1 settlement sheet, printing loan documents on residential transactions, and even printing checks

---

 E T H I C S :   Case Problem

Ann is a real estate legal assistant in a large law firm. Her primary responsibility is to assist two attorneys who represent a bank in the closing of real estate loans. She has developed a good working relationship with the bank's loan officers. In fact, the loan officers send most of their new loans directly to Ann. On receipt from the bank, Ann prepares file opening memorandums for the supervising attorney's signatures.

It is late Wednesday afternoon, and Ann receives a new loan file from the bank as well as a telephone call from the loan officer. The loan officer indicates that the loan has to close no later than Friday and that it is a super priority matter. A conflicts check on the loan reveals that the borrower had several years ago been represented by one of the lawyers in the firm. It appears that there has been no activity with this client for the past three years. Ann calls the attorney to check out the situation but finds that the attorney is on vacation and will not be back until Monday. The attorney's secretary doesn't know anything about the client. Ann decides that the expedient thing to do is to go ahead and open the file and proceed for a closing.

Thursday morning Ann calls the borrower to go over the closing requirements. Once Ann identifies herself and the firm for which she works, the borrower is relieved to know that she works for the firm that represents him. The borrower is cooperative in providing information for the closing.

After receiving all the necessary information, Ann prepares the closing documents and schedules the closing for 3:00 P.M. on Friday. Ann attempts a number of times to meet with her supervising attorney so that she can review the loan documents but is not successful.

On Friday, Ann receives a call from the borrower, who indicates that he has a surprise business appointment out of town and must leave in an hour. He would like for Ann to come to his office and have him sign the papers. Ann immediately goes to the office. When she arrives, she finds that the borrower has left to pick up airline tickets and will not be back for about forty-five minutes. The borrower's secretary asks that the documents be left with her and she would make sure that the borrower signed them before he left town. She would then courier them back over to Ann. Ann agrees and goes back to the office.

Later that afternoon, the documents arrive in Ann's office and none of them have been notarized. Ann calls the secretary to discuss this fact, and the secretary indicates that she saw the borrower sign the documents. She asks Ann to notarize the documents; everything is O.K. Ann, to close the transaction on time, notarizes the documents.

Later, as Ann is putting the package together for transmittal back to the bank client, her supervising attorney stops by. The attorney would like to review the file before the 3:00 P.M. closing. Ann tells her that the closing has already taken place. Ann tells her about the developer's unexpected trip out of town and the trip to his office and the closing at the office. Ann neglects to tell the attorney the part about leaving the documents for signature and her notarization of the documents.

What legal ethics or codes of professional responsibility have been violated in this example?

for disbursement to the seller, purchaser, and lender. Most law firms that do a reasonable volume of residential work own such software applications. Many of the software applications claim that an entire residential loan package can be completed within thirty minutes, which is far less than the usual three or four hours required without a software package. Software applications also assure accuracy not only in making the computations necessary for the closing statement but also in the repetitive use of data in the various closing documents. Once the correct data is entered into the software, it is accurately and correctly redistributed on the various closing documents.

SUMMARY

Many law firms ask the legal assistant to prepare the documents used in a real estate closing transaction. The legal assistant should be familiar not only with what types of forms must be used, but also with the content of these forms. When preparing the forms the legal assistant must be careful not to make mistakes that will change the transaction or require corrective work. It is important that legal documents be carefully reviewed and proofread to minimize mistakes.

KEY TERMS

affidavit

bill of sale

SELF-STUDY EXAMINATION

(Answers provided in Appendix)

1. What statements of fact are included in a title affidavit?

2. When is a corporate resolution required in a closing transaction, and why is it important?

3. You are a legal assistant involved in a real estate sale transaction. The seller of the property is Susan T. Clark. The title examination of the property reveals that there are five judgments against Susan Clark, S. T. Clark, and Sue Clark. You call the seller, Susan T. Clark, and tell her about the judgments. She informs you on the phone that she is not the Susan Clark mentioned in the judgments. What do you do to protect the purchaser in the closing?

4. You are a legal assistant involved in a real estate sale transaction. The sale is to close on September 10. The title examination reports that county real estate taxes have been paid by the seller for the current year in the amount of $1,640. The tax year for the county begins February 1 and ends January 31. You have been asked to calculate the tax proration between purchaser and seller. What is the amount of the tax proration, and on which line of the HUD-1 would the amount appear?

5. You are assisting in a real estate closing transaction. The loan is $80,000 at an interest rate of 12 percent per annum. The loan is closing on March 14, and the lender wants the first payment on the loan to begin on May 1. The lender also requires the borrower to pay in advance all interest accruing during March. How much interest would you collect from the borrower at closing?

6. You are a legal assistant working on a real estate sale transaction. The title examination reports that real estate taxes for the current year are unpaid in the amount of $1,350 and the taxes are due November 15 of the year. The closing is taking place on May 10. The closing also involves a loan in which the lender wants taxes escrowed. The lender's first payment under the note will be July 1. Calculate the tax proration between seller and purchaser. Calculate the amount of taxes to be escrowed for the lender. Are the amounts the same? If not, should they be?

7. You are preparing a title affidavit for a real estate closing. Exhibit A to the affidavit is a legal description of the real property, and Exhibit B is a list of title exceptions to the real property. Where would you get the information to complete Exhibits A and B?

8. You are assisting in a real estate sale transaction. The title examination reports that there is an outstanding loan to Second Bank and Trust on the property. The loan is to be satisfied at closing. You believe the closing will take place on July 10. You obtain from Second Bank and Trust a satisfaction and payoff letter indicating how much money is needed to pay the loan as of July 10. The loan closing is delayed and does not take place until July 15. Is there any additional information you may need from Second Bank and Trust for the July 15 closing?

9. You are assisting in the closing of a sale of a home. The contract price for the home is $86,500. Seller's real estate

broker commission is 6 percent of the sales price and other closing costs are $600. In addition, there is an outstanding loan on the property that is to be paid at closing in the amount of $28,400. In addition, real property taxes for the current year in the amount of $2,150 are unpaid. The tax year is the calendar year, and the closing is taking place on August 15. In preparing the Uniform Settlement Statement, how much net money would the seller take home from the closing?

10. You are assisting in the purchase of a home. The contract purchase price is $115,000. The settlement costs allocated to the purchaser are $3,230. Taxes for the current year in the amount of $1,650 have been paid by the seller. The tax year is the calendar year, and the closing takes place on September 25. The purchaser has paid an earnest money deposit of $5,000 for the property and has obtained a loan to purchase the property for $90,000. You are preparing the Uniform Settlement Statement. How much money, if any, does the purchaser need to bring to closing to consummate the sale?

11. What is the penalty for a false affidavit?

12. What is a same name affidavit and why is it used?

13. What is a bill of sale and what does it do?

14. What information is generally contained in an assignment of leases?

15. What is an affidavit of no material change and why is it used?

ADDENDUM

EXHIBIT 10-10
Sales Contract

January 15,   , 20____

As a result of the efforts of_____Northside Realty Co., Inc._____ ,

a licensed Broker, the undersigned Purchaser agrees to buy, and the undersigned Seller agrees to sell, all that tract or parcel of land, with such improvements as are located thereon, described as follows: all that tract or parcel of land lying and being in Land Lot 359 of the 18th District of Fulton County, Georgia, being Lot 12 of Bassett Hall Subdivision, as per plat recorded in Plat Book 68, Page 79, Fulton County, Georgia, being improved property with a house located thereon known as 5167 Tilly Mill Road, Atlanta, Georgia 30302.

together with all electrical, mechanical, plumbing, air-conditioning, and any other systems or fixtures as are attached thereto and all plants, trees, and shrubbery now on the premises.
The purchase price of said property shall be:

_____One Hundred Thousand and No/100_____ DOLLARS, $_100,000.00_____ ,

to be paid as follows:
    All cash at closing

Purchaser has paid to the undersigned, __One Thousand Dollars -------------------------------- , as Broker,

$_1,000.00_____ ( ) cash (X) check, receipt whereof is hereby acknowledged by Broker, as earnest money, which earnest

money is to be promptly deposited in Broker's escrow account and is to be applied as part payment of purchase price of said property at the time sale is consummated.
    Seller warrants that he presently has title to said property, and at the time the sale is consummated, he agrees to convey good and marketable title to said property to Purchaser by general warranty deed subject only to (1) zoning ordinances affecting said property, (2) general utility easements of record serving said property, (3) subdivision restrictions of record, and (4) leases, other easements, other restrictions and encumbrances specified in this contract. In the event leases are specified in this contract, the Purchaser agrees to assume the Seller's responsibilities thereunder to the tenant and to the Broker who negotiated such leases.
    The Purchaser shall move promptly and in good faith after acceptance of this contract to examine title and to furnish Seller with a written statement of objections affecting the marketability of said title. Seller shall have reasonable time after receipt of such objections to satisfy all valid objections and if Seller fails to satisfy such valid objections within a reasonable time, then at the option of the Purchaser, evidenced by written notice to Seller, this contract shall be null and void. Marketable title as used herein shall mean title which a title insurance company licensed to do business in the State of Georgia will insure at its regular rates, subject only to standard exceptions unless otherwise specified herein.
    Seller and Purchaser agree that such papers as may be necessary to carry out the terms of this contract shall be executed and delivered by such parties at time the sale is consummated.
    Purchaser, its agents, or representatives, at Purchaser's expense and at reasonable times during normal business hours, shall have the right to enter upon the property for the purpose of inspecting, examining (including soil boring), testing, and surveying the property. Purchaser assumes all responsibility for the acts of itself, its agents, or representatives in exercising its rights under this paragraph and agrees to hold Seller harmless for any damages resulting therefrom.
    Seller warrants that when the sale is consummated the improvements on the property will be in the same condition as they are on the date this contract is signed by the Seller, natural wear and tear excepted. However, should the premises be destroyed or substantially damaged before the contract is consummated, then at the election of the Purchaser: (a) the contract may be cancelled, or (b) Purchaser may consummate the contract and receive such insurance as is paid on the claim of loss. This election is to be exercised within ten (10) days after the Purchaser has been notified in writing by Seller of the amount of the insurance proceeds, if any, Seller will receive on the claim of loss; if Purchaser has not been notified within forty-five (45) days subsequent to the occurrence of such damage or destruction, Purchaser may, at its option, cancel the contract.
    In negotiating this contract, Broker has rendered a valuable service for which reason Broker is made a party to enable Broker to enforce his commission rights hereunder against the parties hereto on the following basis: Seller agrees to pay Broker the full commission when the sale is consummated and in the event the sale is not consummated because of Seller's inability, failure or refusal to perform any of the Seller's covenants herein, then the Seller shall pay the full commission to Broker, and Broker, at the option of Purchaser, shall return the earnest money to Purchaser. Purchaser agrees that if Purchaser fails or refuses to perform any of Purchaser's covenants herein, Purchaser shall forthwith pay Broker the full commission; provided that Broker may first apply one-half of the earnest money toward payment of, but not to exceed, the full commission and may pay the balance thereof to Seller as liquidated damages of Seller, if Seller claims balance as Seller's liquidated damages in full settlement of any claim for damages, whereupon Broker shall be released from any and all liability for return of earnest money to Purchaser. If this transaction involves exchange of real estate, the full commission shall be paid in respect to the property conveyed by each party to the other and notice of the dual agency is hereby given and accepted by Seller and Purchaser. The commission on an exchange shall be calculated on the amount on the basis of which each property is taken in such exchange, according to the contract between the parties, and if no value is placed on any property exchange, then according to the reasonable value thereof. In the event of an exchange, each party shall be regarded as Seller as to the property conveyed by each party.
    Commission to be paid in connection with this transaction has been negotiated between Seller and Broker and shall be _____
_____7% of the purchase price._____ .

    Time is of essence of this contract.
    This contract shall inure to the benefit of, and be binding upon, the parties hereto, their heirs, successors, administrators, executors and assigns.
    The interest of the Purchaser in this contract shall not be transferred or assigned without the written consent of Seller.
    This contract constitutes the sole and entire agreement between the parties hereto and no modification of this contract shall be binding unless attached hereto and signed by all parties to this agreement. No representation, promise, or inducement not included in this contract shall be binding upon any party hereto.
    The following stipulations shall, if conflicting with printed matter, control:

(continued)

EXHIBIT 10-10
Sales Contract
(continued)

SPECIAL STIPULATIONS

1. Real Estate taxes on said property shall be prorated as of the date of closing.
2. Seller shall pay State of Georgia property transfer tax.
3. Sale shall be closed on or before __April 25, 20___ .
4. Possession of premises shall be granted by Seller to Purchaser no later than __April 25, 20___
5. Seller warrants that all appliances remaining with the dwelling and the heating and air conditioning systems will be in normal operating condition at time of closing. Purchaser shall have the privileges and responsibility of making inspections of said equipment and systems prior to closing of sale.
6. Seller shall provide at time of closing of the transaction a clearance letter from a licensed pest control operator, certified in wood destroying organisms, certifying the property is free from termites and other wood destroying organisms and from structural damage caused thereby and carrying a guarantee that the property will be treated for a period of one year from the date of issuance of said letter.

* continued

This instrument shall be regarded as an offer by the Purchaser or Seller who first signs to the other and is open for acceptance by the other until _____O'clock ___M., on the ____day of_____,20___; by which time written acceptance of such offer must have been actually received by Broker, who shall promptly notify other party, in writing of such acceptance.

The above proposition is hereby accepted
this _____ day of _____ , 20 ____.

_____
(Purchaser)   Helen Davis

_____
(Purchaser)

_____
(Seller)   Markam Industries, Inc.

_____
(Seller)

By: Northside Realty Co., Inc.
      (Broker)

* continued

7. All kitchen appliances are included in the sales price.
8. This contract is in cooperation with Ajax Realty Co. and the commission is to be divided 50/50.
9. This contract is subject to the Purchaser obtaining a loan in the principal amount of not less than $80,000.00, shall bear interest at a rate not to exceed 11% per annum and a term of not less than 25 years.

OR IN LIEU OF SAID LETTER

Seller shall provide a Termite Contract that is in full force with a licensed pest control company that may be transferred to the Purchaser, providing said contract covers both ADDITIONAL TREATMENT and REPAIR OF DAMAGE.

FORM 203

IVAN ALLEN CO., ATLANTA

To

From

Commerical Sales Contract

ATLANTA REAL ESTATE BOARD
September, 1972

AMERICAN EAGLE MORTGAGE COMPANY

March 7, 20__

Ms. Helen Davis
849 Mentelle Drive, N.E.
Atlanta, Georgia 30308

Re: Mortgage Loan Commitment—$80,000 at 8% for thirty (30) years

Dear Ms. Davis:

American Eagle Mortgage Company (the "Company") is pleased to inform you that it has acted upon your application and has approved a loan to you, subject to all terms and conditions of this letter. The loan will be in the principal sum of $80,000.00 at an annual rate of 8%, to be repaid as follows:

In equal consecutive monthly installments of $588.00 per month for thirty (30) years. Each installment, when paid, shall be applied first to the payment of accrued interest and then to the unpaid principal balance.

The holder may collect a "late charge" not to exceed an amount equal to four percent (4%) of any installment which is not paid within fifteen (15) days of the due date thereof, to cover the extra expenses involved in handling delinquent payments.

The loan proceeds shall be used for the acquisition of improved real estate (the "Property") located at 5167 Tilly Mill Road, Atlanta, Georgia.

The loan shall be secured by a first priority lien on the Property and on all improvements now or hereafter existing thereon. The Company's agreement to make the loan to you is subject to satisfaction of the following conditions, all at your sole cost and expense and in a manner acceptable to the Company.

1. The Company shall procure a standard form ALTA mortgagee's policy of title insurance insuring the loan as a first priority lien against the Property, showing there is to be no other encumbrances against the Property which render it unmarketable.

2. You shall provide the Company prior to closing with a recent plat of survey of the Property, together with a surveyor's certificate in form satisfactory to the Company's title insuror, depicting and certifying all improvements on the Property to be completely within the boundary lines of the Property and to be in compliance with all applicable building or setback line restrictions.

3. You shall provide the Company prior to closing with fire, lightning and extended coverage insurance issued by a company or companies and upon terms acceptable to the Company in at least the sum of $80,000.00. Premiums for such insurance shall be paid by you for not less than one year in advance. All policies shall be issued with a mortgagee clause in favor of and acceptable to the Company and shall be non-cancellable without at least ten (10) days prior written notice to the Company.

4. The Company shall select an attorney to close the loan and to prepare all documents deemed necessary or appropriate by the Company to evidence the loan and to establish the Company's first priority lien against the Property and the Policy. All such loan documents will be in form and substance satisfactory to the Company's closing attorney.

5. All actual fees or expenses (including, without limitation, such closing attorney's fees, title insurance premiums, cost of title examination, abstract of title fee, document preparation fee, cost of survey, appraisal fee, recording fees and intangibles or other taxes) incurred in connection with reviewing your loan application, or with closing, servicing, collecting or cancelling the loan, shall be paid by you.

6. The loan may be assumed by a transferee of the Property, provided the Company gives prior written consent thereto; but any transfer of title to all or any part of the Property whatsoever, or any further encumbrance or other lien imposed against the Property without the Company's prior written consent, will authorize the Company to declare the loan immediately due and payable. Any such assumption, transfer or encumbrance to which the

(continued)

EXHIBIT 10–11
American Eagle
Mortgage Company
Loan Commitment
(continued)

Company shall consent shall be upon such terms and conditions as the Company shall determine and approve.

7. You shall pay a non-refundable commitment fee of $1,000.00 to the Company upon your acceptance of this commitment letter.

8. You shall provide the Company with photographs of all buildings or other structural improvements on the Property prior to closing.

9. You shall pay an appraisal fee to the Company in the amount of $500.00.

10. The loan is to be escrowed for taxes and insurance premiums.

Very truly yours,
AMERICAN EAGLE MORTGAGE COMPANY

By: _____
J. Perry Drake
Treasurer

EXHIBIT 10–12
Title Examination

RE: 5167 Tilly Mill Road, Atlanta, Georgia

A search of the above referenced property as of April 20, 20__ at 5:00 P.M., reveals title to be vested in Markam Industries, Inc., subject to the following objections:

1. Easement between Sam Turner and Georgia Power Company dated August 6, 1959 recorded at Deed Book 2898, page 25, Fulton County Records.

2. Easement between Markam Industries, Inc. and Georgia Power Company dated February 11, 1998 and recorded in Deed Book 5106, page 810 aforesaid records.

3. Deed to Secure Debt from Markam Industries, Inc. to The Southern National Bank dated March 3, 2001 recorded in Deed Book 5508, page 83, aforesaid recording securing the original principal amount of $85,000.00.

4. County taxes have been paid through 20__ but are unpaid for 20__, in the amount of $1,850.00—due on October 1, 20__.

5. City of Atlanta taxes paid through 20__; 20__ due in the amount of $1,560.00 and due on October 1, 20__.

EXHIBIT 10–13
Corporate Resolution

CERTIFICATE

I, FLOYD KNOX, Secretary of MARKAM INDUSTRIES, INC., a Georgia Corporation (the "Company") do hereby certify as follows:

1. Attached hereto as Exhibit "A" is a true and correct copy of resolutions which were duly adopted at a special meeting of the Board of Directors on _____, 20__, at which a quorum was present and acting throughout and which have not been amended, modified, or rescinded in any respect and are in full force and effect from the date hereof.

2. The below-named persons have been duly elected and are qualified and at all times have been and this day are officers of the Company, holding the respective offices below set opposite their names, and signatures set opposite their names are their genuine signatures.

JIM BAXTER
President   _____

FLOYD KNOX
Secretary   _____

(continued)

WITNESS my hand and seal of the Company this _____ day of _____, 20__.

_____ (SEAL)
FLOYD KNOX
Secretary
[CORPORATE SEAL]

EXHIBIT "A"

RESOLVED, that MARKAM INDUSTRIES, INC., a Georgia Corporation (hereinafter called the "Company"), sell that certain real property more particularly described on Exhibit "B" attached hereto and made a part hereof to HELEN DAVIS pursuant to Contract for Sale dated January 15, 20__;

FURTHER RESOLVED, that the President of the Company, JIM BAXTER, is hereby authorized and directed to execute and deliver on behalf of Company any and all documentation required to sell the property to HELEN DAVIS, including but not limited to, any and all warranty deeds, affidavits, bills of sale and closing statements.

EXHIBIT "B"

All that tract or parcel of land lying and being in Land Lot 359 of the 18th District of Fulton County, Georgia, being Lot 12 of Bassett Hall Subdivision as per plat recorded of Plat Book 68, page 79, Fulton County, Georgia Records.

STATE OF GEORGIA   )
)   ss:
COUNTY OF FULTON   )

CERTIFICATE AND AFFIDAVIT OF NON-FOREIGN STATUS

The undersigned is the President of MARKAM INDUSTRIES, INC., a Georgia corporation (the "Transferor"), and is duly authorized to execute this Certificate and Affidavit in his representative capacity on behalf of the Transferor, as well as in his individual capacity;

That the principal place of business, principal office and chief executive office of the Transferor is located at 210 Corporate Square, Atlanta, Fulton County, Georgia 30303;

That the Transferor is a corporation duly organized and validly existing under the laws of the State of Georgia;

That the Transferor is not a "foreign corporation," as such term is defined in the United States Internal Revenue Code of 1986, as amended (the "Code") and Regulations promulgated thereunder, and is not otherwise a "foreign person," as defined in § 1445 of the Code;

That the Transferor's United States taxpayer identifying number is 58-1004212;

That the undersigned is making this Certificate and Affidavit pursuant to the provisions of § 1445 of the Code in connection with the sale of the real property described on Exhibit "A", attached hereto and incorporated herein by reference, by the Transferor to HELEN DAVIS (the "Transferee"), which sale constitutes the disposition by the Transferor of a United States real property interest, for the purpose of establishing that the Transferee is not required to withhold tax pursuant to § 1445 of the Code in connection with such disposition; and

That the undersigned acknowledges that this Certificate and Affidavit may be disclosed to the Internal Revenue Service by the Transferee, that this Certificate and Affidavit is made under penalty of perjury, and that any false statements made herein could be punished by fine, imprisonment, or both.

Under penalty of perjury, I declare that I have examined the foregoing Certificate and Affidavit and hereby certify that it is true, correct, and complete.

(continued)

EXHIBIT 10–14
**Certificate and
Affidavit of Non-
Foreign Status
(continued)**

_____ (SEAL)

JIM BAXTER

Certified, sworn to and subscribed before me this
day of _____ , 20_____ .

_____

Notary Public

My Commission Expires:

_____

[Notarial Seal]

EXHIBIT "A"

All that tract or parcel of land lying and being in Land Lot 359 of the 18th District of Fulton County, Georgia, being Lot 12 of Bassett Hall Subdivision as per plat recorded of Plat Book 68 page 79, Fulton County, Georgia Records.

EXHIBIT 10–15
Owner's Affidavit

STATE OF GEORGIA   )
)   ss:
COUNTY OF FULTON   )

OWNER'S AFFIDAVIT

The undersigned, being duly sworn, states:

That the undersigned is the President of MARKAM INDUSTRIES, INC., a Georgia corporation (the "Company"), and is duly authorized to execute this affidavit in his capacity on behalf of the Company as well as in his individual capacity;

That the principal place of business, principal office, and chief executive office of the Company is located in Fulton County, Georgia and has been located in said County at all times since the formation of the Company;

That the Company is the fee simple title owner of the real property described on Exhibit "A" attached hereto and incorporated herein by reference (the "Property").

That the lines and corners of the Property are clearly marked and there are no disputes concerning the location of said lines and corners;

That no improvements or repairs have been made or contracted for by the Company on the Property during the three (3) months immediately preceding the date of this affidavit, for which there are outstanding bills for labor or services performed or rendered, or for materials supplied or furnished, or incurred in connection with improvements or repairs on the Property, or for the services of architects, surveyors, or engineers in connection with improvements or repairs on the Property;

That, except for the matters set forth on Exhibit "B" attached hereto and incorporated herein by reference, the Property is free and clear of all claims, liens and encumbrances, and there is no outstanding indebtedness for or liens against any equipment or fixtures attached to, installed on, incorporated in, or located on, or otherwise used in connection with the operation or maintenance of, the Property or the improvements thereon;

That there are no persons or other parties in possession of the Property who have a right or claim to possession extending beyond the date hereof;

That there are no suits, proceedings, judgments, bankruptcies, liens, or executions against the Company which affect title to the Property, the improvements thereon or the fixtures attached thereto;

(continued)

EXHIBIT 10-15
Owner's Affidavit
(continued)

That the undersigned is making this affidavit with the knowledge that it will be relied upon by purchasers, attorneys, and title insurance companies interested in the title to the Property.

Sworn to and subscribed before me this _____ day of _____, 20_____ .

_____

Notary Public   JIM BAXTER

My Commission Expires:

_____

[Notarial Seal]

EXHIBIT "A"

All that tract or parcel of land lying and being in Land Lot 359 of the 18th District of Fulton County, Georgia being Lot 12 of Bassett Hall Subdivision as per plat recorded in Plat Book 68 page 79 Fulton County, Georgia Records.

EXHIBIT "B"

1. All taxes for the current year.
2. Easement between Sam Turner and Georgia Power Company dated August 6, 1959, recorded at Deed Book 2898, page 25, Fulton County, Georgia Records.
3. Easement between Markam Industries, Inc., and Georgia Power Company dated February 11, 1998 and recorded at Deed Book 5106, page 810, aforesaid records.
4. Deed to Secure Debt from Markam Industries, Inc., to The Southern National Bank dated March 3, 2001, recorded at Deed Book 5508, page 83, aforesaid records securing the original principal amount of $85,000.00.

EXHIBIT 10-16
Transfer Tax Certificate

PT-61 (Rev. 10/92)				(PLEASE TYPE OR PRINT)

SECTION A - SELLER'S INFORMATION

1. NAME
Markam Industries, Inc.

2. MAILING ADDRESS (STREET & NUMBER)
210 Corporate Square

3. CITY, STATE, ZIP CODE — Atlanta, Georgia 30324 | 4. DATE OF SALE

SECTION B - BUYER'S INFORMATION

1. NAME
Helen Davis

2. MAILING ADDRESS FOR TAX NOTICES, BILLS, ETC. (STREET & NUMBER)
5167 Tilly Mill Road

3. CITY, STATE, ZIP CODE — Atlanta, Georgia 30302 | 4. INTENDED USE [ ] [ ] [ ] [ ] R A C I

SECTION C - PROPERTY INFORMATION

1. LOCATION (STREET, ROUTE, HWY., ETC.) — 5167 Tilly Mill Road | 2. COUNTY — Fulton

3. CITY (IF APPLICABLE) — Atlanta | 4. MAP & PARCEL NUMBER

5. ACRES | 6. DISTRICT — 18 | 7. LAND LOT — 359 | 8. SUB LOT & BLOCK

SECTION D - RECORDING INFORMATION

1. DATE | 2. DEED BOOK | PAGE | 3. PLAT BOOK | PAGE

SECTION E - TAX COMPUTATION

1. Actual value of consideration received by seller (Fill out below only when actual value is not known) — $100,000.00

1a. Estimated fair market value of Real and Personal property conveyed

2. Fair market value of Personal property only conveyed

3. Amount of Liens and Encumbrances not removed by transfer

4. Net Taxable Value (1 or 1a minus 2 minus 3) — $100,000.00

5. TAX DUE at 10¢ per $100 or fraction thereof (Minimum $1.00) — 100.00

SECTION F - CERTIFICATIONS

SELLER: I hereby certify that all the items of information entered on this transfer form PT-61 are true and correct to the best of my knowledge and belief.

Signature _____
(Seller or Authorized Agent)   (Date)

BUYER: I hereby certify that all information on this form is true and correct to the best of my knowledge and belief. I acknowledge that if the above property is taxable and is subdivided or improved during the year of this transfer, that I must return it for taxation the following year, but if there are no changes and I do not elect to file a return, I will be deemed to have returned the property at the same valuation as was finally determined for the year of this transfer. I further acknowledge that this form does not relieve me of the responsibility of filing a return for personal property or of applying for homestead or other exemptions.

Signature _____
(Buyer or Authorized Agent)   (Date)

CLERK OF COURT: I hereby certify that the recording information in Section D is correct and that the tax due in Section E5 is computed correctly based upon the information supplied in Section E by the seller or authorized agent.

Signature _____
(Clerk or Deputy of Superior Court)   (Date)

REVENUE COPY

EXHIBIT 10-17
Warranty Deed

STATE OF GEORGIA

COUNTY OF FULTON

WARRANTY DEED

THIS INDENTURE made this   25th day of   April   20__   by and between
MARKAM INDUSTRIES, INC., a Georgia corporation
party or parties of the first part, hereinafter referred to as "Grantor", and

HELEN DAVIS
party or parties of the second part hereinafter referred to as "Grantee", the words "Grantor" and "Grantee" to
include the neuter, masculine and feminine genders, the singular and the plural;

WITNESSETH:

FOR AND IN CONSIDERATION of the sum of Ten Dollars in hand paid and other good and valuable
consideration delivered to Grantor by Grantee at and before the execution, sealing and delivery hereof, the receipt and
sufficiency of which is hereby acknowledged, Grantor, has and hereby does grant bargain, sell and convey unto
Grantee and the heirs, legal representatives, successors and assigns of Grantee

All that tract or parcel of land lying and being in Land Lot 359 of the 18th
District of Fulton County, Georgia, being Lot 12 of Bassett Hall Subdivision,
as per plat recorded at Plat Book 68, Page 79, Fulton County, Georgia Records.

SUBJECT TO:

Ad valorem taxes for the year 20__ and subsequent years.

Easement between Sam Turner and Georgia Power Company dated August 6, 1959,
recorded at Deed Book 2898, Page 25, Fulton County, Georgia Records.

Easement between Markam Industries, Inc. and Georgia Power Company dated
February 11, 1998 and recorded at Deed Book 5106, Page 810, aforesaid records.

TO HAVE AND TO HOLD said tract or parcel of land, together with any and all of the rights, members and appurtenances thereof to the same being, belonging or in anywise appertaining to the only proper use, benefit and behoof of the
Grantee and the heirs, legal representatives, successors and assigns of Grantee, forever, in fee simple.

GRANTOR SHALL WARRANT and forever defend the right and title to said tract or parcel of land unto the Grantee
and the heirs, legal representatives, successors and assigns of Grantee, against the claims of all persons whomsoever.

IN WITNESS WHEREOF, the Grantor has signed and sealed this deed, the day and year first above written.

Signed, Sealed and Delivered in the presence of: MARKAM INDUSTRIES, INC.

_____   By: _____ (SEAL)
        (Unofficial Witness)   Jim Baxter, President
                                               Attest: _____ (SEAL)
_____   Floyd Knox, Secretary
        (Notary Public)

                                                    [CORPORATE SEAL]

EXHIBIT 10–18
General Warranty
Bill of Sale

STATE OF GEORGIA   )
)   ss:

COUNTY OF FULTON   )

GENERAL WARRANTY BILL OF SALE

In consideration of the sum of Ten and No/100 ($10.00) Dollars, and other good and valuable consideration in hand paid to MARKAM INDUSTRIES, INC., a Georgia corporation (hereinafter referred to as "Seller") by HELEN DAVIS (hereinafter referred to as "Purchaser"), Seller hereby sells and conveys to Purchaser, its successors and assigns, all personal property, appliances and fixtures located on or used in connection with the property described on Exhibit "A" attached hereto and made a part hereof.

Seller hereby convenants with and represents and warrants to Purchaser as follows:

1. That Seller is lawfully seized and possessed of said personal property;

2. That Seller has a right to sell, transfer, and convey the same;

3. That the same is free and clear of any and all encumbrances or security interests;

4. That Seller warrants and forever will defend the title to same against any and all claims whatsoever.

IN WITNESS WHEREOF, Seller, by its duly authorized officers, has hereunto its hand and seal this the _____ day of _____ , 20_____ .

                                              MARKAM INDUSTRIES, INC.,
                                              a Georgia corporation

                                              By: _____ (SEAL)
                                                    JIM BAXTER
                                                    President

                                              Attest: _____ (SEAL)
                                                    FLOYD KNOX
                                                    Secretary

Signed, sealed, and delivered in the presence of this _____ day of _____ , 20_____ .

_____
Unofficial Witness

_____
Notary Public
My Commission Expires:

_____
[Notarial Seal]

EXHIBIT "A"

All that tract or parcel of land lying and being in Land Lot 359 of the 18th District of Fulton County, Georgia being Lot 12 of Bassett Hall Subdivision as per plat recorded of Plat Book 68 page 79, Fulton County, Georgia Records.

EXHIBIT 10-19
Truth-in-Lending Disclosure Statement

TRUTH-IN-LENDING MORTGAGE DISCLOSURE STATEMENT

Lender: AMERICAN EAGLE MORTGAGE COMPANY   **Borrower's Name and Address:**   Helen Davis
5167 Tilly Mill Road
Atlanta, Georgia 30302

APPLICATION #   DATE OF DISCLOSURE

(In this disclosure statement, the words "I," "me," "my," and "mine" refer to each consumer listed above. The words "you," "your," and "lender" refer to American Eagle Mortgage Company

ANNUAL PERCENTAGE RATE The cost of my credit as a yearly rate,	**FINANCE CHARGE** The dollar amount the credit will cost me,	**Amount Financed** The amount of credit provided to me or on my behalf.	**Total of Payments** The amount I will have paid after I have made all payments as scheduled, based on the current annual interest rate
8.25 %	$ 132,680.00	$ 79,000.00	$ 211,680.00

My payment schedule will be:

Number of Payments	Amount of Payments	When Payments Are Due
360	$588.00	First day of each month commencing on June 1, 20__

☐ **Construction Loan:** Interest on the amount of credit advanced during the construction period will be paid for _____ based on the outstanding balance. After the construction period I will pay payments as shown above.

☐ **Variable Rate:**

Security: I am giving you a mortgage on real estate located at
5167 Tilly Mill Road, Atlanta, Georgia 30302

Late Charge: If payment is ____15____ days late, I will be charged ____4____% of the interest and principal payment.
Assumption:
☐ Someone buying my home may be allowed to assume the remainder of the mortgage on the original terms, subject to conditions.
☐ Someone buying my house cannot assume the remainder of the mortgage on the original terms.

Prepayment: If I pay off early, I _____ have to pay a penalty, and I will not be entitled to a rebate of part of the finance charge.
☐ If this space is checked, all above numerical disclosures except for the late charge are estimates.

See contract documents for any additional information about nonpayment default, any required repayment in full before the scheduled date, and prepayment refunds and penalties.
e means an estimate

Recording Fees: $ _____.

Insurance: I may obtain all required property insurance (including any required flood insurance) from anyone I want that is acceptable to the lender.

Itemization of Amount Financed: ($_____) (c minus d):

(a) $_____ Amount given to me directly
(b) $_____ Amount applied to indebtedness of mine with the lender
(c) $_____ Principal amount of loan (total of a + b)
(d) $_____ Prepaid finance charge (itemized below)

$_____ for "points" paid by me
$_____ for_____ days prepaid interest
$_____ for_____

EXHIBIT 10–20
Borrower's Affidavit

STATE OF GEORGIA   )
)   ss:

COUNTY OF FULTON   )

BORROWER'S AFFIDAVIT

The undersigned, being duly sworn, states:

That the undersigned is the fee simple title owner of the real property described on Exhibit "A" attached hereto and incorporated herein by reference (the "Property").

That the lines and corners of the Property are clearly marked and there are no disputes concerning the location of said lines and corners;

That no improvements or repairs have been made or contracted for by the undersigned on the Property during the three (3) months immediately preceding the date of this affidavit, for which there are outstanding bills for labor or services performed or rendered, or for materials supplied or furnished, or incurred in connection with improvements or repairs on the Property, or for the services of architects, surveyors or engineers in connection with improvements or repairs on the Property;

That, except for the matters set forth on Exhibit "B" attached hereto and incorporated herein by reference, the Property is free and clear of all claims, liens, and encumbrances, and there is no outstanding indebtedness for or liens against any equipment or fixtures attached to, installed on, incorporated in or located on, or otherwise used in connection with the operation or maintenance of, the Property or the improvements thereon;

That there are no persons or other parties in possession of the Property who have a right or claim to possession extending beyond the date hereof;

That there are no suits, proceedings, judgments, bankruptcies, liens, or executions against the undersigned which affect title to the Property, the improvements thereon, or the fixtures attached thereto;

That the undersigned is making this affidavit with the knowledge that it will be relied upon by lenders, attorneys, and title insurance companies interested in the title to the Property.

Sworn to and subscribed before me this
day of _____ , 20____ .

_____

Notary Public
My Commission Expires:

_____

[Notarial Seal]

_____

HELEN DAVIS

EXHIBIT "A"

All that tract or parcel of land lying and being in Land Lot 359 of the 18th District of Fulton County, Georgia being Lot 12 of Bassett Hall Subdivision as per plat recorded of Plat Book 68 page 79, Fulton County, Georgia Records.

EXHIBIT "B"

1. All taxes for the current year.
2. Easement between Sam Turner and Georgia Power Company dated August 6, 1959, recorded at Deed Book 2898, page 25, Fulton County, Georgia Records.
3. Easement between Markam Industries, Inc., and Georgia Power Company dated February 11, 1988 and recorded at Deed Book 5106, page 810, aforesaid records.

EXHIBIT 10-21
Note

NOTE

April 25 , 20   Atlanta , Georgia
      [Date]   [City]   [State]

5167 Tilly Mill Road, Atlanta, Georgia 30302
           [Property Address]

1. BORROWER'S PROMISE TO PAY

In return for a loan that I have received, I promise to pay U.S. $ 80,000.00 (this amount is called "Principal"), plus interest, to the order of the Lender. The Lender is AMERICAN EAGLE MORTGAGE COMPANY . I will make all payments under this Note in the form of cash, check or money order.

I understand that the Lender may transfer this Note. The Lender or anyone who takes this Note by transfer and who is entitled to receive payments under this Note is called the "Note Holder."

2. INTEREST

Interest will be charged on unpaid principal until the full amount of Principal has been paid. I will pay interest at a yearly rate of eight (8) %.

The interest rate required by this Section 2 is the rate I will pay both before and after any default described in Section 6(B) of this Note.

3. PAYMENTS

(A) Time and Place of Payments

I will pay principal and interest by making a payment every month.

I will make my monthly payment on the 1st day of each month beginning on June 1 , 20 . I will make these payments every month until I have paid all of the principal and interest and any other charges described below that I may owe under this Note. Each monthly payment will be applied as of its scheduled due date and will be applied to interest before Principal. If, on May 1 , 20 , I still owe amounts under this Note, I will pay those amounts in full on that date, which is called the "Maturity Date."

I will make my monthly payments at ADDRESS OF AMERICAN EAGLE MORTGAGE COMPANY or at a different place if required by the Note Holder.

(B) Amount of Monthly Payments

My monthly payment will be in the amount of U.S. $ 588.00 .

4. BORROWER'S RIGHT TO PREPAY

I have the right to make payments of Principal at any time before they are due. A payment of Principal only is known as a "Prepayment." When I make a Prepayment, I will tell the Note Holder in writing that I am doing so. I may not designate a payment as a Prepayment if I have not made all the monthly payments due under the Note.

I may make a full Prepayment or partial Prepayments without paying a Prepayment charge. The Note Holder will use my Prepayments to reduce the amount of Principal that I owe under this Note. However, the Note Holder may apply my Prepayment to the accrued and unpaid interest on the Prepayment amount, before applying my Prepayment to reduce the Principal amount of the Note. If I make a partial Prepayment, there will be no changes in the due date or in the amount of my monthly payment unless the Note Holder agrees in writing to those changes.

5. LOAN CHARGES

If a law, which applies to this loan and which sets maximum loan charges, is finally interpreted so that the interest or other loan charges collected or to be collected in connection with this loan exceed the permitted limits, then: (a) any such loan charge shall be reduced by the amount necessary to reduce the charge to the permitted limit; and (b) any sums already collected from me which exceeded permitted limits will be refunded to me. The Note Holder may choose to make this refund by reducing the Principal I owe under this Note or by making a direct payment to me. If a refund reduces Principal, the reduction will be treated as a partial Prepayment.

MULTISTATE FIXED RATE NOTE—Single Family—Fannie Mae/Freddie Mac UNIFORM INSTRUMENT   Form 3200   1/01 *(page 1 of 3 pages)*

(continued)

EXHIBIT 10–21
Note (continued)

6. BORROWER'S FAILURE TO PAY AS REQUIRED

(A) Late Charge for Overdue Payments

If the Note Holder has not received the full amount of any monthly payment by the end of __15__ calendar days after the date it is due, I will pay a late charge to the Note Holder. The amount of the charge will be __4__ % of my overdue payment of principal and interest. I will pay this late charge promptly but only once on each late payment.

(B) Default

If I do not pay the full amount of each monthly payment on the date it is due, I will be in default.

(C) Notice of Default

If I am in default, the Note Holder may send me a written notice telling me that if I do not pay the overdue amount by a certain date, the Note Holder may require me to pay immediately the full amount of Principal which has not been paid and all the interest that I owe on that amount. That date must be at least 30 days after the date on which the notice is mailed to me or delivered by other means.

(D) No Waiver By Note Holder

Even if, at a time when I am in default, the Note Holder does not require me to pay immediately in full as described above, the Note Holder will still have the right to do so if I am in default at a later time.

(E) Payment of Note Holder's Costs and Expenses

If the Note Holder has required me to pay immediately in full as described above, the Note Holder will have the right to be paid back by me for all of its costs and expenses in enforcing this Note to the extent not prohibited by applicable law. Those expenses include, for example, reasonable attorneys' fees.

7. GIVING OF NOTICES

Unless applicable law requires a different method, any notice that must be given to me under this Note will be given by delivering it or by mailing it by first class mail to me at the Property Address above or at a different address if I give the Note Holder a notice of my different address.

Any notice that must be given to the Note Holder under this Note will be given by delivering it or by mailing it by first class mail to the Note Holder at the address stated in Section 3(A) above or at a different address if I am given a notice of that different address.

8. OBLIGATIONS OF PERSONS UNDER THIS NOTE

If more than one person signs this Note, each person is fully and personally obligated to keep all of the promises made in this Note, including the promise to pay the full amount owed. Any person who is a guarantor, surety or endorser of this Note is also obligated to do these things. Any person who takes over these obligations, including the obligations of a guarantor, surety or endorser of this Note, is also obligated to keep all of the promises made in this Note. The Note Holder may enforce its rights under this Note against each person individually or against all of us together. This means that any one of us may be required to pay all of the amounts owed under this Note.

9. WAIVERS

I and any other person who has obligations under this Note waive the rights of Presentment and Notice of Dishonor. "Presentment" means the right to require the Note Holder to demand payment of amounts due. "Notice of Dishonor" means the right to require the Note Holder to give notice to other persons that amounts due have not been paid.

10. UNIFORM SECURED NOTE

This Note is a uniform instrument with limited variations in some jurisdictions. In addition to the protections given to the Note Holder under this Note, a Mortgage, Deed of Trust, or Security Deed (the "Security Instrument"), dated the same date as this Note, protects the Note Holder from possible losses which might result if I do not keep the promises which I make in this Note. That Security Instrument describes how and under what conditions I may be required to make immediate payment in full of all amounts I owe under this Note. Some of those conditions are described as follows:

> If all or any part of the Property or any Interest in the Property is sold or transferred (or if Borrower is not a natural person and a beneficial interest in Borrower is sold or transferred) without Lender's prior written consent, Lender may require immediate payment in full of all sums secured by this Security Instrument. However, this option shall not be exercised by Lender if such exercise is prohibited by Applicable Law.

MULTISTATE FIXED RATE NOTE—Single Family—Fannie Mae/Freddie Mac UNIFORM INSTRUMENT   Form 3200   1/01 *(page 2 of 3 pages)*

(continued)

EXHIBIT 10–21
Note (continued)

If Lender exercises this option, Lender shall give Borrower notice of acceleration.   The notice shall provide a period of not less than 30 days from the date the notice is given in accordance with Section 15 within which Borrower must pay all sums secured by this Security Instrument. If Borrower fails to pay these sums prior to the expiration of this period, Lender may invoke any remedies permitted by this Security Instrument without further notice or demand on Borrower.

WITNESS THE HAND(S) AND SEAL(S) OF THE UNDERSIGNED

_____ (Seal)
HELEN DAVIS   - Borrower

_____ (Seal)
                                                                            - Borrower

_____ (Seal)
                                                                            - Borrower

[Sign Original Only]

MULTISTATE FIXED RATE NOTE—Single Family—Fannie Mae/Freddie Mac UNIFORM INSTRUMENT   Form 3200   1/01 *(page 3 of 3 pages)*

EXHIBIT 10-22
Security Deed

After Recording Return To:

_____

_____

_____

_____

_____ **[Space Above This Line For Recording Data]** _____

SECURITY DEED

DEFINITIONS

Words used in multiple sections of this document are defined below and other words are defined in Sections 3, 11, 13, 18, 20 and 21. Certain rules regarding the usage of words used in this document are also provided in Section 16.

(A) **"Security Instrument"** means this document, which is dated __April 25,_____ , __20__ , together with all Riders to this document.

(B) **"Borrower"** is __HELEN DAVIS_____ . Borrower is the grantor under this Security Instrument.

(C) **"Lender"** is __AMERICAN EAGLE MORTGAGE COMPANY_____ . Lender is a _____ organized and existing under the laws of _____ _____ . Lender's address is __10 Piedmont Center, Atlanta,_____ __Georgia 30317_____ . Lender is the grantee under this Security Instrument.

(D) **"Note"** means the promissory note signed by Borrower and dated __April 25, 20___ , _____ . The Note states that Borrower owes Lender __Eighty Thousand and No/100__ Dollars (U.S. $__80,000.00_____) plus interest. Borrower has promised to pay this debt in regular Periodic Payments and to pay the debt in full not later than __May 1, 20___ .

(E) **"Property"** means the property that is described below under the heading "Transfer of Rights in the Property."

(F) **"Loan"** means the debt evidenced by the Note, plus interest, any prepayment charges and late charges due under the Note, and all sums due under this Security Instrument, plus interest.

(G) **"Riders"** means all Riders to this Security Instrument that are executed by Borrower. The following Riders are to be executed by Borrower [check box as applicable]:

☐ Adjustable Rate Rider ☐ Condominium Rider ☐ Second Home Rider
☐ Balloon Rider ☐ Planned Unit Development Rider ☐ Other(s) [specify] _____
☐ 1-4 Family Rider ☐ Biweekly Payment Rider

GEORGIA--Single Family--Fannie Mae/Freddie Mac **UNIFORM INSTRUMENT** Form 3011 1/01 *(page 1 of 16 pages)*

(continued)

EXHIBIT 10–22
Security Deed (continued)

(H) **"Applicable Law"** means all controlling applicable federal, state and local statutes, regulations, ordinances and administrative rules and orders (that have the effect of law) as well as all applicable final, non-appealable judicial opinions.

(I) **"Community Association Dues, Fees, and Assessments"** means all dues, fees, assessments and other charges that are imposed on Borrower or the Property by a condominium association, homeowners association or similar organization.

(J) **"Electronic Funds Transfer"** means any transfer of funds, other than a transaction originated by check, draft, or similar paper instrument, which is initiated through an electronic terminal, telephonic instrument, computer, or magnetic tape so as to order, instruct, or authorize a financial institution to debit or credit an account. Such term includes, but is not limited to, point-of-sale transfers, automated teller machine transactions, transfers initiated by telephone, wire transfers, and automated clearinghouse transfers.

(K) **"Escrow Items"** means those items that are described in Section 3.

(L) **"Miscellaneous Proceeds"** means any compensation, settlement, award of damages, or proceeds paid by any third party (other than insurance proceeds paid under the coverages described in Section 5) for: (i) damage to, or destruction of, the Property; (ii) condemnation or other taking of all or any part of the Property; (iii) conveyance in lieu of condemnation; or (iv) misrepresentations of, or omissions as to, the value and/or condition of the Property.

(M) **"Mortgage Insurance"** means insurance protecting Lender against the nonpayment of, or default on, the Loan.

(N) **"Periodic Payment"** means the regularly scheduled amount due for (i) principal and interest under the Note, plus (ii) any amounts under Section 3 of this Security Instrument.

(O) **"RESPA"** means the Real Estate Settlement Procedures Act (12 U.S.C. §2601 et seq.) and its implementing regulation, Regulation X (24 C.F.R. Part 3500), as they might be amended from time to time, or any additional or successor legislation or regulation that governs the same subject matter. As used in this Security Instrument, "RESPA" refers to all requirements and restrictions that are imposed in regard to a "federally related mortgage loan" even if the Loan does not qualify as a "federally related mortgage loan" under RESPA.

(P) **"Successor in Interest of Borrower"** means any party that has taken title to the Property, whether or not that party has assumed Borrower's obligations under the Note and/or this Security Instrument.

TRANSFER OF RIGHTS IN THE PROPERTY

This Security Instrument secures to Lender: (i) the repayment of the Loan, and all renewals, extensions and modifications of the Note; and (ii) the performance of Borrower's covenants and agreements under this Security Instrument and the Note. For this purpose, Borrower does hereby grant and convey to Lender and Lender's successors and assigns, with power of sale, the following

GEORGIA--Single Family--Fannie Mae/Freddie Mac UNIFORM INSTRUMENT   Form 3011   1/01 *(page 2 of 16 pages)*

(continued)

EXHIBIT 10-22
Security Deed (continued)

described property located in the _____ of
[Type of Recording Jurisdiction]

_____ :
[Name of Recording Jurisdiction]

All that tract or parcel of land lying and being in Land Lot 359 of the 18th District of
Fulton County, Georgia, being Lot 12 of Bassett Hall Subdivision, as per plat recorded in
Plat Book 68, Page 79, Fulton County, Georgia Records, being improved property with a
house located thereon known as 5167 Tilly Mill Road, Atlanta, Georgia 30302.

which currently has the address of ___5167 Tilly Mill Road,_____
                                                        [Street]

__Atlanta_____, Georgia __30302_____ ("Property Address"):
          [City]   [Zip Code]

TO HAVE AND TO HOLD this property unto Lender and Lender's successors and assigns,
forever, together with all the improvements now or hereafter erected on the property, and all
easements, appurtenances, and fixtures now or hereafter a part of the property. All replacements and
additions shall also be covered by this Security Instrument. All of the foregoing is referred to in this
Security Instrument as the "Property."

BORROWER COVENANTS that Borrower is lawfully seised of the estate hereby conveyed
and has the right to grant and convey the Property and that the Property is unencumbered, except
for encumbrances of record. Borrower warrants and will defend generally the title to the Property
against all claims and demands, subject to any encumbrances of record.

THIS SECURITY INSTRUMENT combines uniform covenants for national use and non-
uniform covenants with limited variations by jurisdiction to constitute a uniform security instrument
covering real property.

UNIFORM COVENANTS. Borrower and Lender covenant and agree as follows:
1. **Payment of Principal, Interest, Escrow Items, Prepayment Charges, and Late
Charges.** Borrower shall pay when due the principal of, and interest on, the debt evidenced by the
Note and any prepayment charges and late charges due under the Note. Borrower shall also pay
funds for Escrow Items pursuant to Section 3. Payments due under the Note and this Security
Instrument shall be made in U.S. currency. However, if any check or other instrument received by
Lender as payment under the Note or this Security Instrument is returned to Lender unpaid, Lender
may require that any or all subsequent payments due under the Note and this Security Instrument
be made in one or more of the following forms, as selected by Lender: (a) cash; (b) money order;

GEORGIA--Single Family--Fannie Mae/Freddie Mac UNIFORM INSTRUMENT   Form 3011   1/01 *(page 3 of 16 pages)*

(continued)

EXHIBIT 10-22
Security Deed (continued)

(c) certified check, bank check, treasurer's check or cashier's check, provided any such check is drawn upon an institution whose deposits are insured by a federal agency, instrumentality, or entity; or (d) Electronic Funds Transfer.

Payments are deemed received by Lender when received at the location designated in the Note or at such other location as may be designated by Lender in accordance with the notice provisions in Section 15. Lender may return any payment or partial payment if the payment or partial payments are insufficient to bring the Loan current. Lender may accept any payment or partial payment insufficient to bring the Loan current, without waiver of any rights hereunder or prejudice to its rights to refuse such payment or partial payments in the future, but Lender is not obligated to apply such payments at the time such payments are accepted. If each Periodic Payment is applied as of its scheduled due date, then Lender need not pay interest on unapplied funds. Lender may hold such unapplied funds until Borrower makes payment to bring the Loan current. If Borrower does not do so within a reasonable period of time, Lender shall either apply such funds or return them to Borrower. If not applied earlier, such funds will be applied to the outstanding principal balance under the Note immediately prior to foreclosure. No offset or claim which Borrower might have now or in the future against Lender shall relieve Borrower from making payments due under the Note and this Security Instrument or performing the covenants and agreements secured by this Security Instrument.

2. Application of Payments or Proceeds. Except as otherwise described in this Section 2, all payments accepted and applied by Lender shall be applied in the following order of priority: (a) interest due under the Note; (b) principal due under the Note; (c) amounts due under Section 3. Such payments shall be applied to each Periodic Payment in the order in which it became due. Any remaining amounts shall be applied first to late charges, second to any other amounts due under this Security Instrument, and then to reduce the principal balance of the Note.

If Lender receives a payment from Borrower for a delinquent Periodic Payment which includes a sufficient amount to pay any late charge due, the payment may be applied to the delinquent payment and the late charge. If more than one Periodic Payment is outstanding, Lender may apply any payment received from Borrower to the repayment of the Periodic Payments if, and to the extent that, each payment can be paid in full. To the extent that any excess exists after the payment is applied to the full payment of one or more Periodic Payments, such excess may be applied to any late charges due. Voluntary prepayments shall be applied first to any prepayment charges and then as described in the Note.

Any application of payments, insurance proceeds, or Miscellaneous Proceeds to principal due under the Note shall not extend or postpone the due date, or change the amount, of the Periodic Payments.

3. Funds for Escrow Items. Borrower shall pay to Lender on the day Periodic Payments are due under the Note, until the Note is paid in full, a sum (the "Funds") to provide for payment of amounts due for: (a) taxes and assessments and other items which can attain priority over this Security Instrument as a lien or encumbrance on the Property; (b) leasehold payments or ground rents on the Property, if any; (c) premiums for any and all insurance required by Lender under Section 5; and (d) Mortgage Insurance premiums, if any, or any sums payable by Borrower to Lender in lieu of the payment of Mortgage Insurance premiums in accordance with the provisions of Section 10. These items are called "Escrow Items." At origination or at any time during the term of the Loan, Lender may require that Community Association Dues, Fees, and Assessments, if any,

GEORGIA--Single Family--**Fannie Mae/Freddie Mac UNIFORM INSTRUMENT**   Form 3011   1/01 *(page 4 of 16 pages)*

(continued)

EXHIBIT 10—22
Security Deed (continued)

be escrowed by Borrower, and such dues, fees and assessments shall be an Escrow Item. Borrower shall promptly furnish to Lender all notices of amounts to be paid under this Section. Borrower shall pay Lender the Funds for Escrow Items unless Lender waives Borrower's obligation to pay the Funds for any or all Escrow Items. Lender may waive Borrower's obligation to pay to Lender Funds for any or all Escrow Items at any time. Any such waiver may only be in writing. In the event of such waiver, Borrower shall pay directly, when and where payable, the amounts due for any Escrow Items for which payment of Funds has been waived by Lender and, if Lender requires, shall furnish to Lender receipts evidencing such payment within such time period as Lender may require. Borrower's obligation to make such payments and to provide receipts shall for all purposes be deemed to be a covenant and agreement contained in this Security Instrument, as the phrase "covenant and agreement" is used in Section 9. If Borrower is obligated to pay Escrow Items directly, pursuant to a waiver, and Borrower fails to pay the amount due for an Escrow Item, Lender may exercise its rights under Section 9 and pay such amount and Borrower shall then be obligated under Section 9 to repay to Lender any such amount. Lender may revoke the waiver as to any or all Escrow Items at any time by a notice given in accordance with Section 15 and, upon such revocation, Borrower shall pay to Lender all Funds, and in such amounts, that are then required under this Section 3.

Lender may, at any time, collect and hold Funds in an amount (a) sufficient to permit Lender to apply the Funds at the time specified under RESPA, and (b) not to exceed the maximum amount a lender can require under RESPA. Lender shall estimate the amount of Funds due on the basis of current data and reasonable estimates of expenditures of future Escrow Items or otherwise in accordance with Applicable Law.

The Funds shall be held in an institution whose deposits are insured by a federal agency, instrumentality, or entity (including Lender, if Lender is an institution whose deposits are so insured) or in any Federal Home Loan Bank. Lender shall apply the Funds to pay the Escrow Items no later than the time specified under RESPA. Lender shall not charge Borrower for holding and applying the Funds, annually analyzing the escrow account, or verifying the Escrow Items, unless Lender pays Borrower interest on the Funds and Applicable Law permits Lender to make such a charge. Unless an agreement is made in writing or Applicable Law requires interest to be paid on the Funds, Lender shall not be required to pay Borrower any interest or earnings on the Funds. Borrower and Lender can agree in writing, however, that interest shall be paid on the Funds. Lender shall give to Borrower, without charge, an annual accounting of the Funds as required by RESPA.

If there is a surplus of Funds held in escrow, as defined under RESPA, Lender shall account to Borrower for the excess funds in accordance with RESPA. If there is a shortage of Funds held in escrow, as defined under RESPA, Lender shall notify Borrower as required by RESPA, and Borrower shall pay to Lender the amount necessary to make up the shortage in accordance with RESPA, but in no more than 12 monthly payments. If there is a deficiency of Funds held in escrow, as defined under RESPA, Lender shall notify Borrower as required by RESPA, and Borrower shall pay to Lender the amount necessary to make up the deficiency in accordance with RESPA, but in no more than 12 monthly payments.

Upon payment in full of all sums secured by this Security Instrument, Lender shall promptly refund to Borrower any Funds held by Lender.

GEORGIA--Single Family--Fannie Mae/Freddie Mac UNIFORM INSTRUMENT   Form 3011   1/01 *(page 5 of 16 pages)*

(continued)

EXHIBIT 10-22
Security Deed (continued)

4. Charges; Liens. Borrower shall pay all taxes, assessments, charges, fines, and impositions attributable to the Property which can attain priority over this Security Instrument, leasehold payments or ground rents on the Property, if any, and Community Association Dues, Fees, and Assessments, if any. To the extent that these items are Escrow Items, Borrower shall pay them in the manner provided in Section 3.

Borrower shall promptly discharge any lien which has priority over this Security Instrument unless Borrower: (a) agrees in writing to the payment of the obligation secured by the lien in a manner acceptable to Lender, but only so long as Borrower is performing such agreement; (b) contests the lien in good faith by, or defends against enforcement of the lien in, legal proceedings which in Lender's opinion operate to prevent the enforcement of the lien while those proceedings are pending, but only until such proceedings are concluded; or (c) secures from the holder of the lien an agreement satisfactory to Lender subordinating the lien to this Security Instrument. If Lender determines that any part of the Property is subject to a lien which can attain priority over this Security Instrument, Lender may give Borrower a notice identifying the lien. Within 10 days of the date on which that notice is given, Borrower shall satisfy the lien or take one or more of the actions set forth above in this Section 4.

Lender may require Borrower to pay a one-time charge for a real estate tax verification and/or reporting service used by Lender in connection with this Loan.

5. Property Insurance. Borrower shall keep the improvements now existing or hereafter erected on the Property insured against loss by fire, hazards included within the term "extended coverage," and any other hazards including, but not limited to, earthquakes and floods, for which Lender requires insurance. This insurance shall be maintained in the amounts (including deductible levels) and for the periods that Lender requires. What Lender requires pursuant to the preceding sentences can change during the term of the Loan. The insurance carrier providing the insurance shall be chosen by Borrower subject to Lender's right to disapprove Borrower's choice, which right shall not be exercised unreasonably. Lender may require Borrower to pay, in connection with this Loan, either: (a) a one-time charge for flood zone determination, certification and tracking services; or (b) a one-time charge for flood zone determination and certification services and subsequent charges each time remappings or similar changes occur which reasonably might affect such determination or certification. Borrower shall also be responsible for the payment of any fees imposed by the Federal Emergency Management Agency in connection with the review of any flood zone determination resulting from an objection by Borrower.

If Borrower fails to maintain any of the coverages described above, Lender may obtain insurance coverage, at Lender's option and Borrower's expense. Lender is under no obligation to purchase any particular type or amount of coverage. Therefore, such coverage shall cover Lender, but might or might not protect Borrower, Borrower's equity in the Property, or the contents of the Property, against any risk, hazard or liability and might provide greater or lesser coverage than was previously in effect. Borrower acknowledges that the cost of the insurance coverage so obtained might significantly exceed the cost of insurance that Borrower could have obtained. Any amounts disbursed by Lender under this Section 5 shall become additional debt of Borrower secured by this Security Instrument. These amounts shall bear interest at the Note rate from the date of disbursement and shall be payable, with such interest, upon notice from Lender to Borrower requesting payment.

GEORGIA--Single Family--**Fannie Mae/Freddie Mac UNIFORM INSTRUMENT**   Form 3011   1/01 *(page 6 of 16 pages)*

(continued)

EXHIBIT 10-22
Security Deed (continued)

All insurance policies required by Lender and renewals of such policies shall be subject to Lender's right to disapprove such policies, shall include a standard mortgage clause, and shall name Lender as mortgagee and/or as an additional loss payee. Lender shall have the right to hold the policies and renewal certificates. If Lender requires, Borrower shall promptly give to Lender all receipts of paid premiums and renewal notices. If Borrower obtains any form of insurance coverage, not otherwise required by Lender, for damage to, or destruction of, the Property, such policy shall include a standard mortgage clause and shall name Lender as mortgagee and/or as an additional loss payee.

In the event of loss, Borrower shall give prompt notice to the insurance carrier and Lender. Lender may make proof of loss if not made promptly by Borrower. Unless Lender and Borrower otherwise agree in writing, any insurance proceeds, whether or not the underlying insurance was required by Lender, shall be applied to restoration or repair of the Property, if the restoration or repair is economically feasible and Lender's security is not lessened. During such repair and restoration period, Lender shall have the right to hold such insurance proceeds until Lender has had an opportunity to inspect such Property to ensure the work has been completed to Lender's satisfaction, provided that such inspection shall be undertaken promptly. Lender may disburse proceeds for the repairs and restoration in a single payment or in a series of progress payments as the work is completed. Unless an agreement is made in writing or Applicable Law requires interest to be paid on such insurance proceeds, Lender shall not be required to pay Borrower any interest or earnings on such proceeds. Fees for public adjusters, or other third parties, retained by Borrower shall not be paid out of the insurance proceeds and shall be the sole obligation of Borrower. If the restoration or repair is not economically feasible or Lender's security would be lessened, the insurance proceeds shall be applied to the sums secured by this Security Instrument, whether or not then due, with the excess, if any, paid to Borrower. Such insurance proceeds shall be applied in the order provided for in Section 2.

If Borrower abandons the Property, Lender may file, negotiate and settle any available insurance claim and related matters. If Borrower does not respond within 30 days to a notice from Lender that the insurance carrier has offered to settle a claim, then Lender may negotiate and settle the claim. The 30-day period will begin when the notice is given. In either event, or if Lender acquires the Property under Section 22 or otherwise, Borrower hereby assigns to Lender (a) Borrower's rights to any insurance proceeds in an amount not to exceed the amounts unpaid under the Note or this Security Instrument, and (b) any other of Borrower's rights (other than the right to any refund of unearned premiums paid by Borrower) under all insurance policies covering the Property, insofar as such rights are applicable to the coverage of the Property. Lender may use the insurance proceeds either to repair or restore the Property or to pay amounts unpaid under the Note or this Security Instrument, whether or not then due.

6. Occupancy. Borrower shall occupy, establish, and use the Property as Borrower's principal residence within 60 days after the execution of this Security Instrument and shall continue to occupy the Property as Borrower's principal residence for at least one year after the date of occupancy, unless Lender otherwise agrees in writing, which consent shall not be unreasonably withheld, or unless extenuating circumstances exist which are beyond Borrower's control.

7. Preservation, Maintenance and Protection of the Property; Inspections. Borrower shall not destroy, damage or impair the Property, allow the Property to deteriorate or commit waste

GEORGIA--Single Family--Fannie Mae/Freddie Mac UNIFORM INSTRUMENT   Form 3011   1/01   *(page 7 of 16 pages)*

(continued)

EXHIBIT 10-22
Security Deed (continued)

on the Property. Whether or not Borrower is residing in the Property, Borrower shall maintain the Property in order to prevent the Property from deteriorating or decreasing in value due to its condition. Unless it is determined pursuant to Section 5 that repair or restoration is not economically feasible, Borrower shall promptly repair the Property if damaged to avoid further deterioration or damage. If insurance or condemnation proceeds are paid in connection with damage to, or the taking of, the Property, Borrower shall be responsible for repairing or restoring the Property only if Lender has released proceeds for such purposes. Lender may disburse proceeds for the repairs and restoration in a single payment or in a series of progress payments as the work is completed. If the insurance or condemnation proceeds are not sufficient to repair or restore the Property, Borrower is not relieved of Borrower's obligation for the completion of such repair or restoration.

Lender or its agent may make reasonable entries upon and inspections of the Property. If it has reasonable cause, Lender may inspect the interior of the improvements on the Property. Lender shall give Borrower notice at the time of or prior to such an interior inspection specifying such reasonable cause.

8. Borrower's Loan Application. Borrower shall be in default if, during the Loan application process, Borrower or any persons or entities acting at the direction of Borrower or with Borrower's knowledge or consent gave materially false, misleading, or inaccurate information or statements to Lender (or failed to provide Lender with material information) in connection with the Loan. Material representations include, but are not limited to, representations concerning Borrower's occupancy of the Property as Borrower's principal residence.

9. Protection of Lender's Interest in the Property and Rights Under this Security Instrument. If (a) Borrower fails to perform the covenants and agreements contained in this Security Instrument, (b) there is a legal proceeding that might significantly affect Lender's interest in the Property and/or rights under this Security Instrument (such as a proceeding in bankruptcy, probate, for condemnation or forfeiture, for enforcement of a lien which may attain priority over this Security Instrument or to enforce laws or regulations), or (c) Borrower has abandoned the Property, then Lender may do and pay for whatever is reasonable or appropriate to protect Lender's interest in the Property and rights under this Security Instrument, including protecting and/or assessing the value of the Property, and securing and/or repairing the Property (as set forth below). Lender's actions can include, but are not limited to: (a) paying any sums secured by a lien which has priority over this Security Instrument; (b) appearing in court; and (c) paying reasonable attorneys' fees to protect its interest in the Property and/or rights under this Security Instrument, including its secured position in a bankruptcy proceeding. Securing the Property includes, but is not limited to, making repairs, replacing doors and windows, draining water from pipes, and eliminating building or other code violations or dangerous conditions. Although Lender may take action under this Section 9, Lender does not have to do so and is not under any duty or obligation to do so. It is agreed that Lender incurs no liability for not taking any or all actions authorized under this Section 9.

Any amounts disbursed by Lender under this Section 9 shall become additional debt of Borrower secured by this Security Instrument. These amounts shall bear interest at the Note rate from the date of disbursement and shall be payable, with such interest, upon notice from Lender to Borrower requesting payment.

GEORGIA--Single Family--Fannie Mae/Freddie Mac **UNIFORM INSTRUMENT**   Form 3011   1/01 *(page 8 of 16 pages)*

(continued)

EXHIBIT 10-22
Security Deed (continued)

If this Security Instrument is on a leasehold, Borrower shall comply with all the provisions of the lease. If Borrower acquires fee title to the Property, the leasehold and the fee title shall not merge unless Lender agrees to the merger in writing.

10. Mortgage Insurance. If Lender required Mortgage Insurance as a condition of making the Loan, Borrower shall pay the premiums required to maintain the Mortgage Insurance in effect. If, for any reason, the Mortgage Insurance coverage required by Lender ceases to be available from the mortgage insurer that previously provided such insurance and Borrower was required to make separately designated payments toward the premiums for Mortgage Insurance, Borrower shall pay the premiums required to obtain coverage substantially equivalent to the Mortgage Insurance previously in effect, at a cost substantially equivalent to the cost to Borrower of the Mortgage Insurance previously in effect, from an alternate mortgage insurer selected by Lender. If substantially equivalent Mortgage Insurance coverage is not available, Borrower shall continue to pay to Lender the amount of the separately designated payments that were due when the insurance coverage ceased to be in effect. Lender will accept, use and retain these payments as a non-refundable loss reserve in lieu of Mortgage Insurance. Such loss reserve shall be non-refundable, notwithstanding the fact that the Loan is ultimately paid in full, and Lender shall not be required to pay Borrower any interest or earnings on such loss reserve. Lender can no longer require loss reserve payments if Mortgage Insurance coverage (in the amount and for the period that Lender requires) provided by an insurer selected by Lender again becomes available, is obtained, and Lender requires separately designated payments toward the premiums for Mortgage Insurance. If Lender required Mortgage Insurance as a condition of making the Loan and Borrower was required to make separately designated payments toward the premiums for Mortgage Insurance, Borrower shall pay the premiums required to maintain Mortgage Insurance in effect, or to provide a non-refundable loss reserve, until Lender's requirement for Mortgage Insurance ends in accordance with any written agreement between Borrower and Lender providing for such termination or until termination is required by Applicable Law. Nothing in this Section 10 affects Borrower's obligation to pay interest at the rate provided in the Note.

Mortgage Insurance reimburses Lender (or any entity that purchases the Note) for certain losses it may incur if Borrower does not repay the Loan as agreed. Borrower is not a party to the Mortgage Insurance.

Mortgage insurers evaluate their total risk on all such insurance in force from time to time, and may enter into agreements with other parties that share or modify their risk, or reduce losses. These agreements are on terms and conditions that are satisfactory to the mortgage insurer and the other party (or parties) to these agreements. These agreements may require the mortgage insurer to make payments using any source of funds that the mortgage insurer may have available (which may include funds obtained from Mortgage Insurance premiums).

As a result of these agreements, Lender, any purchaser of the Note, another insurer, any reinsurer, any other entity, or any affiliate of any of the foregoing, may receive (directly or indirectly) amounts that derive from (or might be characterized as) a portion of Borrower's payments for Mortgage Insurance, in exchange for sharing or modifying the mortgage insurer's risk, or reducing losses. If such agreement provides that an affiliate of Lender takes a share of the insurer's risk in exchange for a share of the premiums paid to the insurer, the arrangement is often termed "captive reinsurance." Further:

EXHIBIT 10-22
Security Deed (continued)

(a) Any such agreements will not affect the amounts that Borrower has agreed to pay for Mortgage Insurance, or any other terms of the Loan. Such agreements will not increase the amount Borrower will owe for Mortgage Insurance, and they will not entitle Borrower to any refund.

(b) Any such agreements will not affect the rights Borrower has – if any – with respect to the Mortgage Insurance under the Homeowners Protection Act of 1998 or any other law. These rights may include the right to receive certain disclosures, to request and obtain cancellation of the Mortgage Insurance, to have the Mortgage Insurance terminated automatically, and/or to receive a refund of any Mortgage Insurance premiums that were unearned at the time of such cancellation or termination.

11. **Assignment of Miscellaneous Proceeds; Forfeiture.** All Miscellaneous Proceeds are hereby assigned to and shall be paid to Lender.

If the Property is damaged, such Miscellaneous Proceeds shall be applied to restoration or repair of the Property, if the restoration or repair is economically feasible and Lender's security is not lessened. During such repair and restoration period, Lender shall have the right to hold such Miscellaneous Proceeds until Lender has had an opportunity to inspect such Property to ensure the work has been completed to Lender's satisfaction, provided that such inspection shall be undertaken promptly. Lender may pay for the repairs and restoration in a single disbursement or in a series of progress payments as the work is completed. Unless an agreement is made in writing or Applicable Law requires interest to be paid on such Miscellaneous Proceeds, Lender shall not be required to pay Borrower any interest or earnings on such Miscellaneous Proceeds. If the restoration or repair is not economically feasible or Lender's security would be lessened, the Miscellaneous Proceeds shall be applied to the sums secured by this Security Instrument, whether or not then due, with the excess, if any, paid to Borrower. Such Miscellaneous Proceeds shall be applied in the order provided for in Section 2.

In the event of a total taking, destruction, or loss in value of the Property, the Miscellaneous Proceeds shall be applied to the sums secured by this Security Instrument, whether or not then due, with the excess, if any, paid to Borrower.

In the event of a partial taking, destruction, or loss in value of the Property in which the fair market value of the Property immediately before the partial taking, destruction, or loss in value is equal to or greater than the amount of the sums secured by this Security Instrument immediately before the partial taking, destruction, or loss in value, unless Borrower and Lender otherwise agree in writing, the sums secured by this Security Instrument shall be reduced by the amount of the Miscellaneous Proceeds multiplied by the following fraction: (a) the total amount of the sums secured immediately before the partial taking, destruction, or loss in value divided by (b) the fair market value of the Property immediately before the partial taking, destruction, or loss in value. Any balance shall be paid to Borrower.

In the event of a partial taking, destruction, or loss in value of the Property in which the fair market value of the Property immediately before the partial taking, destruction, or loss in value is less than the amount of the sums secured immediately before the partial taking, destruction, or loss in value, unless Borrower and Lender otherwise agree in writing, the Miscellaneous Proceeds shall be applied to the sums secured by this Security Instrument whether or not the sums are then due.

If the Property is abandoned by Borrower, or if, after notice by Lender to Borrower that the Opposing Party (as defined in the next sentence) offers to make an award to settle a claim for

GEORGIA--Single Family--Fannie Mae/Freddie Mac UNIFORM INSTRUMENT   Form 3011   1/01 *(page 10 of 16 pages)*

(continued)

EXHIBIT 10-22
Security Deed (continued)

damages, Borrower fails to respond to Lender within 30 days after the date the notice is given, Lender is authorized to collect and apply the Miscellaneous Proceeds either to restoration or repair of the Property or to the sums secured by this Security Instrument, whether or not then due. "Opposing Party" means the third party that owes Borrower Miscellaneous Proceeds or the party against whom Borrower has a right of action in regard to Miscellaneous Proceeds.

Borrower shall be in default if any action or proceeding, whether civil or criminal, is begun that, in Lender's judgment, could result in forfeiture of the Property or other material impairment of Lender's interest in the Property or rights under this Security Instrument. Borrower can cure such a default and, if acceleration has occurred, reinstate as provided in Section 19, by causing the action or proceeding to be dismissed with a ruling that, in Lender's judgment, precludes forfeiture of the Property or other material impairment of Lender's interest in the Property or rights under this Security Instrument. The proceeds of any award or claim for damages that are attributable to the impairment of Lender's interest in the Property are hereby assigned and shall be paid to Lender.

All Miscellaneous Proceeds that are not applied to restoration or repair of the Property shall be applied in the order provided for in Section 2.

12. Borrower Not Released; Forbearance By Lender Not a Waiver. Extension of the time for payment or modification of amortization of the sums secured by this Security Instrument granted by Lender to Borrower or any Successor in Interest of Borrower shall not operate to release the liability of Borrower or any Successors in Interest of Borrower. Lender shall not be required to commence proceedings against any Successor in Interest of Borrower or to refuse to extend time for payment or otherwise modify amortization of the sums secured by this Security Instrument by reason of any demand made by the original Borrower or any Successors in Interest of Borrower. Any forbearance by Lender in exercising any right or remedy including, without limitation, Lender's acceptance of payments from third persons, entities or Successors in Interest of Borrower or in amounts less than the amount then due, shall not be a waiver of or preclude the exercise of any right or remedy.

13. Joint and Several Liability; Co-signers; Successors and Assigns Bound. Borrower covenants and agrees that Borrower's obligations and liability shall be joint and several. However, any Borrower who co-signs this Security Instrument but does not execute the Note (a "co-signer"): (a) is co-signing this Security Instrument only to mortgage, grant and convey the co-signer's interest in the Property under the terms of this Security Instrument; (b) is not personally obligated to pay the sums secured by this Security Instrument; and (c) agrees that Lender and any other Borrower can agree to extend, modify, forbear or make any accommodations with regard to the terms of this Security Instrument or the Note without the co-signer's consent.

Subject to the provisions of Section 18, any Successor in Interest of Borrower who assumes Borrower's obligations under this Security Instrument in writing, and is approved by Lender, shall obtain all of Borrower's rights and benefits under this Security Instrument. Borrower shall not be released from Borrower's obligations and liability under this Security Instrument unless Lender agrees to such release in writing. The covenants and agreements of this Security Instrument shall bind (except as provided in Section 20) and benefit the successors and assigns of Lender.

14. Loan Charges. Lender may charge Borrower fees for services performed in connection with Borrower's default, for the purpose of protecting Lender's interest in the Property and rights under this Security Instrument, including, but not limited to, attorneys' fees, property inspection and valuation fees. In regard to any other fees, the absence of express authority in this Security

GEORGIA--Single Family--Fannie Mae/Freddie Mac UNIFORM INSTRUMENT   Form 3011   1/01 *(page 11 of 16 pages)*

(continued)

EXHIBIT 10-22
Security Deed (continued)

Instrument to charge a specific fee to Borrower shall not be construed as a prohibition on the charging of such fee. Lender may not charge fees that are expressly prohibited by this Security Instrument or by Applicable Law.

If the Loan is subject to a law which sets maximum loan charges, and that law is finally interpreted so that the interest or other loan charges collected or to be collected in connection with the Loan exceed the permitted limits, then: (a) any such loan charge shall be reduced by the amount necessary to reduce the charge to the permitted limit; and (b) any sums already collected from Borrower which exceeded permitted limits will be refunded to Borrower. Lender may choose to make this refund by reducing the principal owed under the Note or by making a direct payment to Borrower. If a refund reduces principal, the reduction will be treated as a partial prepayment without any prepayment charge (whether or not a prepayment charge is provided for under the Note). Borrower's acceptance of any such refund made by direct payment to Borrower will constitute a waiver of any right of action Borrower might have arising out of such overcharge.

15. Notices. All notices given by Borrower or Lender in connection with this Security Instrument must be in writing. Any notice to Borrower in connection with this Security Instrument shall be deemed to have been given to Borrower when mailed by first class mail or when actually delivered to Borrower's notice address if sent by other means. Notice to any one Borrower shall constitute notice to all Borrowers unless Applicable Law expressly requires otherwise. The notice address shall be the Property Address unless Borrower has designated a substitute notice address by notice to Lender. Borrower shall promptly notify Lender of Borrower's change of address. If Lender specifies a procedure for reporting Borrower's change of address, then Borrower shall only report a change of address through that specified procedure. There may be only one designated notice address under this Security Instrument at any one time. Any notice to Lender shall be given by delivering it or by mailing it by first class mail to Lender's address stated herein unless Lender has designated another address by notice to Borrower. Any notice in connection with this Security Instrument shall not be deemed to have been given to Lender until actually received by Lender. If any notice required by this Security Instrument is also required under Applicable Law, the Applicable Law requirement will satisfy the corresponding requirement under this Security Instrument.

16. Governing Law; Severability; Rules of Construction. This Security Instrument shall be governed by federal law and the law of the jurisdiction in which the Property is located. All rights and obligations contained in this Security Instrument are subject to any requirements and limitations of Applicable Law. Applicable Law might explicitly or implicitly allow the parties to agree by contract or it might be silent, but such silence shall not be construed as a prohibition against agreement by contract. In the event that any provision or clause of this Security Instrument or the Note conflicts with Applicable Law, such conflict shall not affect other provisions of this Security Instrument or the Note which can be given effect without the conflicting provision.

As used in this Security Instrument: (a) words of the masculine gender shall mean and include corresponding neuter words or words of the feminine gender; (b) words in the singular shall mean and include the plural and vice versa; and (c) the word "may" gives sole discretion without any obligation to take any action.

17. Borrower's Copy. Borrower shall be given one copy of the Note and of this Security Instrument.

GEORGIA--Single Family--**Fannie Mae/Freddie Mac UNIFORM INSTRUMENT**   Form 3011   1/01 *(page 12 of 16 pages)*

(continued)

EXHIBIT 10-22
Security Deed (continued)

18. Transfer of the Property or a Beneficial Interest in Borrower. As used in this Section 18, "Interest in the Property" means any legal or beneficial interest in the Property, including, but not limited to, those beneficial interests transferred in a bond for deed, contract for deed, installment sales contract or escrow agreement, the intent of which is the transfer of title by Borrower at a future date to a purchaser.

If all or any part of the Property or any Interest in the Property is sold or transferred (or if Borrower is not a natural person and a beneficial interest in Borrower is sold or transferred) without Lender's prior written consent, Lender may require immediate payment in full of all sums secured by this Security Instrument. However, this option shall not be exercised by Lender if such exercise is prohibited by Applicable Law.

If Lender exercises this option, Lender shall give Borrower notice of acceleration. The notice shall provide a period of not less than 30 days from the date the notice is given in accordance with Section 15 within which Borrower must pay all sums secured by this Security Instrument. If Borrower fails to pay these sums prior to the expiration of this period, Lender may invoke any remedies permitted by this Security Instrument without further notice or demand on Borrower.

19. Borrower's Right to Reinstate After Acceleration. If Borrower meets certain conditions, Borrower shall have the right to have enforcement of this Security Instrument discontinued at any time prior to the earliest of: (a) five days before sale of the Property pursuant to any power of sale contained in this Security Instrument; (b) such other period as Applicable Law might specify for the termination of Borrower's right to reinstate; or (c) entry of a judgment enforcing this Security Instrument. Those conditions are that Borrower: (a) pays Lender all sums which then would be due under this Security Instrument and the Note as if no acceleration had occurred; (b) cures any default of any other covenants or agreements; (c) pays all expenses incurred in enforcing this Security Instrument, including, but not limited to, reasonable attorneys' fees, property inspection and valuation fees, and other fees incurred for the purpose of protecting Lender's interest in the Property and rights under this Security Instrument; and (d) takes such action as Lender may reasonably require to assure that Lender's interest in the Property and rights under this Security Instrument, and Borrower's obligation to pay the sums secured by this Security Instrument, shall continue unchanged. Lender may require that Borrower pay such reinstatement sums and expenses in one or more of the following forms, as selected by Lender: (a) cash; (b) money order; (c) certified check, bank check, treasurer's check or cashier's check, provided any such check is drawn upon an institution whose deposits are insured by a federal agency, instrumentality or entity; or (d) Electronic Funds Transfer. Upon reinstatement by Borrower, this Security Instrument and obligations secured hereby shall remain fully effective as if no acceleration had occurred. However, this right to reinstate shall not apply in the case of acceleration under Section 18.

20. Sale of Note; Change of Loan Servicer; Notice of Grievance. The Note or a partial interest in the Note (together with this Security Instrument) can be sold one or more times without prior notice to Borrower. A sale might result in a change in the entity (known as the "Loan Servicer") that collects Periodic Payments due under the Note and this Security Instrument and performs other mortgage loan servicing obligations under the Note, this Security Instrument, and Applicable Law. There also might be one or more changes of the Loan Servicer unrelated to a sale of the Note. If there is a change of the Loan Servicer, Borrower will be given written notice of the change which will state the name and address of the new Loan Servicer, the address to which payments should be made and any other information RESPA requires in connection with a notice

GEORGIA--Single Family--Fannie Mae/Freddie Mac UNIFORM INSTRUMENT   Form 3011   1/01 *(page 13 of 16 pages)*

(continued)

EXHIBIT 10-22
Security Deed (continued)

of transfer of servicing. If the Note is sold and thereafter the Loan is serviced by a Loan Servicer other than the purchaser of the Note, the mortgage loan servicing obligations to Borrower will remain with the Loan Servicer or be transferred to a successor Loan Servicer and are not assumed by the Note purchaser unless otherwise provided by the Note purchaser.

Neither Borrower nor Lender may commence, join, or be joined to any judicial action (as either an individual litigant or the member of a class) that arises from the other party's actions pursuant to this Security Instrument or that alleges that the other party has breached any provision of, or any duty owed by reason of, this Security Instrument, until such Borrower or Lender has notified the other party (with such notice given in compliance with the requirements of Section 15) of such alleged breach and afforded the other party hereto a reasonable period after the giving of such notice to take corrective action. If Applicable Law provides a time period which must elapse before certain action can be taken, that time period will be deemed to be reasonable for purposes of this paragraph. The notice of acceleration and opportunity to cure given to Borrower pursuant to Section 22 and the notice of acceleration given to Borrower pursuant to Section 18 shall be deemed to satisfy the notice and opportunity to take corrective action provisions of this Section 20.

21. Hazardous Substances. As used in this Section 21: (a) "Hazardous Substances" are those substances defined as toxic or hazardous substances, pollutants, or wastes by Environmental Law and the following substances: gasoline, kerosene, other flammable or toxic petroleum products, toxic pesticides and herbicides, volatile solvents, materials containing asbestos or formaldehyde, and radioactive materials; (b) "Environmental Law" means federal laws and laws of the jurisdiction where the Property is located that relate to health, safety or environmental protection; (c) "Environmental Cleanup" includes any response action, remedial action, or removal action, as defined in Environmental Law; and (d) an "Environmental Condition" means a condition that can cause, contribute to, or otherwise trigger an Environmental Cleanup.

Borrower shall not cause or permit the presence, use, disposal, storage, or release of any Hazardous Substances, or threaten to release any Hazardous Substances, on or in the Property. Borrower shall not do, nor allow anyone else to do, anything affecting the Property (a) that is in violation of any Environmental Law, (b) which creates an Environmental Condition, or (c) which, due to the presence, use, or release of a Hazardous Substance, creates a condition that adversely affects the value of the Property. The preceding two sentences shall not apply to the presence, use, or storage on the Property of small quantities of Hazardous Substances that are generally recognized to be appropriate to normal residential uses and to maintenance of the Property (including, but not limited to, hazardous substances in consumer products).

Borrower shall promptly give Lender written notice of (a) any investigation, claim, demand, lawsuit or other action by any governmental or regulatory agency or private party involving the Property and any Hazardous Substance or Environmental Law of which Borrower has actual knowledge, (b) any Environmental Condition, including but not limited to, any spilling, leaking, discharge, release or threat of release of any Hazardous Substance, and (c) any condition caused by the presence, use or release of a Hazardous Substance which adversely affects the value of the Property. If Borrower learns, or is notified by any governmental or regulatory authority, or any private party, that any removal or other remediation of any Hazardous Substance affecting the Property is necessary, Borrower shall promptly take all necessary remedial actions in accordance with Environmental Law. Nothing herein shall create any obligation on Lender for an Environmental Cleanup.

GEORGIA--Single Family--**Fannie Mae/Freddie Mac UNIFORM INSTRUMENT**   Form 3011   1/01 *(page 14 of 16 pages)*

(continued)

EXHIBIT 10-22
Security Deed (continued)

NON-UNIFORM COVENANTS. Borrower and Lender further covenant and agree as follows:

22. **Acceleration; Remedies.** Lender shall give notice to Borrower prior to acceleration following Borrower's breach of any covenant or agreement in this Security Instrument (but not prior to acceleration under Section 18 unless Applicable Law provides otherwise). The notice shall specify: (a) the default; (b) the action required to cure the default; (c) a date, not less than 30 days from the date the notice is given to Borrower, by which the default must be cured; and (d) that failure to cure the default on or before the date specified in the notice may result in acceleration of the sums secured by this Security Instrument and sale of the Property. The notice shall further inform Borrower of the right to reinstate after acceleration and the right to bring a court action to assert the non-existence of a default or any other defense of Borrower to acceleration and sale. If the default is not cured on or before the date specified in the notice, Lender at its option may require immediate payment in full of all sums secured by this Security Instrument without further demand and may invoke the power of sale granted by Borrower and any other remedies permitted by Applicable Law. Borrower appoints Lender the agent and attorney-in-fact for Borrower to exercise the power of sale. Lender shall be entitled to collect all expenses incurred in pursuing the remedies provided in this Section 22, including, but not limited to, reasonable attorneys' fees and costs of title evidence.

If Lender invokes the power of sale, Lender shall give a copy of a notice of sale by public advertisement for the time and in the manner prescribed by Applicable Law. Lender, without further demand on Borrower, shall sell the Property at public auction to the highest bidder at the time and place and under the terms designated in the notice of sale in one or more parcels and in any order Lender determines. Lender or its designee may purchase the Property at any sale.

Lender shall convey to the purchaser indefeasible title to the Property, and Borrower hereby appoints Lender Borrower's agent and attorney-in-fact to make such conveyance. The recitals in the Lender's deed shall be prima facie evidence of the truth of the statements made therein. Borrower covenants and agrees that Lender shall apply the proceeds of the sale in the following order: (a) to all expenses of the sale, including, but not limited to, reasonable attorneys' fees; (b) to all sums secured by this Security Instrument; and (c) any excess to the person or persons legally entitled to it. The power and agency granted are coupled with an interest, are irrevocable by death or otherwise and are cumulative to the remedies for collection of debt as provided by Applicable Law.

If the Property is sold pursuant to this Section 22, Borrower, or any person holding possession of the Property through Borrower, shall immediately surrender possession of the Property to the purchaser at the sale. If possession is not surrendered, Borrower or such person shall be a tenant holding over and may be dispossessed in accordance with Applicable Law.

23. **Release.** Upon payment of all sums secured by this Security Instrument, Lender shall cancel this Security Instrument. Borrower shall pay any recordation costs. Lender may charge Borrower a fee for releasing this Security Instrument, but only if the fee is paid to a third party for services rendered and the charging of the fee is permitted under Applicable Law.

24. **Waiver of Homestead.** Borrower waives all rights of homestead exemption in the Property.

GEORGIA--Single Family--Fannie Mae/Freddie Mac UNIFORM INSTRUMENT   Form 3011   1/01 *(page 15 of 16 pages)*

(continued)

EXHIBIT 10-22
Security Deed (continued)

25. Assumption Not a Novation. Lender's acceptance of an assumption of the obligations of this Security Instrument and the Note, and any release of Borrower in connection therewith, shall not constitute a novation.

26. Security Deed. This conveyance is to be construed under the existing laws of the State of Georgia as a deed passing title, and not as a mortgage, and is intended to secure the payment of all sums secured hereby.

BORROWER ACCEPTS AND AGREES to the terms and covenants contained in this Security Instrument and in any Rider executed by Borrower and recorded with it.

IN WITNESS WHEREOF, Borrower has signed and sealed this Security Instrument.

Signed, sealed and delivered in the presence of:

_____   _____(Seal)
Unofficial Witness   HELEN DAVIS   - Borrower

_____   _____(Seal)
                                                                 - Borrower

Notary Public, _____ County

_____ **[Space Below This Line For Acknowledgment]** _____

GEORGIA--Single Family--Fannie Mae/Freddie Mac UNIFORM INSTRUMENT   Form 3011   1/01 *(page 16 of 16 pages)*

EXHIBIT 10-23
HUD-1 Settlement Statement

A. SETTLEMENT STATEMENT

U.S. Department of Housing and Urban Development

OMB No. 2502-0265

B. Type of Loan

1. ___ FHA	2. ___ FmHA	3. _X_ Conv. Unins.	6. File Number	7. Loan Number	8. Mortgage Insurance Case No.#
4. ___ VA	5. ___ Conv. Ins.				

C. NOTE: This form is furnished to give you a statement of actual settlement costs. Amounts paid to and by the settlement agent are shown. Items marked (P.O.C.) were paid outside the closing; they are shown here for information purposes and are not included in the totals.

D. Name and Address of Borrower	E. Name and Address of Seller	F. Name and Address of Lender
HELEN DAVIS 5167 Tilly Mill Road Atlanta, Georgia 30302	MARKAM INDUSTRIES, INC. 210 Corporate Square Atlanta, Georgia 30324	AMERICAN EAGLE MORTGAGE COMPANY 10 Piedmont Center Atlanta, Georgia 30317

G. Property Location	H. Settlement Agent	
5167 Tilly Mill Road Atlanta, Georgia 30324	Place of Settlement	I. Settlement Date 4/25/20___ RD:

J. SUMMARY OF BORROWER'S TRANSACTION:		K. SUMMARY OF SELLER'S TRANSACTION:	
100. Gross Amount Due From Borrower		**400. Gross Amount Due To Seller**	
101. Contract sales price	100,000.00	401. Contract sales price	100,000.00
102. Personal property		402. Personal property	
103. Settlement charges to borrower (line 1400)	5,612.54	403.	
104.		404.	
105.		405.	
Adjustments for items paid by seller in advance		*Adjustments for items paid by seller in advance*	
106. City/town taxes to		406. City/town taxes to	
107. County taxes to		407. County taxes to	
108. Assessments to		408. Assessments to	
109.		409.	
110.		410.	
111.		411.	
112.		412.	
120. GROSS AMOUNT DUE FROM BORROWER	105,612.54	**420. GROSS AMOUNT DUE TO SELLER**	100,000.00
200. Amounts Paid By or In Behalf of Borrower		**500. Reductions In Amount Due To Seller**	
201. Deposit or earnest money	1,000.00	501. Excess Deposit (see instructions) (EM)*	1,000.00
202. Principal amount of new loan(s)	80,000.00	502. Settlement charges to seller (line 1400)	6,103.00
203. Existing loan(s) taken subject to		503. Existing loan(s) taken subject to	
204.		504. Payoff of first mortgage loan	82,460.00
205.		505. Payoff of second mortgage loan	
206.		506. *Earnest Money	
207.		507.	
208.		508.	
209.		509.	
Adjustments for items unpaid by seller		*Adjustments for items unpaid by seller*	
210. City/town taxes 1/1 to 4/25 (115)	491.05	510. City/town taxes 1/1 to 4/25 (115)	491.05
211. County taxes 1/1 to 4/25 (115)	583.05	511. County taxes 1/1 to 4/25 (115)	583.05
212. Assessments to		512. Assessments to	
213.		513.	
214.		514.	
215.		515.	
216.		516.	
217.		517.	
218.		518.	
219.		519.	
220. TOTAL PAID BY/FOR BORROWER	82,074.10	**520. TOTAL REDUCTION AMOUNT DUE SELLER**	90,637.10
300. Cash At Settlement From or To Borrower		**600. Cash At Settlement To or From Seller**	
301. Gross amount due from borrower (line 120)	105,612.54	601. Gross amount due to seller (line 420)	100,000.00
302. Less amounts paid by/for borrower (line 220)	82,074.10	602. Less reduction amount due seller (line 520)	90,637.10
303. CASH FROM BORROWER	23,538.44	603. CASH TO SELLER	9,362.90

(continued)

EXHIBIT 10-23
Settlement Statement (continued)

			PAGE 2
U.S. DEPARTMENT OF HOUSING AND URBAN DEVELOPMENT	**SETTLEMENT STATEMENT**		

L. SETTLEMENT CHARGES: FILE NO.#:	PAID FROM BORROWER'S FUNDS AT SETTLEMENT	PAID FROM SELLER'S FUNDS AT SETTLEMENT
700. TOTAL SALES/BROKER'S COMMISSION based on price $ 100,000.00 @7% = 7,000.00		
Division of commission (line 700) as follows:		
701. $ 3,500.00 to Ajax Realty Co.		
702. $ 3,500.00 to Northside Realty Co., Inc.		6,000.00
703. Commission paid at Settlement $1,000.00 Earnest Money retained by Northside		
704. Realty Co.		
800. ITEMS PAYABLE IN CONNECTION WITH LOAN		
801. Loan Origination Fee 1 % American Eagle Mortgage Company	1,000.00	
802. Loan Discount %		
803. Appraisal Fee to American Eagle Mortgage Company	500.00	
804. Credit Report to		
805. Lender's Inspection Fee to		
806. Mtg. Ins. Application Fee to		
807. Assumption Fee to		
808.		
809.		
810.		
811.		
812.		
813.		
814.		
815.		
900. ITEMS REQUIRED BY LENDER TO BE PAID IN ADVANCE		
901. Interest from 4/25 to 5/1 @ $ 17.53 6 /day	105.18	
902. Mortgage Insurance Premium for to		
903. Hazard Insurance Premium for yrs to		
904.		
905.		
1000. RESERVES DEPOSITED WITH LENDER FOR		
1001. Hazard Insurance 2 mo.@$ 40.00 /mo.	80.00	
1002. Mortgage Insurance mo.@$ /mo.		
1003. City Property Taxes 8 mo.@$ 130.00 /mo.	1,040.00	
1004. County Property Taxes 8 mo.@$ 154.17 /mo.	1,233.36	
1005. Annual Assessments mo.@$ /mo.		
1006. mo.@$ /mo.		
1007. mo.@$ /mo.		
1008. mo.@$ /mo.		
1100. TITLE CHARGES		
1101. Settlement or closing fee to		
1102. Abstract or title search to		
1103. Title examination to		
1104. Title insurance binder to		
1105. Document Preparation to		
1106. Notary Fees to		
1107. Attorney's fees to Law Firm	650.00	
(includes above items No: 1101, 1102, 1103, 1104, 1105 and 1106)		
1108. Title Insurance to Title Company	400.00	
(includes above items No:)		
1109. Lender's coverage $ 80,000.00 ----		
1110. Owner's coverage $ 100,000.00 ----		
1111.		
1112.		
1113.		
1200. GOVERNMENT RECORDING AND TRANSFER CHARGES		
1201. Recording Fees: Deed $ 3.00 ; Mortgage $ 11.00 ; Releases $ 3.00	14.00	3.00
1202. City/county tax/stamps: Deed $; Mortgage $		
1203. State Tax/stamps: Deed $ 100.00 ; Mortgage $ 240.00	240.00	100.00
1204.		
1205.		
1300. ADDITIONAL SETTLEMENT CHARGES		
1301. Survey to Survey Company	350.00	
1302. Pest Inspection to		
1303.		
1304.		
1305.		
1306.		
1307.		
1308.		
1400. **TOTAL SETTLEMENT CHARGES** (enter on lines 103 and 502, Sections J and K)	5,612.54	6,103.00

Condominiums and Cooperatives

"Living together alone in our space."

—Anonymous

OBJECTIVES

After reading this chapter you should be able to:

- Understand the condominium form of property ownership
- Understand the cooperative form of property ownership
- Understand the time-sharing form of property ownership
- Understand the difference between condominium and cooperative forms of ownership
- Understand the requirements for condominium declarations and condominium plats
- Understand the content of the legal documents required to create a condominium

America's first 200 years of growth and settlement as a nation depended, to a large extent, on an abundance of cheap land. Early landowners were able to obtain individual tracts of land on which to construct homes and other improvements. Early development of the country was horizontal, across the surface of the land. Early cities consisted of rows of individually owned homes and businesses. Multifamily housing in the early cities was rental housing with a building being owned by a single landowner and the various apartments or living spaces being leased to tenants. During the late nineteenth century, land, especially that in urban areas, became more expensive, and landowners, including residential landowners, began to build vertically, on the surface of the land. These early "high-rise" apartments were also under single ownership with the living spaces leased to tenants. As the wealth of the tenants grew and these high-rise apartments became more desirable, a new concept of ownership began to develop—the condominium or cooperative. Condominium and cooperative ownership have become popular, and condominiums and cooperatives exist in many states. Some are in high-rise or multistory buildings and some are in low-rise or cluster-detached housing. The condominium and cooperative concept extends beyond residential use. Condominium office buildings are commonplace in many areas.

It is essential, to assist in the representation of a client who is buying, selling, or making a loan on a condominium or cooperative, that a legal assistant understand the basic rules and concepts of condominium and cooperative property ownership.

CONDOMINIUM

The word *condominium* is a combination of two Latin words: *con*, meaning one or more persons, and *dominium*, meaning control over an object or property. Similar to its name, the **condominium** concept of property ownership is a combination of individual and joint ownership. A condominium owner individually owns his or her unit, which usually is located in a multiunit building. In addition, together with the other individual condominium owners, he or she has joint ownership and control over the common property, sometimes referred to as the **common areas** or common elements of the condominium. The common areas usually consist of exterior walls of buildings, stairwells, elevators, walks, yards, roofs, entryways, and so on. In many residential condominiums,

condominium
Form of property ownership in which the owner owns an individual unit in a multiunit building and is a tenant in common with other owners of units in the building in certain common areas.

common areas
Common areas or common elements of a condominium is that portion of the condominium property that is owned in common by all the owners of units in the condominium.

High-Rise Condominium

the common areas may include recreational areas, swimming pools, and, in some country club settings, even a golf course. The common areas are used by all the condominium owners and are jointly owned and maintained by the condominium owners.

The laws that govern and define condominium ownership are both statutory and contractual. All states have passed laws commonly referred to as condominium acts that set forth a comprehensive legal framework for the creation and governance of condominium ownership. In addition to the state regulation, condominium developers prepare a comprehensive set of contractual covenants, known as a **condominium declaration,** that will govern the ownership and control the governance of the condominium. The declaration is recorded, and each condominium owner is bound by its terms.

condominium declaration
Legal document required by state condominium acts to create a condominium.

Birth of a Condominium

A developer can create a condominium either by purchasing an apartment building and converting it into a condominium or by developing and constructing a new condominium. In either situation, the developer is required by state law to prepare for each condominium a condominium declaration that sets forth the rules and regulations of the condominium, a **plat** that shows the location of all individual units as well as the common areas, and to create a condominium homeowners' association that will govern the condominium property on final completion and sale of the units by the developer. The declaration, plat, and homeowners' association must be in place before the project can be considered a condominium and before individual units can be sold.

The declaration, sometimes called master deed or master lease, is the most important legal document in the creation of a condominium. It is prepared and signed by the condominium developer and recorded in the county where the condominium is located. The declaration describes and defines the boundaries of the units and the common areas or elements, creates or provides for the creation of the condominium government, and imposes restrictive covenants on the owners that regulate the use of the units and common areas. Most states' condominium acts require that the declaration contain certain express provisions for the condominium to be

condominium plat
Plat of survey of condominium property required by state condominium acts. The plat must show in sufficient detail the location and dimensions of the real property, as well as all condominium units located on the real property.

properly created. A unit owner may find it difficult to resell or obtain financing on a unit when the declaration is defective and does not comply with state law. An example of state condominium act requirements for the contents of a declaration is shown in Exhibit 11–1 at the end of this chapter.

In general, a condominium declaration contains the following information:

1. Name of the condominium, which in many states is required to contain the word *condominium* or to be followed by the words *a condominium*
2. Legal description of the entire property being submitted to the condominium form of ownership
3. Description or delineation of the boundaries of the individual condominium units, including horizontal, upper, lower, vertical, and lateral boundaries
4. Description or delineation of all common areas, including a designation of limited common areas. A **limited common area** is a common area that, by the declaration, is limited in use to one or more of the condominium owners. For example, an enclosed backyard or patio in a low-rise condominium project may be a limited common area assigned for use only to the property owner whose unit adjoins the patio or enclosed yard. Although the use of the limited common area is assigned only to a particular unit owner, the limited common areas are owned in common by all the owners in the condominium project
5. Creation of a governing body for the condominium or the requirement that one be created. The governing body usually is a nonprofit corporation in which each owner is entitled to one vote. These corporations often are referred to as the condominium association
6. Limitations or restrictions on the power of the condominium
7. Allocation of a share of liability for common area expenses to each condominium unit
8. Statement of all restrictive covenants in the general use of the units and common areas
9. Description of how the condominium can be expanded. It is not unusual for some developers to do phase condominiums. In a phase condominium, the developer may develop only a portion of the condominium to test the market. If the condominium sells, the developer will then add new units over a period of time. The declaration must spell out in detail how this phase of additional units will be accomplished
10. Statement of how the condominium form of ownership can be terminated

An example of a condominium declaration appears as Exhibit 11–2 at the end of this chapter.

A condominium developer, in addition to preparing and recording a declaration, must prepare and record a plat of the condominium improvements. The plat must show in sufficient detail the location and dimensions of the submitted property; the location and dimensions of all structural improvements located on any portion of the submitted property; the intended location and dimensions of all contemplated structural improvements committed to be provided by the declaration; and the location and dimensions of all easements appurtenant to the submitted property or otherwise submitted to the condominium form of ownership. An example of a state condominium act's requirements for a condominium plat appears as Exhibit 11–3 at the end of this chapter.

Articles and Bylaws of a Condominium Association

The internal operations of a condominium are governed by a homeowners' association or **condominium association.** The association takes the legal form of a nonprofit corporation, with each owner of a unit being entitled to a vote in the affairs of the association.

A condominium association, like any other corporation, is governed by two legal documents: the articles of incorporation and bylaws. The articles of incorporation form the basic corporate constitution or charter and are filed with the secretary of state's office in the state where the association is located. The articles of incorporation contain the following information:

- Name of the association
- Purpose of the association
- Period of the duration for the corporation
- Initial directors of the corporation

limited common area
Common area of a condominium that is limited in use to one or more condominium unit owners.

condominium association
Governing body of a condominium, the members of which are owners of condominium units. The condominium association usually is in the form of a nonprofit corporation.

- Registered agent and registered office of the corporation. The registered agent is the person on whom service of process can be served for the corporation, and the registered office is the address for the registered agent
- Criteria for becoming an owner or member of the association and the name of the incorporator. The incorporator usually is the developer or an attorney for the developer

An example of articles of incorporation for a condominium association is shown as Exhibit 11–4 at the end of this chapter.

The bylaws of a condominium association are the rules and regulations by which the association is governed. Bylaws contain more detail about the association than do the articles of incorporation. The bylaws provide for the following:

- Selection of the board of directors
- How meetings are to be held and conducted
- How officers are to be appointed or elected
- How votes are to be counted and the governance of the corporation, whether resolutions must be passed by a simple majority or a three-fourths or two-thirds majority vote
- Regulation of the common elements
- Rights and responsibilities of unit owners
- Assessment and collection of monthly charges and other relevant matters

Bylaws usually are not required to be recorded or filed with a state agency. They must, however, be provided to a purchaser of a unit before the time of purchase. An example of condominium bylaws are set forth as Exhibit 11–5 at the end of this chapter.

A developer usually retains control of the condominium association until such time as either all the units have been sold to purchasers or a percentage of units have been sold. Most condominium associations that provide for this limited period of developer control have two levels of membership in the association: the owner's level of membership, with one vote for each unit owned, and the developer's voting rights, which usually consist of all the voting rights as long as the developer is a member. The developer usually turns over control to the unit owners on the sale of a set number of units, typically not less than 75 percent.

The costs and expenses of operating a condominium are borne by the condominium owners. Expenses include taxes on the individual units, taxes on the common elements, maintenance and repair of the common elements, and insurance.

Taxes on the individual units are paid by the individual unit owners. The units can be returned to the tax authorities for taxes the same as a single-family home or other property. Tax on the common elements, however, is an expense of the association and a joint obligation of all the owners. The repair and maintenance of the common area are also joint responsibilities and expenses of the owners. In addition, most condominium declarations and even some condominium acts require that the insurance on both the units and the common area be under one master policy and that such insurance be the expense of the condominium association and, indirectly, the joint expense of all the owners.

The joint responsibility for paying common area expenses such as taxes, maintenance, and insurance is handled by the use of an **assessment** against each owner's unit to cover that unit owner's share of the common area expenses.

The amount of the assessment is determined by the condominium association. The determination is made based on an operating budget for the year's expenses in regard to the common areas and allocation of this operating budget to the number of units in the association. If a condominium is composed of different-sized units, the owner of a larger unit may be allocated a greater portion of the common area expense assessment than the owner of a smaller unit. The method for imposing assessments is determined both by state law and by condominium declaration.

If a common area assessment is not voluntarily paid by a unit owner, the association may have a lien against the unit for unpaid assessments. This lien, like any other lien, can be enforced by having the unit sold for the purpose of paying the lien. The association, in addition to imposing the lien, can sue an owner directly for nonpayment of delinquent assessments. It has been held in many states that an owner's obligation to pay is unconditional. This means that the owner is obligated to pay the assessment even if the association is not providing all the services required by the association.

assessment
Sum of money owed by a condominium owner for monthly upkeep of the common areas of the condominium.

Unpaid assessments are also imposed on a purchaser of a unit if the assessments are unpaid at the time of purchase. It is prudent, when representing a condominium purchaser, to inquire of the association if assessments are unpaid on the unit being purchased. These unpaid assessments often are not in the form of a lien that is recorded, and therefore, the only method of determining if unpaid assessments exist is to inquire of the association.

Condominium owners also have a joint and several liability for damage or harm caused to person or property in connection with the common areas. This liability is covered by liability insurance that insures both the individual unit owners and the association. In some states, an owner's liability for injury or harm which takes place on the common areas may be limited to the owner's pro rata share of the common area. For example, if an owner has a 2 percent share of the common areas and there is liability caused by negligence, such as a slip and fall at the swimming pool, then this owner's liability for the harm would be limited to 2 percent.

Insurance covering casualty of the condominium improvements is a master policy that insures all unit owners and the condominium association. The insurance covers both the individual units and the common areas. State law and condominium declarations usually require that insurance money be used for restoration of the condominium improvements unless a specified number of homeowners—usually not less than 75 percent—agree not to restore. In the event restoration does not take place, the insurance proceeds would be paid to the owners according to their interest in the condominium. In the event insurance proceeds are insufficient to totally repair or restore the premises, it would be the joint obligation of the owners to contribute money necessary to complete the construction. This contribution could be imposed in the form of an assessment lien, the same as assessments for common area expenses and maintenance.

Representing the Condominium Unit Purchaser or Lender

A legal assistant's involvement with a condominium form of ownership usually takes the form of assisting a purchaser or lender who is buying or making a loan on a condominium unit. The legal assistant, to adequately assist in the representation of this client, must be knowledgeable of the condominium laws in the state where the condominium is located. In addition, the legal assistant should obtain copies of all the condominium documentation, such as the declaration, plat, articles of incorporation, and bylaws of the condominium association, and review them carefully.

The following is a checklist of issues and questions that need to be asked and answered when representing a condominium unit purchaser or lender.

 C H E C K L I S T

Condominium Checklist

☐ 1. The reputation of the condominium developer or builder is related to the success of the developer's projects. A good reputation means that the builder builds good-quality condominium units that usually are trouble-free. The quality of construction in a condominium unit can greatly affect the cost of maintaining the unit and the resale value of the unit.

☐ 2. Does the condominium documentation comply with state law? A condominium declaration that is defective or does not comply with state law can affect the marketability and cloud the title of the condominium unit. Purchasers may not want to purchase property that is not technically in compliance with the state condominium laws, and lenders may decline to make loans on such property. It is possible in some states to obtain an endorsement from a title insurance company ensuring that the condominium has been properly formed and is in compliance with the state condominium act.

☐ 3. Carefully review the assessments while a developer is still in control of the condominium project. Not uncommonly, the developer, while in control, may subsidize the condominium budget and keep assessments artificially low during this period of ownership. It is important to obtain copies of the actual budget, if available, from the developer to determine what the assessments will be once the developer has sold the units and left the project.

❏ 4. Who controls the board of directors? During the development, it is not unusual for the developer to have control over the board of directors. The developer usually retains control until such time as a minimum number of units have been sold, usually not less than 75 percent of the units. Although it is not unusual for a developer to control the association during the period of development, the property owner needs to know when control will be turned over to the owners and to be aware that for a period of time, he or she may have little say in the internal affairs of the association.

❏ 5. Review the restrictions on use of the unit and common areas. A condominium contains restrictive covenants that affect the use of units and the common areas by the owners. These restrictive covenants are enforceable so long as they do not violate some public policy, such as racial discrimination. A potential condominium purchaser must be made aware that these covenants are enforceable and that there probably is someone in the condominium project who enforces them. If a condominium purchaser has trouble with any of the restrictive covenants, he or she needs to second-think the purchase.

❏ 6. Is there any control on the resale of the property? A few condominium declarations contain rights of first refusal restrictions on an owner's ability to resell his or her unit. The right of first refusal usually requires that the owner offer the unit first to the condominium association before it can be resold. The association seldom exercises these rights of first refusal, but this practice can affect an owner's ability to sell the unit or present problems at a closing in the event a notice of the sale was not sent to the association.

COOPERATIVE

The **cooperative** form of ownership, despite its popularity in Europe and other parts of the world, has had limited success in the United States. Cooperatives usually are found in urban areas along the East Coast. In the late 1960s and early 1970s they were used to provide publicly assisted housing. A limited number of these properties can still be found throughout the United States.

> **cooperative**
> Form of ownership of real property in which a corporation owns a multiunit building and leases living space in the building to the shareholders of the corporation.

Cooperative ownership is quite different from condominium ownership. In a cooperative, a corporation owns the land, the building, and all common areas. A person who wants to become an owner purchases from the cooperative corporation shares of stock in the corporation. These shares of stock entitle the person to enter into a long-term lease for his or her cooperative unit with the corporation. A cooperative owner is, in essence, both a tenant under a long-term lease with the corporation and an owner because the person owns shares in the landlord cooperative corporation. The owner participates with other owners, who are also members of the corporation, in the governance of the corporation. The shares of stock and lease are transferable and, therefore, offer a cooperative owner, like a condominium owner, an opportunity to build value in his or her investment. Ownership in a cooperative usually is considered ownership of personal property rather than of real property.

Differences between Condominiums and Cooperatives

The main difference between a cooperative and a condominium is financing. With a condominium, each owner pays his or her own financing and pledges the unit as security for the loan. In cooperative financing, there is a blanket mortgage on all the cooperative property, including the living units and common areas. The cooperative purchaser agrees to pay his or her share of the blanket mortgage payments, which is based on the percentage of ownership of the total cooperative. At the time of purchase, a cooperative owner may also be required to make a substantial downpayment, which typically is greater than a condominium downpayment. A condominium owner usually can purchase a unit with a downpayment of only 10 to 20 percent of the purchase price, whereas it is not unusual for a cooperative owner to have to pay as much as one-third of the purchase price as a downpayment. The master financing of a cooperative versus individual financing of a condominium creates another set of problems for the cooperative owner. A cooperative owner could be making his or her payments each month to the cooperative corporation for his or her share of the common mortgage, but the other cooperative owners could be defaulting on their payment obligations. These collective defaults of other owners could cause the blanket mortgage to go into default and could threaten the foreclosure of the master mortgage on the co-operative owner's home.

Cooperative owners commonly have more restricted rights of resale than do condominium owners. Most condominium owners can resell their units without consent of the condominium association. Cooperative owners usually cannot sell their cooperative interests unless the board of directors of the cooperative corporation approves the new owners. This approval process is necessary because of the collective mortgage and the requirement that the cooperative owners work more closely together in a cooperative effort so that each cooperative owner can prosper and be protected in his or her ownership of a unit.

The financing difficulties and the restrictions on resale have caused the cooperative form of ownership to be less popular than the condominium form of ownership.

TIME-SHARES

time-share
Form of ownership of real property in which an owner owns the property for a short period, usually one or two weeks out of each year. Time-share ownership typically is used for vacation or recreational property.

You like to ski, and each year you go to your favorite ski resort for a week. You enjoy the trip very much and think it might be a good idea to own property in the area of the ski resort. You are hesitant to buy a vacation condominium or home because you will only be using it one or two weeks out of the year. You are not certain if the unit can be rented the other fifty weeks to cover your costs and expenses of ownership. Wouldn't it be nice if you could just buy a condominium or home in the ski area for one or two weeks a year? It is this desire and demand that an industry known as time-sharing was created to satisfy. **Time-share,** or interval ownership, is a popular marketing device for resort developments in the United States. Under a time-sharing arrangement, a person purchases the right to use a home or condominium at a resort area for a limited period each year.

Time-share ownership comes in a number of legal forms. A time-share may be a cooperative in which the developer owns a corporation and each owner of the time-share purchases stock in the corporation. The amount of stock owned by the purchaser permits the owner to use units within the development during a certain period of the year. A time-share may be based on a form of interval ownership in which an owner of a time-share actually owns the unit for a certain time each year. A time-share may also be structured in such a way that the purchaser enters into a tenancy in common arrangement with other time-share owners for the entire resort development. This arrangement permits the owner to use a particular residential unit during a portion of the year.

rescission
Right to terminate a contract.

Time-shares have been subject to abuse and fraud by developers and are heavily regulated by state law. The purchaser of a time-share is entitled to full disclosure concerning all operations of the time-share and is given a period of **rescission** after a contract to buy a time-share has been signed. During this period, usually five to seven days, the purchaser can change his or her mind and terminate the agreement.

 E T H I C S :   Legal Assistant Correspondence

You are a closing legal assistant employed in a busy real estate department of a law firm. Your work requires a great deal of correspondence, and you share a secretary with your supervising attorney. Your secretary has taken a day's vacation and you are working with a temporary secretary. You have a number of letters that need to go out and you notice that the temporary has used firm letterhead for all your correspondence and has typed your name in such a way that it appears you are an attorney for the firm. It is late in the day, and it will take more than an hour to retype the letters. Do you send the letters, or have them retyped?

Many states provide that to the extent necessary to perform functions properly delegated to a legal assistant and to the extent that these functions do not fall within the definition of the practice of law, the legal assistant may correspond on the law firm letterhead in the legal assistant's own name. If a legal assistant in the employ of a member of the bar is permitted by the member to correspond on the law firm letterhead, the legal assistant must clearly identify his or her status by the use of an appropriate designation, such as "paralegal," "legal assistant," or "law clerk." Failure to do so might constitute a representation on the part of the law firm that the legal assistant is a member of the state bar and authorized to practice law within the state.

SUMMARY

The condominium and cooperative forms of property ownership combine individual and joint ownership. A condominium owner individually owns his or her unit and, together with other individual owners, has joint ownership and control over the common property. A cooperative owner has a lease on his or her living unit and owns stock in the cooperative corporation that owns the building in which the unit is located. A legal assistant who represents a purchaser, seller, or lender of condominium or cooperative property must be familiar with all the rules and regulations involving condominiums and cooperatives.

KEY TERMS

assessment	condominium declaration	rescission
common areas	condominium plat	time-share
condominium	cooperative	
condominium association	limited common area	

SELF-STUDY EXAMINATION

(Answers provided in Appendix)

1. T or F. A swimming pool in a condominium development would be a limited common area.

2. T or F. A condominium owner buys stock in a corporation which owns the condominium, and this stock gives the condominium owner a right to live in a condominium unit.

3. T or F. A condominium form of ownership once created can never be terminated.

4. T or F. A governing body of most condominiums is a nonprofit corporation in which each owner is entitled to one vote.

5. T or F. Taxes on the individual condominium units are common expenses paid by the condominium association.

6. T or F. A condominium association can foreclose and sell an owner's condominium unit if the owner fails to pay common area assessments.

7. T or F. A condominium owner's obligation to pay common area assessments is conditioned upon the condominium association's providing services.

8. T or F. Condominiums and cooperatives are the same thing.

9. T or F. A cooperative owner generally does not have any restrictions on the owner's right to resell the cooperative unit.

10. T or F. Most cooperatives are financed by individual mortgages on the individual cooperative owner's unit.

11. What does the owner in a condominium own?

12. Describe briefly some items that would be considered common areas or common elements of a condominium.

13. What is a condominium declaration?

14. What is a limited common area and give an example?

15. The internal operations of a condominium are governed by what organization?

16. Taxes on individual units of a condominium are paid by whom?

17. How is insurance on a condominium generally handled?

18. If you were representing a condominium purchaser, which issues and questions would you be interested in finding answers to?

19. What is a cooperative?

20. How does a cooperative differ from a condominium?

ADDENDUM

Exhibit 11–1	State condominium act requirements for declaration
Exhibit 11–2	Condominium declaration
Exhibit 11–3	State condominium code requirements for condominium plat
Exhibit 11–4	Articles of incorporation for condominium association
Exhibit 11–5	Condominium association bylaws

EXHIBIT 11–1
State Condominium
Act Requirements for
Declaration

44-3-77. Contents of declaration.

(a) The declaration for every condominium shall contain the following:

(1) The name of the condominium, which name shall include the word "condominium" or be followed by the words "a condominium";

(2) The name of the county or counties in which the condominium is located;

(3) A legal description by metes and bounds of the submitted property, including any horizontal, upper and lower, boundaries as well as the vertical, lateral, boundaries;

(4) A description or delineation of the boundaries of the units, including any horizontal, upper and lower, boundaries as well as the vertical, lateral, boundaries;

(5) A description or delineation of any limited common elements showing or designating the unit or units to which each is assigned;

(6) A description or delineation of all common elements that may subsequently be assigned as limited common elements together with a statement that they may be so assigned and a description of the method whereby any such assignments shall be made;

(7) The allocation to each unit of an undivided interest in the common elements;

(8) The allocation to each unit of a number of votes in the association;

(9) The allocation to each unit of a share of the liability for common expenses;

(10) Any limitations or restrictions on the powers of the association and the board of directors;

(11) The name and address of the attorney or other person who prepared the declaration;

(12) A statement of any and all restrictions on the general use of the condominium or a statement that there are no such restrictions; and

(13) Such other matters not inconsistent with this article as the declarant deems appropriate.

(b) If the condominium is an expandable condominium, the declaration shall also contain the following:

(1) The explicit reservation of an option or options to expand the condominium;

(2) A time limit or date not exceeding seven years from the recording of the declaration upon which all options to expand the condominium shall expire together with a statement of any circumstances which will terminate any such option prior to the expiration of the time limit so specified; provided, however, that, if the condominium instruments so provide, the unit owners of units to which two-thirds of the votes in the association appertain, exclusive of any vote or votes appurtenant to any unit or units then owned by the declarant, may consent to the extension of any such option within one year prior to the date upon which the option would otherwise have expired;

(3) A statement of any other limitations on the option or options or a statement that there are no such limitations;

(4) A legal description by metes and bounds of the additional property, including any horizontal, upper and lower, boundaries as well as the vertical, lateral, boundaries;

(5) A statement as to whether portions of the additional property may be added to the condominium at different times, together with any limitations fixing the boundaries of those portions by legal descriptions setting forth the metes and bounds thereof or regulating the order in which they may be added to the condominium, or a statement that there are no such limitations;

(6) A statement of any limitations as to the location of any improvements that may be made on any portions of the additional property or a statement that there are no such limitations;

(7) A statement of the maximum number of units that may be created on the additional property. If portions of the additional property may be added to the condominium and the boundaries of those portions are fixed in accordance with paragraph (5) of this subsection, the declaration shall also state the maximum number of units that may be created on each such portion added to the condominium. If portions of the additional property may be added to the condominium and the boundaries of those portions are not fixed in accordance with paragraph (5) of this subsection, then the

(continued)

declaration shall also state the maximum average number of units per acre that may be created on any such portion added to the condominium;

(8) With regard to the additional property, a statement of whether any units may be created therein that may not be restricted exclusively to residential use and, if so, a statement of the maximum extent thereof or a limitation as to the extent of such nonresidential use;

(9) A statement of the extent to which any structures erected on any portion of the additional property added to the condominium will be compatible with structures on the submitted property in terms of quality of construction, the principal materials to be used, and architectural style or a statement that no assurances are made in those regards;

(10) A description of all other improvements that will be made on any portion of the additional property added to the condominium, or a statement of any limitations as to what other improvements may be made thereon, or a statement that no assurances are made in that regard;

(11) A statement that any units created on any portion of the additional property added to the condominium will be substantially identical to the units on the submitted property, or a statement of any limitations as to what types of units may be created thereon, or a statement that no assurances are made in that regard;

(12) A description of the declarant's reserved right, if any, to create limited common elements within any portion of the additional property or to designate common elements therein which may subsequently be assigned as limited common elements, in terms of the types, sizes, and maximum number of such limited common elements within each such portion, or a statement that no limitations are placed on that right; and

(13) A statement of a formula, ratio, or other method whereby, upon the expansion of any expandable condominium, there shall be reallocated among the units the undivided interests in the common elements, the votes in the association, and the liability for common expenses.

Plats or plans may be recorded with the declaration of any amendment thereto and identified therein to supplement or provide information required to be furnished pursuant to this subsection; and provided, further, that paragraph (8) of this subsection need not be complied with if none of the units on the submitted property are restricted exclusively to residential use.

(c) If the condominium contains any convertible space, the declaration shall also contain a statement of a formula, ratio, or other method whereby, upon the conversion of all or any portion of a convertible space, there shall be allocated among the units created therefrom such undivided interest in the common elements, such number of votes in the association, and such liability for common expenses as previously pertained to such convertible space.

(d) If the condominium is a leasehold condominium, with respect to any ground lease, other lease, or other instrument creating the estate for years, the expiration or termination of which may terminate or reduce the condominium, the declaration shall set forth the county or counties wherein the same are recorded and the deed book and page number where the first page of each such lease or other instrument is recorded. The declaration shall also contain the following:

(1) The date upon which such leasehold or estate for years is due to expire;

(2) A statement of whether any property will be owned by the unit owners in fee simple and, if so, a legal description by metes and bounds of any such property. With respect to any improvements owned by the unit owners in fee simple, the declaration shall contain a statement of any rights the unit owners shall have to remove the improvements after the expiration or termination of the leasehold or estate for years involved or a statement that they shall have no such rights;

(3) A statement of the name and address of the person or persons to whom payments of rent must be made by the unit owners unless such rent is collected from the unit owners as a part of the common expenses; and

(4) A statement of the share of liability for payments under any such lease or other instrument which are chargeable against each unit.

(continued)

(e) Whenever this Code section requires a legal description by metes and bounds of submitted property or additional property, such requirement shall be deemed to include a requirement of a legally sufficient description of any easements that are submitted to this article or that may be added to the condominium, as the case may be. In the case of any such easement, the declaration shall contain the following:

(1) A description of the permitted use or uses;

(2) If the benefit of the easement does not inure to all units and their lawful occupants, a statement of the relevant restrictions and limitations on utilization; and

(3) If any person other than those entitled to occupy any unit may use the easement, a statement of the rights of others to such use.

Notwithstanding any other provision of this subsection, the foregoing requirements may be satisfied by attaching a true copy of any such easement to the declaration.

(f) Whenever this Code section requires a legal description by metes and bounds of submitted property or additional property, such requirement shall be deemed to include a separate legal description by metes and bounds of all property in which the unit owners collectively shall or may be tenants in common or joint tenants with any other persons. No units shall be situated on any such property, however, and the declaration shall describe the nature of the unit owners' estate therein. No such property shall be shown on the same plat or plats showing other portions of the condominium but shall be shown instead on separate plats unless such property is specifically shown and labeled as being owned subject to such a tenancy.

(g) Wherever this article requires a statement of a method for allocation or reallocation of undivided interests in the common elements, votes in the association, and the liability for common expenses, such method shall be so related to the physical characteristics of the units affected or otherwise so stated as to enable any person to determine the interest, vote, or share in such matters pertaining to any particular unit upon such allocation or reallocation. Certain spaces within the units, including, without limitation, attic, basement, and garage space, may but need not be omitted from such calculation or partially discounted by the use of a ratio so long as the same basis of calculation is employed for all units in the condominium. In the event that the declaration allocates or provides for the allocation to any unit of a different share of undivided interests in common elements than is allocated for liability for common expenses, such difference shall be based upon a good faith estimate of the declarant regarding the approximate relative maintenance or other costs occasioning such disparity, and the basis of such determination shall be stated in the declaration; provided, however, that no unit owner or other person may require any reallocation on account of any disparity between actual costs and the determination reflected in the declaration. Subject to the foregoing sentence of this subsection, nothing contained in this article shall be construed to require that the proportions of undivided interest in the common elements, of votes in the association, or of liability for common expenses assigned and allocated to each unit be equal, it being intended that such proportions may be independent. (Ga. L. 1975, p. 609, § 14; Ga. L. 1982, p. 3, § 44.)

EXHIBIT 11-2
Condominium
Declaration

STATE OF _____
COUNTY OF _____

DECLARATION OF CONDOMINIUM
FOR
CLAIREMONT OAKS, A CONDOMINIUM

THIS DECLARATION is made by The Farris Corporation (herein called the "Declarant").

WITNESSETH:

WHEREAS, Declarant is the fee simple owner of that certain tract or parcel of land lying and being in Land Lot 55 of the 6th District of Wayne County, _____(State)_____, as more particularly described in Exhibit "A" attached hereto and incorporated herein by reference, hereinafter called the "Property" subject to the matters set forth on Exhibit "B" attached hereto; and

WHEREAS, certain improvements have been constructed on the Property as shown on the Plat and the Plans which are referenced in Section 5.01(a) and (b) hereof and the matters attached hereto as Exhibit "C"; and

WHEREAS, Declarant has duly incorporated Clairemont Oaks Condominium Association, Inc. as a nonprofit membership corporation under the laws of the State of _____, copies of the Articles of Incorporation, By-Laws and Organizational Meeting being attached hereto as Exhibits "D", "E" and "F"; and

WHEREAS, the Declarant desires to submit the Property to the condominium form of ownership pursuant to the provisions of the _____(State)_____ Condominium Act, as the same is in effect on the date hereof (as amended, hereinafter called the "Act"), the terms, conditions and provisions of which are incorporated herein by express reference, and the terms and conditions hereinafter set out.

NOW, THEREFORE, the Declarant does hereby make, declare and publish its intention and desire to submit, and does hereby submit, the Property to the condominium form of ownership pursuant to, subject to and in accordance with the provisions of the Act and the terms and conditions hereinafter set forth.

ARTICLE 1

Name

1.01 The name of the condominium shall be CLAIREMONT OAKS, A CONDOMINIUM (the "Condominium").

ARTICLE 2

Description of Submitted Property

2.01 The Property is located in Wayne County, _____(State)_____, in Land Lot 55 of the 6th District, and is more particularly described in Exhibit "A" attached hereto and incorporated herein by reference.

2.02 The Property is subject to the easements and other matters which are set forth on Exhibit B" attached hereto and by reference made a part hereof.

ARTICLE 3

Definitions

3.01 The terms defined in Official Code of _____(State)_____, Section _____ shall have the meanings specified therein and wherever they appear in the condominium instruments unless the context otherwise requires.

(continued)

EXHIBIT 11–2
Condominium
Declaration
(continued)

ARTICLE 4

Convertible Space; Expandable Condominium

4.01 Convertible Space. The Condominium does not contain any convertible space.

4.02 Expansion of Condominium. This Condominium shall contain sixty (60) residential units, and is not expandable beyond that amount.

ARTICLE 5

Unit Information and Boundaries

5.01 The buildings and structures situated upon the property are:

(a) located thereon as shown on that certain plat of Clairemont Oaks, A Condominium, dated _____ , prepared by _____ , which plat has been prepared in accordance with Official Code of ____(State)____ , Section _____ and has been filed contemporaneously herewith in Condominium Plat Book _____ , Page _____ , Wayne County, ____(State)____ Records a copy of which is attached hereto as Exhibit "C" (hereinafter said condominium plat as recorded is referred to as the "Plat" or the "Condominium Plat");

(b) divided into sixty (60) residential units intended for independent ownership and use and as substantially shown upon those certain Plans for Clairemont Oaks, dated _____ , by _____ , and filed contemporaneously herewith in the Condominium Floor Plans Cabinet _____ , Folder _____ , _____ County, ____(State)____ Records (hereinafter said plans are referred to as the "Plans" or the "Condominium Plans").

5.02 Unit Number. Each unit shall have the identifying number allocated to it in accordance with the Plat and the Plans.

5.03 Boundaries. The boundaries of the units are the floors, ceilings and walls delineated in the Plans.

5.04 Appurtenant Surfaces. If any chute, flue, duct, conduit, wire, bearing wall, bearing column or any other apparatus lies partially within and partially outside the designated boundaries of a unit, any portions thereof serving only that unit shall be deemed a part of that unit, and any portions thereof serving more than one unit or any portion of the common elements shall be deemed a part of the common elements.

5.05 Subdivision and Partition of Units; Relocation of Boundaries. The boundaries between adjoining units may be relocated from time to time, but no unit may be subdivided for the purpose of creating two or more units therefrom and no owner shall have the right of partition of a unit.

ARTICLE 6

Limited Common Elements

6.01 Generally. Any shutter, awning, window box, doorstep, porch, balcony, patio and any other apparatus designed to serve a single unit shall be deemed to be a limited common element appertaining to that unit exclusively.

ARTICLE 7

Allocation of Undivided Interest in the Common Elements

7.01 The undivided interest in the common elements allocated to each unit is set forth on Exhibit "G" attached hereto and incorporated herein by reference.

ARTICLE 8

Allocation of Votes in the Association

8.01 Generally. The number of votes in the Clairemont Oaks Condominium Association, Inc. for each unit shall be as designated on Exhibit "G" attached hereto.

(continued)

EXHIBIT 11-2
Condominium
Declaration
(continued)

8.02 Method of Voting. The persons entitled to exercise such votes at meetings of the Association, the method by which such votes may be exercised and the rights and obligations generally of members of the Association with regard to voting shall be in accordance with the By-Laws of the Association.

ARTICLE 9

Allocation of Liabilities, Common Expenses and Utility Fees

9.01 Derivation of Amounts. The share of liability for each unit of the common expenses of the Association is shown on Exhibit "D" attached hereto and incorporated herein by reference.

9.02 Liability for Assessments. The owner of each unit shall, by acceptance of a deed from the Declarant or any direct or remote successor-in-interest to Declarant in any unit, be personally liable for and shall pay to the Association:

(a) any assessment with respect to all expenditures made or incurred by or on behalf of the Association in the operation, management and maintenance of the Property, including but not limited to: fees for management and supervision; printing, mailing, office equipment, all legal and accounting fees as required, secretarial and other expenses related to the conduct of the affairs of the Association and the Board of Directors; insurance; all utility charges in connection with the common elements, including gas, electric, water, sewerage and telephone charges; all expenses in connection with maintenance and repair of all common elements; security; and water, sewer, sanitary, gas and electric services and other similar charges for all units.

(b) any assessment, payable monthly or as otherwise billed, for utility fees chargeable to each unit for the providing of electricity, gas and such other utility service as may from time to time be provided to or for the unit.

(c) pursuant to the By-Laws of the Association, assessments may be made more often than annually, may be made for the purpose of defraying, in whole or in part, utilities, operating expenses, the cost of any construction or reconstruction, or unexpected repair or replacement of capital improvements in respect to the common elements.

The Declarant shall be liable for all common area and other assessments and utility fees on units owned by Declarant. The Declarant shall not be liable for any other assessments or expenses provided in this Article 9 of this Declaration prior to the date of the first unit sale.

9.03 Equitable Assessment for Limited Common Area Expenses. Any common expenses which:

(a) are incurred through or occasioned by the use or enjoyment of any common elements which benefits or is intended to benefit less than all the units, shall not be assessed against all the units pursuant to Section 9.01 hereof, but shall be specifically assessed equitably among those units which are so benefited or intended to be benefited; and

(b) are incurred by the conduct of less than all of those entitled to occupy all of the units or by the licensees or invitees of any such unit or units shall be especially assessed against the condominium unit or units, the conduct of any occupant, licensee or invitee of which occasioned any such common expenses.

9.04 Assessment for Exclusive Benefit of Particular Units. Any common expenses which relate to limited common elements assigned to any unit or units and reserved for the exclusive use of those entitled to the use of such unit or units shall be assessed against such unit or units only.

9.05 Lien Rights of Association. The Board of Directors shall have the authority to establish general rules applicable to all units providing that the lien for assessments shall include any one or more of the following: (i) a late or delinquency charge (not in excess of $10.00 or ten percent of the amount of each assessment or installment thereof not paid when due, whichever is greater), (ii) interest on each assessment or installment thereof, and any delinquency or late charge appertaining thereto, from the date the same was first due and payable, at a rate not in excess of ten percent per annum, (iii) the costs of collection, including court costs, the expenses of sale, any expenses required for the protection and preservation of the unit, and reasonable attorneys' fees actually incurred, and (iv) the fair rental value of the condominium unit from the time of the institution of suit until the sale of the condominium unit at foreclosure (or until the judgment rendered in such suit is otherwise satisfied).

(continued)

EXHIBIT 11–2
Condominium
Declaration
(continued)

ARTICLE 10

Association

10.01 Creation. The Declarant has caused the Clairemont Oaks Condominium Association, Inc., to be duly incorporated as a nonprofit membership corporation.

10.02 Powers Generally. The limitations and restrictions on the powers of the Association and on the Board of Directors of the Association are set out in the By-Laws of the Association.

10.03 Enforcement. The Association shall be empowered, in order to enforce compliance with the lawful provisions of the condominium instruments, including any rules or regulations contained in or promulgated in accordance with the By-Laws of the Association, to impose and assess fines and to suspend temporarily the right of use of certain of the common elements.

10.04 Restrictions on Powers. The Association shall have, except to the extent restricted herein, all those powers permitted by the provisions of Official Code of _____(State)_____ , Section _____ , and except to the extent that it may not without the written consent of two-thirds of the unit owners (excluding Declarant) sell or transfer the common elements (excluding the grant of easements for public utilities or for any other public purposes consistent with the intended use of the common elements by the unit owners).

ARTICLE 11

Easements, Covenants and Use of the Condominium

11.01 Purposes. The Condominium is formed for residential purposes only and units shall be occupied and used by the owners thereof only as private residences for the owners and the families, tenants, invitees, and guests of such owners and for no other purposes whatsoever. Without derogating from the generality of the foregoing, no business shall be maintained or conducted in or from any unit.

11.02 Common Elements. All occupants of units and their guests shall have a nonexclusive right to use the common elements for the purposes for which they are intended, subject, however, to the following provisions:

(a) No such use shall enter or encroach upon the lawful rights of other persons; and

(b) The right of the Association to restrict the use and govern the operation of the common elements by promulgating reasonable rules and regulations with respect thereto, including, without limitation, the right to charge reasonable monthly fees for the use thereof by unit owners as the Association deems necessary or appropriate.

11.03 Strict Compliance. The owners of the units shall be entitled to all of the rights but shall be subject to all of the obligations provided for in the Act and all owners shall comply strictly with the provisions of the Condominium instruments including any restrictions, rules or regulations contained in or promulgated in accordance with the By-Laws of the Association.

11.04 Maintenance of Offices. The provisions of Section 10.01 hereof shall not affect the right of the Declarant and its duly authorized agents, representatives and employees to enjoy the easement provided for in Official Code of _____(State)_____ , Section _____ for the maintenance of sales and leasing offices and/or model units on the submitted property.

11.05 Construction Easement. The Property shall be subject to a nonexclusive easement in favor of Declarant and its officers, employees, agents, independent contractors and invitees for entry upon and passage over the Property for purposes of constructing the units and other improvements described herein.

11.06 Utility Easements. There shall be appurtenant to each unit a nonexclusive easement for use of all pipes, wire cables, conduits, utility lines, flues and ducts serving such unit and situated in any other unit. Each unit shall be subject to an easement in favor of other units for use of all pipes, wire, cables, conduits, utility lines, flues and ducts situated in such unit and serving such other units.

(continued)

EXHIBIT 11-2
Condominium
Declaration
(continued)

11.07 Encroachments. If any portion of the common elements now encroaches upon any unit, or if any unit now encroaches upon any other unit or upon any portion of the common element, or if any such encroachment shall occur hereafter as a result of (i) settling of a unit or units; (ii) repair, alteration or reconstruction of the common elements made by or with the consent of the Association; (iii) repair or reconstruction of a unit or units following damage by fire or other casualty; or (iv) condemnation or eminent domain proceedings, a valid easement shall exist for such encroachment and for the maintenance of the same so long as the Property remains subject to the Act.

11.08 Right of Access. The Association shall have the irrevocable right, to be exercised by the Board of Directors, to have access to each unit from time to time during reasonable hours as may be necessary for the maintenance, repair or replacement of any of the common elements therein or accessible therefrom, or for making emergency repairs therein necessary to prevent damage to the common elements or to another unit.

11.09 Maintenance of Common Elements. The necessary work of maintenance, repair and replacement of the common elements and the making of any additions or improvements thereto shall be carried out only as provided in the Act, this Declaration and the By-Laws.

11.10 Prohibited Work. No owner shall do any work which would jeopardize the soundness or safety of the Property, reduce the value thereof or impair any easement or hereditament without in every such case unanimous consent of all other owners being first obtained.

ARTICLE 12

Insurance and Casualty Losses

12.01 Insurance Coverage. The Association shall obtain and maintain in full force and effect, at all times, the following insurance coverages:

(a) Insurance covering all of the insurable improvements on the property (with the exception of improvements and betterments made by the respective unit owners or occupants) and all personal property as may be owned by the Association, against loss or damage by fire and other hazards covered by the standard extended coverage endorsement, and such other risk as from time to time shall be customarily covered with respect to buildings similar in construction, location and use as the units, including, but not limited to, vandalism and malicious mischief in an amount equal to the maximum insurable replacement value thereof (exclusive of excavation and foundations), as determined annually by the Association;

(b) Comprehensive public liability insurance covering all of the common elements and insuring against all damage or liability caused by the acts of the Association, its officers, directors, agents and employees, all unit owners and other persons entitled to occupy any unit or any other portion of the condominium, with liability limits in amounts authorized from time to time by the Association, but in no event less than the amounts required in the Act;

(c) Such other types and amounts of insurance as may from time to time be deemed necessary, desirable or proper, and be authorized by the Association by action of the Board of Directors or in its By-Laws.

12.02 Payment of Insurance Premiums. Premiums for all insurance carried by the Association shall be common expenses and shall be paid by the Association.

12.03 Policy Standards.

(a) All insurance coverage obtained by the Association shall be written in the name of the Association as trustee for, and for the use and benefit of, each of the unit owners and their mortgagees as their interest may appear, and their respective percentages of undivided interest in and to the common elements. Each such insurance policy shall be issued by an insurer authorized under the laws of the State of _____ to do business in ____(State)____ and to issue the coverage provided by the policy, and shall provide for the issuance of a certificate of insurance to each unit owner and its mortgagee, if any, which shall specify the proportionate amount of such insurance attributable to the particular unit owner's interest in the property.

(continued)

EXHIBIT 11–2
Condominium
Declaration
(continued)

(b) The Association shall use its best efforts to cause all of such insurance policies to contain: (i) a waiver of subrogation by the insurer as to any claims against the Association, any officer, director, agent or employee of the Association, the unit owners and their employees, agents, tenants and invitees, and a waiver of any defenses based on co-insurance or on invalidity arising from the acts of the insured; (ii) a waiver by the insurer of its right to repair and reconstruct instead of paying cash; (iii) a provision that the policy cannot be cancelled, invalidated or suspended on account of the conduct of any unit owner or any employee, agent, tenant or invitee of any unit owner, or any officer, director, agent or employee of the Association, without a prior demand in writing and delivered to the Association to cure the defect and the allowance of reasonable time thereafter within which the defect may be cured by the Association, any unit owner or any mortgagee; (iv) a provision that any "other insurance" clause in the policy shall exclude from its scope any policies of the individual unit owners; (v) a provision that the coverage may not be cancelled or substantially modified (including cancellation for nonpayment of premium) without at least thirty days written notice to any and all of the insured thereunder, including mortgagees; and (vi) a provision that the coverage will not be prejudiced by any act or neglect of the owners of the units when said act or neglect is not within the control of the Association, or any failure of the Association to comply with any warranty or condition regarding any portion of the property over which the Association has no control.

12.04 Adjustment of Losses. Exclusive authority to adjust losses under insurance policies obtained by the Association shall be vested in the Association; provided, however, that no mortgagee shall be prohibited from participating in the settlement negotiations, if any, related thereto.

12.05 Individual Insurance by Unit Owners. It shall be the individual responsibility of each unit owner, at its sole cost and expense, to provide, as it sees fit any insurance coverage not required to be maintained by the Association. Any unit owner who obtains an individual insurance policy rejecting any risk as to which insurance is carried by the Association shall file a copy of such individual policy with the Association within thirty days after the purchase thereof.

12.06 Handling of Casualty Insurance Proceeds. All insurance policies purchased by and in the name of the Association shall provide that proceeds covered in casualty loss shall be paid to the Association. The Association shall receive such proceeds as are paid and delivered to it and hold the same in trust for the benefit of the unit owners and their mortgagees as follows:

(a) Proceeds on account of damage to the common elements not involving a unit shall be held to the extent of the undivided interest of each unit owner, for each unit owner, such interest to be equal to the undivided interest of each unit owner in and to the common elements.

(b) Proceeds on account of damage to units (or on account of damage to common elements involving a unit) shall be held for the owners of the damaged units in proportion to the cost of repairing the damage suffered by each unit owner, which cost shall be determined by the Board of Directors.

(c) In the event a mortgagee endorsement has been issued as to any unit under the policy under which such proceeds are paid, the share of that unit owner shall be held in trust for the unit owner and the mortgagee, as their interest may appear. Unless a determination is made not to repair or reconstruct pursuant to Section 12.07(b) hereof, and such proceeds, or such portion thereof as may be required for such purpose, shall be disbursed by the Association as payment of the cost and any expenses of repair or reconstruction, as hereinafter provided. Any proceeds remaining after payment of all cost and expenses of repair or reconstruction shall be common profits.

12.07 Damage and Destruction.

(a) Immediately after any damage or destruction by fire or other casualty to all or any portion of the property covered by insurance written in the name of the Association, the Association shall proceed with the filing and adjustment of all claims and losses arising under such insurance and obtain reliable and detailed estimates of the cost of repair or reconstruction of the damaged or destroyed property. Repair or reconstruction, as used in this paragraph, means repairing or restoring the property to substantially the same condition that existed prior to the fire or other casualty with each unit and the common elements having the same vertical and horizontal boundaries as before the casualty.

(continued)

EXHIBIT 11–2
Condominium
Declaration
(continued)

(b) Any damage or destruction shall be repaired or reconstructed unless: (i) the condominium is terminated pursuant to, subject to and in accordance with the provisions of the Act and this Declaration; (ii) the damaged or destroyed portion of the property is withdrawn from the condominium pursuant to, subject to and in accordance with the provisions of the Act; or (iii) the unit owners of the damaged or destroyed units, if any, and their mortgagees, together with the unit owners of other units to which two-thirds of the votes in the Association appertain and the mortgagees, exclusive of the votes appertaining to any damaged or destroyed units, agree not to repair or reconstruct such damage or destruction, pursuant to, subject to and in accordance with the provisions of the Act. Any such determination shall be conclusively made, if at all, not more than ninety days after the date of the casualty. Should a determination be made to terminate the condominium, as herein provided, then the insurance proceeds paid to the Association and held by it on account of such casualty shall be common profits, to be held and disbursed pursuant to, subject to and in accordance with Section 12.06 hereof. Should a determination be made to withdraw from the condominium the damaged portion of the property or not to repair or reconstruct the damage or destruction, as herein provided, then the insurance proceeds paid to the Association and held by it on account of such casualty shall be disbursed by the Association in accordance with the manner in which such proceeds are held by the Association, pursuant to Section 12.06 hereof. Any remittances with respect to units as to which mortgagee endorsements have been issued on the policies under which the proceeds were paid shall be payable to the unit owner and its mortgagee jointly, as their interest may appear.

(c) If the damage or destruction for which the insurance proceeds are paid is to be repaid and such proceeds are not sufficient to defray the cost thereof, the Association may levy an additional assessment against all unit owners in sufficient amounts to provide funds to pay such excess cost of repair or reconstruction. Further, additional assessments may be made in a like manner and any time during or following the completion of any repair or reconstruction. The proceeds from insurance and assessments, if any, received by the Association hereunder when the damage or destruction is to be repaired or reconstructed shall be disbursed as provided for in Section 12.06 hereof.

12.08 Non-Liability and Indemnity of Officers and Directors of the Association and Declarant. The officers and directors of the Association and Declarant shall not be personally liable to any unit owner for any mistake of judgment or for any other act or omission of any nature whatsoever in administering the Association, except for acts or omission which constitute gross negligence or willful misconduct. The Association shall indemnify and hold harmless each of the officers and directors of the Association and Declarant and their respective legal representatives, successors and assigns, from any liability, cost or expense arising out of any act or omission in administering the Association which is not deemed to be gross negligence or willful misconduct.

ARTICLE 13

Damage or Destruction

13.01 Obligation to Rebuild. In the event of damage to or destruction of the whole or any part of the building, the Association shall repair, rebuild or restore the building or such part as has been damaged or destroyed.

13.02 Compliance With Condominium Instruments. Such reparation, rebuilding or restoration shall be carried out in accordance with the provisions of the Act and the By-Laws of the Association.

ARTICLE 14

Sale or Leasing of Units

14.01 Notice Provisions. Any owner who sells or who leases his unit shall give notice in writing to the Board of Directors of such sale or of such lease stating the name and address of the purchaser or lessee and such other information as the Board may reasonably require. The Board of Directors shall have authority to make and to enforce reasonable rules and regulations in order to enforce this provision, including the right to impose fines constituting a lien upon the unit sold or leased, pursuant to the Act; provided, however, no rule or regulation may create a right of first refusal in the Association

(continued)

EXHIBIT 11–2
Condominium
Declaration
(continued)

or any other third party, this paragraph solely creating the obligation of an owner to give notice to sell or lease. Notice, as required herein, shall be given, in the case of a lease, not later than fifteen (15) days after commencement of the lease and, in the case of a sale, not later than the closing of the sale.

14.02 Leasing Provision. Units may be rented only in their entirety; no fraction or portion may be rented. There shall be no subleasing of units or assignment of leases. With the exception of a lender in possession of a condominium unit following a default in a first mortgage, a foreclosure proceeding, or any deed or other arrangement in lieu of foreclosure, no unit owner shall be permitted to lease his unit for transient or hotel purposes. All leases and lessees are subject to the provisions of the condominium units and rules and regulations adopted pursuant thereto. Any lease agreement shall be required to provide that the terms of a lease shall be subject in all respects to the provisions of the Declaration and By-Laws and that any failure by the lessee to comply with the terms of such documents shall be a default under the lease. All leases shall be in writing. Other than units owned by the Declarant and with the exception of a lender in possession of a condominium unit following a default in a first mortgage, a foreclosure proceeding, or any deed or other arrangement in lieu of foreclosure, all rentals must be for a term of no less than one year. The unit owner must make available to the tenant copies of the Declaration, By-Laws and Rules and Regulations.

14.03 Any unit owner or person having executed a lease or a contract for the purchase of a condominium unit requesting a recordable statement certifying to the receipt by the Association of the notice herein specified, or the waiver of the Association's rights to receive such notice shall be furnished such a statement. Any such statement shall be binding on the Association and every unit owner. Payment of a fee, not exceeding $25.00, may be required as a prerequisite to the issuance of such a statement.

ARTICLE 15

Eminent Domain

15.01 If any portion of the Condominium property is taken by eminent domain, the award shall be allocated as provided in Official Code of _____(State)_____ , Section _____ .

ARTICLE 16

Amendment of Condominium Instruments

16.01 By Owners. The Condominium instruments, including this Declaration, shall be amended only by the agreement of both the owners and mortgagees of units to which two-thirds (2/3) of the votes in the Association appertain, as provided in the By-Laws.

ARTICLE 17

Termination of the Condominium

17.01 Clairemont Oaks, a Condominium, shall be terminated only by the agreement of four-fifths (4/5) of the owners of the units and of all mortgagees of such units unless, in the case of the destruction of the entire development by fire or other casualty, following which the owners of the units decide not to rebuild, in which case the provisions of the By-Laws and the Declaration shall apply.

ARTICLE 18

Control by Declarant

18.01 Generally. The Declarant is hereby authorized in accordance with the By-Laws of the Association, incorporated herein by reference, to appoint and remove any member or members of the Board of Directors and any officer or officers of the Association with or without cause until the first of the following two occur:

(a) The third anniversary of the date of recording of this Declaration, or

(b) The date as of which units to which seventy percent (70%) of the undivided interests in the common elements have been conveyed by Declarant to unit owners other than a person or persons constituting Declarant, or

(continued)

EXHIBIT 11–2
Condominium
Declaration
(continued)

(c) The date as of which the Declarant surrenders the authority to appoint and remove all members of the Board of Directors by express amendment to the Declaration executed and recorded by the Declarant.

ARTICLE 19

Perpetuities

19.01 Should any of the provisions of this Declaration be unlawful, void or voidable for violation of the rule against perpetuities, then such provision shall continue only until twenty-one (21) years after the date that is ninety (90) years from and after the date of this Declaration.

ARTICLE 20

Miscellaneous

20.01 Notices. Notices provided for in the Act, this Declaration or the Articles or By-Laws shall be in writing, and shall be addressed to any unit owner at his/her or their unit at the condominium or at such other address as hereinafter provided. Notices to the Association shall be in writing and addressed to the President of the Association at his or her unit at the condominium, or to such other address as may hereafter be provided for and a written notice of such change of address furnished to all unit owners. Any unit owner may designate a different address for notices to him by giving written notice to the Association. Notices addressed as above shall be deemed delivered three business days after mailing by United States Registered or Certified Mail, or when delivered in person. Upon written request to the Association, the holder of any interest in any unit shall be given a copy of all notices to be given to the owner whose unit is subject to such interest.

20.02 Right to Notice, Attend Meetings and Inspection of Records. The owner of any interest in any unit, including any mortgagee, and any insurer or grantor of such mortgage, in addition to the rights set forth in the Act, shall have the right to inspect the books and records of the Association, including financial records, upon reasonable notice, and the right to attend and speak at any meeting of the Association, provided, however, no person other than a member as such shall have any voting rights. If the owner of any such interest files with the Association a written request, the Association shall have the right to notify such party of any violation by the owner of such unit, provided, however, that in no event shall the Association agree with any such party to furnish such notice unless such party agrees in writing that in no event shall the Association be liable for any claim or damages as a result of any failure to give such notice. Upon written request, any mortgagee shall have the right to receive a financial statement for the immediately preceding fiscal year.

20.03 Headings. The headings, sections and subsections in this Declaration and the Articles and By-Laws are for convenience or reference only and shall not in any way be deemed to limit or construe the intent of the parties or interpret the meaning of any document.

20.04 Number and Gender. As used in this Declaration, the singular shall include the plural, the masculine, feminine and neuter pronouns shall be fully interchangeable, where the context so requires.

20.05 Severability. If any provision of this Declaration or the Articles or By-Laws is held invalid, the validity of the remainder of this Declaration and the Articles and By-Laws shall not be affected thereby, and the remainder thereof shall be construed as if such invalid part was never included herein or therein.

20.06 Rights and Obligations. Each successor in title of the Declarant with respect to any part of the property, by the acceptance of a Deed of Conveyance, accepts the same subject to all restrictions, conditions, covenants, reservations, liens and charges created or reserved by this Declaration. All rights, benefits and privileges hereby imposed shall be deemed and taken to be covenants running with the land, and shall be binding inured to the benefit of any person having any interest or estate in the property, or any portion thereof.

(continued)

EXHIBIT 11–2
Condominium
Declaration
(continued)

ARTICLE 21
Author

21.01 This Declaration was prepared by _____ , with an office address of_____

_____.

IN WITNESS WHEREOF, the Declarant has executed this Declaration under seal on the _____ day of _____ , 20___.

DECLARANT:

Signed, sealed and delivered in the presence of:

THE FARRIS CORPORATION

_____
Unofficial Witness

_____

_____
Notary Public

By: _____
President

County of Appointment:
Expiration of Commission:
[Notary Seal]

Attest: _____
Secretary

[CORPORATE SEAL]

EXHIBIT 11–3
State Condominium
Code Requirements for
Condominium Plat

44-3-83. Recording of plats and plans; contents; completion of structural improvements; certification by registered architect or engineer.

(a) Prior to the first conveyance of a condominium unit, there shall be recorded one or more plats of survey showing the location and dimensions of the submitted property; the location and dimensions of all structural improvements located on any portion of the submitted property; the intended location and dimensions of all contemplated structural improvements committed to be provided by the declaration on any portion of the submitted property; and, to the extent feasible, the location and dimensions of all easements appurtenant to the submitted property or otherwise submitted to this article as part of the common elements. With respect to all such structural improvements, the plats shall indicate which, if any, have not been begun by use of the phrase "Not Yet Begun." No structural improvement which contains or constitutes all or part of any unit or units and which is located on any portion of the submitted property shall be commenced on any portion of the submitted property after the recording of the plats. The declarant shall complete all structural improvements depicted on the plats, subject only to such limitations, if any, as may be expressly stated in the declaration with respect to those labeled "Not Yet Begun" on the plats, provided that, within six months after written notice from the association, the declarant shall be obligated to complete within a reasonable time every structural improvement actually commenced on the submitted property, notwithstanding any provision of the declaration, unless the declarant removes within a reasonable time all portions of any such structural improvement and restores the surface of the land affected thereby to substantially the same condition as that which existed prior to commencement of any such structural improvement; and provided, further, that nothing contained in this sentence shall exempt the declarant from any contractual liability to complete any such structural improvement. If the submitted property consists of noncontiguous parcels, the plats shall indicate the approximate distances between such parcels unless such information is disclosed in the declaration. If, with respect to any portion or portions, but less than all, of the submitted property, the unit owners are to own only a leasehold or estate for years,

(continued)

the plats shall show the location and dimensions of any such portion or portions and shall label each such portion by use of the phrase "Leased Land." To the extent feasible, the plats shall show all easements to which the submitted property or any portion thereof is subject. The plats shall also show all encroachments by or on any operation of the submitted property. In the case of any units which have vertical boundaries lying wholly or partially outside of structures for which plans pursuant to subsection (b) of this Code section are recorded, the plats shall show the location and dimensions of the vertical boundaries to the extent that they are not shown on the plans; and the units or portions thereof thus depicted shall bear their identifying numbers. Each plat shall be certified as to its accuracy and compliance with this subsection by a registered land surveyor. The specification within this subsection of items that shall be shown on the plats shall not be construed to mean that the plats shall not also show all other items customarily shown or required by law to be shown for land title surveys.

(b) There shall be recorded prior to the first conveyance of a condominium unit:

(1) Plans which have been prepared, signed, and sealed by a registered architect or registered engineer of every structure which contains or constitutes all or part of any unit or units located on or within any portion of the submitted property, which plans shall show:

(A) The location and dimensions of the exterior walls and roof of such structures;

(B) The walls, partitions, floors, and ceilings as constitute the horizontal boundaries, if any, and the vertical boundaries of each unit, including convertible space, to the extent that such boundaries lie within or coincide with the boundaries of such structures; and

(C) The identifying numbers of all units or portions thereof depicted on the plans; and

(2) A certification by such architect or engineer to the effect that he has visited the site and viewed the property and that, to the best of his knowledge, information, and belief:

(A) The exterior walls and roof of each structure are in place as shown on the plans; and

(B) Such walls, partitions, floors, and ceilings, to the extent shown on said plans, as constitute the horizontal boundaries, if any, and the vertical boundaries of each unit, including convertible space, have been sufficiently constructed so as to establish clearly the physical boundaries of such unit.

In addition, each convertible space depicted in the plans shall be labeled as such by use of the phrase "CONVERTIBLE SPACE." Unless the condominium instruments expressly provide otherwise, it shall be presumed that, in the case of any unit not wholly contained within or constituting one or more of the structures, the horizontal boundaries extend, in the case of each unit, at the same elevation with regard to any part of such unit lying outside of such structures, subject to the following exception: in the case of any unit which does not lie over any other unit other than basement units, it shall be presumed that the lower horizontal boundary, if any, of that unit lies at the level of the ground with regard to any part of that unit lying outside of the structures.

(b.1) There shall be recorded prior to the first conveyance of a condominium unit plans of every structure which contains or constitutes all or part of any unit or units located on or within any portion of the submitted property and a certification by a registered architect or registered engineer to the effect that he has visited the site and viewed the property and that, to the best of his knowledge, information, and belief:

(1) The foundation, structural members, exterior walls, and roof of each such structure are complete and in place as shown on the plans;

(2) The walls, partitions, floors, and ceilings, to the extent shown on the plans, as constituting or coinciding with the vertical and horizontal boundaries of each unit, including convertible space, within each such structure, are sufficiently complete and in place to establish clearly the physical boundaries of such unit and that such physical boundaries are as shown on the plans; and

(3) Each such structure, to the extent of its stage of completion at that time, is constructed substantially in accordance with such plans.

The plans shall show the location and dimensions of the horizontal boundaries, if any, and the vertical boundaries of each unit to the extent that such boundaries lie within or coincide with the boundaries

(continued)

of such structures, and the units, or portions thereof, thus depicted shall bear their identifying numbers. In addition, each convertible space depicted in the plans shall be labeled as such by use of the phrase "CONVERTIBLE SPACE." Unless the condominium instruments expressly provide otherwise, it shall be presumed that, in the case of any unit not wholly contained within or constituting one or more of the structures, the horizontal boundaries extend, in the case of each unit, at the same elevation with regard to any part of such unit lying outside of such structures, subject to the following exception: in the case of any unit which does not lie over any other unit other than basement units, if shall be presumed that the lower horizontal boundary, if any, of that unit lies at the level of the ground with regard to any part of that unit lying outside of the structures. This subsection shall apply to any condominium created prior to July 1, 1980, or to the expansion of any such condominium.

(c) Prior to the first conveyance of a condominium unit located on any portion of any additional property being or having been added to an expandable condominium, there shall be recorded new plats of survey conforming to the requirements of subsection (a) of this Code section and, with regard to any structures on the property being or having been added, plans conforming to the requirements of subsection (b) of this Code section or certifications, conforming to the certification requirements of subsection (b) of this Code section, of plans previously recorded.

(d) When converting all or any portion of any convertible space into one or more units or limited common elements, the declarant shall record, with regard to the structure or portion thereof constituting that convertible space, plans showing the location and dimensions of the horizontal boundaries, if any, and the vertical boundaries of each unit formed out of such space. The plans shall be certified by a registered architect or registered engineer in accordance with the certification requirements of subsection (b) of this Code section.

(e) When any portion of the submitted property is withdrawn, there shall be recorded a plat or plats showing the portion of the submitted property withdrawn and the remaining submitted property, which plat or plats shall be certified as provided in subsection (a) of this Code section.

EXHIBIT 11-4
Articles of
Incorporation for
Condominium
Association

ARTICLES OF INCORPORATION
OF
CLAIREMONT OAKS CONDOMINIUM ASSOCIATION, INC.

ARTICLE 1

The name of the corporation shall be:

CLAIREMONT OAKS CONDOMINIUM ASSOCIATION, INC.

ARTICLE 2

The corporation is organized pursuant to the provisions of the ____(State)____ Nonprofit Corporation Code.

ARTICLE 3

The corporation shall have perpetual duration.

(continued)

EXHIBIT 11-4
Articles of
Incorporation for
Condominium
Association
(continued)

ARTICLE 4

The corporation shall have no stock or stockholders; it is not organized and shall not operate for profit or pecuniary gain; and no part of the net earnings of the corporation shall inure to the benefit of any member, director, officer of any private individual except that, pursuant to proper authorization, reasonable compensation may be paid for services rendered to or for the corporation affecting one or more of its purposes. No substantial part of the activities of the corporation shall be for carrying on of propaganda, or otherwise attempting to influence legislation, and the corporation shall not participate in or intervene in (including publishing or distributing statements) any political campaign on behalf of any candidate for public office.

ARTICLE 5

The purposes for which the corporation is organized are: to provide for the administration of a condominium to be known as Clairemont Oaks, A Condominium; to provide for the maintenance, repair, replacement and operation of portions of the condominium; to promote the health, safety and welfare of the owners and occupants of the condominium; to exercise all rights and privileges and perform all duties and obligations of the corporation as set forth in the ___(State)___ Condominium Act and in the Declaration for Clairemont Oaks, A Condominium to be recorded in the Office of the Clerk of the Superior Court of Wayne County, ___(State)___; and to perform such related functions as the board of directors of the corporation shall from time to time determine.

ARTICLE 6

In addition to, but not in limitation of, the general powers conferred by law, the corporation shall have the power to own, acquire, construct, operate and maintain property, buildings, structures and other facilities incident thereto; to supplement municipal or governmental services; to fix and collect assessments to be levied against and with respect to the condominium units and the owners thereof which assessments shall be a lien and permanent charge on said units as well as the personal obligation of said owners; to enforce any and all covenants, restrictions and agreements applicable to the condominium; to buy, hold, lease, sell, rent, manage and otherwise deal in property of every kind and description, whether real or personal; to borrow money, issue promissory notes and other obligations and evidences of indebtedness and to secure the same by mortgage, deed, security deed, pledge or otherwise; and, insofar as permitted by law, to do any other thing that, in the opinion of the board of directors, will promote, directly or indirectly, the health, safety, welfare, common benefit or enjoyment of the unit owners and occupants of said units; enhance, preserve or maintain property values within the condominium; enhance, preserve or maintain the appearance of the condominium and its surroundings; or be necessary, proper, useful or incidental to the carrying out of the functions for which the corporation is organized.

ARTICLE 7

The address of the initial registered office of the corporation shall be c/o _____ at _____, and the name of its original agent at such address is _____.

ARTICLE 8

The directors of the corporation shall be elected or appointed at the time and in the manner as provided in the Bylaws of the corporation as the same may from time to time be amended.

(continued)

EXHIBIT 11–4
Articles of
Incorporation for
Condominium
Association
(continued)

ARTICLE 9

The initial board of directors of the corporation shall number _____ (_____) and the name and address of each person who is to serve as a member thereof is as follows:

Name

Address

_____   _____

    _____

_____   _____

    _____

_____   _____

    _____

ARTICLE 10

The corporation shall have one class of members. Each owner of a condominium unit comprising a portion of Clairemont Oaks, A Condominium, shall automatically be a member of the corporation, which membership shall continue during the period of ownership by such unit owner Pursuant to the provisions of the _____(State)_____ Condominium Act, the number of votes in the corporation allocated to each condominium unit is set forth in the Declaration for Clairemont Oaks, A Condominium. Said votes shall be cast under such rules and procedures as may be prescribed in the Bylaws of the corporation, as amended from time to time, or by law.

ARTICLE 11

These Articles of Incorporation may be amended as by law provided pursuant to resolution duly adopted by the board of directors and by at least two-thirds of the votes which members present in person or by proxy at a duly called meeting are entitled to cast; provided, however, that no members shall be entitled to vote on amendments to these Articles of Incorporation for the sole purpose of complying with the requirements of any governmental or quasigovernmental entity authorized to fund or guarantee mortgages on individual condominium units, as such requirements may exist from time to time, which amendments may be adopted only at a meeting of the board of directors upon receiving the vote of a majority of the directors then in office.

ARTICLE 12

The corporation may be dissolved as by law provided pursuant to resolution duly adopted by the board of directors and by at least four-fifths of the votes of the members of the corporation.

ARTICLE 13

The name of the incorporator is _____, whose address is _____.

IN WITNESS WHEREOF, the incorporator has executed these Articles of Incorporation.

_____

(continued)

EXHIBIT 11–4
**Articles of
Incorporation for
Condominium
Association
(continued)**

CONSENT TO APPOINTMENT AS REGISTERED AGENT

To: Secretary of State
     Ex-Officio Corporation
     Commissioner
     State of _____

    I, _____, do hereby consent to serve as registered agent for the corporation Clairemont Oaks Condominium Association, Inc.

    This _____ day of _____, 20_____.

                                          _____

Address of Registered Agent:

_____

_____

_____

EXHIBIT 11–5
**Condominium
Association Bylaws**

BYLAWS OF
CLAIREMONT OAKS CONDOMINIUM ASSOCIATION, INC.

ARTICLE 1

Name and Location

    Section 1. Name. The name of the association is Clairemont Oaks Condominium Association, Inc., a _____(State)_____ nonprofit membership corporation, hereinafter referred to as the "Association."

    Section 2. Location. The principal office of the Condominium shall be located in Wayne County, (State) . Meetings of members and directors may be held at such places within the State of _____, County of Wayne as may be designated from time to time by the Board of Directors.

ARTICLE 2

Definitions

    Section 1. General. The terms used in these Bylaws, unless otherwise specified or unless the context otherwise requires, shall have the meanings specified in Official Code of ____(State)____ , Section _____ and the Declaration for Clairemont Oaks, A Condominium (hereinafter called the "Declaration"). Statutory references shall be construed as meaning the referenced statute or portion thereof as the same may exist from time to time.

(continued)

EXHIBIT 11–5
Condominium
Association Bylaws
(continued)

ARTICLE 3

Membership and Voting Rights

Section 1. Membership. Each unit owner shall automatically be a member of the Association, which membership shall continue during the period of ownership by such unit owner.

Section 2. Voting Rights. The Association shall have one class of voting membership which shall consist of all unit owners. Such owners shall be entitled to exercise voting rights as provided in the __(State)__ Condominium Act, the Declaration and as prescribed herein. The number of votes allocated to each unit is as set forth in the Declaration. When a unit is owned by other than one or more natural persons, the person entitled to cast the vote for such unit shall be designated by a certificate signed by the record owner of such unit and filed with the Secretary. Each such certificate shall be valid until revoked, superseded by a subsequent certificate or a change occurs in the ownership of such unit. When a unit is owned by more than one natural person, they may, without being required to do so, designate the person entitled to cast the vote for such unit as provided above. In the event they do not designate such a person, the following provisions shall apply:

(a) If only one is present at a meeting, the person present shall be counted for purposes of a quorum and may cast the vote for the unit, just as though he owned it individually, and without establishing the concurrence of the absent person or persons.

(b) If more than one of such owners, whether or not all of them, are present at a meeting and concur, any one of the owners may cast the vote for the owners.

(c) If more than one of such owners, whether or not all of them, are present at a meeting and are unable to concur in their decision upon any subject requiring a vote, they shall lose their right to vote on that subject at that meeting.

The votes of the unit owners shall be cast under such rules and procedures as may be prescribed in the Declaration or in these Bylaws, as amended from time to time, or by law.

Section 3. Suspension of Voting Rights. During any period in which a unit owner shall be in default in payment of any assessment, the voting rights of such unit owner may be suspended by the Board of Directors until such assessment has been paid. Such rights of a unit owner may also be suspended, for a period not to exceed 30 days, for violation of any rules and regulations established by the Board of Directors.

ARTICLE 4

Meetings of Unit Owners

Section 1. Annual Meetings. The first annual meeting of the unit owners shall be called by the President upon request of the Declarant and shall be held within 12 months following the incorporation of the Association. Each subsequent regular annual meeting of the owners shall be held on the same day of the same month of each year thereafter unless otherwise provided by the unit owners at any previous meeting. If the day for the annual meeting of the unit owners is a legal holiday, the meeting will be held on the first day following which is not a legal holiday.

Section 2. Special Meetings. Special meetings of the unit owners may be called at any time by the President or by the Board of Directors, or upon written request of the unit owners who are entitled to vote at least _____ (___%) of the votes of the membership.

Section 3. Notice of Meetings. Written notice of each meeting of the unit owners shall be given by, or at the direction of, the Secretary or person authorized to call the meeting at least 21 days in advance of any annual or regularly scheduled meeting, and at least seven days in advance of any other meeting, stating the time, place and purpose of such meeting. Such notice shall be delivered personally or sent by United States mail, postage prepaid, to all unit owners of record at such address or addresses as any of them may have designated, or, if no other address has been so designated, at the address of their respective units. Such notice shall also be sent by United States mail, postage prepaid, to each institutional holder of a first mortgage on a unit having theretofore requested same in writing. Each such holder shall be permitted to designate a representative to attend each such meeting without voice or vote except pursuant to Section 5 of this Article 4.

(continued)

EXHIBIT 11–5
Condominium
Association Bylaws
(continued)

Section 4. Quorum. The presence at the meeting of unit owners and/or proxies entitled to cast more than one-third of the votes of the membership shall constitute a quorum for any action except as otherwise expressly provided in the _____(State)_____ Condominium Act or in the Declaration. If, however, such quorum shall not be present or represented at any meeting, the unit owners and/or proxies entitled to cast a majority of the votes threat shall have the power to adjourn the meeting from time to time, without notice other than announcement at the meeting, until a quorum as aforesaid shall be present or be represented.

Section 5. Proxies. Subject to the provisions of Article 3, Section 2, hereof, at all meetings of the unit owners, each unit owner may vote in person or by proxy. All proxies shall be in writing and filed with the Secretary. Each proxy shall be revocable, shall automatically cease upon conveyance by a unit owner of his unit and shall be effective only for the meeting specified therein and any adjournment thereof.

Section 6. Order of Business. The order of business at all annual meetings of the owners shall be as follows:

(a) Roll call.
(b) Proof of notice of meeting.
(c) Reading of minutes of preceding meeting.
(d) Reports of officers.
(e) Report of Board of Directors.
(f) Reports of committees.
(g) Election of Directors.
(h) Unfinished business.
(i) New business.

Section 7. Decisions of Unit Owners. Unless otherwise expressly provided in the _____(State)_____ Condominium Act, the Declaration or these Bylaws, a majority of the votes cast on any particular issue shall be necessary to adopt decisions at any meeting of the unit owners. When the _____(State)_____ Condominium Act, the Declaration or these Bylaws require the approval or consent of all or a specified percentage of mortgagees and/or other lien holders, no decision or resolution duly adopted by the unit owners shall be effective or valid until such approval or consent shall be obtained. During such time as the Declarant has the right to control the Association pursuant to the provisions of Official Code of _____(State)_____, Section _____, no decision or resolution duly adopted by the unit owners shall be effective or valid until the Declarant's approval or consent shall have been obtained.

Section 8. Conduct of Meetings. The President shall preside over all meetings of the unit owners and the Secretary shall keep the minutes of the meetings and record in a minute book all resolutions duly adopted as well as a record of all transactions occurring at such meetings. The latest edition of Roberts Rules of Order shall govern the conduct of all meetings of the unit owners when not in conflict with the _____(State)_____ Condominium Act, the Declaration or these Bylaws.

ARTICLE 5

Board of Directors

Section 1. Number and Qualifications. Following expiration of the period of the Declarant's right to control the Association pursuant to the provisions of Official Code of _____(State)_____, Section _____, the Board of Directors of the Association shall be composed of three persons. With the exception of those persons appointed as directors by the Declarant pursuant to the provisions of Official Code of _____(State)_____, Section _____, each such person shall be a member of the Association or the spouse of a member.

Section 2. Election and Term of Office. Upon the termination of the Declarant's right to control the Association pursuant to the provisions of Official Code of _____(State)_____, Section _____, the Declarant shall give at least seven days' written notice to each member of a special meeting of the members, to be held not more than 30 days after the date of such termination,

(continued)

EXHIBIT 11–5
Condominium
Association Bylaws
(continued)

to elect a new board of directors. At such meeting, and at each annual meeting thereafter the unit owners shall elect three directors for a term of one year each. Except in the case of death, resignation or removal, each director elected by the members shall serve until the annual meeting at which his term expires and until his successor has been duly elected and qualified. Persons receiving the largest number of votes at any election of directors shall be elected whether or not such number constitutes a majority of the votes cast. Cumulative voting shall not be permitted.

Section 3. Removals; Vacancies. Following expiration of the period of the Declarant's right to control the Association pursuant to the provisions of Official Code of _____(State)_____, Section _____, any director may be removed from the Board of Directors with or without cause, by a majority vote of the unit owners theretofore entitled to elect such director. In the event of death or resignation of a director, his successor shall be selected by the remaining members of the board. In the event of removal of a director, his successor shall be elected by the unit owners theretofore entitled to elect such director. Any such successor shall serve for the unexpired term of his predecessor.

Section 4. Annual Organization Meeting. The first meeting of the Board of Directors following each annual meeting of the unit owners shall be held within ten days thereafter, at such time and place as shall be fixed by the newly elected directors at such annual meeting, and no notice shall be necessary in order legally to constitute such meeting.

Section 5. Regular Meetings. Regular meetings of the Board of Directors may be held at such time and place as shall be determined from time to time by the Board of Directors. Notice of the time and place of regular meetings shall be given to every director by mail or telephone at least three days prior to the date of such meeting.

Section 6. Special Meetings. Special meetings of the Board of Directors may be called by the President on two days notice to every director given by mail or telephone and stating the time, place and purpose of the meeting. Special meetings shall be called by the President or Secretary in like manner and on like notice on the written request of directors entitled to cast at least two votes at such meetings.

Section 7. Waiver of Notice; Action without Meeting. Whenever notice of a meeting of the Board of Directors is required to be given under any provision of these Bylaws, a written waiver thereof, executed by a director before or after the meeting and filed with the Secretary, shall be deemed equivalent to notice to the director executing the same. Attendance at a meeting by the director shall constitute a waiver of notice of such meeting by the director if such director attends the meeting without protesting prior thereto or at the meeting's commencement the lack of notice to him. Neither the business to be transacted at, nor the purpose of, any meeting of the Board of Directors need be specified in any written waiver of notice. Any action required or permitted to be taken at any meeting of the Board of Directors may be taken without a meeting provided that all directors consent to the action in writing and the written consents are filed with the records of the proceedings of the Board of Directors. Such consents shall be treated for all purposes as a vote at a meeting.

Section 8. Voting; Quorum of the Board; Adjournment of Meetings. At all meetings of the Board of Directors, each director shall be entitled to cast one vote. The presence in person of directors representing at least two-thirds of the votes of the Board of Directors shall be a quorum at any Board of Directors meeting and a majority of the votes present and voting shall bind the Board of Directors and the Association as to any matter within the powers and duties of the Board of Directors.

Section 9. Powers and Duties. The Board of Directors shall have the powers and duties necessary for administration of the affairs of the Association and may do all such acts and things except as by law or the Declaration may not be delegated to the Board of Directors by the unit owners. In exercising its powers and duties, the Board of Directors shall take as its standard the maintenance of the general character of the condominium as a residential community of the first class in the quality of its maintenance, use and occupancy. Such powers and duties of the Board of Directors shall be exercised in accordance with and subject to all provisions of the _____(State)_____ Condominium Act, the Declaration and these Bylaws and shall include without limitation powers and duties to:

(a) Operate, care for, maintain, repair and replace the common elements and employ personnel necessary or desirable therefor.

(b) Determine common expenses of the Association.

(continued)

EXHIBIT 11–5
Condominium
Association Bylaws
(continued)

(c) Collect assessments from the unit owners.

(d) Adopt and amend rules and regulations covering the details of the operation and use of the condominium.

(e) Open bank accounts on behalf of the Association and designate the signatories required therefor.

(f) Manage, control, lease as lessor, and otherwise deal with the common elements, including power to make shut-offs of common services and other interruptions of the normal functioning of the buildings to facilitate performance of any maintenance or repair work or the making of additions, alterations or improvements by the Association or the unit owners pursuant to provisions of the Declaration. The Board of Directors shall use reasonable efforts to disrupt the unit owners and occupants as little as possible in exercising such authority to effect shut-offs and other interruptions.

(g) Purchase, lease or otherwise acquire units offered for sale or lease or surrendered by their unit owners to the Association.

(h) Own, sell, lease, encumber, and otherwise deal in, but not vote with respect to, units owned by the Association.

(i) Obtain and maintain insurance for the condominium pursuant to the provisions of the Declaration.

(j) (1) Make additions and improvements to and alterations of the common elements, and (2) make repairs to and restoration of the property after damage or destruction by fire or other casualty, or as a result of condemnation.

(k) Enforce by any legal or equitable remedies available all obligations of the unit owners or any of them to the Association. Such enforcement power shall include, without limitation, the power to levy, as assessments, fines against unit owners for default in the performance of said obligations in such amounts as from time to time the Board of Directors may deem proper in the circumstances, but not in excess of $_____ for any one violation, counting each day a violation continues after notice from the Board of Directors as a separate violation. If any owner fails to pay a fine within ten days after notification thereof, the Board of Directors may levy, as assessments, additional fines to enforce payment of the initial fine.

(l) Appoint auditors of the Association.

(m) Employ a manager or managing agent and delegate thereto any duties of the Board of Directors under subparagraphs (a), (c), (e), (i) and (o) of this Section 9.

(n) Conduct litigation and be subject to suit as to any cause of action involving the common elements or arising out of the enforcement of the provisions of the ___(State)___ Condominium Act, the Declaration or these Bylaws.

(o) Make contracts in connection with the exercise of any of the powers and duties of the Board of Directors.

(p) Take all other actions the Board of Directors deems necessary or proper for the sound management of the condominium and fulfillment of the terms and provisions of the ___(State)___ Condominium Act, the Declaration and these Bylaws.

In the case of those powers and duties specified in the foregoing clauses (d), (g), (h), (j), (l), and (m), the Board of Directors need exercise the same only to the extent, if any, it deems necessary or desirable or is required to do so by vote of the unit owners. The Board of Directors shall not be obligated to take any action or perform any duty imposed upon it requiring an expenditure of funds unless in its opinion it shall have funds of the Association sufficient therefor.

ARTICLE 6

Officers

Section 1. Designation. The Principal officers of the Association shall be the President, the Vice President, the Secretary and the Treasurer, all of whom shall be elected by the Board of Directors. One person may hold the office of Secretary and Treasurer simultaneously. The Board of Directors may appoint an assistant treasurer, an assistant secretary, and such other officers as in its judgment may be necessary. The Vice President may also hold the office of assistant secretary and perform the functions

(continued)

EXHIBIT 11–5
Condominium
Association Bylaws
(continued)

thereof in the absence of the Secretary. The President and Vice President shall be members of the Board of Directors. Any other officers may be, but shall not be required to be, members of the Board of Directors.

Section 2. Election of Officers. The officers of the Association shall be elected annually by the Board of Directors at the organization meeting of each new Board of Directors and shall hold office at the pleasure of the Board of Directors. Any vacancy in an office shall be filled by the Board of Directors at a regular meeting of the Board of Directors, or at any special meeting of the Board of Directors called for such purpose.

Section 3. Removal of Officers. Upon the affirmative vote of a majority of the votes of the Board of Directors, any officer may be removed, either with or without cause, and his successor may be elected at any regular meeting of the Board of Directors, or at any special meeting of the Board of Directors called for such purpose.

Section 4. Multiple Offices. The offices of Secretary and Treasurer may be held by the same person. No person shall simultaneously hold more than one of any of the other offices except in the case of special offices created pursuant to Section 1 of this Article 6.

Section 5. President. The President shall be the chief executive of the Association. He shall preside at all meetings of the unit owners and of the Board of Directors. He shall have all of the general powers and duties which are incident to the office of president of a corporation, including, but not limited to, the power to appoint committees from among the unit owners from time to time as he may, in his sole discretion, deem appropriate to assist in the conduct of the affairs of the Association.

Section 6. Vice President. The Vice President shall take the place of the President and perform his duties whenever the President shall be absent or unable to act. If neither the President nor the Vice President is able to act, the Board of Directors shall appoint some other member of the Board of Directors to act in the place of the President on an interim basis. The Vice President shall also perform such other duties as shall, from time to time, be imposed upon him by the Board of Directors or by the President.

Section 7. Secretary. The Secretary shall keep the minutes of all meetings of the unit owners and of the Board of Directors and shall have charge of such books and papers as the Board of Directors may direct. He shall, in general, perform all the duties incident to the office of secretary of a corporation and such other duties as shall, from time to time, be imposed upon him by the Board of Directors or by the President.

Section 8. Treasurer. The Treasurer shall have the responsibility for Association funds and securities and shall be responsible for keeping full and accurate financial records and books of account showing all receipts and disbursements, and for the preparation of all required financial data; he shall be responsible for the deposit of all monies and other valuable effects in the name of the Association, in such depositories as may from time to time be designated by the Board of Directors, and he shall, in general, perform all the duties incident to the office of treasurer of a corporation and such other duties as shall, from time to time, be imposed upon him by the Board of Directors or by the President.

Section 9. Compensation. Unless otherwise expressly provided by the Board of Directors, no officer shall receive compensation from the Association for acting as such, but shall be entitled to reimbursement from the Association as a common expense for reasonable out-of-pocket disbursements made by him in the performance of his duties. No officer shall be obligated to make any such disbursements.

ARTICLE 7

Officers and Directors: General Provisions

Section 1. Contracts with Interested Parties. No contract or transaction between the Association and one or more of its officers or directors, or between the Association and any other entity in which one or more of the association's officers or directors are officers, directors, partners or trustees, or have a financial interest, shall be void or voidable solely for this reason, or solely because the Association's officer or director is present at or participates in the meeting of the Board of Directors which authorizes the contract or transaction, or solely because his or their votes are counted for such

(continued)

EXHIBIT 11–5
Condominium
Association Bylaws
(continued)

purpose, if (a) the material facts as to his interest and as to the contract or transaction are disclosed or are known to the Board of Directors and the Board of Directors in good faith authorized the contract or transaction by a vote sufficient for such purpose without counting the vote or votes of the interested director or directors; or (b) the material facts as to his interest and as to the contract or transaction are disclosed or are known to the unit owners entitled to vote thereon, and the contract or transaction is specifically approved or ratified in good faith by vote of such unit owners; or (c) the contract or transaction is fair as to the Association as of the time it is authorized, approved or ratified by the Board of Directors or the unit owners. Interested directors may be counted in determining the presence of a quorum at a meeting of the Board of Directors which authorizes the contract or transaction.

Section 2. Indemnification. Pursuant to the provisions of Section 12.08 of the Declaration, the Association shall indemnify its officers and directors to the extent provided in and subject to the limitations of the Declaration.

ARTICLE 8

Books and Records

Section 1. Books and Records. The Association shall keep such books and records as by law provided and shall make same available for inspection by any unit owner, any institutional holder of a first mortgage on a unit and their respective agents and attorneys, for any proper purpose at any reasonable time. In addition, an annual report of the receipts and expenditures of the Association, based upon an audit made by an independent public accountant, shall be rendered by the Board of Directors to all unit owners, and to each institutional holder of a first mortgage on a unit having theretofore requested same in writing, within three months after the end of each fiscal year.

ARTICLE 9

Amendments

Section 1. Amendments. These Bylaws may be amended only by the owners of the units to which two-thirds (2/3) of the votes in the Association cast their vote in person or by proxy at a meeting duly called for such purpose, written notice of which shall be delivered or sent to all unit owners not less than 21 days in advance of the meeting stating the time, place and purpose of such meeting and the subject matter of the proposed amendment or, in lieu of such vote, these Bylaws may be amended by an instrument duly executed by unit owners having at least two-thirds (2/3) of the entire voting interest of all unit owners. Amendments to these Bylaws for the sole purpose of complying with the requirements of any governmental or quasi-governmental entity authorized to fund or guarantee mortgages on individual condominium units, as such requirements may exist from time to time, may be effected by an instrument duly executed by a majority of the directors of the Association. Each such amendment shall be effective when adopted or at such later date as may be specified therein.

ARTICLE 10

Miscellaneous

Section 1. Conflicts. In the event of any conflict between the Declaration and these Bylaws, the Declaration shall control.

Section 2. Association Seal. The Association shall have a seal in circular form having within its circumference the words: _____.

Section 3. Fiscal Year. The fiscal year of the Association shall begin on the first day of January and end on the 31st day of December of every year, except that the first fiscal year shall begin on the date on which the Association was incorporated under the laws of the State of _____.

Surveys and Land Descriptions

Halfway down a bystreet of one of our New England towns stands a rusty wooden house, with seven acutely peaked gables, facing towards various points of the compass, and a huge, clustered chimney in the midst.

—Nathaniel Hawthorne, The House of the Seven Gables

OBJECTIVES

After reading this chapter you will be able to:

- Read and understand three types of land descriptions: government rectangular survey description, platted description, and metes and bounds description
- Review surveys
- Review a land survey for the accuracy of a legal description
- Prepare a legal description from a land survey

In a scene from the classic film *Cocoanuts,* Groucho Marx explains real estate to Chico Marx. Groucho asks Chico if he knows what a lot is. Chico replies, "Yeah, too much." Groucho then says, "I don't mean a whole lot, just a little lot with nothing on it." Chico responds, with all of Chico's logic, "Anytime you gotta too much, you gotta whole lot. A whole lot is too much, too much is a whole lot; same thing."

Regardless of whether you have a whole lot or a small lot with nothing on it, the lot has to be described. Real estate often is described casually, such as the "big white house on the corner of Wilton and Lullwater" or "the Harris farm at the end of the road." The competent practice of real estate law, however, demands that parcels of land be referred to more precisely. Every deed, mortgage, lease, easement, or other document that deals with land must state the exact size and location of the land according to an established system of land description. The purpose of the description is to fix the boundaries of the land and to distinguish the land in question from other land. A description that is too vague will render void any document in which it is incorporated. Therefore, a specific or correct description is called a **legal description,** because it makes the document legal and enforceable. In many states, legal descriptions are prepared by registered land surveyors, and the real estate legal assistant only needs to proofread the description for mistakes. In other states, the preparation of a legal description is the task of an attorney or a legal assistant working under the supervision of an attorney. The land surveyor prepares a survey or drawing of the property showing the various boundaries, and it is the duty of the legal assistant to prepare a written legal description locating and identifying the property's boundaries as shown on the survey.

legal description
Description of real property by a government survey, metes and bounds, or lot numbers of a recorded plat, which description is complete enough that a particular parcel of land can be located and identified.

THE SURVEY

survey
Visual presentation of the physical boundaries of real property. A survey is used to describe real property.

The word **survey** is derived from an old French word meaning "to look over." It refers to the evaluation of real property evidence to locate the physical limits of a particular parcel of land. The real property evidence considered by the surveyor typically consists of physical field evidence, written record evidence, and field measurements. The surveyor, having made an evaluation of the evidence, forms an opinion as to where the lines would be located.

EXHIBIT 12-1
As-Built Survey

SURVEY BY:	SURVEY FOR	
	PROPERTY OF	
	LOT 9 BLOCK B NORTH HIGHLANDS S/D	
	LAND LOT 2 17TH DISTRICT SECTION FULTON COUNTY, GEORGIA	
	SCALE: 1" = 30'	DATE:
	PLAT BOOK 12 PAGE 98	

The surveyor then prepares a map, or plat of survey, to communicate his or her opinion to others. The map or plat is colloquially known as the survey.

A survey may be a boundary survey, which locates the boundaries of the land in question and provides a description of the land. A surveyor may, however, be asked to prepare an **as-built survey.** An as-built survey locates all physical improvements on the land in relation to the boundary lines. On an as-built survey, the surveyor usually locates all fences, walls, driveways, pavements, building structures, and natural features such as streams and ponds. This information is necessary to determine both the presence of features that may limit the value or use of the land and the conformity with local ordinances regarding minimum building setbacks and other requirements. An example of an as-built survey is shown in Exhibit 12–1.

Note that the as-built survey reveals some interesting features of this property. For example, a 36-inch concrete pipe runs underneath the corner of the house. In addition, a sanitary sewer line runs underneath the house. Both the concrete pipe and the sewer line could cause substantial problems for the owner. These features may make it difficult for the owner to obtain a loan

as-built survey
Survey that locates all physical improvements on the land in relation to the boundary lines of the land.

Surveying Crew

on the property or to sell the property. The utility companies that own rights to the concrete pipe and sanitary sewer line also could damage the house if they had to repair the pipe and line.

For purposes of land descriptions, a survey should provide the legal assistant with the following information: (a) the state, county, land district, and section in which the property surveyed is located; (b) an indication of which direction on the survey is north; (c) a point of beginning for a land description; (d) courses and distances for each property line; (e) the name of the surveyor; (f) a scale for distances not shown on the survey; and (g) a legend of abbreviations or symbols used.

PREPARATION OF SURVEYS AND SURVEY STANDARDS

Surveys are generally prepared by professionals known as land surveyors. Land surveyors are generally licensed by the state and must pass certain examinations for competency. Educational requirements generally are a college degree with a major in engineering or mathematics.

Most surveyors prepare surveys based on standards developed jointly by **title insurance** companies and surveyors. These standards are generally referred to as the ALTA/ACSM standards. The ALTA/ACSM standards were last revised in 1999. A copy of the 1999 ALTA/ACSM standards are contained at the end of this chapter as Exhibit 12–18. The ALTA/ACSM requirements contain basic requirements with additional items which can be requested by the client. The more additional items that are required, the more expensive a survey will be, but the survey will also contain a more accurate picture, drawing, or representation of the property. Generally, a client or attorney, when ordering a survey, should provide the surveyor with (a) an accurate legal description of the property; (b) a current **title insurance commitment;** (c) copies of all recorded **easements,** servitudes, and covenants affecting the property; (d) copies of any appurtenant easements; and (e) names and deed data for all adjacent owners.

LAND DESCRIPTIONS

Three types of land description are in use in the United States: (1) government rectangular survey description, (2) platted description, and (3) metes and bounds description.

Government Rectangular Survey Description

When the United States was first being established, a standard system of describing land was needed to make areas of land easy to locate and available for sale by federal land offices. Thomas Jefferson headed a committee that in 1785 devised a method of dividing land into a series of rectangles. The rectangular survey system is used in describing land in Alabama, Alaska, Arizona, Arkansas, California, Colorado, Florida, Idaho, Illinois, Indiana, Iowa, Kansas, Louisiana, Michigan, Minnesota, Mississippi, Missouri, Montana, Nebraska, Nevada, New Mexico, North Dakota, Ohio, Oklahoma, Oregon, South Dakota, Utah, Washington, Wisconsin, and Wyoming (see Exhibit 12–2).

The rectangular survey system is based on sets of two intersecting hypothetical lines: **principal meridians** and **base lines.** Principal meridians are vertical lines that run north and south. Base lines are horizontal lines that run east and west. Using the principal meridians and base lines, a state can be divided into land areas that are easily identified. Within these identifiable areas of land, any particular section or parcel of land can be located.

Principal Meridians

A principal meridian is a surveyor's line that runs due north and south through a particular area or state. Principal meridians are identifiable in terms of their distance in degrees, minutes, and seconds west of the Greenwich meridian. The United States contains thirty-five principal meridians, and each is assigned a name or number for identification purposes. For example, the principal meridians running north and south in the state of Louisiana are called the Louisiana meridian and the St. Helena meridian.

Base Lines

A base line is a surveyor's line that runs due east and west and is identified as being a certain number of degrees north of the equator. Only one base line will cross each principal meridian; therefore, a parcel of land can be described as being a certain distance east or west of a given principal meridian and a certain distance north or south of a given base line.

Township or Range Lines

Using only principal meridians and base lines, the areas of land are still large, and surveying a particular parcel within the areas would be difficult. To simplify the task of identifying a smaller parcel, township and range lines have been established. **Township lines** run east and west at 6-mile intervals parallel with base lines and form strips of land or tiers called townships. Land on either side of the principal meridians is also divided into 6-mile strips by north and south lines called **range lines.** Squares of land formed by the intersecting township lines and range lines make up a grid, with each square within the grid having about 6 miles on each side. These squares, called **townships,** make up the basic units of the rectangular survey system. In theory, each township is 6 miles square and contains 36 square miles; in reality, a slight overage or shortage may exist because of difficulties encountered during surveying.

Correction Lines and Guide Meridians

Because the earth is round, all range lines gradually approach one another to the point where they eventually meet at the north pole. Thus, an accurate survey of a township would show its north boundary line to be about 50 feet shorter than its south boundary line. In the case of the fourth township north of the base line, the difference is four times as great, or about 200 feet. The rectangular survey system uses *correction lines* to compensate for these resulting shortages. Each fourth township line (24 miles) north and south of a base line is designated as a correction line. At each correction line, the east and west range lines are remeasured to the full distance of 6 miles apart. Each correction line serves as a new base line for townships that lie between it and the next correction line. *Guide meridians* are lines running due north and south at 24-mile intervals (every fourth range line) on either side of the principal meridian. They begin at the base line and extend to the first correction line in either direction. Guide meridians are not parallel to the principal meridians or to one another. Combined with the correction lines, these guide meridians divide land territories into areas about 24 miles apart.

Township Squares

A *township square* is identified by using (a) the location of the township's strip in which the township is located; (b) the designation of the range strip; and (c) the name or number of the

---

principal meridians
Imaginary north and south lines used in a government survey system. Meridians intersect the base lines to form a starting point for the measurement of land under that system.

base line
Imaginary east-west survey line used in the government survey system to establish township lines.

township lines
Lines in a government rectangular survey system, that run east and west at 6-mile intervals parallel with base lines and that form strips of land or tiers called townships.

range lines
Division of a state in a government survey system being a 6-mile-wide row of townships running north and south.

township
In a government survey, it is a square tract of land 6 miles on each side, containing 36 square miles.

EXHIBIT 12-2
Methods of Land
Description in the
United States

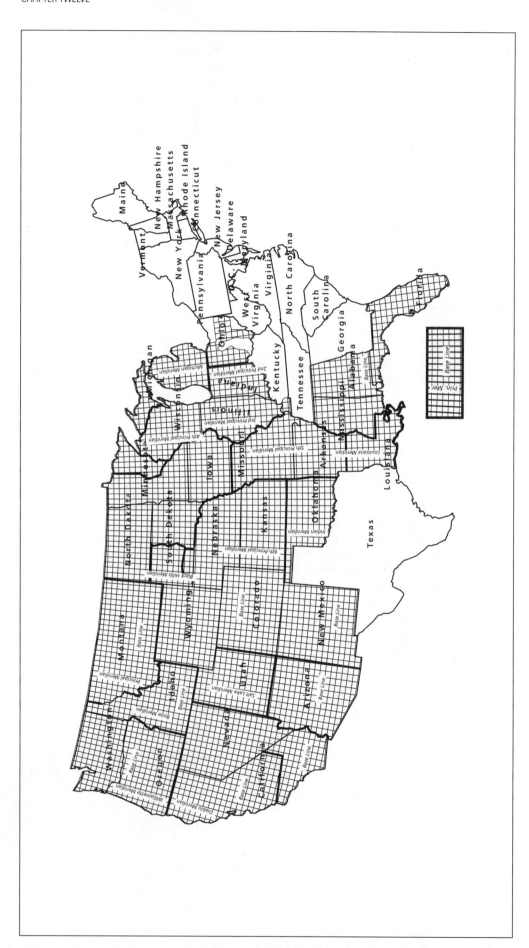

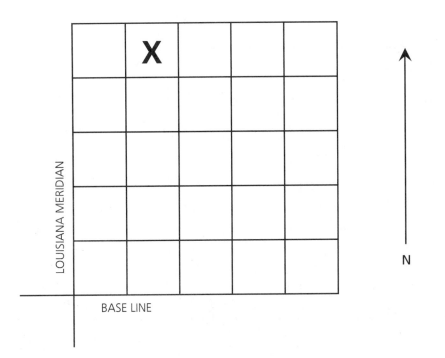

EXHIBIT 12–3
Principal Meridian and
Base Line

closest principal meridian. The first tier of squares immediately adjacent to and parallel with the base line is assigned Township 1, the second tier is assigned Township 2, and so on; therefore, each township in the first tier north of the base line is called Township 1 North of the base line; each in the second row is Township 2 North of the base line, and so on. Likewise, each township square in the first tier south of the base line is called Township 1 South; each township in the second tier is Township 2 South, and so on. Similarly, range numbers are assigned to each tier of township squares running parallel to a principal meridian, beginning with a row immediately adjacent to the principal meridian. Township squares in the first row east of the principal meridian are numbered Range 1 East of a particular principal meridian. Those in the second row east would be identified as Range 2 East, and so on. Similarly, townships located within range lines on the west side of the principal meridian would be identified as Range 1 West, Range 2 West, Range 3 West, and so on.

For example, in Exhibit 12–3, the township marked x is described as Township 5 North, Range 2 East of the Louisiana meridian. It is Township 5 North because the township is located within the fifth strip north of the base line. It is Range 2 East because the township is located within the second strip of land running north and south east of the Louisiana meridian. Finally, references are made to the Louisiana meridian because it is the closest principal meridian. The description can be abbreviated as T5 North, R2 East, Louisiana meridian.

Sections

The 36-mile township square is further subdivided into thirty-six **sections,** each section being 1 mile square and containing about 640 acres. The sections are numbered consecutively from 1 to 36, beginning in the northeast corner or upper right-hand corner of the township and proceeding west and east alternatively through the township, ending in the southeast corner with the number 36 (Exhibit 12–4).

Sections are subdivided into quarter sections and quarter sections can be further divided into halves or quarters. These halves of the quarter sections and quarter-quarter sections can be divided into smaller tracts. Exhibit 12–5 shows a section that has been subdivided. Note that in Exhibit 12–5, the SE 1/4 of the NE 1/4 of the section would be an area of land equal to 40 acres. The S 1/2 of the SW 1/4 of the NE 1/4 would be an area of land equal to 20 acres.

Exhibits 12–5 and 12–6 are helpful in visualizing land descriptions and understanding the rectangular survey system.

section
Division or parcel of land on a government survey comprising 1 square mile, or 640 acres.

EXHIBIT 12-4
Sections in a Township

N

6	5	4	3	2	1
7	8	9	10	11	12
18	17	16	15	14	13
19	20	21	22	23	24
30	29	28	27	26	25
31	32	33	34	35	36

W   E

S

EXHIBIT 12-5
One Section of Land

NW 1/4	NW 1/4 of NE 1/4	NE 1/4 of NE 1/4
	N 1/2 of SW 1/4 of NE 1/4	SE 1/4 of NE 1/4
	S 1/2 of SW 1/4 of NE 1/4	
W 1/2 of SW 1/4	E 1/2 of SW 1/4	N 1/2 of SE 1/4
		S 1/2 of SE 1/4

EXHIBIT 12–6
A Section

A SECTION OF LAND	ACRES	LINEAR CHAINS (1 Chain= 66 feet)	LINEAR RODS (1 Rod = 16 1/2 feet)	LINEAR FEET	SQUARE MILE
ONE FULL SECTION	640	80	320	5,280	1
QUARTER SECTION	160	40	160	2,640	1/2
QUARTER QUARTER SECTION	40	20	80	1,320	1/4
QUARTER QUARTER QUARTER SECTION	10	10	40	660	1/8
QUARTER QUARTER QUARTER QUARTER SECTION	21/2	5	20	330	1/16
QUARTER QUARTER QUARTER QUARTER QUARTER SECTION	5/8	21/2	10	165	1/32

Practice Note in Reading Government Rectangular Survey Descriptions

A government rectangular survey description is read backward. That is, you read from the end of the description to the beginning to determine the location and size of the property. For example, consider the following description:

> The North 1/2 of the Northeast 1/4 of the Southeast 1/4 of Section 5, Township 3 North, Range 2 East of the Louisiana Principal Meridian.

To locate this tract of land from the description above, you read the description starting with the end. First search for the Louisiana principal meridian on the map of the United States. Then on a regional map, find the township in which the property is located by counting two range strips east to the Louisiana meridian and three townships north of its corresponding base line. After locating section 5 of the township on the map, divide the section into quarters, the southeast quarter into quarters, and then the northeast 1/4 of the southeast 1/4 into halves. The north half of the northeast 1/4 of the southeast 1/4 is the property in question. The property contains 20 acres. The description can be abbreviated as N 1/2, NE 1/4, SE 1/4 of Section 5, T 3N, R 2E, of the Louisiana principal meridian.

Platted Description

The platted, or short form, description describes a piece of land by reference to a recorded survey or plat. The first requirement for a platted legal description is that a land surveyor prepare a **plat** showing the dimensions and boundaries of the land. The plat is then recorded in the county records where the land is located. Platted descriptions commonly are used in single-family home subdivisions, condominiums, and industrial parks. The local custom in some areas also may dictate that almost all property be platted.

plat
Survey of real property that often is recorded.

A legal assistant preparing a platted legal description need only make reference to the plat, indicating the book and page numbers where the plat has been recorded. Example 12–1 is an example of a platted legal description.

EXAMPLE 12-1

ALL THAT TRACT or parcel of land lying and being in Land Lot 106 of the 18th district of DeKalb County, Georgia, and being Lot 3, Block A, Unit 1 of Farris Subdivision as shown on Plat of Subdivision recorded at Plat Book 10, Page 84, DeKalb County, Georgia Records.

Practice Note on Platted Description

The platted legal description refers to a certain lot being shown on a certain plat recorded in a certain plat book and page within the county. For the legal description to be correct, the land being described must in fact appear as designated in the brief reference. It is a good idea to obtain a copy of the recorded plat to make certain that the property is adequately and correctly described.

The requirements for a platted description are as follows:

- Land lot
- District
- County
- State
- Subdivision name and lot, block, and unit numbers
- Recorded reference to plat book and page numbers

Metes and Bounds Description

A metes and bounds description sets forth and completely describes the boundary lines of the land. Example 12–2 is an example of a metes and bounds description. The survey from which it was taken is shown in Exhibit 12–7.

EXAMPLE 12-2

ALL THAT TRACT OR PARCEL OF LAND lying and being in Land Lot 99 of the 17th District of Fulton County, Georgia, and being more particularly described as follows:

TO FIND THE TRUE POINT OF BEGINNING, commence at a point formed by the intersection of the northerly side of Buckhead Avenue (a 60-foot right-of-way) and the easterly side of Peachtree Road; thence run east along the aforementioned right-of-way line of Buckhead Avenue a distance of 293.8 feet to an iron pin found and the TRUE POINT OF BEGINNING; thence running north 00 degrees 52 minutes 00 seconds west a distance of 82.13 feet to a nail found; thence north 21 degrees 48 minutes 38 seconds east a distance of 14.84 feet to a nail found on the southeasterly right-of-way line of Bolling Way; thence along the right-of-way line of Bolling Way north 37 degrees 19 minutes 27 seconds east a distance of 98.20 feet to a nail found; thence south 86 degrees 24 minutes 30 seconds east a distance of 13.5 feet to a nail found; thence south 00 degrees 52 minutes 00 seconds east a distance of 167.80 feet to an iron pin found on the northerly right-of-way line of Buckhead Avenue; thence south 86 degrees 02 minutes 22 seconds west along the northerly right-of-way line of Buckhead Avenue a distance of 80.0 feet to the TRUE POINT OF BEGINNING.

course
In a metes and bounds legal description, it is the direction of a property boundary line.

distance
In a metes and bounds legal description, it is the length of a property boundary line, usually measured in feet and hundredths of a foot (example: 82.13 feet).

Each boundary line, or "call," is described by a course and a distance. The **course** is the direction in which the boundary line travels, and the **distance** is the length of the boundary line. For example, the first call in Exhibit 12–7 measuring the eastern boundary of the property as it leaves Buckhead Avenue is north 00°52′00″ west 82.13 feet. The course of the call is northwest, and the distance of the call is 82.13 feet.

A metes and bounds description usually begins with an introduction that locates the land in a general part of the state. For example, the state of Georgia is subdivided into counties, and a county is further subdivided into land districts, and some districts are divided into sections. Within districts and sections are land lots that range from 40 to 490 acres. The boundaries of the counties, districts, sections, and land lots are all made definite by government survey. An example of an introduction to a metes and bounds description in Georgia is shown in Example 12–3.

EXHIBIT 12-7
Metes and
Bounds Survey

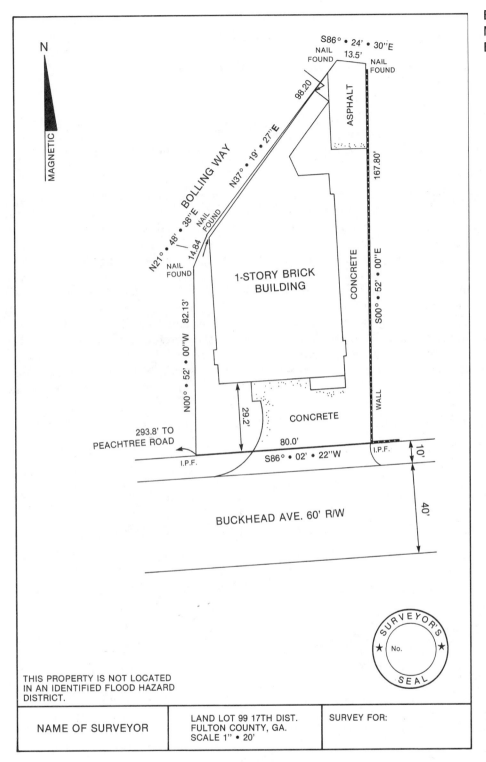

EXAMPLE 12-3

All that tract or parcel of land lying and being in Land Lot 99 of the 17th District of Fulton County, Georgia, and being more particularly described as follows:

Each metes and bounds description must begin somewhere, and that somewhere is called the point of beginning, or beginning point. The beginning point must be precise or the entire description will be incorrect; it must be a definitely ascertainable point and a point that can be located on the ground. Therefore, a beginning point must be either (a) at a known point (a monument, man-made or natural), such as a land lot corner, street corner, street intersection,

intersection of the street with a railroad, or intersection of a street with a stream; or (b) a certain course and distance from a monument. The beginning point for the survey in Exhibit 12–7 and the legal description above is the intersection of two streets, Buckhead Avenue and Peachtree Road. The beginning point is described in Example 12–4.

EXAMPLE 12–4

TO FIND THE TRUE POINT OF BEGINNING, commence at a point formed by the intersection of the northerly side of Buckhead Avenue (60-foot right-of-way) and the easterly side of Peachtree Road; thence run East along the aforementioned right-of-way line of Buckhead Avenue a distance of 293.8 feet to an iron pin found and the TRUE POINT OF BEGINNING.

Review the other sample metes and bounds legal descriptions at the end of this chapter and see how each of the beginning points was obtained. It is incorrect to say as a beginning point, "Begin at an iron pin (found on a certain street)" or "Begin at a point (on a certain street)" because there are an infinite number of iron pins or points along that street.

Once the beginning point has been fixed, the metes and bounds description proceeds along a series of calls, each **call** being a course and distance describing a boundary line of the land. Each of these calls is located on the survey by the land surveyor. A review of the legal description and the survey in Exhibit 12–7 as well as the sample legal descriptions and surveys at the end of this chapter show how the course and distances have been described. The course (the direction) of a boundary line usually is done by course bearings. These bearings are based on true north or true south compass readings, and each course is based on a north-south direction. The compass directions are based on a 360-degree radius, for which there are four 90-degree quadrants: northwest, northeast, southeast, and southwest (Exhibit 12–8). Each quadrant has 90 degrees; each

call
Course and distance describing a boundary line of land in a metes and bounds land description

EXHIBIT 12–8
Quadrants of Compass

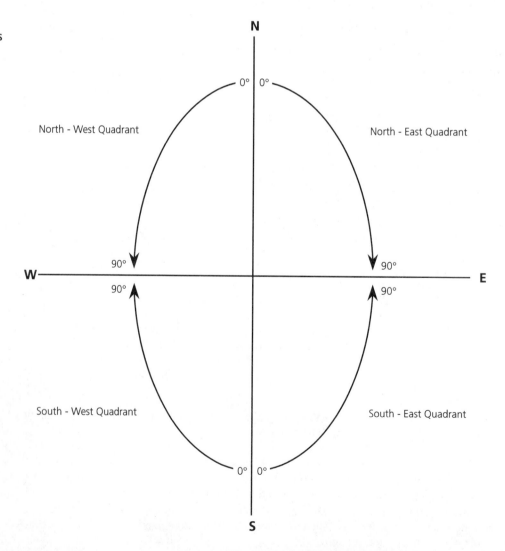

degree has sixty minutes; and each minute has sixty seconds. For example, a line that is north 10°50′26″ west is a line that is 10°50′26″ west of due north and is a line that would be found in the northwest quadrant of the compass.

The distance of a call usually is measured in feet or hundredths of feet. A call that is 56.8 feet is 56 and 80/100ths of a foot in length. In some parts of the country, especially in rural areas, the distances may be measured in rods and chains. A rod is 16.5 feet. A chain is 100 links, with each link being 0.66 feet; so the entire chain is 66 feet. It is rare for a distance to be given in yards.

Curved Property Lines

Not all property can be measured in straight lines, and many times a metes and bounds description involves a curved land boundary. Whenever a legal description involves a curve, the land surveyor should give the following information concerning each curve: (a) the arc distance of the curve; (b) the radius distance of the curve; (c) the chord course (**chord** being a straight line drawn from the beginning point of the arc to the ending point of the arc); and (d) the distance of the chord (Exhibit 12–9).

A legal assistant who has been given the arc distance, the radius distance of the curve, and the chord course and distance can prepare a land description involving a curved boundary. An example of a curved land description taken from Exhibit 12–9 is shown in Example 12–5.

chord
Straight line drawn from the beginning point of an arc to the ending point of an arc.

EXAMPLE 12–5

THENCE, along the arc of a curve an arc distance of 583.49 feet to a point (said curve having a radius of 583.44 feet and being subtended by a chord bearing north 39°16′12″ east, a chord distance of 559.48 feet).

Measurement of Courses by Angles

Sometimes surveyors use angles to measure the exact direction of a property line instead of or in addition to bearings.

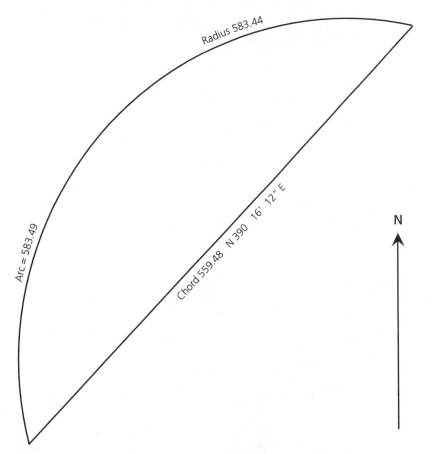

EXHIBIT 12–9
Elements of Curved Property Description

A circle has 360 degrees (each degree has sixty minutes and each minute has sixty seconds), and this is the basis for angles used in legal descriptions. The only thing an angle has in common with the bearings is the use of the terms *degrees, minutes,* and *seconds;* a line running northeasterly at an interior angle of 60°14′30″ is not the same thing as a line running north 60°14′30″ east.

An angle runs from the last described course and is either interior (inside the property boundary) or exterior (outside the property boundary).

When reviewing a survey in which angles are used to describe courses, think of a property corner as an intersection of two lines. At the point of intersection, draw a circle, using that point as a center of the circle. The arc of the circle within the property boundary is the interior angle, and the arc outside the property boundary is the exterior angle.

At one corner of the example shown in Exhibit 12–10, there is an interior angle of 85 degrees and an exterior angle of 275 degrees; at another corner, there is an interior angle of 270 degrees and an exterior angle of 90 degrees. The calls would be any one of the following: thence north at an interior angle of 85 degrees (exterior angle of 275 degrees from the last described course); thence east at an interior angle of 85 degrees (exterior angle of 275 degrees from the last described course); thence south at an interior angle of 270 degrees (exterior angle 90 degrees) from the last described course; thence east at an interior angle of 270 degrees (exterior angle 90 degrees) from the last described course.

When angles are used, the interior-exterior angles are always the same, even though the property lines are described from different directions. Most surveyors locate only one interior-exterior angle at a corner, not necessarily both; but a circle always has 360 degrees, and the omitted angle can easily be computed if necessary.

Closure

A metes and bounds description must close. This means that the legal description starts at the beginning point, follows each boundary line by course and distance, and ends back at the beginning point. If the land description does not close, it is defective.

Practice Notes on Metes and Bounds Description

The basic requirements for a metes and bounds legal description are (a) identification of land lot, district, section, county, and state in which the property is located; (b) definite beginning

EXHIBIT 12–10
Measurement of Courses by Angles

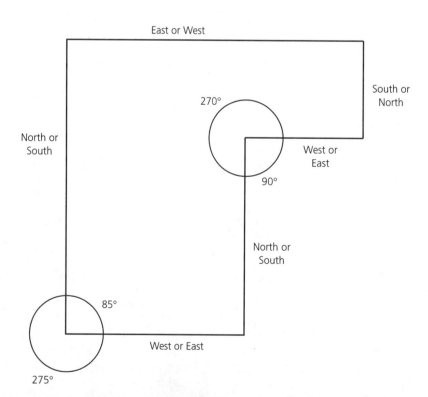

point; (c) compass direction and distances from one point to the next; and (d) return to the beginning point.

A metes and bounds legal description usually cannot be prepared without a survey. Most surveyors locate the beginning point on the survey and also give a course and distance for each property boundary line. The main problem in the metes and bounds description is carelessness: mistakes in reading the survey and omission of a boundary line description. It is a good practice to proofread a metes and bounds description with another person. The other person should read the legal description and the person responsible for the legal description should proof what is being read on the survey. Then roles should be swapped: the other person should read the survey and the person responsible for the description should proof the description.

PRACTICE TIPS FOR REVIEWING A SURVEY _____

One of the duties of a real estate legal assistant is to assist the attorney in the review of a survey. A survey review is generally conducted in connection with a transaction involving a sale or a loan secured by real property. Generally the client for whom the survey is being reviewed will either be a purchaser of the real property being surveyed or a lender who is making a loan secured by the real property.

A legal assistant, when reviewing a survey, should have a survey, a title commitment or title report, a survey checklist, and several colored marking pens. Most law firms have developed their own survey review checklist; however, one is attached as Exhibit 12–19. Generally when reviewing a survey it is acceptable to write or mark on the survey. A legal assistant should order several copies so that clean copies of the survey can be given to the client.

The legal assistant should review the survey carefully to determine if the surveyor has provided the basic information on the survey. Basic survey information includes a north arrow indicating which direction is north and a legend describing any symbols the surveyor used to mark different items on the survey. In addition, a survey should be dated and contain the surveyor's seal, and in many states should be personally signed by the surveyor.

One of the key objectives when reviewing a survey is to determine if the survey description of the property matches the description contained in either the deed from the current owner or the title insurance commitment. Most surveys will contain a printed legal description of the property, and the description contained on the boundary lines of the property. The legal assistant should locate the boundary on the survey and highlight the boundary to identify it. If the description for the property is a metes and bounds, the legal assistant should trace each course and distance around the boundary from the point of beginning following each boundary until returning to the point of beginning. If there is insufficient information on the survey to permit the legal assistant to trace the legal description, then the survey may be defective. If the legal description is a platted description referring to platted lots, the legal assistant should locate the plat information and recording on the survey and match it with the legal description in the deed or title commitment. It is important that the survey legal description match the legal description used in the title insurance commitment and the legal documents used for the transaction. If there are differences between the legal descriptions in survey and the title insurance commitment, an investigation needs to be done to determine why the differences exist and then any discrepancies need to be resolved. The legal assistant should confer with the attorney if he or she finds a difference between the survey description and the title insurance commitment description.

Another objective in a survey review is to locate on the survey each easement or other encumbrance shown in the title insurance commitment. The survey should show the recording number of each easement and the location of the easement on the survey. If the easements mentioned in the title commitment cannot be located on the survey, an inquiry needs to be made as to why these easements were not found. Occasionally, a surveyor will indicate by notes on the survey that certain easements cannot be located. These easements may be blanket easements covering the entire property, or the descriptions on the easements were so vague that the surveyor could not determine where they were located.

The location of any improvements on the property and a review of the survey to determine if there are encroachments either onto the property or from the property is an important objective when reviewing a survey. It is important to locate all buildings and other improvements and to trace around the property boundary to see that the improvements do not encroach onto an adjoining neighbor's property or over or upon easements located on the survey. It is also important to determine if improvements on adjacent properties do not encroach upon the property being surveyed. Any encroachments located by the legal assistant should be brought to the attention of the attorney to determine if the encroachments constitute a serious problem.

Most property is serviced by utilities, so the survey should locate evidence of these utilities. The survey should be reviewed carefully to ensure that utility services such as electricity, water, storm sewer, sanitary sewer, telephone lines, and gas are shown and that the property is connected to such utilities.

In addition to utilities, a means of vehicular access to the property is important. A survey should show all adjacent streets, roads, and highways and indicate whether the accesses are public or private. The survey should be reviewed carefully to determine whether the property has access to a public street. The driveways and curb cuts drawn on the survey should be studied to determine how vehicles drive onto and leave the property from the public street.

Other issues to review on a survey include setback lines, which may be required by private restrictions or **zoning** regulations. The setback line requirements generally provide that improvements must be located a certain distance from the street or from the boundary of the property. If the improvements violate the setback lines, this could result in noncompliance of zoning or a violation of a restrictive covenant. Any encroachments or violations of setback lines should be brought to the attention of the attorney to determine if they are serious encroachments.

Surveyors should indicate whether the property is located in a flood hazard area. If this is the case, flood insurance may be required. The legal assistant should carefully review the survey and notes to determine if any of the property is located in a flood hazard zone.

zoning
Legitimate police power of governments to regulate the use of real property.

 E T H I C S :   Competency

You are a legal assistant with a small general practice firm that represents clients in a number of areas, including real estate. You are working with an attorney on a complicated real property transaction. The land description for the property is complicated. The attorney you work with remarks to you that she is not very good at drafting land descriptions. She mentions that because you received formal legal assistant training, you should be skilled in this area, and she requests that you do the land description. She does not know that you also have difficulty preparing land descriptions. You know that if you prepare the description, even though your supervising attorney will review it, it is questionable whether the attorney will be knowledgeable enough to catch any mistakes. Should you draft the land description and hope for the best?

The American Bar Association's Code of Professional Responsibility provides that a lawyer should represent a client competently. An attorney should strive to become and remain proficient in his or her practice and should accept employment only in matters in which he or she is or intends to become competent to handle. Although a legal assistant is not directly regulated by the American Bar Association's Code of Professional Responsibility, an ethical and professional legal assistant should act with competence and proper care in assisting attorneys in the representation of clients. When a legal assistant undertakes the duty of assisting an attorney in the representation of a client, the legal assistant should use proper care to safeguard the client's interest. If the legal assistant is working in an area beyond his or her competence but in which he or she is expected to become competent, it is the legal assistant's duty to diligently undertake the work and to study whatever is necessary to perform the work competently. Legal assistants should take pride in their professional endeavors. Their obligation to act competently requires a higher motivation to be a professional.

In this factual situation, the legal assistant should either decline to prepare the description and explain to the attorney his or her difficulty in preparing descriptions of this type or seek help from other members of the firm to see if someone else in the firm is competent in this area of practice. The legal assistant may also obtain help from title insurance companies, surveyors, or other professionals who may be willing to assist the legal assistant in gaining an understanding of the skills and tasks required to prepare the land description.

SUMMARY

A survey is an important part of any real estate transaction. A surveyor describes the boundaries of the property and either provides a legal description or a means for preparing a legal description of the real property. In addition, the land survey will also locate all improvements on the property and show any encroachment of improvements onto adjacent properties or encroachments of improvements from adjacent properties onto the surveyed property. The surveyor will also locate easements, utilities, means of access, and other important features of the property being surveyed.

Surveys are generally prepared by professional licensed surveyors according to standards developed by the survey profession and the title insurance industry.

Real estate legal assistants come in daily contact with surveys and will use these surveys to either prepare or proof legal descriptions, and to determine if the property, as represented on the survey, satisfies all the expectations and requirements of the client. A full knowledge of land descriptions and survey requirements is important to enable the legal assistant to fully assist an attorney in a real estate transaction.

KEY TERMS

as-built survey	easement	survey
base line	legal description	title insurance
call	plat	title insurance commitment
chord	principal meridians	township
course	range lines	township lines
distance	section	zoning

SELF-STUDY EXAMINATION

(Answers provided in Appendix)

1. T or F. A boundary survey without any warranties as to accuracy is called an "as-built" survey.

2. T or F. All states use a government rectangular survey system.

3. T or F. Base lines run east and west.

4. T or F. A township's square is divided into 36 sections.

5. T or F. A metes and bounds call will contain both a course and a distance.

6. T or F. The length between two points on a metes and bounds description is called a course.

7. T or F. A survey should indicate which direction is north on the survey by including a north arrow.

8. T or F. A metes and bounds description describes a parcel of land by reference to a recorded survey or plat.

9. T or F. A straight line between the beginning and ending points of a curve is called a chord.

10. T or F. An arc distance and a chord distance will always be the same.

11. List the types of land description.

12. A base line has what relationship to a meridian line in a government rectangular survey?

13. How many acres are found in the North 1/2 of a NW 1/4 of a SE 1/4 of a section?

14. What are the basic requirements for a platted description?

15. How does the course of a boundary line differ from the distance of a boundary line?

16. What information should the land surveyor give concerning a curved property line?

17. What is meant by the statement that "a metes and bounds description must close"?

ADDENDUM

Exhibit 12–11	Platted description survey
Exhibit 12–12	Metes and bounds description (including curves with descriptions)
Exhibit 12–13	Metes and bounds survey with use of interior angles
Exhibit 12–14	Metes and bounds survey—E. Ponce de Leon property
Exhibit 12–15	Metes and bounds survey—Mohawk Trail property
Exhibit 12–16	Metes and bounds survey—West Pine Valley Road property
Exhibit 12–17	Metes and bounds survey with legal description—Willow Creek property
Exhibit 12–18	ALTA/ACSM 1999 Survey Standards
Exhibit 12–19	Survey Review Checklist

EXHIBIT 12-11
Platted Description Survey

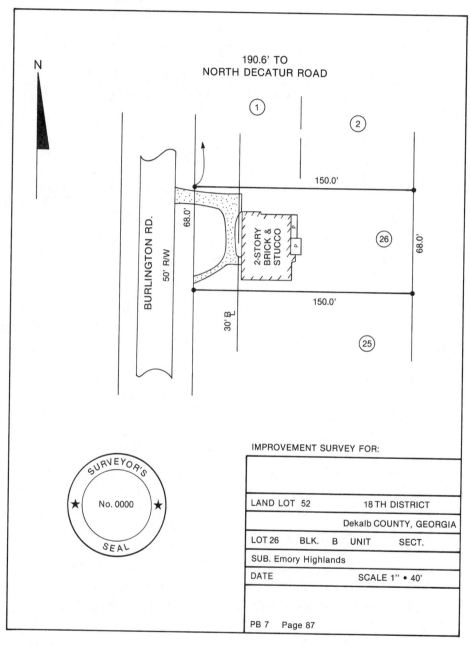

ALL THAT TRACT or parcel of land lying and being in Land Lot 52 of the 18th District of DeKalb County, Georgia, being Lot 26, Block B, Emory Highlands, according to plat recorded in Plat Book 7 at page 87, in the office of the Clerk of the Superior Court of DeKalb County, Georgia.

EXHIBIT 12-12
Metes and Bounds Description (Including Curves with Descriptions)

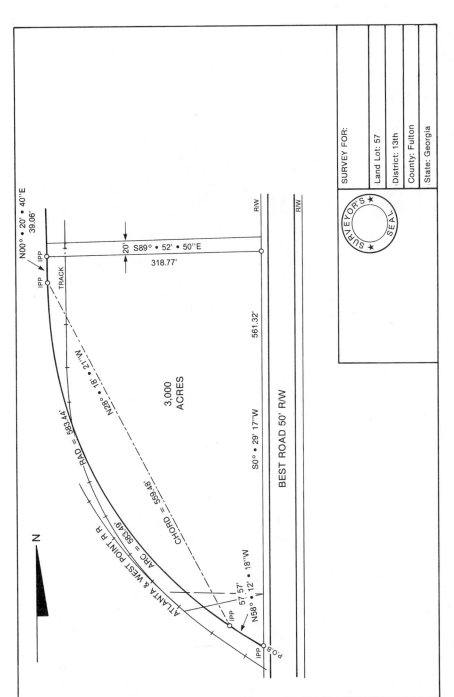

ALL THAT TRACT or parcel of land lying and being in Land Lot 57 of the 13th District of Fulton County, Georgia, and being more particularly described as follows:

BEGIN at an iron pin at the intersection of the western right-of-way at Best Road (50-foot right-of-way) and the northeastern right-of-way of the Atlanta & West Point Railroad; thence, run north 58 degrees 12 minutes 18 seconds west 57.57 feet to an iron pin placed; thence, run in a northwesterly direction along the arc of a curve an arc distance of 583.49 feet to an iron pin (said curve having a radius of 583.44 feet and being subtended by a chord bearing north 28 degrees 18 minutes 21 seconds west, a chord distance of 559.48 feet); thence, north 00 degrees 20 minutes 40 seconds east 39.06 feet to an iron pin; thence, south 89 degrees 52 minutes 50 seconds east 318.77 feet to an iron pin located on the western right-of-way of Best Road; thence, run along the western right-of-way of Best Road south 00 degrees 29 minutes 17 seconds west 561.32 feet to the POINT OF BEGINNING.

EXHIBIT 12-13
Metes and Bounds Survey with Use of Interior Angles

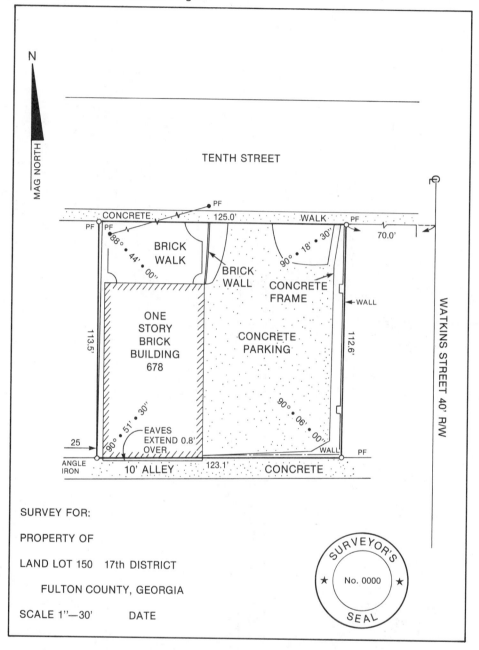

ALL THAT TRACT or parcel of land lying and being in Land Lot 150 of the 17th District of Fulton County, Georgia, and being more particularly described as follows:

BEGINNING at an iron pin found on the south side of 10th Street 70 feet west of the center line of Watkins Street (having a 40-foot right-of-way) as measured along the south side of 10th Street; thence south and forming an interior angle of 90 degrees 18 minutes 30 seconds from 10th Street 112.6 feet to a 3-inch steel fence post on the north side of an alley; thence, west along the north side of said alley and forming an interior angle of 90 degrees 06 minutes from the preceding call 123.1 feet to a 3-inch steel fence post; thence north and forming an interior angle of 90 degrees 51 minutes 30 seconds from the preceding call 113.5 feet to a 3-inch steel fence post on the south side of 10th Street; thence east along the south side of 10th Street and forming an interior angle of 88 degrees 44 minutes from the preceding call 125 feet to the point of BEGINNING; said property being known as 678 10th Street, N.W., according to the present system of numbering houses in the City of Atlanta, and being formerly known as Lots 4, 5, 6, 7 and 8, Block G of the Joe E. Brown Co. as per plat recorded in Plat Book 7, pages 86 and 87, Fulton County, Georgia Records; and being the same property shown on a plat of survey dated April 30, 1987.

TOGETHER WITH all of Grantor's right, title and interest, if any, in and to the ten (10) foot alley located along the rear line of the above-described property.

EXHIBIT 12-14
Metes and Bounds Survey—E. Ponce de Leon Property

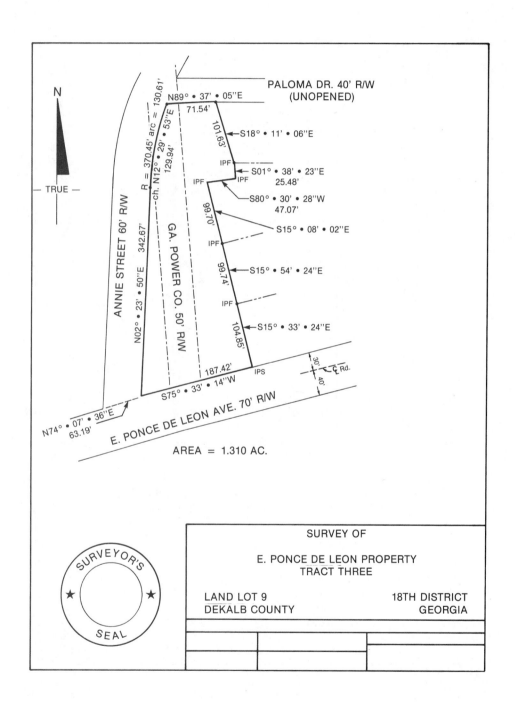

N
— TRUE —

PALOMA DR. 40' R/W
(UNOPENED)

N89° • 37' • 05"E
71.54'

S18° • 11' • 06"E
101.63'

IPF
S01° • 38' • 23"E
25.48'

IPF   IPF
S80° • 30' • 28"W
47.07'

S15° • 08' • 02"E
99.70'

IPF
S15° • 54' • 24"E
99.74'

IPF
S15° • 33' • 24"E
104.85'

R = 370.45' arc = 130.61'
ch. N12° • 29' • 53"E 129.94'

N02° • 23' • 50"E 342.67'

ANNIE STREET 60' R/W

GA. POWER CO. 50' R/W

187.42'   IPS
S75° • 33' • 14"W

30'
40'   ℄ Rd.

N74° • 07' • 36"E
63.19'

E. PONCE DE LEON AVE. 70' R/W

AREA = 1.310 AC.

SURVEY OF

E. PONCE DE LEON PROPERTY
TRACT THREE

LAND LOT 9   18TH DISTRICT
DEKALB COUNTY   GEORGIA

SURVEYOR'S SEAL

EXHIBIT 12-15
Metes and Bounds Survey—Mohawk Trail Property

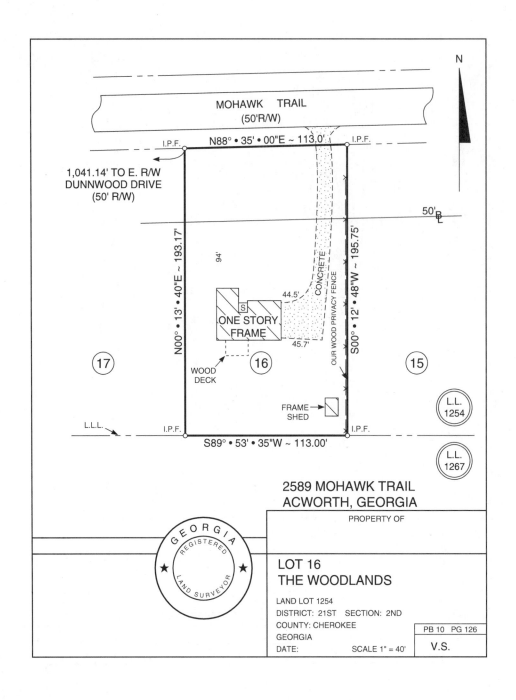

EXHIBIT 12–16
Metes and Bounds Survey—West Pine Valley Road Property

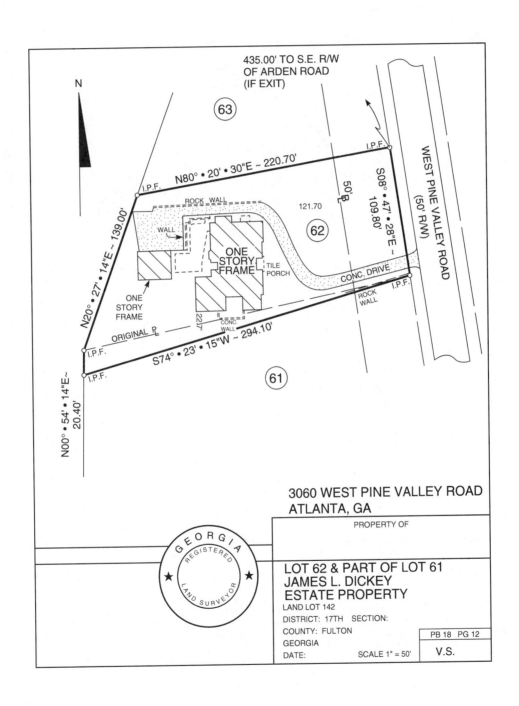

EXHIBIT 12-17
Metes and Bounds Survey with Legal Description—Willow Creek Property

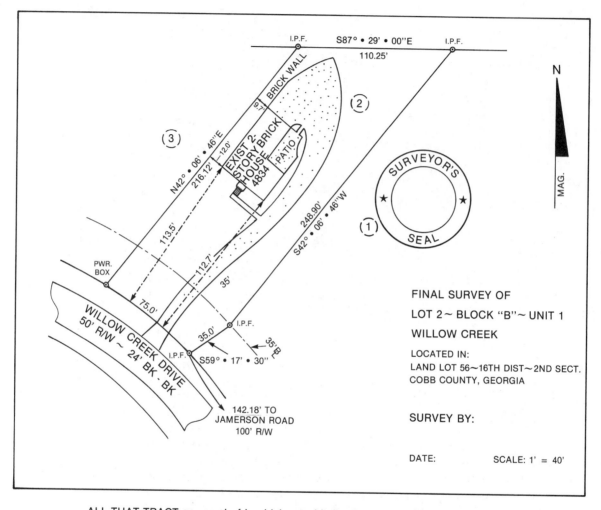

FINAL SURVEY OF

LOT 2 ~ BLOCK "B" ~ UNIT 1

WILLOW CREEK

LOCATED IN:
LAND LOT 56~16TH DIST~2ND SECT.
COBB COUNTY, GEORGIA

SURVEY BY:

DATE: SCALE: 1' = 40'

ALL THAT TRACT or parcel of land lying and being in Land Lot 56 of the 16th District, 2nd Section, Cobb County, Georgia, and being more particularly described as follows:

BEGIN at an iron pin found on the northeastern right-of-way of Willow Creek Drive (50-foot right-of-way), said iron pin being located 142.18 feet northwest of the intersection of the northeastern right-of-way of Willow Creek Drive with the northern right-of-way of Jamerson Road (100-foot right-of-way); run thence in a northwesterly direction along the northeasterly right-of-way of Willow Creek Drive 75.0 feet to a power box; run thence North 42°06'46" East 261.12 feet to an iron pin found; thence run South 87°29'00" West 110.25 feet to an iron pin found; thence run South 24°06'46" West 248.90 feet to an iron pin found; run thence South 59°17'03" West 35.0 feet to an iron pin found being the POINT OF BEGINNING.

EXHIBIT 12–18
ALTA/ACSM 1999
Survey Standards

MINIMUM STANDARD DETAIL REQUIREMENTS
for ALTA/ACSM LAND TITLE SURVEYS
as adopted by
American Land Title Association
American Congress on Surveying & Mapping
and
National Society of Professional Surveyors

It is recognized that members of the American Land Title Association (ALTA) have specific needs, peculiar to title insurance matters, which require particular information for acceptance by title insurance companies when said companies are asked to insure title to land without exceptions as to the many matters which might be discoverable from survey and inspection and not be evidenced by the public records. In the general interest of the public, the surveying profession, title insurers and abstracters, ALTA, the American Congress on Surveying and Mapping (ACSM) and the National Society of Professional Surveyors, Inc. (NSPS) jointly promulgate and set forth such details and criteria for standards. It is understood that local variations may require local adjustments to suit local situations, and often must be applied. It is recognized that title insurance companies are entitled to rely on the survey furnished to them being of the appropriate professional quality, both as to completeness and as to accuracy. It is equally recognized that for the performance of a survey, the surveyor will be provided with appropriate data which can be relied upon in the preparation of the survey.

For a survey of real property and the plat or map of the survey to be acceptable to a title insurance company for purposes of insuring title to said real property free and clear of survey matters (except those matters disclosed by the survey and indicated on the plat or map), certain specific and pertinent information shall be presented for the distinct and clear understanding between the client (insured), the title insurance company (insurer), and the surveyor (the person professionally responsible for the survey). These requirements are:

1. The client shall request the survey or arrange for the survey to be requested and shall provide a written authorization to proceed with the survey from the person responsible for paying for the survey. Unless specifically authorized in writing by the insurer, the insurer shall not be responsible for any costs associated with the preparation of the survey. The request shall specify that an "ALTA/ACSM LAND TITLE SURVEY" is required, meeting the then-current accuracy standards jointly adopted by ALTA, ACSM and NSPS. The request shall also designate which of the optional items listed in Table A are to be incorporated. The request shall set forth the record description of the property. Complete copies of the record description of the property, any record easements benefitting the property, the record easements or servitudes and covenants affecting the property ("Record Documents"), documents of record referred to in the Record Documents, and any other documents containing desired appropriate information affecting the property being surveyed and to which the survey shall make reference shall be provided to the surveyor for notation on the plat or map of survey.

2. The plat or map of such survey shall bear the name, address, telephone number, and signature of the professional land surveyor who made the survey, his or her official seal and registration number, the date the survey was completed and the dates of all revisions, and the caption "ALTA/ACSM Land Title Survey" with the certification set forth in paragraph 8.

3. An "ALTA/ACSM LAND TITLE SURVEY" shall be in accordance with the then-current "Accuracy Standards for Land Title Surveys" ("Accuracy Standards") as adopted, from time to time, by the American Congress on Surveying and Mapping, the National Society of Professional Surveyors, and the American Land Title Association and incorporated herein by reference.

4. On the plat or map of an "ALTA/ACSM LAND TITLE SURVEY," the survey boundary shall be drawn to a convenient scale, with that scale clearly indicated. A graphic scale, shown in feet or meters or both, shall be included. A north arrow shall be shown and when practicable, the plat or map of survey shall be oriented so that north is at the top of the drawing. Symbols or abbreviations used shall be identified on the face of the plat or map by use of a legend or other means. If necessary for

(continued)

EXHIBIT 12-18
ALTA/ACSM 1999
Survey Standards
(continued)

clarity, supplementary or exaggerated diagrams shall be presented accurately on the plat or map. The plat or map shall be a minimum size of 8 1/2 by 11 inches.

5. The survey shall be performed on the ground and the plat or map of an "ALTA/ACSM LAND TITLE SURVEY" shall contain, in addition to the required items already specified above, the following applicable information:

(a) All data necessary to indicate the mathematical dimensions and relationships of the boundary represented, with angles given directly or by bearings, and with the length and radius of each curve, together with elements necessary to mathematically define each curve. The point of beginning of the surveyor's description shall be shown as well as the remote point of beginning if different. A bearing base shall refer to some well-fixed bearing line, so that the bearings may be easily re-established. All bearings around the boundary shall read in a clockwise direction wherever possible. The North arrow shall be referenced to its bearing base and should that bearing base differ from record title, that difference shall be noted.

(b) When recorded bearings or angles or distances differ from measured bearings, angles or distances, both the record and measured bearings, angles, and distances shall be clearly indicated. If the record description fails to form a mathematically closed figure, the surveyor shall so indicate.

(c) Measured and record distances from corners of parcels surveyed to the nearest right-of-way lines of streets in urban or suburban areas, together with recovered lot corners and evidence of lot corners, shall be noted. The distances to the nearest intersecting street shall be indicated and verified. Names and widths of streets and highways abutting the property surveyed and widths of rights of way shall be given. Any use contrary to the above shall be noted. Observable evidence of access (or lack thereof) to such abutting streets or highways shall be indicated. Observable evidence of private roads shall be so indicated. Streets abutting the premises, which have been described in Record Documents, but not physically opened, shall be shown and so noted.

(d) The identifying titles of all recorded plats, filed maps, right of way maps, or similar documents which the survey represents, wholly or in part, shall be shown with their appropriate recording data, filing dates and map numbers, and the lot, block, and section numbers or letters of the surveyed premises. For non-platted adjoining land, names, and recording data identifying adjoining owners as they appear of record shall be shown. For platted adjoining land, the recording data of the subdivision plat shall be shown. The survey shall indicate platted setback or building restriction lines which have been recorded in subdivision plats or which appear in a Record Document which has been delivered to the surveyor. Contiguity, gores, and overlaps along the exterior boundaries of the surveyed premises, where ascertainable from field evidence or Record Documents, or interior to those exterior boundaries, shall be clearly indicated or noted. Where only a part of a recorded lot or parcel is included in the survey, the balance of the lot or parcel shall be indicated.

(e) All evidence of monuments shall be shown and noted to indicate which were found and which were placed. All evidence of monuments found beyond the surveyed premises on which establishment of the corners of the surveyed premises are dependent, and their application related to the survey shall be indicated.

(f) The character of any and all evidence of possession shall be stated and the location of such evidence carefully given in relation to both the measured boundary lines and those established by the record. An absence of notation on the survey shall be presumptive of no observable evidence of possession.

(g) The location of all buildings upon the plot or parcel shall be shown and their locations defined by measurements perpendicular to the boundaries. If there are no buildings erected on the property being surveyed, the plat or map shall bear the statement, "No buildings." Proper street numbers shall be shown where available.

(h) All easements evidenced by a Record Document which have been delivered to the surveyor shall be shown, both those burdening and those benefitting the property surveyed, indicating recording information. If such an easement cannot be located, a note to this effect shall be included. Observable evidence of easements and/or servitudes of all kinds, such as those created by roads; rights-of-way; water courses; drains; telephone, telegraph, or electric lines; water, sewer, oil or gas

EXHIBIT 12–18
ALTA/ACSM 1999
Survey Standards
(continued)

pipelines on or across the surveyed property and on adjoining properties if they appear to affect the surveyed property, shall be located and noted. If the surveyor has knowledge of any such easements and/or servitudes, not observable at the time the present survey is made, such lack of observable evidence shall be noted. Surface indications, if any, of underground easements and/or servitudes shall also be shown.

(i) The character and location of all walls, buildings, fences, and other visible improvements within five feet of each side of the boundary lines shall be noted. Without expressing a legal opinion, physical evidence of all encroaching structural appurtenances and projections, such as fire escapes, bay windows, windows and doors that open out, flue pipes, stoops, eaves, cornices, areaways, steps, trim, etc., by or on adjoining property or on abutting streets, on any easement or over setback lines shown by Record Documents shall be indicated with the extent of such encroachment or projection. If the client wishes to have additional information with regard to appurtenances such as whether or not such appurtenances are independent, division, or party walls and are plumb, the client will assume the responsibility of obtaining such permissions as are necessary for the surveyor to enter upon the properties to make such determinations.

(j) Driveways and alleys on or crossing the property must be shown. Where there is evidence of use by other than the occupants of the property, the surveyor must so indicate on the plat or map. Where driveways or alleys on adjoining properties encroach, in whole or in part, on the property being surveyed, the surveyor must so indicate on the plat or map with appropriate measurements.

(k) As accurately as the evidence permits, the location of cemeteries and burial grounds (i) disclosed in the process of researching title to the premises or (ii) observed in the process of performing the field work for the survey, shall be shown.

(l) Ponds, lakes, springs, or rivers bordering on or running through the premises being surveyed shall be shown.

6. As a minimum requirement, the surveyor shall furnish two sets of prints of the plat or map of survey to the title insurance company or the client. If the plat or map of survey consists of more than one sheet, the sheets shall be numbered, the total number of sheets indicated and match lines be shown on each sheet. The prints shall be on durable and dimensionally stable material of a quality standard acceptable to the title insurance company. At least two copies of the boundary description prepared from the survey shall be similarly furnished by the surveyor and shall be on the face of the plat or map of survey, if practicable, or otherwise attached to and incorporated in the plat or map. Reference to date of the "ALTA/ACSM LAND TITLE SURVEY," surveyor's file number (if any), political subdivision, section, township and range, along with appropriate aliquot parts thereof, and similar information shown on the plat or map of survey shall be included with the boundary description.

7. Water boundaries necessarily are subject to change due to erosion or accretion by tidal action or the flow of rivers and streams. A realignment of water bodies may also occur due to many reasons such as deliberate cutting and filling of bordering lands or by avulsion. Recorded surveys of natural water boundaries are not relied upon by title insurers for location of title.

When a property to be surveyed for title insurance purposes contains a natural water boundary, the surveyor shall measure the location of the boundary according to appropriate surveying methods and note on the plat or map the date of the measurement and the caveat that the boundary is subject to change due to natural causes and that it may or may not represent the actual location of the limit of title. When the surveyor is aware of changes in such boundaries, the extent of those changes shall be identified.

8. When the surveyor has met all of the minimum standard detail requirements for an ALTA/ACSM Land Title Survey, the following certification shall be made on the plat:

To (name of client), (name of lender, if known), (name of title insurance company, if known), (name of others as instructed by client):

This is to certify that this map or plat and the survey on which it is based were made in accordance with "Minimum Standard Detail Requirements for ALTA/ACSM Land Title Surveys," jointly

EXHIBIT 12–18
ALTA/ACSM 1999
Survey Standards
(continued)

established and adopted by ALTA, ACSM and NSPS in 1999, and includes items ___ of Table A thereof. Pursuant to the Accuracy Standards as adopted by ALTA, NSPS, and ACSM and in effect on the date of this certification, undersigned further certifies that (Surveyor to complete certificate with the appropriate ONE of the following three phrases)

- the Positional Uncertainties resulting from the survey measurements made on the survey do not exceed the allowable Positional Tolerance.
- the survey measurements were made in accordance with the "Minimum Angle, Distance, and Closure Requirements for Survey Measurements Which Control Land Boundaries for ALTA/ACSM Land Title Surveys."
- proper field procedures, instrumentation, and adequate survey personnel were employed in order to achieve results comparable to those outlined in the "Minimum Angle, Distance, and Closure Requirements for Survey Measurements Which Control Land Boundaries for ALTA/ACSM Land Title Surveys."

Date: _____ (signed) _____ (seal)

Registration No.

Adopted by the American Land Title Association on October 6, 1999.
Adopted by the Board of Direction, American Congress on Surveying and Mapping on October 20, 1999.
Adopted by the Board of Directors, National Society of Professional Surveyors on October 19, 1999.
American Land Title Association, 1828 L St., N.W., Suite 705, Washington, D.C. 20036.
American Congress on Surveying and Mapping, 5410 Grosvenor Lane, Bethesda, MD 20814.
National Society of Professional Surveyors, 5410 Grosvenor Lane, Bethesda, MD 20814.

TABLE A
OPTIONAL SURVEY RESPONSIBILITIES AND SPECIFICATIONS

NOTE: The items of Table A must be negotiated between the surveyor and client. It may be necessary for the surveyor to qualify or expand upon the description of these items, e.g. in reference to item 6, there may be a need for an interpretation of a restriction. The surveyor cannot make a certification on the basis of an interpretation.

If checked, the following optional items are to be included in the ALTA/ACSM LAND TITLE SURVEY:

1. __X__ Monuments placed (or a reference monument or witness to the corner) at all major corners of the boundary of the property, unless already marked or referenced by an existing monument or witness to the corner.
2. __X__ Vicinity map showing the property surveyed in reference to nearby highway(s) or major street intersection(s).
3. __X__ Flood zone designation (with proper annotation based on Federal Flood Insurance Rate Maps or the state or local equivalent, by scaled map location and graphic plotting only).
4. __X__ Land area as specified by the client.
5. _____ Contours and the datum of the elevations.
6. __X__ Identify and show if possible, setback, height, and floor space area restrictions of record or disclosed by applicable zoning or building codes (in addition to those recorded in subdivision maps). If none, so state.
7. __X__ (a) Exterior dimensions of all buildings at ground level
   (b) Square footage of:
   __X__   (1) exterior footprint of all buildings at ground level
   __X__   (2) gross floor area of all buildings; or
   __X__   (3) other areas to be defined by the client
   (c) Measured height of all buildings above grade at a defined location. If no defined location is provided, the point of measurement shall be shown.
8. __X__ Substantial, visible improvements (in addition to buildings) such as signs, parking areas or structures, swimming pools, etc.

(continued)

9. __X__ Parking areas and, if striped, the striping and the type (eg., handicapped, motorcycle, regular, etc.) and number of parking spaces.

10. __X__ Indication of access to a public way such as curb cuts and driveways.

11. _____ Location of utilities (representative examples of which are shown below) existing on or serving the surveyed property as determined by:

_____ (a) Observed evidence

__X__ (b) Observed evidence together with plans and markings provided by client, utility companies, and other appropriate sources (with reference as to the source of information)

  • railroad tracks and sidings;

  • manholes, catch basins, valve vaults or other surface indications of subterranean uses;

  • wires and cables (including their function) crossing the surveyed premises, all poles on or within ten feet of the surveyed premises, and the dimensions of all crosswires or overhangs affecting the surveyed premises; and

  • utility company installations on the surveyed premises.

12. _____ Governmental Agency survey-related requirements as specified by the client.

13. __X__ Names of adjoining owners of platted lands.

14. _____ Observable evidence of earth moving work, building construction or building additions within recent months.

15. __X__ Any changes in street right of way lines either completed or proposed, and available from the controlling jurisdiction. Observable evidence of recent street or sidewalk construction or repairs.

16. _____ Observable evidence of site use as a solid waste dump, sump or sanitary landfill.

17. _____

_____

EXHIBIT 12-18
ALTA/ACSM 1999
Survey Standards
(continued)

SURVEY REVIEW CHECKLIST

Date: _____

File name: _____

Reviewed by: _____

Survey date: _____ Last Revision _____

Surveyor: _____ Phone _____

Prepared for: _____

Type of Survey: _____

Title Report Reference: _____

SURVEY REQUIREMENTS

1. _____ Scale

2. _____ Basis of bearings

3. _____ North arrow

4. _____ Legend

5. _____ Signed, sealed, and dated

6. _____ Property description and location:

EXHIBIT 12-19
Survey Review
Checklist

(continued)

EXHIBIT 12–19
Survey Review
Checklist (continued)

A. _____ Legal Description (on survey; match title commitment): _____

_____ Description closes: _____

B. _____ Boundaries: _____

_____ point of commencement/point of beginning shown (and description returns to POB)

_____ corners set

_____ iron pins placed at deflection points

_____ curves (length and arc or radius, tangent)

_____ monuments found

_____ azimuth base line shown

_____ platted property: lots, blocks, section and recording numbers of plat

_____ platted property; metes and bounds match plat

C. _____ Adjoining properties (noted with any overlaps or gaps shown): _____

D. _____ Multiple parcels contiguous: _____

7. _____ Easements and other physical encumbrances shown on title (locate all with corresponding number of title commitment; include appurtenant easements):

_____

_____

8. _____ Improvements:

A. _____ Building and structures (height, area, perimeter dimensions; frame, roof and exterior
finish): _____

B. _____ Other improvements or physical objects (fences—determine ownership and issues,
rockeries, landscaping, planter boxes, out-buildings): _____

9. _____ Encroachments (improvements over easements/boundaries; subject property onto adjoiner, adjoiner onto subject property): _____

10. _____ Access:

A. _____ Roads (adjoining streets, highways, alleys—public vs. private, right-of-ways; labeled,
distance to property and restrictions shown): _____

B. _____ Ingress and egress (curb cuts and driveways): _____

11. _____ Utilities (locate electricity, sewer—storm and sanitary, telephone, water, gas; all connected
to public utility lines either through public street or easement over private adjoiner):

_____

12. _____ Storm drainage ponds and systems (if any; easement for runoff): _____

13. _____ Parking (number and size of spaces): _____

14. _____ Building setback lines: _____

15. _____ Street address (of each building): _____

16. _____ Area of land and area of buildings: _____

17. _____ Water (locate including flow direction all creeks, rivers, ponds, bays, lakes adjacent to or
on property, or within flood plain or flood prone area): _____

18. _____ Cemeteries (if any): _____

(continued)

EXHIBIT 12-19
Survey Review
Checklist (continued)

19. _____ Vicinity sketch (show closest thoroughfare intersection): _____

20. _____ Field notes on survey: _____

21. _____ Flood Hazard Area Certification (map number, zone): _____

22. _____ Certification (compare with requirement; client named): _____

23. _____ Other: _____

Leases

"And Summer's lease hath all too short a date."

—William Shakespeare, Sonnet 18

OBJECTIVES

After reading this chapter you will be able to:

- Review a commercial lease and understand its key provisions
- Define the various methods to compute rent under a lease
- Understand the legal differences between an assignment of lease and a sublease
- Recognize a landlord's remedies for a tenant's default under a lease
- Recognize a tenant's remedies for a landlord's default under a lease

lease
Legal document that transfers possession of real property from one party to another. The lease also may contain numerous terms and conditions involving the use and possession of the property.

residential lease
A lease for the possession and use of a residence such as an apartment or a house.

commercial lease
A lease for the possession and use of a business or commercial enterprise such as a retail store, warehouse, or office.

Legal assistants often are involved in the preparation and review of **leases.** Although in many instances a legal assistant is furnished with either a preprinted form or a form prepared by a law firm to review or to use as a guide in the preparation of the new lease, it is important that the legal assistant understand the legal theories and concepts of leases as well as be aware of the general provisions found in most leases.

A lease may be a **residential lease** for use in a residential situation for the possession and use of an apartment or house. A lease may also be a **commercial lease** and used in a commercial setting for the possession and use of a business or commercial enterprise such as a retail store, warehouse, or an office. Because of the legal expense involved, most legal assistants are involved in the preparation and review of commercial leases. For this reason, most of the discussion in this chapter pertains to commercial leases. Many of the issues discussed, however, have equal application to a residential apartment or home lease. Examples of residential and commercial lease forms are included at the end of this chapter.

COMMON LAW AND LEASES

The English common law treated a lease as a combination of property and contract law. Because a lease transfers possession and, in some cases, is an estate for years, it is deemed to be a conveyance of real property. In addition, leases contain numerous terms and conditions that involve the use and possession of the property. In this respect, the lease is a contract and enforceable according to the general terms of contract law.

The common law of leases made a major departure from contract law in holding that lease covenants were independent. This meant that the landlord's promises were independent from the tenant's, and the failure of one party (such as a landlord) to perform its obligations was not an excuse for the other party, the tenant, not to perform. For example, a lease may require the landlord to provide basic utility services to the premises and the tenant to pay rent.

The landlord refuses or fails to provide utility services. Does this excuse the tenant from its obligation to pay rent? The common law theory of independent covenants said no. The tenant must continue to pay rent even though the landlord refuses to perform its obligations. The tenant is left with the remedy of suing the landlord to perform or to compensate the tenant for damages caused by nonperformance. Historically, the common law theory of independent lease covenants has worked to the disadvantage of the tenant. Many states, especially in the area of residential leases, have radically modified the independent theory of lease covenants. For example, many states impose in residential leases a warranty of habitability on the landlord. This means that the landlord warrants to the tenant that the premises are capable of human habitation. This usually means that the landlord must provide basic utility services, such as water, sewer, and heat. In the event the premises prove not to be habitable, this excuses the tenant from payment of rent. Nevertheless, the common law theory of independent covenants is the law in most states as it pertains to commercial leases.

COMMERCIAL LEASE PROVISIONS

A legal assistant who is involved in the preparation and review of a commercial lease must be familiar with the various terms commonly found in commercial leases.

Parties to Lease

The parties to a lease are **landlord** and **tenant,** or **lessor** and **lessee.** The landlord usually is the fee owner of the property. In making the lease, the landlord is transferring the possession and use of the property to the tenant. The landlord must have title to the property to grant the lease, and the title must be sufficient to cover the lease term. For example, a landlord who had only a life estate in the property could not necessarily grant a lease for twenty years. If the landlord died during the twenty years, the lease would terminate when the landlord's title terminated.

A lease also is subject to all the landlord's title defects. It is prudent in many cases, when representing a tenant, to examine the landlord's title before entering into the lease. A tenant should pay particular attention to any zoning or restrictive covenants that may affect the use of the leased property. Another area of concern for the tenant is any prior mortgages that may exist on the property. A mortgage that is in existence at the time the lease is entered into is senior to the lease. If the loan payments are not made and the mortgage is foreclosed, the lease will terminate. This could place a tenant at a great disadvantage, not to mention tremendous expense, in moving or renegotiating the terms of the lease with the purchaser at the foreclosure sale.

The tenant under the lease is the party to whom possession and use of the property are being transferred. Particular attention is paid to the financial ability of a tenant. It is crucial that the tenant have the ability to perform all the lease covenants. In many cases, it may be necessary that corporate tenants obtain a **lease guaranty** from the principal shareholders of the corporation, or a subsidiary corporation obtain a guaranty from the parent corporation, to assure financial ability.

Premises

A lease must describe the property that is being rented. The property being rented in a lease often is referred to as the **premises.** Legal assistants should pay careful attention when preparing or reviewing a lease to make sure that the premises described are exactly those that are being transferred to the tenant and that the landlord intends to transfer. Important questions in a premises clause are (a) where is the premises located? (b) what is the size of the premises? and (c) how is the size of the premises to be determined or confirmed? If the lease covers other premises, such as hallways, streets, bathrooms, or parking privileges, all this should be described and covered in the lease. Many times a lease of real property includes the use of certain personal property; if so, the personal property should be described and listed within the lease.

The location of the premises within a building or project should already be the subject of the parties negotiated understanding by the time the legal assistant starts to prepare or review the lease. The only real concern should be to review the lease to make sure that the lease accurately documents that understanding. A comparable degree of specificity and precision should be used in leases in describing the premises as is used in conveyancing documents such as a deed. The lease should, at a minimum, provide a method whereby the precise size and location of the premises can be (or will be) determined and verified. Legal descriptions, plats of survey, plans and specifications, street addresses, and suite members are all used under different circumstances (and in different combinations) to accomplish this task.

---

landlord or lessor
Generally the owner of real property who transfers possession and use of the real property under a lease to a tenant or lessee.

tenant or lessee
Person who receives possession and use of property pursuant to a lease.

lease guaranty
A legal document that obligates the maker of the document to perform the obligations of a tenant under the lease including, but not limited to, the payment of the rent by the tenant to the landlord.

premises
Land and the buildings located on the land. The term often is used to describe real property covered by a lease.

Shopping Mall

In many situations, the premises will be space that is to be built in a proposed office building or shopping center. When the space is to be built, the tenant should be provided a reasonable means and opportunity to review and confirm the landlord's stated square footage. Many leases contain a provision that the landlord's architect will measure the premises when they are completed, and the determination of the landlord's architect will be binding on both parties. The lease may provide the tenant with a procedure for objecting or contesting the landlord's architect's measurement.

Use

The use the tenant intends to make of the premises should be specified in the lease. The tenant wants a specific use identified in the lease and permission to use the premises for any lawful purpose. A landlord, on the other hand, probably wants to be more restrictive and require that the tenant's use of the premises be only that use set forth in the lease and no other use without prior written consent of landlord.

Term

With respect to the term of a lease, the better practice is to set out the exact commencement and termination dates, rather than merely state a term of years. To the extent renewal options are part of the transaction, this clause also should describe with specificity the term and type of notice required to exercise the renewal option. The length of the term of the lease usually is the subject of the parties' negotiated understanding, and in reviewing a lease, this point should only have to be verified by the legal assistant.

Possession and Commencement of the Rent

A lease should provide for a precise beginning and ending date. The lease may provide that possession will begin in the future. Many developers, when constructing new shopping centers or office buildings, prelease the property before the time of completion. A lease that provides for future possession should clearly state that the lease becomes effective when signed, but possession will be delayed until a date in the future. The exact time of possession should be carefully described within the lease. As a practical note, a date of possession can be crucial to a tenant. Most tenants are at some other location and will have to go to the expense of closing that location and moving to the new premises. If, for some reason, possession is delayed, this can cause a disruption of business and considerable expense. A tenant may try to negotiate a provision that requires the landlord to pay an amount of money for each day possession is late.

Rent

Rent is the sum of money the tenant pays to the landlord for the use and possession of the premises. It usually is payable in advance and in installments. Rent can be paid at any interval (e.g., annually, semiannually, daily, weekly, monthly). In most commercial and residential properties, the landlord's mortgage on the leased premises has payment due monthly, and because the landlord uses the rent to make the payments, rent is due monthly.

A tenant has a contractual obligation to pay rent. This obligation continues even if the tenant has transferred its interest to the premises or has vacated the premises. The obligation to pay rent, as earlier discussed, usually is independent of the landlord's promises and covenants under the lease. Even though the landlord may be in default under the lease, a tenant must still pay the rent.

rent
Money paid by a tenant to a landlord for the use and possession of property pursuant to a lease.

Percentage Rent

Rent typically is paid in a fixed amount of dollars and is due and payable on a certain day of the month. Rent, however, may be based on a percentage of sales; this type of rental provision commonly is found in retail store leases. A **percentage rent** clause provides that a percentage of the gross sales sold from the premises will be the amount of the rent. Many leases provide for a minimum rent, or base rent, to be paid plus a percentage of sales over a certain amount. These leases are percentage sales leases with a minimum base of sales guaranteed. For example, if the landlord believes that the tenant will sell $1 million in merchandise from the location in a given year and the landlord wants a 3 percent percentage rent, the landlord will ask that $30,000 of rent (3 percent of $1 million) be payable in twelve equal installments of $2,500 per month. The rent figure is expressed in the lease as a fixed $2,500 per month together with 3 percent of all sales in excess of $1 million.

A percentage rent clause permits a landlord to earn additional rental income based on the amount of a retail tenant's gross sales or net sales from the premises. Such clauses usually are drafted to calculate the tenant's percentage rent obligations on an annual basis. The reason percentage rent has traditionally been due on an annual basis is because each lease year or calendar year (depending on which annual period is used in a given lease) must occur and conclude, and the final gross sales figures must be calculated before the actual percentage rent obligation for the year can be determined. It is not uncommon for leases today to provide for quarterly or even monthly payments of percentage rent. Such payments during the year are stated as payments "made against" the tenant's obligation for percentage rent, which is subject to a final determination. If necessary, a payment adjustment of some amount will be made after the close of the annual period.

Some of the key terms in percentage rent clauses are (a) a percentage rent rate; (b) the percentage rent breakpoint; (c) the amount and definition of gross sales; (d) the amount and nature of permitted exclusions or deductions from gross sales; and (e) the procedure or mechanism for verifying and, if necessary, adjusting payments of percentage rent.

Percentage rent rate and percentage breakpoint are concepts that are interrelated with the base rent obligation. A percentage rent rate is a mutually agreed on amount of the tenant's total annual gross sales that the tenant owes as percentage rent. This amount customarily is stated as a percentage. Different segments of the retail industry appeared to have settled on the "appropriate" percentage rate for their kind of store through negotiations over the years, and no attempt is made here to comment on what rate is appropriate for any given tenant.

The **percentage breakpoint** is the level of gross sales made during the year at which the percentage rent obligation commences. Thereafter, the percentage rent rate applies to all additional gross sales above the breakpoint. The two concepts are interrelated to the base rent

percentage rent
Rent based on a percentage of sales from a specific location. Percentage rent often is found in retail store leases.

percentage breakpoint
Level of gross sales made during a year at which time a percentage rent obligation will commence.

because a natural percentage rent breakpoint is an amount determined by dividing the base rent by the percentage rent rate expressed as a number instead of a percentage.

Required inclusions in gross sales and permitted exclusions or deductions from gross sales are fundamental to the percentage rent clause. The starting point of most lease forms is that the proceeds received from or attributed to everything and anything sold for cash or on credit (including lay-away sales, credit card sales, and sales paid for by checks that ultimately are no good) should be included in gross sales.

Most retailers and landlords agree that some or most of the following items should be excluded or deducted from gross sales: (a) the amount of any sales of fixtures, equipment, and property that is not carried as inventory; (b) sale price merchandise sold to tenant's employees at a discount; (c) the amount of any finance, insurance, or service charges on credit sales; (d) charges to customers for making deliveries or repairs to merchandise; (e) the amount of any cash or credit refund made on any sale in which the merchandise sold or some part thereof is thereafter returned by the purchaser and accepted by the tenant; and (f) any sums collected and paid out by the tenant for any sale or excise tax based on gross sales to the extent such taxes have been included in the gross sales price.

Regardless of whether the tenant is paying percentage rent on a monthly, quarterly, or annual basis, the tenant is obligated to provide a written statement of its gross sales for such a period within a prescribed number of days after the period closes. Timing requirements for reports should be reviewed with the tenant to be sure that they comport with the tenant's current practice of keeping books. Similarly, many percentage rent clauses delineate the specific kinds of books and records of gross sales (including the kinds of cash registers, cash register tapes, and sales slips required) that must be kept and maintained by the tenant and made available to the landlord so that the accuracy of the tenant's report of gross sales can be verified. These details must be reviewed and accepted by the tenant. Finally, many percentage clauses require the tenant to keep its books and records of gross sales at the premises. This may not be workable with a tenant who has multiple locations. Most landlords will, in such circumstances, permit the tenant to keep its records at a central office but will require the tenant to produce them at the premises after an agreed notice (five or ten days) requesting such production has been given by the landlord to the tenant.

Many leases also require that annual statements of gross sales either be audited by an independent certified public accountant or be certified as true and correct by the chief financial officer of the tenant, at the landlord's option. Because most tenants would not go to the expense of such an audit for their own purpose, a tenant may negotiate to limit the applicability of this requirement to situations in which the tenant's annual statement of gross sales for a prior annual period has been understated by a certain percentage (e.g., 3 percent or 5 percent), which is mutually agreed to be sufficiently indicative of improper or poor record-keeping practices to trigger the audit obligation.

Most percentage lease provisions permit the landlord to inspect or audit the tenant's books and records of gross sales. If the inspection discloses an understatement of percentage rents by a certain percentage (e.g., 3 percent or 5 percent) or more, the tenant bears the cost of the audit. If either the tenant's preparation of its annual statement of gross sales or the landlord's audit of the tenant's records of gross sales reveals that an overpayment has occurred, most leases provide that the tenant will receive a credit against percentage rent thereafter due.

A lease that contains a percentage rent clause may have a covenant that the tenant will operate and actively conduct the business from the premises. Retail leases often establish the hours the store must be open, such as 10 A.M. through 9 P.M. Monday through Saturday. Percentage sales leases may contain restrictions on assignment and subletting. A percentage sales lease may contain a **radius clause.** A radius clause prohibits a tenant from opening another store within a certain geographical radius of the leased premises. This is a way of protecting a market area for the location and ensuring a particular volume of sales. Example 13–1 shows a percentage rent clause.

radius clause
Clause contained in a lease that prohibits a tenant from operating another retail store or business within a certain geographical radius of the leased premises.

EXAMPLE 13–1

Percentage Rent

(a) In addition to Minimum Rent, Tenant shall pay to Landlord a sum equal to the amount, if any, by which _____ (_____%) percent of Tenant's gross sales for any whole or partial lease year exceeds the Minimum Rent payable for such lease year (hereinafter referred to as "Percentage Rent"). Percentage

Rent shall be due and payable on or before the tenth (10th) day of each calendar month during the term hereof and on or before the tenth (10th) day of the first (1st) calendar month following the termination hereof. On or before the tenth (10th) day of each calendar month during the term hereof, Tenant shall furnish Landlord with a written statement certified to be correct by Tenant showing the amount of gross sales in the Premises from the beginning of the lease year to the end of the previous calendar month or portion thereof. If, by the end of any such preceding calendar month, _____ (____%) percent of the gross sales in the Premises shall have exceeded the Minimum Rent payable for such lease year, Tenant shall pay Landlord the Percentage Rent due hereunder on the basis of such sales less the aggregate of Percentage Rent previously paid by Tenant during the lease year.

(b) The term "gross sales" as used herein shall be construed to include the entire sales price, whether for cash or otherwise, of all merchandise sold (including gift and merchandise certificates) and services rendered, and all other receipts whatsoever of all business conducted in or from the Premises whether made by Tenant or any permissible subtenant, concessionaire or licensee. Each sale upon installment or credit shall be treated as a sale for the full price in the month during which such sale was made, and there shall be no deduction from gross sales for uncollected or noncollectable credit accounts. Gross sales shall not include sums collected and paid out for any sales or retail excise tax imposed by any duly constituted governmental authority.

(c) Tenant shall maintain at the Premises and shall cause any permissible subtenants, concessionaires or licensees to keep and maintain accurate books and records which shall disclose separately for each business day of the term all information required to determine gross sales (including but not limited to inventories and receipts of merchandise, telephone and mail order slips, all federal, state and local sales tax returns, records of daily bank deposits of the entire receipts from transactions in, at, or from the Premises, sales slips, daily dated cash register tapes, sales books and bank statements). Such books and records shall be open to inspection and audit at the Premises by Landlord or its duly authorized agents at any time within two years following the close of the lease year in question. If such audit shall disclose a deficiency in rent, Tenant shall promptly pay such deficiency. If such audit shows gross sales to be understated by two (2%) percent or more, Tenant shall pay the cost of such audit in addition to any deficiency and if such audit shows gross sales to be understated by five (5%) percent or more, Landlord shall have the right to terminate this Lease upon five (5) days' written notice to Tenant, in addition to any other remedies provided for Tenant's default hereunder. Tenant shall keep and preserve said records for not less than twenty-five (25) months after the close of each lease year.

(d) Tenant shall submit to Landlord on or before the thirtieth (30th) day following the end of the lease year a complete statement signed by Tenant and either certified under oath by a duly authorized officer of Tenant or certified by a Certified Public Accountant, showing accurately and in reasonable detail the amount of gross sales made by Tenant and any permissible sublessees, concessionaires, or licensees, upon and within the Premises during the preceding lease year.

Use Clauses

(a) Use.

(a) Tenant covenants and agrees to use the Premises only for the Permitted Uses and for no other purposes; to operate its business in the Premises under the Tenant's Trade Name (or such other trade name as is adopted by a majority of stores operating under the Trade Name); and to conduct its business at all times in a dignified manner and in conformity with the highest standards of practice obtaining among superior type stores, shops or concerns dealing in the same or similar merchandise and in such manner as to produce the maximum volume of Gross Sales and to help establish and maintain a high reputation for the Shopping Center.

(b) Tenant covenants and agrees to continuously and uninterruptedly use, occupy, and operate for retail sales purposes all of the Premises other than such minor portions thereof as are reasonably required for storage and office purposes; to use such storage and office space only in connection with the business conducted by Tenant in the Premises; to furnish and install all trade fixtures and permitted signs; to carry a full and complete stock of seasonable merchandise; to maintain an adequate number of trained personnel for efficient service to customers; to open for business and remain open continuously during the entire Term from at least 10:00 A.M. to 9:30 P.M. Mondays through Saturdays and 12:30 P.M. to 5:30 P.M. Sundays, and to light its display windows and signs during those hours and on those days when the covered mall is kept illuminated by Landlord (but Tenant shall not be obligated to keep the same illuminated beyond 11:00 P.M. on any day). Tenant shall, if not in conflict with any governmental requirements, and provided that (i) at least one Department Store is open on such day and (ii) Landlord shall agree to cause the Shopping Center to remain open for such hours, also open for business for additional hours.

(b) Radius Clause.

Except for existing stores, Tenant shall not, nor shall any officer, director, shareholder, affiliate, franchisee or licensee or the like of Tenant, directly or indirectly operate, manage or have any interest in any other store or other facility for the sale at retail of merchandise or services similar to what is permitted under "Permitted Use" within _____ miles of the Shopping Center. Without limiting Landlord's remedies in the event Tenant should violate this covenant, Landlord may, at its option, include the Gross Sales of such other store in the Gross Sales transacted in the Premises for the purpose of computing Percentage Rent due hereunder. In the event Landlord so elects, all of the provisions of Section _____ hereof (relating to Tenant's records) shall be applicable to all records pertaining to such other store.

Gross versus Net Lease

gross lease
Lease wherein the tenant pays rent only; the operating expenses of the leased premises, such as taxes, utility costs, and insurance, are paid by the landlord.

net rent lease
Lease in which the tenant is responsible for all expenses of the leased premises, such as utilities, taxes, and insurance.

Lease rent may be gross or net. A **gross lease** is one under which the tenant pays rent only; the ordinary and necessary operating expenses of the premises, such as taxes, utility costs, and insurance, are paid by the landlord.

In a **net rent lease,** the tenant pays a fixed amount of money to the landlord that is net to the landlord, and the tenant is responsible for all expenses of the property, such as utilities, taxes, and insurance.

Exhibits 13–1 and 13–2 show the duties of landlord and tenant under both a gross lease and a net lease. Some leases may be a hybrid between the pure gross and the pure net lease. These leases may obligate the tenant to pay a fixed amount of rent to the landlord and then to pay certain escalations in the expenses of the property. It is not uncommon for leases of this type to contain tax escalation, insurance escalation, and operating expense escalation provisions. These provisions operate on a theory that the landlord is responsible for the amount of taxes, insurance premiums, and operating expenses during the first year of the lease. All increases in taxes, insurance, and operating expenses that occur during the term of the lease will be paid by the tenant. Sample provisions of a tax, insurance, and operating expense escalation clauses are set forth in Example 13–2.

EXAMPLE 13–2

Tenant shall pay upon demand, as additional rental during the term of this Lease, or any extension or renewal thereof, the amount by which all taxes, insurance premiums insuring the improvements and charges to maintain the common area, exceed the cost of all taxes, insurance premiums and

EXHIBIT 13–1
Landlord and Tenant's Duties under a Residential Apartment Lease (Gross Lease)

Tenant's Duties	Landlord's Duties
1. Pay rent to landlord.	1. Duty of quiet enjoyment.
2. Keep interior of property in good repair.	2. Keep property and common area in good repair.
3. Assign or sublet the lease only with landlord's consent.	3. Insure property and common area.
4. Surrender premises in original condition less ordinary wear and tear at the end of the lease.	4. Pay taxes.

EXHIBIT 13–2
Landlord and Tenant's Duties and Obligations under a Commercial Lease (Net Lease)

Tenant's Duties	Landlord's Duties
1. Pay rent to landlord.	1. Insure exterior of property.
2. Pay percentage interest of real estate taxes.	2. Maintain roof and exterior walls.
3. Pay percentage interest of insurance premiums.	3. Quiet enjoyment.
4. Maintain the interior and exterior of the property.	
5. Insure tenant's contents.	
6. Assign or sublet the premises only with landlord's consent.	
7. At the termination of the lease surrender the premises in the original condition less ordinary wear and tear.	

common area charges for the year _____. In the event the Premises are less than the entire property assessed for such taxes, insurance and common area charges for any such year, then the assessment for any such year applicable to the Premises shall be determined by proration on the basis that the rental floor area of the Premises bear to the rental floor area of the entire property assessed. Tenant's pro-rata portion of the increased taxes, insurance premiums or common area charges, as provided herein, shall be payable within fifteen (15) days after receipt of notice from Landlord as to the amount due.

Rent Escalation Clauses

During periods of inflation, a lease may require an adjustment in the tenant's rent by tying rent to an inflation-based index, such as the consumer price index (CPI). The tenant's rent increases as the index increases. The use of an inflator index protects the landlord's purchasing power of the rent dollar.

A CPI clause typically is an annual rental adjustment mechanism that uses some versions of the CPI or some other governmental or independently determined inflation-measuring statistic to determine the amount of each annual increase in the base or minimum rent. When reviewing a CPI clause, one should be careful to determine when the clause first "kicks in" if it is a "one-way or two-way escalator" and if potential adjustments are limited, or "capped."

Many (if not most) CPI clauses are drafted to operate on a calendar basis, and the effect of this fact must be considered.

If a tenant's lease term commences in the middle or latter part of a calendar year, then the first adjustment (with a CPI) usually is drafted to be effective "as of January 1," even if not determined until sometime thereafter. This arguably occurs prematurely because the tenant has not received the benefit of a year (or close to a year) of base rental payments at the original amount. A reasonable compromise that accommodates both landlord and tenant is to leave the adjustment mechanism intact as far as how it operates and what measuring period (e.g., calendar year) it uses but to have the first adjustment be postponed until the first anniversary of the commencement date of the lease instead of January 1. Subsequent adjustments can be treated similarly and be effective as of subsequent anniversary dates of the lease.

A CPI clause should adjust the minimum rate downward if the CPI declines over the relative measuring period. Although the historical trends of the past several decades belie the likelihood of this occurring, there is no conceptual reason why adjustment should not operate in both directions.

Tenants may try to limit the amount of any potential increase for any single measuring period. This usually is accomplished with language that establishes a ceiling, or cap, on any single adjustment by fixing it at no more than an agreed percentage (e.g., 4 percent or 5 percent of the prior year's adjusted base rent). Tenants also may try to limit the total "life-time adjustments" (to some agreed on percentage) of the original scheduled minimum rent. A sample CPI clause is shown in Example 13–3.

EXAMPLE 13-3

The annual rental hereunder shall be increased by an amount equal to the product of a (a) $_____ X (b) the difference expressed as a percentage between the Consumer Price Index, as hereinbelow defined, published for the month of _____ of the year _____.

"Consumer Price Index," as used herein, shall be the "Consumer Price Index for all urban consumers, U.S., City average, all items (1967) equal 100" issued by the U.S. Bureau of Labor Statistics. If the Consumer Price Index, published by the U.S. Bureau of Labor Statistics is discontinued, then the Consumer Price Index published by the U.S. Department of Commerce shall be used (with proper adjustment); and if the U.S. Department of Commerce Index is discontinued, then Landlord and Tenant shall in good faith agree on a suitable substitute.[1]

Another mechanism used to adjust base rent is a negotiated "set," or "bump," increase. Under this provision, the minimum rent usually is scheduled to increase a predetermined amount effective as of each anniversary date of the commencement date of the lease term.

---

[1]Phillip G. Skinner, *Office and Retail Leases—Representing the Smaller Tenant.* Real Property Law Institute (1988): Institute of Continuing Legal Education in Georgia, pp. 8.1–8.63. Used by permission.

Maintenance and Alterations of Premises

Most leases prohibit a tenant from conducting any use or making any modification that would in any way (a) violate a certificate of occupancy, (b) make void or voidable any insurance in force with respect to the premises or make it impossible to obtain such insurance, (c) cause structural injury to all or any part of the premises or to any improvements constructed thereon, and (d) constitute a public or private nuisance. Under appropriate circumstances, the landlord may want to consider granting the tenant the right to make nonstructural additions and modifications after receiving prior notice and detail concerning these additions or modifications. Most leases provide that all modifications, additions, or improvements made by the tenant to the premises shall be done in compliance with all applicable building codes and zoning ordinances and that the tenant shall permit no mechanics' liens to be filed against the premises. Example 13–4 shows a maintenance and alteration provision.

EXAMPLE 13–4

Tenant shall not make or suffer to be made any alterations, additions, or improvements in, on, or to the premises or any part thereof without the prior written consent of Landlord; and any such alterations, additions, or improvements in, on, or to said premises, except to Tenant's movable furniture and equipment, shall immediately become Landlord's property and, at the end of the Term hereof, shall remain on the premises without compensation to Tenant. In the event Landlord consents to the making of any such alterations, additions, or improvements by Tenant, the same shall be made by Tenant, at Tenant's sole cost and expense, in accordance with all applicable laws, ordinances, and regulations and all requirements of Landlord's and Tenant's insurance policies, and in accordance with plans and specifications approved by Landlord, and any contractor or person selected by Tenant to make the same and all subcontracts must first be approved in writing by Landlord, or, at Landlord's option, the alteration, addition or improvement shall be made by Landlord for Tenant's account and Tenant shall reimburse Landlord for the cost thereof upon demand. Upon the expiration or sooner termination of the Term, Tenant shall upon demand by Landlord, at Tenant's sole cost and expense, forthwith and with all due diligence remove any or all alterations, additions, or improvements made by or for the account of Tenant, designated by Landlord to be removed, and Tenant shall forthwith and with due diligence, at its sole cost and expense, repair and restore the premises to their original condition.

Most leases also identify the party obligated for repairs, maintenance, and general management of the premises. Items such as foundations, roofs, utility systems, and other major structural mechanical components usually are maintained by the landlord. All other items, including any items that benefit only the premises, usually are maintained and repaired by the tenant.

Most leases provide that the tenant will not permit any lien to be filed with respect to the premises or the building, and in the event such lien is filed based on work performed for or materials supplied to the tenant, the tenant will cause the lien to be satisfied, bonded, or discharged immediately.

Insurance

Most leases impose on a tenant the requirement to carry appropriate kinds of insurance coverage in amounts with a carrier specified in the lease. A commercial tenant's insurance obligation should, at a minimum, encompass fire and extended coverage and comprehensive public liability insurance, including property damage. The tenant may be required to insure not only contents but the actual premises as well. This is especially true in a freestanding structure in which the tenant leases the entire premises. Any policies of insurance required to be obtained by the tenant pursuant to the terms of the lease should provide by endorsement that losses are payable to the landlord and tenant as their respective interest appear. In addition, each policy required under the lease should contain an agreement by the insurer that such policy will in no event be canceled without at least thirty days' prior written notice to each party. The lease may permit the landlord to pay any insurance premiums not promptly paid by the tenant and to assess that cost to the tenant.

In addition, most lease provisions release and hold harmless both the landlord and the tenant from each other's actions in regard to the cause of any casualty to the premises that is covered by insurance. This release and hold harmless impairs an insurance company's right of **subrogation.** An insurance company has a right when it pays a claim to be subrogated or substituted to the party paid and obtain any rights this party may have against the party causing the accident to recover damages. For example, a tenant negligently starts a fire on the premises that causes substantial damage. The insurance carrier pays the landlord the cost of the damage. The insurance carrier then is subrogated or substituted in place of the landlord to proceed against the tenant and recover for the tenant's negligence in destruction of the premises.

When a lease holds both parties harmless from any action that may damage the premises covered by insurance, this release and hold harmless impairs the insurance company's right of subrogation. When subrogation is impaired, an insurance company does not have to pay a claim under the policy. It is easy to see how this situation can create a serious problem. If subrogation is impaired under the policy, then the insurance company pays no claim for the damage, and if the landlord and tenant have already waived rights against each other, the landlord or tenant has no right to recover for the damage either. The damage, therefore, is unrecoverable, and the expense of it must be borne totally by the landlord or the tenant. This potentially dangerous problem can be resolved by having the insurance company waive its rights of subrogation. This is routinely done, and waivers of subrogation oftentimes are already built into the "boiler plate" terms and conditions of a commercial insurance policy. The legal assistant, when reviewing a lease that includes hold harmless language, should review all the appropriate insurance policies to make sure that the right of subrogation has been waived by the insurance carrier.

subrogation
Right to be substituted to the rights of another person. For example, an insurance carrier who pays a claim to the insured is given the rights of the insured to proceed against any party who caused the damage resulting in the claim.

Damage or Destruction to the Premises

Under common law, a lease continued even after the premises had been damaged and destroyed, and the tenant was obligated to continue paying rent. The common law rule has been changed by statute in many states and often is changed within the lease agreement. It is not unusual for a lease to contain a fire damage clause that provides that the lease will terminate or rent will abate if the building or premises are destroyed by fire. Leases do provide, however, that a tenant is obligated for any damage that the tenant causes to the premises by the tenant's negligence or intentional conduct.

It also should be noted that many leases obligate a tenant to return the premises in the same condition as the tenant received it. This affirmative obligation would require the tenant to keep the premises in good repair throughout the term of the lease and to even protect it against casualties caused by fire or other risk.

A lease typically provides that if there is substantial destruction to the premises, either the landlord or the tenant may terminate the lease. The lease also provides that if there is partial or temporary destruction to the premises, the lease will not be terminated and the premises will be restored; the rent, however, will abate (not be due and payable) during the period of restoration or will abate in proportion to the amount of the premises that cannot be used. For example, a tenant leases 10,000 square feet of space. A fire causes 1,000 square feet of the space to be unusable, but the remaining 9,000 is usable. Under the restoration and abatement provisions in most leases, a tenant would only be responsible for 90 percent of the rent during the restoration of the 1,000 square feet of damaged space.

Obligation of Repair

Under common law, a landlord was not responsible for repair of the premises. The tenant leased the premises "as is," with full obligations to repair. The common law not only made the landlord not responsible for the repair of the premises, but also the landlord was not responsible for any injuries caused by the condition of the premises or the lack of repair. An exception to the common law rule was that a landlord was responsible for hidden defects that were known to exist. A hidden defect is a defect that the landlord knew about but did not disclose to the tenant and is a defect that the tenant would not discover on reasonable investigation or inspection of the property.

This common law rule is still followed in many states. Under certain types of leases, such as residential leases, state statutes have made the landlord responsible for defective premises.

Under these statutes, the tenant does have an obligation to make the landlord aware of defects and to give the landlord a reasonable time to repair defects before the landlord will be responsible for any injuries caused by the defects. A landlord also usually is responsible for injuries and accidents that occur in the common premises under the landlord's possession and control, such as hallways, stairs, and parking lots.

Condemnation and Eminent Domain

A lease ordinarily provides for what happens in the event that a specified amount of the leased premises is taken by condemnation, eminent domain, or other governmental right. If this happens, the landlord or the tenant usually has an option to terminate the lease. In the event an election to terminate is not made, the rent is apportioned in accordance with the proportion of the premises remaining tenable.

Default

Most leases contain provisions that indicate what shall constitute an event of default under the lease. At minimum, a tenant will be in default under the lease if the tenant (a) fails to pay any installment of rent or any other sum payable by the tenant under the lease, within a certain number of days after the due date; (b) fails to perform or observe any covenant, term, or condition under the lease, which failure continues for a certain period of days beyond the period of time necessary to cure if diligently pursued; (c) fails to continue its business as a going concern or tenant vacates or abandons the premises; and (d) fails to maintain certain evidence of financial stability.

Landlord's Remedies for Tenant's Default

A landlord's basic remedies for a tenant's default are to (a) sue the tenant for performance, (b) terminate the lease and sue for damages, and (c) dispossess the tenant and sue for damages. A landlord may sue a tenant for performance in the event of a default on the lease. For example, a landlord may sue a tenant for the rent, although this may require a suit brought each month, or the landlord may permit the rent to accumulate for a period of time before bringing suit. A landlord may sue a tenant for a nonmonetary default and ask the tenant to perform, or the landlord may cure the default and sue for reimbursement of the expense. For example, a landlord may sue a tenant to remove an unauthorized sign placed on the premises or the landlord may remove the sign and sue the tenant for the cost of removal.

A landlord has the right to terminate the lease and evict a tenant for the tenant's default. Once the lease is terminated, rental under the lease ceases and the landlord may only recover damages. The damage usually is the amount calculated by what the rent for the remainder of the term would have been less a reasonable rent that could be obtained for the remainder of the term by releasing the premises.

Most leases provide that a landlord may evict and remove a tenant from possession of the premises and not terminate the lease. The landlord then may act as the tenant's agent for purposes of reletting or releasing the space. The tenant remains responsible for the rent less any new rent received through reletting.

A lease may provide that the landlord has the right to serve notice of termination on the tenant that will accelerate all rent and other costs and charges reserved to the landlord under the lease.

An accelerated rent remedy is a provision whereby all the future, unearned rent is accelerated and made immediately due and payable at the election of the landlord in the event that an uncured event of default occurs under the lease.

A typical default paragraph may provide that on receipt of a termination notice, the tenant will peacefully quit and surrender the premises.

Landlord's Right to Perform Tenant's Obligations

Most leases grant the landlord the right to perform any duties and obligations required of the tenant pursuant to the lease and to charge the cost of such performance to the tenant. The right to perform includes the ability to make payment of any sums due and payable by the tenant under the lease on default by the tenant, such as obligations of the tenant to pay taxes or insurance. Most leases provide that any performance rendered by the landlord does not constitute a waiver of the tenant's default, thereby depriving the landlord of the right to exercise its other remedies under the lease for tenant's default.[2]

A lease provision covering the tenant's default and the landlord's remedies appears in Example 13–5.

EXAMPLE 13–5

The following events shall be deemed to be events of default by Tenant under this Lease:

(1) Tenant shall fail to pay when or before due any sum of money, becoming due to be paid to Landlord hereunder, whether such sum be any installment of the rental herein reserved, any other amount treated as additional rental hereunder, or any other payment or reimbursement to Landlord required herein, whether or not treated as additional rental hereunder, and such failure shall continue for a period of five (5) days from the date such payment was due; or

(2) Tenant shall fail to comply with any term, provision or covenant of this Lease other than failing to pay when or before due any sum of money becoming due to be paid to Landlord hereunder, and shall not cure such failure within twenty (20) days (forthwith, if the default involves a hazardous condition) after written notice thereof to Tenant; or

(3) Tenant shall abandon any substantial portion of the leased premises; or

(4) Tenant shall fail to vacate the leased premises immediately upon termination of this Lease, by lapse of time or otherwise, or upon termination of Tenant's right to possession only; or

(5) If, in spite of the provisions hereof, the interest of Tenant shall be levied upon under execution or be attached by process of law or Tenant shall fail to contest diligently the validity of any lien or claimed lien and give sufficient security to landlord to insure payment thereof or shall fail to satisfy any judgment rendered thereon and have the same released, and such default shall continue for ten (10) days after written notice thereof to Tenant.

(b) Upon the occurrence of any such events of default described in this paragraph or elsewhere in this Lease, Landlord shall have the option to pursue any one or more of the following remedies without any notice or demand whatsoever:

(1) Landlord may, at its election, terminate this Lease or terminate Tenant's right to possession only, without terminating the Lease.

(2) Upon any termination of this Lease, whether by lapse of time or otherwise, or upon any termination of Tenant's right to possession without termination of this Lease, Tenant shall surrender possession and vacate the leased premises immediately, and deliver possession thereof to Landlord, and Tenant hereby grants to Landlord full and free license to enter into and upon the leased premises in such event with or without process of law and to repossess Landlord of the leased premises as of Landlord's former estate and to expel or remove Tenant and any others who may be occupying or within the leased premises and to remove any and all property therefrom, without being deemed in any manner guilty of trespass, eviction or forcible entry or detainer, and without incurring any liability for any damage resulting therefrom, Tenant hereby waiving any right to claim damage for such re-entry and expulsion and without relinquishing Landlord's right to rent or any other right given to Landlord hereunder or by operation of law.

(3) Upon termination of this Lease, whether by lapse of time or otherwise, Landlord shall be entitled to recover as damages, all rental, including any money treated as additional rental hereunder, and other sums due and payable by Tenant on the date of termination, plus the sum of (i) an amount equal to the then-present value of the rental, including any amounts treated as additional rental hereunder, and other sums provided herein to be paid by Tenant for the residue of the stated term hereof, less the fair rental value of the leased premises for such residue (taking into account the time and expense necessary to obtain a replacement tenant or tenants, including expenses hereinafter described in subparagraph (b)(4) relating to recovery of the leased premises, preparation for reletting and for reletting itself), and (ii) the cost of performing any other covenants which would have otherwise been performed by Tenant.

(4)(i) Upon any termination of Tenant's right to possession only without termination of the Lease, Landlord may, at Landlord's option, enter into the leased premises, remove Tenant's signs and other evidences of tenancy, and take and hold possession thereof as provided in subparagraph (b)(2) above, without such entry and possession terminating the Lease or releasing Tenant, in whole or in part, from any obligation, including Tenant's obligation to pay the rental, including any amounts

---

[2]Carleton Richard Kemph, "Drafting Commercial Leases," *Real Estate Law Journal* 10 (1981): 99–111. Used by permission of Warren, Gorham & Lamont, Inc.

treated as additional rental, hereunder for the full Term. In any such case, Tenant shall pay forthwith to Landlord if Landlord so elects, a sum equal to the entire amount of the rental, including any amounts treated as additional rental hereunder, for the residue of the stated Term hereof, plus any other sums provided herein to be paid by Tenant for the remainder of the Lease Term;

(ii) Landlord may, but is not required to relet the leased premises, or any part thereof, for such rent and upon such terms as Landlord in its sole discretion shall determine (including the right to relet the leased premises for a greater or lesser term than that remaining under this Lease, the right to relet the leased premises as a part of a larger area, and the right to change the character and use made of the leased premises) and Landlord shall not be required to accept any substitute tenant offered by Tenant or to observe any instructions given by Tenant about such reletting. In any such case, Landlord may make repairs, alterations and additions in or to the leased premises, and redecorate the same to the extent Landlord deems necessary or desirable, and Tenant shall, upon demand, pay the cost thereof, together with Landlord's expenses for reletting including, without limitation, any broker's commission incurred by Landlord. If the consideration collected by Landlord upon any such reletting plus any sums previously collected from Tenant are not sufficient to pay the full amount of all rental, including any amounts treated as additional rental hereunder and other sums reserved in this Lease for the remaining Term hereof, together with the costs of repairs, alterations, additions, redecorating, and Lessor's expenses of reletting and the collection of the rental accruing therefrom (including attorneys' fees and broker's commissions), Tenant shall pay to Landlord the amount of such deficiency upon demand and Tenant agrees that Landlord may file suit to recover any sums falling due under this section from time to time.

(5) Landlord may, at Landlord's option, enter into and upon the leased premises, with or without process of law, if Landlord determines in its sole discretion that Tenant is not acting within a commercially reasonable time to maintain, repair or replace anything for which Tenant is responsible hereunder and correct the same, without being deemed in any manner guilty of trespass, eviction or forcible entry and detainer and without incurring any liability for any damage resulting therefrom and Tenant agrees to reimburse Landlord, on demand, as additional rental, for any expenses which Landlord may incur in thus effecting compliance with Tenant's obligations under this Lease.

(6) Any and all property which may be removed from the leased premises by Landlord pursuant to the authority of the Lease or of law, to which Tenant is or may be entitled, may be handled, removed and stored, as the case may be, by or at the direction of Landlord at the risk, cost and expense of Tenant, and Landlord shall in no event be responsible for the value, preservation or safekeeping thereof. Tenant shall pay to Landlord, upon demand, any and all expenses incurred in such removal and all storage charges against such property so long as the same shall be in Landlord's possession or under Landlord's control. Any such property of Tenant not retaken by Tenant from storage within thirty (30) days after removal from the leased premises shall, at Landlord's option, be deemed conveyed by Tenant to Landlord under this Lease as by a bill of sale without further payment or credit by Landlord to Tenant.

(c) Pursuit of any of the foregoing remedies shall not preclude pursuit of any of the other remedies herein provided or any other remedies provided by law (all such remedies being cumulative), nor shall pursuit of any remedy herein provided constitute a forfeiture or waiver of any rental due to Landlord hereunder or of any damages accruing to Landlord by reason of the violation of any of the terms, provisions and covenants herein contained. No act or thing done by Landlord or its agents during the Term shall be deemed a termination of this Lease or an acceptance of the surrender of the leased premises, and no agreement to terminate this Lease or accept a surrender of said premises shall be valid unless in writing signed by Landlord. No waiver by Landlord of any violation or breach of any of the terms, provisions and covenants herein contained shall be deemed or construed to constitute a waiver of any other violation or breach of any of the terms, provisions and covenants herein contained. Landlord's acceptance of the payment of rental or other payments hereunder after the occurrence of an event of default shall not be construed as a waiver of such default, unless Landlord so notifies Tenant in writing. Forebearance by Landlord in enforcing one or more of the remedies herein provided upon an event of default shall not be deemed or construed to constitute a waiver of such default or of Landlord's right to enforce any such remedies with respect to such default or any subsequent default. If, on account of any breach or default by Tenant in Tenant's obligations under the terms and conditions of this Lease, it shall become necessary or appropriate for Landlord to employ or consult with an attorney concerning or to defend any of Landlord's rights or remedies hereunder, Tenant agrees to pay reasonable attorneys' fees so incurred.

(d) Without limiting the foregoing, to the extent permitted by law, Tenant hereby: (i) appoints and designates the leased premises as a proper place for service of process upon Tenant, and agrees that service of process upon any person apparently employed by Tenant upon the leased premises or leaving process in a conspicuous place within the leased premises shall constitute personal service of such process upon Tenant (provided, however, Landlord does not hereby waive the right to serve Tenant with process by any other lawful means); (ii) expressly waives any right to trial by jury; and (iii) expressly waives the service of any notice under any existing or future law of the State of Georgia applicable to landlords and tenants.

Landlord's Lien

Some leases provide that a landlord has a lien against the personal effects of a tenant stored on the leased premises to secure the performance of the tenant under the lease. This lien often is created as a security interest and is perfected by the filing of the Uniform Commercial Code financing statement. If the tenant defaults, the landlord has the right to repossess the tenant's personal property and sell it to pay the tenant's obligations under the lease.

Grace Periods

Most landlords are willing to accept a five- to ten-day notice and cure period for monetary defaults such as failure to pay rent, taxes, or other expenses required of the tenant. Many landlords, however, request that such a notice and cure as to monetary defaults be limited to an obligation to provide such a notice an agreed number of times (e.g., two or three times in any twelve consecutive-month period). This provision prevents a repeat offender from taking advantage of the notice requirement by repeatedly paying monetary obligations only after notices of default have been received.

Other defaults under the lease that are nonmonetary often are more difficult to cure because the requirements for cure may not be solely within the control of the tenant. For example, a lease obligates a tenant to operate its business in full compliance of all health, safety, and fire codes. The tenant installs electrical equipment that requires part of the premises to be rewired. The rewiring is not approved by the building inspector. The tenant is in default under the lease and must not only have the wiring replaced but also schedule another inspection. A longer period of notice and cure (usually twenty or thirty days) is commonplace for nonmonetary defaults.

Tenant's Remedies for Landlord's Default

As previously mentioned, the covenants of a commercial lease are independent, so that a tenant does not have the right to offset or not pay the rent due to a landlord's default under the lease. This leaves the tenant with only the remedy of suing the landlord to perform or for damages caused by nonperformance.

Quiet Enjoyment

Most leases provide that the landlord covenants that the tenant will peacefully and quietly enjoy the premises without hindrance or interference by the landlord for the entire duration of the lease term, subject to each party's performance of the provisions of the lease.[3] A sample of a quiet enjoyment provision is shown in Example 13–6.

EXAMPLE 13–6

Landlord agrees that if Tenant shall perform all the covenants and agreements herein required to be performed by Tenant, Tenant shall, subject to the terms of this Lease, at times during the continuance of this Lease, have the peaceable and quiet enjoyment and possession of the Demised Premises.

Surrender the Premises

Most leases provide that on expiration or termination of the lease, the tenant will peacefully and quietly surrender the premises in the original condition, less ordinary wear and tear. The tenant usually has a right to remove trade fixtures at the termination of the lease. This right to

---

[3]Ibid.

remove trade fixtures, however, often is limited to the following provisions: (a) the tenant can remove trade fixtures before the termination of the lease; (b) the trade fixtures cannot be removed if the tenant is in default; and (c) the tenant must repair all damage to the premises caused by the removal of the trade fixtures. Most leases provide that if trade fixtures remain in the premises on termination of the lease, the landlord has the right to remove the trade fixtures and store them. The landlord has no liability for any damage caused to the trade fixtures during the removal and storage, and the landlord can recover from the tenant the cost of such removal and storage. A sample provision regarding surrender of the premises is shown in Example 13–7.

EXAMPLE 13-7

(a) Tenant shall, at least one hundred eighty (180) days before the last day of the Lease Term, give to Landlord a written notice of intention to surrender the premises on that date, but nothing contained therein or in the failure of Tenant to give such notice shall be construed as an extension of the Term, or as consent of Landlord to any holding over by Tenant.

(b) At the end of the Term, or any renewal thereof, or other sooner termination of this Lease, the Tenant peaceably will deliver to the Landlord possession of the premises, together with all improvements or additions upon or belonging to the same, by whomsoever made, in the same condition as received, or first installed, ordinary wear and tear, damage by fire, earthquake, act of God or the elements alone excepted. Tenant may, upon the termination of this Lease, remove all movable furniture and equipment belonging to Tenant, at Tenant's sole cost, title to which shall be in the name of Tenant until such termination, repairing any damage caused by such removal. Property not so removed shall be deemed abandoned by the Tenant, and title to the same shall thereupon pass to Landlord. Upon request by Landlord, unless otherwise agreed to in writing by Landlord, Tenant shall remove, at Tenant's sole cost, any or all permanent improvements or additions to the premises installed by or at the expense of Tenant and all movable furniture and equipment belonging to Tenant which may be left by Tenant and repair any damage resulting from such removal.

(c) The voluntary or other surrender of this Lease by Tenant, or a mutual cancellation thereof, shall not work a merger, and shall, at the option of the Landlord, terminate all or any existing subleases or subtenancies or may, at the option of Landlord, operate as an assignment to it of any or all such subleases or subtenancies.

Estoppel Certificate

estoppel certificate
Written statement signed by either a landlord or a tenant swearing to certain facts concerning a lease.

It is not unusual for a lease to provide that the tenant shall, on request, provide to the landlord or to a person at the landlord's direction a sworn statement of facts concerning the lease, commonly referred to as an **estoppel certificate.** An institutional lender that is making a loan to the landlord and taking the premises as security will request estoppel certificates from the tenants. A purchaser of the premises from the landlord will likewise request estoppel certificates from the tenants. The estoppel certificates normally refer to an annexed true copy of the lease and should include a confirmation that (a) the lease is in full force and effect; (b) the lease has not been supplemented, amended, or modified in any respect; (c) no default under the lease exists and no event has occurred that, with the giving of notice and/or lapse of time, would become a default under the lease; and (d) there are no defenses, setoffs, recoupments, claims, or counterclaims of any nature by or on behalf of such party against the other.[4] An estoppel certificate is shown as Exhibit 13–3 at the end of this chapter.

Memorandum of Lease

Most leases are not recorded. In some instances, to protect the tenant's interest in the lease or if the lease contains certain additional provisions such as options to purchase the premises by the tenant, a memorandum of lease is recorded. A memorandum of lease includes all operative terms of the lease as well as any purchase options, renewals, and first refusals of additional space. Recording a memorandum in the real property records in which the premises are fully located protects the tenant against a landlord who might otherwise release or wrong-

---

[4] Ibid.

fully convey the premises to a bona fide purchaser having no notice of the tenant's rights.[5] An example of a short-form memorandum lease provision is set forth in Example 13–8. An example of a short-form memorandum prepared for recordation is shown in Exhibit 13–4 at the end of this chapter.

EXAMPLE 13-8

SHORT FORM LEASE. LESSOR and LESSEE hereby agree to enter into a Short-Form Lease setting out (a) the names of the parties hereto, (b) the description of Demised Premises as the same appears in Exhibit A hereof (c) the dates of this Lease Agreement and of its initial and extension or renewal terms and (d) LESSEE's rights upon termination of this Lease Agreement; such Short-Form Lease shall be in writing, duly executed by all the parties hereto on the date hereof or at any time thereafter as prepared and requested by either party hereof, and shall be properly attested and acknowledged for recording in Ohio.

Limitation on the Landlord's Liability

Landlords in commercial leases strive to minimize personal liability. It is not unusual for the lease to provide that the landlord is not responsible for any damage done to the tenant or to the tenant's property or personal effects because of the landlord's failure to perform the landlord's obligations under the lease and that any recovery for any liability of whatever nature under the lease can only be made against the landlord's interest in the premises. This type of provision protects the landlord but does leave the tenant in a precarious situation of not being able to recover for any of the landlord's defaults under the lease.

A limitation of landlord's liability clause may contain an exception for the landlord's intentional misconduct or gross negligence.[6]

ASSIGNMENTS, SUBLETTING, OR MORTGAGING OF THE LEASED PREMISES

The general rule is that a tenant may assign, sublet, or mortgage his or her interest in the lease. An **assignment,** by definition, is when the tenant transfers all of his or her interest under the lease and retains nothing. A **sublet** is when a tenant transfers only a portion of his or her interest under the lease and the tenant retains some interest. For example, if a tenant leased the premises for five years, a sublet may be when he or she transfers possession for only two of those five years. Another example might be a tenant who has leased 10,000 square feet of space and in turn sublets 5,000 square feet of this space to another person.

Restrictions on assignment or subletting of the lease are strictly construed. This means that if the lease prohibits only assignments, then subletting is permissible. If the lease prohibits only subletting, then assignments are permissible. It is not unusual for leases to provide that both assignments and subletting are prohibited or can only take place with the landlord's prior written consent.

An assignment or sublet in violation of a lease restriction could result in the lease being in default. If the landlord accepts rent from an assignee, or subtenant, after a nonauthorized assignment, the landlord may waive its right to declare the lease in default.

The original tenant, after an assignment or sublet, remains responsible on the lease for rent and other lease obligations unless the lease provides otherwise.

An assignee of a lease has the responsibility for rent as long as the assignee is in possession and is responsible for lease covenants that run with the land. Although the definition and interpretation of lease covenants that run with the land vary from state to state, they usually include any type of use restrictions. An assignee, by express agreement, can be required to assume all obligations under the lease. An express assumption of all lease obligations makes the assignee as responsible as the original tenant. The assumption of lease covenants by an

assignment
With regard to a lease, it is when the tenant transfers all of his or her interest under the lease and retains nothing.

sublet
In regard to a lease, it is when the tenant transfers only a portion of his or her interest under the lease and the tenant retains some interest.

[5]Ibid.
[6]Ibid.

PROFILE

LIZBETH F. HENDERSON

What do you like best about your work?

Although I have been a real estate paralegal for twenty years, I find that no two projects are the same, and I am constantly learning new things and meeting new challenges. I am fortunate to work for a firm with an expansive real estate practice, so I have the opportunity to work on a wide variety of commercial real estate transactions including shopping center and apartment development and loan and timber transactions. For the most part, I work without direct day-to-day supervision and enjoy responding to client needs and requests directly.

What is the greatest challenge that you face in your area of work?

The greatest challenge I face is prioritizing the work of the many attorneys with whom I work. I not only find it difficult to juggle deadlines but also to recognize and incorporate the different attorney working styles with client demands. In addition, although new technology has in many ways made our jobs easier, it has also made quick deadlines the norm. With the use of overnight delivery, faxes, and e-mails, clients and attorneys alike anticipate that your work will be done quickly as well as efficiently.

What advice do you have for would-be paralegals in your area of work?

The best advice I can give to anyone who would like to become a commercial real estate paralegal is to try to find a position with a law firm or company that does a wide breadth of real estate work. The many facets of the commercial real estate industry will give a paralegal the opportunity to work in different areas with different clients, which keeps your job interesting and challenging. It is also important to ask a lot of questions. Tap into the experience of attorneys as well as senior paralegals, as they are a wealth of information and knowledge.

What are some tips for success as a paralegal in your area of work?

Staying organized and keeping on top of deadlines are the most important things a real estate paralegal can do. You become invaluable if you remind attorneys and clients of upcoming deadlines. Give them every opportunity to develop confidence in your abilities. Become familiar with the computer system you will be working with, especially the document management system, because you will find that there is a form for almost every document you will be asked to prepare. Finally, try to do all of your post-closing work as quickly after a closing as possible—otherwise it becomes easy to neglect.

Liz Henderson is a commercial real estate paralegal specialist in the Atlanta office of Sutherland, Asbill & Brennan, LLP, a large nationally recognized law firm with offices in Washington, D.C., New York, Austin, Texas, and Tallahassee, Florida. Liz received her paralegal certificate from the National Center for Paralegal Training after graduating with a B.A. degree in communications from Rollins College in Winter Park, Florida. Before joining Sutherland, Asbill & Brennan, Liz worked at Alston & Bird in Atlanta and Botein, Hays & Sklar in New York.

---

assignee, however, does not release the original tenant. The landlord can sue both the original tenant and the assignee in the event of a default.

A subtenant or sublessee has no responsibility to the original landlord under the lease for either rent or any of the lease covenants. A sublessee is responsible only to the tenant and responsible only pursuant to the terms of the sublease. Great care should be taken when drafting subleases to make sure that the sublease does not conflict with the main lease and that the tenant has full rights to enforce performance of the main lease covenants against the sublessee. This is important because the original tenant is responsible to the landlord for any acts of the subtenant under the sublease. Example 13–9 shows an assignment and subletting provision.

EXAMPLE 13–9

(a) Tenant shall not sell, assign, encumber or otherwise transfer by operation of law or otherwise this Lease, or any interest herein, nor shall Tenant sublet the premises or any portion thereof, or suffer any other person to occupy or use the premises or any portion thereof, without the prior written consent of Landlord as provided herein, nor shall Tenant permit any lien to be placed on the

Tenant's interest by operation of law. Tenant shall, by written notice, advise Landlord of its desire from and after a stated date (which shall not be less than thirty (30) days nor more than ninety (90) days after the date of Tenant's notice) to sublet the premises or any portion thereof for any part of the Term ("Subletting Notice"); and supply Landlord with such information, financial statements, verifications and related materials as Landlord may request or desire to evaluate the written request to sublet or assign. In such event, Landlord shall have the right, to be exercised by giving written notice to Tenant (Landlord's "Termination Notice") within ten days after receipt of Tenant's Subletting Notice, to terminate this Lease as to the portion of the premises described in Tenant's Subletting Notice and this Lease shall thereupon be terminated with respect to the portion of the premises therein described as of the date stated in Tenant's Notice. Tenant's Subletting Notice shall state the name and address of the proposed subtenant, and Tenant shall deliver to Landlord a true and complete copy of the proposed sublease with such Notice. If such Subletting Notice shall indicate that Tenant desires to sublet all of the premises and Landlord shall give its Termination Notice with respect thereto, this Lease shall terminate on the date stated in Tenant's Subletting Notice. If, however, this Lease shall terminate pursuant to the foregoing with respect to less than all the premises, the rental, as defined and reserved hereinabove and as adjusted pursuant to Paragraph 2, shall be adjusted on a pro rata basis according to the number of square feet retained by Tenant, and this Lease as so amended shall continue thereafter in full force and effect. If Landlord, upon receiving Tenant's Subletting Notice with respect to any of the premises, shall not exercise its right to terminate, Landlord will not unreasonably withhold its consent to Tenant's subletting the premises as requested in such Subletting Notice. Tenant shall, at Tenant's own cost and expense, discharge in full any outstanding commission obligation on the part of Landlord with respect to this Lease, and any commissions which may be due and owing as a result of any proposed assignment or subletting, whether or not the Lease is terminated pursuant hereto and rented by Landlord to the proposed subtenant or any other tenant.

(b) Any subletting or assignment hereunder by Tenant shall not result in Tenant being released or discharged from any liability under this Lease. As a condition to Landlord's prior written consent as provided for in this paragraph, the assignee or subtenant shall agree in writing to comply with and be bound by all of the terms, covenants, conditions, provisions and agreements of this Lease, and Tenant shall deliver to Landlord promptly after execution, an executed copy of each sublease or assignment and an agreement of said compliance by each sublessee or assignee.

(c) Landlord's consent to any sale, assignment, encumbrance, subletting, occupation, lien or other transfer shall not release Tenant from any of Tenant's obligations hereunder or be deemed to be a consent to any subsequent occurrence. Any sale, assignment, encumbrance, subletting, occupation, lien or other transfer of this Lease which does not comply with the provisions of this Paragraph shall be void.

A tenant may mortgage the leasehold interests or rights under a lease. The mortgage is subject to the terms of the lease and will terminate if the lease terminates. It is not unusual for lenders who take as security a tenant's obligation under a lease to enter into an agreement with the landlord to provide that the landlord will not terminate the lease unless notice is given to the leasehold mortgagee and the leasehold mortgagee has a right to cure all defaults. It also is important in representing leasehold mortgagees to obtain permission from the landlord to foreclose the mortgage and to accept an assignment of the lease and take over possession of the premises. A landlord often will agree and will recognize anyone who forecloses the leasehold mortgage as the new tenant under the lease. These agreements are called **attornment and nondisturbance agreements.** A form of attornment and nondisturbance agreement can be found at the end of this chapter as Exhibit 13–5.

The landlord also can mortgage its interest in the fee. The landlord's mortgage will be either subordinate or superior to the lease, depending on the time the mortgage was placed on the premises. The mortgage on the premises at the time the lease was entered into will be superior and the mortgage that was placed on the premises after the lease will be subordinate. These rules can change by contract and lease provision. It is not unusual for leases to provide an automatic subordination that states that the lease will be subordinate to any mortgage on the premises, regardless of when it is placed. Example 13–10 shows a subordination clause.

EXAMPLE 13–10

Tenant's rights shall be subject to any bona fide mortgage or deed of trust which is now, or may hereafter be, placed upon the Premises by Landlord. Tenant shall, if requested by Landlord, execute a separate agreement reflecting such subordination.

attornment and nondisturbance agreement
An agreement usually entered into between a tenant and a holder of a mortgage on the leased premises wherein each party agrees to recognize the other in the event of a foreclosure of the mortgage. The mortgage holder also agrees not to terminate the lease or disturb the tenant's possession in the event of a foreclosure of the mortgage.

A superior mortgage on the leased premises creates a problem for the tenant if the mortgage is foreclosed because the lease will terminate. A tenant often will try to obtain attornment agreements from the landlord's mortgagee, asking the mortgagee to agree that if it forecloses and the tenant is not in default under the lease, the lender will honor the lease.

Special Sublease Issues

A valid sublease effects no change in the relation between the landlord and the tenant and creates no new relation between the landlord and the subtenant. The tenant remains liable to the landlord for any breach of the prime lease. The landlord cannot collect rent directly from the subtenant, and the subtenant cannot bring an action to compel the landlord to comply with its obligations on the prime lease with respect to the subleased premises or to collect damages from the landlord resulting from such breach. Any default by the tenant on the prime lease that results in termination of the prime lease by the landlord automatically terminates the sublease.

Because of the lack of privity between landlord and subtenant, the subtenant's rights to remain in the space are at the sufferance first of the tenant and then of the landlord. If the tenant incurs financial problems and defaults on the prime lease, the subtenant's rights terminate with those of the tenant. If the subtenant does not have a covenant of quiet enjoyment from the tenant, the subtenant has no recourse against the tenant.

Provisions Normally Contained in a Sublease

A sublessor should be careful to stipulate that the term of the sublease ends at some period before termination of the prime lease. A sublessor should seek to avoid any liability for a breach by the prime landlord of its obligations under the prime lease and indemnification for any expenses that it incurs in enforcing the landlord's obligations under the prime lease to the benefit of the sublessee. In addition, the sublessor may desire to make more restrictive certain terms of the prime lease as they apply between the sublessor and the sublessee, such as the right to further sublease and to reduce the periods for making rental payments and curing breaches so that such periods will terminate before the time that the tenant is obligated to perform under the prime lease. For example, if under the prime lease the tenant has a ten-day notice and right to cure for failure to make rent payments on time, the tenant may want to provide in a sublease that sublessee has only five days from notice to make rent payments. This provides the tenant with an additional five days after default by the sublessee to pay the rent under the prime lease without causing a default of the prime lease. A sublessor may want to stipulate that insurance required to be maintained by the sublessee name both the sublessor and the prime landlord as insured and contain waiver of subrogation to both. The sublessor will want all covenants and provisions of the prime lease to be carried over into the sublease. The sublessor may seek indemnification for damages incurred by reason of the sublessee's action or inaction that creates a violation of the prime lease.

The sublessee should attempt to include the following provisions in the sublease: (a) a covenant of quiet enjoyment and an indemnification from the sublessor against damages incurred by reason of the sublessor's action or inaction in violation of the prime lease; and (b) a condition precedent to the effectiveness of the sublease that the prime landlord consents to the sublease and that the prime landlord enter into a nondisturbance agreement with the sublessee. This nondisturbance agreement provides that in the event there is a default under the prime lease, the landlord will honor the sublease according to its terms.

A sublessee may want a covenant that the sublessor shall be liable to cure any breach by the prime landlord, or the sublessor shall diligently commence and prosecute a suit against the prime landlord to force the landlord to perform under the prime lease.[7]

Lease Guaranty

It is not unusual for a tenant's obligation under a lease to be guaranteed by some other party. This may happen when the tenant is a corporation with little or no assets or an individual with-

---

[7]Jerome Berkman, "Negotiable Issues in Commercial Subleases," *Real Estate Law Journal* 13 (1984) 28–44. Used by permission of Warren, Gorham & Lamont, Inc.

out substantial financial reserve. For example, a landlord may require that the principal share-holders of a corporate tenant guarantee the tenant's performance under the lease. A form of lease guaranty can be found at the end of this chapter as Exhibit 13–6.

A lease guaranty usually is unconditional, and the guarantor agrees to perform all obligations of the tenant under the lease, including but not limited to all monetary obligations of the tenant such as payment of rent, taxes, insurance, utilities, or maintenance charges as well as all other obligations of the tenant, such as maintenance and repair obligations. It is not unusual for a guaranty to be limited in term. The major risks of tenant default normally are in the early years of the lease. It is common for a guaranty of a long-term lease to be applicable only to the first few years of the lease. For example, a subsidiary corporation enters into a ten-year lease with a landlord. The landlord may negotiate with the parent corporation to guarantee the first three years of the subsidiary's obligations under the lease.

Most guarantors agree to pay all costs of collection or enforcement of the guaranty, including attorney's fees and court costs.

Uniform Residential Landlord and Tenant Act

The common law rules regarding the landlord and tenant relationship have been modified in a number of states for leases of residential property by the passage of either part or all of the Uniform Residential Landlord and Tenant Act (URLTA). URLTA can be considered consumer legislation since it has the effect of tempering or modifying some of the harsher effects of common law regarding landlord and tenant relationship. URLTA attempts to balance the playing field between landlords and tenants in residential situations by giving the tenants more rights than they would otherwise have under the general common law. Some examples of this moderation of the common law are hereafter discussed.

URLTA requires an obligation of good faith in landlord and tenant dealings. This means that every duty under URLTA and every act that must be performed as a condition precedent to the exercise of relief under URLTA imposes an obligation of good faith in its performance or enforcement. An example of this obligation of good faith is that URLTA prohibits a retaliatory eviction by a landlord because a tenant has made complaints to public authorities about the condition of the premises or has made complaints to the landlord about its obligation to repair the premises.

Under URLTA, rent is generally payable monthly and is due at the beginning of each month. Unless the rental agreement fixes a definite term, the tenancy is a month-to-month tenancy. If the rental agreement provides for a term longer than one year it is effective for only one year.

A lease may also be enforceable even though it may not be fully signed by both the landlord and the tenant. An acceptance of rent without reservation by a landlord gives the rental agreement the same effect as if it had been signed and delivered by the landlord. Possession of the premises and payment of rent by a tenant without reservation gives the rental agreement the same effect as if it had been signed and delivered by the tenant.

URLTA prohibits certain provisions in a rental agreement. For example, the rental agreement may not provide that the tenant:

1. Agrees to waive or forgo rights or remedies under URLTA
2. Authorizes any person to confess judgment on a claim arising out of the rental agreement
3. Agrees to pay the landlord's attorneys' fees
4. Agrees to the exculpation or limitation of any liability of a landlord arising under law or to indemnify the landlord for that liability or the cost connected therewith

URLTA also provides that if a landlord deliberately uses a rental agreement containing provisions known by the landlord to be prohibited, the tenant may recover in addition to his or her actual damages an amount up to three months' periodic rent and reasonable attorneys' fees.

URLTA provides that a landlord may not command or receive a security deposit in an amount in excess of one months' rent. It also provides that upon termination of the lease, the security deposit held by the landlord may be applied to the payment of accrued rent and the amount of damages that a landlord has suffered by reason of the tenant's noncompliance with certain terms of the lease. An itemization of costs must be given by the landlord in a written notice to the tenant together with the amount due within fourteen days after termination of the lease.

URLTA provides for a comprehensive division of landlord and tenant responsibilities concerning the use and occupancy of the premises. URLTA imposes a duty on the landlord to keep the premises in good repair, particularly as it materially affects the health and safety of the tenant. A tenant may terminate the lease for the landlord's failure to keep the premises in good repair. A willful or negligent failure on the part of the landlord to provide heat, hot water, or other essential services gives the tenant a right to terminate the lease.

A landlord's remedy to elect to terminate or evict a tenant for failure of the tenant to perform under a lease has also been modified from common law and is regulated under URLTA. Under URLTA, a landlord cannot terminate a lease because of the tenant's default without a written notice to the tenant stating the default and giving the tenant thirty days to cure the default.

A copy of the Uniform Residential Landlord and Tenant Act including a list of states that have adopted portions of the act can be found at the following Web sites:

http://rental-housing.com/rental/URLTA.htm

http://www.law.cornell.edu/uniform/vol7.html

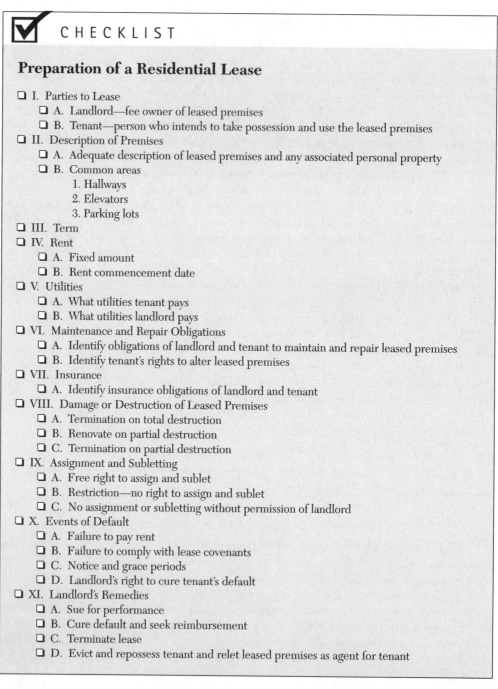

✓ CHECKLIST

Preparation of a Residential Lease

- ☐ I. Parties to Lease
  - ☐ A. Landlord—fee owner of leased premises
  - ☐ B. Tenant—person who intends to take possession and use the leased premises
- ☐ II. Description of Premises
  - ☐ A. Adequate description of leased premises and any associated personal property
  - ☐ B. Common areas
    - 1. Hallways
    - 2. Elevators
    - 3. Parking lots
- ☐ III. Term
- ☐ IV. Rent
  - ☐ A. Fixed amount
  - ☐ B. Rent commencement date
- ☐ V. Utilities
  - ☐ A. What utilities tenant pays
  - ☐ B. What utilities landlord pays
- ☐ VI. Maintenance and Repair Obligations
  - ☐ A. Identify obligations of landlord and tenant to maintain and repair leased premises
  - ☐ B. Identify tenant's rights to alter leased premises
- ☐ VII. Insurance
  - ☐ A. Identify insurance obligations of landlord and tenant
- ☐ VIII. Damage or Destruction of Leased Premises
  - ☐ A. Termination on total destruction
  - ☐ B. Renovate on partial destruction
  - ☐ C. Termination on partial destruction
- ☐ IX. Assignment and Subletting
  - ☐ A. Free right to assign and sublet
  - ☐ B. Restriction—no right to assign and sublet
  - ☐ C. No assignment or subletting without permission of landlord
- ☐ X. Events of Default
  - ☐ A. Failure to pay rent
  - ☐ B. Failure to comply with lease covenants
  - ☐ C. Notice and grace periods
  - ☐ D. Landlord's right to cure tenant's default
- ☐ XI. Landlord's Remedies
  - ☐ A. Sue for performance
  - ☐ B. Cure default and seek reimbursement
  - ☐ C. Terminate lease
  - ☐ D. Evict and repossess tenant and relet leased premises as agent for tenant

❑ XII. Tenant's Remedies for Landlord's Default
    ❑ A. Withhold rent
    ❑ B. Sue to enforce
    ❑ C. Sue for money damages
    ❑ D. Cure default and offset costs against rent
❑ XIII. Quiet Enjoyment
❑ XIV. Surrender of Leased Premises
    ❑ A. Tenant must vacate before lease term expires
❑ XV. Holding Over
    ❑ A. Tenant is deemed to be month-to-month tenant
    ❑ B. Tenant to pay same rent as during rent term
    ❑ C. Tenant pays additional rent during holdover period

A form of residential lease can be found at the end of the chapter in Exhibit 13–7.

Preparation of Commercial Lease

❑ I. Purpose of Lease
    ❑ A. Retail space
    ❑ B. Office space
    ❑ C. Retail space—shopping center
❑ II. Parties to Lease
    ❑ A. Landlord—fee owner of lease premises
    ❑ B. Tenant—entity that intends to take possession and use the property
    ❑ C. Broker—party to lease to enforce commission rights
❑ III. Description of Property to Be Leased
    ❑ A. Adequate description of leased premises and any associated personal property
    ❑ B. Common area property
        1. Hallways
        2. Elevators
        3. Parking lots
        4. Mall
        5. Restaurants
❑ IV. Term
    ❑ A. Fixed term
    ❑ B. Option renewals
    ❑ C. Term to commence in future
        1. Open for business
        2. Fixed future date
        3. Procedure and remedies for unavailability of space at commencement of term
❑ V. Use
    ❑ A. Specified use
    ❑ B. Any lawful purpose
❑ VI. Rent
    ❑ A. Fixed amount
    ❑ B. Percentage rent
        1. What is included
        2. Definition of gross sales
        3. Exclusions from gross sales
        4. Record keeping
        5. When is percentage rent payable
        6. Landlord's right to audit and inspect books
        7. Agreement to operate
        8. Radius clause
    ❑ C. Rent escalation (tax, insurance, expenses)
    ❑ D. Gross rent
    ❑ E. Net rent
    ❑ F. Inflators (CPI Index)
    ❑ G. When is rent due

☑ C H E C K L I S T

- ❏ VII. Maintenance and Alterations
  - ❏ A. Identify obligations of landlord and tenant to maintain and repair premises
  - ❏ B. Identify tenant's rights to alter premises
  - ❏ C. Alterations and maintenance to be lien-free
- ❏ VIII. Insurance
  - ❏ A. Allocate responsibilities for insurance between landlord and tenant
  - ❏ B. Waiver of subrogation in insurance policies
- ❏ IX. Damage or Destruction to Premises
  - ❏ A. Termination on total destruction
  - ❏ B. Rent abatement on partial destruction
  - ❏ C. Termination on partial destruction
- ❏ X. Condemnation—Eminent Domain
  - ❏ A. Termination on total taking
  - ❏ B. Abatement of rent on partial taking
  - ❏ C. Termination on partial taking
  - ❏ D. Allocation of condemnation award between landlord and tenant
- ❏ XI. Assignment and Subletting
  - ❏ A. Free right to assign and sublet
  - ❏ B. Restriction—no right to assign and sublet
  - ❏ C. No assignment or subletting without permission of landlord
- ❏ XII. Subordination and Nondisturbance
  - ❏ A. Lease period
  - ❏ B. Lease subordinate to mortgages
  - ❏ C. Lease subordinate to mortgages but with attornment and subordination agreement
- ❏ XIII. Events of Default
  - ❏ A. Failure to pay rent
  - ❏ B. Failure to comply with lease covenants
  - ❏ C. Notice and grace period
  - ❏ D. Landlord's right to cure tenant's default
  - ❏ E. Tenant's payment of all expenses of enforcement of lease
    - 1. Attorney's fees
    - 2. Court costs
    - 3. Reimbursement to landlord for expenses to cure or remedy default
- ❏ XIV. Landlord's Remedies
  - ❏ A. Sue for performance
  - ❏ B. Cure default and seek reimbursement
  - ❏ C. Terminate lease
  - ❏ D. Evict and repossess tenant and relet premises as agent for tenant
  - ❏ E. Accelerate rent
  - ❏ F. Landlord's lien against tenant's personal property to secure payment of rent
- ❏ XV. Tenant's Remedies for Landlord's Default
  - ❏ A. Sue to enforce
  - ❏ B. Sue for money damages
  - ❏ C. Cure default and offset cost against rent
  - ❏ D. Withhold rent
- ❏ XVI. Quiet Enjoyment
- ❏ XVII. Surrender of Premises
  - ❏ A. Tenant must vacate before lease term expires
  - ❏ B. Tenant may remove trade fixtures
    - 1. If tenant is not in default
    - 2. Repair damage to premises caused by removal
    - 3. Remove before termination of lease
- ❏ XVIII. Holding Over
  - ❏ A. Tenant is deemed to be month-to-month tenant
  - ❏ B. Tenant to pay same rent as during lease term
  - ❏ C. Tenant pays additional rent for holdover period

❑ XIX. Estoppel Certificate
    ❑ A. Tenant obligated to give estoppel certificate on landlord's demand
        1. To purchasers of leased premises
        2. Mortgage lender
❑ XX. Short-Form Lease
    ❑ A. Short-form lease to be prepared
    ❑ B. Short-form lease to be recorded
    ❑ C. No recordation of total lease
❑ XXI. Limitation on Landlord's Liability
    ❑ A. No liability for landlord's failure to perform
    ❑ B. Liability limited to recovery against the leased premises
    ❑ C. Total landlord's liability
    ❑ D. Landlord liability for intentional misconduct or gross negligence
❑ XXII. Other Lease Considerations
A form of small commercial retail space lease can be found at the end of this chapter in
Exhibit 13–8.

 E T H I C S : Legal Needs of the Poor

Attorneys have always considered it a professional obligation to volunteer legal services for the poor. The rules of professional responsibility and conduct that govern attorneys in most states require a public service obligation as part of the ethical requirements of being an attorney. This obligation, often called pro bono participation, taken from the Latin phrase *pro bono publico*, which means "for the public good," should not be limited just to attorneys. A paralegal should consider voluntary pro bono participation as a necessary part of his or her professional life.

One of the major problems of the American justice system is the unmet civil legal needs of the poor. The right to legal counsel in civil cases usually is provided by a number of quasi-governmental or voluntary associations that usually depend on full-time paid staff and volunteers to provide the necessary legal services.

Pro bono participation can provide the legal assistant with an opportunity to develop and improve skills in an area in which the legal assistant specializes. Many poor have landlord-tenant problems, and therefore, a knowledge of lease law can be applied by a legal assistant in a pro bono situation. The pro bono experience may also offer the legal assistant an opportunity to work in areas of the law in which he or she would not otherwise have the opportunity.

SUMMARY

Leasing is an important aspect of the real estate business. As the chapter points out, there are many issues to be considered in a lease transaction. Although lease negotiations are not adversarial in nature, it is obvious that a landlord and tenant do not have mutual interests in negotiating the lease. It is not always possible to please all the parties in a lease transaction, and even in the fairest and most reasonable of leases, some provisions favor the landlord and some favor the tenant. When reviewing or preparing a lease, the legal assistant should keep in mind the effect of any lease provision on the client. Knowledge and experience are the essential ingredients to becoming competent in the area of lease transactions.

KEY TERMS

assignment	lease	radius clause
attornment and nondisturbance agreement	lease guaranty	rent
	net rent lease	residential lease
commercial lease	percentage breakpoint	sublet
estoppel certificate	percentage rent	subrogation
gross lease	premises	tenant or lessee
landlord or lessor		

SELF-STUDY EXAMINATION

(Answers provided in Appendix)

1. T or F. Failure of a landlord to perform its obligations under a lease is a legal excuse for the tenant not to pay rent.

2. T or F. Rent is generally payable in arrears.

3. T or F. A lease in which the tenant pays rent plus all expenses of the premises is known as a gross lease.

4. T or F. A landlord generally has the right to terminate a lease upon a tenant's default.

5. T or F. A tenant after an assignment or sublet is released from its responsibility under the lease.

6. T or F. A subtenant is responsible to the original landlord for all lease covenants.

7. T or F. Foreclosure of a prior mortgage on the leased premises will terminate the lease.

8. T or F. A transfer of a tenant's complete interest in a lease is known as a sublet.

9. T or F. A transfer of a tenant's complete interest in a lease is known as an assignment.

10. T or F. An attornment is a sworn statement of facts concerning a lease.

11. Explain the theory of independent covenants in lease law.

12. What is the difference between an assignment and a sublease?

13. Briefly describe the difference between a gross rent lease and a net rent lease.

14. What title concerns should a tenant have when entering into a lease with a landlord?

15. Briefly discuss the basic remedies of a landlord for a tenant's default under a lease.

16. Identify briefly and discuss the basic remedies of a tenant for a landlord's default under a lease.

17. What is a lease guaranty and when would it be used by a landlord?

ADDENDUM

Exhibit 13–3   Estoppel certificate
Exhibit 13–4   Short-form memorandum
Exhibit 13–5   Subordination, attornment, and nondisturbance agreement

Exhibit 13–6   Guaranty of lease
Exhibit 13–7   Home or apartment lease
Exhibit 13–8   Small commercial retail space lease

EXHIBIT 13–3
Estoppel Certificate

Date:

Re:

Gentlemen:

     It is our understanding that _____
_____ (hereinafter called "Purchaser") intends to purchase the above-captioned premises, and as a condition precedent, such Purchaser requires that this certification be made by the undersigned (hereinafter called "Tenant").

     1. Tenant presently leases approximately _____ square feet of retail space located on the above-referenced Property, pursuant to the terms and provisions of that certain Lease Agreement dated _____, by and between _____, as Landlord and Tenant as Lessee, a copy of said Lease being attached hereto and made a part hereof as Exhibit "A" (the "Lease").

     2. Said Lease is in full force and effect and Tenant is primarily liable as Lessee thereunder, and the documents attached hereto as Exhibit "A" constitute a full, complete and accurate copy of said Lease, and said Lease has not been modified, supplemented or amended in any way, and there are no other promises, obligations, understandings, agreements, or commitments between Landlord and Tenant with respect to said Property other than as expressly set forth in said Lease.

     3. All contingencies and conditions precedent to the commencement, effectiveness, validity and enforceability of said Lease have been satisfied, and Tenant hereby ratifies said Lease. All duties of an inducement nature and all work required under said Lease to be performed by Landlord have been satisfactorily completed in accordance with the provisions of said Lease, and Tenant claims no off-

(continued)

EXHIBIT 13–3
Estoppel Certificate
(continued)

sets, rebates, concessions, abatements, recoupments, or defenses against or with respect to rent, additional rent, or other sums payable under the terms of said Lease, and there are no breaches or defaults under the terms of said Lease, and no event has occurred which, with the passage of time or the giving of notice or both, shall constitute a default by Landlord or Tenant under the terms of said Lease.

4. The base monthly rental presently payable by Tenant under the terms of said Lease is ($_____) Dollars per month, which monthly rental installments have been paid to Landlord through _____ and no other rent has been prepaid to Landlord or any other party, and there has been a security deposit in the amount of ($_____) Dollars paid to and presently held by Landlord with respect to said Lease.

5. The Lease Term pursuant to said Lease commenced on _____, and shall expire on _____.

6. Tenant has no interest, rights or claims with respect to said Property other than the interest, rights, or claims arising out of or with respect to said Lease.

7. Tenant is a corporation and is in good standing with the State of _____, and has full authority to execute the within document.

8. The undersigned officers of Tenant have full authority to execute and deliver this certificate as agents for and on behalf of Tenant.

9. Tenant is presently in actual, full and complete physical occupancy and possession of said Property, and Tenant has accepted said Property as suitable for all uses and purposes contemplated or intended under said Lease.

10. Upon acquisition of said Property by Purchaser, Tenant shall attorn to Purchaser and recognize Purchaser as Tenant's Lessor and Landlord pursuant to said Lease.

Very truly yours,

By: _____

EXHIBIT 13–4
Short–Form Memorandum

Memorandum of Lease Agreement

THIS MEMORANDUM OF LEASE AGREEMENT ("Memorandum") is entered into as of this 23rd day of March, 20___ by and between HARROLD ROBERTS AND THOMAS CLARK, whose address is 235 East Paces Ferry Road, Stanton, Ohio 60315 (collectively "Lessor"), and ACME CORPORATION, whose address is 6065 Roswell Road, Suite 120, Stanton, Ohio 60305 ("Lessee").

Recitals

By Lease Agreement dated March 23, 20___ ("Lease Agreement"), Lessor has leased to Lessee certain real property located at 5 West Paces Ferry Road, according to the present numbering system in Stanton, Knox County, Ohio, and being more particularly described on Exhibit A attached hereto and incorporated herein by reference, together with all buildings, structures, driveways, parking areas and all other improvements now or hereafter located thereon ("Demised Premises").

TO HAVE AND TO HOLD the Demised Premises for an initial term of approximately ten (10) years and three (3) months commencing on the date of the Lease Agreement and expiring approximately on July 31, 20___, together with the option to extend the initial term for one (1) additional term of five (5) years commencing immediately upon the expiration of the initial term, all on the terms and conditions contained in the Lease Agreement, which terms and conditions are made a part hereof by reference.

Pursuant to the terms of Paragraph 18 of the Lease Agreement, Lessor has the right, after the fifth (5th) anniversary of the Commencement Date of the Initial Term, to terminate the Lease Agreement under certain circumstances. In the event of any such termination, Lessee has an option, under certain circumstances, to lease space in the new development located on the property of which the Demised Premises are a part, under the terms and conditions set forth in that Paragraph of the Lease Agreement.

In addition to the terms referred to above, the Lease Agreement contains numerous other terms, covenants and conditions which affect the Demised Premises, and notice is hereby given that reference

EXHIBIT 13–4
Short-Form
Memorandum
(continued)

should be had to the Lease Agreement directly with respect to the details of such terms, covenants and conditions. Copies of the Lease Agreement are kept at the offices of Lessor and Lessee at the addresses set forth above. This Memorandum does not alter, amend, modify or change the Lease Agreement or the exhibits thereto in any respect. It is executed by the parties solely for the purpose of being recorded in the public records of Knox County, Ohio, and it is the intent of the parties that it shall be so recorded and shall give notice of and confirm the Lease Agreement and exhibits thereto and all of its terms to the same extent as if all of the provisions of the Lease Agreement and exhibits thereto were fully set forth herein. The Lease Agreement and all exhibits thereto are hereby incorporated by reference in this Memorandum and the parties hereby ratify and confirm the Lease Agreement as if said Lease Agreement were being presently re-executed by both parties and being recorded. In the event of any conflict between the provisions of the Memorandum and the Lease Agreement, the provisions of the Lease Agreement shall control.

IN WITNESS WHEREOF, Lessor and Lessee have set their hands and seals herewith and have caused this instrument to be executed in their names and their seals to be affixed hereunto by duly authorized officials thereof, the day and year first above written.

LESSOR:

_____ (SEAL)

HARROLD ROBERTS

_____ (SEAL)

THOMAS CLARK

LESSEE:

ACME CORPORATION, an Ohio
Corporation

By: _____

its President

[CORPORATE SEAL]

EXHIBIT 13–5
Subordination,
Attornment, and
Nondisturbance
Agreement

THIS AGREEMENT is made as of _____, 20__, by and among _____, a _____ ("Lessor"), whose address is _____, and _____, a _____ ("Lessee"), whose address is _____, and _____ , a _____ corporation ("Lender"), whose address is _____.

A. The Property.

The term "Property," as used herein, shall mean the real property situated in the County of _____, State of _____, legally described in Exhibit "A" attached hereto and by this reference made a part hereof, together with all buildings, structures, improvements and fixtures now or hereafter located thereon, and together with all easements and other rights appurtenant thereto.

B. The Lease.

Pursuant to the terms and provisions of a lease dated _____, between Lessor and Lessee (the "Lease"), for a term of _____, the Property has been leased to Lessee.

C. The Loan; Security Documents; Security Deed.

Lessor proposed to borrow certain sums from Lender to be evidenced by a promissory note. Lessor proposes to encumber the Property as security for payment of its obligations to Lender and, for such purpose, shall enter into various instruments and documents (collectively the "Security Documents"), including without limitation a Deed to Secure Debt and Security Agreement (the "Security Deed") from

(continued)

Lessor to Lender and an Assignment of Leases and Rents (the "Collateral Assignment"), which Security Deed and Collateral Assignment will be recorded in the real property records of _____ County.

D. Purposes.

In connection with the above-mentioned transactions, Lessor and Lessee have agreed to offer certain assurances and representations to the Lender, and all parties agree to provide for (i) the subordination of the Lease to the Security Documents; (ii) the continuation of the Lease notwithstanding any foreclosure of the Security Deed subject to certain conditions; and (iii) Lessee's attornment to the Lender or to such other parties as may acquire title to the Property as a result of any foreclosure or any conveyance of the Property in lieu of foreclosure.

AGREEMENT

NOW, THEREFORE, in consideration of the mutual terms and provisions hereinafter contained and other good and valuable consideration received by any party from any other, the receipt and sufficiency of which are hereby acknowledged, the parties agree as follows:

1. Notices of Default to Lender.

Notwithstanding anything to the contrary in the Lease, Lessee shall personally deliver or mail to Lender, at Lender's address set forth above, written notice of any default under the Lease by Lessor, and if within the time provided in the Lease for curing thereof by Lessor, Lender performs or causes to be performed all such obligations with respect to which Lessor is in default which can be cured by the payment of money, any right of Lessee to terminate the Lease by reason of such default shall cease and be null and void.

2. Subordination of Lease to Security Documents.

Lessee hereby subordinates its leasehold estate in the Property and all of Lessee's right under the Lease to the Security Documents and to all extensions, renewals, modifications, consolidations and replacements thereof, to the full extent of all obligations secured or to be secured thereby including interest thereon and any future advances thereunder.

3. Non-Disturbance of Lessee.

Lender agrees that, for so long as Lessee shall perform and satisfy all obligations of Lessee under the Lease in accordance with its terms, neither the Lease nor Lessee's rights pursuant thereto shall be disturbed or affected by any foreclosure of the Security Deed or conveyance in lieu of foreclosure. Lender's obligations under this Section 3 shall be null and void if Lessee shall, at any time, default in the timely performance of the Lessee's obligations under the Lease of this Agreement and not cure such default within the time, if any, allowed in the Lease.

4. Lender as Landlord after Foreclosure.

In the event that the Lender (or any other party) shall acquire title to the Property or shall succeed to Lessor's interest in the Lease, whether through foreclosure of the Security Deed, conveyance in lieu of foreclosure, or otherwise, Lender (or such other party) shall thereupon, and without the necessity of attornment or other act or agreement, be substituted as Lessee's landlord under the Lease, and shall be entitled to the rights and benefits and subject to the obligations thereof; provided that neither Lender nor any other party shall be:
    (a) liable for any act or omission of any prior landlord under the Lease (including Lessor); or
    (b) subject to any offsets or defenses which Lessee might have against any prior landlord (including Lessor); or
    (c) bound by Lessee's payment of any rent or additional rent beyond the then current rent period to any prior landlord under the Lease (including Lessor); or
    (d) bound by any amendment, modification, extension or supplement of the Lease made without Lender's prior written consent; or
    (e) bound by any representations or warranties made by any prior landlord under the Lease (including Lessor) whether such representations are set forth in the lease or in any other writing or were

(continued)

EXHIBIT 13–5
Subordination,
Attornment, and
Nondisturbance
Agreement
(continued)

EXHIBIT 13—5
Subordination,
Attornment, and
Nondisturbance
Agreement
(continued)

made orally, regardless of the knowledge of Lender or such other party of the existence and substance of any such representations or warranties;

and Lessee hereby agrees to attorn to and recognize such Lender (or such other party) as Lessee's landlord.

5. Payment of Rent upon Default.

Lessee has been advised that the Security Documents give Lender the right to collect rent and other sums payable under the Lease directly from Lessee upon the occurrence of a default thereunder, and that upon the receipt from Lender of notice of any such default, Lessee will thereafter pay all rent and other sums payable under the Lease directly to Lender (or as Lender shall direct) as they become due and payable.

6. Application of Insurance and Condemnation Proceeds.

Lessee has been advised that the insurance and condemnation provisions of the Security Documents give Lender certain rights to require that insurance and condemnation proceeds be applied to payment of the indebtedness secured thereby and not to restoration or rebuilding; and Lessee hereby waives any terms of such Lease with respect to the application of insurance and condemnation proceeds which are inconsistent with the terms of the Security Documents.

7. Estoppel.

Lessee hereby certifies to Lender as follows:

(a) Lessee is the lessee under the Lease, a true and correct copy of which, together with any amendments thereto, is attached hereto;

(b) Except as set forth in the amendment(s), if any, attached hereto, the Lease has not been amended, modified or supplemented and the Lease is in full force and effect;

(c) All of the improvements contemplated by the Lease have been entirely completed as required therein, the leased premises and the improvements thereon have been accepted by Lessee with Lessee in occupancy thereof and all sums, if any, payable by Lessor to Lessee in connection with the construction of such improvements have been paid in full and all conditions precedent to Lessee's obligations under the Lease have occurred;

(d) The term of the Lease commenced on _____, 20___, and will end, if not sooner terminated according to the terms of the Lease, on _____, 20___;

(e) Rent commenced to accrue under the Lease on _____, and there are presently no offsets or credits against rents thereunder and no payments are due from Lessor to Lessee under the Lease;

(f) Lessee has not prepaid (and will not prepay) any rent which is not yet due and payable under the Lease and no concessions, rebates, allowances or other considerations for free or reduced rent in the future have been granted;

(g) Lessee acknowledges that the Lease and the rentals thereunder have been (or will be) pledged to Lender and that Lessee has no knowledge of any assignment, hypothecation or pledge of the Lease or of any rentals thereunder, other than to Lender;

(h) Lessee has no knowledge of (a) any present defaults of the Lessor under the Lease or (b) any present condition or state of facts which by notice or the passage of time, or both, would constitute a default by Lessor under the Lease; and

(i) The party executing this agreement on behalf of Lessee is fully authorized and empowered to do so.

8. Binding Effect.

The provisions of this Agreement shall be covenants running with the Property, and shall be binding upon and shall inure to the benefit of the parties hereto and their respective heirs, representatives, successors and assigns.

(continued)

    IN WITNESS WHEREOF, the parties hereto have executed and sealed this Agreement as of the day and year first above written.

LESSOR:
[Individual]

_____ (SEAL)

Signed, sealed and delivered this

_____ (SEAL)

_____ day of _____,

20___, in the presence of:

[corporation or partnership]

_____

_____

Witness

By: _____

_____

Title: _____

Notary Public

[CORPORATE SEAL]

My Commission Expires:

_____

LESSEE:

[Notarial Seal]

[Individual]

_____ (SEAL)

_____ (SEAL)

[corporation or partnership]

Signed, sealed and delivered this _____

_____

day of _____, 20___, in the

By: _____

presence of:

Title: _____

_____

[CORPORATE SEAL]

Witness

_____

Notary Public

My Commission Expires:

_____

[Notarial Seal]

LENDER:

By: _____

Name: _____

Title: _____

Attest: _____

Name: _____

Title: _____

[CORPORATE SEAL]

(continued)

EXHIBIT 13-5
Subordination,
Attornment, and
Nondisturbance
Agreement
(continued)

**EXHIBIT 13-5
Subordination,
Attornment, and
Nondisturbance
Agreement
(continued)**

Signed, sealed and delivered this _____
day of _____, 20__, in the
presence of:

_____
Witness

_____
Notary Public
My Commission Expires:

_____
[Notarial Seal]

**EXHIBIT 13-6
Guaranty of Lease**

For and in consideration of the leasing by _____
_____ (referred to as "Landlord"), of certain Premises
(hereinafter referred to as the "Premises") to _____
_____ (hereinafter
referred to as "Tenant"), pursuant to the terms and provisions of that certain Lease Agreement
dated _____ by and between Landlord and Tenant (hereinafter collectively referred to as the
"Lease"), and in further consideration of the sum of Ten and No/100 Dollars ($10.00) to the under-
signed paid by Landlord, the receipt and sufficiency of which are hereby acknowledged, the undersigned (hereinafter collectively referred to as "Guarantor") hereby unconditionally guarantees to
Landlord the full and prompt payment of any and all rents, percentage rent, if any, or additional
rental (hereinafter collectively referred to as "rent") payable by Tenant under the Lease, and hereby
further guarantees the full and timely performance and observance of all of the covenants and
terms therein provided to be performed and observed by Tenant; and Guarantor, to the same extent
as Tenant, hereby agrees that if default or breach shall at any time be made by Tenant in the payment of rent under the Lease, or if Tenant should default in the performance and observance of any
of the covenants and terms contained in the Lease, Guarantor shall pay the rent and any arrears
thereof, to Landlord, and shall faithfully perform and fulfill all such covenants and terms of the
Lease, and shall forthwith pay to Landlord all damages that may arise or are incident to or in con-
sequence of any default or breach by Tenant under the Lease, and/or by the enforcement of this
Guaranty, including without limitation, all attorneys' fees, court costs, and other expenses and costs
incurred by Landlord.

  This Guaranty shall be enforceable by Landlord in a joint action against Guarantor and Tenant
or in a separate and independent action against Guarantor without the necessity of any suit, action, or proceeding by Landlord of any kind or nature whatsoever against Tenant because of Tenant's
default or breach under the Lease, and without the necessity of any other notice or demand to
Guarantor to which Guarantor might otherwise be entitled, all of which notices Guarantor hereby
expressly waives; without limiting the generality of the foregoing, Guarantor hereby expressly
waives any statutory right pursuant to _____ to require Landlord to take action against Tenant.
Guarantor hereby agrees that the validity of this Guaranty and the obligations of Guarantor here-

(continued)

EXHIBIT 13-6
Guaranty of Lease
(continued)

under shall not be terminated, affected, diminished, or impaired by reason of the assertion or the failure to assert by Landlord against Tenant any of the rights or remedies reserved to Landlord pursuant to the provisions of the Lease or any other remedy or right which Landlord may have at law or in equity or otherwise, the obligations of Guarantor being independent of the obligations of Tenant under the Lease.

Guarantor hereby further covenants and agrees that this instrument constitutes a continuing guaranty, and the liability of Guarantor hereunder shall in no way be affected, modified, or diminished by reason of any assignment, renewal, modification, or extension of the Lease or any modification or waiver of or change in any of the covenants and terms of the Lease by agreement of Landlord and Tenant, or by any unilateral action or either Landlord or Tenant, or by any extension of time that may be granted by Landlord to Tenant or any indulgence of whatever kind granted to Tenant, or any dealings or transactions or matter or thing occurring between Landlord and Tenant, including without limitation, any adjustment, compromise, settlement, accord and satisfaction, or release, or any bankruptcy, insolvency, reorganization, arrangement, assignment for the benefit of creditors, receivership, or trusteeship affecting Tenant. Guarantor does hereby expressly waive any suretyship defense it may have by virtue of any statute, law, ordinance of any state or other governmental authority, and further waives any and every defense of tenant, including, without limitation, any defense arising by reason of any disability of Tenant or by reason of the cessation from any cause whatsoever of the liability of Tenant.

In the event that other agreements similar to this Guaranty are executed from time to time by other entities or persons with respect to the Lease, this Guaranty shall be cumulative of any such other agreements to the effect that the liabilities and obligations of Guarantor hereunder shall be joint and several with those of each other such guarantor, and the liabilities and obligations of Guarantor hereunder shall in no event be affected or diminished by reason of any such other agreement.

All of Landlord's rights and remedies under the Lease or under this Guaranty are intended to be distinct, separate, and cumulative and no such right and remedy therein or herein is intended to be to the exclusion of or a waiver of any other.

Guarantor hereby expressly waives presentment, demand for performance, notice of nonperformance, protest, notice of protest, notice of dishonor, and notice of acceptance.

Landlord may, without notice, assign this Guaranty in whole or in part, and/or may assign all of its interests in and to the Lease, and, in such event, each and every successive assignee of the Lease and/or of this Guaranty shall have the right to enforce this Guaranty, by suit or otherwise, for the benefit of such assignee as fully as if such assignee were named herein.

Guarantor warrants and represents that they have the legal right and capacity to execute this Guaranty. This Guaranty shall be governed by and construed in accordance with the laws of the State of _____ .

This Guaranty shall be binding upon Guarantor and the successors, heirs, executors, and administrators of Guarantor, and shall inure to the benefit of Landlord, Landlord's representatives, successors, and assigns. If more than one party shall execute this Guaranty, all such parties shall be jointly and severally obligated hereunder and are herein collectively referred to as "Guarantor."

IN WITNESS WHEREOF, Guarantor have executed, sealed, and delivered this Guaranty, this _____ day of _____, 20__.

_____ (SEAL)

_____ (SEAL)

EXHIBIT 13-7
Home or Apartment
Lease

THIS AGREEMENT, made this   day of   , 20   , among

(hereinafter referred to as "Lessor")
to as "Lessee"), and   (hereinafter referred
                                                                      (hereinafter referred to as "Agent").

WITNESSETH: That in consideration of the mutual covenants hereinafter set forth, the parties do hereby covenant and agree as follows:

Premises and Term
1.   Lessor does hereby lease to Lessee and Lessee does hereby lease from Lessor Apartment No.   (hereinafter referred to as "Premises") in Lessor's apartment house situated at

in metropolitan Atlanta,   County, Georgia, according to the present system of numbering buildings in metropolitan

Atlanta,   County, Georgia, for a term commencing on the   day of   , 20   , and ending at

midnight on the   day of   , 20

Rental
2.   Lessee shall pay to Lessor, through   at its office in Atlanta, Georgia, promptly on the first day of each month in advance during the term of this Lease, a monthly rental of $ If such rental is not received by the fifth day of each month, Lessee shall pay to Agent a late charge in the amount of 10% of the monthly rental; Lessee shall also pay Agent a charge for any returned checks of Lessee in the amount of $5.00 for each returned check.

Security Deposit
3.   Lessee herewith deposits with Agent the sum of $ (hereinafter referred to as "Security Deposit") as evidence of good faith on the part of Lessee in the fulfillment of all the terms of this Lease, which Security Deposit shall be held by Lessor during the term of this Lease or any renewal thereof and for fifteen days thereafter. Lessor shall have the right to use said Security Deposit to pay, as fully as possible, the expense of any unpaid rentals, of any accumulated late charges or returned check charges, of any unreturned keys, as well as the expense of repairing any damage to Premises, except reasonable wear and tear occurring from normal use of Premises. Lessor's right to recover additional sums from Lessee for damages to Premises shall not be limited by the amount of said Security Deposit. In no event shall Lessee be entitled to apply the Security Deposit to any rental payment due hereunder.

Utilities
4.   Lessor shall furnish Lessee with the utilities checked as follows: ☐ cold water; ☐ hot and cold water; ☐ heat; ☐ all utilities for use in Premises. Lessor shall not be responsible for failure to furnish such utilities if the failure to do so is due to any cause beyond Lessor's control. Lessee shall pay all bills for utilities other than those checked hereinabove and used by Lessee in Premises, but all utilities shall be used only for ordinary household purposes. Lessee shall make a written request for any repairs or services to such utilities to Agent or any representative of Lessor at Premises, except in an extreme emergency in which event such notice may initially be given by telephone and later confirmed in writing. Lessor shall not be obligated to furnish any utilities paid for by Lessor to Premises at any time at which Lessee is in default hereunder. Lessor shall not be responsible for stopped-up plumbing, drains or disposals where such stoppage is caused by the introduction of foreign objects not intended for sewer disposal, and Lessee shall pay on demand all charges for repair of such stoppage.

Occupancy
5.   Premises will be occupied only by the following adults and minors:

No persons other than those named above (occasional overnight guests excepted) shall occupy or share Premises with Lessee. In no event shall more persons than the number of persons listed above occupy Premises.

Pets
6.   Pets may be permitted at the discretion of Agent and Lessor; provided that such pets do not constitute a nuisance to other tenants and provided that Lessee deposits with Lessor an additional damage deposit of $. Lessee recognizes that "reasonable wear and damage" as specified in this Lease does not include damage caused by pets and that Lessor's judgment shall be the sole factor in determining such pet damage. Pets must be on leash when outside of Premises and cannot be tied to anything outside of Premises. Lessee shall be limited to one dog or cat weighing not more than twenty-five pounds. Pets must be approved by Agent and Lessor, and such approval is contingent upon Lessee's observance of the foregoing conditions of this Lease and can be withdrawn at any time.

Extension Terms
7.   Unless another Lease is signed by the parties hereto or unless written notice of termination is given by either party at least thirty calendar days before expiration of the term of this Lease, this Lease shall be automatically extended on a year-to-year basis after the expiration of the initial term hereof without the execution of any new Lease or other instrument whatsoever. If Lessor desires to increase the rental payable hereunder for any such upcoming extension term hereof, Lessor shall give Lessee notice of such increased rental at least thirty days prior to the commencement of such extension term and, unless Lessee promptly otherwise notifies Lessor or Agent, then Lessor and Lessee shall enter in a new lease for such extension term at such increased rental. If Lessee does promptly notify Lessor or Agent that Lessee shall not accept such increased rental, then the term of this Lease shall not be extended and shall terminate as set forth herein.

Lessor's Failure to Give Possession
8.   Lessor shall not be liable to Lessee for failure to deliver possession of Premises at the commencement of the term of this Lease, but Lessor shall use Lessor's best efforts to give Lessee timely possession of Premises; if failure to do so is caused by any tenant holding over, Lessor will use all customary means to oust the old tenant. Lessee may secure a transfer of and prosecute in Lessee's name any cause of action which Lessor may have against such tenant holding over, and Lessee shall be entitled to retain all amounts recovered in such action.

Use of Premises; Maintenance; Indemnity
9.   Premises shall be used as Lessee's residence only and for no other purposes whatsoever; nor shall Premises be used in violation of any laws, ordinances, restrictions or regulations of any governmental body, nor so as to create a nuisance, nor to vitiate or increase the rate of insurance thereon. Lessee accepts Premises in its present condition and as suited for residential use by Lessee. Lessor shall not be required to make any repairs or improvements to Premises, except that, after receipt of written notice from Lessee of any damage or defect rendering Premises unsafe or untenantable, Lessor shall remedy such defective condition or, if the damaged or defective Premises is unfit for occupancy and if Lessor decides not to repair Premises, then upon written notice from Lessor to Lessee this Lease shall terminate, with rent prorated and any balance due Lessee refunded. Lessee shall be liable for, indemnify and hold Lessor and Agent harmless for any claim of damage or injury to the person or property of Lessee, Lessor's other tenants and any other party whatsoever, if such damage or injury be due to the act or neglect of Lessee, any guest of Lessee or anyone in Lessee's control or employ or brought into Premises by Lessee or if such damage or injury be due to any failure of Lessee to report in writing to Lessor any such defective condition. Lessee shall maintain Premises in good condition and repair and shall do no damage thereto. If Premises are rendered untenantable by fire, storm, earthquake or other casualty whatsoever, this Lease shall terminate as of the date of such destruction or damage and rental shall be accounted for as of that date.

Assignment and Subletting
10.   Lessee shall not assign this Lease or sublet Premises or any part thereof or secure a replacement for Lessee hereunder without first obtaining the written approval of Lessor or Agent.

Fixtures and Furniture
11.   Lessee may (if not in default hereunder), prior to the termination of this Lease, remove all fixtures, personalty and equipment which Lessee has placed in Premises; provided that Lessee restores Premises to its condition prior to the installation of such fixtures. Lessor shall not be liable for any loss of or damage to any property whatsoever, and Lessee shall at all times cause Lessee's fixtures, personalty and equipment to be insured in amounts satisfactory to Lessee.

Agent's Commission
12.   Agent's commission under this Lease shall be paid by Lessor under the terms of a separate agreement between Lessor and Agent. If any rent owing under this Lease is collected by or through an attorney at law, Lessee agrees to pay fifteen per cent of the total amount so collected as attorney's fees. Lessee hereby waives and assigns to Lessor all homestead rights and exemptions which Lessee may have under any law as against any obligation owing under this Lease.

(continued)

EXHIBIT 13-7
Home or Apartment Lease (continued)

Lessee's Conduct; Common Areas; Inspection 13. Lessee, Lessee's family and guests shall not act in a disorderly, boisterous nor unlawful manner and shall not disturb the rights, comforts or convenience of other persons in the building or complex in which Premises is located. The swimming pool, if any, and all other common areas will be used only in compliance with present and future written rules and regulations furnished to Lessee or posted in the common areas, and such pool and common areas are to be used wholly at the risk of the persons making use thereof. Lessor reserves the right to control the method, manner, and time of parking in parking spaces and to control and limit the entry to Premises by agents, messengers, delivery men, solicitors and salesmen. If Lessee or any member of Lessee's family or guest is present in Premises, then Lessor, Lessor's representatives or servicemen may enter Premises at all reasonable times for any reasonable business purpose. If such parties are not present in Premises, then Lessor's representatives or servicemen may enter Premises at all reasonable times (so long as written notice of such entry is left in the apartment after such entry) for the following purposes: repairs, extermination, preventive maintenance, failure to return tools or appliances within prescribed time, emergency, safety or fire inspections and building inspection by fire marshals, mortgage lenders, prospective purchasers or residents or insurance agents.

Lessee's Transfer 14. In the event Lessee is transferred or obtains employment outside of the Metropolitan Atlanta area (such Metropolitan Atlanta area being defined for the purposes of this Lease as any point within sixty miles in any direction from the intersection of Marietta and Peachtree Streets in downtown Atlanta, Fulton County, Georgia), then Lessee shall be released from further obligations under this Lease after Lessee completes the following conditions precedent to such release: (a) Lessee shall provide Agent with written notice of Lessee's intention to seek such release hereunder by virtue of such transfer or new employment at least thirty calendar days prior to termination hereof, and (b) such notice shall be valid only if accompanied by an affidavit from Lessee's employer confirming such transfer or new employment and by Lessee's payment of all rentals and charges whatsoever due under this Lease, including without limitation charges for any damage and repairs to Premises which are the obligation of Lessee under this Lease, and (c) Lessee shall release all Lessee's rights to any Security Deposit made under this Lease as liquidated damages for such cancellation of this Lease. This provision is for the benefit of Lessee, and the foregoing conditions hereof must be strictly complied with by Lessee in order to effectuate such release hereunder.

Premature Cancellation 15. This Lease shall be prematurely cancelled by Lessor as of the first day of any month during the term hereof, if (a) Lessee has given Agent written notice of such desired cancellation at least thirty calendar days prior thereto, and (b) if such notice is accompanied by Lessee's payment of all rental and other charges whatsoever hereunder, including without limitation charges for any damage and repairs to Premises which are the obligation of Lessee under this Lease, due up to such proposed date of cancellation of this Lease and by payment of liquidated damages for such premature cancellation in the amount of one additional month's rental hereunder. In such event any Security Deposit posted by Lessee shall be retained by Lessor as additional liquidated damages hereunder.

Termination and Reletting by Lessor or Agent 16. If Lessee defaults for three calendar days after written notice from Lessor or Agent of default by Lessee in the payment of rental due or otherwise defaults under any term, conditionor provision of this Lease; or if Lessee fails to reimburse Lessor for any damages, repairs or plumbing service costs when due under this Lease; or if Lessee shall abandon Premises; or if Lessee or any other occupant or guest in Premises shall violate or fail to comply with any term, condition or provision of this Lease or any of the Apartment Rules and Regulations hereinafter set forth in this Lease, as such rules may be reasonably changed or additional rules imposed and Lessee notified thereof, then Lessor or Agent shall have the option to either terminate this Lease by written notice to Lessee or, without terminating this Lease, to enter upon and take possession of Premises, removing all persons and property therefrom and, as Lessee's agent, to rerent Premises at the best price obtainable by reasonable effort, without advertisement and by private negotiations and for any term Lessor or Agent deems proper; Lessee shall be liable to Lessor for any deficiency between all rental due hereunder and the price obtained by Lessor on such reletting. Such termination shall not release Lessee from liability for any unpaid rentals under this Lease, past or future.

Surrender of Premises 17. Whenever under the terms hereof Lessor is entitled to possession of Premises, Lessee shall at once surrender Premises to Lessor and shall remove all of Lessee's effects therefrom; and Lessor may forthwith re-enter Premises and repossess itself thereof, removing all persons and effects therefrom and using such force as may be necessary, without being guilty of forcible entry or detainer, trespass or other tort. Lessee shall not remain in possession of Premises after the expiration of the final term of this Lease. Any holding of Premises by Lessee after the expiration of this Lease (except pursuant to a new lease, or the expiration hereof as provided in paragraph #7 hereof) shall not constitute a tenant-at-will interest on behalf of Lessee, but Lessee shall be a tenant at sufferance. Unless this Lease is extended pursuant to provision of paragraph #7, there shall be no renewal or extension of this Lease by operation of law or otherwise.

Service of Notices 18. Lessee hereby appoints as Lessee's agent to receive service of all dispossessory or other legal proceedings and notices thereunder,and all notices required under this Lease, the person occupying Premises at the time such notice is given, and, if no person be occupying the same, then such service or notice may be made by attaching the same on the front entrance to Premises. A copy of all notices under this Lease shall also be sent to Lessee's last known address if different from Premises.

Signs; Carding 19. Lessee shall place no signs, placards, or other advertisements of any character on Premises. Lessor may card Premises "For Rent" at any time within sixty days prior to the expiration of this Lease and during such sixty day period may exhibit Premises to prospective tenants.

Storage and Garage 20. If Lessor makes available to Lessee any storage space or garage outside Premises, anything placed therein by Lessee shall be stored wholly at the risk of Lessee, and Lessor shall have no responsibility in respect thereof. If Lessor makes available to Lessee any space for use as a garage or for parking cars, Lessor shall not be responsible for any damage to or loss of any vehicle stored or parked therein, nor for any part or accessory of such vehicle, nor for any property of any kind stored or left in said garage or vehicle.

Keys 21. All keys issued to Lessee hereunder shall be returned or the replacement cost thereof paid by Lessee when Lessee vacates Premises.

Definitions 22. "Lessor" as used in this Lease shall include Lessor, Lessor's heirs, executors, administrators, legal representatives, assigns and successors in title to Premises; "Lessee" shall include Lessee, Lessee's heirs, executors, administrators, legal representatives and, if this Lease shall be validly assigned or sublet, shall also include Lessee's assignees and sub-lessees. "Agent" shall include Agent, successors and assigns. Lessor, Lessee and Agent include male, female, singular, plural, corporation, partnership or individual, as may fit the particular parties. The captions used herein are merely descriptive of some matters contained therein and do not necessarily describe the contents of each paragraph.

Miscellaneous 23. Except for the commission agreement between Lessor and Agent referred to hereinabove, this Lease contains the entire agreement of the parties and no representation, inducement, promises or agreements, oral or otherwise, between the parties not embodied herein shall be of any force or effect. No failure of Lessor to exercise any power given Lessor hereunder, or to insist upon strict compliance by Lessee of any obligation hereunder, including without limitation any acceptance of partial payments of rental or other amounts due hereunder, and no custom or practice of the parties at variance with the terms hereof, shall constitute a waiver of Lessor's right to demand exact compliance with the terms hereof. Time is of the essence of this agreement. Lessee's rights under this Lease shall be subject to any bona fide mortgage or deed to secure debt which is now or may hereafter be placed upon Premises.

Special Stipulations In so far as the following special stipulations conflict with any of the foregoing provisions of this Lease, the following shall control.

IN WITNESS WHEREOF, the parties have executed or caused this Lease to be executed by authorized officials in duplicate, the day and year first above written.

Individually and as Agent for Lessor

BY: ______________________ X ______________________ (SEAL)
Lessee

RULES AND REGULATIONS OF APARTMENTS

Lessee shall:

1. Not obstruct sidewalks, courts, entry passage, halls, and stairways, nor allow children to loiter or play in them, nor use them for any purpose except ingress and egress, nor leave bicycles or other vehicles therein. Children shall confine their playing to area designated by Lessor.
2. Not cover or obstruct skylights and windows that reflect or admit light to public space.
3. Not use water closets, drains or other plumbing apparatus for any other purposes than those for which they were constructed and not throw sweepings, rubbish, rags, ashes or other substances therein.
4. Be responsible for damage to plumbing, cooling, or heating apparatus, and other equipment from misuse by Lessee.
5. Throw nothing out of the windows or doors, or down the passage, or skylight of the building.
6. Close windows when it rains or snows, and be responsible for any injury to premises or other tenants due to failure so to do.
7. Not alter premises nor change any partition, door, or window, nor add locks thereto, nor paint, paper, bore or screw upon or in the walls, ceiling, floors, woodwork or plaster.
8. Keep whole all glass, locks and trimmings in or upon the door and windows, and immediately replace or repair such thereof as may be broken or out of order under the direction and to the satisfaction of the Lessor.
9. Erect no awnings or shades outside or inside the windows unless approved by Lessor or his agent.
10. Confine his use of porches or balconies in that portion thereof directly in front of his apartment if any and shall keep them clean and shall not use them for storage purposes.
11. Discontinue all phonographs, television, pianos, radios and other musical devices at eleven o'clock P.M. and shall not practice on musical instruments at any time, nor give music lessons, vocal or instrumental, at any time.
12. Preserve perfect order at all times and permit no boisterous conduct.
13. Observe such other and reasonable rules as Lessor in his judgment may from time to time promulgate for the safety, care and cleanliness of the premises, the building, and for the preservation of good order therein.
14. Not hang washing, clothing, bed covers or linen from the windows, or porches, or in any yard space, except that, if any, which Lessor may provide for the specific purpose.
15. Not place flower pots, boxes or other receptacles in hallways or in windows, or porch railings or where they may possibly cause injury to any person, nor place any objects in windows, hallways, or porch railings deemed unsightly by Lessor.
16. No water beds shall be allowed in Premises.
17. No two wheel motor vehicles, nor any tearing down or repairing of any motor vehicles whatsoever, nor any storage or abandonment of inoperative motor vehicles shall be allowed in Premises or on any part of Lessor's real property on which Lessee's Apartment is located.

EXHIBIT 13–8
Small Commercial Retail Space Lease

_____ , 20 ____

THIS LEASE, made this _____ day of _____, 20 ____, by and between _____
first party, (hereinafter called "Landlord"); and _____, second party, (hereinafter
called "Tenant"); and _____ third party, (hereinafter called "Agent");

WITNESSETH:

Premises

1. The Landlord, for and in consideration of the rents, covenants, agreements and stipulations hereinafter mentioned, provided for and contained, to be paid, kept and performed by the Tenant, has leased and rented, and by these presents leases and rents, unto the said Tenant, and said Tenant hereby leases and takes upon the terms and conditions which hereinafter appear, the following described property (hereinafter called "Premises"), to wit:

and being known as _____
No easement for light or air is included in the Premises.

Term

2. The Tenant shall have and hold the Premises for a term of _____ beginning on the _____ day of
_____ 20 ____, and ending on the _____ day of _____
20 ____ , at midnight, unless sooner terminated as hereinafter provided.

Rental

3. Tenant agrees to pay to Landlord, by payments to _____ Agent of Landlord, who negotiated this Lease, at the office of
Agent in Atlanta, Georgia, an annual rental in the amount of $_____, which shall be paid promptly on the first day of each
month in advance during the term of this Lease, in equal monthly installments of $_____.

Agent's Commission

4. Agent has rendered Landlord and Tenant a valuable service by assisting in the creation of the Landlord-Tenant relationship hereunder. For this reason, Agent is made a party to this Lease and is given a special lien on the interest of the Landlord and the interest of the Tenant in the Premises in order to enable Agent to enforce its commission rights against the Premises as well as against the other parties hereto as herein provided and as otherwise provided by law or equity. The commission to be paid in conjunction with the creation of the aforesaid Landlord-Tenant relationship by this Lease has been negotiated between Landlord and Agent, and Landlord hereby agrees to pay Agent, as compensation for Agent's services in procuring this Lease and creating the aforeseaid Landlord-Tenant relationship, as follows:

If the Tenant becomes a tenant at will or at sufferance pursuant to Paragraph 25 hereof, or if the term of this Lease is extended or if this Lease is renewed or if a new lease is entered into between Landlord and Tenant covering either the Premises, or any part thereof, or covering any other premises as an expansion of, addition to, or substitution for, the Premises, regardless of whether such premises are located adjacent to or in the vicinity of the Premises, Landlord, in consideration of Agent's having assisted in the creation of the Landlord-Tenant relationship, agrees to pay Agent Additional Commissions as set forth below; it being the intention of the parties that Agent shall continue to be compensated so long as the parties hereto, their successors and/or assigns continue the relationship of Landlord and Tenant which initially resulted from the efforts of Agent, whether relative to the Premises or any expansion thereof, or addition thereto or substitution therefor, or relative to any other premises leased by Landlord to Tenant from time to time, whether the rental therefore is paid under this Lease or otherwise:

Landlord, with the consent of Tenant, hereby authorizes Agent to deduct its commission from each rental payment it collects from Tenant; but nothing herein shall relieve Landlord from his obligation to pay to Agent his commission if Tenant fails to pay any rental payment.

Agent agrees that, in the event Landlord sells the Premises, and upon Landlord's furnishing Agent with an agreement signed by Purchaser assuming Landlord's obligations to Agent under this Lease, Agent will release original Landlord from any further obligations to Agent hereunder. Tenant agrees that if this Lease is assigned by him he will secure from assignee an agreement in writing recognizing the assignment of the commissions owed to Agent and agreeing to pay rental to Agent during the continuation of the Landlord-Tenant relationship between or among said assignee, its successors and/or assigns, and Landlord, its successors and/or assigns, whether relative to the Premises or any expansion thereof or substitution therefor, or relative to any other property leased by Landlord to Tenant from time to time, whether rental therefor is paid under this Lease or otherwise. Voluntary cancellation of this Lease shall not nullify Agent's right to collect the commission due for the remaining term of this Lease and the provisions contained hereinabove relative to Additional Commissions shall survive any cancellation or termination of this Lease. In the event that the Premises are condemned, or sold under threat of and in lieu of condemnation, Agent shall, on the date of receipt by Landlord of the condemnation award or sale proceeds, be paid Agent's commission, reduced to its present cash value at the then existing legal rate of interest, which would otherwise be due to the end of the term contracted for under paragraph 2 above.

Purchase of Property by Tenant

5. In the event that Tenant acquires title to the Premises or any part thereof, or any other premises as an expansion of, addition to, or substitution for, the Premises, at any time during the term of this Lease, any renewals thereof, or within six months after the expiration of the term hereof or the extended term hereof, then Landlord shall pay Agent a commission on the sale of the Premises in lieu of any further commissions which otherwise would have been due under this Lease.

Such commission, as negotiated between parties, is to be _____

Utility Bills

6. Tenant shall pay all utility bills, including, but not limited to water, sewer, gas, electricity, fuel, light, and heat bills, for the Premises, and Tenant shall pay all charges for garbage collection services or other sanitary services rendered to the Premises or used by Tenant in connection therewith. If Tenant fails to pay any of said utility bills or charges for garbage collection or other sanitary services, Landlord may pay the same, and such payment shall be added to and become part of the next rental payment due under this Lease.

Use of Premises

7. Premises shall be used for _____
purposes and no other. Premises shall not be used for any illegal purposes, nor in any manner to create any nuisance or trespass, nor in any manner to vitiate the insurance or increase the rate of insurance on premises.

Abandonment of the Premises

8. Tenant agrees not to abandon or vacate the Premises during the period of this Lease and agrees to use the Premises for the purposes herein leased until the expiration hereof.

Repairs by Landlord

9. Landlord agrees to keep in good repair the roof, foundations, and exterior walls of the Premises (exclusive of all glass and exclusive of all exterior doors), and underground utility and sewer pipes outside the exterior walls of the building, except repairs rendered necessary by the negligence of Tenant, its agents, employees or invitees. Landlord gives to Tenant exclusive control of the Premises and shall be under no obligation to inspect said Premises. Tenant shall promptly

(continued)

EXHIBIT 13–8
Small Commercial Retail Space Lease (continued)

report in writing to Landlord any defective condition known to it which Landlord is required to repair, and failure so to report such conditions shall make Tenant responsible to Landlord for any liability incurred by Landlord by reason of such conditions.

Repairs by Tenant

10. Tenant accepts the Premises in their present condition and as suited for the uses intended by Tenant. Tenant shall, throughout the initial term of this Lease and any extension or renewal thereof, at its expense, maintain in good order and repair the Premises, including the building, heating and air conditioning equipment (including but not limited to replacement of parts, compressors, air handling units and heating units), and other improvements located thereon, except those repairs expressly required to be made by Landlord hereunder. Tenant further agrees to care for the grounds around the building, including the mowing of grass, paving, care of shrubs and general landscaping. Tenant agrees to return the Premises to Landlord at the expiration, or prior to termination, of this Lease in as good condition and repair as when first received, natural wear and tear, damage by storm, fire, lightning, earthquake or other casualty alone excepted.

Tax Escalation

11. Tenant shall pay upon demand, as additional rental during the term of this Lease and any extension or renewal thereof, the amount by which all taxes (including, but not limited to, ad valorem taxes, special assessments and any other governmental charges) on the Premises for each tax year exceed all taxes on the Premises for the tax year ______. In the event the Premises are less than the entire property assessed for such taxes for any such tax year, then the tax for any such year applicable to the Premises shall be determined by proration on the basis that the rentable floor area of the Premises bears to the rentable floor area of the entire property assessed. If the final year of the lease term fails to coincide with the tax year, then any excess for the tax year during which the term ends shall be reduced by the pro rata part of such tax year beyond the lease term. If such taxes for the year in which the Lease terminates are not ascertainable before payment of the last month's rental, then the amount of such taxes assessed against the property for the previous tax year shall be used as a basis of determining the pro rata share, if any, to be paid by Tenant for that portion of the last lease year. Tenant's pro rata portion of increased taxes, as provided herein, shall be payable within fifteen days after receipt of notice from Landlord or Agent as to the amount due. The Agent's commission shall not apply to any such additional rental resulting from the provisions of this paragraph unless billing and collection thereof is handled by Agent at the request of the Landlord.

Destruction of or Damage to Premises

12. If the Premises are totally destroyed by storm, fire, lightning, earthquake or other casualty, this Lease shall terminate as of the date of such destruction, and rental shall be accounted for as between Landlord and Tenant as of that date. If the Premises are damaged but not wholly destroyed by any such casualties, rental shall abate in such proportion as use of the Premises has been destroyed, and Landlord shall restore Premises to substantially the same condition as before damage as speedily as is practicable, whereupon full rental shall recommence.

Indemnity

13. Tenant agrees to, and hereby does, indemnify and save Landlord harmless against all claims for damages to persons or property by reason of Tenant's use or occupancy of Premises, and all expenses incurred by Landlord because thereof, including attorney's fees and court costs. Supplementing the foregoing and in addition thereto, Tenant shall during all terms of this Lease, and any extension or renewal thereof, and at Tenant's expense maintain in full force and effect comprehensive general liability insurance with limits of $500,000.00 per person and $1,000,000.00 per accident, and property damage limits of $100,000.00, which insurance shall contain a special endorsement recognizing and insuring any liability accruing to Tenant under the first sentence of this Paragraph 13; such insurance policy shall contain a clause expressly waiving any right of the insurer of subrogation against Landlord. Prior to the commencement of the term of this Lease, Tenant shall furnish Landlord with a certificate of such insurance which shall show the waiver of subrogation, and the endorsement required hereby. Such certificate shall provide that Landlord will be given ten (10) days written notice prior to cancellation or expiration of the insurance evidenced thereby.

Governmental Orders

14. Tenant agrees, at his own expense, promptly to comply with all requirements of any legally constituted public authority made necessary by reason of Tenant's occupancy of the Premises. Landlord agrees promptly to comply with any such requirements if not made necessary by reason of Tenant's occupancy. It is mutually agreed, however, between Landlord and Tenant, that if in order to comply with such requirements, the cost to Landlord or Tenant, as the case may be, shall exceed a sum equal to one year's rent, then Landlord or Tenant who is obligated to comply with such requirements may terminate this Lease by giving written notice of termination to the other party, by registered mail, which termination shall become effective sixty (60) days after receipt of such notice, and which notice shall eliminate necessity of compliance with such requirement by party giving such notice unless party receiving such notice of termination shall, before termination becomes effective, pay to party giving notice all cost of compliance in excess of one year's rent, or secure payment of said sum in manner satisfactory to party giving notice.

Condemnation

15. If the whole of the Premises, or such portion thereof as will make the Premises unusable for the purposes herein leased, be condemned by any legally constituted authority for any public use or purpose, then in either of said events the term hereby granted shall cease from the date when possession thereof is taken by public authorities, and rental shall be accounted for as between Landlord and Tenant as of said date. Such termination, however, shall be without prejudice to the rights of either Landlord or Tenant to recover compensation and damage caused by condemnation from the condemnor. It is further understood and agreed that neither the Tenant nor Landlord shall have any rights in any award made to the other by any condemnation authority notwithstanding the termination of the Lease as herein provided. Landlord agrees to pay to Agent, from the award made to Landlord under condemnation, the balance of lease commissions, reduced to their present cash value, as provided in paragraph 4 hereof, and Agent may become a party to the condemnation proceeding for the purpose of enforcing its rights under this paragraph.

Assignment and Subletting

16. Tenant may sublease portions of the Premises to others provided such sublessee's operation is a part of the general operation of Tenant and is under the supervision and control of Tenant, and provided such operation is within the purposes for which the Premises shall be used. Except as provided in the preceding sentence, Tenant shall not, without the prior written consent of Landlord endorsed hereon, assign this Lease or any interest hereunder, or sublet the Premises or any part thereof, or permit the use of the Premises by any party other than Tenant. Consent to any assignment or sublease shall not impair this provision, and all later assignments or subleases shall be made likewise only on the prior written consent of Landlord. Assignee of Tenant, at option of Landlord, shall become directly liable to Landlord for all obligations of Tenant hereunder, but no sublease or assignment by Tenant shall relieve Tenant of any liability hereunder.

Removal of Fixtures

17. Tenant may (if not in default hereunder) prior to the expiration of this Lease, or any extension or renewal thereof, remove all fixtures and equipment which he has placed in the Premises, provided Tenant repairs all damage to the Premises caused by such removal.

Events of Default

18. The happening of any one or more of the following events (hereinafter any one of which may be referred to as an "Event of Default") during the term of this Lease, or any renewal or extension thereof, shall constitute a breach of this Lease on the part of the Tenant: (1) Tenant fails to pay the rental as provided for herein; (2) Tenant abandons or vacates the Premises; (3) Tenant fails to comply with or abide by and perform any other obligation imposed upon Tenant under this Lease; (4) Tenant is adjudicated bankrupt; (5) a permanent receiver is appointed for Tenant's property and such receiver is not removed within sixty (60) days after written notice from Landlord to Tenant to obtain such removal; (6) Tenant, either voluntarily or involuntarily, takes advantage of any debtor relief proceedings under any present or future law, whereby the rent or any part thereof is, or is proposed to be, reduced or payment thereof deferred; (7) Tenant makes an assignment for benefit of creditors; or (8) Tenant's effects are levied upon or attached under process against Tenant, which is not satisfied or dissolved within thirty (30) days after written notice from Landlord to Tenant to obtain satisfaction thereof.

Remedies Upon Default

19. Upon the occurrence of any Event of Default, Landlord may pursue any one or more of the following remedies, separately or concurrently, without any notice (except as specifically provided hereafter) and without prejudice to any other remedy herein provided or provided by law: (a) if the Event of Default involves nonpayment of rental, and Tenant fails to cure such default within ten days after receipt of written notice thereof from Landlord, or if the Event of Default involves a default in performing any of the terms or provisions of this Lease other than the payment of rental, and Tenant fails to cure such default within thirty (30) days after the receipt of written notice of default from Landlord, Landlord may terminate this Lease by giving written notice to Tenant and, upon such termination, shall be entitled to recover from the Tenant damages in an amount equal to all rental which is then due and which would otherwise have become due throughout the remaining term of this Lease, or any renewal or extension thereof (as if this Lease had not been terminated); or (b) if the Event of Default involves any matter other than those set forth in item (a) of this Paragraph 19, the Landlord may terminate this Lease by giving written notice to Tenant, and upon such termination, shall be entitled to recover from the Tenant damages in an amount equal to all rental which is then due and which would otherwise have become due throughout the remaining term of this Lease, or any renewal or extension thereof (as if this Lease had not been terminated); or (c) upon any Event of Default, Landlord may give to Tenant written notice of such default and advise Tenant that unless such default is cured within ten days after receipt of such notice, the entire amount of the rental for the remainder of the term of this Lease, or any renewal or extension thereof, shall immediately become due an payable upon the expiration of the ten day period, and thereafter, unless all the terms and provisions of this Lease are fully complied with by the Tenant within said ten-day period, the entire amount of said rental shall thereupon become immediately due and payable without further notice to Tenant; or (d) upon any Event of Default, Landlord, as Tenant's agent, without terminating this Lease may enter upon and rent the Premises, in whole or in part, at the best price obtainable by reasonable effort, without advertisement and by private negotiations and for any term Landlord deems proper, with Tenant being liable to Landlord for the deficiency, if any, between Tenant's rent hereunder and the price obtained by Landlord on reletting; provided, however, that Landlord shall not be considered to be under any duty by reason of this provision to take any action to mitigate damages by reason of Tenant's default.

Exterior Signs

20. Tenant shall place no signs upon the outside walls or roof of the Premises except with the written consent of the Landlord. Any and all signs placed on the Premises by Tenant shall be maintained in compliance with rules and regulations governing such signs, and the Tenant shall be responsible to Landlord for any damage caused by installation, use, or maintenance of said signs. Tenant, upon the expiration of this Lease, and any extension or renewal thereof, shall remove said signs and agrees upon removal of said signs to repair all damage incident to such removal.

Entry for Carding, etc.

(continued)

EXHIBIT 13-8
Small Commercial
Retail Space Lease
(continued)

reasonable hours to exhibit same to prospective purchasers or tenants and to make repairs required of Landlord under the terms hereof, or to make repairs to Landlord's adjoining property, if any.

Effect of Termination of Lease

22. No termination of this Lease prior to the normal ending thereof, by lapse of time or otherwise, shall affect Landlord's right to collect rent for the period prior to termination thereof.

Mortgagee's Rights

23. Tenant's rights shall be subject to any bona fide mortgage or deed to secure debt which is now, or may hereafter be, placed upon the Premises by Landlord. Tenant shall, if requested by Landlord, execute a separate agreement reflecting such subordination.

No Estate in Land

24. This Lease shall create the relationship of Landlord and Tenant between the parties hereto; no estate shall pass out of Landlord. Tenant has only a usufruct, not subject to levy and sale, and not assignable by Tenant except by Landlord's consent.

Holding Over

25. If Tenant remains in possession of the Premises after expiration of the term hereof, with Landlord's acquiescence and without any express agreement of parties, Tenant shall be a tenant at will at the rental rate which is in effect at end of Lease; and there shall be no renewal of this Lease by operation of law. If Tenant remains in possession of the Premises after expiration of the term hereof without Landlord's acquiescence, then Tenant shall be a tenant at sufferance and, commencing on the date following the date of such expiration, the monthly rental payable under Paragraph 3 hereof shall, for each month or fraction thereof during which Tenant so remains in possession, be twice the monthly rental otherwise payable under Paragraph 3 hereof.

Attorney's Fees and Homestead

26. If any rent or other sum owing under this Lease is collected by or through an attorney at law, Tenant agrees to pay fifteen percent (15%) thereof as attorneys' fees. Tenant waives all homestead rights and exemptions which he may have under any law as against any obligation owing under this Lease. Tenant hereby assigns to Landlord his homestead exemption.

Rights Cumulative

27. All rights, powers and privileges conferred hereunder upon parties hereto shall be cumulative and not restrictive of those given by law.

Service of Notice

28. Tenant hereby appoints as his agent to receive service of all dispossessory or distraint proceedings and notices hereunder, and all notices required under this Lease, the person in charge of the Premises at the time, or occupying the Premises; and if no person is in charge of, or occupying the Premises, then such service or notice may be made by attaching the same on the main entrance to the Premises. A copy of all notices under this Lease shall also be sent to Tenant's last known address, if different from the Premises.

Waiver of Rights

29. No failure of Landlord to exercise any power given Landlord hereunder, or to insist upon strict compliance by Tenant of his obligations hereunder, and no custom or practice of the parties at variance with the terms hereof shall constitute a waiver of Landlord's right to demand exact compliance with the terms hereof.

Disclosure of Ownership

30. The owner of the Premises is _____ .

whose address is _____

and the person authorized to manage the Premises is _____ , whose address is

_____

Service of process and demands and notices as to the Landlord shall be made on _____ , whose address is

_____

who is authorized to acknowledge the receipt of same.

Limitation on Agent's Services

31. Agent is a party to this Lease solely for the purpose of enforcing his rights under Paragraph 4 of this Lease, and it is understood by all parties hereto that Agent is acting solely in the capacity as agent for Landlord, to whom Tenant must look as regards all covenants, agreements and warranties herein contained, and that Agent shall never be liable to Tenant in regard to any matter which may arise by virtue of this Lease. It is understood and agreed that the commissions payable to Agent under Paragraph 4 of this Lease are compensation solely for Agent's services in assisting in the creation of the Landlord-Tenant relationship hereunder; accordingly, Agent is not obligated hereunder on account of payment of such commissions, to furnish any management services for the Premises.

Time of Essence

32. Time is of the essence of this Lease.

Definitions

33. "Landlord" as used in this Lease shall include first party, his heirs, representatives, assigns and successors in title to the Premises. "Tenant" shall include second party, his heirs and representatives, and if this Lease shall be validly assigned or sublet, shall include also Tenant's assignees or sublessees, as to the Premises covered by such assignment or sublease. "Agent" shall include third party, his successors, assigns, heirs and representatives. "Landlord," "Tenant," and "Agent" include male and female, singular and plural, corporation, partnership or individual, as may fit the particular parties.

Special Stipulations

In so far as the following stipulations conflict with any of the foregoing provisions, the following shall control:

This Lease contains the entire agreement of the parties hereto and no representations, inducements, promises or agreements, oral or otherwise, between the parties, not embodied herein, shall be of any force or effect.

IN WITNESS WHEREOF, the parties herein have hereunto set their hands and seals, in triplicate, the day and year first above written.

Signed, sealed and delivered as
to Landlord, in the presence of:

_____   _____ (SEAL)
                                            (Landlord)

_____   _____ (SEAL)
Notary Public   (Landlord)

Signed, sealed and delivered as
to Tenant, in the presence of:

_____   _____ (SEAL)
                                            (Tenant)

_____   _____ (SEAL)
Notary Public   (Tenant)

Signed, sealed and delivered as
to Agent, in the presence of:

_____   By: _____ (SEAL)

_____
Notary Public

Answers to Self-Study Examinations

CHAPTER 1

1. T
2. F
3. F
4. T
5. T
6. F
7. F
8. T
9. T
10. F

11. Personal property and real property.
12. (a) possession of the property, (b) use of the property, and (c) power of disposition.
13. Land, airspace, mineral rights, and water.
14. (a) inheritance, (b) devise, (c) gift, (d) contract and sale, or (e) adverse possession.
15. Waste is the failure to exercise ordinary care and prudence for the preservation or protection of property that results in a permanent injury to the value of the property. The importance of waste in a life estate is that if the life estate owner commits waste, the life estate will terminate, even though the measuring life is still alive.
16. The property, on Bob's death, would go to Carol's heirs. Carol's interest does not require that Carol survive Bob.
17. Rules of adverse possession vary from state to state. Typically, the possessor must possess the property for a period ranging from seven to twenty years. Possession must be adverse, which means without the consent or permission of the true owner. Possession must be public, continuous, peaceful, exclusive, and uninterrupted.
18. The court will consider the following:
    (a) The manner in which the item is attached to the real property. The more permanent the attachment, the more likely that the court will find the item is a fixture.
    (b) The character of the item and its adaptation to real property. If it is clear that the item has been specifically constructed or fitted with a view to its location and use in a particular building, then the item is more likely to be a fixture.
    (c) The intention of the parties. If it is clear from the circumstances surrounding the attachment of the item to the building or home that the parties intended for it to be a fixture and part of real property, the item is likely to be a fixture.
19. A "reversion" interest is the future property interest held by the fee simple grantor after a life estate has been granted. For example, Aaron, the fee simple owner of property, transfers a life estate in the property to Bob. Aaron retains a reversion interest in the property, which means that on Bob's death, the property will revert back to Aaron.
20. Fee simple absolute ownership interest is ownership forever. The property is freely inheritable and has indefinite duration. An estate for years is ownership of property for a definite period. An estate for years has a definite beginning and ending date and terminates on the expiration of its term.
21. The categories of water sources are (a) groundwater; (b) surface water; and (c) water that accumulates in a river, stream, or natural lake.
22. Under the riparian rights doctrine, an owner of riparian land has the right to use the water equally with other owners of riparian lands.
23. Under the appropriation or prior appropriation water rights doctrine, the right to use the water is given to the landowner who uses the water first.
24. The elements of valid appropriation are (a) intent to apply water to a beneficial use, (b) an actual diversion of water from a natural source, and (c) application of the water to a beneficial use within a reasonable time.
25. An inheritance is a transfer of property from a previous owner who died without a will. A devise is a transfer of property from a previous owner who died with a will.

CHAPTER 2

1. T	2. F
3. F	4. T
5. T	6. T
7. F	8. F
9. T	10. F

11. The four unities are interest, title, time, and possession. In other words, each owner's interest must constitute an identical interest (e.g., fee simple life estate), accrue by the same conveyance (deed or will), commence at the same time, and be held in the same undivided possession.

12. Tenancy in common has three main differences from joint tenancy with right of survivorship. These differences are (a) there is no special language needed to create a tenancy in common, (b) ownership in a tenancy in common does not have to be equal shares, and (c) there is no right of survivorship in a tenancy in common.

13. Both the tenancy by the entirety and community property involve property that is jointly owned by husband and wife. The main difference between the two is that a tenancy by the entirety is created by a conveyance or grant and community property is created by operation of law. To create a tenancy by the entirety, it is necessary that property be conveyed to a husband and wife. Community property, by operation of law, holds that a husband and wife each own an undivided one-half interest in the community property. Another difference is that in a tenancy by the entirety, the married couple is deemed to own the property and the individual spouses are not deemed to own any individual interest in the property. Community property is deemed to be held equally by the spouses.

14. Dower is an interest in real property of the husband that the law in some states gives to the widow to provide the widow with a means of support after the husband's death. A dower interest is either a life estate or a fee simple interest and in an undivided fraction of the real property that the husband owned during the marriage.

15. A common owner who pays more than his or her share of the common expenses has a right to reimbursement from the other co-owners for their proportionate share of the amount paid. This right to reimbursement is known as the "right of contribution." The right of contribution is important to an owner because it is the method to enforce that all common owners pay their fair share of expenses and obligations.

16. The main advantage to both of these agreements is to determine between the parties the ownership rights of various properties. These agreements resolve disputes of property ownership that may arise at the time of divorce or on sale of the property.

17. The owners of the property are Carol, an undivided one-third, and Stewart, an undivided two-thirds, as tenants in common. The property originally was owned by Juan, Jane, and Susan, as joint tenants with the right of survivorship, each owning an undivided one-third interest. Juan, during the lifetime of the joint ownership, transfers his interest in the property to Carol. This transfer from Juan to Carol terminates the survivorship feature as to Carol's undivided one-third interest. At this stage, Carol is a tenant in common with Jane and Susan who are still joint tenants with the right of survivorship. After Juan's transfer to Carol, Jane dies and wills her interest in the property to Barbara. Jane's will will not take effect because the survivorship feature will preempt the will, and Jane's interest in the property will be transferred to Susan. At this stage, the owners of the property are Carol, an undivided one-third interest, and Susan, an undivided two-thirds interest, as tenants in common. On Susan's death, her will of the property to Stewart will take effect. Stewart will become co-owner of the property with Carol.

18. It would appear that a deed that transfers property to David Farris, Mary Farris, and John Farris with no other indication would create a tenancy in common. It would also be assumed that each have an equal, or one-third interest in the property.

19. To purchase 100 percent of the property that is co-owned, it is necessary for a purchaser to enter into a contract with all the co-owners of the property and to receive a deed from all the co-owners of the property at the time of closing. In regard to the particular question asked in question 19, it would be necessary for the purchaser to have a contract signed by Samuel Seller, Susan Seller, and Sarah Seller as well as the deed of transfer at the time of the closing.

20. The answer to question 20 depends on the form of ownership held by Robert Black and Margo Black. If Robert Black and Margo Black own the property as tenants in common or as joint tenants with right of survivorship or as community property, the creditor who has made a loan to Robert Black will be able to enforce its debt against Robert Black's undivided interest in the property. On the other hand, if Robert Black and Margo Black own the property as tenancy by the entirety, a creditor of a single tenant by the entirety cannot attach the entirety property for the satisfaction of the debt, and this would prevent the creditor from having a lien on any interest of the property.

21. The survivorship feature of a joint tenancy provides that as each joint tenant dies, his or her interest in the property will pass to the surviving joint tenants and will not pass by inheritance or will of the deceased joint tenant.

22. A common owner of a tenancy in common is generally entitled to a share of rent or income in the same percentage as the tenant's ownership of the property. That is, a tenant who has a one-fourth interest in a tenancy in common property would be entitled to one-fourth of the rent or income produced from the property.

23. Property may be partitioned voluntarily by the common owners or by a court proceeding.

24. Community property provides that during marriage all property individually or jointly acquired by the husband or wife is held by them as community property. The community property is created by operation of law, not by operation of grant.

25. Property owned prior to marriage and property acquired by gift, devise, or descent is generally not considered to be community property.

CHAPTER 3

1. F
2. T
3. T
4. F
5. T
6. F
7. T
8. T
9. F
10. F

11. Zoning regulations, building codes, subdivision regulations, environmental protection laws, power of eminent domain, and taxation.

12. The general rule is that a lien claim dates from the time work is first performed and the materials first furnished. The importance of priority is that the lien claimant's right to be paid takes precedence over any party who acquires an interest in the property after the lien has attached to the property. For example, work is first performed on March 1 and a lien claim takes effect as of March 1. The property owner then borrows money and pledges a mortgage on the property dated April 1. The April 1 mortgage will be junior to the lien claim, and if the property is sold to satisfy debts, the lien claimant will be paid first.

13. The main legal issue is whether the owner has been provided with necessary procedural safeguards such as (a) a hearing and an opportunity to be represented by counsel, (b) whether the use for which the private property is to be taken is a proper public use, and (c) whether the property owner has been paid fair market value for the property being taken.

14. Private restrictive covenants are enforced by injunction or by a suit for money damages.

15. A judgment lien is a money debt that attaches to real property. The property owner should be concerned about judgment liens because if they are not paid, the property can be sold to satisfy the lien.

16. An easement may be created by (a) express grant, (b) implication, (c) prescription, or (d) necessity.

17. Parcel A is the servient tenement and parcel B is the dominant tenement.

18. An easement by necessity is an easement created by state law to prevent a property owner from being landlocked. Easement by necessity grants to an otherwise landlocked landowner the right to acquire an easement over a neighbor's property to gain access to a public road. The easement requires that fair compensation be paid to the landowner of the condemned easement. A prescriptive easement is an easement created when a person uses property without the permission of the owner for a period of time. Prescriptive easements are similar to adverse possession, and once obtained, they do not require compensation to be paid to the owner of the burdened property.

19. No.

20. A deed of trust on property to be encumbered by an easement has priority over the easement. Failure to pay the debt secured by the deed of trust and a foreclosure of the deed of trust could result in a termination of the easement. The real estate developer should be concerned about the First Bank and Trust deed of trust, since a foreclosure will terminate the necessary driveway easement. The developer can be protected by obtaining from First Bank and Trust a consent and agreement that a foreclosure of the deed of trust will not terminate the easement.

21. An encumbrance is generally thought of as a negative thing for a property owner.

22. The main objective of zoning is to improve living and working conditions in a congested area and to prevent the liberties of one property owner from interfering with the rights of another.

23. Implied easements are based upon a theory that when real property is conveyed, that conveyance contains whatever is necessary for the beneficial use and enjoyment of the real property or retains whatever is necessary for the beneficial use and enjoyment of real property retained by the grantor.

24. Easements may be terminated by (a) expiration of express term, (b) abandonment, (c) merger, (d) foreclosure of prior liens, or (e) express release or termination.

25. A license is generally considered not a property interest but a mere permission to perform certain acts upon another's land.

26. A Phase I environmental assessment requires an environmental engineer to review government regulatory data concerning the property and the surrounding area. The regulatory data usually include any state or county list of hazardous generators and an examination of the public records to determine if environmental liens have been filed. The review also requires a search of the United States EPA database for a list of hazardous waste generators, transporters, and storage treatment facilities. An environmental engineer will also look to see if there are any underground storage tanks either on the property or within a reasonable vicinity of the property, which might lead to contamination of the property. The environmental engineer will inspect the property and look for any evidence of toxic materials, including the storage, handling, and disposal thereof. The Phase I report will generally indicate whether there is any concern regarding contamination of the property, which may require additional tests. Additional testing is generally referred to as a Phase II environmental assessment. A Phase II environmental assessment involves the environmental engineer obtaining soil and water samples from the property. These soil and water samples are then analyzed in a laboratory to determine if they obtain elements of contamination in excess of the limits considered normal by federal and state government standards.

27. The innocent purchaser defense under CERCLA provides an exception to the joint and separate liability for cleanup costs under the Superfund law. It provides that anyone who purchases or makes a loan on contaminated property who at the time of the acquisition or making of the loan was not aware that the property was contaminated will not be liable for the cost of cleanup of the contamination. To avail oneself of the innocent party defense, a person must (1) have no actual knowledge of the contamination at the time of the purchase or making a loan, and (2) have undertaken at the time of acquisition or making of the loan an inquiry into the previous ownership and uses of the property consistent with good commercial or customary practice. A Phase I environmental examination may satisfy this requirement.

CHAPTER 4

1. F	2. F
3. T	4. T
5. T	6. F
7. T	8. F
9. T	10. T

11. The original Statute of Frauds was enacted in England in 1677 to prevent fraudulent practices of proving oral contracts in court. The Statute of Frauds requires that certain contracts be in writing to be enforceable. Contracts for the sale of land or an interest in land are required by the Statute of Frauds to be in writing. Each state has its own Statute of Frauds.

12. The remedies are money damages, specific performance, and rescission.

13. A real estate broker earns a real estate commission if the broker produces a person who is ready, willing, and able to purchase the property at the price and on the terms required by the seller in the listing agreement.

14. The measure of damages for breach of real estate contract is the difference between contract price and fair market value at the time of the breach. The seller in question 14 would not be entitled to any money damages from the purchaser who did not perform. If the property has a fair market value higher than the purchase price, the seller has not been damaged by the purchaser's failure to perform.

15. A contract does not exist until there has been a mutual agreement of the parties, which in the case of a real estate contract means that both the purchaser and the seller must be in complete agreement on what is to be purchased and the price to be paid. For example, in question 15, the seller has offered to sell the home to the purchaser for $75,000. The purchaser's response to purchase the home for $65,000 is a counteroffer. The counteroffer terminates the initial offer to sell for $75,000. The counteroffer in turn is rejected by the seller. The purchaser then increases the counteroffer to $75,000, but the counteroffer must be accepted by the seller before there is a contract.

16. A real estate contract must reflect the negotiation of the buyer and seller and capture their agreements in writing. The contract dictates the rights and responsibilities of the parties and establishes a blueprint for the closing of the purchase and sale.

17. A "time is of the essence" provision in the contract makes dates for performance critical dates. If something is not performed by a certain date, then the party may be in default if time is of the

essence. If the "time is of the essence" phrase is not contained in the contract, the general rule is the time limits set forth in the contract are not strictly enforceable. The parties may be permitted to perform within a reasonable period after the dates specified in the contract.

18. At minimum, the contract should touch on the following aspects of seller financing: (a) security for the note, (b) priority of the lien created by the security, (c) when installment payments are due under the note, (d) late penalties for payments not timely made, (e) prepayment penalty or privileges, (f) the obligation to be due on the subsequent sale by the purchaser of the property, (g) interest rates payable, (h) maintenance of insurance on the insured property, (i) personal liability of the purchaser, (j) the amount of the note and the exact method by which the note will be determined at closing, and (k) copies of the proposed seller financing documents, note, and mortgage should be attached as exhibits to the contract.

19. The following items usually are prorated in a real estate contract: (a) real estate taxes, (b) interest on any assumable mortgages, (c) lease income, and (d) expenses in the maintenance and operation of the property.

20. (a) Favor seller
    (b) Favor seller
    (c) Favor purchaser
    (d) Favor purchaser
    (e) Neutral provision with a slight bias in favor of seller

21. The legal capacity to contract means that the parties to the contract are responsible for their promises, and the law will make them bound by their promises.

22. A mutual agreement requires that the parties agree on the same thing, the same terms, and at the same time.

23. A listing agreement is an agreement entered into by an owner of property and a real estate broker, giving the broker the authority to sell the property.

24. The closing is the date on which the parties perform all of their obligations under the contract. In some states, the closing is sometimes referred to as a settlement.

25. The risk of loss generally shifts from seller to purchaser at the time the real estate contract is entered into. The parties, however, may agree in the contract that risk of loss remains with seller until closing.

26. An agent owes certain duties and responsibilities to a principal. These are (a) duty to follow the instructions of the principal, (b) duty to exercise reasonable care and skill in the performance of the agent's duties, (c) duty to disclose all matters that the agent becomes aware of relating to the agency relationship, and (d) a duty to account for any money belonging to the principal which comes into the agent's possession.

27. A principal owes certain duties and obligations to the agent. These duties are (a) a duty to compensate the agent for his or her work, (b) a duty to reimburse the agent for any expenditures that the agent has reasonably incurred in connection with the performance of the agency, and (c) a duty to indemnify the agent against any third-party claims that may be made against the agent due to his or her performance under the agency agreement.

CHAPTER 5

1. T	2. T
3. F	4. F
5. T	6. T
7. F	8. F
9. T	10. T

11. A quitclaim deed does not contain any warranties.

12. Generally only the grantor signs a deed.

13. The general requirements for witnesses of a signature on a deed are that the witnesses be disinterested (i.e., not the grantor/grantee to the deed) and that the witnesses actually see the grantor sign. In some states the witness may need to be a notary public.

14. The law of the state where the real property is located generally controls the form as well as the formal requirements of a deed.

15. A grantee of a deed need not be competent.

16. A general warranty deed is an absolute warranty regarding the property that includes warranties for what predecessors in title may have done. A limited warranty deed warrants only against lawful claims of people by, through, or under the grantor. The grantor in a limited warranty deed does not warrant against the actions of any predecessors in title.

17. The basic requirements of a valid deed are (a) written instrument, (b) competent grantor, (c) identity of the grantee, (d) words of conveyance, (e) adequate description of land, (f) consideration, (g) signature of grantor, (h) witnesses, and (i) delivery of the completed deed to the grantee.

18. A quitclaim deed conveys whatever title the grantor has. If the grantor has marketable title, the quitclaim deed will convey marketable title.

19. A general warranty deed contains six covenants or warranties: (a) covenant of seizen, (b) covenant of right to convey, (c) covenant against encumbrances, (d) covenant of further assurance, (e) covenant of quiet enjoyment, and (f) covenant of warranty.

20. The deed must be signed by Samuel Adams.

21. The formal parts of a deed are (a) caption, (b) premises or preamble, (c) granting clause, (d) description, (e) habendum, (f) warranty clause, and (g) testimonium.

22. Most states do not prohibit the spouse of a grantor from witnessing the grantor's signature. Therefore, Timothy White can witness the deed. Aretha Greene, who is the grantee of the deed, is an interested party and cannot witness Ruth White's signature. A legal assistant may witness Ruth White's signature.

23. The covenants of seizen, right to convey, and against encumbrances are called present covenants because if they are breached, it is at the time the deed is delivered. The immediate grantee (original purchaser or recipient of the land) is the only person who can sue for breach of a present covenant. The present covenants are not transferable when the land is subsequently sold. Covenants of further assurance, quiet enjoyment, and warranty are called future covenants because they may be breached at some time in the future. Future covenants are transferable and run with the land. Any owner of the land has standing to sue for breach of a future covenant contained in a general warranty deed.

24. A purchaser of real property would prefer to receive a general warranty deed. A general warranty deed is the best type of deed and contains six covenants or warranties made by the grantor of the deed. These covenants or warranties protect the purchaser against a number of possible title problems with the property being transferred.

25. Possession of the deed by the grantee is a presumption of delivery. Possession of a deed by the grantor is presumption of nondelivery. Recordation of a deed in the public records is presumption of delivery. All these presumptions are rebuttable if facts can be shown to the contrary.

CHAPTER 6

1. T	2. T
3. F	4. T
5. F	6. T
7. F	8. T
9. F	10. T

11. An open-end or dragnet mortgage is a mortgage that is given to secure any and all debt between the mortgagor and the mortgagee, including past debt, present debt, and even future debt incurred after the mortgage is given.

12. The purchaser of real property subject to a mortgage does not have personal liability for the payment of the mortgage. The purchaser of real property who assumes the mortgage has personal liability to pay the mortgage.

13. The main risk inherent in a second-mortgage loan is that the first prior mortgage will not be paid and a foreclosure will result. A foreclosure of the prior mortgage will have the effect of terminating the second-mortgage lien on the property.

14. The filing of a bankruptcy acts as an automatic injunction to any attempts to foreclose on the bankrupt debtor's property.

15. The general rule of law is that an alteration of the note without a guarantor's consent releases the guarantor from his or her guaranty. It is recommended that Gooden Earth, as guarantor, consent to the extension of the note and agree that the extension shall not in any way affect his guaranty.

16. The types of things you would include in an estoppel certificate to be signed by a first mortgagee are (a) attach a true and correct copy of the note and first mortgage, (b) state the outstanding unpaid principal balance of the note, (c) state that the borrower is not in default under the note, (d) state that the making of a second mortgage will not constitute an event of default under the note and mortgage, and (e) agree to give to the second-mortgage holder notice of any defaults under the first mortgage and an opportunity to cure or correct such defaults before foreclosure.

17. A legal assistant holding excess proceeds from a foreclosure sale should not pay the money over to an alleged holder of a second mortgage. The best course of action is for the money to be interpled into court so that the proper parties entitled thereto can be determined.

18. The requirements for a valid mortgage are (a) names of the parties, (b) words of conveyance or grant, (c) valid description of the property conveyed, (d) description of the debt being secured, (e) proper execution and attestation, and (f) effective delivery to the lender.

19. A valid foreclosure sale terminates the property owner–debtor's interest in the property. A valid foreclosure sale also has the effect of terminating any interests in the property that were created after the date of the foreclosed mortgage.

20. A promissory note is an obligation to pay money. A guaranty is an obligation of a person other than the debtor to guarantee the payment of the debtor's note.

21. The parties to a promissory note are the maker, the party who promises to pay, and the payee, the party to whom the promise is made.

22. A guaranty of a note must be written.

23. The three basic security instruments given to secure a note in connection with a real estate loan are (a) mortgage, (b) deed of trust, or (c) security deed.

24. The parties to a deed of trust are (a) the owner of the property, (b) the lender, and (c) a trustee who holds title for the benefit of the lender.

25. An interpleader is a proceeding by which money is paid into a court and the debtor and all junior mortgage holders who may have an interest in the money are notified of the proceeding. The lender is released of any obligation upon payment of the money into court.

26. The method of protecting a creditor's security interest in personal property is by filing a UCC-1 financing statement. If the financing statement is properly filed, the creditor's security interest will be protected against subsequent purchasers or creditors who deal with the personal property.

27. The information required in a UCC-1 financing statement includes a debtor's name and address, secured party's (creditor's) name and address, description of the personal property, and a description of the real property where the personal property is located. It must be described with specificity so it can be identified. The debtor must be correctly identified in the financing statement.

CHAPTER 7

1. F	2. T
3. F	4. F
5. T	6. F
7. T	8. T
9. F	10. F

11. Actual notice occurs when a purchaser has direct knowledge or information about title matters. Actual notice includes any facts that the purchaser can see with his or her own eyes, any facts that the purchaser learns about the property, or any information the circumstances of which should put the purchaser on duty to conduct an investigation that would lead to the finding of certain facts in regard to the property.

    Constructive notice is a presumption of law that charges the purchaser with responsibility of learning about all title matters that would result from an inspection of the property or an examination of the public real property records.

12. A full discussion of the recording statutes is contained on pages 166 and 167.

13. A bona fide purchaser for value rule states than anyone who purchases property in good faith for valuable consideration without notice of any claim to or interest in the property by any other party takes the property free and clear of any claims to or interests in the property by other parties.

14. A grantor index is an alphabetical index by last name of all people who are grantors of a real property interest within the county in a given year. The grantor index will have a list of sellers, borrowers, mortgagors, grantors of easements, and so on.

    The grantee index is an alphabetical index by last name of all people who are grantees of any property interest within the county in a given year. The grantee index will have a list of purchasers, holders of mortgages and security deeds, easement holders, tenants, holders of liens, and so on.

15. Alice does not have a right to stop Jose from using his prescriptive easement over the road. Alice, as a bona fide purchaser for value, will take subject to any title matters that she has actual or constructive notice of. The road was clearly visible from an inspection of the property, and therefore, she has actual notice of the road if she had inspected the property and constructive notice, since Alice has an obligation to inspect the property.

16. The mortgage held by Sam is enforceable against the apartment complex. Because the mortgage, although it was not recorded, was mentioned in a deed that was recorded, the mortgage was therefore properly entered into the real property records and provided constructive notice for all subsequent purchasers of the apartment complex, including John.

17. It would be easier to find a recorded mortgage from Alice Owner to Sam Seller by looking under Alice Owner's name in the grantor index.

18. Information needed by a title examiner to do a title examination is as follows: (a) name of current owner of property, which will be the seller under the contract; (b) a complete legal description of the property being bought and sold; and (c) a survey of the property, if available.

19. A pending suit that may affect title to the property will not constitute notice to a bona fide purchaser for value unless a notice of lis pendens is filed. Therefore, the purchaser, to protect rights against subsequent purchasers of the property, would need to file a lis pendens.

20. The following information is contained in a grantor or grantee index entry: (a) name of grantor, (b) name of grantee, (c) date of instrument, (d) date of recording of instrument, (e) nature of the instrument (e.g., deed, mortgage, easement), (f) brief description of the property conveyed, and (g) place where the instrument can be found so that it can be examined and read (record book and page reference).

21. An unrecorded document that is referenced or mentioned in a recorded document would give constructive notice to a bona fide purchaser for value.

22. The recording of a real estate document such as a deed or mortgage is important because it gives constructive notice to a subsequent bona fide purchaser for value.

23. Title examinations are generally conducted in the courthouse of the county in which the property is located.

24. When reviewing deeds, easements, or mortgages an examiner usually does the following: (a) note the identity of the parties to the instrument, the date the instrument was signed and the date it was filed; (b) examine the signature and witnessing requirements; (c) make a notation of what estate was being conveyed, fee simple, or life estate; and (d) pay particular attention to any covenants or other requirements that may be set out in the instrument.

25. A lis pendens is a notice that there is a lawsuit pending regarding the title to the real property.

CHAPTER 8

1. T	2. T
3. F	4. F
5. F	6. F
7. T	8. T
9. F	10. T

11. Three safeguards that assure good title are (a) general warranty deed of conveyance, (b) title examination before conveyance, and (c) title insurance.

12. A list of risks covered by an ALTA owner's policy are found on pages 182 and 183, and a full discussion of insurance provisions of an ALTA owner's policy can be found on pages 182 and 183.

13. Exclusions from coverage on a title insurance policy are standard and will be the same from policy to policy. The exclusions from coverage are not waiveable by the title insurance company. Exceptions to coverage vary from policy to policy, depending on each title that is being insured. The exceptions to coverage can, in some situations, be waived by the title insurance company.

14. Schedule B contains a list of title matters that are not insured against in the title policy. The title insurance company provides no insurance for matters shown on Schedule B. It is important to review Schedule B to make sure that a client is willing to purchase or take a loan on the property with the Schedule B exceptions.

15. A title commitment is the agreement by a title insurance company to issue a title insurance policy once certain conditions have been met. Title insurance is essentially a postclosing matter; that is, you cannot ensure that a person owns a property until he or she in fact does own property, nor that a lender has a mortgage on the property until in fact the loan has been made and the mortgage recorded. A title commitment, however, is a preclosing item that illustrates to the legal assistant and attorney exactly how the title insurance policy will appear once the closing has taken place.

16. Title insurance only insures title as of an effective date (i.e., the effective date of the policy). It is important that the effective date for an owner's policy be the date of the recordation of the deed into the owner, and that for a loan policy, the effective date be the date of the recordation of the mortgage.

17. Kim Buyer may purchase an owner's policy in the amount of $125,000. Acme Loan Company may purchase a loan policy in the amount of $105,000.

18. Owner's policies are not transferable; therefore, B. Thatcher has no claim against the title insurance purchased by T. Sawyer. The situation would be different if B. Thatcher had inherited the property from T. Sawyer on T. Sawyer's death because heirs of an insured are deemed to have a continued coverage under an owner's policy of title insurance.

19. An effective date of December 26 on an owner's policy when the deed was not recorded until January 5 is an incorrect effective date. The correct effective date should be January 5.

20. The parties in possession exception may be deleted by providing the title insurance company with one or both of the following: (a) survey of the property showing no parties in possession, and (b) an affidavit from the owner that there are no parties in possession other than the owner.

21. Schedule A to an ALTA owner's title insurance policy generally sets forth the following information: (a) date of the policy, (b) amount of the insurance, (c) identity of the insured, (d) description of the property being insured, and (e) estate or interest insured.

22. Information generally contained on Schedule B to an ALTA owner's title insurance policy are the list of exceptions to coverage.

23. The standard title exceptions found on Schedule B are (a) rights or claims of parties in possession not shown by public record; (b) encroachments, overlaps, boundary line disputes, and any other matters that would be disclosed by an accurate survey and inspection of the premises; (c) easements or claim of easements not shown by public records; (d) any lien or right to lien for services, labor, or materials furnished; and (e) taxes or special assessments not shown as existing liens by the public records.

24. A title insurance policy generally makes an exception for rights or claims of parties in possession because a title insurance company does not make an inspection of the property.

25. Schedule B, Section 1 of a title commitment sets forth the requirements that must be met before the transaction closes in order for the title insurance to be issued.

CHAPTER 9

1. T	2. F
3. F	4. F
5. T	6. T
7. F	8. T
9. T	10. T

11. A real estate contract sets forth the obligations of the purchaser and seller in regard to the transaction. The contract will set forth the names of the parties, a legal description of the property, purchase price of the property, the amount of the earnest money, the date for closing, and what documents the respective seller and purchaser must furnish to each other at the closing. It is the main document to review to prepare a sale closing checklist.

12. A mortgage loan commitment is a contract to issue a mortgage loan. A mortgage loan commitment will give to the legal assistant the amount of the loan, interest rate, term of the loan, repayment terms, prepayment terms, full description of the security or collateral for the loan, and a list of requirements that must be satisfied before the lender is willing to close and fund the loan.

13. The minimum documentation a seller must furnish at a real estate closing may vary from transaction to transaction, but at bare minimum, a seller must provide a purchaser with the following: (a) a deed transferring ownership of the property, and (b) an owner's title affidavit.

14. The minimum documentation a purchaser must furnish at a real estate closing will vary from transaction to transaction, but at minimum, the purchaser should provide good funds in the amount of the purchase price for the property and proof of insurance on the improvements.

15. At minimum, a surveyor will need the following information: (a) legal description of the property to be surveyed, (b) any information regarding previous surveys, (c) correct names of the purchasers as they appear on the survey, (d) the correct name of the lending institution as it appears on the survey, and (e) any special purchaser/lender requirements for a survey.

16. The value of most real property is in improvements located on the property. The insurance of these improvements is important to the loan transaction. A mortgagee loss payable clause is an endorsement to a hazard insurance policy naming a mortgagee and its address. The policy will provide that any losses under the policy will be payable to the mortgagee, either solely or jointly with the owner of the property.

17. Real estate closings are complicated matters and often involve the preparation of many documents. A checklist is a good method of determining in the beginning the scope of the work that is required and is a good method of making sure that all documents and due diligence requirements have been satisfied.

18. As a general rule, a loan cannot be prepaid before its maturity unless permission is granted in the loan documents. Many institutional lenders do not want a prepayment before maturity, and therefore only permit a prepayment on the payment of a premium. A prepayment premium is a charge of money that must be paid to prepay a loan before maturity. Late charges are a penalty assessed for a late payment of a monthly installment of a loan.

19. The six steps of a real estate closing are (a) file creation; (b) information gathering; (c) document preparation; (d) the closing; (e) disbursement, recording, and transmittal of the closing package; and (f) final close out.

20. Both residential and commercial real estate closings involve the same type of documentation and, in essence, the same process (i.e., transfer of ownership of real property or the closing of a loan on real property). Sometimes commercial transactions are easier because the people involved are experienced. Often the legal techniques used for commercial closings are more sophisticated and the documentation more prone to negotiation and tailored to the transaction at hand.

CHAPTER 10

1. A title affidavit is a statement of facts swearing to the following: (a) the affiant owns the real property described in the affidavit; (b) the boundary lines of the real property are certain and not in dispute; (c) the affiant has a right to possession of the real property; (d) there are no liens, encumbrances, easements, or leases affecting the real property unless they are identified in the affidavit; (e) there are no judgments, bankruptcies, or other restrictions against the affiant owner of the real property; and (f) the affidavit is being made by the affiant with knowledge that it will be relied on by purchasers, lenders, and title insurance company involved with the real property.

2. A corporate resolution is required in any closing transaction if either the purchaser or the seller is a corporation. A corporate resolution is important because it authorizes the sale or purchase of real property on behalf of the corporation and empowers certain officers of the corporation to sign the purchase and sale documents.

3. To protect the purchaser at closing from any judgments that may be imposed on the property against the seller, it would be necessary to obtain an affidavit from Susan T. Clark swearing that she is not Susan Clark, S. T. Clark, or Sue Clark referred to in the judgments. It would also be necessary to discuss this matter with the title insurance company and make sure that the title insurance company is willing to insure the property free and clear of these judgments with the affidavit from Susan T. Clark.

4. $996.78, and it would appear on lines 107 and 407 of the HUD-1. The calculation is determined as follows: The tax amount equals $1,640 divided by 365 days, equals $4.49 per day. Based on a tax year of February 1, which ends on January 31, September 10 is the 222nd day of the tax year. $4.49 times 222 days equals $996.78.

5. The amount of interest to be collected from the borrower at closing is $480.06. This calculation is derived by taking the amount of the loan, $80,000, times the interest rate of 12 percent, which equals $9,600 of interest per year. You would then divide the $9,600 by a 360-day year or 365-day year. Dividing $9,600 by a 360-day year equals $26.67 interest per day. The lender would require that interest be collected on the date of closing, March 14, through the end of March, which would equal eighteen days. Eighteen days times $26.67 equals $480.06.

6. The amount of the tax proration between seller and purchaser would be $481 credit to the purchaser. This credit is calculated by taking $1,350 divided by 365 days to arrive at $3.70 each day. The $3.70 daily tax bill is then multiplied times 130 days (May 10 being the 130th day of the year) and equals $481.

   Taxes to be escrowed by the lender would be $787.50. This calculation is made by taking the tax bill of $1,350 and dividing it by 12, which equals $112.50 each month. The lender will receive $112.50 for the month on July 1, August 1, September 1, October 1, and November 1, or five months before the time the bill is due. For the lender to have enough money to pay the taxes on November 15, the lender will have to collect seven months of escrow of $112.50 each at closing.

   The prorations between seller and purchaser and the amount to be escrowed with lender are not the same amount. The two computations are for two totally different reasons, and therefore it would be extremely rare if they would be the same amount.

7. Information to complete Exhibit A to a title affidavit would either come from the title examination or from a legal description prepared from a survey of the property. A list of title exceptions appearing as Schedule B would come from the title examination or from a title commitment.

8. Because the satisfaction payoff letter from Second Bank and Trust is good only through July 10, and the closing has been delayed and does not take place until July 15, it will be necessary to obtain an updated payment letter from Second Bank and Trust for the additional five day's interest due in July.

9. Net money due to the seller at closing would be $50,972.97. This amount is determined by subtracting from the purchase price of $86,500 the following expenses: (a) the real estate commission, $5,190; (b) closing costs, $600; (c) payment of prior loan, $28,400; and (d) tax proration, $1,337.03, for a total of $35,527.03. The real estate commission is determined by multiplying 6 percent times $86,500 to get $5,190. Closing costs of $600 and the payment of the prior loan of $28,400 were given

in the example. Real estate taxes must be prorated with a credit to the purchaser. Taxes are $2,150 divided by 365 days equals $5.89 per day. August 15 is the 227th day of the year, and therefore the credit to the purchaser is $1,337.03.

10. The purchaser must bring to closing the sum of $23,668.44. This computation is arrived at as follows: (a) contract price, $115,000; (b) closing costs, $3,230; (c) purchaser's share of the tax proration, $438.44; and (d) gross amount due is $118,668.44. Subtract from the gross amount of $118,668.44 the $5,000 previously paid earnest money and the $90,000 loan proceeds to arrive at a balance of $23,668.44. The tax proration is calculated by taking the tax bill for the year of $1,650 and dividing it by 365 days, equaling $4.52 per day. Because the taxes have been paid by the seller, the purchaser owes the seller the amount of money for the taxes from September 25 through the end of the year, or 97 days. Ninety-seven days times $4.52 equals $438.44.

11. The penalty for a false affidavit is perjury.

12. A same name affidavit is used any time an owner of property is referred to in the chain of title in more than one way.

13. A bill of sale transfers ownership to personal property.

14. Information generally contained in an assignment of leases would be (a) a list of leases assigned, and (b) indemnities between the assignor and assignee regarding defaults under the leases either prior to or after the assignment.

15. An affidavit of no material change certifies that no change has taken place in the buyer's financial condition from the date of loan application to loan closing.

CHAPTER 11

1. F	2. F
3. F	4. T
5. F	6. T
7. F	8. F
9. F	10. F

11. An owner in a condominium owns his or her condominium unit, as well as an undivided share in the condominium common area.

12. Common areas in a condominium usually consist of exterior walls of buildings, stairwells, elevators, walks, yards, roofs, entryways, and, in some situations, recreational areas such as swimming pools or tennis courts.

13. A condominium declaration is a contractual set of covenants that govern the ownership and control of the condominium.

14. A limited common area is an area limited to use by one or more condominium owners. An example might be an enclosed backyard or patio.

15. The internal operations of condominiums are generally governed by a condominium association.

16. A condominium owner generally pays taxes assessed on his or her individual condominium unit.

17. Insurance on a condominium is generally handled by a master policy that insures the entire condominium.

18. Issues and questions that would be relevant to a condominium purchaser are (a) reputation of the condominium developer; (b) does the condominium documentation comply with state law; (c) how are the assessments assessed and who controls the budget; (d) who controls the board of directors of the association; (e) a review of all restrictions on the use of the unit and common areas; and (f) is there any control on resale of the property.

19. A cooperative is a form of ownership in which a corporation owns residential property and the shareholders of the corporation are entitled to lease apartments within the property.

20. A cooperative is different from a condominium in that the cooperative unit owners own only shares in the cooperative corporation and a lease to their individual units.

CHAPTER 12

1. F	2. F
3. T	4. T
5. T	6. F
7. T	8. F
9. T	10. F

11. The types of land descriptions are (a) government rectangular survey, (b) platted, and (c) metes and bounds.

12. A base line is a surveyor line that runs due east and west and is identified as being a certain number of degrees north of the equator. Its relationship with a meridian is that only one base line will cross each principal meridian. Therefore, a parcel of land can be described as being a certain distance east or west of a given principal meridian at a certain distance north or south of a given base line.

13. 20 acres.

14. The basic requirements for a platted description are (a) land lot, (b) district, (c) county, (d) state, (e) subdivision, (f) lot and unit number, and (g) recorded reference to plat book and page numbers.

15. The course of a boundary line is the direction in which the boundary line travels and the distance is the length of the line.

16. The land surveyor should give the following information concerning each curved line: (a) the arc distance of the curve, (b) the radius distance of the curve, (c) the course of the chord, which is a straight line drawn from the beginning point of the arc to the ending point of the arc, and (d) the distance of the chord.

17. A metes and bounds description must close. This means that the legal description starts at a beginning point, follows each boundary line by course and distance, and ends back at the beginning point.

CHAPTER 13

1. F		2. F	
3. F		4. T	
5. F		6. F	
7. T		8. F	
9. T		10. F	

11. The theory of independent covenants states that a breach of promises or covenants by one party to a lease does not excuse the other party from performance from its promises or covenants. This means that if the landlord defaults under a lease, the tenant is not excused from paying rent. Historically, the theory of independent lease covenants has worked to the disadvantage of the tenant. Some states, especially in the area of residential leases, have modified the independent theory of lease covenants.

12. An assignment of a lease is the transfer by a tenant of all of his or her interest under the lease, with the tenant retaining nothing. A sublet is the transfer by a tenant of only a portion of the interest under the lease, with the tenant retaining some interest.

13. A gross lease is one in which the tenant pays rent to the landlord but all ordinary and necessary operating expenses for the premises, such as taxes, utilities, costs, and insurance, are paid by the landlord. In a net rent lease, the tenant pays a fixed amount of rent money to a landlord that is net to the landlord and the tenant is responsible for all expenses of the property, such as utilities, taxes, and insurance.

14. A lease is subject to all of the landlord's title defects. A tenant should examine the landlord's title to make sure the landlord owns the property, and the property does not have any restrictive covenants, which would affect the use of the leased property by the tenant. Another area of concern for the tenant is any prior mortgages. A mortgage that is in existence at the time a lease is entered into is senior to the lease and if the mortgage is foreclosed, the lease will terminate.

15. Basic remedies for a tenant's default under the lease are (a) sue the tenant for performance, (b) terminate the lease and sue for damages, or (c) dispossess the tenant and sue for the rental payments under the lease.

16. Generally a tenant does not have the right to withhold rent because of a landlord's default under a lease. A tenant has the remedy of suing the landlord for performance and for any damage caused by the landlord's nonperformance. The default of a landlord generally does not give the tenant the right to terminate the lease. The URLTA, where applicable, may modify these rules.

17. A lease guaranty is a situation where some person or entity other than the tenant guarantees the tenant's performance under the lease. A landlord might use a lease guaranty in a situation where the landlord is leasing the property to a corporate tenant with few assets. The landlord may ask the principal shareholder of the corporate tenant to guarantee the corporate tenant's obligations under the lease. A guaranty may also be used in a situation where a subsidiary of a corporation is the tenant. The landlord may ask that the parent corporation guarantee the subsidiary's performance under the lease.

actual notice Title matters that a purchaser has direct knowledge or information about.

ad valorem taxes Taxes assessed against real property, usually measured by the value of the real property being taxed.

adverse possession Method of acquiring ownership to real property by possession for a statutory time period.

affidavit Written statement of fact that is sworn to by the person making the statement under oath as a true statement of facts.

appropriation In regard to water law, doctrine stating that water belongs to the person who first makes beneficial use of it.

appurtenant easement Easement created to benefit a particular parcel of real property. The easement transfers automatically with a transfer of the ownership of the real property benefited by the easement.

as-built survey Survey that locates all physical improvements on the land in relation to the boundary lines of the land.

assessment Sum of money owed by a condominium owner for monthly upkeep of the common areas of the condominium.

assignment With regard to a lease, it is when the tenant transfers all his or her interest under the lease and retains nothing.

attornment and nondisturbance agreement An agreement usually entered into between a tenant and a holder of a mortgage on the leased premises wherein each party agrees to recognize the other in the event of a foreclosure of the mortgage. The mortgage holder also agrees not to terminate the lease or disturb the tenant's possession in the event of a foreclosure of the mortgage.

base line Imaginary east-west survey line used in the government survey system to establish township lines.

bill of sale Legal document that transfers ownership to personal property.

bona fide purchaser for value Person who purchases real property in good faith for valuable consideration without notice of any claim to or interest in the real property by any other party.

building codes Public laws that regulate methods and materials to be used in the construction of improvements.

call Course and distance describing a boundary line of land in a metes and bounds land description.

caption Portion of the deed that indicates the county and state in which the deed was signed by the grantor.

cashier's check Check issued by a bank, the payment of which is guaranteed by the full faith and credit of the bank.

CERCLA Also known as Superfund, is federal legislation which created a trust fund designed to finance the activities of the Environmental Protection Agency and gave the Environmental Protection Agency the authority to recover clean-up costs

for contaminated properties from the responsible parties for the contamination.

certified check Personal check in which the bank certifies that the funds are in the account and that the check will be honored on presentment for payment.

chain of title Historical sequence of all owners to a particular tract of real property beginning with the original owner and all successive owners who have derived their title from the original owner.

chord Straight line drawn from the beginning point of an arc to the ending point of an arc.

closing Consummation of a real estate purchase and sale transaction.

closing Date set forth in a real estate contract on which the parties agree to perform all the promises of the contract. The date on which ownership of the real property is transferred from seller to purchaser and the purchaser pays the seller the purchase price for the real property.

commercial lease A lease for the possession and use of a business or commercial enterprise such as a retail store, warehouse, or office.

common areas Common areas or common elements of a condominium is that portion of the condominium property that is owned in common by all the owners of units in the condominium.

community property law Rule of law in states following the civil law of Spain and France, which provides that real property acquired during marriage is owned equally by the husband and wife.

condition precedent Condition in a contract that must be satisfied in accordance with the terms of the contract before one or both of the parties are required to perform their contractual obligations.

condominium Form of property ownership in which the owner owns an individual unit in a multiunit building and is a tenant in common with other owners of units in the building in certain common areas.

condominium association Governing body of a condominium, the members of which are owners of condominium units. The condominium association usually is in the form of a nonprofit corporation.

condominium declaration Legal document required by state condominium acts to create a condominium.

condominium plat Plat of survey of condominium property required by state condominium acts. The plat must show in sufficient detail the location and dimensions of the real property, as well as all condominium units located on the real property.

consideration   Something of value given to make the promises in a contract enforceable.

constructive notice   A presumption of law that charges a person with notice of all title matters that can be discovered from an inspection of the real property or an examination of public real property records.

contract   Agreement between two or more persons consisting of a promise, or mutual promises that the law will enforce or the performance of which the law recognizes as a duty.

contribution   Right for a co-owner of real property to receive reimbursement from other co-owners for their share of expenses that are common to the real property.

conversion   Act of taking a person's property without a legal right to do so.

conveyance   Act of transferring ownership from one person to another.

conveyance   Transfer of title or ownership to real property from one person to another by deed. The terms may be used to include assignment, lease, mortgage, or encumbrance of real property.

cooperative   Form of ownership of real property in which a corporation owns a multiunit building and leases living space in the building to the shareholders of the corporation.

course   In a metes and bounds legal description, it is the direction of a property boundary line.

curtesy   Interest in real property of the wife that the law in some states gives to the surviving husband at the time of the wife's death.

deed of trust   Legal document that conveys title to real property to a trustee who holds the title as security for a debt to a lender.

deed to secure debt   Legal document that conveys title to real property to a lender to secure a debt.

deed   Written document that transfers ownership of real property from one person to another.

devise   Conveyance of real property by means of a last will and testament.

distance   In a metes and bounds legal description, it is the length of a property boundary line, usually measured in feet and hundredths of a foot (example: 82.13 feet).

dominant tenement   Parcel of land benefited by an appurtenant easement.

dower   Widow's interest in real property of her husband that provides a means of support after the husband's death.

due on sale clause   Clause found in a mortgage that prohibits the sale of the real property described in the mortgage without the lender's consent. A sale in violation of this provision is a default of the mortgage.

earnest money   Money paid by the purchaser at the time the real estate contract is signed. The money may be used as a downpayment on the purchase price or may be retained by the seller for damages in the event the purchaser defaults on the contract.

easement   Right granted to a nonowner of real property to use the real property for a specific purpose; for example, a right

given to an electric utility company to locate an electric line on real property.

easement by necessity   Easement for access to a public street that is necessary for the use and enjoyment of the property benefited by the easement.

easement in gross   Easement granting the owner of the easement the right to use real property for a particular purpose. The easement does not benefit a parcel of real property owned by the owner of the easement.

elective share   Right given to a widow in many states to elect, at her husband's death, to receive either dower or some ownership (fee simple) share of her husband's real property.

eminent domain   Power of government to take private property for public use.

encumbrance   Claim, lien, charge, or liability attached to and binding real property that may exist in another person to the diminishment of the value of the real property or that interferes with the use of the real property by the owner.

endorsement   Method of transferring ownership of a promissory note.

escrow   Agreement that requires the deposit of a document or money into the possession of a third party to be held by that party until certain conditions are fulfilled.

estate at will   Estate of real property the duration of which is for an indefinite period. An estate at will can be terminated at the will of the parties.

estate for years   Estate of real property the duration of which is for a definite period.

estoppel certificate lease   Written statement signed by either a landlord or a tenant swearing to certain facts concerning a lease.

estoppel certificate (mortgage loan)   A written statement, generally signed by the holder of a first mortgage and given to the holder of a second mortgage, swearing as to certain facts concerning the first mortgage loan. The estoppel certificate may also obligate the first mortgage holder to notify the second mortgage holder in the event of a default under the first mortgage loan.

execution   Signature of a party to a legal document. The act of signing a legal document.

express authority   Authority that has clearly been given by a principal to an agent.

fee simple absolute   Estate of real property with infinite duration and no restrictions on use.

fee simple determinable   Estate of real property with potential infinite duration. The ownership of a fee simple determinable is subject to a condition the breach of which can result in termination of the estate. A fee simple determinable automatically expires on the nonoccurrence or occurrence of a condition.

fee simple on condition subsequent   Estate of real property with a potential infinite duration. The ownership of a fee simple on condition subsequent is subject to a condition the breach of which can result in termination of the estate. A fee simple on condition subsequent continues in existence until an action is brought to recover the property.

fiduciary A person who holds a special relationship of confidence and trust to a principal and owes to the principal a duty to exercise all of the affairs of the principal in good faith and with loyalty.

fixture Item of personal property that becomes real property because of its attachment to the land or a building.

foreclosure Sale brought by a holder of a mortgage, deed of trust, or security deed of the real property conveyed in the instrument for the purposes of paying the debt secured by the real property.

general warranty deed Deed containing full warranty of title.

grantee index Alphabetical index of the public real property records that lists the last name of all people who are grantees of real property interest during a given year within the county.

grantee Person in whom real property has been transferred by deed.

grantor index Alphabetical index of the public real property records that lists the last name of all people who are grantors of real property interest during a given year within the county.

grantor Transferor of real property by deed.

gross lease Lease wherein the tenant pays rent only; the operating expenses of the leased premises, such as taxes, utility costs, and insurance, are paid by the landlord.

guarantor Person who signs a guaranty promising to pay the debt of another person.

guaranty Legal document that obligates the maker of the document to pay the debt of another person.

habendum Clause found in a deed that indicates what estate in real property is being transferred by the deed.

holder Person who is the owner of a promissory note.

implied authority Authority that is implied by law to be those things necessary and proper for an agent to carry out the duties of an agency.

implied easement Easement created by the conduct of the parties to the easement, not by written agreement.

inheritance Ability to acquire ownership to real property because of one's kinship to a deceased property owner.

interpleader Judicial proceeding in which money is paid into the court and all parties who claim an interest in the money are allowed to process their claims to the money in the court proceeding.

joint tenancy with right of survivorship Ownership of real property by two or more persons. Joint tenants with the right of survivorship hold equal interest in the real property, and on the death of any owner, the deceased owner's interest in the real property will pass to the surviving owner.

judgment Money debt resulting from a lawsuit. Judgments are liens on real property owned by the judgment debtor.

landlord or lessor Generally the owner of real property who transfers possession and use of the real property under a lease to a tenant or lessee.

lease Legal document that transfers possession of real property from one party to another. The lease also may contain numerous terms and conditions involving the use and possession of the property.

lease guaranty A legal document that obligates the maker of the document to perform the obligations of a tenant under the lease including, but not limited to, the payment of the rent by the tenant to the landlord.

legal description Description of real property by a government survey, metes and bounds, or lot numbers of a recorded plat, which description is complete enough that a particular parcel of land can be located and identified.

license Authority or permission to do a particular act or series of acts on another person's land.

lien Money debt attached to real property. The holder of the lien can sell the real property to pay the debt.

life estate Estate of real property the duration of which is measured by the life or lives of one or more persons.

limited common area Common area of a condominium that is limited in use to one or more condominium unit owners.

limited or special warranty deed Deed wherein the grantor covenants and warrants only against the lawful claims of people claiming by, through, or under the grantor.

liquidated damages Amount of money agreed on by the parties to a contract to be the damages in the event of a default of the contract.

lis pendens Notice recorded in the real property records that informs that a lawsuit affecting title to real property described in the notice has been filed and is pending.

listing agreement Agreement entered into between an owner and a real estate broker retaining the real estate broker to assist the owner in selling real property.

loan closing Consummation of a loan secured by real property.

loan commitment Contract between a borrower and a lender to make and accept a mortgage loan secured by real property. The loan commitment sets forth the terms, requirements, and conditions for the mortgage loan.

maker Party to a promissory note who promises to pay money.

marketable title Title to real property that is free from doubt and enables the owner to hold the real property in peace; free from the hazard of litigation or adverse claims.

mechanics' or materialmen's lien Lien imposed by law on real property to secure payment for work performed or materials furnished for the construction, repair, or alteration of improvements on the real property.

mortgage Legal document that creates an encumbrance on real property to secure a debt.

mortgagee Person who receives a mortgage.

mortgagee loss payable clause Endorsement to a policy of fire and hazard insurance whereby the owner of the insured property and the insurance company agree that any and all proceeds payable under the policy are to be paid directly to the lender who has a mortgage on the insured property.

mortgagee or loan policy Policy of title insurance that insures the interest of a mortgagee or lender to the title of real property.

mortgagor Person who signs a mortgage pledging real property to secure a debt.

net rent lease Lease in which the tenant is responsible for all expenses of the leased premises, such as utilities, taxes, and insurance.

open-end or dragnet clause Mortgage provision that provides that the mortgage will secure any and all debt between the mortgagor and the mortgagee, including past debt, present debt, and even future debt incurred after the mortgage is signed.

option A contract by which an owner of property, usually called the optionor, agrees with another person, usually called the optionee, that the optionee shall have the right to buy the owner's real property at a fixed price within a certain time on agreed terms and conditions.

owner's policy Policy of title insurance that insures an owner's title to real property.

parol evidence rule Rule of evidence that provides that a written agreement is the best and only evidence of the agreement between the parties and that the parties are not permitted to bring in oral testimony regarding other agreements concerning the transaction.

partition Method by which co-owners of real property can divide the common property into separate ownerships. Partition may be by voluntary agreement of the co-owners or by court action.

payee Party to a promissory note to whom a promise to pay money has been made.

percentage breakpoint Level of gross sales made during a year at which time a percentage rent obligation will commence.

phase I An examination of real property to determine if it contains environmental contamination.

phase II A more intensive environmental examination of property usually including the testing of soil and water for evidence of contamination.

plat Survey of real property that often is recorded.

plat index Index of all plats that have been recorded within the county within a given year.

possession Occupation of land evidenced by visible acts such as an enclosure, cultivation, the construction of improvements, or the occupancy of existing improvements.

power of attorney Written document authorizing another person to act as one's agent.

preamble Portion of the deed that sets forth the parties to the deed and the date of the deed.

premises Land and the buildings located on the land. The term often is used to describe real property covered by a lease.

prenuptial agreement Agreement entered into by a married couple that, among other things, outlines an agreement between the couple regarding the division and ownership of property in the event of separation or divorce.

prescriptive easement Easement created when a person uses real property for a period of time without the owner's permission.

principal A person who hires an agent to act on his or her behalf. A principal is generally responsible for the acts of the agent.

principal meridians Imaginary north and south lines used in a government survey system. Meridians intersect the base lines to form a starting point for the measurement of land under that system.

promissory note Legal document that contains a promise by one party to pay money to another party.

quitclaim deed Deed that contains no warranties of title. A quitclaim deed transfers only the interest that the grantor has in the land and not the land itself.

radius clause Clause contained in a lease that prohibits a tenant from operating another retail store or business within a certain geographical radius of the leased premises.

range lines Division of a state in a government survey system being a 6-mile-wide row of townships running north and south.

receiver Third party appointed by a court to take possession of real property in the event of a mortgage default. A receiver acts as a caretaker for the property.

record title holder Owner of real property as shown on the deed records from a title examination of the property.

recording statutes State statutes that regulate the recordation of real property documents.

redemption Right of a property owner to buy back his or her property after a foreclosure.

rent Money paid by a tenant to a landlord for the use and possession of property pursuant to a lease.

rescission Remedy for default of a real estate contract wherein the contract is terminated and the defaulting party must reimburse the injured party for expenses incurred in connection with the contract.

residential lease A lease for the possession and use of a residence such as an apartment or a house.

riparian rights Rights of the owners of lands adjoining streams, rivers, and lakes relating to the water and its use.

section Division or parcel of land on a government survey comprising 1 square mile, or 640 acres.

servient tenement Parcel of land on which an appurtenant easement is located.

specific performance Remedy for breach of real estate contract that requires a defaulting party to perform the promises under the contract.

sublet In regard to a lease, it is when the tenant transfers only a portion of his or her interest under the lease and the tenant retains some interest.

subrogation Right to be substituted to the rights of another person. For example, an insurance carrier who pays a claim to the insured is given the rights of the insured to proceed against any party who caused the damage resulting in the claim.

survey Visual presentation of the physical boundaries of real property. A survey is used to describe real property.

tacking Combination of possession periods by different adverse possessors.

tenancy by the entirety Ownership of real property by a husband and wife. The husband and wife are treated as a single owner, and neither the husband nor the wife can transfer the property without the other's consent.

tenancy in common Co-ownership of real property by two or more persons. Each owner's interest in the property is capable of inheritance.

tenant or lessee Person who receives possession and use of property pursuant to a lease.

testimonium Portion of the deed that the grantor signs and the signature is witnessed or notarized.

time is of the essence Provision contained in a contract that requires strict performance of the contract by the date or dates provided therein.

time-share Form of ownership of real property in which an owner owns the property for a short period, usually one or two weeks out of each year. Time-share ownership typically is used for vacation or recreational property.

title endorsement Amendment to a title insurance policy that generally modifies existing coverage or adds special coverage to the policy.

title examination Examination of the real property records to determine the ownership to a particular tract of real property.

title insurance Contract to indemnify the insured against loss through defects in the title to real property.

title insurance commitment Commitment or contract by a title insurance company to issue a title insurance policy.

township In a government survey, it is a square tract of land 6 miles on each side, containing 36 square miles of land.

township lines Lines in a government rectangular survey system, that run east and west at 6-mile intervals parallel with base lines and that form strips of land or tiers called townships.

usury Interest rates that are determined to be in excess of the maximum permitted by law.

warranty or covenant Promise that a fact is true or that an event will take place.

waste Action or nonaction that causes a loss of value to real property.

will Legal document by which a person disposes of his or her property. A will takes effect on the death of the property owner.

zoning Legitimate police power of government to regulate the use of real property.